Literatures of Latin America

From Antiquity to the Present

Edited and with introductions by

Willis Barnstone

DISTINGUISHED PROFESSOR OF SPANISH
AND COMPARATIVE LITERATURE

INDIANA UNIVERSITY

Prentice
Hall

Upper Saddle River, New Jersey 07458

Library of Congress Cataloging-in-Publication Data

Literatures of Latin America / edited and with
introductions by Willis Barnstone.
    p. cm.
    Previously published as part of: Literatures of Asia, Africa, and Latin America. 1999.
    Includes bibliographical references and index.
    ISBN 0-13-061360-6
    1. Latin American Literature—Translations into English. 2. Indian Literature—Latin
America—Translations into English. 3. Latin America—Literatures—Translations into
English. I. Barnstone, Willis II. Literatures of Asia, Africa, and Latin America.

PQ7087.E5 L58 2003
808.8'0098—dc21
                            2002022667

Editor-in-Chief: Leah Jewell
Senior Acquisitions Editor: Carrie Brandon
Editorial Assistant: Jennifer Migueis
Managing Editor: Ann Marie McCarthy
Production Liaison: Fran Russello
Project Manager: Linda B. Pawelchak

Prepress and Manufacturing Buyer:
  Sherry Lewis
Interior Design: Delgado Design, Inc.
Cover Design: Robert Farrar-Wagner
Cover Image Credit: Willis Barnstone
Marketing Manager: Rachel Falk

This text is derived from *Literatures of Africa, Asia, and Latin America* by Willis Barnstone
and Tony Barnstone.

Acknowledgments begin on page 464, which constitutes a continuation of this copyright page.

This book was set in 10/12 New Baskerville by Lithokraft II and was printed and bound
by The Courier Companies. The cover was printed by Phoenix Color Corp.

This book is dedicated to Roberto González-Echevarría

© 2003 by Pearson Education, Inc.
Upper Saddle River, New Jersey 07458

Printed in the United States of America
10 9 8 7 6 5 4 3 2 1

ISBN 0-13-061360-6

Pearson Education LTD, *London*
Pearson Education Australia PTY. Limited, *Sydney*
Pearson Education Singapore, Pte. Ltd
Pearson Education North Asia Ltd, *Hong Kong*
Pearson Education Canada Ltd, *Toronto*
Pearson Educación de Mexico, S.A. de C.V.
Pearson Education—Japan, *Tokyo*
Pearson Education Malaysia, Pte. Ltd
Pearson Education, *Upper Saddle River, New Jersey*

CONTENTS

Section 2 ■ Discovery, Conquest, and the Colonies 106

Section 3 ■ Nineteenth and Twentieth Centuries 188

Poetry

Prose Nonfiction

Fiction

Literatures of Latin America brings together literary, religious, and philosophical traditions from two continents and the Caribbean. Each of these regions has given us important writings, some of them dating back as far as the first millennium B.C. Until recently, historically speaking, we have been essentially ignorant of the major writers of Latin America, and in particular have known virtually nothing of precolumbian texts. Recent decades of assiduous translation, however, have made the larger world of Latin American literature accessible in English, connecting us to an enormous past and present of creative endeavor. Particularly in our multicultural society, with peoples of every background, it is vital to reveal the great traditions of Latin America, and to do so in fresh, excellent literary translation, or in their original English texts, as in the case of postcolonial writers, such as Nobel Prize–winning novelist V. S. Naipaul and Nobel Prize–winning poet Derek Walcott. *Literatures of Latin America* presents a hemispheric view of literature and civilization. The picture that emerges is of two continents in a splendor of creativity and of a migration of languages and literary forms.

The great written documents of antiquity root us as readers in a past of cultural particularity, cultural marriage, and universal themes and have offered superb new models for modern and postmodern writers. Whereas early in the twentieth century, the major foreign models for American literature came from France, in the post–World War II period the poets and novelists from Latin America have clearly been revealed in magnificent translations and have profoundly changed the ways that North American authors write. We live in a time when it is no less common for American poets to count Nobel Prize authors Pablo Neruda and Octavio Paz as major influences than it is for them to see their verse springing from Walt Whitman and T. S. Eliot. The new generation of American novelists looks to metafiction, magic realism, and the fantastic in the great recent Latin American authors such as Julio Cortázar, Jorge Luis Borges, and Gabriel García Márquez, another Nobel laureate. In the current ferment of translation, a well-read lover of literature is as likely to be reading César Vallejo as Paul Celan, as likely to be reading the Caribbean novelist Jamaica Kincaid as Ernest Hemingway. As in the Spanish saying "the world is a handkerchief" (*el mundo es un pañuelo*), the major literatures of Latin America and the Caribbean are now intimately accessible.

Literatures of Latin America has been designed to present teachers and students with a textbook representative of the finest works of Latin American and Caribbean literature, one that is amenable to many different teaching approaches. This book includes a wealth of materials in order to give teachers choices that they can tailor to their own preferences, needs, and expertise. This capaciousness will allow students to read around in authors, periods, and traditions that particularly excite them, supplementing assigned reading and providing an essential source book for their individual research. Teaching such a broad spectrum of texts may be challenging, and with this in mind I have supported the literary texts with a full apparatus: a general introduction, section introductions, subsection introductions, and extensive headnotes. These supporting materials provide broad and specific contexts, placing literary texts within important cultural, linguistic, and historical movements. In addition, the headnotes include up-to-date bibliographies to guide students for further research.

Translations have been selected primarily for their literary quality because I firmly believe that it is a disservice to students, professors, and authors to present a great work of literature in an English translation that does not read as literature. The depth and quality of these texts demand excellent translations so that students and professors may encounter them in a form that preserves their artistic integrity and delight. The translators featured here are among the finest in their fields, and many are themselves prominent writers. They include W. S. Merwin, Mark Strand, Gordon Brotherston, Elizabeth Bishop, Robert Bly, Paul Blackburn, Anthony Kerrigan, James Merrill, Nathaniel Tarn, Gregory Rabassa, Richard Wilbur, Clayton Eshleman, James Wright, and Philip Levine, among others. My one rule has been to include no translation that is merely adequate. In a sense, then, this text is a showcase for the art of literary translation, and my hope has been to compile an anthology that students will want to take home with them and read long after the course is completed.

In addition to literary texts, *Literatures of Latin America* includes selections from religious and philosophical texts that have literary merit, such as Native American hymns, creation myths, shaman narrations, cures, chronicles, and exorcisms. These beautiful texts also provide a cosmological and cultural context for literary movements. Extensive headnotes and introductions trace out religious movements and influence, giving students a broad overview of world religions, which have often inspired and been an essential part of world literatures.

The book also includes important examples of the secular essay, including precolumbian historical annals; the log of Christopher Columbus; colonial histories and letters by Bartolomé de las Casas, Bernal Díaz del Castillo, the Inca Garcilaso de la Vega, and Sor Juana Inés de la Cruz. These essays are themselves of immense literary importance and at the same time provide political, philosophical, historical, and biographical supplements to the literary selections. In addition to providing context for the literary selections, the essays provide students with a valuable resource for writing and researching their own essays.

"You can never step in the same river twice," writes Heraclitus, the Presocratic Greek philosopher. Time is such a river, but so is language, which flows from our mouths and is the medium of culture and society. How can one detain the evanescent essence of human communication—language? Like the Irish bog men preserved for centuries in peat or the marvelously conserved mummies of Egypt, humanity is preserved by writing. And there is wonder in what reaches us from antiquity. Like a bead of amber containing a prehistoric insect caught in midcrawl, each word deciphered from Mayan or Nahuatl glyphs is precious. Ancient coins unearthed still retain monetary value, but we esteem them even more for their worth as microcosms of vanished worlds. This is the value to be found in ancient writing as well. An inexpressible pathos of lost love is found in the intimate words of a Quechua folksong, "I have lost my dove. / Wandering I call to her in a loud voice. / Everyone who finds me says, / 'Why did you love her?'" Grand drama is experienced in reading the log of Christopher Columbus, sailing with him for two months over uncharted seas, seeing him calm the mutinous crew, glimpsing with him at last a light in the night, which he describes as "like a little wax candle bobbing up and down," and then in reading the next entry, "At dawn we saw naked people." Extraordinarily moving and revealing is the response of the Aztec priests to the Franciscan missionaries sent from Rome to convert them to Christianity: "We don't believe. We don't mock. . . . / It is enough that we have done penance, / that we are ruined, / that we are forbidden and stripped of power. / Make of us / the thing that most suits you. / This is all we have to reply, / Señores."

These texts stretch from antiquity to the present and, despite cultural differences, reveal throughout the universality of life-and-death experience. In every century and place, writers have recorded visions of the origins and end of the world, of the supernatural permeating ordinary life and afterlife, as in the cosmologies and cosmogonies of the Quiche-Maya religious epic *Popol Vuh* and of the Quechua Huarochiri manuscript. Writers, religions, and philosophies have always tried to answer basic questions of origin, presence, and destiny and at the same time have given us intimate records of the self and the phenomenal world. The world's authors have observed the known and speculated on the unknown. *Literatures of Latin America* is a record of their questioning and achievement. It encompasses a vast precinct of human knowledge, hemispheric in scope, given to us by the writers of antiquity and by their heirs, our contemporaries, who continue to extend, innovate, and astound, from Mexico to Argentina.

I would like to thank Roberto González-Echevarría for advice on Cuban and Latin American writers. Gordon Brotherston coedited the translations in the precolumbian section and translated many of the readings in that section. I greatly appreciate his help in putting together a selection from this underrepresented province of world literature. I would like to thank Erika Embry, David Livingston, and Ayame Fukuda for their essential help in research, typing, organization, and the thousand small tasks that a project such as this entails. Ayame Fukuda provided essential research help and also cowrote several introductions.

I would also like to acknow-ledge the following reviewers: Ali Jimale Ahmed, Queens College; Peter Edmunds, Lansing (MI) Community College; Lydia Liv, University of California, Berkeley; Michael Palencia Roth,

University of Illinois; Herman Rapaport, University of Iowa; and Lois
Parkinson Zamora, University of Houston.

—WILLIS BARNSTONE

General Introduction

■

In 1839, two explorers, John Lloyd Stephens, an American archeologist, and Frederick Catherwood, an English architect and archeological artist, were in the almost impenetrable jungles of Honduras, looking for the fabled Mayan ruins of Copán. The nineteenth-century explorer Charles Gallenkamp describes their moment of encounter when they found themselves

> in the midst of wonders exceeding their wildest expectations. Scattered about were gigantic sculptured monoliths and altars, some standing erect, others fallen over broken, their surfaces richly carved with masks, animals, human figures, and inscriptions. Huge pyramid-shaped structures reached up through the trees, scarcely visible under a thick mantle of rubble and vegetation. . . . Grotesque heads of jaguars, serpents, and mythical creatures had fallen from their facades—images of unknown gods in whose veneration the once-magnificent temples had been erected . . . wherever Stephens and Catherwood looked they saw miracles frozen in its crumbled monuments.[1]

An earlier traveler remarked, "The genii who attended on King Solomon seem to have been the artists."[2] Three centuries earlier, the Spanish chronicler Bernal Díaz del Castillo described Cortés's first view of Tenochtitlán, the Aztec capital in Mexico (now Mexico City), stating that Cortés and his men also marveled before the splendor of temples, towers, crowded bridges, and great causeways and wondered whether it was all a dream.

The Maya city of Copán, along with magnificent Tikal, Palenque, Uxmal, and Chichén Itzá, had actually disappeared into the concealing safety yet slow decay of the jungle four centuries before the Spanish conquerors reached Mesoamerica. But even in a period of decline, there was still much Indian culture to dazzle the Spaniards, particularly in Mexico City, where Montezuma and the Aztecs were at the pinnacle of their power. The Spanish mission was to seize the material wealth of the empire, to convert the natives from their "devilish idolatry" to the "true faith" of Catholicism, and to build new cities throughout Spanish America, which the Spaniards did with enormous energy. Since the temples and written documents that preserved the Maya past were perceived as the greatest obstacles to the imposition of Christianity, temples were razed throughout "New Spain" and the great Maya and Aztec codices were burned wherever they

---

1. Charles Gallenkamp, *Maya: The Riddle and Rediscovery of a Lost Civilization* (3rd rev. ed.) (New York: Viking, 1985), 28.
2. Ibid.

could be discovered. The most ardent destroyer was a young Franciscan monk, Diego de Landa (1524–1579). At the age of twenty-five, he traveled the Yucatán, cleansing the pagans of their native religion by means of fire and torture. In Maní, southeast of Mérida, he discovered the greatest repository of ancient hieroglyphic books. He burned it. One of the few surviving Maya works to escape the Inquisitional fires of the church, the epic *Popol Vuh* from the Guatemalan highlands, is a genesis and cosmology of the Quiche-Maya and a monument of world literature. Paradoxically, the same ardent friar was to become the Bishop of Yucatán and write *The Relation of Things in the Yucatán,* the most important ethnological account of the area from the colonial period.

Despite the angry flames of religious arrogance and bigotry, diverse writings from the precolumbian periods survived, many of them oral narrations and songs recorded by churchmen in native tongue—as was the *Popol Vuh*— or in Spanish translation in the early days after the conquest. In recent decades, most of the obstacles to deciphering Maya hieroglyphs have been overcome, and the stones and remaining fragments of codices have revealed their secrets. Moreover, works in Native American languages have continued to be written in the Americas. Despite tribal and linguistic differences, we have seen Native American writings as part of a larger phenomenon of civilization in the Americas prior to and contemporaneous with the European presence.

With the conquest complete, Spanish became the tongue of chronicle and literature. New World literature begins with the discoverers and first historians, and so Columbus and Amerigo Vespucci, the geographer whose name gave us the unifying word America, were among the first authors. In his *The Royal Commentaries of Peru,* Garcilaso de la Vega Inca (1539–1695), the son of a Spanish father and Inca princess mother, was the perfect writer to transform oral memory into a history of the Incas. Living the latter part of his life in Spain, Garcilaso published his *Commentaries* there and introduced Europe to the history and fable of one of the great precolumbian cultures. The foremost literary writer of the Spanish Americas was the Mexican nun Sor Juana Inés de la Cruz (1648/51–1695). Of Spanish Catholic and Native American origin, Sor Juana wrote European secular sonnets in the Spanish Golden Age manner as well as Christian mystery plays, yet she also heard and understood songs in Nahuatl (the Aztec tongue) in her native village. Sor Juana's "First Dream" is the single most important and extended metaphysical poem in all Europe or the Americas.

In the nineteenth century, two Argentine writers emerged, the statesman Domingo Faustino Sarmiento (1811–1888) and the epic poet José Hernández (1834–1886), who made the gaucho the symbol of the wild outlaw hero. Two decades later, the Cuban journalist and poet José Martí (1853–1895) wrote revolutionary lyrics for the common man and woman. But the major nineteenth-century author was the Brazilian Machado de Assis (1867–1907), who in dramatic, ironic novellas captured the drama and absurdity of Brazilian middle-class lives.

Latin American writing reached its zenith, however, with the publications of the Argentine parabalist, fiction writer, and poet Jorge Luis Borges (1899–1986). Along with Kafka and Joyce, Borges is one of the masters, innovators, and highly imitated writers of twentieth-century world literature. His younger counterparts, authors of the Latin American novel who developed and extended Borges's fantasy and magic realism, have taken over modern world literature. As the epithet the "boom novel" suggests, there was (and continues to be) an explosion of interest around the globe when the great men and women fiction writers from Latin America appeared on the scene. Beginning with Borges, who is their "fantastic" father, Julio Cortázar and Manuel Puig from Argentina, Gabriel García Márquez from Colombia, José Donoso and Isabel Allende from Chile, Mario Vargas Llosa from Peru, Juan Rulfo and Carlos Fuentes from Mexico, Alejo Carpentier, Guillermo Cabrera Infante, and Reinaldo Arenas from Cuba have made the novel from Latin America the most translated work in the world. The bestselling novel *Like Water for Chocolate* by the Mexican novelist Laura Esquivel is one of the latest artistic wonders to come out of Latin America. In her engaging, experimental, historical, and enthralling novel, she has given us, in concise and specific speech, a drama of women and men in the panorama of the early twentieth century.

There have been great poets from Latin America—the Chileans Gabriela Mistral and Pablo Neruda, Octavio Paz from Mexico (all three Nobel Prize laureates), the Peruvian César Vallejo and the Brazilian Carlos Drummond de Andrade. These poets have been abundantly and excellently translated by the best poets in the English language and consequently have had a profound effect on the development of poetry in English. Before World War II, it was to France that American and British poets went for models. So T. S. Eliot found Jules Laforgue and Tristan Corbiere when he wanted to introduce a waste land city life into American poetry; Wallace Stevens went to the French symbolist poets, especially Mallarmé; and the humor and typographical trickery of e. e. cummings is inconceivable without the earlier *Calligrammes* of the French poet Guillaume Apollinaire. But after World War II, it was the Russian, Greek, Spanish, and Spanish American poets who replaced the French. Since Spanish is a language accessible to many English-speaking readers (unlike Russian and Modern Greek), our leading poets, W. S. Merwin, Robert Bly, Denise Levertov, Robert Lowell, Richard Wilbur, and Mark Strand have translated from the Spanish. Elizabeth Bishop, the leading woman poet of her generation, lived for more than a decade in Brazil. She not only translated Drummond de Andrade (1902–) and João Cabral de Melo Neto (1920–) but coedited with Mark Strand an anthology of very important contemporary Brazilian poets with magnificent translations by American poets.

From the Caribbean, we also have many world-famous authors, such as the French-writing poet Aimé Césaire (1913–), whose surreal writings link Caribbean Martinique with Paris and Africa; the East Indian Trinidadian V. S. Naipaul (1932–), the 2001 recipient of the Nobel Prize in literature, whose novels and reportage link his island with London, India, and Africa; and the 1992 Nobel poet Derek Walcott (1924–) from Saint Lucia, whose epic poem *Omeros* owes its sources to Homeric Greek, to Africa, and to his Carib islands.

The twentieth century ends with the dissolution of cultural borders. As Asia and Africa have become part of our reading habit, so too have Latin America and the Caribbean. From Boston and New York all the way down to Borges's gaucho pampas and Pablo Neruda's southernmost Chilean mountains near the Arctic circle, we now witness the reality of the writers in all the Americas.

SECTION

1

Native American Literature of Precolumbian and Later Periods

■

EDITED BY GORDON BROTHERSTON AND WILLIS BARNSTONE

INTRODUCTION

Before Columbus set sail, literature had been evolving in the Americas for thousands of years, along with agriculture (plant genetics), medicine, mathematics, astronomy, architecture, weaving, metallurgy, and many other orders of knowledge. This great endeavor, which is largely unrivaled anywhere, was the work of peoples whose survivors are today commonly referred to as American Indians or Native Americans. Modern analysis of their languages, as of their blood, confirms their long occupation of America, north and south, and that they were and are the true authors of culture in their continent.

ᦂ ᦂ ᦂ ᦂ ᦂ ᦂ ᦂ ᦂ ᦂ ᦂ ᦂ ᦂ ᦂ ᦂ ᦂ ᦂ ᦂ ᦂ

In 1492, the Old World from which Columbus set sail was customarily thought of as threefold, with Asia, Europe, and Africa respectively in first, second, and third positions. America came to be perceived as the "fourth part of the world" *(quarta orbis pars)*, or simply the "Fourth World." In recent decades, this term has been adopted by George Manuel and other Native Americans. It helps to establish a comparability among all four worlds, in terms of their "cumulative history," when in practice, America has been more thoroughly dispossessed than the other three. For, despite native resistance that continues even today, Columbus announced a destruction of people and culture so violent and cynical as to defy belief.

Fourth-World texts, Native Americans' accounts of themselves and their place, constitute a great neglected chapter of world literature. Based on and transcribed in part from scripts and recording systems developed in the first millennium B.C. or earlier, these texts range from cosmogony—the story of the world ages and the epic of human emergence told from one end of the continent to the other—to history and annals, from poetry to law. Yet throughout we find the same literary recurrence to the guardian mountains of creation, the bird messengers, and the revered plants that sustain humankind—manioc, maize or corn in all its colors, beans, squash, potatoes, quinoa, to mention but a few. Paramount among these texts stands the *Popol Vuh,* written by the Quiche-Maya in the sixteenth century in what is now Guatemala. Its ingenuity as a text and the scale of the knowledge it encodes as a genesis make it a classic not just of the Fourth World but of world literature. In turn, this literary wealth has become an ever more immediate source for Americans writing in imported languages such as Portuguese, Spanish, French, and English. An exemplary case is that of the Guatemalan Miguel Angel Asturias, who won the Nobel Prize thanks to *Hombres de maíz* (1949; *Men of Maize)*, a novel that draws profoundly on the *Popol Vuh.*

Encompassing no more than a fraction of major Fourth-World texts, the selections here focus on seven language traditions, which range geographically over the Andes and the rainforest of South America, then Mexico and Mesoamerica. Each of these traditions lives today along with a wealth of texts that lead us back to the great American story of genesis. As the language of the former Inca empire, Tahuantinsuyu, Quechua has had a continuous visible presence for us since the sixteenth century, when it was first transcribed into the alphabet. The same is true of the languages that survived from the empires of Mesoamerica, Nahuatl (the language of the Aztecs and their Toltec forebears), and lowland and highland Maya.

Generally Fourth-World texts first entered the Western tradition already in translation, through the reports of missionaries and conquistadors and the works of early historians, native and European. From the start, there was an appreciation of their literary qualities, as in Ixtlilxochitl's commentary in Spanish on the lyrics of his ancestor Nezahualcoyotl, or Montaigne's famous remark on the "Anacreontic" style of a poem in Tupi-Guarani (a major South American language not represented here). J. G. Herder's *Stimmen der*

Völkern in Liedern (1797), one of the first attempts to anthologize world literature, included Quechua hymns and poems, and in the following century D. G. Brinton published a range of texts in the nine volumes of his remarkable *Library of Aboriginal American Literature* (1882–1890). Yet only in the last three or four decades have many key works been edited and translated adequately for the first time, especially into English, which had lagged notably behind German, French, and Spanish. In the process, anthropology and literature have intelligently conjoined, as will be apparent from many of the more recent translations included here by Edmonson, Rothenberg, Tarn, Tedlock, Guss, Burns, and several others. At the same time, the verse tradition of both Nahuatl and Quechua, once the languages of Aztec and Inca, have repeatedly attracted the attentions of translators who are poets in their own right.

Within each language section, the arrangement is broadly chronological and ends with work of recent years that often bears an author's name. The longer Quechua and Nahuatl sections draw on a wealth of sixteenth-century texts transcribed from Inca and Aztec antecedents, where dates of transcription or publication are often unhelpful, and a more thematic sequence has been preferred. Here, the opening pieces are chosen to reflect the moment of encounter with Europe.

—Gordon Brotherston

Quechua Language

Known in various dialects, for example, the northern Quichua, Quechua is the major American language to have survived from precolumbian times. It was the common tongue *(runasimi)* of the Inca empire Tahuantinsuyu or "Four Districts" that centered on Cuzco. Today, it is spoken by more than ten million people in the Andean countries that once made up Tahuantinsuyu (Peru, Bolivia, northern Argentina, Ecuador, southern Colombia), and it has been declared a second official language in Peru and Ecuador. Native and Spanish historians mention several Quechua texts, for example, hymns to the deity Viracocha, that in the sixteenth century were transcribed from the Inca recording medium, the knotted-string *quipu,* whole libraries of which were burnt by the European invaders. Quechua is also renowned for its vigorous tradition in drama and music, a cycle of Inca kingship plays, and a rich repertoire of poetry and song that continues into this century and affirms resistance to modern assaults on native lands, economy, and language.

Only a few Quechua poems have found their way to literary translation into English, which presumably reproduces the quality and beauty of the original version. Just as the Spanish Arabist Juan García Gómez translated poetry of Arabic Spain into Spanish and thereby for the first time gave

Spanish writers (particularly Federico García Lorca) a real awareness of their Moorish past, so the translation of even a few Native American poems into Spanish brings alive the silent literature of the Americas. From the Spanish, two of America's best and most skillful poets and poet translators, Mark Strand and W. S. Merwin, have given us a taste of Quechuan lyrics. Those familiar with popular song of many civilizations in all continents will easily recognize common thematic and prosodic elements that appear and reappear in the world's oral and written poetry.

FURTHER READING: *18 Poems from the Quechua.* Translated by Mark Strand, 1971. W. S. Merwin. *Selected Translations: 1948–1968,* 1968.

—Gordon Brotherston and editors

■ Apu Inca Atawallpaman (Sixteenth Century) *Peru* (poem)

TRANSLATED BY W. S. MERWIN

Although he satisfied Pizarro's inordinate demands for gold as ransom, the Inca emperor Atahuallpa was nonetheless murdered by the conquistadors in Cajamarca in 1533. The shock was felt throughout the four districts of Tahuantinsuyu, as numerous native texts testify, including dramas that continued the Inca kingship cycle and are still performed in the Andes today. This lament closely resembles speeches made in those dramas yet has a strong elegiac quality of its own.

from *The Elegy for the Great Inca Atawallpa*

. . . You all by yourself fulfilled
  Their malignant demands,
But your life was snuffed out
  In Cajamarca.

Already the blood has curdled   5
  In your veins,
And under your eyelids your sight
  Has withered.
Your glance is hiding in the brilliance
  Of some star.   10

Only your dove suffers and moans
    And drifts here and there.
Lost in sorrow, she weeps, who had her nest
    In your heart.

                               15

The heart, with the pain of this catastrophe,
    Shatters.
They have robbed you of your golden litter
    And your palace.
All of your treasures which they have found   *20*
    They have divided among them.

Condemned to perpetual suffering,
    And brought to ruin,
Muttering, with thoughts that are elusive
    And far away from this world,   *25*
Finding ourselves without refuge or help,
    We are weeping,
And not knowing to whom we can turn our eyes,
    We are lost.

Oh sovereign king,   *30*
    Will your heart permit us
To live scattered, far from each other,
    Drifting here and there,
Subject to an alien power,
    Trodden upon?

                               35

Discover to us your eyes which can wound
    Like a noble arrow;
Extend to us your hand which grants
    More than we ask,
And when we are comforted with this blessing   *40*
    Tell us to depart.

■ The Huarochiri Manuscript (1608)
Peru (prose narration)

TRANSLATED BY FRANK SALOMON AND GEORGE URIOSTE

Often referred to as the "Popol Vuh of the Andes," this remarkable text comes from Huarochiri, which lies between the old Inca capital Cuzco and the coastal capital Lima established by the Spanish. It threads through its thirty-one chapters the story of the American world ages that end in flood, eclipse, volcanic fire, and hurricane. It was recorded as part of the Jesuit-trained Francisco de Avila's efforts to extirpate native religion, and it deals explicitly with the relative status of Viracocha, the deity imposed by Cuzco, and local gods like Paria Caca, who features in the world age story and becomes the principal *huaca* or shrine mountain of the region. This accounts for the rather irreverent account of Viracocha's behavior in which he adopts undignified subterfuge in order to impregnate a woman at the same time that he raises the structures of civilization.

Only a few native documents deal with the forty-year Spanish invasion of the vast Inca empire. Among the most valuable of these is the sixteenth-century Quechua text known as the Huarochiri Narrative. It consists of oral and written reports gathered by Francisco de Avila in the area around Huarochiri, Checa, and Yauyos (on the road from Lima to Cuzco). In chapter 2, we hear a version of parthenogenesis that is closely related to the origins of the Inca state. In the early heroic days of the gods, it is said, Viracocha both founded the towns of the state and established himself as superior to other gods who represented only local interests. At first, less prepossessing than they, he nonetheless ousts them "in his wisdom" and reveals himself as nothing less than a solar father, "enlightening the earth," like his later representative, the Sapa Inca.

The tale is filled with humorous ironies that humanize the gods and universalize them as the insecure yet arrogant gods of every civilization. Clearly, the mother is ashamed of the godman who claims to be the father, and she feels pity for her child. Viracocha, like a spurned Zeus, attempts to impress the virgin mother with his potential magnificence. While the other gods tremble, he dons a golden suit (Zeus resorted to golden rain in his seduction); then (like the sungod Apollo, who was spurned by Daphne), he uses his power to light up the world.

FURTHER READING: *The Huarochiri Manuscripts: A Testament of Ancient and Colonial Andean Religion.* Translated by Frank Salomon, 1991.

Chapter 1

HOW THE IDOLS OF OLD WERE, AND HOW THEY WARRED AMONG THEMSELVES, AND HOW THE NATIVES EXISTED AT THAT TIME

In ancient times, there were *huacas* named Yana Namca and Tuta Namca.

Later, another *huaca* named Huallallo Caruincho defeated them.

After he defeated them, he ordered the people to bear two children and no more.

He would eat one of them himself.

The parents would raise the other, whichever one was loved best.

Although people did die in those times, they came back to life exactly on the fifth day.

And as for their foodstuffs, they ripened exactly five days after being planted.

These villages and all the others like them were full of Yunca.

When a great number of people had filled the land, they lived miserably, scratching and digging the rock faces and ledges to make terraced fields.

These fields, some small, others large, are still visible today on all the rocky heights.

And all the birds of that age were perfectly beautiful, parrots and toucans all yellow and red.

Later, at the time when another *huaca* named Paria Caca appeared, these beings and all their works were cast out to the hot Anti lands by Paria Caca's actions.

Further on we'll speak of Paria Caca's emergence and of his victories.

There was another *huaca* named Cuni Raya.

Regarding him, we're not sure whether he existed before Paria Caca or maybe after him.

However, Cuni Raya's essential nature almost matches Vira Cocha's,[1] for when people worshiped this *huaca,* they would invoke him, saying,

"Cuni Raya Vira Cocha,

You who animate mankind,
Who charge the world with being,
All things are yours!
Yours the fields and yours the people."

And so long ago, when beginning anything difficult, though they couldn't see Vira Cocha, the ancients used to throw coca leaves to the ground, talk to him, and worship him before all others, saying,

"Help me remember how,
Help me work it out,
Cuni Raya Vira Cocha!"

And the master weaver would worship and call on him whenever it was hard for him to weave.

---

1. Because of his alleged importance as a supreme deity, comparable to the Christian God, Vira Cocha has become the subject of a large and frequently misleading literature. Here, however, this deity's role has little to do with the Christian concept of God and a lot in common with the pan–New World concept of a Trickster, whose buffoonery is at the same time a force making and remaking the world.

For that reason, we'll write first about this *huaca* and about his life, and later on about Paria Caca.

Chapter 2

HOW CUNI RAYA VIRA COCHA ACTED IN HIS OWN AGE. THE LIFE OF CUNI RAYA VIRA COCHA. HOW CAUI LLACA GAVE BIRTH TO HIS CHILD, AND WHAT FOLLOWED

A long, long time ago, Cuni Raya Vira Cocha used to go around posing as a miserably poor and friendless man, with his cloak and tunic all ripped and tattered. Some people who didn't recognize him yelled, "You poor lousy[2] wretch!"

Yet it was this man who fashioned all the villages. Simply by speaking he made the fields, and finished the terraces with walls of fine masonry. As for the irrigation canals, he channeled them out from their sources simply by tossing down the flower of a reed called *pupuna*.

After that, he went around performing all kinds of wonders, putting some of the local *huacas* to shame with his cleverness.

Once there was a female *huaca* named Caui Llaca.

Caui Llaca had remained a virgin.

Since she was very beautiful, every one of the *huacas* and *villcas*[3] longed for her. "I've got to sleep with her!" they thought.

But she never consented.

Once this woman, who had not allowed any male to fondle[4] her, was weaving beneath a *lúcuma* tree.

Cuni Raya, in his cleverness, turned himself into a bird and climbed into the *lúcuma*.

---

2. Lice have a peculiar double meaning; Marie-France Souffez (1986), relying partly on findings by Christopher Donnan and Maria Rostworowski, notes that in Mochica imagery of shamanism the lice growing on a shaman's body emblematize the many people her or his power can sustain. Latent wealth hidden in apparent squalor is a common attribute of Huarochiri protagonists.

3. Internal evidence (chap. 31, sec. 417) suggests that in the Huarochiri context it means a person who has entered into the society of *huacas* by achievement or marriage. In the *Tratado* (Arguedas and Duviols 1966: 209), the word *villca* is translated "a very important *cacique*" (*cacique muy principal;* see also Zuidema 1973: 19). In Huánchor village in 1621, the founding hero Huánchor was mummified and housed underneath a *huaca* called Huanchorvilca (Arguedas and Duviols 1966: 264). Overall, the implication seems to be that a *villca* is a human being who partakes of a *huaca*'s status.

4. *chancaycochicuspa* "fondle": Gonçález Holguín ([1608] 1952:94) glosses related verbs as meaning "to stroke or touch lightly." Similar verbs in modern Quechua usually sound sexually piquant.

He put his semen into a ripened fruit and dropped it next to the woman.

The woman swallowed it down delightedly.

Thus she got pregnant even though she remained untouched by man.

In her ninth month, still a virgin, she gave birth just as other women give birth.

And for one year she nursed her child at her breast, wondering, "Whose child could this be?"

In the fullness of the year, when the youngster was crawling around on all fours, she summoned all the *huacas* and *villcas* to find out who was the child's father.

When the *huacas* heard the message, they were overjoyed, and they came dressed in their best clothes, each saying to himself, "It's me!" "It's me she'll love!"

This gathering took place at Anchi Cocha, where the woman lived.

When the *huacas* and *villcas* had taken their seats there, that woman addressed them:

"Behold, gentlemen and lords. Acknowledge this child. Who made me pregnant?"[5] One by one she asked them:

"Was it you?"

"Was it you?"

But nobody answered, "The child is mine."

The one called Cuni Raya Vira Cocha had taken his seat at the edge of the gathering. Since he looked like a friendless beggar, and since so many handsome men were present, she spurned him and didn't question him. She thought, "How could my baby possibly be the child of that beggar?"

Since no one had said, "The child is mine," she first warned the *huacas*, "If the baby is yours, it'll crawl up to you," and then addressed the child:

"Go, identify your father yourself!"

The child began at one end of the group and crawled along on all fours without climbing up on anyone, until reaching the other end, where its father sat.

On reaching him the baby instantly brightened up and climbed onto its father's knee.

When its mother saw this, she was indignant: "Atatay, what a disgrace! How could I have given birth to the child of a beggar?" she said. And taking only her child, she headed straight for the ocean.

---

5. *yumahuarcanquichic* "made me pregnant": The root is yumay "sperm." "The literal sense is "inseminated me."

Then, while all the local *huacas* stood in awe, Cuni Raya Vira Cocha put on his golden garment. He started to chase her at once, thinking, "She'll be overcome by sudden desire for me."

"Sister Caui Llaca!" he called after her. "Here, look at me! Now I'm really beautiful!" he said, and he stood making his garment glitter.[6]

Caui Llaca didn't even turn her face back to him.

"Because I've given birth to the child of such a ruffian, such a mangy beggar, I'll just disappear into the ocean," she said. She headed straight out into the deep sea near Pacha Camac, where even now two stones that clearly look like people stand.

And when she arrived at what is today her dwelling, she turned to stone.

Yet Cuni Raya Vira Cocha thought, "She'll see me anyway, she'll come to look at me!" He followed her at a distance, shouting and calling out to her.

First, he met a condor.

"Brother, where did you see that woman?" he asked him.

"Right near here. Soon you'll find her," replied the condor.

Cuni Raya Vira Cocha said to him,

"You'll live a long life. You alone will eat any dead animal from the wild mountain slopes, both guanacos and vicuñas, of any kind and in any number. And if anybody should kill you, he'll die himself."

Farther on, he met a skunk.

"Sister, where did you meet that woman?" he asked.

"You'll never find her now. She's gone far away," replied the skunk.

When she said this, he cursed her hatefully, saying,

"Because of what you've told me, you'll never go around in the daytime. You'll only walk at night, stinking disgustingly. People will be revolted by you."

Next he met a puma.

"She just passed this way. She's still nearby. You'll soon reach her," the puma told him.

Cuni Raya Vira Cocha spoke to him, saying,

"You'll be well beloved. You'll eat llamas, especially the llamas of people who bear guilt. Although people may kill you, they'll wear you on their heads during a great festival and set you to dancing. And then when they

---

6. If Cuni Raya is indeed a water deity, as Rostworowski (1977) persuasively argues, his glittering garment may be a metaphor for water sparkling in sunlight.

bring you out annually they'll sacrifice a llama first and then set you to dancing."

Then he met a fox.

"She's already gone way far away. You'll never find her now," that fox told him.

When the fox said this, he replied,

"As for you, even when you skulk around keeping your distance, people will thoroughly despise you and say, 'That fox is a sneak thief.' When they kill you, they'll carelessly throw you away and your skin, too."

Likewise he met a falcon.

"She's just passed this way. You'll soon find her," said the falcon.

He replied.

"You're greatly blessed. When you eat, you'll eat the hummingbird first, then all other birds. When people kill you, the man who has slain you will have you mourned with the sacrifice of a llama. And when they dance, they'll put you on their heads so you can sit there shining with beauty."

And then he met some parakeets.

"She's already gone far away. You'll never find her now," the parakeets told him.

"As for you, you'll travel around shrieking raucously," replied Cuni Raya Vira Cocha. "Although you may say, 'I'll spoil your crops!' when people hear your screaming they'll chase you away at once. You'll live in great misery amidst the hatred of humans."

And so he traveled on. Whenever he met anyone who gave him good news, he conferred on him good fortune. But he went along viciously cursing those who gave him bad news.

When he reached the seashore, he went straight over it. Today people say, "He was headed for Castile," but in the old days people said, "He went to another land, another world," and he turned back toward Pacha Camac.

He arrived at the place where Pacha Camac's two daughters lived, guarded by a snake.

Just before this, the two girls' mother had gone into the deep sea to visit Caui Llaca. Her name was Urpay Huachac.

While Urpay Huachac was away, Cuni Raya Vira Cocha seduced one girl, her older daughter.

When he sought to sleep with the other sister, she turned into a dove and darted away.

That's why her mother's name means 'Gives Birth to Doves.'

At that time there wasn't a single fish in the ocean.

Only Urpay Huachac used to breed them, at her home, in a small pond.

It was these fish, all of them, that Cuni Raya angrily scattered into the ocean, saying, "Why did she visit Caui Llaca, the woman of the ocean depths?"

Ever since, fish have filled the sea.

Then Cuni Raya Vira Cocha fled along the seashore.

When Urpay Huachac's daughters told her how he'd seduced them, she got furious and chased him.

As she followed him, calling him again and again, he waited for her and said, "Yes?"

"Cuni, I'm just going to remove your lice," she said, and she picked them off.

While she picked his lice, she caused a huge abyss.

Chapter 4

HOW THE SUN DISAPPEARED FOR FIVE DAYS. IN WHAT FOLLOWS WE SHALL TELL A STORY ABOUT THE DEATH OF THE SUN

In ancient times the sun died.[7]

Because of his death it was night for five days.

Rocks banged against each other.

Mortars and grinding stones began to eat people.

Buck llamas started to drive men.

Here's what we Christians think about it: We think these stories tell of the darkness following the death of our Lord Jesus Christ.

Maybe that's what it was.

Afterward, man began to multiply once more.

That's the reason there are people until today.

Regarding this story, we Christians believe it refers to the time of the Flood.

But they believe it was Villca Coto mountain that saved them.

---

7. Like various New World mythologies, Andean myths both ancient and modern include a motif of successive deaths and replacements of suns. Juan Ossio believes this chapter and Guaman Poma's scheme of "ages" are related to Montesinos's mid-seventeenth-century account of an Andean myth about successive suns equated to millennia (Ossio 1973: 188). Many modern Andeans interpret precolumbian structures as the houses of people who lived before the current sun arose.

Chapter 5

HOW IN ANCIENT TIMES PARIA CACA APPEARED ON A MOUNTAIN NAMED CONDOR COTO IN THE FORM OF FIVE EGGS, AND WHAT FOLLOWED. HERE WILL BEGIN THE ACCOUNT OF PARIA CACA'S EMERGENCE

In preceding chapters we have recounted the lives lived in ancient times.

Nevertheless, we don't know the origins of the people of those days.

These people, who lived in that era, spent their lives warring and conquering each other. For their leaders, they recognized only the strong and the rich.

We speak of them as the Purum Runa, 'people of desolation.'

It was at this time that the one called Paria Caca was born in the form of five eggs on Condor Coto mountain.

A certain man, and a poor friendless one at that, was the first to see and know the fact of his birth; he called Huatya Curi, but was also known as Paria Caca's son.

Now we'll speak of his discovery, and of the many wonders he performed.

They say that fellow called Huatya Curi subsisted by baking potatoes in earth pits, eating the way a poor man does, and people named him the "Baked Potato Gleaner."

At that time there was another man named Tamta Ñamca, a very rich and powerful lord.

Both his own house and all his other houses looked like *cassa* and *cancho* feather-weavings, for they were thatched with wings of birds. His llamas were yellow llamas, red and blue llamas; he owned llamas of every hue.

Seeing that this man lived so well, people who came from all the villages paid him homage and worshiped him.

For his part, he pretended to be very wise and spent his life deceiving a lot of people with the little he really knew.

Then this man called Tamta Ñamca, who pretended to be so wise, even to be a god, contracted a really horrible disease.

His illness went on for a great many years, and in time people talked. "How can a man who knows so much, who's so powerful, be so sick?" they said.

Just like the Spaniards who, on such occasions, summon experts and doctors, Tamta Ñamca, hoping to recover, summoned all sorts of shamans and wise men.

But no one could diagnose his disease.

Just then Huatya Curi was coming from the vicinity of Ura Cocha, and he went to sleep on the mountain by which we descend to Sieneguella.

While he was sleeping, a fox who'd come from down below and one who'd come from up above met face to face there. One fox asked the other, "Brother, how are things in Upper Villca?"

"What's good is good. But a lord in Anchi Cocha, a *villca* as a matter of fact, one who claims to know a lot, to be a god himself, is terribly ill. All the wise men who found their way to him are wondering, 'Why's he so ill?' No one can identify his sickness. But his disease is this: while his wife was toasting maize, a grain of muro maize popped from the griddle and got into her private part.

"She picked it out and served it to a man to eat. Because of having served it, she became a sinner in relation to the man who ate it." (Nowadays they reckon that act tantamount to being an adulteress.)

"As a result of this fault," he told the fox who'd come from down below, "a snake has made its dwelling on top of that magnificent house and is eating them up. What's more, a toad, a two-headed one, lives under their grinding stone. And nobody is aware of these devouring animals."

Then he asked, "And how are people doing in Lower Villca, brother?"

The other fox answered similarly, saying, "There's a woman, the offspring of a great lord and a *villca,* who almost died because of a penis."

As the foxes were telling each other these tidings, the man called Huatya Curi heard that the great lord who pretended to be a god was ill.

This great man had two daughters.

He had joined the elder daughter to a fellow *ayllu* member who was very rich. [He married her.]

The poor man called Huatya Curi came to that lord while he was still ill.

When he arrived, he went around asking surreptitiously, "Isn't someone sick in this town?"

"It's my father who's sick," replied the younger daughter.

Huatya Curi answered, "Let's get together. For your sake I'll cure your father."

The young woman didn't agree right away.

She told her father, "Father, there's a poor man here. He came and said to me, 'I'll cure your father.'"

All the wise men who were sitting there burst into laughter when they heard these words, and said, "If we ourselves can't cure him, how can this nobody make him well?"

But that lord wanted a cure so badly that he called for Huatya Curi. "Let him come, never mind what sort of man he is," he said.

When the great lord summoned him, Huatya Curi entered and said, "Father, if you want to get well, I'll make you well. But you have to give me your daughter."

Overjoyed, Tamta Ñamca replied, "Very well then!"

But when his older daughter's husband heard this proposition he flew into a rage. "How dare he join her, the sister-in-law of such a powerful man as me, to a nobody like that?"

Huatya Curi began his cure by saying, "Father, your wife is an adulteress. Because she's an adulteress, a sinner, she's made you ill. As for what's eating you, it's the two snakes that dwell on top of this magnificent house of yours. And there's a toad, too, a two-headed one, that lives under your grinding stone.

"Now we'll kill them all. Then you'll get well. After you recover, you must worship my father above all things. He'll be born tomorrow or the day after. And as for you, you're not such a powerful man. If you were really powerful, you wouldn't be sick."

The rich man was astonished when Huatya Curi said this.

And when Huatya Curi said, "Now I'll take apart this gorgeous house of his," he became distraught.

And his wife started yelling, "This nobody, this crook, is slandering me! I'm no adulteress!"

Nonetheless the sick man wanted his health back very badly, and he let his house be dismantled.

Then Huatya Curi removed the two snakes and killed them. Next he clearly explained the facts to the rich man's wife: just how a grain of muro maize had popped out and gotten in her private part, and how she, after picking it out, had served it to a man.

After that, the woman confessed everything. "It's all true," she said.

Next he had the grinding stone lifted.

A toad, a two-headed one, came out from under it and fled to Anchi Cocha ravine.

It exists in a spring there to this day.

When people come to that spring, it either makes them disappear or else drives them crazy.

Once Huatya Curi finished all these deeds, the ailing man got well.

After Tamta Ñamca's recovery, on the day that had been foretold, Huatya Curi went for the first time to Condor Coto mountain.

It was there that the one called Paria Caca dwelled in the form of five eggs.

All around him a wind rose up and began to blow.

In earlier times no wind had been observed.

Just before he went there on the appointed day, the man who'd recovered his health gave him his unmarried daughter.

While the two of them were traveling in the vicinity of that mountain they sinned together.[8]

As soon as that elder brother-in-law heard they'd sinned together he set out to compete against Huatya Curi.

"I'll bring deep shame on that beggarman," he muttered.

And so one day that man challenged him, saying, "Brother, let's have it out in a contest, whatever kind. How dare a nobody like you marry the sister-in-law of a powerful man like me?"

That poor man agreed, and went to inform his father Paria Caca.

"Very well then. Whatever he tells you, come to me right away," his father replied.

The contest between them was like this.

One day the challenger said, "Let's have a drinking and dancing contest."

So that poor man Huatya Curi went to inform his father.

His father Paria Caca advised him, "Go to that mountain over there. There you'll pretend to be a guanaco and lie down as if dead. Early in the morning a fox with his skunk wife will come there to see me."

"They'll bring their maize beer in a small long-necked jar and they'll also bring along their drum. When they spot you, a dead guanaco, they'll set their things on the ground, and as soon as the fox puts down his pan-pipes, they'll start to eat you. Then turn back into a man, scream so loud it hurts their ears, and run away. When they scamper off forgetting their possessions, you'll take them and go to the contest."

The poor man did as he was told.

The rich man was the first to dance in the contest.

His wives, who numbered almost two hundred, danced along with him, and after they were done the poor man entered by himself, with only his wife, just the two of them.

As they entered through the doorway, as they danced to the skunk's drum he'd brought along, the earth of that whole region quaked.

With this, he beat them all.

Next, they began drinking.

Huatya Curi went with just his wife to sit at the head of the group, exactly as guests do until today.

And all of those people who were sitting there served him drink after drink without giving him a break.

Even though he drank every bit of it he sat there with no problem.

---

8. *hochallicorcan* "they sinned together": *hochalliy*, like *pincay* "private part" (literally, "shame"), is a shame-oriented term of Quechua lexicon and Christian mentality. The verb root employed seems to have meant a ceremonial debt or obligation (it is still used in this sense), but Christian missionaries chose it as the translation for "sin."

Then it was his turn. He began to serve the maize beer he'd brought in that little long-necked jar, and everybody ridiculed him. "How could he possibly fill so many people from such a tiny jar?" they said.

But when he began to serve, starting from the head of the gathering, they dropped down drunk in no time, one after another.

The next day, since Huatya Curi had won, the other man wanted a different contest.

This contest was all about outdoing each other in splendid costumes decorated with the exquisite feather-weavings called *cassa* and *cancho*.

So Huatya Curi again went to his father.

His father gave him a snow garment.

In that garment he dazzled all the people's eyes and won the contest.

Then the challenger said, "Let's compete in putting on puma skins."

That man wanted to win by wearing the puma skins he had.

The poor man, following his father's advice, went to a spring early in the morning and brought back a red puma skin.

He danced. And while he was dancing in that red puma, a rainbow appeared in the sky, like the rainbow that appears in the sky today.

Next the rich man wanted to compete at house-building.

Since that man had access to many people, he almost finished a large house in a single day.

The poor man just laid down the foundations and then strolled around all day long with his wife.

That night all kinds of birds, snakes, and other animals of the land walled the house.

The next day, seeing it already finished, the challenger was awestruck.

Likewise Huatya Curi won at roofing the house. All the guanacos and vicuñas brought his thatching straw.

As for the other man, while his materials were being transported on llamas, Huatya Curi availed himself of a bobcat's help. He lay in ambush for them by a cliff, stampeded them, and destroyed them by making them fall over it.

By this trick he won again.

After winning all these contests, the poor man spoke just as his father had advised: "Brother, we've competed so many times now, always agreeing to your rules. Now you agree to my rules."

"Very well then," the rich man agreed.

Huatya Curi said, "Now, with blue tunics! And let our breechclouts be of white cotton! That's how we'll dance!"

"Very well then," the rich man agreed.

The rich man, since he'd danced first from the beginning, went ahead and danced first.

As he was dancing, Huatya Curi charged down on him from outside screaming. That man panicked, turned into a brocket deer, and ran away.

And his wife followed him, saying, "I'll die with my own old man!"

Then that poor man flew into a rage: "Go, idiot! You two have victimized me so much, I'll kill you!" he said, and he chased after them.

Chasing them, he caught the wife on the road to Anchi Cocha and stood her upside down on her head. "People coming from up above and those coming from down below will gape at your private parts as they pass by," he said.

And right then and there she turned to stone instantly.

This stone, just like a woman's legs with thighs and a vagina, stands there until today.

Even now people put coca on top of it when they undertake something.

But the man who'd turned into a brocket deer climbed up a mountain and disappeared.

(Now, in ancient times, brocket deer used to eat human beings.

Later on, when brocket deer were very numerous, they danced, ritually chanting, "How shall we eat people?"

Then one of their little fawns made a mistake and said, "How shall people eat us?"

When the brocket deer heard this they scattered.

From then on brocket deer became food for humans.)

After Huatya Curi finished all these deeds, Paria Caca flew forth from the five eggs in the shape of five falcons.

These five falcons turned into humans and they began to roam around.

And at that time, hearing all about the things people had done, about how that man called Tamta Ñamca had said, "I am a god," and about how the man had himself worshiped, Paria Caca went into a rage over all these sins of theirs. Rising up as rain, he flushed them all away to the ocean, together with all their houses and their llamas, sparing not a single one.

At that time, too, there was something called the Pullao, which bridged like an arch Llantapa mountain[9] and another mountain called Vichoca.[10]

That thing called the Pullao was a gigantic tree.

Monkeys, toucans, and birds of all colors used to live on it.

These animals, too, all of their kind, he swept to the sea.

After he finished these feats, Paria Caca ascended to the place that's known today as Upper Paria Caca.

---

9. Llantapa mountain today is 14 km southwest of Llacsa Tambo (if the latter is modern Llaquistambo) (IGM 1970–1971).

10. Modern Guichuca peak, 4,000 m above sea level, 14 km southwest of Llantapa.

■ Zithuwa Hymns (1575?) *Peru*

The Zithuwa Hymns to the gods and divine powers were performed in Cuzco as part of the Inca "cleansing" ritual. Urban and hierarchic, they recall the Twenty Sacred Hymns in Nahuatl performed at the Aztec capital in Tenochtitlán. There is an important difference here, however: all events are subject to the overarching power of the patriarchal deity Viracocha, the herder who protects his flock, his llama-people. In the Americas, this pastoral scheme, like the economy that underpinned it, was in fact particular to the Andes.

Harvest

Viracocha, ancient Viracocha,
skilled creator,
who makes and establishes:
Below on earth
may they eat,   5
may they drink,
you say.
For those you set in place,
those you made,
may food be plentiful.   10
May there be
potatoes, maize,
all kinds of food,
you say, who command and increase.
They shall not suffer,   15
and not suffering, do your will.
May there be no frost, no hail.
Keep them in peace.

TRANSLATED BY J. H. ROWE

Sister Rain

Fair princess,
your brother has broken your jar.
That is why
it thunders and lightens.

So princess,   5
you give us falling rain
or hail and snow.

Viracocha,
earth-establisher, earth maker,
for this duty   *10*
has established and made you.

TRANSLATED BY GORDON BROTHERSTON, AFTER TRANSLATION BY
GARCILASO DE LA VEGA INCA

■ Afu Ollantay (1770) *Peru* (song)

TRANSLATED BY MARK STRAND

Known in several late-eighteenth-century copies, *Afu Ollantay* deals
with the unsuccessful rebellion of Ollantay, a prince from the District
(Suyu) of Anti, against the authority of the Inca in Cuzco. It is also the story
of Ollantay's love for an Inca princess, thwarted by the edict that the royal
family may marry only among themselves. In celebrating Inca power and
statesmanship, the play belongs to the cycle of Inca kingship drama that
lives on still in parts of the Andes and which, at the time of Tupac Amaru's
rising against the Spanish (1780), was fiercely suppressed. This extract is a
song of the type that was sung in the fields to scare birds away from the
crops and was then adapted to the taste of the Cuzco court—and of numerous writers since (it appears, for example, in Peter Shaffer's *The Royal
Hunt of the Sun*). It is a small play within a play that warns Ollantay away
from the princess.

Song

Stop, don't eat now,
my little dove,
on the princess's land,
my little dove.
Don't try to eat,   *5*
my little dove,
the tempting corn,
my little dove.
The kernels are white,
my little dove,   *10*
the ears are still thin,
my little dove.
You won't be nourished,
my little dove,

the leaves are still tender,   *15*
my little dove.
Gluttons get caught,
my little dove,
and so will you,
my little dove.   *20*
I'm picking a quarrel,
my little dove,
for your own good,
my little dove.
Look at the quail,   *25*
my little dove,
there he hangs,
my little dove.
Ask your heart,
my little dove,   *30*
consult your feathers,
my little dove.
He was destroyed,
my little dove,
for pecking grain,   *35*
my little dove.
And that's what happens,
my little dove,
to careless birds,
my little dove.   *40*

■ Folk Songs and Poems (Sixteenth to Twentieth Centuries) *Peru, Bolivia, Ecuador*

In communal life throughout Bolivia, Peru, and Ecuador, Quechua continues to be the medium of songs, a point aptly illustrated at the start of this century in *Tarmpa Pacha Huaray* (1905), edited in Peru by dissident Quechuans, proud of their language and its literary tradition. Their effort was followed by the D'Harcourts' monumental study of Inca music (1925) and by the major anthologies of Basadre (1938), Arguedas (1938, 1949), Lara (1947), and others. Many of the pieces in these collections are in pre-Hispanic modes—that directly recall antecedents recorded in the sixteenth century by Guaman Poma, Garcilaso El Inca, and other historians. Found in Guaman Poma, "War Song," for example, is still sung today; the knotted rope in "Pastoral" is the Inca quipu; and the strength invoked in "A Woman Goes to the Fields" is that of the ancient demon-spirit zupay.

Like a Feather in the Air

My mother gave me my being,
    Ay!
In the middle of a rain cloud,
    Ay!
So that I would weep like rain,   5
    Ay!
So that I would go round like a cloud,
    Ay!
Wandering from door to door
    Ay!   10
Like a feather in the air,
    Ay!

TRANSLATED BY W. S. MERWIN (ARAWI)

I Have Lost My Dove

I have lost my dove.
Wandering, I call to her in a loud voice.
Everyone who finds me says,
"Why did you love her?"
    Where have you flown?   5
Who have you left here to console me?
Like a dove whose wings have been cut off
I will die walking back and forth.
    Come back, dove whom I cherished.
How long must I wait for you?   10
In the nest, where we should be,
Now the birds of night raise their moans.

TRANSLATED BY W. S. MERWIN (ARAWI)

Where Are You

Where are you where are you going
they say
and we still have to go on

sun and moon go past
    and go past   5
    six months to get from Cuzco to Quito
at the foot of Tayo we'll rest

fear nothing
lord Inca fear nothing
we're going with you we'll get there together   10

TRANSLATED BY W. S. MERWIN (INCA) (1979; AFTER BASADRE 1938)

War Song

We shall drink from the traitor's skull,
we shall wear his teeth as a necklace,
of his bones we shall make flutes,
of his skin we shall make a drum;
later, we'll dance.   5

TRANSLATED BY MARK STRAND (CUZCO)

To This Song

To this song
you will sleep.
At midnight
I shall come.

TRANSLATED BY MARK STRAND

Song

Prince

Because you're a star
          yes
you shine at night
          yes
under the sun's fire   5
          yes
I'll never see you
          yes

Princess

If I'm a star
          no   10
open your heart
          no
and under the sun's fire
          no

half-close your eyes   *15*
    no

Prince
You seem to call
    yes
only in moonlight
    yes   *20*
and when I come near
    yes
you change into snow
    yes

Princess
If I seem to call   *25*
    no
please come quickly
    no
if I change into snow
    no   *30*
toss me your fire
    no

Prince
When my fire burns you
    yes
you change into dew   *35*
    yes
are you the wind
    yes
or are you a dream
    yes   *40*

Princess
If you think I am dew
    no
bring your lips near
    no
though I may be a dream   *45*
    no
don't ever lose me
    no

TRANSLATED BY MARK STRAND

I Am Raising a Fly

I am raising a fly
with wings of gold,
I am raising a fly
with burning eyes.

It brings death   5
in its eyes of fire,
brings death
in its hair of gold,
in its beautiful wings.

I am raising it   10
in a green bottle;
nobody knows
if it drinks,
nobody knows
if it eats.   15

It wanders at night
like a star,
and wounds to death
with its glowing red,
with its eyes of fire.   20

In its eyes of fire
it brings love,
its blood
shines in the night,
the love it brings   25
in its heart.

Insect of night,
fly of death,
loving it so,
I am raising it   30
in a green bottle.

And that is all,
that is all.
Nobody knows
if I give it   35
something to drink,
if I give it
something to eat.

TRANSLATED BY MARK STRAND

Doesn't your heart hurt

doesn't your heart hurt
don't you want to cry
you, my precious flower
you, my queen,
you, my princess   5
see how justice takes me off in spate
and imprisons me
when I glimpse your mantle
when I see your dress
the day does not exist for me   10
in this night I awake to know
it will never dawn;
I think that you,
my queen, my señora,
don't remember me   15
I'm eaten up
by the puma and the fox of the zancay
I'm alone,
disheartened and lost, my lady.

TRANSLATED BY GORDON BROTHERSTON (AFTER BASADRE,
FROM *GUAMAN POMA*)

Poems for a Carnival

1

That's the big
boss's house
shining with the money
studded in it
rolls of bank notes   5
papered on it
his cows even
shit gold

2

The carnival was
a sad old man it was
under the bridge
sniffing around he was

I saw him with his
such'i fish moustache
in his bag
two eggs there were
I tried to grab them
but hollow they were

5

10

3

The politicians from the valley
have no mouths
being without mouths
they peck with their nails

TRANSLATED BY GORDON BROTHERSTON (AFTER LARA)

■ Folk Tales (Twentieth Century) *Peru*

Like songs, tales continue to be told in Quechua throughout the former Tahuantinsuyu, many of them strongly reminiscent of those told in classic texts like the Huarochiri Manuscript. Basadre (1938) and Arguedas (1949) are prominent among their collectors.

Ichi the Dwarf

TRANSLATED BY W. S. MERWIN

In Qjelle Huanca the earth opened and a dwarf popped out. He was naked and his hair was bright red like a fire. He sat down on a stone, and for the fun of it he brandished his lighted hair. His little lively eyes, like small coals, stared at the landscape in wonder, and because it was cold he began to cry like a suckling pig.

Then that little dwarf began to leap around among the rocks and crags and his scarlet hair caught in the thick leaves and fig branches and tangled him. At midnight he beat his belly like a drum and the raw sound rebounded from hill to hill. In the quiet afternoons he blew on his pipe and the flute warbled and trilled, but what he liked best of all was to frighten the men working in the fields. Whenever he found them gathering wood he would growl, he would give a low growl.

He sang, too, under the ground, and his songs went up into the air in the same way that the water of the marshes turns into clouds. When dawn rose into the heavens the far away songs of the little dwarf Ichi woke the children, and the calves lowed sweetly.

Carib Languages

In its several varieties, Cariban speech belongs to the sea named for it—the Caribbean—where it is all but extinct, and to northern South America, where is it still strong, especially in the Guyana highlands that stand between the Orinoco and Amazon river systems. Found in the uppermost reaches of the Orinoco in southern Venezuela is Makiritare or Yekuana Carib, which names itself *Soto* ("the people"). Through contacts made over the last half century or so, this Soto tradition has provided texts that superbly exemplify rainforest teaching about the creation of the world and human perception. Chief among them are *Watunna,* a cosmogony and history, and its companion piece *Medatia.*

■ Watunna: An Orinoco Creation Cycle (1950) *Venezuela* (oral creation myth)

TRANSLATED BY DAVID M. GUSS

Only recently published in translation, *Watunna* stands as one of the great cosmogonies of the rainforest, indeed of the Fourth World as a whole, and readily bears comparison with the *Popol Vuh* in the scope and the subtlety of its construction. It takes us from the beginnings of time, the ages of great floods and repeated metamorphosis, up to the invasion of the rainforest that is occurring today. The flight of the watersnake Huiio reveals the origins of the "plumed serpent" motif integral to American accounts of evolution; and, at the first harvest, it confirms the summit of human achievement to have been agriculture, focused in this case on manioc, the staple crop in the conuco or field-garden of the tropical forest.

The *Watunna* is a sacred oral tradition that unites a Cariban-speaking tribe called Makiritare, who live along the rivers in the Guayana highlands of southern Venezuela. This Venzuelan creation cycle, transcribed by Marc de Civrieux, is an account of the earth's genesis, with all the imagination, symbolism, and moral authority of the world's great creation and fertility myths. However, it is not the tale of magnificent gods who are uniquely chosen and powerful and rule the entire earth. Rather, it is the moving story of the miracle creation work of poor Native American gods in an impoverished isolated basin area of the Orinoco River. The birds, like angel instructors, come to a dry earth, bring knowledge and hope, and at the same time establish social proprieties for living the good life in a region that they cause to be generated with abundant trees, fruit, and crops. After the miracles of huge mountains, enormous yucca trees, and great new rivers, there appears the outlaw Jaguar, who robs food and stores his loot in a cave for his private use. Jaguar must be punished so that the people can live with food and in peace. Jaguar, who robs, is not forgiven, unlike the young demigod Kuchi, who originally stole fruit and the seed of trees to bring them to earth for the benefit of humanity. The humble, skinned-alive Kuchi, a Promethean and Eve-like figure, will have his body restored to its former condition and be forgiven—unlike Prometheus, who suffers eternal physical dismemberment for bringing fire to the earth, and Eve, who forever bears the sin of offending Heaven for having brought knowledge to humanity.

FURTHER READING: *Watunna: An Orinoco Creation Cycle.* Translated and edited by David M. Guss (1950), transcribed by Marc de Civrieux.

Kuchi, Who Brought Trees and Fruit to the Dirt Earth

Those old people were very poor now. They had no food. There weren't any trees on the Earth. They had no *conucos*. They ate dirt and nothing else. They sent their children out to gather it in *tudi*. They just ate dirt. There was no water.

It had been different in the beginning. Iamankave, the Yuca Mistress, the food keeper, she lived in the highest part of the Sky. She always sent a *damodede* with armfuls of cassava for them.

"Where do you come from?" they would ask.

"From far away," he'd say. And he gave them the cassava and left.

Iyako, the veinticuatro ant, used to come down to Earth all the time. He brought them water. "Where do you come from?" they would ask. He didn't answer. He just gave them the water and went on his way.

Then Odosha came. When he came, he ruined everything. He brought evil and sickness. Now that cassava man didn't come back anymore. Neither did that ant with the water. Hunger and thirst came.

One day, a man said: "I know the ant's road. I'm going to find water again."

That man was named Dariche. He turned into a swift. He flew off. He grew smaller and smaller in the clouds. He disappeared. Then he came back with the water. They say that he went to Akuenaña in the highest Sky, that he stole the water from Lake Akuena.

He brought it to the Kashishare (Casiquiare). He made a great pool there. They call it the Old Water. There was no water on the Earth before that. The Orinoco and the Ventuari didn't exist yet. There weren't any rivers.

Now there was just that water by the Casiquiare far away from here. It didn't run. It was all in one place, still. Dariche brought the Old Water. The old people went off to look for it. They walked and walked. When they got there they were tired. They didn't find anything but a smelly old pond.

Then another man said: "I know the cassava road. I'll go look for it again."

His name was Kuchi. Now we'll tell the story of that man.

"I know," he said. "I know the way."

He knew it. He was wise. "Once I dreamed I went to Iamankave's house in Heaven." That's what he said.

That man turned into Kuchi, the kinkajou. Then he went to Heaven. He left his body on Earth for the kinkajous of today. He was the first one, the grandfather of them all. Now that man went up to the Sky, climbing and climbing. He grew very small. You couldn't see him at all anymore. He arrived at Iamankave's house at the top of Heaven. He saw a huge *kanawa* full of *mañoco* hanging in the doorway. Near the house, in the garden, he saw the giant food tree surrounded by a fence. It was Iamankave's garden. Now he hid so Iamankave wouldn't see him.

A boy named Wedama came out of the house. He was Iamankave's son, Kuchi's friend.

Kuchi called him. "I came to find food," he said.

"You're here. Okay. Let's hide. Come with me." That's what the boy said.

He turned into a swallow. He flew over the fence, up to the top of the branches. Kuchi turned into a kinkajou. He jumped over the fence. He climbed up the trunk. They flew, they climbed up to the fruit. There was every kind of fruit up on that tree. It was the Yuca Mother. Each branch was different and filled with another kind of food.

As they ate, they shook up the wasps. They had their nest there. They guarded the tree. They were flying around now, screaming: "Someone's here! Someone's stealing the food!"

Now the Yuca Mistress knew. She came running out to see what was happening.

She came up there. The swallow hid. Kuchi ran. As he ran, he hid a little piece of that tree beneath his nail. He went on running. He couldn't get away. The Yuca Mistress caught him. She skinned him. Then she hung him on the fence without a skin.

"I'm going to die," Kuchi thought. He had a powerful, wise sister. She lived in the Sky Place. He called and called, asking her for help. The sister came. Her name is Iumakawa.

When she came, she said to him: "You stole the food. That's why you're hanging here without any skin. You got what you deserved."

"We're hungry on Earth. That's why I stole it," he said. "Help me. I'm going to die here without any skin."

His sister helped him. She asked the Yuca Mistress to forgive him.

"He was hungry," she said. "He came from the Earth. There's no food there. He's my brother. That's why I'm asking you."

First the Mistress said: "He robbed the food. His punishment is fair." Then she said: "Okay. I'll forgive him." And she gave Iumakawa Kuchi's skin back. She healed her brother. She made him like new again. Now he jumped up. He ran. He went back down to Earth. He had a splinter of the tree hidden beneath his nail.

When he returned, he was like a man again. He sat down on his shaman's bench, without speaking, without doing anything, just thinking and nothing else. He waited until night. When night came, he pulled the splinter out from under his nail and planted it.

That was far away in Dodoima (Mount Roraima). During the night, the yuca began to sprout. You couldn't see it. When dawn came, there was a tall, tall tree with many branches and all sorts of fruit. "It's done," said Kuchi. He ate. He was happy when the dawn came. That was the beginning of our food, the Dodoima tree, when the people were hungry.

Dodoima was the first tree. Now we see it as a very tall mountain. Many wild fruits still grow there. No one plants them. They just grow as reminders.

Kamaso heard about it. That man lived in Kamaso wochi (Kamaso's Savanna). "Good," he said. "Kuchi has planted food in Dodoima. That's too far away. The people there can eat now. We don't have anything to eat but dirt. All we have are stories."

Kamaso sent a messenger to Roraima. She was a woman named Edenawadi. She walked for days and came to the East. She spoke with Kuchi. She asked for a yuca shoot to plant here. "Okay," said Kuchi. He gave her the shoot.

Then Edenawadi headed back toward the sunset. On her way, night fell. The night found her in a place called Uaiante (Auyan Tepui). When she arrived there, Edenawadi sat down. She planted the shoot. She dreamed of yuca, food, different fruits. When the sun came up, there was a shoot, just one little shoot. Three little green yuca leaves and nothing else. It didn't grow like a tree. It didn't have different fruits. That soil was no good.

Edenawadi picked up her shoot. She started walking toward the sunset again. When night came, she planted the yuca, in Kuntinama. Nothing. The next night in Metakuni. Nothing. The next night in Arahame. Nothing. Now she came to her house in Kamaso wochi. She gave the shoot to Kamaso. Many people came to see. They were shouting with joy: "Our food's arrived!" Kamaso planted it during the night. He sang and sang. When the sun came up, there was just one shoot. There wasn't any fruit. "This soil's no good," he said. They all went away, sad, like before, looking for dirt to eat.

There was Madunawe. She was a woman too. She lived in Wade's house in Truma achaka. She was kin to Wade.

When the news came, Wade shook with joy: "Kuchi, yuca, Dodoima, Kamaso, Edenawadi!" When the news came, he called the woman named Madunawe.

"We have good soil here," he said. "Let's ask for the shoot."

"Good," answered Madunawe. "We'll plant it."

It was nighttime when the woman planted the shoot in the black soil. All the fruits, palms, trees, vines, every green thing there is on the Earth today, was born in one night, when that woman planted the yuca.

When day came, the tree was tallllllll. They called it Marahuaka. The branches, the leaves, the fruits of Marahuaka covered the entire Earth. It was like a roof. Each branch was budding and sprouting and bearing fruit, turning into another and another and another, and every one with a different food. It was all the yuca. All the plants, all the fruits we know today began there. It was just one tree with many branches. It wouldn't stop sprouting. Every time it was something different.

The people came to look at Marahuaka. When they came, they were hungry. They were sick and thin. Now they shouted: "Marahuaka! Our food has come!"

Some were laughing. Others wept as the tree went on sprouting. There wasn't anything else. There was no food, no water, nothing on the Earth. That's what the old ones say. I didn't see it.

First they were happy, then sad. With empty stomachs, they opened up their arms, their mouths, their eyes. They just looked at the fruit. It was up there in the sky. "What'll we do now? How can we get it?" asked one after another with their arms and mouths and eyes open. They were really sad as they stood there and looked.

Now a branch full of *cucurito* came crashing down.

"Ahhhhhhh!" they shouted. "Here comes our food."

When the branch fell, it killed someone. It fell on the head of a boy, Wade's son.

Now a branch full of *pijiguao* fell.

"Ahhhh!" they shouted. "Our food!"

When it fell, it landed right on the nose of Odoma, the paca. He ran off screaming and yelling. He had his face crushed. The pacas are still that way today, with flat faces. That's the reason why. You can see them.

Then another branch fell, and another and another. They were falling all over. The people got crushed, killed.

They just ran, terrified. They didn't know where to go. The whole Earth was covered. Wherever they went, fruit was falling, crushing them.

That's what they say.

Semenia, the Bird Who Showed How to Plant

Wanadi was still living here on Earth, in Wade's house. They gathered around him, weeping, asking for help.

Wanadi said: "Okay. Now I'll make new people. I'll make birds to help you. They'll have wings to fly up to the branches. They'll get the fruit."

At that time there were no birds. That was in the beginning.

Wanadi stuck a few rows of sticks in the earth and looked at them. He sat down in front of them, smoking. He played his maraca. He sang. He thought.

That's the way he made his new people for the harvest, his new people called birds. When they wanted to, they turned into birds and flew. Then they changed back into people like us again.

Now the birds made ladders out of vines. Some went climbing up them like people. They climbed up the vines. Others flew up to the branches like birds. Now they started gathering the fruit. The old people watched them from the ground. They wove *tudi*. The birds began to come. They were carrying the fruit. It was heavy. It started to slip and fall. It killed people like before.

"That's no good," said one of the birds. "We'll plant. We'll cultivate the earth. We can help. We're strong, us birds. Let's stop this gathering and cut down the tree. Then we'll plant in the earth."

That was the chief of the birds. His name is Semenia. He was wise. He showed us how to plant. They cut the trees down. That's how they make *conucos*. That's how they plant. The old people didn't know that. They only knew how to gather wild fruit, like monkeys. When Semenia came, he showed them how to cut down trees to make *conucos*. When they cut down the Marahuaka tree, they fed the earth. Semenia showed them how to work to get their food.

There were two who didn't want to obey. They didn't want to work. They were called Mado, the jaguar, and Wachedi, the tapir.

"Who's that giving orders now?" they asked. "Everyone's obeying. Well, we don't want to work or obey. When we're hungry, we just find our food and eat it, that's all. We're not going to have anything to do with those people."

They went looking for fallen fruit. They ate. They gorged themselves. What was left they were going to hide. They thought: "We two are the biggest ones on Earth. The others are so small. Semenia is tiny. How can we obey him? How can we share?"

They hid the food in caves. They went back to get more. They weren't thinking of the others. They were their own chiefs. They worked alone. They didn't want to share because they were so hungry. They didn't listen to Semenia when he said: "First we work together; then we celebrate. We'll divide the food later."

In the old days Semenia was our chief. They said: "Why's he chief?"

The people watched them. Semenia watched them. "That's no good," he said. "Those two are hiding food. They don't want to live with us. They've forgotten we're here. They're making fun of us. Now we'll punish them."

Then he called for them. At first they didn't want to come. Then everyone circled around them, staring at them. They were afraid. Then they went to see Semenia.

"You're working?" he asked.

"Oh, yeh. We're working," they answered.

"Good. That's why I called. We all work together. Now we're thirsty. There's no water here. You're going to go to the Casiquiare to get water for us."

"Okay," they said. They were scared now. The others were watching them.

Semenia gave them a strainer to carry the water in. It was a trick. You can't carry water in a strainer. They were both idiots. They didn't catch on.

"Okay," they said. They went walking and walking, far off there on the Casiquiare trail to get water with a strainer.

Semenia wanted hunger and misery to stop. That's why he came with his new people, with the birds. Wanadi made them. The people were living in hunger and misery because of Odosha. They were listening to Odosha. They weren't together. There was no order, no justice. They were all selfish. They had no chiefs. Each one just found his own dirt and ate it. They didn't worry about anyone else. They never thought about the others.

Semenia made himself chief to teach us. He showed us how to work. He punished the ones that didn't want to live like people, like brothers. He brought food, rain, fertility and obedience for everyone. He showed them what to do. Now we have food again. We're happy despite Odosha. Semenia was Wanadi's messenger, our first chief in the beginning.

When Jaguar and Tapir left, Semenia said: "Now we'll cut it down."

Four toucans came up. They were like people in the beginning. They brought some good axes to cut down Marahuaka. They hit the trunk. Their axes bounced off. The tree was thick. The wood was hard. The tree wouldn't go down. The axes couldn't cut it. Now they turned into birds, toucans with long, hard beaks. They were their axes now. They tried to peck the tree down. Nothing. They couldn't do it. The first toucan broke the edge of his beak. That's the way the toucans are now, with beaks like saws. Then another toucan came up, and another and another. Nothing. Then the woodpeckers came. Wanadi came up to peck like Wanadi tonoro. Semenia came as a Semenia bird. Waraihai and Sumunuadi came too. They went at the tree with their beaks. They cut all day. At night, they rested. They slept. When the sun rose, they got up. The tree was intact again as if nothing had happened.

"What are we going to do?" they asked. "We can't go to sleep. Our cuts just close up. We're just wasting our time. We'll never finish."

Semenia said: "We won't cut this way anymore, all at the same time. We'll take turns now. One will cut and the others will rest."

So that's what they did. There was always one cutting, day and night. The cut didn't close. They kept on cutting deeper and deeper, first one, then the other. They just kept on cutting. They slept too, first one, then the other. They didn't get tired. Peck . . . peck . . . peck . . . peck. They pecked like that for days.

Now one of them came up. He gave the last blow. It was Wanadi. He was happy. "It's done!" he shouted.

It really was done. It was completely cut.

They all turned to look. They were frightened. "It's going to fall now. Which way is it going to fall? Which way should we run?"

Marahuaka didn't fall. It just stood there, hanging from the Sky in silence. It was just there. It wouldn't budge.

They all stood there looking.

"What was all that work for?" That tree just wouldn't fall. They couldn't understand it.

Now they called Kadiio, the squirrel. "Run up there and see what's happening."

"Okay," said Kadiio. And he went running up to see. Then he came back down. "It's tangled up there in the Sky," he said. "The branches are caught. They look like roots up there. That's why it's hanging. It's stuck."

Semenia gave him an axe. "Go up and cut it."

Kadiio cut Marahuaka. He cut it up there in Heaven. It was an upside down tree, with its roots on top.

Then the great Marahuaka tree finally fell. The entire Earth shook. Branches, fruit, palms, seeds, everything fell. It felt like the sky was falling. It was like the end of the world.

They hid in caves. They huddled together. They shut their eyes. They were afraid.

Then they came out. When they came out it was raining everywhere. They didn't know what it was. It was the first rain. It fell from Heaven in waterfalls and rapids. It poured down from Heaven out of Marahuaka's cut roots.

"Rain," said Semenia. "Now we can plant."

The water looked for a way through the Earth. Now new paths, the rivers, were born. The Orinoco, Fhadamu, Kunukunuma, Antawari, Merewari, Metakuni, Kuntinama, and others, many others. All the rivers were born. They called them the New Water. They ran like snakes across the Earth.

The earth became very soft for planting. Now the women gathered cuttings, shoots, sprouts, seeds. They gathered them in the rain to plant.

Now four waterfalls came down from the top of Marahuaka, from the cliffs: Motasha, Iamo, Namanama, and Kuhuaka. They were born on the green Earth and they opened beautiful ways.

In Kushamakari, three waterfalls were searching for paths, Auakosho, Iukati, and Matuhushi. They ran along pulling up stones and shooting out foam. You couldn't recognize the Earth anymore from the beginning.

Now there were buds everywhere. The Earth became green. The forest bloomed, our *conucos* blossomed. The forest filled with trees. Our *conucos* filled with yuca.

Marahuaka's trunk broke into three pieces. We call them Marahuaka huha, Marahuaka huih and Atawashiho. They turned into stone when they fell. Now they're mountains, the three parts of the highest mountain on Earth. They're there as reminders. It was that day that our food came.

Kadiio fell down too, onto one of the Duida's peaks. Now he lives there, hidden. He's the master of that peak they call Kadiio ewiti.

The people were happy; happy together in their *conuco*. The yuca grew quickly. All of a sudden it was there. Now the men rested. That's what Semenia told them. Now the women worked. That's how we still do it. We don't forget that way. The men clear the *conuco*, like Marahuaka in the beginning. The women plant and harvest and prepare it.

Now they came carrying *wuwa* filled with yuca. Then the men worked again. They wove baskets, strainers, trays, presses. They carved graters and *kanawa*. Those are their jobs. The women harvest, carry, grate, press, cook the cassava. They make *iarake* in the *kanawa*.

"That's good," said Semenia. Then he said: "Let's dance. Let's sing and eat and drink. Now we'll remember."

It was the first harvest festival. The Conuco Song, that's what they call it, *Adahe ademi hidi*, that's its name.

Now they played the momi bark horns and Semenia sang. Wanadi and Wade sang too. They remembered everything. They didn't forget anything: Kuchi, Dodoima, Kamaso, Marahuaka, how they planted, how they cleared. *Watunna*, that's what we call the memory of our beginning.

Just as they sang, we sing now.

The *aichudiaha*, the old ones of today, they know the ancient ways. They sing and teach the young ones what Semenia did. They teach us how to work so that our food returns. They sing about how Jaguar and Tapir were punished.

It's always the same, now as before. The way we ate once, we do over and over again. We obey. We remember. The old ones sing beautifully. We just repeat.

Now those people who came to help in the beginning, those people that Wanadi made to cut down Marahuaka, said goodby.

As they were dancing and singing, they turned into birds of every color. They flew off. The air was filled with feathers, all red and green and yellow and blue. It was beautiful. Now the Water Mother, Huiio, the Great Snake, came leaping out of the water and shot into the air.

"I want my crown," she said, looking for birds and feathers for her crown. Huiio threw her great body into the sky. Many birds came. She covered herself with feathers. She was the rainbow. They called it *wasudi*.

"Good. It's done," the birds said. "Let's leave now."

Then they disappeared. They went to Heaven. They just left their bodies on the Earth for the birds of today. You couldn't see the rainbow anymore. It went to live in Lake Akuena.

Semenia went off as a bird too. He looked like the Wanadi bird. He was kin to Wanadi. Now he's the master of the Earth's food.

Okay. That's it.

Glossary

Adekato   The *akato's* journey, which is recounted to its body in the form of dreams. The *adekato* is a dangerous journey, for whenever it leaves the body, the akato may be captured by Odosha.

Aichuriaha   The "aichuri," or "song man," referring to the keeper of the *Watunna*. Neither a hereditary nor paid position, there is in every village a small group of elders who guard and perpetuate this tradition.

Aiuku   A hallucinogenic snuff made from the seeds of a large, leguminous tree (*Anadenanthera peregrina*), aiuku is found throughout the South American rain forest and is variously known as ñopo, yopo, and vilca.

Akato   The body's companion spirit or double, which descends from heaven to occupy it upon birth. All *akato* are eternal and upon the body's death return to live in heaven once again.

Akene   The water of Lake Akuena, which has the power of immortality, derived in part from the *kaahi* plant that grows along its shores.

Chakara   The shaman's medicine pouch in which he stores a variety of magic herbs, power stones and tobacco.

Conuco   The large slash and burn gardens found throughout the greater Amazon region.

Ennemadi   The fifth house of heaven, where the masters of the *wiriki* crystals dwell.

Hadewa   The master of the seventh house of heaven, Hadewa is identified as a fish and is very likely the father-in-law of Wanadi, the culture hero who married the daughter of the master of fish.

Höhöttu   The ferruginous pygmy owl, *Glaucidium brasilianum phalaenoides,* who lives in the sixth house of heaven with Mudo and Tawadi and forms, along with them, the great trinity of shaman's helpers.

Huhai   (pronounced fhufhai) Shaman.

Huiio   A supernatural anaconda with a feathered crown who lives in the rapids with her mawadi people, Huiio is the mistress of all water and the mother of everything in it.

Iarake   The most important alcoholic beverage of the Makiritare, made with fermented yuca.

Iukuta   The principal Makiritare beverage made from cassava and water and drunk in great quantities at every meal.

Kaahi   A hallucinogenic made from a *Banisteriopsis* vine, *kaahi* among the Makiritare is restricted to the *huhai* who uses it to travel to heaven to make contact with the invisible world. One of the most wide-spread hallucinogens in native South America, it is also known as caapi, yage, and ayahuasca, the "dead man's vine."

Koiohiña   The dark, cavelike region of the universe where Odosha and his Odoshankomo dwell.

Maraka   The shaman's gourd rattle, whose great magical properties are attributed to the *wiriki* crystals inside of it.

Mawadi   Supernatural anaconda, extremely feared for their custom of kidnapping women, overturning canoes, and causing floods.

Motadewa   The shamanic or secret name of heaven.

Mudo   The great potoo, *Nyctibius grandis,* who is Wanadi's brother and one of the three great bird spirits living in the sixth heaven.

Nuna   The moon, who is an evil cannibal spirit that spends all its time searching for *akato* and *huhai* travelling between earth and heaven.

Odosha   The master of evil and the incarnation of all negative forces in the universe, Odosha lives with his people, the Odoshankomo, in dark caves in a land called Koiohiña and is involved in a constant struggle to dominate the earth.

Setawa Kaliana   The "*huhai's* masters," who dwell in ladekuna hana, the second house of heaven, these spirits are said to be related to the Kaliana, or Sape Indians, of the Paragua River. It is the image of the Setawa Kaliana shamans, seated back to back in meditation, which is carved at the top of every maraca.

Shiriche The stars, both those we see in our own sky and the invisible ones dwelling in Shiriche Kumenadi at the top of heaven.

So'to A human being or person, defined as any member of the Makiritare tribe or one who speaks its language.

Tawadi The nacunda nighthawk, *Podager nacunda,* who dwells with Mudo and Höhöttu in the sixth heaven, Matawahuña.

Wanadi God, culture hero and proto-shaman all in one, Wanadi is the unknowable, unseen force ("light") in heaven, who since his farewell has taken no part in the affairs of humans. Created by Shi, the sun, it was Wanadi who established order as it is known today.

Watunna The complete, sacred narrative tradition of the Makiritare.

Wiriki Small quartz crystals (by which Wanadi himself was created); all shamans, upon initiation, must travel to heaven to find these "power stones," which are then put in their maraca along with the roots of the shaman's drugs, *aiuku* and *kaahi.* The Makiritare claim that a long time ago, all people were created from *wiriki.*

Maya Language

Maya is the name used by speakers themselves, a million or so in number, to denote the language of the lowlands that include Peten and the Yucatán peninsula. This is the domain of the great cities of the Classic Period (300–900), such as Copán, Tikal, and Palenque, whose hieroglyphic inscriptions record the Maya language phonetically. Today, these Maya are divided by the national frontiers of Mexico, Guatemala, Belize, Honduras, and El Salvador. Transcribed in part from hieroglyphic script, the corpus of Maya texts is dominated by the tradition of the Chilam Balam books, which has been kept alive into this century in Chumayel and several Yucatecan towns and which defends the old calendar against the conventions and values imported by foreigners (*dzulob*).

■ The Chilam Balam Book of Chumayel (1780) *Mexico* (religious narration)

The core of these books is the calendrical cycle known as the *kahlay katunob,* or Katun Count, which corresponds to a period of 260 years (of 360 days each). The Katun Count texts have a direct antecedent in the Maya hieroglyphic books and inscriptions, and they went on to regulate life after the Spanish invasion in a system that rotated political power among the Yucatecan towns after which these Chilam Books are named, such as Chumayel, Mani, Tizimin, Kaua, Oxcutzcab, and Ixil. Here the count of thirteen named katuns (e.g., 2 Ahau, or 13 Ahau) is the model for history and prognosis, for cosmogony, and for the prophecies of individual "speakers" or priests (*chilam*). Even riddles were incorporated into this corpus, as the means of examining pretenders to office in the katun system of government.

The Interrogation of the Chiefs

This is the examination which takes place in the katun which ends today. The time has arrived for examining the knowledge of the chiefs of the towns, to see whether they know how the ruling men came, whether they have explained the coming of the chiefs, of the head-chiefs, whether they are of the lineage of rulers, whether they are of the lineage of chiefs, that they may prove it.

This is the first question which will be asked of them: he shall ask them for his food "Bring the sun." This is the word of the head-chief to the chiefs. "Bring the sun, my son, bear it on the palm of your hand to my plate. A lance is planted, a lofty cross, in the middle of its heart. A green jaguar is seated over the sun to drink its blood." Of Zuyua is the wisdom. This is what the sun is which is demanded of them: a very large fried egg. This is the lance and the lofty cross planted in its heart of which he speaks: it is the benediction. This is what the green jaguar is which is set over it to drink its blood: it is a green chile-pepper, is the jaguar. This is the language of Zuyua.

This is the second question that will be asked of them: let them go and get the brains of the sky, so the head-chief may see how large they are. "It is my desire to see them; let me see them." This is what he would say to them. This is what the brains of the sky are: it is copal gum.[1]

This is the third question which will be asked of them: let them construct a large house. Six *thils* is its length: one such measure is that of its upright timbers. This is what the large house is: it is a very large hat set on the floor. He shall be told to mount a very large white horse. White shall be his mantle and his cape, and he shall grasp a white rattle in his hand, while he rattles it at his horse. There is coagulated blood on the rosette of his rattle, which comes out of it. This is what the white horse is: it is a stirrup of henequen fiber. This is the white rattle mentioned, and the white cape: they are a Plumeria flower and a white wreath. This is the coagulated blood on the rosette of the rattle, which is demanded of them: it is the gold in the middle, because it is blood which comes from the veins of the fatherless and motherless orphan.

---

1. The gum of the copal (*Protium copal* Engl.) was the principal incense used by the Maya. The thick clouds of smoke may have suggested the convolutions of the brain.

This is the fourth question which will be asked of them: Let them go to his house and then they shall be told: "When you come, you shall be visible at midday. You shall be children again, you shall creep again. When you arrive, your little dog shall be just behind you. This little dog of yours carries with its teeth the soul of our holy mistress,[2] when you come with it." This is what the second childhood at midday is, which is mentioned to him. He shall go where he casts a shadow, this is what is called creeping. Then he shall come to the house of the head-chief. This is what his little dog is which is demanded of him: it is his wife. This is what the soul of our holy mistress is: it is an enormous thick wax candle.

This is the fifth question which will be asked of them. They shall be told to go and get the heart of God the Father in heaven. "Then you shall bring me thirteen layers[3] wrapped up in a coarse white fabric." This is the heart of God the Father, of which they are told: it is a bead of precious stone. This is what the covering of thirteen layers is, which is mentioned. It is an enormous tortilla. Thirteen layers of beans are in it. This is what the coarse white fabric is, it is a white mantle. This shall be demanded of them, as signified in the language of Zuyua.

This is the sixth question which will be asked of them: to go and get the branch of the *pochote* tree, and a cord of three strands, and a living liana. This he will relish. "My food for tomorrow. It is my desire to eat it." It is not bad to gnaw the trunk of the *pochote* tree, so they are told. This is what the trunk of the *pochote* tree is: it is a lizard. This is the cord of three strands, the tail of an iguana. This is the living liana, it is the entrails of a pig. This is the trunk of the *pochote* tree, the base of the tail of a lizard.

This is the seventh question which will be asked of them. They shall be told: "Go and gather for me those things which plug the bottom of the cenote, two white ones, two yellow ones. I desire to eat them." These are the things which plug the bottom of the cenote, which are demanded of them. They are two white and two yellow jícamas.[4] These are the things to be understood in order to become chiefs of the town, when they are brought before the ruler, the first head-chief.

These are the words. If they are not understood by the chiefs of the towns, ill-omened is the star adorning the night. Frightful is its house. Sad is the havoc[5] in the courtyards of the nobles. Those who die are those who do not understand; those who live will understand it. This competitive test

---

2. Our holy mistress (*ca cilich colel*) is a term usually applied to the Holy Virgin.

3. Probably a reference to the thirteen heavens of the Maya cosmos.

4. *Pachyrhizus erosus* (L.) Urban. The Maya name, *chicam*, appears to be derived from the Nahuatl jícama, and this edible root may have been introduced by the Toltecs.

5. *Bulcum*, a misfortune frequently associated in these pages with swarming flies.

shall hang over the chiefs of the towns; it has been copied so that the severity may be known in which the reign is to end.

TRANSLATED BY RALPH ROYS

How Human Time Begins

It was set out this way by the first
      sage Melchisedek, the first
      prophet Napuctum, sacerdote,
      the first priest.
This is the song of how the *uinal*   5
      was realized, before the world
      was.
He started up from his inherent
      motion alone.
His mother's mother and her   10
      mother, his mother's sister and
      his sister-in-law, they all said:
How shall we say, how shall we
      see, that man is on the road?
These are the words they spoke as   15
      they moved along, where there
      was no man.
When they arrived in the east they
      began to say:
Who has been here? These are   20
      footprints. Get the rhythm of
      his step.
So said the Lady of the world,
and our Father, Dios, measured his
      step.   25
This is why the count by footstep
      of the whole world, *xoc lah cab*
      oc, was called *lahca oc* "12 Oc."
This was the order born through 13
      Oc,   30
when the one foot joined its
      counter print to make the
      moment of the eastern
      horizon.
Then he spoke its name when the   35
      day had no name
as he moved along with his

mother's mother and her
    mother, his mother's sister and
    his sister-in-law.   *40*
The *uinal* born, the day so named,
    the sky and earth,
the stairway of water, earth, stone,
    and wood, the things of sea
    and earth realized.   *45*
Chuen, the day he rose to be a
    day-ity and made the sky and
    earth.
Eb, he made the first stairway. It
    ebbs from heaven's heart,   *50*
the heart of water, before there was
    earth, stone, and wood.
Ben, the day for making
    everything, all there is,
the things of the air, of the sea, of   *55*
    the earth.
Ix, he fixed the tilt of the sky and
    earth.
Men, he made everything.
Cib, he made the number one   *60*
    candle
and there was light in the absence
    of sun and moon.
Caban, honey was conceived
    when we had not a caban.   *65*
Etznab, his hands and feet were
    set, he sorted minutiae on the
    ground.
Cauac, the first deliberation of
    hell.   *70*
Ahau, evil men were assigned to
    hell out of respect for Ds.
that they need not be noticed.
Imix, he construed stone and
    wood;   *75*
he did this within the face of the
    day.
Ik, occurred the first breath;
it was named Ik because there was
    no death in it.   *80*
Akbal, he poured water on the
    ground;
this he worked into man.

Kan, he "canned" the first anger
      because of the evil he had   *85*
      created.
Chicchan, he uncovered the evil
      he saw within the town.

Cimi, he invented death;
as it happened the father Ds.   *90*
      invented the first death

Lamat, he invented the seven
      great seas.
Muluc, came the deluge and the
      submersion of everything   *95*
before the dawning. Then the
      father Ds. invented the word
when there was no word in heaven,
      when there was neither stone
      nor wood.   *100*
Then the twenty deities came to
      consider themselves in
      summation and said:
Thirteen units plus seven units
      equals one.   *105*
So said the *uinal* when the word
      came in, when there had been
      no word,
and this led to the question by the
      day Ahau, ruler,   *110*
Why was the meaning of the word
      not opened to them
so that they could declare
      themselves?
Then they went to heaven's heart   *115*
      and joined hands.

TRANSLATED BY GORDON BROTHERSTON AND ED DORN

The Three Invasions

They didn't want to join the foreigners
Christianity was not their desire
they didn't want another tax

Those with their sign in the bird
those with their sign in the stone, flat worked stone   *5*

those with their sign in the jaguar — three emblems —:
four times four hundred *hab* was the period of their lives
plus fifteen score *hab* before that period ended
because they knew the rhythm of the days in themselves.

Whole the moon whole the *hab*   *10*
whole the day whole the night
whole the breath when it moved too whole the blood too
when they came to their beds their mats their thrones;
rhythm in their reading of the good hours
rhythm in their search for the good days   *15*
as they observed the good stars enter their reign
as they watched the reign of the good stars begin
Everything was good.

For they kept sound reason
there was no sin in the holy faith of their lives   *20*
there was no sickness they had no aching bones
they had no high fever they had no smallpox
they had no burning chest they had no bellyache
they had no chest disease they had no headache
The course of mankind was ciphered clearly.   *25*

Not what the foreigners arranged when they came here
Then shame and terror were preferred
carnal sophistication in the flowers of Nacxit Xuchit and his circle
no more good days were shown to us
this was the start of the two-day chair, the two-day rule   *30*
this was the start of our sickness also
there were no good days for us, no more sound reason.
At the end of the loss of our vision and of our shame
everything will be revealed.
There was no great priest no lord speaker no lord priest   *35*
with the change of rulers when the foreigners came
The priests they set down here were lewd
they left their sons here at Mayapan
These in turn received their affliction from the foreigners called
      the Itza.
The saying is: since foreigners came three times   *40*
three score *hab* is the age to get us exempted from tax
The trouble was the aggression of those men the Itza
we didn't do it we pay for it today
But there is an agreement at last to make us and the foreigners
      unanimous
Failing that we have no alternative to war   *45*

TRANSLATED BY GORDON BROTHERSTON AND ED DORN

Last Words

This alone is the word
I, Chilam Balam, have interpreted the word
of the true god of all places in the world
in every part of the world it is heard, oh father
of sky and earth. Splendid indeed is his word in heaven 5
oh father, his rule over us, over our souls.
Yet as thrice the offspring of animals are the old men
of the younger brothers of the land. Snarled minds, hearts dead
in carnal sophistication, who too often turn back, who
propagate Nacxit Xuchit through the sophistication of his circle 10
the two-day rulers, lustful on their thrones
lustful in their sophistication. Two-day men, their words
two-day their seats, their bowls, their hats
the day crime, the night crime, hoods of the world.
They turn back their necks, they wink their eyes, they drool 15
        at the mouth
before our own representatives, oh father. See,
when they come the foreigners bring no truth.
Yet great secrets are told by the sons of the men
and the women of seven ruined houses 20
        Who is the prophet
who is the priest who shall read
the word of this book

TRANSLATED BY GORDON BROTHERSTON AND ED DORN

■ Ritual of the Bacabs (1650) *Mesoamerica* (shaman cure)

TRANSLATED BY GORDON BROTHERSTON

Containing cures in the mainstream tradition of American shamanism, the texts in this manuscript originate entirely in the pre-Hispanic period and were written down in the alphabet around 1600. In addition to the usual shamanic appeal to birds, fourfold sky-bearers (bacabs), colors and winds, we find a peculiarly Maya emphasis on calendar dates, strikingly the "4 Ahau" date with which the current Mesoamerican era began in 3114 B.C.

This Is to Cool Burning Fever and to Cool Fire, the Ailment Fire

My foot's coolness, my hand's coolness,
  as I cooled this fire.
Fivefold my white hail, my black hail, yellow hail,
  as I cool the fire.
Thirteenfold my red cloth, my white cloth, black cloth,   5
  yellow cloth,
  when I answered the strength of this fire.
A black fan my emblem,
  as I answered the strength of this fire.
With me comes the white water maize,   10
  and I answered the strength of this fire.
With me comes the white water lily,
  and I have answered the strength of this fire.
Just now I settled my foot's coolness, my hand's coolness.
  Amen.   15

■ X-Kolom-Che (Eighteenth Century) *Mexico* (song)

TRANSLATED BY ANN LONDON

Originally from the village of Dzitbalche in Campeche, this manuscript was found in Mérida in 1942; it contains fifteen songs (*kay*) and its orthography (e.g., *z* for *c*) is eighteenth century. The thirteenth song (*X'okoot-kay h'ppum-t-huul*), translated here, directly invokes pre-Hispanic ritual through the prowess of the archer.

The Archer's Dance Song

Look,
    stalker, mountain hunter,
once,
      twice
we're going to dance/hunt   5
    up to where the trees begin
three times in all.

Keep your head up
    look around

          don't make any mistakes that
          will lose you the game.

Were you careful to?
      1. file down your arrowhead
      2. stretch your bowstring tight
      3. resin the feathers with *catzim*   15
         down to the endknob of your arrowshaft
      4. smear the fat from a stag in rut
         on the power of your arm
         on the power of your foot
         on your knees   20
         on your balls
         on your ribs
         on your chest
         over your heart

NOW   25

          dance three times around
          the painted stone shaft

THERE

          where the young man is
          lashed   30
          virile, virgin, perfect

first time around

second time around
          take your bow
          fit the arrow   35
          aim at his chest
             but don't shoot with all your strength
             or tear into his flesh too deep

          let him suffer a little while

because this is the way   40

          Lord God
          wanted it.

The next time
          you dance around the (painted blue) shaft
          shoot him   45
again

          you must do this thing without
          a break in the dance because
          that is how the good fighters,
          the ones with shields, do it   50

men who were chosen
to please
the eyes of
Lord God

As soon as the sun looks out   55
over the eastern woods
comes
the song of the archer

They do it all
the shieldbearers   60
the fighters

Quiche-Maya Language

One of the several highland Maya languages spoken by majority popula-
tions in Chiapas and Guatemala, Quiche also names a kingdom whose
western frontier with the Aztec tribute empire coincides with that between
Guatemala and Mexico today. The term *Qui-che* means people of the trees
or woods and as such approximates the Nahuatl Cuauh-temellan from
which the very name Guatemala derives. The object of murderous military suppression in recent years, the town and province of Quiche remain
unsubdued. Written alphabetically by native scribes soon after the European invasion, Quiche-Maya has the distinction of being the language
of the *Popol Vuh*, by common consent the greatest work of early American
literature.

■ Popol Vuh (1558) *Guatemala, Mexico* (religious narration)

As the book (*vuh*) of counsel, community, or the woven mat (*pop*), this
text offers the fullest known American account of the world ages and the
birth of humankind. Though written in the alphabet and "within Christianity," in the interests of a particular clan of the Quiche, it is grand enough to
deserve the title "bible of America," and it builds on the deepest foundations in geology and biology in affirming its political claim. At the very start,
energy switches between the feather-snake, iridescent in the water below,
and Sky Heart, the "hurricane" One Leg above, and then moves through
four "sproutings and humiliations" in time and space. It reveals the world
ages and their endings. The mud men of the first age were too sloppy and
reverted to fish in the flood water; those of the second were too stiff
and perished when the "face of the earth was darkened" in eclipse. Next,

under the protection of hairy mammal ancestors, the Twins defeat the egg-laying bird-reptile family of Seven Parrot, whose saurian sons play like volcanoes with the earth's crust. Consequently, the Twins are able to usurp their elder half brothers, who become monkeys and whose mother Alligator Macaw lacked the genetic advantage given to the Twins by their mother Blood Woman, daughter of the bony lord of the underworld Xibalba. Finally, Xibalba itself is overcome through the Twins' epic defeat of its rulers, and after they have walked into the sky as sun and moon, the people of this era are created from maize.

Preamble: Silence of Sea and Sky

And now we shall name the name of the father of Hunahpu and Xbalanque. Let's drink to him, and let's just drink to the telling and accounting of the begetting of Hunahpu and Xbalanque. We shall tell just half of it, just a part of the account of their father. Here follows the account.

These are the names: One Hunahpu and Seven Hunahpu, as they are called.

And these are their parents: Xpiyacoc, Xmucane. In the blackness, in the night, One Hunahpu and Seven Hunahpu were born to Xpiyacoc and Xmucane.

And this One Hunahpu had two children, and the two were sons, the firstborn named One Monkey and the second named One Artisan.

And this is the name of their mother: she is called Xbaquiyalo, the wife of One Hunahpu. As for Seven Hunahpu, he has no wife. He's just a partner and just secondary; he just remains a boy.

They are great thinkers and great is their knowledge. They are the midmost seers, here on the face of the earth. There is only good in their being and their birthright. They taught skills to One Monkey and One Artisan, the sons of One Hunahpu. One Monkey and One Artisan became flautists, singers, and writers; carvers, jewelers, metalworkers as well.

And as for One and Seven Hunahpu, all they did was throw dice and play ball, every day. They would play each other in pairs, the four of them together. When they gathered in the ball court for entertainment a falcon would come to watch them, the messenger of Hurricane, Newborn Thunderbolt, Raw Thunderbolt. And for this falcon it wasn't far to the earth here, nor was it far to Xibalba; he could get back to the sky, to Hurricane, in an instant.

The four ballplayers remained here on the face of the earth after the mother of One Monkey and One Artisan had died. Since it was on the road to Xibalba that they played, they were heard by One Death and Seven Death, the lords of Xibalba:

"What's happening on the face of the earth? They're just stomping and shouting. They should be summoned to come play ball here. We'll defeat them, since we simply get no deference from them. They show no respect, nor do they have any shame. They're really determined to run right over us!" said all of Xibalba, when they all shared their thoughts, the ones named One and Seven Death. They are great lawgivers.

And these are the Lords over Everything, each lord with a commission and a domain assigned by One and Seven Death:

There are the lords named House Corner and Blood Gatherer. And this is their commission: to draw blood from people.

Next are the lordships of Pus Master and Jaundice Master. And this is their domain: to make people swell up, to make pus come out of their legs, to make their faces yellow, to cause jaundice, as it is called. Such is the domain of Pus Master and Jaundice Master.

Next are the lords Bone Scepter and Skull Scepter, the staff bearers of Xibalba; their staffs are just bones. And this is their staff-bearing: to reduce people to bones, right down to the bones and skulls, until they die from emaciation and edema. This is the commission of the ones named Bone Scepter and Skull Scepter.

Next are the lords named Trash Master and Stab Master. This is their commission: just to catch up with people whenever they have filth or grime in the doorway of the house, the patio of the house. Then they're struck, they're just punctured until they crawl on the ground, then die. And this is the domain of Trash Master and Stab Master, as they are called.

Next are the lords named Wing and Packstrap. This is their domain: that people should die in the road, just "sudden death," as it is called. Blood comes to the mouth, then there is death from vomiting blood. So to each of them his burden, the load on his shoulders: just to strike people on the neck and chest. Then there is death in the road, and then they just go on causing suffering, whether one is coming or going. And this is the domain of Wing and Packstrap.

Such are those who shared their thoughts when they were piqued and driven by One and Seven Hunahpu. What Xibalba desired was the gaming equipment of One and Seven Hunahpu: their kilts, their yokes, their arm guards, their panaches and headbands, the costumes of One and Seven Hunahpu.

And this is where we shall continue telling of their trip to Xibalba. One Monkey and One Artisan, the sons of One Hunahpu, stayed behind. Their mother died—and, what is more, they were to be defeated by Hunahpu and Xbalanque.

And now for the messengers of One and Seven Death: "You're going, you Military Keepers of the Mat, to summon One and Seven Hunahpu. You'll tell them, when you arrive:

"'They must come,' the lords say to you. "Would that they might come to play ball with us here. Then we could have some excitement with them. We are truly amazed at them. Therefore they should come," say the lords, "and they should bring their playthings, their yokes and arm guards should come, along with their rubber ball," say the lords,' you will say when you arrive," the messengers were told.

And these messengers of theirs are owls: Shooting Owl, One-legged Owl, Macaw Owl, Skull Owl, as the messengers of Xibalba are called.

There is Shooting Owl, like a point, just piercing.

And there is One-legged Owl, with just one leg; he has wings.

And there is Macaw Owl, with a red back; he has wings.

And there is also Skull Owl, with only a head alone; he has no legs, but he does have wings.

There are four messengers, Military Keepers of the Mat in rank.

And when they came out of Xibalba they arrived quickly, alighting above the ball court where One and Seven Hunahpu were playing, at the ball court called Great Abyss at Carchah. The owls, arriving in a flurry over the ball court, now repeated their words, reciting the exact words of One Death, Seven Death, Pus Master, Jaundice Master, Bone Scepter, Skull Scepter, House Corner, Blood Gatherer, Trash Master, Stab Master, Wing, Packstrap, as all the lords are named. Their words were repeated by the owls.

"Don't the lords One and Seven Death speak truly?"

"Truly indeed," the owls replied. "We'll accompany you. 'They're to bring along all their gaming equipment,' say the lords."

"Very well, but wait for us while we notify our mother," they replied.

And when they went to their house, they spoke to their mother; their father had died:

"We're going, our dear mother, even though we've just arrived. The messengers of the lord have come to get us:

"'They should come,' he says,' they say, giving us orders. We'll leave our rubber ball behind here," they said, then they went to tie it up under the roof of the house. "Until we return—then we'll put it in play again."

They told One Monkey and One Artisan:

"As for you, just play and just sing, write and carve to warm our house and to warm the heart of your grandmother." When they had been given their instructions, their grandmother Xmucane sobbed, she had to weep.

"We're going, we're not dying. Don't be sad," said One and Seven Hunahpu, then they left.

After that One and Seven Hunahpu left, guided down the road by the messengers.

And then they descended the road to Xibalba, going down a steep cliff, and they descended until they came out where the rapids cut through, the roaring canyon narrows named Neck Canyon. They passed through there, then they passed on into the River of Churning Spikes. They passed through countless spikes but they were not stabbed.

And then they came to water again, to blood: Blood River. They crossed but did not drink. They came to a river, but a river filled with pus. Still they were not defeated, but passed through again.

And then they came to the Crossroads, but here they were defeated, at the Crossroads:

Red Road was one and Black Road another.

White Road was one and Yellow Road another.

There were four roads, and Black Road spoke:

"I am the one you are taking. I am the lord's road," said the road. And they were defeated there: this was the Road of Xibalba.

And then they came to the council place of the lords of Xibalba, and they were defeated again there. The ones seated first there are just manikins, just woodcarvings dressed up by Xibalba. And they greeted the first ones:

"Morning, One Death," they said to the manikin. "Morning, Seven Death," they said to the woodcarving in turn.

So they did not win out, and the lords of Xibalba shouted out with laughter over this. All the lords just shouted with laughter because they had triumphed; in their hearts they had beaten One and Seven Hunahpu. They laughed on until One and Seven Death spoke:

"It's good that you've come. Tomorrow you must put your yokes and arm guards into action," they were told.

"Sit here on our bench," they were told, but the only bench they were offered was a burning-hot rock.

So now they were burned on the bench; they really jumped around on the bench now, but they got no relief. They really got up fast, having burned their butts. At this the Xibalbans laughed again, they began to shriek with laughter, the laughter rose up like a serpent in their very cores, all the lords of Xibalba laughed themselves down to their blood and bones.

"Just go in the house. Your torch and cigars will be brought to your sleeping quarters," the boys were told.

After that they came to the Dark House, a house with darkness alone inside. Meanwhile the Xibalbans shared their thoughts:

"Let's just sacrifice them tomorrow. It can only turn out to be quick; they'll die quickly because of our playing equipment, our gaming things," the Xibalbans are saying among themselves.

This ball of theirs is just a spherical knife. White Dagger is the name of the ball, the ball of Xibalba. Their ball is just ground down to make it smooth; the ball of Xibalba is just surfaced with crushed bone to make it firm.

And One and Seven Hunahpu went inside Dark House. And then their torch was brought, only one torch, already lit, sent by One and Seven Death, along with a cigar for each of them, also already lit, sent by the lords. When these were brought to One and Seven Hunahpu they were cowering, here in the dark. When the bearer of their torch and cigars arrived, the torch was bright as it entered; their torch and both of their cigars were burning. The bearer spoke:

"'They must be sure to return them in the morning—not finished, but just as they look now. They must return them intact,' the lords say to you," they were told, and they were defeated. They finished the torch and they finished the cigars that had been brought to them.

And Xibalba is packed with tests, heaps and piles of tests.

This is the first one: the Dark House, with darkness alone inside.

And the second is named Rattling House, heavy with cold inside, whistling with drafts, clattering with hail. A deep chill comes inside here.

And the third is named Jaguar House, with jaguars alone inside, jostling one another, crowding together, with gnashing teeth. They're scratching around; these jaguars are shut inside the house.

Bat House is the name of the fourth test, with bats alone inside the house, squeaking, shrieking, darting through the house. The bats are shut inside; they can't get out.

And the fifth is named Razor House, with blades alone inside. The blades are moving back and forth, ripping, slashing through the house.

These are the first tests of Xibalba, but One and Seven Hunahpu never entered into them, except for the one named earlier, the specified test house.

And when One and Seven Hunahpu went back before One and Seven Death, they were asked:

"Where are my cigars? What of my torch? They were brought to you last night!"

"We finished them, your lordship."

"Very well. This very day, your day is finished, you will die, you will disappear, and we shall break you off. Here you will hide your faces: you are to be sacrificed!" said One and Seven Death.

And then they were sacrificed and buried. They were buried at the Place of Ball Game Sacrifice, as it is called. The head of One Hunahpu was cut off; only his body was buried with his younger brother.

"Put his head in the fork of the tree that stands by the road," said One and Seven Death.

And when his head was put in the fork of the tree, the tree bore fruit. It would not have had any fruit, had not the head of One Hunahpu been put in the fork of the tree.

This is the calabash tree, as we call it today, or "the head of One Hunahpu," as it is said.

And then One and Seven Death were amazed at the fruit of the tree. The fruit grows out everywhere, and it isn't clear where the head of One Hunahpu is; now it looks just the way the calabashes look. All the Xibalbans see this, when they come to look.

The state of the tree loomed large in their thoughts, because it came about at the same time the head of One Hunahpu was put in the fork. The Xibalbans said among themselves:

"No one is to pick the fruit, nor is anyone to go beneath the tree," they said. They restricted themselves; all of Xibalba held back.

It isn't clear which is the head of One Hunahpu; now it's exactly the same as the fruit of the tree. Calabash tree came to be its name, and much was said about it. A maiden heard about it, and here we shall tell of her arrival.

And here is the account of a maiden, the daughter of a lord named Blood Gatherer.

And this is when a maiden heard of it, the daughter of a lord. Blood Gatherer is the name of her father, and Blood Woman is the name of the maiden.

And when he heard the account of the fruit of the tree, her father retold it. And she was amazed at the account:

"I'm not acquainted with that tree they talk about. '"Its fruit is truly sweet!" they say,' I hear," she said.

Next, she went all alone and arrived where the tree stood. It stood at the Place of Ball Game Sacrifice:

"What? Well! What's the fruit of this tree? Shouldn't this tree bear something sweet? They shouldn't die, they shouldn't be wasted. Should I pick one?" said the maiden.

And then the bone spoke; it was here in the fork of the tree:

"Why do you want a mere bone, a round thing in the branches of a tree?" said the head of One Hunahpu when it spoke to the maiden. "You don't want it," she was told.

"I do want it," said the maiden.

"Very well. Stretch out your right hand here, so I can see it," said the bone.

"Yes," said the maiden. She stretched out her right hand, up there in front of the bone.

And then the bone spit out its saliva, which landed squarely in the hand of the maiden.

And then she looked in her hand, she inspected it right away, but the bone's saliva wasn't in her hand.

"It is just a sign I have given you, my saliva, my spittle. This, my head, has nothing on it—just bone, nothing of meat. It's just the same with the head of a great lord: it's just the flesh that makes his face look good. And when he dies, people get frightened by his bones. After that, his son is like his saliva, his spittle, in his being, whether it be the son of a lord or the son of a craftsman, an orator. The father does not disappear, but goes on being fulfilled. Neither dimmed nor destroyed is the face of a lord, a warrior, craftsman, orator. Rather, he will leave his daughters and sons. So it is that I have done likewise through you. Now go up there on the face of the earth; you will not die. Keep the word. So be it," said the head of One and Seven Hunahpu—they were of one mind when they did it.

This was the word Hurricane, Newborn Thunderbolt, Raw Thunderbolt had given them. In the same way, by the time the maiden returned to her home, she had been given many instructions. Right away something was generated in her belly, from the saliva alone, and this was the generation of Hunahpu and Xbalanque.

And when the maiden got home and six months had passed, she was found out by her father. Blood Gatherer is the name of her father.

And after the maiden was noticed by her father, when he saw that she was now with child, all the lords then shared their thoughts—One and Seven Death, along with Blood Gatherer:

"This daughter of mine is with child, lords. It's just a bastard," Blood Gatherer said when he joined the lords.

"Very well. Get her to open her mouth. If she doesn't tell, then sacrifice her. Go far away and sacrifice her."

"Very well, your lordships," he replied. After that, he questioned his daughter:

"Who is responsible for the child in your belly, my daughter?" he said.

"There is no child, my father, sir; there is no man whose face I've known," she replied.

"Very well. It really is a bastard you carry! Take her away for sacrifice, you Military Keepers of the Mat. Bring back her heart in a bowl, so the lords can take it in their hands this very day," the owls were told, the four of them.

Then they left, carrying the bowl. When they left they took the maiden by the hand, bringing along the White Dagger, the instrument of sacrifice.

"It would not turn out well if you sacrificed me, messengers, because it is not a bastard that's in my belly. What's in my belly generated all by itself when I went to marvel at the head of One Hunahpu, which is there at the Place of Ball Game Sacrifice. So please stop: don't do your sacrifice, messengers," said the maiden. Then they talked:

"What are we going to use in place of her heart? We were told by her father:

'Bring back her heart. The lords will take it in their hands, they will satisfy themselves, they will make themselves familiar with its composition. Hurry, bring it back in a bowl, put her heart in the bowl.' Isn't that what we've been told? What shall we deliver in the bowl? What we want above all is that you should not die," said the messengers.

"Very well. My heart must not be theirs, nor will your homes be here. Nor will you simply force people to die, but hereafter, what will be truly yours will be the true bearers of bastards. And hereafter, as for One and Seven Death, only blood, only nodules of sap, will be theirs. So be it that these things are presented before them, and not that hearts are burned before them. So be it: use the fruit of a tree," said the maiden. And it was red tree sap she went out to gather in the bowl.

After it congealed, the substitute for her heart became round. When the sap of the croton tree was tapped, tree sap like blood, it became the substitute for her blood. When she rolled the blood around inside there, the sap of the croton tree, it formed a surface like blood, glistening red now, round inside the bowl. When the tree was cut open by the maiden, the so-called cochineal croton, the sap is what she called blood, and so there is talk of "nodules of blood."

"So you have been blessed with the face of the earth. It shall be yours," she told the owls.

"Very well, maiden. We'll show you the way up there. You just walk on ahead; we have yet to deliver this apparent duplicate of your heart before the lords," said the messengers.

And when they came before the lords, they were all watching closely:

"Hasn't it turned out well?" said One Death.

"It has turned out well, your lordships, and this is her heart. It's in the bowl."

"Very well. So I'll look," said One Death, and when he lifted it up with his fingers, its surface was soaked with gore, its surface glistened red with blood.

"Good. Stir up the fire, put it over the fire," said One Death.

After that they dried it over the fire, and the Xibalbans savored the aroma. They all ended up standing here, they leaned over it intently. They found the smoke of the blood to be truly sweet!

And while they stayed at their cooking, the owls went to show the maiden the way out. They sent her up through a hole onto the earth, and then the guides returned below.

In this way the lords of Xibalba were defeated by a maiden; all of them were blinded.

And here, where the mother of One Monkey and One Artisan lived, was where the woman named Blood Woman arrived.

And when the Blood Woman came to the mother of One Monkey and One Artisan, her children were still in her belly, but it wasn't very long before the birth of Hunahpu and Xbalanque, as they are called.

And when the woman came to the grandmother, the woman said to the grandmother:

"I've come, mother, madam. I'm your daughter-in-law and I'm your child, mother, madam," she said when she came here to the grandmother.

"Where do you come from? As for my last born children, didn't they die in Xibalba? And these two remain as their sign and their word: One Monkey and One Artisan are their names. So if you've come to see my children, get out of here!" the maiden was told by the grandmother.

"Even so, I really am your daughter-in-law. I am already his, I belong to One Hunahpu. What I carry is his. One Hunahpu and Seven Hunahpu are alive, they are not dead. They have merely made a way for the light to show itself, madam mother-in-law, as you will see when you look at the faces of what I carry," the grandmother was told.

And One Monkey and One Artisan have been keeping their grandmother entertained: all they do is play and sing, all they work at is writing and carving, every day, and this cheers the heart of their grandmother.

And then the grandmother said:

"I don't want you, no thanks, my daughter-in-law. It's just a bastard in your belly, you trickster! These children of mine who are named by you are dead," said the grandmother.

"Truly, what I say to you is so!"

"Very well, my daughter-in-law, I hear you. So get going, get their food so they can eat. Go pick a big netful of corn, then come back—since you are already my daughter-in-law, as I understand it," the maiden was told.

"Very well," she replied.

After that, she went to the garden; One Monkey and One Artisan had a garden. The maiden followed the path they had cleared and arrived there in the garden, but there was only one clump, there was no other plant, no second or third. That one clump had borne its ears. So then the maiden's heart stopped:

"It looks like I'm a sinner, a debtor! Where will I get the netful of food she asked for?" she said. And then the guardians of food were called upon by her:

"Come thou, rise up, come thou, stand up:
Generous Woman, Harvest Woman,
Cacao Woman, Cornmeal Woman,
thou guardian of the food of One Monkey, One Artisan,"
said the maiden.

And then she took hold of the silk, the bunch of silk at the top of the ear. She pulled it straight out, she didn't pick the ear, and the ear reproduced itself to make food for the net. It filled the big net.

And then the maiden came back, but animals carried her net. When she got back she went to put the pack frame in the corner of the house, so it would look to the grandmother as if she had arrived with a load.

And then, when the grandmother saw the food, a big netful:

"Where did that food of yours come from? You've leveled the place! I'm going to see if you've brought back our whole garden!" said the grandmother.

And then she went off, she went to look at the garden, but the one clump was still there, and the place where the net had been put at the foot of it was still obvious.

And the grandmother came back in a hurry, and she got back home, and she said to the maiden:

"The sign is still there. You really are my daughter-in-law! I'll have to keep watching what you do. These grandchildren of mine are already showing genius," the maiden was told.

Now this is where we shall speak of the birth of Hunahpu and Xbalanque.

And this is their birth; we shall tell of it here.

Then it came to the day of their birth, and the maiden named Blood Woman gave birth. The grandmother was not present when they were born; they were born suddenly. Two of them were born, named Hunahpu and Xbalanque. They were born in the mountains, and then they came into the house. Since they weren't sleeping:

"Throw them out of here! They're really loudmouths!" said the grandmother.

After that, when they put them on an anthill, they slept soundly there. And when they removed them from there, they put them in brambles next.

And this is what One Monkey and One Artisan wanted: that they should die on the anthill and die in the brambles. One Monkey and One Artisan wanted this because they were rowdyish and flushed with jealousy. They didn't allow their younger brothers in the house at first, as if they didn't even know them, but even so they flourished in the mountains.

And One Monkey and One Artisan were great flautists and singers, and as they grew up they went through great suffering and pain. It had cost them suffering to become great knowers. Through it all they became flautists, singers, and writers, carvers. They did everything well. They simply knew it when they were born, they simply had genius. And they were the successors of their fathers who had gone to Xibalba, their dead fathers.

Since One Monkey and One Artisan were great knowers, in their hearts they already realized everything when their younger brothers came into being, but they didn't reveal their insight because of their jealousy. The anger in their hearts came down on their own heads; no great harm was done. They were decoyed by Hunahpu and Xbalanque, who merely went out shooting every day. These two got no love from the grandmother, or from One Monkey and One Artisan. They weren't given their meals; the meals had been prepared and One Monkey and One Artisan had already eaten them before they got there.

But Hunahpu and Xbalanque aren't turning red with anger; rather, they just let it go, even though they know their proper place, which they see as clear as day. So they bring birds when they arrive each day, and One Monkey and One Artisan eat them. Nothing whatsoever is given to Hunahpu and Xbalanque, either one of them. All One Monkey and One Artisan do is play and sing.

And then Hunahpu and Xbalanque arrived again, but now they came in here without bringing their birds, so the grandmother turned red:

"What's your reason for not bringing birds?" Hunahpu and Xbalanque were asked.

"There are some, our dear grandmother, but our birds just got hung up in a tree," they said, "and there's no way to get up the tree after them, our dear grandmother, and so we'd like our elder brothers to please go with us, to please go get the birds down," they said.

"Very well. We'll go with you at dawn," the elder brothers replied.

Now they had won, and they gathered their thoughts, the two of them, about the fall of One Monkey and One Artisan:

"We'll just turn their very being around with our words. So be it, since they have caused us great suffering. They wished that we might die and disappear—we, their younger brothers. Just as they wished us to be slaves here, so we shall defeat them there. We shall simply make a sign of it," they said to one another.

And then they went there beneath a tree, the kind named yellowwood, together with the elder brothers. When they got there they started shooting.

There were countless birds up in the tree, chittering, and the elder brothers were amazed when they saw the birds. And not one of these birds fell down beneath the tree:

"Those birds of ours don't fall down; just go throw them down," they told their elder brothers.

"Very well," they replied.

And then they climbed up the tree, and the tree began to grow, its trunk got thicker.

After that, they wanted to get down, but now One Monkey and One Artisan couldn't make it down from the tree. So they said, from up in the tree:

"How can we grab hold? You, our younger brothers, take pity on us! Now this tree looks frightening to us, dear younger brothers," they said from up in the tree. Then Hunahpu and Xbalanque told them:

"Undo your pants, tie them around your hips, with the long end trailing like a tail behind you, and then you'll be better able to move," they were told by their younger brothers.

"All right," they said.

And then they left the ends of their loincloths trailing, and all at once these became tails. Now they looked like mere monkeys.

After that they went along in the trees of the mountains, small and great. They went through the forests, now howling, now keeping quiet in the branches of trees.

Such was the defeat of One Monkey and One Artisan by Hunahpu and Xbalanque. They did it by means of their genius alone.

And when they got home they said, when they came to their grandmother and mother:

"Our dear grandmother, something has happened to our elder brothers. They've become simply shameless, they're like animals now," they said.

"If you've done something to your elder brothers, you've knocked me down and stood me on my head. Please don't do anything to your elder brothers, my dear grandchildren," the grandmother said to Hunahpu and Xbalanque. And they told their grandmother:

"Don't be sad, our dear grandmother. You will see the faces of our elder brothers again. They'll come, but this will be a test for you, our dear grandmother. Will you please not laugh while we test their destiny?" they said.

And then they began playing. They played "Hunahpu Monkey."

And then they sang, they played, they drummed. When they took up their flutes and drums, their grandmother sat down with them, then they played, they sounded out the tune, the song that got its name then. "Hunahpu Monkey" is the name of the tune.

And then One Monkey and One Artisan came back, dancing when they arrived.

And then, when the grandmother looked, it was their ugly faces the grandmother saw. Then she laughed, the grandmother could not hold back her laughter, so they just left right away, out of her sight again, they went up and away in the forest.

"Why are you doing that, our dear grandmother? We'll only try four times; only three times are left. We'll call them with the flute, with song. Please hold back your laughter. We'll try again," said Hunahpu and Xbalanque.

Next they played again, then they came back, dancing again, they arrived again, in the middle of the patio of the house. As before, what they did was delightful; as before, they tempted their grandmother to laugh. Their grandmother laughed at them soon enough. The monkeys looked truly ridiculous, with the skinny little things below their bellies and their tails wiggling in front of their breasts. When they came back the grandmother had to laugh at them, and they went back into the mountains.

"Please, why are you doing that, our dear grandmother? Even so, we'll try it a third time now," said Hunahpu and Xbalanque.

Again they played, again they came dancing, but their grandmother held back her laughter. Then they climbed up here, cutting right across the building, with thin red lips, with faces blank, puckering their lips, wiping their mouths and faces, suddenly scratching themselves. And when the grandmother saw them again, the grandmother burst out laughing again, and again they went out of sight because of the grandmother's laughter.

"Even so, our dear grandmother, we'll get their attention."

So for the fourth time they called on the flute, but they didn't come back again. The fourth time they went straight into the forest. So they told their grandmother:

"Well, we've tried, our dear grandmother. They came at first, and we've tried calling them again. So don't be sad. We're here—we, your grandchildren. Just love our mother, dear grandmother. Our elder brothers will be remembered. So be it: they have lived here and they have been named; they are to be called One Monkey and One Artisan," said Hunahpu and Xbalanque.

So they were prayed to by the flautists and singers among the ancient people, and the writers and carvers prayed to them. In ancient times they turned into animals, they became monkeys, because they just magnified themselves, they abused their younger brothers. Just as they wished them to be slaves, so they themselves were brought low. One Monkey and One Artisan were lost then, they became animals, and this is now their place forever.

Even so, they were flautists and singers; they did great things while they lived with their grandmother and mother.

$$* \quad * \quad *$$

And here is the beginning of the conception of humans, and of the search for the ingredients of the human body. So they spoke, the Bearer, Begetter, the Makers, Modelers named Sovereign Plumed Serpent:

"The dawn has approached, preparations have been made, and morning has come for the provider, nurturer, born in the light, begotten in the light.

Morning has come for humankind, for the people of the face of the earth," they said. It all came together as they went on thinking in the darkness, in the night, as they searched and they sifted, they thought and they wondered.

And here their thoughts came out in clear light. They sought and discovered what was needed for human flesh. It was only a short while before the sun, moon, and stars were to appear above the Makers and Modelers. Broken Place, Bitter Water Place is the name: the yellow corn, white corn came from there.

And these are the names of the animals who brought the food: fox, coyote, parrot, crow. There were four animals who brought the news of the ears of yellow corn and white corn. They were coming from over there at Broken Place, they showed the way to the break.

And this was when they found the staple foods.

And these were the ingredients for the flesh of the human work, the human design, and the water was for the blood. It became human blood, and corn was also used by the Bearer, Begetter.

And so they were happy over the provisions of the good mountain, filled with sweet things, thick with yellow corn, white corn, and thick with pataxte and cacao, countless zapotes, anonas, jocotes, nances, matasanos, sweets—the rich foods filling up the citadel named Broken Place, Bitter Water Place. All the edible fruits were there: small staples, great staples, small plants, great plants. The way was shown by the animals.

And then the yellow corn and white corn were ground, and Xmucane did the grinding nine times. Corn was used, along with the water she rinsed her hands with, for the creation of grease; it became human fat when it was worked by the Bearer, Begetter, Sovereign Plumed Serpent, as they are called.

After that, they put it into words:

the making, the modeling of our first mother-father,
with yellow corn, white corn alone for the flesh,
food alone for the human legs and arms,
for our first fathers, the four human works.

It was staples alone that made up their flesh.

These are the names of the first people who were made and modeled.
This is the first person: Jaguar Quitze.
And now the second: Jaguar Night.
And now the third: Mahucutah.
And the fourth: True Jaguar.

And these are the names of our first mother-fathers. They were simply made and modeled, it is said; they had no mother and no father. We have named the men by themselves. No woman gave birth to them, nor were they begotten by the builder, sculptor, Bearer, Begetter. By sacrifice alone, by genius alone they were made, they were modeled by the Maker, Modeler,

Bearer, Begetter, Sovereign Plumed Serpent. And when they came to fruition, they came out human:

> They talked and they made words.
> They looked and they listened.
> They walked, they worked.

They were good people, handsome, with looks of the male kind. Thoughts came into existence and they gazed; their vision came all at once. Perfectly they saw, perfectly they knew everything under the sky, whenever they looked. The moment they turned around and looked around in the sky, on the earth, everything was seen without any obstruction. They didn't have to walk around before they could see what was under the sky; they just stayed where they were.

As they looked, their knowledge became intense. Their sight passed through trees, through rocks, through lakes, through seas, through mountains, through plains. Jaguar Quitze, Jaguar Night, Mahucutah, and True Jaguar were truly gifted people.

And then they were asked by the builder and mason:

"What do you know about your being? Don't you look, don't you listen? Isn't your speech good, and your walk? So you must look, to see out under the sky. Don't you see the mountain-plain clearly? So try it," they were told.

And then they saw everything under the sky perfectly. After that, they thanked the Maker, Modeler:

> "Truly now,
> double thanks, triple thanks
> that we've been formed, we've been given
> our mouths, our faces,
> we speak, we listen,
> we wonder, we move,
> our knowledge is good, we've understood
> what is far and near,
> and we've seen what is great and small
> under the sky, on the earth.
> Thanks to you we've been formed,
> we've come to be made and modeled,
> our grandmother, our grandfather,"

they said when they gave thanks for having been made and modeled. They understood everything perfectly, they sighted the four sides, the four corners in the sky, on the earth, and this didn't sound good to the builder and sculptor:

"What our works and designs have said is no good:

'We have understood everything, great and small,' they say." And so the Bearer, Begetter took back their knowledge:

"What should we do with them now? Their vision should at least reach nearby, they should see at least a small part of the face of the earth, but what they're saying isn't good. Aren't they merely 'works' and 'designs' in their very names? Yet they'll become as great as gods, unless they procreate, proliferate at the sowing, the dawning, unless they increase."

"Let it be this way: now we'll take them apart just a little, that's what we need. What we've found out isn't good. Their deeds would become equal to ours, just because their knowledge reaches so far. They see everything," so said

> the Heart of Sky, Hurricane,
> Newborn Thunderbolt, Raw Thunderbolt,
> Sovereign Plumed Serpent,
> Bearer, Begetter,
> Xpiyacoc, Xmucane,
> Maker, Modeler,

as they are called. And when they changed the nature of their works, their designs, it was enough that the eyes be marred by the Heart of Sky. They were blinded as the face of a mirror is breathed upon. Their eyes were weakened. Now it was only when they looked nearby that things were clear.

And such was the loss of the means of understanding, along with the means of knowing everything, by the four humans. The root was implanted.

And such was the making, modeling of our first grandfather, our father, by the Heart of Sky, Heart of Earth.

And then their wives and women came into being. Again, the same gods thought of it. It was as if they were asleep when they received them, truly beautiful women were there with Jaguar Quitze, Jaguar Night, Mahucutah, and True Jaguar. With their women there they became wider awake. Right away they were happy at heart again, because of their wives.

> Celebrated Seahouse is the name of the wife of Jaguar Quitze.
> Prawn House is the name of the wife of Jaguar Night.
> Hummingbird House is the name of the wife of Mahucutah.
> Macaw House is the name of the wife of True Jaguar.

So these are the names of their wives, who became ladies of rank, giving birth to the people of the tribes, small and great.

TRANSLATED BY DENNIS TEDLOCK

The End of the Doll People

> This is the root of the former word.
> > Here is Quiche by name.
> Here we shall write then,
> > We shall start out then, the former words,

The beginnings 5
    And the taproots
Of everything done in the Quiche town,
    The tribe of the Quiche people.
So this is what we shall collect then,
    The decipherment, 10
The clarification,
    And the explanation
Of the mysteries
    And the illumination
By Former, 15
    And Shaper;
Bearer
    And Engenderer are their names,

Hunter Possum
    And Hunter Coyote, 20
Great White Pig
    And Coati,
Majesty
    And Quetzal Serpent,
The Heart of the Lake 25
    And the Heart of the Sea,
Green Plate Spirit
    And Blue Bowl Spirit, as it is said,
Who are likewise called,
    Who are likewise spoken of 30
As the Woman with Grandchildren
    And Man with Grandchildren,
Xpiacoc
    And Xmucane by name,
Shelterer 35
    And Protector,
Great-Grandmother
    And Great-Grandfather,
As it is said
    In Quiche words. 40
Then they said everything
    And did it furthermore,
In the bright existence
    And bright words.
This we shall write already within the word of God, 45

Already in Christianity.
We shall save it
    Because there is no longer
A sight of the Book of Counsel,

A sight of the bright things come   *50*
      from beside the sea,
The description of our shadows,
      A sight of the bright life, as it is called.
There was once the manuscript of it,
      And it was written long ago,   *55*
Only hiding his face is the reader of it,
      The meditator of it.
Great was its account
      And its description
Of when there was finished   *60*
      The birth
Of all of heaven
      And earth:
      The four humiliations,
The knowledge   *65*
      Of the four punishments,
The rope of tying together,
      The line of tying together,
The womb of heaven,
      The womb of earth.   *70*
Four creations,
      Four humiliations, it was told,

By the Former
      And Shaper,
The Mother   *75*
      And Father
Of Life
      And Mankind,
The Inspirer
      And Heartener,   *80*
Bearer
      And Heartener
Light
      And the Race,
Children of the Mother of Light,   *85*
      Sons of the Father of Light,
The Meditator,
      The Thinker
Of everything,
      Whatever exists: *90*
Heaven,
      Earth,
Lake,
      And Sea

II

Here is the description
      Of these things:
Truly it was yet quiet,
      Truly it was yet stilled.
It was quiet.   5
      Truly it was calm.
Truly it was solitary
      And it was also still empty, the womb of heaven.

III

These are truly then the first words,
      The first utterances.
There was not one person yet,
      One animal,
(Deer,)   5
      Bird,
Fish,
      Crab,
Tree,
      Rock,   10
Hole,
      Canyon,
Meadow
      Or forest.
All by itself the sky existed.   15
      The face of the earth was not yet visible.
All by itself the sea lay dammed,
      And the womb of heaven,
Everything.
      There was nothing whatever   20
Silenced
      Or at rest.
Each thing was made silent,
      Each thing was made calm,
Was made invisible,   25

      Was made to rest in heaven.
There was not, then, anything in fact
      That was standing there.
Only the pooled water,
      Only the flat sea.   30
All by itself it lay dammed.
      There was not, then, anything in fact that might have existed.
It was just still.
      It was quiet

In the darkness,   *35*
    In the night.
All alone the Former
    And Shaper,
Majesty,
    And Quetzal Serpent,   *40*
The Mothers
    And Fathers
Were in the water.
    Brilliant they were then,
And wrapped in quetzal   *45*
    And dove feathers.
Thence came the name
    Of Quetzal Serpent.
Great sages they were
    And great thinkers in their essence,   *50*
For indeed there is Heaven
    And there is also the Heart of Heaven.
That is the name
    Of the deity, it is said.

IV

So then came his word here.
    It reached
To Majesty
    And Quetzal Serpent
There in the obscurity,   *5*
    In the nighttime.
It spoke to Majesty
    And Quetzal Serpent, and they spoke.
Then they thought;
    Then they pondered.   *10*
Then they found themselves;
    They assembled
Their words,
    Their thoughts.
Then they gave birth—   *15*
    Then they heartened themselves.
Then they caused to be created
    And they bore men.
Then they thought about the birth,
    The creation   *20*
Of trees
And the birth of life
    And humanity
In the obscurity,

In the nighttime   25
Through him who is the Heart of Heaven,
    Leg by name.
Leg Lightning is the first,
    And the second is Dwarf Lightning.
Third then is Green Lightning,   30
     So that the three of them are the Heart of Hearts
Then they came to Majesty
    And Quetzal Serpent, and then was the invention
Of light
    And life.   35
"What if it were planted?
    Then something would brighten—
A supporter,
    A nourisher.
So be it.   40
    You must decide on it.
There is the water to get rid of,
    To be emptied out,
To create this,
    The earth   45
And have it surfaced
    And levelled
When it is planted,
    When it is brightened—
Heaven   50
    And earth.
But there can be no adoration
    Or glorification
Of what we have formed,
    What we have shaped.   55
Until we have created a human form,
    A human shape," so they said.
So then this the earth was created by them.
    Only their word was the creation of it.
To create the earth, "Earth," they said.   60
    Immediately it was created.
It was just like a cloud,
    Like a mist then,
The creation then,
    The whirlwind.   65
Then the mountain was asked to come from the water.
    Straightaway there were great mountains.
Just their power,
    Just their magic
Caused the making then,   70

The invention
Of mountains
    And valleys.
At a stroke there were also created cedar groves on them
    And pine forests on them.   75
So Quetzal Serpent then rejoiced,
    "It is good that you have come,
Oh Heart of Heaven,
    Oh Leg,
And you, Dwarf Lightning   *80*
    And Green Lightning.
Our forming is successful,
    And our shaping," they said.
And once they had created
    The earth,   85
The mountains
    And valleys,
The paths of the waters were unravelled
    And they proceeded to twist along among the hills.
So the rivers then became more divided   90
    As the great mountains were appearing.
And thus was the creation of the earth
    When it was created by him
Who is the Heart of Heaven,
    The Heart of Earth,   95
As they are called.
    And they were the first to think of it.
The sky was rounded out there
    And the earth was rounded out in the water,

And thus it was invented as they thought,   *100*
    As they reflected
On its perfection,
    Its being made by them.

V

Then they thought further
    Of the wild animals,
Guardians of the forest,
    And all the population of the wild:
Deer,   5
    Birds,
Panthers,
    Jaguars,
Serpents,
    Rattlers,   *10*

Yellowmouths,
    Guardians of plants.
The Mother said this,
    And the Father:
"Should it only be still,   *15*
    Or should it not be silent
Under the trees
    And shrubs?
Indeed, it would be good if there were
    Guardians for them," they said,   *20*
And when they thought
    And talked,
At a stroke there came to be
    And were created
Deer   *25*
    And birds.
Then they awarded homes also to the deer
    And birds.
"You, Deer, on the rivers
    And in the canyons   *30*
Will you sleep then.
    There will you be then,
In the grass,
    In the fruits.
In the wilderness   *35*
    Will you multiply yourselves then.
On all fours your walk,
    Your gait will be,"
They were told,
    And then they designated   *40*
The homes of the little birds
    And the big birds.
"You, oh Birds, in the trees,
    In the bushes
Make your homes then,   *45*
    Make your houses then.
Multiply there then,
    Increase then
On the branches of trees,
    On the branches of shrubs,"   *50*
The deer were told,
    And the birds.
When they had done
    Their creating,
They gave them everything: their nests   *55*
    And lairs.

And so the homes
    Of the animals were the earth.
They gave it, the Mother
    And Father.   60
There was completed
    The assignment
Of all the deer
    And birds.

VI

Then also they were told, the deer
    And birds
By Former
    And Shaper,
The Mother   5
    And Father,
"Talk, then,
    Call, then.
Don't warble;
    Don't cry.   10
Make yourselves understood
    To each other
In each species,
    In each grouping,"
The deer were told,   15
    And the birds,
Panthers,
    Jaguars,
Serpents,
    (And snakes).   20
"Now then, pronounce
    Our names.
Worship us, your Mother
    And your Father.
Now then, say this: 25
    Leg,
Dwarf Lightning,
    Green Lightning,
The Heart of Heaven,
    The Heart of Earth,   30
Former,
    Shaper,
Mother
    And Father.
Talk then,   35
    And call to us.

Worship us,"
    They were told.
But they did not succeed in talking like men.
    They just pretended to.   *40*
They just rattled;
    And they just croaked.
The form of their speech did not emerge.
    Differently they made cries, each one apart.
When Former heard it   *45*
    And Shaper,
"It is not yet arranged
    So they can talk,"
They repeated

    To each other.   *50*
"They do not succeed in pronouncing
    Our names,
Although we are their Former
    And we are their Shaper.
It isn't good," they repeated   *55*
    To each other,
They the Mother
    And Father.
And they were told,
    "Just change yourselves,   *60*
Because it is not yet successful
    Since you do not speak.
We shall therefore change
    Our word.
Your food,   *65*
    Your nourishment,
Your sleeping places,
    Your lairs,
What has been yours
    Has now become   *70*
The canyons
    And the wilderness,
Because our worship has not been achieved;
    You do not yet call upon us.
Indeed there is,   *75*
    Or there should be
A worshipper,
    A praiser whom we shall yet make
Who will just take your places,

    And your flesh will just be eaten.   *80*
So be it then,

And there may you serve,"
They were told.
    So they were commanded—
The little animals   *85*
    And big animals who are upon the earth.
And then it was necessary for them to try their luck again.
It was necessary for them to make another attempt,
And it was necessary for them to arrange again for worship.
For they couldn't catch their speech among themselves.   *90*
For it couldn't be understood,
    As it wasn't made that way.
And so their flesh was humbled.
    They served.
They were eaten.   *95*
    They were killed,
The animals that were here on the face of the earth.
    And so there was another effort
To form man,
    To shape man   *100*
By the Former
    And Shaper,
The Mother
    And Father.
"Let us just try again.   *105*
    Already it has approached
The planting,
    The brightening.
Let us make a supporter for us,
    A nourisher for us.   *110*
How then can we be called upon
    And be remembered upon the earth?
We have already tried with the first of our formings
    Our shapings.
We did not attain our being worshipped   *115*
    And being glorified by them.
And so let us try now
    To make
A praiser,
    A worshipper,   *120*
A supporter,
    A nourisher," they said.
For then there was the forming
    And the working
Of earth   *125*
    And mud.
Its body they made,

But it didn't look good to them.
It just kept coming apart.
    It was just absorbent.   *130*
It was just soggy;
    It was just damp.
It was just crumbling
    And it was just dissolving.
Its head wasn't rounded.   *135*
    Its face was just one sided.
Its eyes were just veiled
    And couldn't be looked into.
As soon as it spoke
    It made no sense.   *140*
Just all at once it dissolved in the water.
    "It wasn't strong," they said then,
Former
    And Shaper.
"It looks wet.   *145*
    If it should just get wet
It couldn't walk
    And it couldn't be made to multiply.
So be it.
    Its mind is dark there," they said.   *150*
And so they destroyed it.
    They overthrew again
What they had formed,
    They had shaped.
And they said again,   *155*
    "What are there that we can make
That may succeed then,
    That may be intelligent then,
Worshipping us,
    And calling upon us?" they said.   *160*
Then they thought further
    And just called upon
Xpiacoc
    And Xmucane,
Hunter Possum   *165*
    And Hunter Coyote.
"They can try again their divination,
    Their creation," they told each other—
The Former
    And Shaper.   *170*
And so they spoke to Xpiacoc
    And Xmucane.
And indeed it was proposed to them,

The far seers,
The Grandmother of Day,   *175*
       The Grandmother of Light.
They were addressed by the Former
       And Shaper.
These are the names of Xpiacoc
       And Xmucane.   *180*

VII

And there spoke also
       Leg
With Majesty
       And Quetzal Serpent.
Then they spoke to the Sun Priest   *5*
       And the Shaper, the far seers,
"It must be sought
       And it will just be found
So that then again we can shape man,
       So that we can form man again then,   *10*
As a supporter
       And nourisher.
We shall be called upon,
       And we shall be remembered.
Then there may be support   *15*
       In words,
Ancestress of Grandchildren,
       Ancestor of Grandchildren,
Our Grandmother,
       Our Grandfather,   *20*
Xpiacoc
       And Xmucane.
If you plow it
       And it is then planted
Then it will brighten into   *25*
       Our being called upon,
Our being supported,
       Our being remembered
By the formed people,
       The shaped people,   *30*
The doll people.
       The made up people.
Do it then.
       So be it.
Manifest you   *35*
       Your names,

Hunter Possum,
 Hunter Coyote,
Grandmother,
 Grandfather,   *40*
Great Pig,
 Great Coati,
Gemcutter,
 Jeweller,
Carver,   *45*
 Sculptor,
Green Plate Spirit,
 Blue Bowl Spirit,
Incense Maker,
 Craftsman,   *50*
Grandmother of Day,
 Grandmother of Light.
Be called upon by what we form,
 What we shape.
Cast with the corn;   *55*
 With the tz'ite beans operate,
And it will just come
 To pass
That we elaborate
 And that we chisel out   *60*
His mouth
 And his face for him,"
They declared
 To the Sun Priests.
And then indeed was their throwing, *65*
 Their divining,
That they cast with corn
 And with tz'ite—
The Sun
 And Shaper.   *70*
And then spoke a Grandmother
 And a Grandfather to them.
There was the Grandfather:
 He was the tz'ite man.
Xpiacoc was his name.   *75*
 There was the Grandmother,
Sun Priest,
 The Shaper,
At his feet,
 Xmucane was her name.   *80*
And they said
 As they began to divine,

> "*Just look around*
> > *And just find it,*
> You say.   *85*
> > Our ear hears
> Your speaking
> > What may have been said.
> *Just find the wood to be worked*
> > *And to be carved*   *90*
> *By the Former*
> > *And Shaper.*
> *Indeed this will be a nourisher*
> > *And supporter*
> When it is planted then,   *95*
> > When it brightens then.
> Oh, Corn,
> > Oh, Tz'ite,
> Oh, Sun,
> > Oh, Shaper,   *100*
> Join now
> > And be coupled"

TRANSLATED BY MUNRO EDMUNSON

Nahuatl Language

Once the lingua franca of the area known as Mesoamerica, Nahuatl names most of its present-day states, such as Mexico, Guatemala, Cuzcatlán (the old name of El Salvador), and Nicaragua. It was inherited from Toltec and other predecessors by the Aztecs or Mexica, the major political power in the area when Cortés arrived in 1519. Based initially on folding books written in the iconic script of Mesoamerica, the literature in Nahuatl is vast and includes annals, histories, cosmogonies, epics, poems, hymns, prayers, letters, and petitions. Spoken by a million or more people in Mexico, it has recently undergone a literary renaissance.

■ Tlatelolco Annals (1528) *Mexico* (chronicles)

The annals of Tlatelolco, the twin city of the Aztec capital Tenochtitlán, span the twelfth century to 1528. In them, local historians tell how the Spaniards were at first welcomed there in the year 1 Reed (1519), before being expelled on account of their barbaric behavior. In the year 3 Reed (1521), the Spaniards and their Tlaxcalán allies returned, built a fleet to control the lake that surrounded the capital, and besieged it. At the very end, the battle shifted from Tenochtitlán to Tlatelolco, where the emperor Cuauhtemoc finally surrendered to Hernán Cortés.

All This Happened among Us

TRANSLATED BY GORDON BROTHERSTON

And all this happened among us. We saw it. We lived through it with
    an astonishment worthy of tears
and of pity for the pain we suffered.
On the roads lie broken shafts and torn hair,
houses are roofless, homes are stained red,   5
worms swarm in the streets, walls are spattered with brains.
The water is reddish, like dyed water;
we drink it so, we even drink brine;
the water we drink is full of saltpetre.
The wells are crammed with adobe bricks.   *10*

Whatever was still alive was kept between shields, like precious treasure, between shields, until it was eaten.

We chewed on hard *tzompantli* wood, brackish *zacatl* fodder, chunks of adobe, lizards, vermin, dust and worms.

We eat what was on the fire, as soon as it is done we eat it together right by the fire.

We had a single price; there was a standard price for a youth, a priest, a boy and a young girl. The maximum price for a slave amounted to only two handfuls of maize, to only ten tortillas. Only twenty bundles of brackish fodder was the price of gold, jade, mantles, quetzal plumes; all valuables fetched the same low price. It went down further when the Spaniards set up their battering engine in the market place.

Now, Cuauhtemoc orders the prisoners to be brought out; the guards don't miss any. The elders and chiefs grab them by their extremities and Cuauhtemoc slits open their bellies with his own hand.

■ The Aztec Priests' Speech (1524) *Mexico* (poem)

TRANSLATED BY GORDON BROTHERSTON AND EDWARD DORN

In 1524, twelve Franciscan missionaries were sent from Rome to urge the Aztec priesthood to convert to Christianity. Their efforts provoked this considered reply, the record of which was revised and polished in 1564 by Nahuatl scribes from Tlatelolco and other centers. It opens on a note of humility and courtesy, like the welcome first offered by Moctezuma to Cortés in 1519. The speaker then rehearses the claims made by the Christians on their own behalf, which gives them an ironic air. Yet his concern is professional: the Aztecs no more want to demolish the friars than they themselves wish to be demolished. Knowing that both parties have been "cast in a corner" by the secular authority Cortés ("our sovereign here"), they say they prefer not to unsettle things "with what we say amongst ourselves." What they reveal of their own religion is imaged as three "gifts," proper to the priesthood itself, the maize farmer, and the warrior. This last statement defends a political tradition older than Teotihuacán, which reaches back to the start of the era and the first named city of Mesoamerica, the lowland Tula of Quetzalcoatl, and the ancient Toltecs.

What we say here is for its own reason
beyond response and against our future.

Our revered lords, sirs, dear ones,
take rest from the toil of the road,
you are now in your house and in your nature.   5
Here we are before you, subjected,
in the mirror of yourselves.
Our sovereign here has let you come,
you have come to rule
as you must in your own place.   10
Where is it you come from,
how is it that your gods have been scattered
from their municipal centres?
Out of the clouds, out of the mist,
out of ocean's midst you have appeared.   15
The Alldeity takes form in you,
in your eye, in your ear, in your lips.
So, as we stand here,
we see, we address,
the one through whom everything lives,   20
the night, the Wind,
whose representatives you are.

And we have felt the breath, the word
of our lord the Alldeity
which you have brought with you.   25
The speaker of the world sent you because of us.
Here we are, amazed by this.
You brought his book with you, his script,
heaven's word, the word of god.

And now what? How is it,   30
what are we supposed to say,
what shall we present to your ears?

Can it be said we are anything at all?
We are small subjects.

We are just dirt,   35
no good,
pressed, reduced to want;
furthermore our sovereign here
mistook us consistently
and has cast us into a corner.   40

But we refute the logo of the Alldeity.

We are down to our skulls in this and we fall over
into the river, into the abyss.
Anger and wrath
will be attracted to our behaviour.   45
Maybe this is our moment; perhaps this is ruin.
In any case, we shall be dispirited.
Where do we go from here
in our subjection,
reduced, mortalized?   50
Cut us loose,
because the gods have died.
But you don't have to feel any of this.

Our dear lords,
we share some of it all.   55
Now we open a little
the store, the treasure casket,
for our sovereign here.

You say
we don't know   60
the Alldeity of heaven and earth.
You say our gods are not original.
That's news to us
and it drives us crazy.

It's a shock and a scandal.   65
Our ancestors came to earth
and spoke quite differently.

They gave us
their law
and they believed,   70
they served, and they taught honour among gods;
they taught the whole service.
That's why we eat earth before them;
that's why we draw our blood and do penance;
and why we burn copal and kill the living.   75
They were the Lifelord
and they became our only subject.
When and where? — In the eldest Darkness.

They gave us
our supper and our breakfast,   80
all things to drink and eat,
maize and beans, purslane and sage.
And we beg them
for thunder rain and water
on which the earth thrives.   85
They are the rich ones
and they have more than simply what it takes;
they are the ones with the stuff,
all ways and all means, forever,
the greenness of growth.   90
Where and how? — In Tlalocan
hunger is not their experience,
nor sickness, and not poverty.

They also gave
inner manliness, kingly valour   95
and the acquisitions of the hunt:
the insignia of the lip, the knotting of the mantle,
loin-cloth and mantle,
Flower and aromatic leaf, jade,
quetzal plumes, and the godshit you call gold.   100
When and where? It is a long tradition.
Do you know
when the emplacement of Tula came, of Uapalcalco,
of Xuchatlappan, of Tamoanchan
of Yoalli ichan, of Teotihuacan?   105
They were the world-makers who founded
the mat of power, the seat of rule.
They gave

authority and entity,
fame and honour.   *110*
And should we now destroy the old law,
Toltec law, Chichimec law,
Colhua law,
Tepanec law,
on which the heart of being flows,   *115*
from which we animate our selves,
through which we pass to adulthood,
from which flows our cosmology
and the manner of our prayer?

Oooh! Señores Nuestros,   *120*
do nothing;
don't do anything to your population.
It can only bring more ruin,
it can only bring more ruin to the old ones,
our elders, from whom man and woman have grown.   *125*

Let us not
anger the gods;
let us not invite their hunger.
Do not unsettle this population.
Why should we agitate them   *130*
with what we say among us?
If you want peace
don't force the people
to see we are put aside.

Let's think about this.   *135*
We don't believe. We don't mock.
We may offend you,
for here stand
the citizens,
the officials,   *140*
the chiefs,
the trustees and rulers of this entire world.

It is enough that we have done penance,
that we are ruined,
that we are forbidden and stripped of power.   *145*
To remain here is to be imprisoned.
Make of us
the thing that most suits you.
This is all we have to reply,
Señores.   *150*

■ Twenty Sacred Hymns (1554) *Mexico*

The highest form of Nahuatl poetry, these hymns were recorded by the Franciscan friar Bernardino de Sahagún around 1559 just north of Tenochtitlán. He attached them to the Florentine Codex but left them untranslated for fear of their demonic power. Their subjects include the Mexica or Aztec war god Huitzilopochtli, who was "born on his shield," and whose temple stood atop the main pyramid in Tenochtitlán, alongside that of the raingod Tlaloc; the Mother of the Gods Tonantzín, the prototype of the Virgin of Guadalupe; the Chichimec patron Mixcoatl or "Cloud-Snake"; the guardians of childbirth; and Cinteotl and other maize deities. An idea of the complex language of these hymns can be gleaned from the term *jaguar-snake* (oceló-coatl) that is applied to Tlaloc. In the visual language of the ancient books, this name evokes his thunder and lightning, as the roar of the jaguar and the strike of the snake. Moreover, in ritual arithmetic Tlaloc's mask is Sign XIX, the sum of the Signs Jaguar (XIV) and Snake (V).

Tlaloc (Hymn 3)

CHORUS In Mexico the god is being asked for a loan
    among the paper banners in four directions
    now is the time for weeping

PRIEST I am prepared   I take to the courtyard
    the bundles of bloodthorns of my god   5
    you are my commander magic prince
    and you are the one who makes our flesh
    you are the very first one   the offerings
    can only cause you shame

TLALOC But if someone causes me shame   10
    it is because he didn't know me
    you are my fathers my elder priesthood
    the Jaguar Snake
    the Jaguar Snake

PRIEST From Tlalocan in a jade boat   15
    Acatonal comes out
    extend yourself in Poyauhtlan
    with rattles of mist he is taken to Tlalocan

VICTIM *My brother, Tozcuecuexi,*
    I am going forever it's the time of weeping   20
    send me to wherever it is
    under his command   I have already said

to the frightening prince I am going forever
it is time for weeping
over four years me shall be carried on the wind   25
unknown to others by you it is told
to the place of the unfleshed
In the house of Quetzal plumes
transformation is effected
it is the due of the one who vivifies men   30

CHORUS Extend yourself in Poyauhtlan
    with rattles of mist he is taken to Tlalocan

TRANSLATED BY GORDON BROTHERSTON AND EDWARD DORN

To the Mother of the Gods (Hymn 4)

Oh, golden flower opened up
    she is our mother
whose thighs are holy
    whose face is a dark mask.
She came from Tamoanchan,   5
    the first place
where all descended
    where all was born.
Oh, golden flower flowered
    she is our mother   10
whose thighs are holy
    whose face is a dark mask.
She came from Tamoanchan
Oh, white flower opened up
    she is our mother   15
whose thighs are holy
    whose face is a dark mask.
She came from Tamoanchan,
    the first place
where all descended   20
    where all was born.
Oh, white flower flowered
    she is our mother
whose thighs are holy
    whose face is a dark mask.   25
She came from Tamoanchan.

*　　*　　*

She lights on the round cactus,
    she is our mother

the dark obsidian butterfly.
    Oh, we saw her as we wandered   *30*
across the Nine Plains,
    she fed herself with deers' hearts.
She is our mother,
    the goddess earth.
    She is dressed   *35*
in plumes
    she is smeared with clay.
In all four directions of wind
    the arrows are broken.
They saw you as a deer   *40*
    in the barren land.
those two men, Xiuhnel and Mimich.

TRANSLATED BY EDWARD KISSAM

To Ease Birth (Hymn 12)

in the house with the tortoise chair
    she will give birth to the pearl
        to the beautiful feather

in the house of the goddess who sits on a tortoise
    she will give birth to the necklace of pearls   *5*
        to the beautiful feathers we are

there she sits on the tortoise
    swelling to give us birth

on your way on your way
    child be on your way to me here   *10*
        you whom I made new

come here child   come be pearl
    be beautiful feather

TRANSLATED BY ANSELM HOLLO

For Eating Unleavened Tamales (Hymn 14)

1
the flower
    my heart
        it opened
at midnight
    that lordly hour   *5*

she has arrived
        Tlaçolteotl
           our mother
               goddess desire

2

in the birth house
in the flower place
on the day called 'one flower'
    the maize god is born

in the vapor and rain place   5
    where we go angling for jewel-fish

    where we too make our young

3

soon day   red sky
quechol-birds in the flowers

4

down here on earth
    you rise in the market place and say
I am the lord Quetzalcoatl

let there be gladness among the flowering trees
    and the quechol-bird tribes   5
who are the souls of the brave

may they rejoice
    hear the word of our lord
the quechol-bird's word

'your brother whom we mourn   10
    will never be killed again
never again will the poison dart strike him'

5

maize flowers
    white and yellow
I have brought from the flower place

see there is the lord of the jewel land
    playing ball in his holy field   5

there he is the old dog god
        Xolotl

6

now go look if Piltzintecutli
    lord fertility himself
has yet lain down in the dark house
        in the house where it grows dark

o Piltzintli Piltzintli   5
    yellow feathers
you glue all over yourself

on the ball-playing field you lie down
    and in the dark house where it grows dark

7

here comes a merchant

a vassal of Xochiquetzal
    mistress of Cholula

(heart o heart
    I fear the maize god is still on his way)   5

a merchant a man from Chacalla
    sells turquoise spikes for your ears
and turquoise bands for your arms

8

the sleeper the sleeper he sleeps

with my hand I have rolled him to sleep

9

here
        the woman
here
        am I
here
           asleep

TRANSLATED BY ANSELM HOLLO, AFTER EDWARD SELER

■ Legend of the Suns (1558) *Mexico* (epic poem)

Completed in the last year of Tenochtitlán's fifty-two-year calendar cycle, this manuscript prefaces its history of highland Tula with a long account of the world ages or "Suns" that inhere in our present Era Four-Ollin (*Ollin* means rubber, elasticity, movement, earthquake; and from it is derived the

name Olmec, the "rubber people" of Mesoamerica's earliest civilization). In
the bridging epic sequence, Quetzalcoatl the traveler in the council of the
gods makes the great descent to the underworld, like the Quiche Twins, and
enters the Food mountain as an ant in order that the people of this era may
be created and fed. For his part, the invalid Nanahuatl sacrifices himself so
that the sun and moon (both male) may be set in motion.

Quetzalcoatl Descends to Mictlan

And then Quetzalcoatl goes to Mictlan, the Dead Land.
He approached the Lord and Lady of Mictlan and said:
"What I have come for is the precious bones which you possess;
I have come to fetch them."
And he was asked: 5
"What do you want to do with them, Quetzalcoatl!"
And he answered:
"What worries the gods is who shall live on earth."
And the Lord of Mictlan then said:
"All right. Blow this conch and carry the bones four times round my 10
 jade circle."
But the conch is totally blocked up.
Quetzalcoatl summons the worms, they hollow it out.

The large and the small bees force their way through.
He blows it; the sound reaches the Lord of Mictlan.

And the Lord of Mictlan next said to him: 15
"All right, take them."
But to his vassals, the Micteca, he said:
"Tell him, o gods, he should leave them here."
But Quetzalcoatl answered:
"No, I'm taking them with me." 20
And then his nahual said to him:
"Just tell them: 'I've left them here.'"
And so he said, he shouted to them:
"I have left them here."
But then he really went back up, clutching the precious bones, 25
male bones on one side, female on the other.
He took them and wrapped them up, and took them with him.
And the Lord of Mictlan again spoke to his vassals:
"O gods, is Quetzalcoatl really taking the bones? Dig him a pit."
They dug him one; he stumbled and fell in. 30
And Quails menaced him and he fainted.

He dropped the precious bones and the Quails tore and pecked at them.
And then Quetzalcoatl came to and weeps and says to his nahual:
"O my nahual, what now?"
And the reply came: 35
"What now? Things went badly; let it be."

When he had brought it there it was ground up
by the woman named Quilaztli, by Cihuacoatl.
Then she placed the meal in a jade bowl and Quetzalcoatl dropped blood
on it by piercing his member.   40
Then all the gods named here did penance like
the Bridger, the Tiller,
the Emerger, the Earth-firmer,
the Plunger, the Shooter:
Quetzalcoatl.   45
And they said:
"The servants of the gods are born." For indeed they did penance for us.

Then they said: "What shall they eat? The gods must find food";
and the ant fetched the maize kernels
from the heart of the Food Mountain.   50
Quetzalcoatl met the ant and said:
"Tell me where you went to find them?"
He asked repeatedly but it didn't answer.
Then it said: "Over there, pointing."
And he accompanied it,   55
becoming a black ant himself.
They both went in
and carried off the maize to Tamoanchan.
The gods chewed it
and put it in our mouths to strengthen us.   60

TRANSLATED BY GORDON BROTHERSTON

The Fifth Sun

This sun is named 4 Movement. We who live today have this one, it's our
sun, though what's here is merely its signification, because the sun fell into
the fire, the spirit oven, at Teotihuacan.

It's the same as the sun of Topiltzin, Quetzalcoatl of Tollan. And before
it was the sun, its name was Nanahuatl, whose home was yonder in Tamoanchan.

Eagle, jaguar, falcon, wolf. 6 Wind, 6 Flower: both are names of the sun.
Now, here is what is called the spirit oven. For four years it burned.

Well then, Tonacateuctli and Xiuhteuctli summoned Nanahuatl. They said to him, "You are the one who must keep the sky and the earth."

And then he was very sad. He said, "What are they saying? There are gods, and I am a worthless invalid!"

They also summoned 4 Flint, the moon. The ones who summoned him were Tlalocanteuctli and Nappateuctli.

And so Nanahuatl fasts. He takes his spines and his needles. Then he gives thorns to the moon, and they do penance.

Then Nanahuatl bathes first. Afterward the moon bathes.

His needles are plumes, his spines are jade. He uses jade as incense.

And when four days have gone by, they feather Nanahuatl, and they chalk him. Then he goes off to fall in the fire, and 4 Flint meanwhile sings and dances for him like a woman.

So Nanahuatl went off to fall in the fire. But the moon only went to fall in the ashes.

And so he went off. And he was able to grab the eagle and carry it along.

But he could not carry the jaguar. It just stood next to the fire and jumped over it. That's how it became spotted. At that time the falcon became smoke-colored. At that time the wolf was singed. These three were unable to go with him.

Well, when he got to the sky, Tonacateuctli and Tonacacihuatl bathed him. Then they sat him in a *quechol* chair. Then they adorned his head with a red border.

Then he tarries in the sky for four days. And then he appears on 4 Movement.

But he spent four days without moving, just staying in place.

Then the gods say, "Why doesn't he move?" Then they send the blade falcon, who goes and tells the sun that it has come to question him. It tells him, "The gods are saying, 'Ask him why he doesn't move.'"

Then the sun said, "Why? Because I'm asking for their blood, their color, their precious substance."

Then the gods hold council. And then Tlahuizcalpanteuctli grows angry. He says, "Well, why is this? I'll shoot him! He must not stay put!"

Then he shoots him. But he failed to hit him.

Meanwhile the sun is shooting at Tlahuizcalpanteuctli, and he succeeds in hitting him because his arrows are like shafts of flame. And then the nine layers covered up his face.

This Tlahuizcalpanteuctli is the frost.

Then all the gods get together. Titlacahuan, Huitzilopochtli, and the women Xochiquetzal, Yapalliicue, Nochpalliicue. And there in Teotihuacan they all died a sacrificial death. So then the sun went into the sky.

And then goes the moon, who had fallen only in the ashes. And when he got to the edge of the sky, Papaztac came and broke his face with a rabbit pot.

And then at a crossroads he met the *tzitzimime,* the *coleletin,* and they said to him, "Come here." They detained him for a long while, dressing him all in rags.

And so it was the sun of 4 Movement that appeared at that time. And at that time, too, he established nightfall.

TRANSLATED BY JOHN BIERHORST

■ Cuauhtitlán Annals (1570) *Mexico* (chronicles)

TRANSLATED BY GORDON BROTHERSTON

The annals of Cuauhtitlán, a town just north of Tenochtitlán give an unbroken count of years from the seventh century, when the Chichimecs first began to emerge from their homeland Seven Caves (Chicomoztoc, some distance to the northwest), up to the arrival of the Spaniards nine centuries later. In its early stages, the authors insert flashbacks that recall how the era itself began millennia ago, having emerged from the cataclysms of the world ages: these correspond exactly to the ones depicted on the giant Sunstone carving of Tenochtitlán and also match the sequence given in the *Popol Vuh.* We also learn in detail about the rise and fall of highland Tula around the tenth century, and how its ruler One Reed was driven out and finally burned himself in the east. Of outstanding brilliance (D. H. Lawrence drew on it in *The Plumed Serpent*), this last passage was made to echo the flight of Quetzalcoatl told in the Florentine Codex, and Jerome Rothenberg, in fact, added it to his translation of that source.

The Five Suns

The first Sun to be founded
has the Sign Four Water.
it is called Water Sun.
Then it happened
that water carried everything away
everything vanished
the people were changed into fish.

The second Sun to be founded
has the Sign Four Jaguar.
it is called Jaguar Sun.
Then it happened
that the sky collapsed

the Sun did not follow its course at midday
immediately it was night
and when it grew dark   15
the people were torn to pieces.
In this Sun giants lived.
The old ones said
the giants greeted each other thus:
"Don't fall over," for whoever fell,   20
fell forever.

The third Sun to be founded
has the Sign Four Rain.
it is called Rain Sun.
It happened then that fire rained down.   25
those who lived there were burned.
And they say that then tiny stones rained down and spread
the fine stones that we can see
the *tezontli* boiled into stone
and the reddish rocks were twisted up.   30

The fourth Sun.
Sign Four Wind,
is called Wind Sun.
Then the wind carried everything away.
The people all turned into monkeys   35
and went to live in the forests.

The fifth Sun.
Sign Four Ollin.
is called Earthquake Sun
because it started into motion.   40
The old ones said
in this Sun there will be earthquakes and general hunger
from which we shall perish.

■ Florentine Codex (1579) *Mexico* (poetry, prose)

The many diverse texts gathered in the Codex served as source material for Bernardino de Sahagún's *History of the Things of New Spain* (ca. 1580). Arranged in twelve books, they offer an encyclopedic range of information about ancient Mexico, in such matters as the origins of the gods and the story of Tula (Book 3), rulers and administration (Book 6), and human types and professions (Book 10).

The Toltecs Were Certainly Rich (Book III)

the toltecs were certainly rich
food was not scarce enough to sell
their vegetables were large
melons for example mostly too fat to get your arms round
maize ears millstone size   5
and they actually *climbed*
      their amaranth plants
cotton came ready dyed
in colours like crimson saffron pink violet leaf-green azure
      verdigris orange umbra grey rose-red and coyote yellow   10
it all just grew that way

they had all kinds of valuable birds
blue cotingas quetzals turpials red-spoonbills
which could talk and sang in tune
jade and gold were low-priced popular possessions   15
they had chocolate too, fine cocoa flowers everywhere

the toltecs did not in fact lack anything
no one was poor or had a shabby house
and the smaller maize ears they used as fuel
to heat their steam baths with   20

TRANSLATED BY GORDON BROTHERSTON AND EDWARD DORN

The Deadly Dance (Book III)

That shaman, owl man,
      dressed himself in shining yellow feathers
once he had won.
      Then he planned that the people
should come together and dance.   5
      So the cryer went to the hill
and announced it,
      and called to all the people.
Everyone in the country around heard him
      and left quickly for   10
Texcalapa, that place in the rocky country.
      They all came,
both nobles and the people,
      young men and young women,
so many they could not be counted,   15
      there were so many.
And then he began his song.

He beats his drum,
again and again.
        They begin to join in the dance.   20
They leap into the air,
        they join hands weaving themselves together,
whirling around, and there is great happiness.
The chant wavers
        up and breaks into the air,   25
returns as an echo from the distant hills
        and sustains itself.
He sang it, he thought of it,
        and they answered him.
As he planned, they took it from his lips.   30
It began at dusk
        and went on halfway to midnight.
And when the dance
        they all did together
reached its climax,   35
        numbers of them hurled themselves from the cliffs
into the gulleys.
        They all died and became stones.
Others, who were on the bridge over the canyon,
        the shaman broke it   40
under them
        though it was stone.
They fell in the rapids
        and became stones.
The Toltecs   45
        never understood what happened there,
they were drunk with it,
        blind,
and afterwards gathered many times there to dance.
Each time,   50
        there were more dead,
        more had fallen from the heights
into the rubble,
        and the Toltecs destroyed themselves.

TRANSLATED BY EDWARD KISSAM

The Artist (Book X)

The artist: disciple, abundant, multiple, restless.
The true artist: capable, practicing, skillful;
maintains dialogue with his heart, meets things with his mind.

The true artist: draws out all from his heart,
works with delight, makes things with calm, with sagacity,   5
works like a true Toltec, composes his objects, works dexterously,
    invents;
arranges materials, adorns them, makes them adjust.

The carrion artist: works at random, sneers at the people,
makes things opaque, brushes across the surface of the face of things,
works without care, defrauds people, is a thief.   10

TRANSLATED BY DENISE LEVERTOV

■ Cantares Mexicanos (Sixteenth Century)
Mexico (songs)

Orphan Song

where is the dios
for whom we live?
where are you?
your sad friends await you
with songs they are grieving   5
with flowers they seek you
they feel pain
searching for your soul
strength, honour, ay!

I say and think   10
if this is orphanhood
what will console my heart
what will ease my sorrow
I who am from Huexotzinco
if my father is gone   15
if my mother is gone
let them be waiting for me
to ease my heart
and the great pain of orphanhood, ay

I note that others here   20
are happy and make merry
they have their capes and jewels
and I suffer
what will make me happy
what will give me pleasure   25
leaving the others here

the lords intertwine
friendship intertwines
the nobility, ay
will come from here, from there   30
yet I want and wish for earthly things
what will make me happy
what will give me pleasure
leaving the others here

you who are the tloque   35
you who are the nahuaque
we here amuse you
and what is to be had from you
who is being served
if you consider us as flowers   40
if we your friends wither?

like precious obsidian you splinter us
like painted script you erase us
everything here goes to the place of the dead
the place where we all disappear   45

as what do you, one god, consider us
that we are born
and die like this?
where shall we disappear to
we the common people?   50
where shall we really go?

hence I weep
for you refuse to act
ypalnemohuani
the jade breaks   55
the quetzal plumes rip
you poke fun
as what, how do you consider us
blotting us out here
destroying us   60

ay what mischance
ypalnemohuani is poking fun
it is a dream to say he is our brother
our hearts convert to the faith
really dios pokes fun   65

hence I weep and grieve
for I was left an orphan
among strangers here on earth
what does your heart desire ypalnemohuani?

let your anger cease   *70*
let orphanhood be glorious
beside you
who are dios and want me dead

TRANSLATED BY LUIS REYES AND GORDON BROTHERSTON

Could It Be True We Live on Earth?

by Nezahualcoyotl

Could it be true we live on earth?
On earth forever?

Just one brief instant here.

Even the finest stones begin to split,
even gold is tarnished,   *5*
even precious bird-plumes
shrivel like a cough.

Just one brief instant here.

TRANSLATED BY EDWARD KISSAM

Death and Rebirth of Tula

At Tula stood the beamed sanctuary,
only the snake columns still stand,
our prince Nacxitl has gone, has moved away.
  Our vanguard is wept for with conches;
  he is going to his destruction in Tlapallan.   *5*

He was there in Cholula,
made an end at Mount Poyauhtecatitlan,
crossed the water at Acallan.
  Our vanguard is wept for with conches;
  he is going to his destruction in Tlapallan.   *10*

I come to the frontier with winged finery,
the lord who pierces and the victim.
  My fine-plumed lord has gone away
  has left me, 10-Flower, an orphan.

The pyramid burst apart hence my tears   15
the sacred sand whirled up hence my desolation.
    My fine-plumed lord has gone away
    has left me, 10-Flower, an orphan.

Tlapallan is where you are expected
is where you are destined to rest;   20
you are moving on, my fine-plumed lord,
destined for Xicalanco.
Still yet, still yet. . . .
    Your house will always be there, your gates
    your palace will always be there.   25
    You left them orphaned here at the Tula frontier.

You wept endlessly, great lord;
    your house will always be there, your gates
    your palace will always be there.
    You left them orphaned here at the Tula frontier.   30
Stone and wood, you painted them
in the city of Tula.
    Where you ruled, our prince Nacxitl,
    your name will never be destroyed;
    your people will always cry for you.   35

The turquoise house and the snake house, you built them
in the city of Tula.
    Where you ruled, our prince Nacxitl,
    your name will never be destroyed;
    your people will always cry for you.   40
As white and yellow maize I am born,
The many-coloured flower of living flesh rises up
and opens its glistening seeds before the face of our mother.
In the moisture of Tlalocan, the quetzal water-plants open their
    corollas.
I am the work of the only god, his creation.   45

    Your heart lives in the painted page,
    you sing the royal fibres of the book,
    you make the princes dance,
    there you command by the water's discourse.
He created you,   50
he uttered you like a flower,
he painted you like a song:
a Toltec artist.
The book has come to the end:
your heart is now complete.   55

Here through art I shall live for ever.   *60*
Who will take me, who will go with me?
Here I stand, my friends.
A singer, from my heart I strew my songs,
my fragrant songs before the face of others.
I carve a great stone, I paint thick wood   *65*
my song is in them.

It will be spoken of when I have gone.
I shall leave my song-image on earth.
       My heart shall live, it will come back,
          my memory will live and my fame.   *70*
I cry as I speak and discourse with my heart.
Let me see the root of song,
let me implant it here on earth so it may be realized.
       My heart shall live, it will come back,
          my memory will live and my fame.   *75*
The Prince Flower gently breathes his aroma,
our flowers are uniting.
       My song is heard and flourishes.
       My implanted word is sprouting,
          our flowers stand up in the rain.   *80*
The Cocoa flower gently opens his aroma,
the gentle Peyote falls like rain.
       My song is heard and flourishes.
       My implanted word is sprouting,
          our flowers stand up in the rain.

                    TRANSLATED BY GORDON BROTHERSTON

Three Nahuatl Poems

One by one I proclaim your songs:
       I bind them on, gold crabs, as if they were anklets:
       like emeralds I gather them.
Clothe yourself in them: they are your riches.
       Bathe in feathers of the quetzal,   *5*
your treasury of birds, plumes, black and yellow,
the red feathers of the macaw
beat your drums about the world:
deck yourself out in them: they are your riches.

                    TRANSLATED BY WILLIAM CARLOS WILLIAMS

Where am I to go, whither?
    The road's there, the road to Two-Gods.
    Well, who checks men here,
here where all lack a body,
at the bottom of the sky?   5
Or, maybe, it is only on Earth
that we lose the body?
    Cleaned out, rid of it completely,
His House: there remains none on this earth!
Who is it that said: 10
Where find them? our friends no longer exist!

TRANSLATED BY WILLIAM CARLOS WILLIAMS

Will he return will Prince Cuautli ever return?
Will Ayocuan, the one who drove an arrow into the sky?
Shall these two yet gladden you?
    Events don't recur: we vanish once only.
Hence the cause of my weeping: 5
Prince Ayocuan, warrior chief
governed us harshly.
His pride waxed more, he grew haughty
here among men.
    But his time is finished . . .   10
he can no longer come to bow down before Father and Mother. . . .
This is the reason for my weeping:
He has fled to the place where all lack a body.

TRANSLATED BY WILLIAM CARLOS WILLIAMS

■ Yancuic Tlahtolli: The New Word (1990)
Mexico (poem)

TRANSLATED BY GORDON BROTHERSTON

    J. Fausto Hernández Hernández's poem appeared in Martínez Hernández's monolingual anthology of Nahuatl poetry published in Tlaxcala (1987). The person addressed could be either father or mother; hardship has driven both sexes to find work in the cities, especially in the northern Veracruz area from which this poem comes.

Bird

by J. Fausto Hernández Hernández

Bird, you went, and lost your head
Why did you not return to your nest?
Where in truth are you?
Where, my fellow bird?
Where shall I find you?   5
Then towards evening I find you
they hurt you and now you are ill
it's a sin what they did to you precious bird
now you will no longer be able to return, fellow of mine
and now what will there be in your nest?   10
the babies await you
they await since they are hungry and cold
they cry and endlessly await you

2

Discovery, Conquest, and the Colonies

■

INTRODUCTION

For Europe, the discovery of the New World was, as "New World" implies, an astonishing encounter with oceans, many populated islands, and two new continents. No discovery of place, even of a second moon or alternate solar system, could have rivaled the significance of those enormous unexplored Americas, which made the last years of the fifteenth and the entire sixteenth century the age of discovery for the sea-going nations of Europe. The old restrictive circles of knowledge were broken. The English poet John Donne (1572–1631) woke as a young man in his bedroom, looked out the window to the ports across the seas to an amazing light, presence, and mystery; he called out to his America as if addressing a new lover who would bequeath him youth, life, and hope: "Oh my America, my new found lande / . . . How blest am I in this discovering thee" ("Elegie: To His Mistris Going to Bed"). Curiosity, enthusiasm, dreams, religious mission, and greed led adventurers, colonizers, and missionary priests to risk

᪥ ᪥ ᪥ ᪥ ᪥ ᪥ ᪥ ᪥ ᪥ ᪥ ᪥ ᪥ ᪥ ᪥ ᪥ ᪥

the waters between old Europe and the virgin terrains of the Native American (whose civilizations were actually as old as Athens and Rome). The discoverers, who were Italian, Spanish, Portuguese, Dutch, and English, eventually brought their languages to the far lands they would conquer and inhabit. The colonizers would also bring slaves from Africa to augment their workforce of conscripted Indians, thereby introducing new peoples, languages, and cultures into the ethnic mix of the newfound continents, now consisting of West Europeans, Native Americans, and Africans.

The first to record the New World was its discoverer, Christopher Columbus (1451–1506), an Italian in the hire of the Spanish monarchy. Columbus, as revealed in his ship's log, was a fabulist and a dreamer who first cast the Americas into the mold of a "New World," a virgin territory, an undiscovered and unexplored land inhabited by a gentle and innocent people. These romantic terms are undermined by the other motives revealed in his log—warlike imperialism, missionary zeal, and hunger for gold. The cost of discovery to the Native Americans, however, was the vast destruction of their writings, cultural integrity, and independence. The preceding section is a selection from what has survived.

In this next section, we cover the writings of the discoverers, conquistadors, and people of the colonies. After Columbus came the chroniclers, who walked with the conquerors and recorded the adventures and tragedies, followed by critics of the conquerors, such as the Spanish missionary Bartolomé de las Casas (1474–1566), who in his monumental *History of the Indies* decried Native American slavery. Then followed the ethnographers, historians, poets, and fabulists of the New World literatures, including the Inca Garcilaso de la Vega (1539–1616), son of a Spanish conquistador and an Inca princess, who through oral sources preserved an Inca version of his people's history and religion. Garcilaso's extensive and elegant writings clarified the fact that while the New World was new to Europe (as China and Japan once seemed new to the West), to Native American inhabitants the New World was their own, their very old and familiar, world, with complex and diverse cultures, each of which implied a long prehistory prior to the conquest. Finally come the writers of Latin America and the Caribbean.

■ Christopher Columbus (1451?–1506)
Italy/Spain/Española (ship's log)

TRANSLATED BY ROBERT H. FUSON

The Italian explorer Christopher Columbus, in the service of the Catholic monarchs Queen Isabella and King Ferdinand of Spain, set out in 1492 from Spain for China and Japan by sailing to the west. Convinced that the world was round—as was any literate seaman of his age—he hoped thereby to find a shorter route to Asia. Columbus proposed that the traditional slow wagons of the Silk Road, carrying valuable spices, silks, and other goods from central and eastern Asia to Europe, be replaced by ships sailing directly to Asia's eastern shores, which he calculated lay about three thousand miles west of Lisbon. He promised his royal patrons great economic gains. So in 1492, the same year that saw Spain's reconquest of Andalusia from the Moors, the expulsion or forced conversion of Spanish Jews, and the unification of Spain, the Spanish monarchs backed Columbus's wild venture of sailing west to find the East. Between Columbus and Asia, however, was a continent, soon to be called America in honor of Amerigo Vespucci, Columbus's fellow Italian cartographer and explorer. On landing in Hispaniola, Columbus thought, or wished to think, that he was indeed in Asia, on islands off the subcontinent of India: hence the West Indies, Indians, and many related misnomers, which trace their etymological origin to the Hindus River from which India also took its name.

It is said that Columbus was born Cristofero Colombo in Genoa, Italy, in 1451. Yet the date and place of his birth remain in doubt. Columbus (or Cristóbal Colón, the Spanish name he went by most of his life) concealed and confused his personal background. Many places claim him, including the Greek island of Chios, a former Genoese colony; Catalan Mallorca, which satisfies those Spanish historians who claim a concealed Spanish-Jewish or convert background; and even Galicia, a Portuguese-speaking part of Spain. As a young man, the talented navigator attempted to convince John II of Portugal and later the Spanish and English courts to finance his venture. After the capture of Granada from the Moors, Isabella agreed to commission Columbus to organize a voyage in the name of Spain, and on August 3, 1492, he sailed from Palos de la Frontera in Andalusian Spain, with three small ships under his command—the *Santa María*, the *Pinta*, and the *Niña*. After landing on a small island in the Bahamas and exploring Cuba, he reached Hispaniola on December 5. Soon, his flagship *Santa María* was wrecked, and after taking captives and some cultural objects from his discovered world, he hurried back to Spain on the *Niña*. He left behind a colony of some forty crew members (who, he found on his second voyage, had been killed). In Spain, he was welcomed as a hero and his royal patrons declared him to be "Admiral of the Ocean Sea" and "Governor of All Territories Discovered and to Be Discovered."

In his writings about the discovery, Columbus reflects an idyllic point of view, although in them we may surmise, and elsewhere learn, that the discovery and conquest also were to bring extermination to the Arawak Indian population of Hispaniola. With and after Columbus came a radical alteration of the discovered world. Although Columbus himself never encountered the highly developed societies that Cortés was to meet and demolish, his initial explorations, the goal of which was to acquire wealth and slaves, all in the name of nation and religion, set in motion the world's ancient and modern habit of conquest and destruction. In the Spain of his day, while the Holy Inquisition was busy cleansing the country of heresy by burning both "converts" and old Christians suspected of religious insincerity, its monarchs were dispatching captains and priests to spread the Christian faith to peoples it considered pagan and idolatrous. The lustful dream of gold and the entry of armies of conquistador and inquisitor into the New World ultimately led to the virtual obliteration of the architectural, sculptural, and written records of past and contemporaneous civilizations of the Americas. Whereas the Incas and Aztecs were at a high point, the Olmec and Maya city states had long since been abandoned by the time Spain set foot in Mesoamerica. But past and present were annihilated wherever they were found. William Prescott's famed histories of the conquests of Peru and Mexico, albeit written in the nineteenth century, describe in great detail the extinction of the foremost New World civilizations.

As in the chronicles recorded by later conquistadors and their scribes, Columbus's initial response to the newly sighted lands was amazement. His word pictures of the Indies were noble and beautiful just as medieval depictions sanctified the cruel and devastating Crusades as courageous and noble pilgrimages to the Holy Land. Those green islands that Columbus came upon—the Bahamas, Cuba, and Hispaniola (Española)—the explorer romantically perceived as new Gardens of Eden. Their description in his journal and letters evokes the marvelous, not unlike Pliny's *Natural Histories,* Marco Polo's wonders along the Silk Road to Asia, and the chivalric novels of the late Middle Ages and early Renaissance that, a century later, were to madden and illumine the mind of Spain's famous internal explorer, Don Quijote de la Mancha. And like Quijote, who saw windmills as monsters in Spain's heartland, Columbus found sirens singing in the Caribbean, guardian Amazons armored with plates of copper in Martinique; he told of men with tails and heard nightingales singing across the islands where no nightingales were. Closer to reality, he found naked "timid" Indians (he was the first to use the term *indios* from which English "Indian" derives); quick huge canoes; gum mastic (*chicle*) that reminded him of the lake of gum on the Greek island of Chios (Homer's reputed birthplace); and bears, fabrics, rhubarb, cinnamon, and golden jewelry. The gold, with its specific wonders, did not disinterest him or his royal sponsors. In exchange for help, he promised his highnesses as much gold as they would want and as much cotton, spice, and slaves as they would command.

In October 1493, fitted out with a fleet of seventeen ships and some fifteen hundred colonists, Columbus sailed from Cádiz on his second voyage to what he called the "other world." He made landfall on the Lesser Antilles, the Leeward Islands, and Puerto Rico; surveyed Cuba; and colonized Hispaniola, leaving his brother Bartolomew in charge. After some three years, he returned to Spain, with few possessions to justify his dream and promise of great wealth and with a sickly crew disgruntled by their meager earnings. His third voyage in 1498 was personally calamitous. He was obliged to carry convicts aboard his ships as the new colonists. He reached the mouth of the Orinoco River in present-day Venezuela. In 1500, after reports of terrible conditions in the colonies, Isabella and Ferdinand sent an independent governor to arrest Governor Columbus, who was accordingly brought back to Spain in chains.

On arrival, Columbus was quickly freed, but by then, with other navigators having explored the coasts of South America, including Amerigo Vespucci, Columbus's name had lost its currency. With difficulty, he convinced the court to support a fourth voyage. Anxious to redeem his reputation by finding Asia, or at least a quick passage to it beyond those islands he had discovered, in 1502 Columbus set out on his fourth voyage into the western seas. He reached his Indies where, through trade, he obtained many gold masks and gold pendants. Continuing his discoveries, enduring storms, swarms of mosquitoes, and more disease, he finally struck the coast of Honduras, where he coasted south, experiencing further terrible hardships, until he reached the Gulf of Darien. He attempted to sail to the colony at Hispaniola, but he was marooned for about a year in Jamaica. His rescue was delayed by Governor Ovando of Hispaniola, who feared that Columbus might seize his post. During his time on Jamaica, by looking at his almanac he was able to predict an eclipse on February 29, 1504; when the eclipse occurred, he told the Indians he would intercede to restore the dying sun in exchange for desperately needed food, which was thereupon provided him and his mutinous crew. After waiting about a year for his reluctant rescue, he returned to Spain in 1504, his greater hopes all but abandoned.

In his last few years of poverty and failing health, the former Admiral of the Ocean Sea requested the king to restore his name and a fair share of trade profits. He failed in his solicitations. For his epoch and continent, Christopher Columbus, with what scholars have shown to be an unsurpassed skill in dead reckoning, had indeed charted a way to the "other world." He left us the fact of exploration—with all its positive and negative implications—and his writings. The navigator died in his modest dwelling in Valladolid, Spain, in 1506.

In his writing, Columbus described his version of what Jean Jacques Rousseau was to call the "noble savage" and his work was a model for later utopias. In reality, he and those who followed were to bring abundant Old World distopias to the New World—destruction, disease, death, and slavery to native inhabitants of Columbus's America, along with Western civilization, its financial and social hierarchies, and its imposed religions. From a literary point of view, Columbus was an innovator; and in his journal and his significant writings, he was a living and courageous Odysseus, recording his voyages, explorations, and ventures into the geography of the unknown.

FURTHER READING: Columbus, Christopher. *Journals and Other Documents on the Life and Voyages of Christopher Columbus,* 1963; *The Four Voyages of Columbus to the New World: Letters.* Edited and translated by J. M. Cohen, 1969; *The Log of Christopher*

Columbus. Translated by Robert H. Fuson, 1992; *The Four Voyages of Columbus: A Documentary History.* Translated and edited by Cecil Jane, 1988; *Book of the Wonders of the World,* 1988. Bradford, Ernle Dusgate Selby. *Christopher Columbus,* 1973. Morison, Samuel Eliot. *Admiral of the Ocean: Christopher Columbus,* 1942. Sable, Martin Howard. *Columbus, Marrano Discoverer from Mallorca,* 1992.

from The Log of Christopher Columbus

The Outward Voyage 3 August to 10 October 1492

In the Name of Our Lord Jesus Christ

Most Christian, exalted, excellent, and powerful princes, King and Queen of the Spains and of the islands of the sea, our Sovereigns: It was in this year of 1492 that Your Highnesses concluded the war with the Moors who reigned in Europe. On the second day of January, in the great city of Granada, I saw the royal banners of Your Highnesses placed by force of arms on the towers of the Alhambra, which is the fortress of the city. And I saw the Moorish king come to the city gates and kiss the royal hands of Your Highnesses, and those of the Prince, my Lord. Afterwards, in that same month, based on the information that I had given Your Highnesses about the land of India and about a Prince who is called the Great Khan, which in our language means "King of Kings," Your Highnesses decided to send me, Christopher Columbus, to the regions of India, to see the Princes there and the peoples and the lands, and to learn of their disposition, and of everything, and the measures which could be taken for their conversion to our Holy Faith.

I informed Your Highnesses how this Great Khan and his predecessors had sent to Rome many times to beg for men learned in our Holy Faith so that his people might be instructed therein, and that the Holy Father had never furnished them, and therefore, many peoples believing in idolatries and receiving among themselves sects of perdition were lost.

Your Highnesses, as Catholic Christians and Princes devoted to the Holy Christian faith and to the spreading of it, and as enemies of the Muslim sect and of all idolatries and heresies, ordered that I should go to the east, but not by land as is customary. I was to go by way of the west, whence until today we do not know with certainty that anyone has gone.

Therefore, after having banished all the Jews[1] from all your Kingdoms and realms, during this same month of January Your Highnesses ordered me to

---

1. The General Edict on the expulsion of the Jews from Spain was actually issued on March 31, 1492. This complicated situation, which evolved over the course of many years, is carefully analyzed by Simon Wiesenthal in *The Secret Mission of Christopher Columbus.*

go with a sufficient fleet to the said regions of India. For that purpose I was granted great favors and ennobled; from then henceforward I might entitle myself *Don* and be High Admiral of the Ocean Sea and Viceroy and perpetual Governor of all the islands and continental land that I might discover and acquire, as well as any other future discoveries in the Ocean Sea. Further, my eldest son shall succeed to the same position, and so on from generation to generation for ever after.

I left Granada on Saturday, the 12th day of the month of May in the same year of 1492 and went to the town of Palos, which is a seaport. There I fitted out three vessels, very suited to such an undertaking. I left the said port well supplied with a large quantity of provisions and with many seamen on the third day of the month of August in the said year, on a Friday, half an hour before sunrise. I set my course for the Canary Islands of Your Highnesses, which are in the Ocean Sea, from there to embark on a voyage that will last until I arrive in the Indies and deliver the letter of Your Highnesses to those Princes, and do all that Your Highnesses have commanded me to do.

To this end I decided to write down everything I might do and see and experience on this voyage, from day to day, and very carefully. Also, Sovereign Princes, besides describing each night what takes place during the day, and during the day the sailings of the night, I propose to make a new chart for navigation, on which I will set down all the sea and lands of the Ocean Sea, in their correct locations and with their correct bearings. Further, I shall compile a book and shall map everything by latitude and longitude. And above all, it is fitting that I forget about sleeping and devote much attention to navigation in order to accomplish this. And these things will be a great task.

Sunday, 2 September 1492

I arrived this morning in Gomera without incident. There are many fine Spaniards on this island, including Doña Beatriz de Pedraza y Bobadilla, the mistress of the island. These Spaniards swear under oath that every year they see land to the west, where the sun sets. I remember that when I was in Portugal, in 1484, a man came from the island of Madeira to ask the King for a caravel to go to the land that he had seen in the west. Also, people in the Azores say that they see land to the west every year. All these people see this land to the west under the same conditions and report it to be about the same size.

Monday, 3 September 1492

When I went to Grand Canary to help Martín Alonso with his rudder, I left a dozen men on Gomera under the command of Pedro Gutiérrez. As an officer of the royal household, he is most experienced in obtaining supplies and is well qualified in the areas of food acquisition and storage.

Gutiérrez has already acquired all the wood and water necessary for the voyage, which I estimate will last 21 days. However, to be on the safe side, in case of contrary winds or currents, I ordered Gutiérrez to prepare for a voyage of 28 days. I anticipate no problem in replenishing our supplies when we reach the Indies.

Wednesday, 5 September 1492

The ships have been loaded, and all is ready for the voyage. Tonight I shall order a special service of thanksgiving; at sunrise I will lift anchors to begin the journey westward.

Thursday, 6 September 1492

Shortly before noon I sailed from the harbor at Gomera and set my course to the west. I am somewhat disturbed by word I received this morning from the captain of a caravel that came to Gomera from the island of Hierro.[2] He reported that a Portuguese squadron of three caravels is in the vicinity of Hierro, apparently with orders to prevent me from departing the Canaries. There could be some truth in this, for King John[3] must be angry that I went over to Castile.

Sunday, 9 September 1492

(Most of this entry [except for course, speed and distance notations] has been interpolated from Fernando's Historie.)

This day we completely lost sight of land, and many men sighed and wept for fear they would not see it again for a long time. I comforted them with great promises of lands and riches. To sustain their hope and dispel their fears of a long voyage, I decided to reckon fewer leagues than we actually made. I did this that they might not think themselves so great a distance from Spain as they really were. For myself I will keep a confidential accurate reckoning.

Monday, 10 September 1492

Today I made 180 miles at a speed of $7\frac{1}{2}$ knots. I recorded only 144 miles in order not to alarm the sailors if the voyage is lengthy.

---

2. *Hierro* ("iron") is the Spanish name, but the Portuguese *Ferro* is more often used on charts today. Columbus always used *Hierro*.

3. King John II of Portugal (João II). Spain and Portugal were at peace, but the Portuguese would have been concerned with a Spanish expedition to their West African claims. This may have been the reason why there was a Portuguese squadron in the area.

Saturday, 15 September 1492

I sailed to the west day and night for 81 miles, or more. Early this morning I saw a marvelous meteorite fall into the sea 12 or 15 miles away to the SW. This was taken by some people to be a bad omen, but I calmed them by telling of the numerous occasions that I have witnessed such events. I have to confess that this is the closest that a falling star has ever come to my ship.

Sunday, 16 September 1492

The weather is like April in Andalucia, with mild breezes, and the mornings are a delight. The only thing lacking is the call of the nightingales. We have begun to see large patches of yellowish-green weed, which seems to have been torn away from some island or reef. I know that the weed has not come from the mainland because I make the mainland to be farther on.

Monday, 17 September 1492

I held my course to the west and made, day and night, 150 miles or more, but I only logged 141 miles. I have a favorable current. I saw a great deal of weed[4] today—weed from rocks that lie to the west. I take this to mean that we are near land. The weed resembles stargrass, except that it has long stalks and shoots and is loaded with fruit like the mastic tree. Some of this weed looks like river grass, and the crew found a live crab in a patch of it. This is a sure sign of land, for crabs are not found even 240 miles from shore.

The sea is less salty by half[5] than it is in the Canaries, and the breezes are more gentle. Everyone is cheerful, and the *Pinta,* the fastest sailing vessel, went ahead as fast as it could in order to sight land.

Tuesday, 18 September 1492

I sailed day and night more than 165 miles, but I recorded only 144 miles. The sea has been as smooth as the river at Sevilla. Martín Alonso Pinzón, who had sailed ahead yesterday in the *Pinta,* a very fast sailer, lay-to for me to come up. He told me that he saw a great flight of birds moving westward. He hoped to sight land last night; that is why he was going so fast. He is a fine captain and very resourceful, but his independence disturbs me somewhat. I trust that this tendency to strike out on his own does not continue, for we can ill afford to become separated this far from home.

---

4. Columbus was entering the Sargasso Sea; any weed of the genus *Sargassum* is called "sargasso weed" or simply "sargassum."

5. There is no basis for this comment.

Thursday, 20 September 1492

The sailors caught a little fish, and we saw much weed of the kind I have already mentioned, even more than before, stretching to the north as far as you can see. In a way this weed comforted the men, since they have concluded that it must come from some nearby land. But at the same time, it caused some of them great apprehension because in some places it was so thick that it actually held back the ships. Since fear evokes imaginary terrors, the men thought that the weed might become so thick and matted that there might happen to them what is supposed to have happened to St. Amador, when he was trapped in a frozen sea that held his ship fast.

Sunday, 23 September 1492

The crew is still grumbling about the wind. When I get a wind from the SW or west it is inconstant, and that, along with a flat sea, has led the men to believe that we will never get home. I told them that we are near land and that is what is keeping the sea smooth. Later, when the sea made up considerably without wind, they were astonished. I saw this as a sign from God, and it was very helpful to me. Such a sign has not appeared since Moses led the Jews out of Egypt, and they dared not lay violent hands on him because of the miracle that God had wrought. As with Moses when he led his people out of captivity, my people were humbled by this act of the Almighty.

Monday, 24 September 1492

I returned to my westerly course and made about 43½ miles, logging only 36. A tern came to the ship, and I saw many petrels.

I am having serious trouble with the crew, despite the signs of land that we have and those given to us by Almighty God. In fact, the more God shows the men manifest signs that we are near land, the more their impatience and inconstancy increases, and the more indignant they become against me. All day long and all night long those who are awake and able to get together never cease to talk to each other in circles, complaining that they will never be able to return home. They have said that it is insanity and suicidal on their part to risk their lives following the madness of a foreigner. They have said that not only am I willing to risk my life just to become a great Lord, but that I have deceived them to further my ambition. They have also said that because my proposition has been contradicted by so many wise and lettered men who considered it vain and foolish, they may be excused for whatever might be done in the matter. Some feel that they have already arrived where men have never dared to sail and that they are not obliged to go to the end of the world, especially if they are delayed anymore and will not have sufficient provisions to return. I am told by a few trusted men (and these are few in number!) that if I persist in going onward, the best course of action will be to throw me into the sea some night. They will then affirm that I fell overboard while taking the position of the North Star with my quadrant.[6] Since I am a foreigner, little or no account will be asked of the matter, but rather, there will be a great many who will swear that God had given me my just desserts on account of my rashness. I know that the men are taking these complaints to the Pinzóns and that the Pinzóns have sided with them.

Inasmuch as most of these people are from Palos and the surrounding area, they stick together, and I know that Martín Alonso cannot be trusted. He is a skilled mariner, but he wants the rewards and honors of this enterprise for himself. He is always running ahead of the fleet, seeking to be the first to sight land. But I am fully aware that I must use him, for his support is too great among the men. I am also confident that if I lose command, the fleet will never reach the Indies and will probably never get back to Spain. With God's help I shall persevere.

The Discovery of the Bahamas
11 to 27 October 1492

Thursday, 11 October 1492

I sailed to the WSW, and we took more water aboard than at any other time on the voyage. I saw several things that were indications of land. At one time a large flock of sea birds flew overhead, and a green reed was found floating near the ship. The crew of the *Pinta* spotted some of the same reeds and some other plants; they also saw what looked like a small board or plank. A stick was recovered that looks manmade, perhaps carved with an iron tool. Those on the *Niña* saw a little stick covered with barnacles. I am certain that many things were overlooked because of the heavy sea, but even these few made the crew breathe easier; in fact, the men have even become cheerful. I sailed 81 miles from sunset yesterday to sunset today. As is our custom, vespers were said in the late afternoon, and a special thanksgiving was offered to God for giving us renewed hope through the many signs of land He has provided.

After sunset I ordered the pilot to return to my original westerly course, and I urged the crew to be ever-vigilant. I took the added precaution of doubling the number of lookouts, and I reminded the men that the first to sight land would be given a silk doublet as a personal token from me. Further, he would be given an annuity of 10,000 maravedíes from the Sovereigns.

---

6. An "improved," lightweight mariner's astrolabe.

About 10 o'clock at night, while standing on the sterncastle, I thought I saw a light to the west. It looked like a little wax candle bobbing up and down. It had the same appearance as a light or torch belonging to fishermen or travellers who alternately raised and lowered it, or perhaps were going from house to house. I am the first to admit that I was so eager to find land that I did not trust my own senses, so I called for Pedro Gutiérrez, the representative of the King's household, and asked him to watch for the light. After a few moments, he too saw it. I then summoned Rodrigo Sánchez of Segovia, the comptroller of the fleet, and asked him to watch for the light. He saw nothing, nor did any other member of the crew. It was such an uncertain thing that I did not feel it was adequate proof of land.

The moon, in its third quarter, rose in the east shortly before midnight. I estimate that we were making about 9 knots and had gone some 67½ miles between the beginning of night and 2 o'clock in the morning. Then, at two hours after midnight, the *Pinta* fired a cannon, my prearranged signal for the sighting of land.

I now believe that the light I saw earlier was a sign from God and that it was truly the first positive indication of land. When we caught up with the *Pinta*, which was always running ahead because she was a swift sailer, I learned that the first man to sight land was Rodrigo de Triana, a seaman from Lepe.

I hauled in all sails but the mainsail and lay-to till daylight. The land is about 6 miles to the west.

Friday, 12 October 1492

(Log entry for 12 October is combined with that of 11 October.)

At dawn we saw naked people, and I went ashore in the ship's boat, armed, followed by Martín Alonso Pinzón, captain of the *Pinta,* and his brother, Vincente Yáñez Pinzón, captain of the *Niña.* I unfurled the royal banner and the captains brought the flags which displayed a large green cross with the letters F and Y at the left and right side of the cross. Over each letter was the appropriate crown of that Sovereign. These flags were carried as a standard on all of the ships. After a prayer of thanksgiving I ordered the captains of the *Pinta* and *Niña,* together with Rodrigo de Escobedo (secretary of the fleet), and Rodrigo Sánchez of Segovia (comptroller of the fleet) to bear faith and witness that I was taking possession of this island for the King and Queen. I made all the necessary declarations and had these testimonies carefully written down by the secretary. In addition to those named above, the entire company of the fleet bore witness to this act. To this island I gave the name *San Salvador,*[7] in honor of our Blessed Lord.

---

7. Samana Cay. For a more extensive discussion of the various landfall theories, see Epilogue.

No sooner had we concluded the formalities of taking possession of the island than people began to come to the beach, all as naked as their mothers bore them, and the women also, although I did not see more than one very young girl. All those that I saw were young people, none of whom was over 30 years old. They are very well-built people, with handsome bodies and very fine faces, though their appearance is marred somewhat by very broad heads and foreheads, more so than I have ever seen in any other race. Their eyes are large and very pretty, and their skin is the color of Canary Islanders or of sunburned peasants, not at all black, as would be expected because we are on an east-west line with Hierro in the Canaries. These are tall people and their legs, with no exceptions, are quite straight, and none of them has a paunch. They are, in fact, well proportioned. Their hair is not kinky, but straight, and coarse like horsehair. They wear it short over the eyebrows, but they have a long hank in the back that they never cut. Many of the natives paint their faces; others paint their whole bodies; some, only the eyes or nose. Some are painted black, some white, some red; others are of different colors.

The people here called this island *Guanahaní* in their language, and their speech is very fluent, although I do not understand any of it. They are friendly and well-dispositioned people who bare no arms except for small spears, and they have no iron. I showed one my sword, and through ignorance he grabbed it by the blade and cut himself. Their spears are made of wood, to which they attach a fish tooth at one end, or some other sharp thing.

I want the natives to develop a friendly attitude toward us because I know that they are a people who can be made free and converted to our Holy Faith more by love than by force. I therefore gave red caps to some and glass beads to others. They hung the beads around their necks, along with some other things of slight value that I gave them. And they took great pleasure in this and became so friendly that it was a marvel. They traded and gave everything they had with good will, but it seems to me that they have very little and are poor in everything. I warned my men to take nothing from the people without giving something in exchange.

This afternoon the people of San Salvador came swimming to our ships and in boats made from one log. They brought us parrots, balls of cotton thread, spears, and many other things, including a kind of dry leaf[8] that they hold in great esteem. For these items we swapped them little glass beads and hawks' bells.

---

8. The "dry leaves" are not actually mentioned until the October 15 entry. At that time Columbus tells us that these highly prized dry leaves were offered to him on 12 October. It is reasonable, then, that the tobacco was part of "the many other things" cited in the Log entry.

Many of the men I have seen have scars on their bodies, and when I made signs to them to find out how this happened, they indicated that people from other nearby islands come to San Salvador to capture them; they defend themselves the best they can. I believe that people from the mainland come here to take them as slaves. They ought to make good and skilled servants, for they repeat very quickly whatever we say to them. I think they can easily be made Christians, for they seem to have no religion. If it pleases Our Lord, I will take six of them to Your Highnesses when I depart, in order that they may learn our language.

Saturday, 13 October 1492

I have been very attentive and have tried very hard to find out if there is any gold here. I have seen a few natives who wear a little piece of gold hanging from a hole made in the nose. By signs, if I interpret them correctly, I have learned that by going to the south, or rounding the island to the south, I can find a king who possesses a lot of gold and has great containers of it. I have tried to find some natives who will take me to this great king, but none seems inclined to make the journey.

Sunday, 14 October 1492

At daybreak I ordered the small boats to be made ready, that is, put in tow behind, and I went along the island to the NNE, to see the other part of the east and the villages. Soon I saw two or three of them, and the people came to the beach, shouting and praising God. Some brought us water; others, things to eat. Others, seeing that I did not care to go ashore, jumped into the sea and swam out to us. By the signs they made I think they were asking if we came from Heaven. One old man even climbed into the boat we were towing, and others shouted in loud voices to everyone on the beach, saying, "Come see the men from Heaven; bring them food and drink." Many men and women came, each one with something. They threw themselves on the sand and raised their hands to the sky, shouting for us to come ashore, while giving thanks to God. I kept going this morning despite the pleas of the people to come ashore, for I was alarmed at seeing that the entire island is surrounded by a large reef. . . .

Also, I wanted to see if I could find a suitable place to build a fort. I saw a piece of land that looked like an island, even though it is not, with six houses on it. I believe that it could be cut through and made into an island in two days. I do not think this is necessary, however, for these people are very unskilled in arms. Your Highnesses will see this for yourselves when I bring to you the seven that I have taken. After they learn our language I shall return them, unless Your Highnesses order that the entire population be taken to Castile, or held captive here. With 50 men you could subject everyone and make them do what you wished.

Tuesday, 16 October 1492

At daybreak I went ashore in the small boat. People met us on the beach. There were many people, and they went naked and in the same condition as those of San Salvador. They let us go anywhere we desired and gave us anything we asked.

I decided not to linger very long at Santa María de al Concepción, for I saw that there was no gold there and the wind freshened to a SE crosswind. . . .

Not only was there a shifting wind and no gold here, I was also afraid that all the men from San Salvador would escape if I did not move on and get farther away. I wanted to go to another large island that I determined lay to the west.

Judging by the clouds and the signs made by the men from San Salvador, this large island to the west was about 27 miles distant. They said that there is a lot of gold there and that the people wear it on their arms, legs, ears, noses, and necks. I do not know if this is another ruse of theirs or not, for I am beginning to believe that all they want to do is escape and they will tell me anything I want to hear.

Sunday, 21 October 1492

At 10 o'clock in the morning I arrived at *Cabo del Isleo* and anchored, as did the other two ships. After having eaten, I went ashore and found no settlement except one house. I found no one; the inhabitants must have fled in fear, for all their housewares were left behind. I did not permit my men to touch a thing, and I went with my captains to see the island. If the other islands are very green and beautiful and fertile, this is much more, with great and green groves of trees. There are some large lakes and above and around them is the most wonderful wooded area. The woods and vegetation are as green as in April in Andalucía, and the song of the little birds might make a man wish never to leave here. The flocks of parrots that darken the sun and the large and small birds of so many species are so different from our own that it is a wonder. In addition, there are trees of a thousand kinds, all with fruit according to their kind, and they all give off a marvelous fragrance. I am the saddest man in the world for not knowing what kind of things these are because I am very sure that they are valuable. I am bringing a sample of everything I can.

Wednesday, 24 October 1492

At midnight I weighed anchors from the island of Isabela, from *Cabo del Isleo* which is in the north part, in order to go to the island of Cuba, which the Indians tell me is very large and has much commerce; gold, spices, ships, and merchants.

The Indians indicated that I should sail to the SW to get to Cuba, and I believe them because all my globes and world maps seem to indicate that the island of Japan is in this vicinity and I am sure that Cuba and Japan are one and the same.

The Discovery of Cuba
28 October to 5 December 1492

Tuesday, 30 October 1492

I departed Río de Mares to the NW, and after having gone 45 miles, I saw a cape covered with palms and named it the *Cabo de Palmas*.[9] The Indians who were in the *Pinta* said that behind that cape was a river, from which it was four days' journey to Cuba. The captain of the *Pinta* understood that Cuba was a city, and that it was on the mainland, a very large land that extends far to the north. He also understood that the king of Cuba was at war with the Great Khan, whom they call *Cami* and whose country or city they call *Faba* and many other names. . . .

I must try to go to the Great Khan, for he is in the vicinity or at the city of Cathay, which is the city of the Great Khan. This is a very great city, according to what I was told before leaving Spain.

This entire country is low and beautiful, and the sea is very deep.

Sunday, 4 November 1492

I also understand that, a long distance from here, there are men with one eye and others with dogs' snouts who eat men. On taking a man they behead him and drink his blood and cut off his genitals.

Tuesday, 6 November 1492

Last night the two men I had sent inland to see the country returned and told me how they had gone 36 miles, to a village of 50 houses where there were a thousand inhabitants, as a great many live in one house. These houses are like very large pavilions.

The Spaniards said that the Indians received them with great solemnity, according to Indian custom, and all the men and women came to see them and lodged them in the best houses. The Indians touched them and kissed their hands and feet in wonderment, believing that we Spaniards came

---

9. Palm Cape (Cape of Palms); now known as *Punta Uvero*.

from Heaven, and so my men led them to understand. The Indians gave them to eat what they had.

The men said that on their arrival, the most distinguished persons in the village took them on their shoulders and carried them to the principal house and gave them two chairs in which to sit, and all the Indians seated themselves on the floor around them. These were most peculiar chairs. Each was made in one piece and in a strange shape, resembling a short-legged animal[10] with a tail as broad as the seat. This tail lifted up to make a back to lean against. These seats are called *dujos* or *duchos* in their language.

The Indians who had gone with my men, that is, the one from Guanahaní and the one from here, told the people how the Christians lived and how we were good people. Afterwards the men left, and the women seated themselves in the same manner around them, kissing their hands and feet, trying to see if they were of flesh and bone like themselves. The women pleaded with them to stay there longer, at least for five days.

My men showed the Indians the cinnamon and pepper and other spices I had given them, and they were told by signs that there were many such spices nearby to the SE, but that they did not know if they had those things there in their own village. Having seen that there were no rich cities, my men returned to *Puerto de Mares*. . . .

All that these people have they will give for a very ridiculous price; they gave one great basket of cotton for the end of a leather strap. These people are very free from evil and war. All the men and women are as naked as their mothers bore them. It is true that the women wear a cotton swatch only large enough to cover their private parts and no more. They are modest, nevertheless, and are not as dark as the people of the Canaries.

I have to say, Most Serene Princes, that if devout religious persons knew the Indian language well, all these people would soon become Christians. Thus I pray to Our Lord that Your Highnesses will appoint persons of great diligence in order to bring to the Church such great numbers of peoples, and that they will convert these peoples, just as they have destroyed those[11] who would not confess the Father, Son, and Holy Spirit. And after your days, for we are all mortal, you will leave your realms in a very tranquil state, free from heresy and wickedness, and you will be well received before the Eternal Creator, Whom may it please to grant you a long life and a great increase of larger realms and dominions, and the will and disposition to

---

10. The animal chair was the *dujo*. Several excellent ones are on display in the Museo del Hombre Dominicano, Santo Domingo, Dominican Republic.

11. Columbus is referring to the defeat of the Moors, not to the expulsion of the Jews.

spread the Holy Christian religion, as you have done up until this time. Amen.

Today I will launch the ship and prepare to depart Thursday, in the name of God, to go to the SE and seek gold and spices and discover land.

Sunday, 11 November 1492

It appears to me that it would be well to take some of these people dwelling by this river to the Sovereigns, in order that they might learn our language and we might learn what there is in this country. Upon return they may speak the language of the Christians and take our customs and Faith to their people. I see and know that these people have no religion whatever, nor are they idolaters, but rather, they are very meek and know no evil. They do not kill or capture others and are without weapons. They are so timid that a hundred of them flee from one of us, even if we are merely teasing. They are very trusting; they believe that there is a God in Heaven, and they firmly believe that we come from Heaven. They learn very quickly any prayer we tell them to say, and they make the sign of the cross. Therefore, Your Highnesses must resolve to make them Christians. I believe that if this effort commences, in a short time a multitude of peoples will be converted to our Holy Faith, and Spain will acquire great domains and riches and all of their villages. Beyond doubt there is a very great amount of gold in this country. These Indians I am bringing say, not without cause, that there are places in these islands where they dig gold and wear it around the neck, in the ears, and on the arms and the legs—and these are very heavy bracelets. Also, there are precious stones and pearls, and an infinite quantity of spices.

Wednesday, 14 November 1492

Your Highnesses will have to pardon me for repeating myself concerning the beauty and fertility of this land, but I can assure you that I have not told a hundredth part. Some of the mountains appear to reach Heaven and are like points of diamonds; others of great height seem to have a table on top; and the sea is so deep that a ship can approach some of them right up to the base. They are all covered with forests and are without rocks.

Thursday, 22 November 1492

Last night I sailed south by east, with the wind east and almost calm. About 3 in the morning it blew NNE. I was still going to the south in order to see the country that lay in that direction, but when the sun rose I found myself as far away as yesterday because of the contrary currents; the land was a distance of 30 miles from me.

Last night, after Martín Alonso departed for the east and the island of Babeque, I could see him for a long time, until he was 12 miles away. I sailed all night toward the land, but took in some of the sails and even showed a light because it seemed that Pinzón was coming toward me. The night was very clear and the light wind favorable for him to sail in my direction if he had so chosen.

Friday, 23 November 1492

I sailed all this day toward the land to the south, always with light wind, and the current never letting me reach land. At sunset I was as far away from land as I was in the morning. The wind was ENE and favorable to sail south, but it was almost calm. Beyond the cape, visible in the distance, is another land or cape that extends to the east. The Indians aboard call this Bohío and say it is very large and has people there with one eye in the forehead, as well as others they call cannibals,[12] of whom they show great fear. When they saw I was taking that course, they were too afraid to talk. They say that the cannibals eat people and are well armed. I believe there is some truth in this, although if they are armed they must be an intelligent people. Perhaps these people may have captured some of the other Indians; when the captives did not return to their own country, it was said that they were eaten. The Indians we have encountered believed the same thing at first about us Christians.

Monday, 26 November 1492

All the people I have encountered up until this time greatly fear the people of Caniba or Canima, whom they say live on this island of Bohío. This island appears to be very large, and I believe that the people on it go and take the other Indians and their lands and houses, because the ones I have seen are very cowardly and know nothing about arms. It is for these reasons that I think the Indians I am taking with me are not accustomed to settling on the coast. The Indians with me continued to show great fear because of the course I was taking and kept insisting that the people of Bohío had only one eye and the face of a dog, and they fear being eaten. I do not believe any of this. I feel that the Indians they fear belong to the domain of the Great Khan.

---

12. *Canibales*, the people of *Caniba* who eat other people. This is the first recorded usage of this term, which is a Taino Indian word.

Tuesday, 27 November 1492

Yesterday at sunset I arrived in the vicinity of Cabo de Campana, but did not anchor even though the sky was clear and the wind light and there were five or six wonderful harbors to the leeward. Whenever I enter one of these harbors, I am detained by sheer pleasure and delight as I see and marvel at the beauty and freshness of these countries, and I do not want to be delayed in pursuing what I am engaged upon. For all these reasons, I stood off the coast last night and beat about until day. . . .

After sailing 1½ miles along the same bay, I saw to the south a very remarkable harbor, and to the SE some incredibly beautiful land, similar to a rolling valley surrounded by mountains. There was a lot of smoke and a number of large villages there, and the land was intensely cultivated. Because of this I decided to enter this harbor and see if I could communicate with these people. If I have praised other harbors, then this one deserves more, along with the land and surroundings and the temperate climate and the population. It is a beautiful place, with pines and palms and a rolling plain extending to the SSE. There are low, smooth mountains on the plain and many streams flowing from the mountains. It is the most beautiful thing in the world.

I anchored the ship and jumped into the boat in order to take soundings in the harbor, which is shaped like a small hammer. When I was facing the entrance to the south, I found the mouth of a river that was wide enough for a galley to enter and so situated that it could not be seen until it was reached. Within a boat's length of the entrance it was 5 fathoms and 8 fathoms in depth.

As I went along the river it was marvelous to see the forests and greenery, the very clear water, the birds, and the fine situation, and I almost did not want to leave this place. I told the men with me that, in order to make a report to the Sovereigns of the things they saw, a thousand tongues would not be sufficient to tell it, nor my hand to write it, for it looks like an enchanted land. I want many other persons who are prudent and have the proper credentials to see this, so as to be certain that they do not praise these things less than I do.

I do not need to write how great the benefits will be from here. It is certain, Lords and Princes, that where there are such lands there must be an infinite quantity of profitable things.

And I certify to Your Highnesses that it does not seem to me that there can be more fertile countries under the sun, or any more temperate in heat and cold, with a greater abundance of good, pure water—unlike those rivers of Guinea, which are all pestilent. Praise be to Our Lord, so far there has not been a single one of my people who has had a headache or who has been in bed because of sickness, except for one old man through pain from kidney stones, from which he has suffered all his life—and even he became well at the end of two days. I say this in regard to all three ships. So may it please God that Your Highnesses may send learned men here, or that they shall come, and they will see that everything I say is true.

I say that Christendom will enter into negotiations, but most of all with Spain, to which all these lands should be subject. And I say that Your Highnesses must not allow any foreigner to set foot here or trade, except Catholic Christians, since it was the beginning and the end of this enterprise that it should be for the increase and the glory of the Christian religion. No one should come to these regions who is not a good Christian.

The Discovery of Española 6 December 1492 to 15 January 1493

Sunday, 16 December 1492

Coming from the coast of the Isla Española, I sailed close to the wind, because later, by 9 o'clock the next morning, the wind blew from the east. In the middle of that bay I found a canoe with a solitary Indian in it. I wondered how he was able to keep himself afloat when there was such a high wind. I brought him and his canoe on board and pleased him greatly by giving him glass beads, hawks' bells, and brass rings. I took him in the ship to a coastal village 12 miles distant. I found a good anchorage there next to the village, which appeared to be newly constructed, for all the houses were new. I let the Indian go ashore in his canoe and trusted that he would spread the word that we Christians are good people. They already knew this, however, from information they had received where my six men had gone before; soon more than 500 men came to the beach, where they gathered near the ships, for we were anchored very near to the shore. After a little while, their King came.

One by one, and in small groups, they came to the ship without bringing anything with them, although some of them wore grains of very fine gold in their ears and noses, which they gave away willingly. I ordered that everyone be treated honorably because they are the best and gentlest people in the world, and above all because I have great hope in Our Lord that Your Highnesses will convert all of them to Christianity and they will all belong to you, for I regard them as yours now.

I saw that they all showed respect for the King, who was on the beach. I sent him a gift, which he received with much ceremony. He is a young man, about 21 years of age. He had an old governor or advisor and other counselors who advised him and spoke for him. He himself said very few words. One of the Indians with me spoke with the King and told him how we had come from Heaven, and that we were searching for gold and wished to see the island of Babeque. He replied that this was good, and that there was a great deal of gold on that island. He showed my master-at-arms who had delivered my gift, the course that must be followed to reach Babeque and said that it could be reached in two days' time from where we were anchored. He also said that if we needed anything in his country, he would give it to us willingly.

The King and all the others went about as naked as they were born, and the women, too, without any shyness, and they are the handsomest men and women I have found up until now. They are exceedingly white, and if they wore clothing and were protected from the sun and the air they would be almost as white as the people in Spain. . . .

Your Highnesses may rest assured that these lands are so extensive and good and fertile, and especially these of this Isla Española, that there is no one who can describe it, and no one who can believe it if he does not see it. And Your Highnesses may believe that this island and all the others are as much yours as is Castile, and all that is needed here is to build a town and order the Indians to do your bidding. I, with the people I have with me, who are not many in number, could go through all these islands without any opposition. I have already seen three of my sailors go ashore where there is a great number of Indians, and the Indians have all fled without anyone wishing to do them any harm. They have no arms and are naked, and have no knowledge of arms and are very timid. A thousand of them would not face three Christians, and so they are suitable to be governed and made to work and sow and do everything else that shall be necessary, to build villages and be taught to wear clothing and to observe our customs.

Tuesday, 18 December 1492

Today I traded for only a small quantity of gold, but I learned from an old man that there were many islands in the vicinity—at a distance of 300 miles or more, according to what I was able to make out—in which a lot of gold is found. I was told that on some of these islands there is so much gold that the whole island is gold. On others they gather it and sift it with sieves and melt it to make bars, and work it in a thousand ways. I was shown, by signs, how this is done. The old man indicated to me the course to take to get to those islands and the place where they may be found. I decided to go there, and if the old man had not been one of the principal persons belonging to the king, I would have taken him along. If I had known the language, I would have begged him to accompany me, and I believe that we are on such good terms that he would have gone along of his own free will. But since I already consider that these people belong to the Sovereigns of Castile, it is not right to offend them. So I decided to leave him alone.

I placed a very large cross in the center of the plaza of that village, and the Indians assisted me greatly in this work. They said prayers and worshipped it, and from their actions I trust in the Lord that all these islands are to be Christianized.

Tuesday, 25 December 1492—Christmas Day

I sailed in a light wind yesterday from La Mar de Santo Tomás to Punta Santa, and at the passing of the first watch, 11 o'clock at night, I was 3 miles east of the point. I decided to lie down to sleep because I had not slept for two days[13] and one night. Since it was calm, the sailor who was steering the ship also decided to catch a few winks and left the steering to a young ship's boy, a thing which I have always expressly prohibited throughout the voyage. It made no difference whether there was a wind or calm; the ships were not to be steered by young boys.

I felt secure from shoals and rocks because on Sunday, when I had sent the boats to that King, they had gone a good 10 miles to the east of Punta Santa, and the sailors had seen this entire coast and the shoals that extend from Punta Santa a good 9 miles to the ESE, and they saw where we could pass. This is something I had not done before on this voyage.

Our Lord willed that at midnight, when the crew saw me lie down to rest and also saw that there was a dead calm and the sea was as in a bowl, they all lay down to sleep and left the helm to that boy. The currents carried the ship upon one of these banks. Although it was night, the sea breaking on them made so much noise that they could be heard and seen at a 3-mile distance. The ship went upon the bank so quietly that it was hardly noticeable.[14] When the boy felt the rudder ground and heard the noise of the sea, he cried out. I jumped up instantly; no one else had yet felt that we were aground. Then the master of the ship, Juan de la Cosa,[15] who was on watch, came out. I ordered him to rouse the crew, to launch the small boat we carry on our stern, and to take an anchor and cast it at the stern. The master and many others jumped into the small boat, and I assumed they were going to follow my orders. Instead, their only thoughts were to escape to the *Niña*, which was 1½ miles to the windward. The crew of the *Niña* would not receive them, which was correct, and therefore they returned to the ship. But the boat from the *Niña* reached the ship before my own boat did!

---

13. Columbus had been extremely busy with the multitude of Indians coming and going, and he probably did a little celebrating on Christmas Eve, just before the grounding. Too much "partying" may be the simple explanation of the accident that was to follow.

14. Columbus used the term *banco* (bank), where the *Santa María* grounded, not his term for coral reef (*restinga de piedras*). The ship appears to have missed the reef, where the waves made the noise Columbus heard, and gently eased into a sand bank. The ship was not really damaged very much, merely hopelessly stuck.

15. Juan de la Cosa, owner of the *Santa María,* was the same man who made (or compiled) the famous chart of the New World in 1500. He sailed again with Columbus on the second voyage; made an expedition to South America with Alonso de Ojeda and Amerigo Vespucci (1499); and was the pilot for Rodrigo de Bastidas in 1500–1501 (when Vasco Nuñez de Balboa was aboard and the coast between Cartagena, Colombia, and Porto Belo, Panama, was first explored). In 1504 he returned to Santo Domingo to serve as Ojeda's lieutenant in the colonization of what is now Colombia (called *Nueva Andalucía*). In 1509, in a fight with the Caribs, Juan de la Cosa died from a poisoned arrow.

When I saw that some of my own crew were fleeing and that the sea was becoming more shallow, with my ship broadside to it, I did the only thing I could. I ordered the mast cut and the ship lightened as much as possible, to see if it could be refloated. But the water became even more shallow, and the ship settled more and more to one side. Although there was little or no sea, I could not save her. Then the seams opened, though she remained in one piece.

I took my crew to the *Niña* for their safety, and as there was a light land breeze and still half the night ahead of us, and since I did not know how far the banks extended, I beat about till daybreak and then went inside the bank to the ship. I also dispatched Diego de Arana, master-at-arms of the fleet, and Pedro Gutiérrez, representative of the Royal Household, to take the small boat and go directly to the King that had last Saturday invited me to his village. I instructed them to beg the King to come to this harbor with his boats.

The village of this King is about 5 miles beyond this bank. My men told me that the King wept when he heard of the disaster. He sent all his people from the village with many large canoes to help us unload the ship.

Wednesday, 26 December 1492

Today at sunrise the King of this country came to the *Niña*, where I was, and almost in tears told me not to be dismayed because he would give me whatever he had. He had already given two very large houses to my men, and he would give us more if we needed them. And yesterday he gave us as many canoes as we needed and the labor to unload the ship, and not even a breadcrumb was taken. They are so loyal and so respectful of the property of others, and this King is even more honest than the others. . . .

The King dined with me on the *Niña* and afterwards went ashore with me, where he paid me great honor. Later we had a meal with two or three kinds of ajes, served with shrimp, game, and other foods they have, including their bread; which they call *cazabe*.[16] Then the King took me to see some groves of trees near the houses, and fully 1,000 people, all naked, went with us. The King was already wearing a shirt and a pair of gloves which I had given him, and he was more excited about the gloves than anything else that had been given him.

By his manner of eating, his decent behavior, and his exceptional cleanliness, he showed himself to be of good birth.

After the meal we remained at the table for some time, and we were brought some herbs with which to rub our hands—I believe they use these to soften the skin. We were also given water for our hands. Later, after we had eaten,

---

16. Manioc bread. For a more extensive discussion of roots and breads, see Epilogue.

the Indians took me to the beach, and I sent for a Turkish bow and a handful of arrows. I had a man from my company who was a skilled archer shoot the arrows. Inasmuch as the King did not know what arms are, since his people neither possess nor use them, the demonstration impressed him very much. This all came about because we had had a conversation about the people of Caniba, whom they call *Caribes,*[17] who come to seize them and who carry bows and arrows without iron tips. Nowhere in these lands is there knowledge of iron or steel, nor of any other metal except gold and copper, and I have seen very little of the latter. I told the King by signs that the Sovereigns of Castile would order the destruction of the Caribes, commanding the Caribes to be brought before them with their hands tied.

I ordered that a lombard and a musket be fired, and the King was spellbound when he saw the effect of their force and what they penetrated. When the people heard the shots, they fell to their knees. They brought me a large mask, which had large pieces of gold in the ears and eyes and in other places, which the King himself presented to me. He placed this, along with other jewels of gold, on my head and around my neck. They also gave many things to the men with me. I derived a great deal of pleasure and consolation from these things, and when I realized that this mitigated the trouble and affliction I had experienced by losing the ship, I recognized that Our Lord had caused me to run aground at this place so that I might establish a settlement here. And so many things came to hand here that the disaster was a blessing in disguise. Certainly, if I had not run aground here, I would have kept out to sea without anchoring at this place because it is situated inside a large bay containing two or three banks of shoals. Neither would I have left any of my people here on this voyage; even if I had desired to leave them, I could not have outfitted them well enough, nor given them enough ammunition, provisions, and materials for a fort. It is quite true that many of the people with me have pleaded with me to permit them to remain here.

Now I have ordered that a tower and a fortress be constructed, very well built, with a large moat. This is not because I believe this to be necessary with these Indians, for I am sure that I could subjugate the entire island—which I believe is larger than Portugal with twice the population—with the men that I have in my company. These Indians are naked, unarmed, and cowardly beyond help. But it is right that this tower be built, and what must be, must be. Since these Indians are so far from Your Highnesses, it is necessary that the people here know your people and what they can do, in order that the Indians may obey Your Highnesses with love and fear.

---

17. First mention of these feared cannibals using the name by which they are known today. Native to South America, they had followed the Taino migrations northward through the Lesser Antilles to Puerto Rico. By 1492 they were raiding Española. Their name also survives in the name Caribbean Sea.

The men remaining have timbers with which to construct the fortress and provisions of bread and wine for more than a year, as well as seeds for sowing, and the ship's boat. I am leaving a caulker, a carpenter, a gunner, and a caskmaker among the many men who desire zealously to serve Your Highnesses and who will please me greatly if they find the mine where the gold comes from. Thus, everything that has happened was for this purpose, that this beginning may be made.

All this was the will of God: the ship's running aground so easily that it could not be felt, with neither wind nor wave; the cowardice of the ship's master and some of the crew (who were mostly from his part of Spain), who refused my order to cast the stern anchor to draw the ship off and save it; the discovery of this country.

I hope to God that when I come back here from Castile, which I intend on doing, that I will find a barrel of gold, for which these people I am leaving will have traded, and that they will have found the gold mine, and the spices, and in such quantities *that within three years*[18] *the Sovereigns will prepare for and undertake the conquest of the Holy Land. I have already petitioned Your Highnesses to see that all the profits of this, my enterprise, should be spent on the conquest of Jerusalem, and Your Highnesses smiled and said that the idea pleased them, and that even without this expedition they had the inclination to do it.*

Sunday, 6 January 1493

After midday the wind blew strongly from the east, and I ordered a sailor to climb to the top of the mast to look out for shoals. He saw the *Pinta* approaching from the east,[19] and she came up to me. Because the water was so shallow, I was afraid to anchor, so I retraced my course 30 miles to Monte Cristi, and the *Pinta* went with me.

Martín Alonso Pinzón came aboard the *Niña* to apologize, saying that he had become separated against his will. He gave many reasons for his departure, but they are all false. Pinzón acted with greed and arrogance that night when he sailed off and left me, and I do not know why he has been so disloyal and untrustworthy toward me on this voyage. Even so, I am going to ignore these actions in order to prevent Satan from hindering this voyage, as he has done up until now.

An Indian, among those I had commended to Pinzón, told Pinzón that on the island of Babeque there was a great quantity of gold; since the *Pinta* was light and swift, he wished to withdraw and go by himself, leaving me.

---

18. Author's italics. According to John Boyd Thacher, this is Columbus' Grand Design: the conquest of the Holy Land, financed by the wealth obtained from the enterprise.

19. Since departing the fleet on 21 November, the *Pinta* had sailed to Babeque (Great Inagua Island) and thence to a location east of Monte Cristi on the island of Española.

Wednesday, 9 January 1493

At midnight I raised sails with the wind SE and sailed to the ENE. I reached a point I named *Punta Roja*,[20] which is exactly east of Monte Cristi some 45 miles. In the shelter of this point I anchored at 3 o'clock in the afternoon. I dared not depart from there at night because of the many reefs.

In this country there are many tortoises; the sailors captured some of them that had come ashore to lay their eggs at Monte Cristi. They are very large, like great wooden shields. Yesterday, when I was going to the Río del Oro, I saw three sirens[21] that came up very high out of the sea. They are not as beautiful as they are painted, since in some ways they have a face like a man. I have seen them on other occasions in Guinea on the coast of Manegueta.[22] Tonight, in the name of Our Lord, I will start on my journey without further delay for any reason, since I have found what I have sought. Also, I do not wish to have more trouble with this Martín Alonso until Your Highnesses learn the news of this voyage and what he has done. Then I will not suffer from the evil actions of persons without virtue, who, with little regard, presume to follow their own wills in opposition to those who did them honor.

The Homeward Voyage 16 January to 15 March 1493

Wednesday, 16 January 1493

Three hours before dawn I departed the gulf, which I have named the *Golfo de las Flechas*,[23] first with a land breeze and then with a west wind. I turned the prow to the east by north, in order to go to the Isla de Caribe, where the people are whom the inhabitants of all these islands and countries fear so greatly. This is because the Caribes cross all these seas in their countless canoes and eat the men they are able to capture. One of the four Indians I took yesterday in the Puerto de las Flechas[24] has shown me the course. After we had gone about 48 miles, the Indians indicated to me that the island lay to the SE. I wanted to follow that course and ordered the sails trimmed, but after we had gone 6 miles the wind again blew very favorably for going to Spain. I noted that the crew were becoming dismayed because we had departed from a direct course for home; and as both ships were taking in a great deal of water, they had no help save that of God. I was compelled to abandon the course that I believe was taking me to the island; I returned to the direct course for Spain, NE by east, and held it until sunset, 36 miles. The Indians told me that on this course I would find the island of

---

20. Red Point; now known as *Punta Cabo Isabela*.

21. The common manatee, known in Spanish as *sirena* until the Taino word *manatí* came into use after Columbus, thence into English.

22. Malagueta Coast of Liberia and Sierra Leone.

23. Gulf of the Arrows; now known as *Puerto Rincón*. See note for Sunday, 13 January.

24. Port of the *golfo de las Flechas* (gulf of the Arrows).

Matinino, which is inhabited only by women. I would like to carry five or six of them to the Sovereigns, but I doubt if the Indians know the course well, and I am not able to delay because of the danger with the leaking caravels. I am certain that there is such an island, and that at a certain time of year men come to these women from the Isla de Caribe, which is 30 or 36 miles from us; if the women give birth to a boy they send him to the island of the men, and if a girl they keep her with them.

Thursday, 21 February 1493

(Part of this entry is under the Log entry of 22 February.)

The sacred theologians and learned philosophers were quite correct when they said that the earthly Paradise is at the end of the Orient, because it is a most temperate place. Those lands which I have now discovered are at the end of the Orient.

■ Bartolomé de las Casas (1474–1566) *Spain/Mexico* (history)

TRANSLATED BY GEORGE SANDERLIN

The Spanish missionary and historian Bartolomé de las Casas has been called the Apostle of the Indies. His role was to awaken the Spanish authorities to the genocide of the *indios* in New Spain. Las Casas arrived in Hispaniola in 1492, only ten years after Christopher Columbus landed there on his first voyage. He became a priest in 1510 and shortly thereafter worked the rest of his life to improve the conditions of the Indian. He did so within the confines of the Catholic church, which is to say, he accepted that pagan "idols" had to be eliminated, both physically and in the hearts of the Indian and did not object to the zealous destruction of religious art objects and documents. His enormous contributions lay in his efforts to provide a better life for the forced native converts to the church. To that end, Las Casas labored against slavery as practiced under the *encomienda*, a food-for-work economic system first used to obtain cheap labor from the Moors in reconquered Spain and then transplanted to the New World.

Theoretically, the encomienda obliged the landowner to protect the Indians, instructing them in the Christian faith in return for which the Indian laborers paid tribute. In practice, it was a form of economic slavery and quickly led to the decimation of the Indians in the West Indies. The encomienda was also the law in continental America, especially in Mexico and Guatemala—then called New Spain. Although the crown and the Dominican order of monks made some efforts to suppress it, the encomienda persisted until 1542, when the "New Laws," promulgated by Las Casas, outlawed forced labor and debt peonage. But encomienda died slowly and was ultimately replaced by the *repartimiento,* another system of distributing land on which Indians worked under forced labor conditions. In reality, though the words changed, the practice of economic serfdom continued in Mexico and Central America well into the twentieth century. Formal slavery itself was not outlawed in Portuguese-settled Brazil until 1888.

Bartolomé de las Casas was the leading figure in all the colonial period in creating awareness of and change in the conditions of the Indian. He spent his life writing and petitioning the Spanish government in Spain, Mexico, and Peru to abolish the virtual slavery of the Indians, who had become forced laborers on the estates of Spanish landholders. He also published descriptions of massacres and maltreatment in his *Very Brief Account of the Destruction of the Indies,* a book that was translated into many languages and countered the Black Legend. The Black Legend was at once a detailed description of massacres and maltreatment and, in the eyes of the deniers of these events, a phrase to indicate a false "legendary" accusation. Las Casas came to the defense of the Native Americans, arguing that Indians are rational beings with souls, and he campaigned against their forced labor in gold and silver mines, where they were dying in droves. He suggested that they be replaced by bringing in African slaves, who he thought had no souls and whose death would be of less consequence. He quickly withdrew his suggestion with regard to Africans. Las Casas spent his life battling all parties for better treatment of the Indian population, and he succeeded in bringing into being the New Laws. These laws to protect the Indians were altered and ignored, but at the very least they kept alive the question of the plight of the Indian serf. As an observer of the societies of Indians and an early anthropologist, he spent many years writing his monumental *Historia de las Indias* (History of the Indies).

FURTHER READING: Las Casas, Bartolomé de. *Very Brief Account of the Destruction of the Indies,* 1522; *Devastation of the Indies,* 1974; *Historia de las Indias (History of the Indies),* 1875–1876; *Tears of the Indians: Selected Works of Bartolomé de las Casas.* Edited by John Phillips, 1953; *Bartolomé de las Casas: A Selection of His Writings,* 1971.

from **The Horrors of the Conquest**

The Conquest of Cuba

At this time, when it was known in the island of Jamaica that Diego Velázquez had gone to settle and pacify . . . the island of Cuba, Juan de Esquivel, the deputy in Jamaica, agreed to send one Pánfilo de Narváez, a native of Valladolid . . . with thirty Spaniards, to aid Diego Velázquez — or else they bestirred themselves and asked permission to go there. All were archers, with their bows and arrows, in the use of which they were more practiced than the Indians.

This Pánfilo de Narváez was a man with an air of authority, tall of stature, and rather fair-haired, tending toward red. He was honorable and wise, but not very prudent; good company, with good habits, valiant in fighting against the Indians and would perhaps have been valiant against other peoples—but above all he had this defect, that he was very careless. . . .

With his band of bowmen he was well received by Diego Velázquez. . . . Velázquez promptly gave them shares of Indians, as if these were heads of cattle, so that the Indians would serve them, although they had brought some Jamaican Indians to do that wherever they went. Diego Velázquez made this Narváez his chief captain and always honored him in such a way that, after Velázquez, Narváez held first place in that island.

A few days later I went there, the said Diego Velázquez having sent for me because of our past friendship in this island of Hispaniola. We went together, Narváez and I, for about two years, and secured the rest of that island, to the detriment of all of it, as will be seen.

[Las Casas tells how Velázquez terrorized the natives of eastern Cuba, near Cape Maisí, executed the chieftain Hatuey, and went on to Baracoa. Narváez landed at the Gulf of Guacayanabo, on the south coast near Maisí, and, on orders from Velázquez, invaded the province of Camagüey, in central Cuba.]

The Spaniards entered the province of Camagüey, which is large and densely populated . . . and when they reached the villages, the inhabitants had prepared as well as they could cassava bread from their food; what they called *guaminiquinajes* from their hunting; and also fish, if they had caught any.

Immediately upon arriving at a village, the cleric Casas would have all the little children band together; taking two or three Spaniards to help him, along with some sagacious Indians of this island of Hispaniola, whom he had brought with him, and a certain servant of his, he would baptize the children he found in the village. He did this throughout the island . . . and there were many for whom God provided holy baptism because He had predestined them to glory. God provided it at a fitting time, for none or almost none of those children remained alive after a few months. . . .

When the Spaniards arrived at a village and found the Indians at peace in their houses, they did not fail to injure and scandalize them. Not content with what the Indians freely gave, they took their wretched subsistence from them, and some, going further, chased after their wives and daughters, for this is and always has been the Spaniards' common custom in these Indies. Because of this and at the urging of the said father, Captain Narváez ordered that after the father had separated all the inhabitants of the village in half the houses, leaving the other half empty for the Spaniards' lodging, no one should dare go to the Indians' section. For this purpose, the father would go ahead with three or four men and reach a village early; by the time the Spaniards came, he had already gathered the Indians in one part and cleared the other.

Thus, because the Indians saw that the father did things for them, defending and comforting them, and also baptizing their children, in which affairs he seemed to have more command and authority than others, he received much respect and credit throughout the island among the Indians. Further, they honored him as they did their priests, magicians, prophets, or physicians, who were all one and the same.

Because of this . . . it became unnecessary to go ahead of the Spaniards. He had only to send an Indian with an old piece of paper on a stick, informing them through the messenger that those letters said thus and so. That is, that they should all be calm, that no one should absent himself because he would do them no harm, that they should have food prepared for the Christians and their children ready for baptism, or that they should gather in one part of the village, and anything else that it seemed good to counsel them—and that if they did not carry these things out, the father would be angry, which was the greatest threat that could be sent them.

They performed everything with a very good will, to the best of their ability. And great was the reverence and fear which they had for the letters, for they saw that through these what was being done in other, distant regions was known. It seemed more than a miracle to them. . . .

The Spaniards thus passed through certain villages of that province on the road they were taking. And because the folk of the villages . . . were eager to see such a new people and especially to see the three or four mares being taken there, at which the whole land was frightened—news of them flew through the island—many came to look at them in a large town called Caonao, the penultimate syllable long. And the Spaniards, on the morning of the day they arrived at the town, stopped to breakfast in a riverbed that was dry but for a few small pools. This riverbed was full of whetstones, and all longed to sharpen their swords on them [and did]. When they had finished their breakfast, they continued on the road to Caonao.

Along the road for two or three leagues there was an arid plain, where one found oneself thirsty after any work; and there certain Indians from the villages brought them some gourds of water and some things to eat.

They arrived at the town of Caonao in the evening. Here they found many people, who had prepared a great deal of food consisting of cassava bread and fish, because they had a large river close by and also were near the sea. In a little square were 2,000 Indians, all squatting because they have this custom, all staring, frightened, at the mares. Nearby was a large *bohio,* or large house, in which were more than 500 other Indians, close-packed and fearful, who did not dare come out.

When some of the domestic Indians the Spaniards were taking with them as servants (who were more than 1,000 souls . . .) wished to enter the large house, the Cuban Indians had chickens ready and said to them: "Take these—do not enter here." For they already knew that the Indians who served the Spaniards were not apt to perform any other deeds than those of their masters.

There was a custom among the Spaniards that one person, appointed by the captain, should be in charge of distributing to each Spaniard the food and other things the Indians gave. And while the captain was thus on his mare and the others mounted on theirs, and the father himself was observing how the bread and fish were distributed, a Spaniard, in whom the devil is thought to have clothed himself, suddenly drew his sword. Then the whole hundred drew theirs and began to rip open the bellies, to cut and kill those lambs—men, women, children, and old folk, all of whom were seated, off guard and frightened, watching the mares and the Spaniards. And within two credos, not a man of all of them there remains alive.

The Spaniards enter the large house nearby, for this was happening at its door, and in the same way, with cuts and stabs, begin to kill as many as they found there, so that a stream of blood was running, as if a great number of cows had perished. Some of the Indians who could make haste climbed up the poles and woodwork of the house to the top, and thus escaped.

The cleric had withdrawn shortly before this massacre to where another small square of the town was formed, near where they had lodged him. This was in a large house where all the Spaniards also had to stay, and here about forty of the Indians who had carried the Spaniards' baggage from the provinces farther back were stretched out on the ground, resting. And five Spaniards chanced to be with the cleric. When these heard the blows of the swords and knew that the Spaniards were killing the Indians—without seeing anything, because there were certain houses between—they put hands to their swords and are about to kill the forty Indians . . . to pay them their commission.

The cleric, moved to wrath, opposes and rebukes them harshly to prevent them, and having some respect for him, they stopped what they were going to do, so the forty were left alive. The five go to kill where the others were killing. And as the cleric had been detained in hindering the slaying of the forty carriers, when he went he found a heap of dead, which the Spaniards had made among the Indians, which was certainly a horrible sight.

When Narváez, the captain, saw him he said: "How does Your Honor like what these our Spaniards have done?"

Seeing so many cut to pieces before him, and very upset at such a cruel event, the cleric replied: "That I commend you and them to the devil!"

The heedless Narváez remained, still watching the slaughter as it took place, without speaking, acting, or moving any more than if he had been marble. For if he had wished, being on horseback and with a lance in his hands, he could have prevented the Spaniards from killing even ten persons.

Then the cleric leaves him, and goes elsewhere through some groves seeking Spaniards to stop them from killing. For they were passing through the groves looking for someone to kill, sparing neither boy, child, woman, nor old person. And they did more, in that certain Spaniards went to the road to the river, which was nearby. Then all the Indians who had escaped with wounds, stabs, and cuts—all who could flee to throw themselves into the river to save themselves—met with the Spaniards who finished them.

Another outrage occurred which should not be left untold, so that the deeds of our Christians in these regions may be observed. When the cleric entered the large house where I said there were about 500 souls—or whatever the number, which was great—and saw with horror the dead there and those who had escaped above by the poles or woodwork, he said to them:

"No more, no more. Do not be afraid. There will be no more, there will be no more."

With this assurance, believing that it would be thus, an Indian descended, a well-disposed young man of twenty-five or thirty years, weeping. And as the cleric did not rest but went everywhere to stop the killing, the cleric then left the house. And just as the young man came down, a Spaniard who was there drew a cutlass or half sword and gives him a cut through the loins, so that his intestines fall out. . . .

The Indian, moaning, takes his intestines in his hands and comes fleeing out of the house. He encounters the cleric . . . and the cleric tells him some things about the faith, as much as the time and anguish permitted, explaining to him that if he wished to be baptized he would go to heaven to live with God. The sad one, weeping and showing pain as if he were burning in flames, said yes, and with this the cleric baptized him. He then fell dead on the ground. . . .

Of all that has been said, I am a witness. I was present and saw it; and I omit many other particulars in order to shorten the account.

"Are Not the Indians Men?"

When Sunday and the hour to preach arrived . . . Father Fray Antonio de Montesinos ascended the pulpit and took as the text and foundation of his sermon, which he carried written out and signed by the other friars: "I am the voice of one crying in the desert." After he completed his introduction and said something concerning the subject of Advent, he began to emphasize the aridity in the desert of Spanish consciences in this island, and the ignorance in which they lived; also, in what danger of eternal damnation they were, from taking no notice of the grave sins in which, with such apathy, they were immersed and dying.

Then he returns to his text, speaking thus: "I have ascended here to cause you to know those sins, I who am the voice of Christ in the desert of this island. Therefore it is fitting that you listen to this voice, not with careless attention, but with all your heart and senses. For this voice will be the strangest you ever heard, the harshest and hardest, most fearful and most dangerous you ever thought to hear."

This voice cried out for some time, with very combative and terrible words, so that it made their flesh tremble, and they seemed already standing before the divine judgment. Then, in a grand manner, the voice . . . declared what it was, or what that divine inspiration consisted of: "This voice," he said, "declares that you are all in mortal sin, and live and die in it, because of the cruelty and tyranny you practice among these innocent peoples.

"Tell me, by what right or justice do you hold these Indians in such a cruel and horrible servitude? On what authority have you waged such detestable wars against these peoples, who dwelt quietly and peacefully on their own land? Wars in which you have destroyed such infinite numbers of them by homicides and slaughters never before heard of? Why do you keep them so oppressed and exhausted, without giving them enough to eat or curing them of the sicknesses they incur from the excessive labor you give them, and they die, or rather, you kill them, in order to extract and acquire gold every day?

"And what care do you take that they should be instructed in religion, so that they may know their God and creator, may be baptized, may hear Mass, and may keep Sundays and feast days? Are these not men? Do they not have rational souls? Are you not bound to love them as you love yourselves? Don't you understand this? Don't you feel this? Why are you sleeping in such a profound and lethargic slumber? Be assured that in your present state you can no more be saved than the Moors or Turks, who lack the faith of Jesus Christ and do not desire it."

■ Bernal Díaz del Castillo (1496–1560)
Spain/Mexico (chronicle)

TRANSLATED BY J. M. COHEN

The soldier-chronicler Bernal Díaz del Castillo recorded Cortés's entry into Tenochtitlán, the fabled Aztec capital of Mexico, and the meeting of Hernán Cortés with the Aztec king Montezuma, whom Cortés ultimately executed in his conquest of Mexico. Díaz, like Columbus, was mesmerized by the almost dreamlike vision that moments of discovery of the New World gave to its Old World viewers. So, when he caught sight of gigantic Tenochtitlán (today's Mexico City), he too wondered whether it was not a dream or some enchanted place recounted in the same chivalric novel, *Amadís de Gaula,* that had addled the brains of the poor burgher Alonso Quijano to make him believe that he was a great knight called Don Quijote. The more normal tone of Castillo's great chronicle is, however, neither that of the dreamer nor of Cortés and his high officers, but of the common soldier. He had been there and experienced the marches, battles, and astonishments of the ordinary soldier. In his old age, retired to what is now Guatemala, he wrote his *Natural History of the Indies.* Emir Rodríguez Monegal writes, "The freshness of his style make[s] his book one of the greatest historical narratives of the Renaissance." Monegal goes on to characterize it as an oral history, put together like a novel. Of the many chronicles and histories of the invasion into the New World, the "true history of the conquest" by Bernal is foremost for its clarity, vigor, and narrative fervor.

FURTHER READING: *True History of the Conquest of New Spain*, 1632.

from *True History of the Conquest of New Spain*

The Entrance into Mexico

Early next day we left Iztapalapa with a large escort of these great *Caciques*, and followed the causeway, which is eight yards wide and goes so straight to the city of Mexico that I do not think it curves at all. Wide though it was, it was so crowded with people that there was hardly room for them all. Some were going to Mexico and others coming away, besides those who had come out to see us, and we could hardly get through the crowds that were there. For the towers and the cues were full, and then came in canoes from all parts of the lake. No wonder, since they had never seen horses or men like us before!

With such wonderful sights to gaze on we did not know what to say, or if this was real that we saw before our eyes. On the land side there were great cities, and on the lake many more. The lake was crowded with canoes. At intervals along the causeway there were many bridges, and before us was the great city of Mexico. As for us, we were scarcely four hundred strong and we well remembered the words and warnings of the people. Huexotzinco and Tlascala and Tlamanalco, and the many other warnings we had received to beware of entering the city of Mexico, since they would kill us as soon as they had us inside. Let the interested reader consider whether there is not much to ponder in this narrative of mine. What men in all the world have shown such daring? But let us go on.

We marched along our causeway to a point where another small causeway branches off to another city called Coyoacan and there, beside some towerlike buildings, which were the shrines, we were met by many more *Caciques* and dignity in very rich cloaks. The different chieftains wore different brilliant liveries, and the causeways were full of them. Montezuma had sent these great *Caciques* in advance to receive us, and as soon as they came before Cortes they told him in their language that we were welcome, and as a sign of peace they touched the ground with their hands and kissed it.

There we halted for some time while Cacamatzin, the lord of Texcoco, and the lords of Iztapalapa, Tacuba, and Coyoacan went ahead to meet the great Montezuma, who approached in a rich litter, accompanied by other great lords and feudal *Caciques* who owned vassals. When we came near to Mexico, at a place where there were some other small towers, the great Montezuma descended from his litter, and these other great *Caciques* supported him beneath a marvelously rich canopy of green feathers, decorated with gold work, silver, pearls, and *chalchihuites,* which hung from a sort of border. It was a marvellous sight. The great Montezuma was magnificently clad, in their fashion, and wore sandals of a kind for which their name is *cotaras,*[1] the soles of which are of gold and the upper parts ornamented with precious stones. And the four lords who supported him were richly clad also in garments that seem to have been kept ready for them on the road so that they could accompany their master. For they had not worn clothes like this when they came out to receive us. There were four other great *Caciques* who carried the canopy above their heads, and many more lords who walked before the great Montezuma, sweeping the ground on which he was to tread, and laying down cloaks so that his feet should not touch the earth. Not one of these chieftains dared to look him in the face. All kept their eyes lowered most reverently except those four lords, his nephews, who were supporting him.

When Cortes saw, heard, and was told that the great Montezuma was approaching, he dismounted from his horse, and when he came near to Montezuma each bowed deeply to the other. Montezuma welcomed our Captain, and Cortes, speaking through Doña Marina, answered by wishing him very good health. Cortes, I think, offered Montezuma his right hand, but Montezuma refused it and extended his own. Then Cortes brought out a necklace which he had been holding. It was made of those elaborately worked and coloured glass beads called *margaritas,* of which I have spoken, and was strung on a gold cord and dipped in musk to give it a good odour. This he hung around the great Montezuma's neck, and as he did so attempted to embrace him. But the great princes who stood round Montezuma grasped Cortes' arm to prevent him, for they considered this an indignity.

Then Cortes told Montezuma that it rejoiced his heart to have seen such a great prince, and that he took his coming in person to receive him and the repeated favours he had done him as a high honour. After this Montezuma made him another complimentary speech, and ordered two of his nephews who were supporting him, the lords of Texcoco and Coyoacan, to go with us and show us our quarters. Montezuma returned to the city with the other two kinsmen of his escort, the lords of Cuitlahuac and Tacuba; and all those grand companies of *Caciques* and dignitaries who had come with him returned also in his train. And as they accompanied their lord we observed them marching with their eyes downcast so that they should not see him, and keeping close to the wall as they followed him with great reverence. Thus space was made for us to enter the streets of Mexico without being pressed by the crowd.

---

1. Actually a Cuban word: the Mexican word was *cactli.*

Who could now count the multitude of men, women, and boys in the streets, on the roof-tops and in canoes on the waterways, who had come out to see us? It was a wonderful sight and, as I write, it all comes before my eyes as if it had happened only yesterday.

They led us to our quarters, which were in some large houses capable of accommodating us all and had formerly belonged to the great Montezuma's father, who was called Axayacatl. Here Montezuma now kept the great shrines of his gods, and a secret chamber containing gold bars and jewels. This was the treasure he had inherited from his father, which he never touched. Perhaps their reason for lodging us here was that, since they called us *Teules* and considered us as such, they wished to have us near their idols. In any case they took us to this place, where there were many great halls, and a dais hung with the cloth of their country for our Captain, and matting beds with canopies over them for each of us.

On our arrival we entered the large court, where the great Montezuma was awaiting our Captain. Taking him by the hand, the prince led him to his apartment in the hall where he was to lodge, which was very richly furnished in their manner. Montezuma had ready for him a very rich necklace, made of golden crabs, a marvellous piece of work, which he hung round Cortes's neck. His captains were greatly astonished at this sign of honour.

After this ceremony, for which Cortes thanked him through our interpreters, Montezuma said: 'Malinche, you and your brothers are in your own house. Rest awhile.' He then returned to his palace, which was not far off.

We divided our lodgings by companies, and placed our artillery in a convenient spot. Then the order we were to keep was clearly explained to us, and we were warned to be very much on the alert, both the horsemen and the rest of us soldiers. We then ate a sumptuous dinner which they had prepared for us in their native style.

So, with luck on our side, we boldly entered the city of Tenochtitlán or Mexico on 8 November in the year of our Lord 1519.

The Stay in Mexico

When the great Montezuma had dined and was told that our Captain and all of us had finished our meal some time ago, he came to our quarters in the grandest state with a great number of princes, all of them his kinsmen. On being told of his approach, Cortes came into the middle of the hall to receive him. Montezuma then took him by the hand, and they brought chairs made in their fashion and very richly decorated in various ways with gold. Montezuma requested our Captain to sit down, and both of them sat, each on his own chair.

Then Montezuma began a very good speech, saying that he was delighted to have such valiant gentlemen as Cortes and the rest of us in his house and his kingdom. That two years ago he had received news of a Captain who had come to Champoton, and that last year also he had received a report of another Captain who had come with four ships. Each time he had wished to see them, and now that he had us with him he was not only at our service but would share all that he possessed with us. He ended by saying that we must truly be the men about whom his ancestors had long ago prophesied, saying that they would come from the direction of the sunrise to rule over these lands, and that he was confirmed in this belief by the valour with which we had fought at Champoton and Tabasco and against the Tlascalans, for lifelike pictures of these battles had been brought to him.

Cortes replied through our interpreters that we did not know how to repay the daily favours we received from him, and that indeed we did come from the direction of the sunrise, and were vassals and servants of a great king called the Emperor Charles, who was ruler over many great princes. Having heard news of Montezuma and what a great prince he was, the Emperor, he said, had sent us to this country to visit him, and to beg them to become Christians, like our Emperor and all of us, so that his soul and those of all his vassals might be saved. Cortes promised to explain to him later how this could be, and how we worship the one true God and who He is, also many other good things which he had already communicated to his ambassadors Tendile, Pitalpitoque, and Quintalbor.

The great Montezuma had some fine gold jewels of various shapes in readiness which he gave to Cortes after this conversation. And to each of our captains he presented small gold objects and three loads of cloaks of rich feather work; and to us soldiers he gave two loads of cloaks each, all with a princely air. For in every way he was like a great prince. After the distribution of presents, he asked Cortes if we were all brothers and vassals of our great Emperor; and Cortes answered that we were brothers in love and friendship, persons of great distinction, and servants of our great king and lord. Further polite speeches passed between Montezuma and Cortes, but as this was the first time he had visited us and we did not want to tire him, the conversation ended.

Montezuma had ordered his stewards to provide us with everything we needed for our way of living: maize, grindstones, women to make our bread, fowls, fruit, and plenty of fodder for the horses. He then took leave of us all with the greatest courtesy, and we accompanied him to the street. However, Cortes ordered us not to go far from our quarters for the present until we knew better what conduct to observe.

Next day Cortes decided to go to Montezuma's palace. But first he sent to know whether the prince was busy and to inform him of our coming. He took four captains with him: Pedro de Alvarado, Juan Velazquez de Leon, Diego de Ordaz, and Gonzalo de Sandoval, and five of us soldiers.

When Montezuma was informed of our coming, he advanced into the middle of the hall to receive us, closely surrounded by his nephews, for no other chiefs were allowed to enter his palace or communicate with him except upon important business. Cortes and Montezuma exchanged bows, and clasped hands. Then Montezuma led Cortes to his own dais, and setting him down on his right, called for more seats, on which he ordered us all to sit also.

Cortes began to make a speech through our interpreters, saying that we were all now rested, and that in coming to see and speak with such a great prince we had fulfilled the purpose of our voyage and the orders of our lord the King. The principal things he had come to say on behalf of our Lord God had already been communicated to Montezuma through his three ambassadors, on that occasion in the sandhills when he did us the favour of sending us the golden moon and sun. We had then told him that we were Christians and worshipped one God alone, named Jesus Christ, who had suffered His passion and death to save us; and that what they worshipped as gods were not gods but devils, which were evil things, and if they were ugly to look at, their deeds were uglier. But he had proved to them how evil and ineffectual their gods were, as both the prince and his people would observe in the course of time, since where we had put up crosses such as their ambassadors had seen, they had been too frightened to appear before them.

The favour he now begged of the great Montezuma was that he should listen to the words he now wished to speak. Then he very carefully expounded the creation of the world, how we are all brothers, the children of one mother and father called Adam and Eve; and how such a brother as our great Emperor, grieving for the perdition of so many souls as their idols were leading to hell, where they burnt in living flame, had sent us to tell him this, so that he might put a stop to it, and so that they might give up the worship of idols and make no more human sacrifices—for all men are brothers—and commit no more robbery or sodomy. He also promised that in the course of time the King would send some men who lead holy lives among us, much better than our own, to explain this more fully, for we had only come to give them warning. Therefore he begged Montezuma to do as he was asked.

As Montezuma seemed about to reply, Cortes broke off his speech, saying to those of us who were with him: 'Since this is only the first attempt, we have now done our duty.'

'My lord Malinche,' Montezuma replied, 'these arguments of yours have been familiar to me for some time. I understand what you said to my ambassadors on the sandhills about the three gods and the cross, also what you preached in the various towns through which you passed. We have given you no answer, since we have worshipped our own gods here from the beginning and know them to be good. No doubt yours are good also, but do not trouble to tell us any more about them at present. Regarding the creation of the world, we have held the same belief for many ages, and for this reason are certain that you are those who our ancestors predicted would come from the direction of the sunrise. As for your great King, I am in his debt and will give him of what I possess. For, as I have already said, two years ago I had news of the Captains who came in ships, by the road that you came, and said they were servants of this great king of yours. I should like to know if you are all the same people.'

Cortes answered that we were all brothers and servants of the Emperor, and that they had come to discover a route and explore the seas and ports, so that when they knew them well we could follow, as we had done. Montezuma was referring to the expeditions of Francisco Hernandez de Cordoba and of Grijalva, the first voyages of discovery. He said that ever since that time he had wanted to invite some of these men to visit the cities of his kingdom, where he would receive them and do them honour, and that now his gods had fulfilled his desire, for we were in his house, which we might call our own. Here we might rest and enjoy ourselves, for we should receive good treatment. If on other occasions he had sent to forbid our entrance into his city, it was not of his own free will, but because his vassals were afraid. For they told him we shot out flashes of lightning, and killed many Indians with our horses, and that we were angry *Teules*, and other such childish stories. But now that he had seen us, he knew that we were of flesh and blood and very intelligent, also very brave. Therefore he had a far greater esteem for us than these reports had given him, and would share with us what he had.

We all thanked him heartily for his signal good will, and Montezuma replied with a laugh, because in his princely manner he spoke very gaily: 'Malinche, I know that these people of Tlascala with whom you are so friendly have told you that I am a sort of god or *Teule*, and keep nothing in any of my houses that is not made of silver and gold and precious stones. But I know very well that you are too intelligent to believe this and will take it as a joke. See now, Malinche, my body is made of flesh and blood like yours, and my houses and palaces are of stone, wood, and plaster. It is true that I am a great king, and have inherited the riches of my ancestors, but the lies and nonsense you have heard of us are not true. You must take them as a joke, as I take the story of your thunders and lightnings.'

Cortes answered also with a laugh that enemies always speak evil and tell lies about the people they hate, but he knew he could not hope to find a more magnificent prince in that land, and there was good reason why his fame should have reached our Emperor.

While this conversation was going on, Montezuma quietly sent one of his nephews, a great *Cacique*, to order his stewards to bring certain pieces of gold, which had apparently been set aside as a gift for Cortes, and ten loads of fine cloaks which he divided: the gold and cloaks between Cortes and the four captains, and for each of us soldiers two gold necklaces, each worth ten pesos, and two loads of cloaks. The gold that he then gave us was worth in all more than a thousand pesos, and he gave it all cheerfully, like a great and valiant prince.

As it was now past midday and he did not wish to be importunate, Cortes said to Montezuma: 'My lord, the favours you do us increase, load by load, every day, and it is now the hour of your dinner.' Montezuma answered that he thanked us for visiting him. We then took our leave with the greatest courtesy, and returned to our quarters, talking as we went of the prince's fine breeding and manners and deciding to show him the greatest respect in every way, and to remove our quilted caps in his presence, which we always did.

The great Montezuma was about forty years old, of good height, well proportioned, spare and slight, and not very dark, though of the usual Indian complexion. He did not wear his hair long but just over his ears, and he had a short black beard, well-shaped and thin. His face was rather long and cheerful, he had fine eyes, and in his appearance and manner could express geniality or, when necessary, a serious composure. He was very neat and clean, and took a bath every afternoon. He had many women as his mistresses, the daughters of chieftains, but two legitimate wives who were *Caciques* in their own right, and when he had intercourse with any of them it was so secret that only some of his servants knew of it. He was quite free from sodomy. The clothes he wore one day he did not wear again till three or four days later. He had a guard of two hundred chieftains lodged in rooms beside his own, only some of whom were permitted to speak to him. When they entered his presence they were compelled to take off their rich cloaks and put on others of little value. They had to be clean and walk barefoot, with their eyes downcast, for they were not allowed to look him in the face, and as they approached they had to make three obeisances, saying as they did so, 'Lord, my lord, my great lord!' Then, when they had said what they had come to say, he would dismiss them with a few words. They did not turn their backs on him as they went out, but kept their faces towards him and their eyes downcast, only turning round when they had left the room. Another thing I noticed was that when other great chiefs came from distant lands about disputes or on business, they too had to take off their shoes and put on poor cloaks before entering Montezuma's apartments; and they were not allowed to enter the palace immediately but had to linger for a while near the door, since to enter hurriedly was considered disrespectful.

For each meal his servants prepared him more than thirty dishes cooked in their native style, which they put over small earthenware braziers to prevent them from getting cold. They cooked more than three hundred plates of the food the great Montezuma was going to eat, and more than a thousand more for the guard. I have heard that they used to cook him the flesh of young boys. But as he had such a variety of dishes, made of so many different ingredients, we could not tell whether a dish was of human flesh or anything else, since every day they cooked fowls, turkeys, pheasants, local partridges, quail, tame and wild duck, venison, wild boar, marsh birds, pigeons, hares and rabbits, also many other kinds of birds and beasts native to their country, so numerous that I cannot quickly name them all. I know for certain, however, that after our Captain spoke against the sacrifice of human beings and the eating of their flesh, Montezuma ordered that it should no longer be served to him.

Let us now turn to the way his meals were served, which was like this. If it was cold, they built a large fire of live coals made by burning the bark of a tree which gave off no smoke. The smell of the bark from which they made these coals was very sweet. In order that he should get no more heat than he wanted, they placed a sort of screen in front of it adorned with the figures of idols worked in gold. He would sit on a soft low stool, which was richly worked. His table, which was also low and decorated in the same way, was covered with white tablecloths and rather long napkins of the same material. Then four very clean and beautiful girls brought water for his hands in one of those deep basins that they call *xicales*.[1] They held others like plates beneath it to catch the water, and brought him towels. Two other women brought him maize-cakes.

When he began his meal they placed in front of him a sort of wooden screen, richly decorated with gold, so that no one should see him eat. Then the four women retired, and four great chieftains, all old men, stood beside him. He talked with them every now and then and asked them questions, and as a great favour he would sometimes offer one of them a dish of whatever tasted best. They say that these were his closest relations and advisers and judges of lawsuits, and if he gave them anything to eat they ate it standing, with deep reverence and without looking in his face.

Montezuma's food was served on Cholula ware, some red and some black. While he was dining, the guards in the adjoining rooms did not dare to speak or make a noise above a whisper. His servants brought him some of every kind of fruit that grew in the country, but he ate very little of it. Sometimes they brought him in cups of pure gold a drink made from the cocoaplant, which they said he took before visiting his wives. We did not take much notice of this at the time, though I saw them bring in a good fifty large jugs of this chocolate, all frothed up, of which he would drink a little. They always served it with great reverence. Sometimes some little humpbacked dwarfs would be present at his meals, whose bodies seemed almost to be broken in the middle. These were his jesters. There were other Indians who told him jokes and must have been his clowns, and others who sang and danced, for Montezuma was very fond of music and entertainment and would reward his entertainers with the leavings of the food and chocolate. The same four women removed the tablecloths and again most reverently brought him water for his hands. Then Montezuma would talk to these four old chieftains about matters that interested him, and they would take their leave with great ceremony. He stayed behind to rest.

As soon as the great Montezuma had dined, all the guards and many more of his household servants ate in their turn. I think more than a thousand plates of food must have been brought in for them, and more than two thousand jugs of chocolate frothed up in the Mexican style, and infinite quantities of fruit, so that with his women and serving-maids and breadmakers and chocolate-makers his expenses must have been considerable.

---

1. Gourds.

One thing I had forgotten to say is that two more very handsome women served Montezuma when he was at table with maize-cakes kneaded with eggs and other nourishing ingredients. These maize-cakes were very white, and were brought in on plates covered with clean napkins. They brought him a different kind of bread also, in a long ball kneaded with other kinds of nourishing food, and *pachol* cake, as they call it in that country, which is a kind of wafer. They also placed on the table three tubes, much painted and gilded, in which they put liquidamber[2] mixed with some herbs which are called tobacco. When Montezuma had finished his dinner, and the singing and dancing were over and the cloths had been removed, he would inhale the smoke from one of these tubes. He took very little of it, and then fell asleep.

I remember that at that time his steward was a great *Cacique* whom we nicknamed Tapia, and he kept an account of all the revenue that was brought to Montezuma in his books, which were made of paper—their name for which is *amal*—and he had a great house full of these books. But they have nothing to do with our story.

Montezuma had two houses stocked with every sort of weapon: many of them were richly adorned with gold and precious stones. There were shields large and small, and a sort of broadsword, and two-handed swords set with flint blades that cut much better than our swords, and lances longer than ours, with five-foot blades consisting of many knives. Even when these are driven at a buckler or a shield they are not deflected. In fact they cut like razors, and the Indians can shave their heads with them. They had very good bows and arrows, and double and single-pointed javelins as well as their throwing-sticks and many slings and round stones shaped by hand, and another sort of shield that can be rolled up when they are not fighting, so that it does not get in the way, but which can be opened when they need it in battle and covers their bodies from head to foot. There was also a great deal of cotton armour richly worked on the outside with different coloured feathers, which they used as devices and distinguishing marks, and they had casques and helmets made of wood and bone which were also highly decorated with feathers on the outside. They had other arms of different kinds which I will not mention through fear of prolixity, and workmen skilled in the manufacture of such things, and stewards who were in charge of these arms.

Let us pass on to the aviary. I cannot possibly enumerate every kind of bird that was in it or describe its characteristics. There was everything from the royal eagle, smaller kinds of eagles, and other large birds, down to multi-coloured little birds, and those from which they take the fine green feathers they use in their feather-work. These last birds are about the size of our magpies, and here they are called *quetzals*. There were other birds too which have feathers of five colours: green, red, white, yellow, and blue, but

---

2. The gum of a native tree.

I do not know what they are called. Then there were parrots with different coloured plumage, so many of them that I have forgotten their names. There were also beautifully marked ducks, and bigger ones like them. At the proper season they plucked the feathers of all these birds, which then grew again. All of them were bred in this aviary, and at hatching time the men and women who looked after them would place them on their eggs and clean their nests and feed them, giving each breed of birds its proper food.

In the aviary there was a large tank of fresh water, and in it was another type of bird on long stilt-like legs with a red body, wings, and tail. I do not know its name, but in Cuba birds rather like them are called *ypiris*. Also in this tank there were many other kinds of water birds.

Let us go on to another large house where they kept many idols whom they called their fierce gods, and with them all kinds of beasts of prey, tigers and two sorts of lion, and beasts rather like wolves which they call *adives*,[3] and foxes and other small animals, all of them carnivores, and most of them bred there. They were fed on deer, fowls, little dogs, and other creatures which they hunt and also on the bodies of the Indians they sacrificed, as I was told.

I have already described the manner of their sacrifices. They strike open the wretched Indian's chest with flint knives and hastily tear out the palpitating heart which, with the blood, they present to the idols in whose name they have performed the sacrifice. Then they cut off the arms, thighs, and head, eating the arms and thighs at their ceremonial banquets. The head they hang up on a beam, and the body of the sacrificed man is not eaten but given to the beasts of prey. They also had many vipers in this accursed house, and poisonous snakes which have something that sounds like a bell in their tails. These, which are the deadliest snakes of all, they kept in jars and great pottery vessels full of feathers, in which they laid their eggs and reared their young. They were fed on the bodies of sacrificed Indians and the flesh of the dogs that they bred. We know for certain, too, that when they drove us out of Mexico and killed over eight hundred and fifty of our soldiers, they fed those beasts and snakes on their bodies for many days, as I shall relate in due course. These snakes and wild beasts were dedicated to their fierce idols, and kept them company. As for the horrible noise when the lions and tigers roared, and the jackals and foxes howled, and the serpents hissed, it was so appalling that one seemed to be in hell.

I must now speak of the skilled workmen whom Montezuma employed in all the crafts they practised, beginning with the jewellers and workers in silver and gold and various kinds of hollowed objects, which excited the admiration of our great silversmiths at home. Many of the best of them lived in a town called Atzcapotzalco, three miles from Mexico. There were other skilled craftsmen who worked with precious stones and *chalchihuites*, and

---

3. Bernal Díaz is mistaken here. This is an Arabic word for jackal, quite commonly used in Spain.

specialists in feather-work, and very fine painters and carvers. We can form some judgement of what they did then from what we can see of their work today. There are three Indians now living in the city of Mexico, named Marcos de Aquino, Juan de la Cruz, and El Crespillo, who are such magnificent painters and carvers that, had they lived in the age of the Apelles of old, or of Michael Angelo, or Berruguete in our own day, they would be counted in the same rank.

Let us go on to the women, the weavers and sempstresses, who made such a huge quantity of fine robes with very elaborate feather designs. These things were generally brought from some towns in the province of Cotaxtla, which is on the north coast, quite near San Juan de Ulua. In Montezuma's own palaces very fine cloths were woven by those chieftains' daughters whom he kept as mistresses; and the daughters of other dignitaries, who lived in a kind of retirement like nuns in some houses close to the great *cue* of Huichilobos, wore robes entirely of featherwork. Out of devotion for that god and a female deity who was said to preside over marriage, their fathers would place them in religious retirement until they found husbands. They would then take them out to be married.

Now to speak of the great number of performers whom Montezuma kept to entertain him. There were dancers and stilt-walkers, and some who seemed to fly as they leapt through the air, and men rather like clowns to make him laugh. There was a whole quarter full of these people who had no other occupation. He had as many workmen as he needed, too, stone-cutters, masons, and carpenters, to keep his houses in repair.

We must not forget the gardens with their many varieties of flowers and sweet-scented trees planted in order, and their ponds and tanks of fresh water into which a stream flowed at one end and out of which it flowed at the other, and the baths he had there, and the variety of small birds that nested in the branches, and the medicinal and useful herbs that grew there. His gardens were a wonderful sight, and required many gardeners to take care of them. Everything was built of stone and plastered; baths and walks and closets and rooms like summerhouses where they danced and sang. There was so much to see in these gardens, as everywhere else, that we could not tire of contemplating his great riches and the large number of skilled Indians employed in the many crafts they practised.

When we had already been in Mexico for four days, and neither our Captain nor anyone else had left our quarters except to visit these houses and gardens, Cortes said it would be a good thing to visit the large square of Tlatelolco and see the great *cue* of Huichilobos. So he sent Aguilar, Doña Marina, and his own young page Orteguilla, who by now knew something of the language, to ask for Montezuma's approval of this plan. On receiving his request, the prince replied that we were welcome to go, but for fear that we might offer some offence to his idols he would himself accompany us with many of his chieftains. Leaving the palace in his fine litter, when he had gone about half way, he dismounted beside some shrines, since he considered it an insult to his gods to visit their dwelling in a litter. Some of the great chieftains then supported him by the arms, and his principal vassals walked before him, carrying two staves, like sceptres raised on high as a sign that the great Montezuma was approaching. When riding in his litter he had carried a rod, partly of gold and partly of wood, held up like a wand of justice. The prince now climbed the steps of the great *cue*, escorted by many *papas*, and began to burn incense and perform other ceremonies for Huichilobos.

Let us leave Montezuma, who had gone ahead as I have said, and return to Cortes and our soldiers. We carried our weapons, as was our custom, both by night and day. Indeed, Montezuma was so used to our visiting him armed that he did not think it strange. I say this because our Captain and those of us who had horses went to Tlatelolco mounted, and the majority of our men were fully equipped. On reaching the market-place, escorted by the many *Caciques* whom Montezuma had assigned to us, we were astounded at the great number of people and the quantities of merchandise, and at the orderliness and good arrangements that prevailed, for we had never seen such a thing before. The chieftains who accompanied us pointed everything out. Every kind of merchandise was kept separate and had its fixed place marked for it.

Let us begin with the dealers in gold, silver, and precious stones, feathers, cloaks, and embroidered goods, and male and female slaves who are also sold there. They bring as many slaves to be sold in that market as the Portuguese bring Negroes from Guinea. Some are brought there attached to long poles by means of collars round their necks to prevent them from escaping, but others are left loose. Next there were those who sold coarser cloth, and cotton goods and fabrics made of twisted thread, and there were chocolate merchants with their chocolate. In this way you could see every kind of merchandise to be found anywhere in New Spain, laid out in the same way as goods are laid out in my own district of Medina del Campo, a centre for fairs, where each line of stalls has its own particular sort. So it was in this great market. There were those who sold sisal cloth and ropes and the sandals they wear on their feet, which are made from the same plant. All these were kept in one part of the market, in the place assigned to them, and in another part were skins of tigers and lions, otters, jackals, and deer, badgers, mountain cats, and other wild animals, some tanned and some untanned, and other classes of merchandise.

There were sellers of kidney-beans and sage and other vegetables and herbs in another place, and in yet another they were selling fowls, and birds with great dewlaps,[4] also rabbits, hares, deer, young ducks, little dogs, and other such creatures. Then there were the fruiterers; and the women who sold cooked food, flour and honey cake, and tripe, had their part of the market. Then came pottery of all kinds, from big water-jars to little jugs, displayed in its own place, also honey, honey-paste, and other sweets like

---

4. Turkeys.

nougat. Elsewhere they sold timber too, boards, cradles, beams, blocks, and benches, all in a quarter of their own.

Then there were the sellers of pitch-pine for torches, and other things of that kind, and I must also mention, with all apologies, that they sold many canoe-loads of human excrement, which they kept in the creeks near the market. This was for the manufacture of salt and the curing of skins, which they say cannot be done without it. I know that many gentlemen will laugh at this, but I assure them it is true. I may add that on all the roads they have shelters made of reeds or straw or grass so that they can retire when they wish to do so, and purge their bowels unseen by passers-by, and also in order that their excrement shall not be lost.

But why waste so many words on the goods in their great market? If I describe everything in detail I shall never be done. Paper, which in Mexico they call *amal*, and some reeds that smell of liquidamber, and are full of tobacco, and yellow ointments and other such things, are sold in a separate part. Much cochineal is for sale too, under the arcades of that market, and there are many sellers of herbs and other such things. They have a building there also in which three judges sit, and there are officials like constables who examine the merchandise. I am forgetting the sellers of salt and the makers of flint knives, and how they split them off the stone itself, and the fisherwomen and the men who sell small cakes made from a sort of weed which they get out of the great lake, which curdles and forms a kind of bread which tastes rather like cheese. They sell axes too, made of bronze and copper and tin, and gourds and brightly painted wooden jars.

We went on to the great *cue*, and as we approached its wide courts, before leaving the market-place itself, we saw many more merchants who, so I was told, brought gold to sell in grains, just as they extract it from the mines. This gold is placed in the thin quills of the large geese of that country, which are so white as to be transparent. They used to reckon their accounts with one another by the length and thickness of these little quills, how much so many cloaks or so many gourds of chocolate or so many slaves were worth, or anything else they were bartering.

Now let us leave the market, having given it a final glance, and come to the courts and enclosures in which their great *cue* stood. Before reaching it you passed through a series of large courts, bigger I think than the Plaza at Salamanca. These courts were surrounded by a double masonry wall and paved, like the whole place, with very large smooth white flagstones. Where these stones were absent everything was whitened and polished, indeed the whole place was so clean that there was not a straw or a grain of dust to be found there.

When we arrived near the great temple and before we had climbed a single step, the great Montezuma sent six *papas* and two chieftains down from the top, where he was making his sacrifices, to escort our Captain; and as he climbed the steps, of which there were one hundred and fourteen, they tried to take him by the arms to help him up in the same way as they helped Montezuma, thinking he might be tired, but he would not let them near him.

The top of the *cue* formed an open square on which stood something like a platform, and it was here that the great stones stood on which they placed the poor Indians for sacrifice. Here also was a massive image like a dragon, and other hideous figures, and a great deal of blood that had been spilled that day. Emerging in the company of two *papas* from the shrine which houses his accursed images, Montezuma made a deep bow to us all and said: 'My lord Malinche, you must be tired after climbing this great *cue* of ours.' And Cortes replied that none of us was ever exhausted by anything. Then Montezuma took him by the hand, and told him to look at his great city and all the other cities standing in the water, and the many others on the land round the lake; and he said that if Cortes had not had a good view of the great market-place he could see it better from where he now was. So we stood there looking, because that huge accursed *cue* stood so high that it dominated everything. We saw the three causeways that led into Mexico: the causeway of Iztapalapa by which we had entered four days before, and that of Tacuba along which we were afterwards to flee on the night of our great defeat, when the new prince Cuitlahuac drove us out of the city (as I shall tell in due course), and that of Tepeaquilla.[5] We saw the fresh water which came from Chapultepec to supply the city, and the bridges that were constructed at intervals on the causeways so that the water could flow in and out from one part of the lake to another. We saw a great number of canoes, some coming with provisions and others returning with cargo and merchandise; and we saw too that one could not pass from one house to another of that great city and the other cities that were built on the water except over wooden drawbridges or by canoe. We saw *cues* and shrines in these cities that looked like gleaming white towers and castles: a marvelous sight. All the houses had flat roofs, and on the causeways were other small towers and shrines built like fortresses.

Having examined and considered all that we had seen, we turned back to the great market and the swarm of people buying and selling. The mere murmur of their voices talking was loud enough to be heard more than three miles away. Some of our soldiers who had been in many parts of the world, in Constantinople, in Rome, and all over Italy, said that they had never seen a market so well laid out, so large, so orderly, and so full of people.

But to return to our Captain, he observed to Father Bartolome de Olmedo, whom I have often mentioned and who happened to be standing near him: 'It would be a good thing, I think, Father, if we were to sound Montezuma as to whether he would let us build our church here.' Father Bartolome answered that it would be a good thing if it were successful, but

---

5. Guadalupe.

he did not think this a proper time to speak of it, for Montezuma did not look as if he would allow such a thing.

Cortes, however, addressed Montezuma through Doña Marina: 'Your lordship is a great prince and worthy of even greater things. We have enjoyed the sight of your cities, and since we are now here in your temple, I beg of you to show us your gods and *Teules.*' Montezuma answered that first he would consult his chief *papas;* and when he had spoken to them he said that we might enter a small tower, an apartment like a sort of hall, in which there were two altars with very rich wooden carvings over the roof. On each altar was a giant figure, very tall and very fat. They said that the one on the right was Huichilobos, their war-god. He had a very broad face and huge terrible eyes. And there were so many precious stones, so much gold, so many pearls and seed-pearls stuck to him with a paste which the natives made from a sort of root, that his whole body and head were covered with them. He was girdled with huge snakes made of gold and precious stones, and in one hand he held a bow, in the other some arrows. Another smaller idol beside him, which they said was his page, carried a short lance and a very rich shield of gold and precious stones. Around Huichilobos' neck hung some Indian faces and other objects in the shape of hearts, the former made of gold and the latter of silver, with many precious blue stones.

There were some smoking braziers of their incense, which they call copal, in which they were burning the hearts of three Indians whom they had sacrificed that day; and all the walls of that shrine were so splashed and caked with blood that they and the floor too were black. Indeed, the whole place stank abominably. We then looked to the left and saw another great image of the same height as Huichilobos, with a face like a bear and eyes that glittered, being made of their mirror-glass, which they call *tezcat*. Its body, like that of Huichilobos, was encrusted with precious stones, for they said that the two were brothers. This Tezcatlipoca, the god of hell, had charge of the Mexicans' souls, and his body was surrounded by figures of little devils with snakes' tails. The walls of this shrine also were so caked with blood and the floor so bathed in it that the stench was worse than that of any slaughter-house in Spain. They had offered that idol five hearts from the day's sacrifices.

At the very top of the *cue* there was another alcove, the woodwork of which was very finely carved, and here there was another image, half man and half lizard, encrusted with precious stones, with half its body covered in a cloak. They said that the body of this creature contained all the seeds in the world, and that he was the god of seedtime and harvest. I do not remember his name.[6] Here too all was covered with blood, both walls and altar, and the stench was such that we could hardly wait to get out. They

---

6. This was probably Tlaltecuhtli.

kept a very large drum there, and when they beat it the sound was most dismal, like some music from the infernal regions, as you might say, and it could be heard six miles away. This drum was said to be covered with the skins of huge serpents. In that small platform were many more diabolical objects, trumpets great and small, and large knives, and many hearts that had been burnt with incense before their idols; and everything was caked with blood. The stench here too was like a slaughter-house, and we could scarcely stay in the place.

Our Captain said to Montezuma, through our interpreters, with something like a laugh: 'Lord Montezuma, I cannot imagine how a prince as great and wise as your Majesty can have failed to realize that these idols of yours are not gods but evil things, the proper name for which is devils. But so that I may prove this to you, and make it clear to all your *papas,* grant me one favour. Allow us to erect a cross here on the top of this tower, and let us divide off a part of this sanctuary where your Huichilobos and Tezcatlipoca stand, as a place where we can put an image of Our Lady'—which image Montezuma had already seen—'and then you will see, by the fear that your idols have of her, how grievously they have deceived you.'

Montezuma, however, replied in some temper (and the two *papas* beside him showed real anger): 'Lord Malinche, if I had known that you were going to utter these insults I should not have shown you my gods. We hold them to be very good. They give us health and rain and crops and weather, and all the victories we desire. So we are bound to worship them and sacrifice to them, and I beg you to say nothing more against them.'

On hearing this and seeing Montezuma's fury, our Captain said no more on the subject but observed cheerfully: 'It is time for your Majesty and ourselves to depart.' Montezuma replied that this was so, but that he had to pray and offer certain sacrifices on account of the great *tatacul*—that is to say sin—which he had committed in allowing us to climb his great *cue* and in being instrumental in letting us see his gods and in the dishonour we had done them by our abuse. Therefore before he left he must pray and worship.

'If that is so, my lord,' Cortes answered, 'I ask your pardon.' And we went down the steps, of which there were a hundred and fourteen, as I said. As some of our soldiers were suffering from pustules or running sores, their thighs pained them as they went down.

I will now give my impression of the *cue's* surroundings. Do not be surprised, however, if I do not describe them as accurately as I might, for I had other thoughts in my head at the time than that of telling a story. I was more concerned with my military duties and the orders my Captain had given me. But to come to the facts, I think the site of the great *cue* was equal to the plots of six large town houses at home. It tapered from the base to the top of the small tower where they kept their idols. Between the middle of this tall *cue* and its highest point there were five holes like loopholes for cannon, but open and unprotected. But as there are many *cues* painted on the banners of the conquerors, including my own, anyone who has seen them can gather what a *cue* looked like from the outside. I heard a report that, at the time when this great *cue* was built, all the inhabitants of that mighty city placed offerings of gold and silver and pearls and precious stones in the foundations, and bathed them in the blood of prisoners of war whom they had sacrificed. They also put there every kind of seed that grew in their country, so that their idols should give them victories and riches and great crops. Some curious readers may ask how we came to know that they had thrown gold and silver and precious *chalchihuites* and seeds into the foundation of the *cue*, and watered them with the blood of Indian victims, seeing that the building was erected a thousand years ago. My answer is that after we conquered that great and strong city and divided the ground we decided to build a church to our patron and guide St James in place of Huichilobos' *cue*, and a great part of the site was taken for the purpose. When the ground was excavated to lay a foundation, gold and silver and *chalchihuites*, and pearls, seed-pearls, and other precious stones were found in great quantities; and a settler in Mexico who built on another part of the site found the same. The officers of His Majesty's Treasury demanded this find as rightfully belonging to the King, and there was a lawsuit about it. I do not remember what the outcome was, only that they asked for information from the *Caciques* and dignitaries of Mexico, and from Guatemoc who was then alive, and they affirmed that all the inhabitants of Mexico had thrown jewels and other things into the foundations, as was recorded in their pictures and records of ancient times. The treasure was therefore preserved for the building of St James's church.

Let me go on to describe the great and splendid courts in front of Huichilobos, on the site where that church now stands, which was called at that time Tlatelolco. I have already said that there were two masonry walls before the entrance to the *cue*, and the court was paved with white stones like flagstones, and all was whitened, burnished and clean. A little apart from the *cue* stood another small tower which was also an idol-house or true hell, for one of its doors was in the shape of a terrible mouth, such as they paint to depict the jaws of hell. This mouth was open and contained great fangs to devour souls. Beside this door were groups of devils and the shapes of serpents, and a little way off was a place of sacrifice, all bloodstained and black with smoke. There were many great pots and jars and pitchers in this house, full of water. For it was here that they cooked the flesh of the wretched Indians who were sacrificed and eaten by the *papas*. Near this place of sacrifice there were many large knives and chopping-blocks like those on which men cut up meat in slaughter-houses; and behind that dreadful house, some distance away, were great piles of brushwood, beside which was a tank of water that was filled and emptied through a pipe from the covered channel that comes into the city from Chapultepec. I always called that building Hell.

Crossing the court you came to another *cue*, where the great Mexican princes were buried. This also contained many idols and was full of blood and smoke. It too had doorways with hellish figures; and beside it was another *cue,* full of skulls and large bones arranged in an orderly pattern, and so numerous that you could not count them however long you looked. The skulls were in one place and the bones in separate piles. Here there were more idols, and in every building or *cue* or shrine were *papas* in long black cloth robes and long hoods.

To proceed, there were other *cues,* a short distance away from that of the skulls, which contained other idols and sacrificial altars decorated with horrible paintings. These idols were said to preside over the marriages of men. But I will waste no more time on the subject of idols. I will only say that all round that great court there were many low houses, used and occupied by the *papas* and other Indians who were in charge of them. On one side of the great *cue* there was another, much bigger pond or tank of very clean water which was solely devoted to the service of Huichilobos and Tezcatlipoca, and the water for this tank was also supplied by covered pipes that came from Chapultepec. Near by were the large buildings of a kind of nunnery where many of the daughters of the inhabitants of Mexico dwelt in retirement until the time of their marriage. Here there were two massive female idols who presided over the marriages of women, and to which they offered sacrifices and feasts in order that they should get good husbands.

I have spent a long time talking about the great *cue* of Tlatelolco and its courts. I will conclude by saying that it was the biggest temple in Mexico, though there were many other fine ones, for every four or five parishes or districts supported a shrine with idols: and since there were many districts I cannot keep a count of them all. I must say, however, that the great *cue* in Cholula was higher than that in Mexico, for it had a hundred and twenty steps. The idol at Cholula, as I heard, had a great reputation, and people made pilgrimages to it from all over New Spain to obtain pardons. This was the reason why they had built it such a magnificent *cue.* It was differently planned from that of Mexico, but also had great courts and a double wall. The *cue* of the city of Texcoco was very high too, having a hundred and seventeen steps, and fine wide courtyards, again of a different shape from the others. Absurd though it was, every province had its own idols, and those of one province or city were of no help in another. Therefore they had infinite numbers of idols and sacrificed to them all.

When we were all tired of walking about and seeing such a diversity of idols and sacrifices, we returned to our quarters, still accompanied by the many *Caciques* and dignitaries whom Montezuma had sent with us.

When our Captain and the Mercedarian friar realized that Montezuma would not allow us to set up a cross at Huichilobos' *cue* or build a church there, it was decided that we should ask his stewards for masons so that we could put up a church in our own quarters. For every time we had said mass since entering the city of Mexico we had had to erect an altar on tables and dismantle it again.

The stewards promised to tell Montezuma of our wishes, and Cortes also sent our interpreters to ask him in person. Montezuma granted our request and ordered that we should be supplied with all the necessary material. We had our church finished in two days, and a cross erected in front of our lodgings, and mass was said there each day until the wine gave out. For as Cortes and some other captains and a friar had been ill during the Tlascalan campaign, there had been a run on the wine that we kept for mass. Still, though it was finished, we still went to church every day and prayed on our knees before the altar and images, firstly because it was our obligation as Christians and a good habit, and secondly so that Montezuma and all his captains should observe us and, seeing us worshipping on our knees before the cross—especially when we intoned the Ave Maria— might be inclined to imitate us.

It being our habit to examine and inquire into everything, when we were all assembled in our lodging and considering which was the best place for an altar, two of our men, one of whom was the carpenter Alonso Yañez, called attention to some marks on one of the walls which showed that there had once been a door, though it had been well plastered up and painted. Now as we had heard that Montezuma kept his father's treasure in this building, we immediately suspected that it must be in this room, which had been closed up only a few days before. Yañez made the suggestion to Juan Velazquez de Leon and Francisco de Lugo, both relatives of mine, to whom he had attached himself as a servant; and they mentioned the matter to Cortes. So the door was secretly opened, and Cortes went in first with certain captains. When they saw the quantity of golden objects—jewels and plates and ingots—which lay in that chamber they were quite transported. They did not know what to think of such riches. The news soon spread to the other captains and soldiers, and very secretly we all went in to see. The sight of all that wealth dumbfounded me. Being only a youth at the time and never having seen such riches before, I felt certain that there could not be a store like it in the whole world. We unanimously decided that we could not think of touching a particle of it, and that the stones should immediately be replaced in the doorway, which should be blocked again and cemented just as we had found it. We resolved also that not a word should be said about this until times changed, for fear Montezuma might hear of our discovery.

Let us leave this subject of the treasure and tell how four of our most valiant captains took Cortes aside in the church, with a dozen soldiers who were in his trust and confidence, myself among them, and asked him to consider the net or trap in which we were caught, to look at the great strength of the city and observe the causeways and bridges, and remember the warnings we had received in every town we had passed through that Huichilobos had counselled Montezuma to let us into the city and kill us there. We reminded him that the hearts of men are very fickle, especially among the Indians, and begged him not to trust the good will and affection that Montezuma was showing us, because from one hour to another it might change. If he should take it into his head to attack us, we said, the stoppage of our supplies of food and water, or the raising of any of the bridges, would render us helpless. Then, considering the vast army of warriors he possessed, we should be incapable of attacking or defending ourselves. And since all the houses stood in the water, how could our Tlascalan allies come in to help us? We asked him to think over all that we had said, for if we wanted to preserve our lives we must seize Montezuma immediately, without even a day's delay. We pointed out that all the gold Montezuma had given us, and all that we had seen in the treasury of his father Axayacatl, and all the food we ate was turning to poison in our bodies, for we could not sleep by night or day or take any rest while these thoughts were in our minds. If any of our soldiers gave him less drastic advice, we concluded, they would be senseless beasts charmed by the gold and incapable of looking death in the eye.

When he had heard our opinion, Cortes answered: 'Do not imagine, gentlemen, that I am asleep or that I do not share your anxiety. You must have seen that I do. But what strength have we got for so bold a course as to take this great lord in his own palace, surrounded as he is by warriors and guards? What scheme or trick can we devise to prevent him from summoning his soldiers to attack us at once?'

Our captains (Juan Velazquez de Leon, Diego de Ordaz, Gonzalo de Sandoval, and Pedro de Alvarado) replied that Montezuma must be got out of his palace by smooth words and brought to our quarters. Once there, he must be told that he must remain as a prisoner, and that if he called out or made any disturbance he would pay for it with his life. If Cortes was unwilling to take this course at once, they begged him for permission to do it themselves. With two very dangerous alternatives before us, the better and more profitable thing, they said, would be to seize Montezuma rather than wait for him to attack us. Once he did so, what chance would we have? Some of us soldiers also remarked that Montezuma's stewards who brought us our food seemed to be growing insolent, and did not serve us as politely as they had at first. Two of our Tlascalan allies had, moreover, secretly observed to Jeronimo de Aguilar that for the last two days the Mexicans had appeared less well disposed to us. We spent a good hour discussing whether or not to take Montezuma prisoner, and how it should be done. But our final advice, that at all costs we should take him prisoner, was approved by our Captain, and we then left the matter till next day. All night we prayed God to direct events in the interests of His holy service.

Next morning two Tlascalan Indians arrived very secretly with letters from Villa Rica containing the news of an attack by the Mexicans at a place called Almeria, in which one of our men and the Constable's horse had been killed, as well as many Totonacs. Moreover the Constable Escalante himself and six more men had died of their wounds after returning to Villa Rica. Now all the hill towns and Cempoala and its dependencies were in revolt. They refused to bring food or serve in the fort; whereas hitherto our men had been respected as *Teules,* now after this disaster Mexicans and Totonacs alike were behaving like wild beasts. They could not control the Indians in any way, and did not know what measures to take.

God knows the distress this news caused us. It was the first defeat we had suffered in New Spain, and misfortunes, as the reader will see, were now descending upon us.

■ The Inca Garcilaso de la Vega (1539–1616) *Peru/Spain* (history)

TRANSLATED BY HAROLD V. LIVERMORE

The illegitimate son of a conquistador and an Inca princess, the Inca Garcilaso is the first American-born writer of distinction in the New World. With him begins American letters in its most profoundly ethnic and literary modes. With Garcilaso, a child of Europe and America, begins the indigious literature in Spanish of the New World. Garcilaso was born in the high Andes city of Cuzco, the ancient capital of the Inca kingdom. Because he was a "half-caste" and illegitimate, he was denied his father's name and was baptized Gómez Suárez de Figueroa. His father was Sebastián de Garcilaso, of the family of Garcilaso de la Vega, the great Spanish Renaissance poet. For the literatures of the Americas, Garcilaso was the perfect interpreter and stylist for the postconquest period, carrying with him a knowledge of Spain and its language as well as his more favored knowledge of Inca reality, history, and legend, which he gave to us in elegant Spanish prose.

Schooled in Peru, in 1560 he went to Spain to complete his education. In Andalusia, he was protected by his paternal uncle and assumed his family name, adding Inca to it to display his Inca heritage. He was unable, however, to assume control of his father's confiscated estate and fortune. In Spain, he led a full literary life and produced three significant books. He edited and compiled *La Florida* (1605), the work of the explorer Hernando de Soto. He translated from Italian into Spanish *Dialoghi d'Amore,* a key Neoplatonic work by the exiled Spanish Jew León Hebreo. Hebreo's original dialogues, early in the sixteenth century, with their mystical lexicon for spiritual love, were, along with the Song of Songs, the principal source for the poetry and commentaries of the Spanish mystical poet Saint John of the Cross. His third book was his literary treasure, *The Royal Commentaries* (1609 and 1617).

In the *Commentaries,* Garcilaso used all the available sources of an educated, well-connected exile in Spain. Schooled in Quechua as a young man, he wrote to his royal Inca relatives for information. He also preserved his own memory of an oral tradition of narration, which had been essential to his Peruvian youth. In the "histories," he recreated Inca glory. He could not know then that the Incas, whose recorded culture dated back to the twelfth century, were not the first Indian civilization in Peru, but, rather, the last in a series of civilizations, and that, for example, the famous, beautiful Peruvian textiles long preceded the Inca period. He did preserve the Inca version of his people's history and religion, reminding Spain that Peru had been ruled by the Sons of the Sun, *los Hijos del Sol.* In later years, the Spanish censors held the book hostage; and when it was permitted publication, the word "Royalty" was removed from the title. The volume was retitled *General History of Peru*—in the manner of the Spanish chronicles of conquest. The grand interior, however, remained untouched, and the majestic quality shone on virtually every page.

FURTHER READING: The Inca Garcilaso de la Vega. *The Dialogues of Love,* 1590; *The Royal Commentaries,* 1609, II, 1617.

from *The Royal Commentaries of Peru*

The Idolatry of the Indians and the Gods They Worshipped before the Incas

For the better understanding of the idolatry, way of life, and customs of the Indians of Peru, it will be necessary for us to divide those times into two periods. First we shall say how they lived before the Incas, and then how the Inca kings governed, so as not to confuse the one thing with the other, and so that the customs and gods of one period are not attributed to the other. It must therefore be realized that in the first age of primitive heathendom there were Indians who were little better than tame beasts and others much worse than wild beasts. To begin with their gods, we may say that they were of a piece with the simplicity and stupidity of the times, as regards the multiplicity of gods and the vileness and crudity of the things the people worshipped. Each province, each tribe, each village, each quarter, each clan, each house had gods different from the rest, for they considered that other people's gods, being busy with other people's affairs, could not help them, but they must have their own. Thus they came to have so great a variety of gods, which were too numerous to count. They did not understand, as the gentile Romans did, how to create abstract gods such as Hope, Victory, Peace, and so on, for their thoughts did not rise to invisible things, and they worshipped what they saw some in one way and others in another. They did not consider whether the things they worshipped were worthy of their worship and they had no self-respect, in the sense of refraining from worshipping things inferior to themselves. They only thought of distinguishing themselves from one another, and each from all the rest. Thus they worshipped grasses, plants, flowers, trees of all kinds, high hills, great rocks and nooks in them, deep caves, pebbles, and little pieces of stone of various colors found in rivers and streams, such as jasper. They worshipped the emerald, especially in the province now called Puerto Viejo. They did not worship diamonds or rubies because these stones did not exist there. Instead they worshipped various animals, some for their ferocity, such as the tiger, lion, and bear: and consequently, regarding them as gods, if they chanced to meet them, they did not flee but fell down and worshipped them and let themselves be killed and eaten without escaping or making any defence at all. They also worshipped other animals for their cunning, such as the fox and monkeys. They worshipped the dog for its faithfulness and nobility, the wild cat for its quickness, and the bird they call *cuntur* for its size; and some natives worshipped eagles, because they boast of descending from them and also from the *cuntur.* Other peoples adored hawks for their quickness and ability in winning their food. They adored the owl for the beauty of its eyes and head; the bat for the keenness of its sight—it caused them much wonder that it could see at night. They also adored many other birds according to their whims. They adored great snakes for their monstrous size and fierceness (some of those in the Antis are about twenty-five or thirty feet long and as thick round as a man's thigh). They also considered other smaller snakes—where there were none so big as in the Antis—to be gods, and they adored lizards, toads, and frogs. In a word, there was no beast too vile and filthy for them to worship as a god, merely in order to differ from one another in their choice of gods, without adoring any real god or being able to expect any benefit from them. They were very simple in everything, like sheep without a shepherd. But we need not be surprised that such unlettered and untaught people should have fallen into these follies, for it is well known that the Greeks and Romans, who prided themselves so greatly on their learning, had thirty thousand gods when their empire was at its height.

The Great Variety of Other Gods They Had

There were many other Indians of various nations in this first period who chose their gods with rather more discrimination than these. They worshipped certain objects that were beneficial, such as streaming fountains and great rivers, which they argued gave them water to irrigate their crops.

Others adored the earth and called it "mother," because it gave them its fruits. Others the air they breathed, saying that men lived by it; others fire, because it warmed them and they cooked their food with it. Others worshipped a ram, because of the great flocks reared in their region; others the great chain of the Sierra Nevada, because of its height and wonderful grandeur and because many rivers used for irrigation flow from it; others maize or *sara,* as they call it, because it was their usual bread; others other cereals or legumes, according to what grew most abundantly in their provinces.

The coastal Indians, in addition to an infinity of other gods they had, even including those already mentioned, generally worshipped the sea, which they called *Mamacocha,* or "Mother Sea," implying that it was like a mother to them in sustaining them with its fish. They also worshipped the whale on account of its monstrous greatness. Besides these cults, which were common to the whole coast, various provinces and regions worshipped the fish most commonly caught there, holding that the first fish that was in the upper world (their word for heaven) was the origin of all other fish of the kind they ate and that it took care to send them plenty of its children to sustain their tribe. Thus in some provinces they worshipped the sardine, which they killed in greater quantity than any other fish, in others the skate, in others the dogfish, in others the goldfish for its beauty, in others the crab and other shellfish for lack of anything better in their waters or because they could not catch or kill anything else. In short, they worshipped and considered gods any fish that was more beneficial to them than the rest. So they had for gods not only the four elements, each separately, but also the compounds and forms of them, however vile and squalid. Other tribes, such as the Chirihuanas and the people of Cape Passau (that is, the southernmost and northernmost provinces of Peru) felt no inclination to worship anything, high or low, either from interest or fear, but lived and still live exactly like beasts, because the doctrine and teaching of the Inca kings did not reach them.

The Kinds of Sacrifices They Made

The cruelty and barbarity of the sacrifices of that ancient idolatry were of a piece with the vileness and crudity of its gods. For in addition to ordinary things such as animals and the fruits of the earth, they sacrificed men and women of all ages taken captive in the wars they waged on one another. Among some tribes their inhuman cruelty exceeded that of wild beasts. Not satisfied with sacrificing their captured foes, in case of need they offered up their own children. They performed these sacrifices of men and women, lads and children by opening their breasts while they were still alive and plucking out their hearts and lungs. The idol that had bidden the sacrifice was then sprinkled with still-warm blood, after which the same heart and lungs were examined for omens to show if the sacrifice had been acceptable or not. In either case the heart and lungs were burnt as an offering before the idol until they were consumed, and the victim of the sacrifice was eaten with the greatest pleasure and relish, and not the less merrymaking and rejoicing, even though it might have been their own child.

Padre Blas Valera, as appears from many parts of his torn papers, had the same design as we have in much of what he wrote. He divided the periods, ages, and provinces so as to show clearly the customs of each tribe. Thus in one of his mutilated notebooks he writes as follows, using the present tense, for the people he speaks of still practice these inhumanities:

> Those who live in the Antis eat human flesh: they are fiercer than tigers, have neither god nor law, nor know what virtue is. They have no idols nor likenesses of them. They worship the Devil when he represents himself in the form of some

animal or serpent and speaks to them. If they make a prisoner in war or otherwise and know that he is a plebeian of low rank, they quarter him and give the quarters to their friends and servants to eat or to sell in the meat market. But if he is of noble rank, the chiefs foregather with their wives and children, and, like ministers of the devil, strip him, tie him alive to a stake, and cut him to pieces with flint knives and razors, not so as to dismember him, but to remove the meat from the fleshiest parts, the calves, thighs, buttocks, and fleshy parts of the arms. Men, women, and children sprinkle themselves with the blood, and they all devour the flesh very rapidly, without cooking it or roasting it thoroughly or even chewing it. They swallow it in mouthfuls so that the wretched victim sees himself eaten alive by others and buried in their bellies. The women, crueller than the men, anoint the nipples of their breasts with the unfortunate victim's blood so that their babies may suck it and drink it with their milk. This is all done in a place of sacrifice with great rejoicing and lightheartedness until the man dies. They then finish eating the flesh together with all his inner parts, no longer as hitherto as a feast or delight, but as a matter of the greatest divinity. Thenceforward they regard the flesh with great veneration and eat it as a sacred thing. If while they were tormenting the unfortunate fellow he showed any signs of suffering in his face or body or gave any groan or sigh, they break his bones to pieces after having eaten the flesh, entrails, and tripes, and throw them scornfully into the fields or river. But if he has shown himself firm, composed, and fierce under torture, when they have eaten the flesh and inner parts they dry the bones and sinews in the sun and set them on the top of hills and hold them and worship them as gods, and offer sacrifices to them. These are the idols of these savages. The empire of the Incas did not reach them, nor so far has that of the Spaniards, so they remain in this state to this day. This race of terrible and cruel men came from the Mexican area and peopled Panama and Darien and all the great forests that stretch to the kingdom of New Granada and in the other direction to Santa Marta.

This is all quoted from Padre Blas Valera, who vividly describes such devilries and assists us to give an idea of what happened in those primitive times, and still endures.

There were other Indians less cruel in their sacrifices, who, though they used human blood, did not kill victims, but obtained it by bleeding their arms and legs, according to the importance of the sacrifice: for the most solemn occasions they extracted it from the root of the nose between the eyebrows. This bleeding was common among the Indians of Peru, even after the Incas came, both for their sacrifices (and one kind especially which we shall presently describe), and in case of illness attended by serious headache. Other types of sacrifice were common to all the Indians (those mentioned above were practiced in some provinces and not in others). Those generally used were of animals such as sheep, ewes, lambs, rabbits, partridges and other birds, tallow, the herb they value so highly called *cuca* [coca], maize and other seeds, and vegetables, and scented woods, and similar things, according to what each tribe produced and thought would please its gods, and taking into account the nature of the latter, whether they were animals or birds, and carnivorous or not. They offered up what they usually saw them eat and what seemed to be most agreeable to their taste. This shall suffice so far as our account of the sacrifices of that ancient heathendom is concerned.

The Life and Government of the Ancient Indians, and the Things They Ate

These gentiles were as barbarous in the style of their houses and villages as in their gods and sacrifices. The more civilized had villages without squares or any order in their streets and houses, but rather after the fashion of a den of wild beasts. Others, because of the wars they waged on one another, dwelt on ridges or high rocks, like fortresses, where they would be least molested by their enemies; others in huts scattered over the fields, valleys, and river bottoms as each happened to find convenient for food and dwellings. Others lived in underground caves, in nooks in the rocks, in hollow trees, each as he happened to find a home, since he was not able to make one. Some of them, like those of Cape Passau and the Chirihuanas and other tribes not conquered by the Inca kings, remain in that state of primitive savagery. They are the most difficult to reduce both to the service of the Spaniards and to Christianity, for as they never had any doctrine, they are irrational beings, who only had a language to make themselves understood within their own tribe, and so live like animals of different kinds which do not meet or deal or communicate between one another.

In these villages and dwelling places the ruler was whoever was boldest and had the will to govern the rest. As soon as he became master, he treated his vassals tyrannically and cruelly, using them as slaves, taking their wives and daughters at will, and making war on his rivals. In some areas they flayed captives and used their skins to cover drums and to terrify their enemies, who, they said, would fly at once on hearing the skins of their relatives. They led a life of banditry, stealing, killing, and burning villages. Thus there arose a multiplicity of chiefs and petty kings, of whom some were good and treated their people well, maintaining peace and justice. The Indians in their simplicity worshipped these as gods for their goodness and nobility, realizing that they were different from and opposed to the horde of tyrants. Elsewhere they lived without rulers or governors, and were unable to form a republic of their own to settle and regulate their lives. They lived in great simplicity like sheep, doing neither good nor harm, though this was due more to ignorance and lack of malice, than to excess of virtue.

In many areas the Indians were so simple and stupid in their way of dressing and covering their bodies that their attempts at dress were laughable. Elsewhere they were astonishingly savage and barbarous in their food and eating; and in many places the two things were found together. In the hottest and consequently most fertile areas they sowed little or nothing, but lived on herbs, roots, wild fruit, and other vegetables that the earth yielded spontaneously or with little improvement from them. As none of them desired more than to sustain their natural lives, they were satisfied with little. In many parts they were extremely fond of human flesh and so greedy that, when they were killing an Indian, they would drink his blood through the wound they had given him before he died: they did the same if they were quartering him, sucking his blood and licking their hands so as not to lose a drop. They had public markets for human flesh, and in order not to waste it they made sausages and polonies of gut which they filled with meat. Pedro de Cieza (ch. xxvi) confirms this and saw it with his own eyes. The passion reached such a pitch with them that they did not spare their own sons by foreign captives taken in war whom they took as concubines. Their children by these women were carefully brought up to the age of twelve or thirteen, and then eaten, and the mothers too, when they were past childbearing. Furthermore, they would spare the lives of many male Indian captives, give them wives from their tribe—the tribe of the victors—bring up the children as their own, and, when they were youths, eat them. It was in fact a cannibals' seminary. They spared none on account of parentage or upbringing, which usually breed affection even among animals of quite various and opposite kinds, as we can affirm from some we have seen and others we have heard about. But among these savages neither the one nor the other availed: they killed the children they had begotten, and the relatives they had reared for the purpose of eating them, treating the parents the same when they no longer served to breed children, without any regard for their close relationship. There was a tribe so strongly addicted to devouring human flesh that they buried their dead in their stomachs. As soon as the deceased had breathed his last, his relatives gathered round and ate him roasted or boiled, according to the amount of flesh he still had: if little, boiled, if much, roasted. Afterwards they assembled the bones and gave them a funeral with great mourning, burying them in crannies in rocks or hollow trees. They had no gods and no conception of worshipping, and are still in the same state. The consumption of human flesh is commoner among Indians of the hot regions than among those of the cold.

In cold and sterile regions where the earth did not bear fruit, roots, and herbs spontaneously, they sowed maize and vegetables, obliged by necessity; but they did this without regard to time or season. They fished and hunted with the same primitive savagery as they displayed in other things.

How They Dressed in Those Ancient Times

Their dress was so indecent that it is rather a subject for silence and secrecy than for discussion and description. But as history obliges one to set down the whole truth, I must beg the modest to turn a deaf ear to this part, and if they censure me in this way, I shall consider their disfavor justified. In this first period the Indians dressed like animals, for they wore no more

clothing than the skin nature had given them. Many of them, out of ingenuity or for love of adornment, had a thick string girded round their bodies. They thought that was clothing enough, and we must not go beyond,
for it is improper. In 1560, on my way to Spain, I met five Indians in the
street in Cartagena without any clothes at all, and they did not walk abreast
but one behind the other like cranes, although they had mingled with
Spaniards for so many years.

The women went in the same dress, naked. When married they wore a
string round the body with a cotton rag about a yard square hanging like an
apron from it. Where they could not or would not spin or weave, they made
it of the barks or leaves of trees. This covered their modesty. Maidens also
wore a string girdle, and instead of the apron they wore something else to
show they were maidens. But out of proper respect for our hearers, we had
better keep to ourselves what remains to be said. Suffice it to say that this
was the dress and costume of the hot regions, so that as regards decency,
they resembled irrational beasts, and it can be imagined from this bestiality
in adorning their persons alone how brutal they would be in everything
else — these Indians of heathen times before the empire of the Incas.

In cold regions they were more decently clad, not indeed out of decency, but obliged by the cold. They covered themselves with skins of animals
and a sort of blanket they made of wild hemp and a long, pliable, soft straw
that grows in the fields. With these contrivances they covered their nakedness as well as they could. Other tribes had a greater sense of propriety and
wore clumsily made cloaks, ill-spun and worse-woven, of wool or wild hemp
called cháhuar. They wore them fastened about the neck and girded to the
body, and were thus adequately covered. The dress we have mentioned
used in primitive times in the hot lands — that is going naked — was found
by the Spaniards in many regions never conquered by the Incas, and is still
today found in many places conquered by the Spaniards, where the Indians
are such brutes that they will not dress, except for those who have close intercourse with Spaniards in their houses and wear clothes more because
the Spaniards insist on it than from any choice or modesty of their own.
The women refuse just as much as the men, and Spaniards often chaff
them about their indecency and unwillingness to spin, and ask if they don't
dress because they won't spin, or if they don't spin because they won't
dress.

The Origin of the Inca Kings of Peru

While these peoples were living or dying in the manner we have seen, it
pleased our Lord God that from their midst there should appear a morning
star to give them in the dense darkness in which they dwelt some glimmer-
ings of natural law, of civilization, and of the respect men owe to one another. The descendants of this leader should thus tame those savages and
convert them into men, made capable of reason and of receiving good doctrine, so that when God, who is the sun of justice, saw fit to send forth the

light of His divine rays upon those idolaters, it might find them no longer in their first savagery, but rendered more docile to receive the Catholic faith and the teaching and doctrine of our Holy Mother the Roman Church, as indeed they have received it—all of which will be seen in the course of this history. It has been observed by clear experience how much prompter and quicker to receive the Gospel were the Indians subdued, governed, and taught by the Inca kings than the other neighboring peoples unreached by the Incas' teachings, many of which are still today as savage and brutish as before, despite the fact that the Spaniards have been in Peru seventy years. And since we stand on the threshold of this great maze, we had better enter and say what lay within.

After having prepared many schemes and taken many ways to begin to give an account of the origin and establishment of the native Inca kings of Peru, it seemed to me that the best scheme and simplest and easiest way was to recount what I often heard as a child from the lips of my mother and her brothers and uncles and other elders about these beginnings. For everything said about them from other sources comes down to the same story as we shall relate, and it will be better to have it as told in the very words of the Incas than in those of foreign authors. My mother dwelt in Cuzco, her native place, and was visited there every week by the few relatives, both male and female, who escaped the cruelty and tyranny of Atahuallpa (which we shall describe in our account of his life). On these visits the ordinary subject of conversation was always the origin of the Inca kings, their greatness, the grandeur of their empire, their deeds and conquests, their government in peace and war, and the laws they ordained so greatly to the advantage of their vassals. In short, there was nothing concerning the most flourishing period of their history that they did not bring up in their conversations.

From the greatness and prosperity of the past they turned to the present, mourning their dead kings, their lost empire, and their fallen state, etc. These and similar topics were broached by the Incas and Pallas on their visits, and on recalling their departed happiness, they always ended these conversations with tears and mourning, saying: "Our rule is turned to bondage" etc. During these talks, I, as a boy, often came in and went out of the place where they were, and I loved to hear them, as boys always do like to hear stories. Days, months, and years went by, until I was sixteen or seventeen. Then it happened that one day when my family was talking in this fashion about their kings and the olden times, I remarked to the senior of them, who usually related these things: "Inca, my uncle, though you have no writings to preserve the memory of past events, what information have you of the origin and beginnings of our kings? For the Spaniards and the other peoples who live on their borders have divine and human histories from which they know when their own kings and their neighbors' kings began to reign and when one empire gave way to another. They even know how many thousand years it is since God created heaven and earth. All this and much more they know through their books. But you, who have no books, what memory have you preserved of your antiquity? Who was the first of our

Incas? What was he called? What was the origin of his line? How did he begin to reign? With what men and arms did he conquer this great empire? How did our heroic deeds begin?"

The Inca was delighted to hear these questions, since it gave him great pleasure to reply to them, and turned to me (who had already often heard him tell the tale, but had never paid as much attention as then) saying:

"Nephew, I will tell you these things with pleasure: indeed it is right that you should hear them and keep them in your heart (this is their phrase for 'in the memory'). You should know that in olden times the whole of this region before you was covered with brush and heath, and people lived in those times like wild beasts, with no religion or government and no towns or houses, and without tilling or sowing the soil, or clothing or covering their flesh, for they did not know how to weave cotton or wool to make clothes. They lived in twos and threes as chance brought them together in caves and crannies in rocks and underground caverns. Like wild beasts they ate the herbs of the field and roots of trees and fruits growing wild and also human flesh. They covered their bodies with leaves and the bark of trees and animals' skins. Others went naked. In short, they lived like deer or other game, and even in their intercourse with women they behaved like beasts, for they knew nothing of having separate wives."

I must remark, in order to avoid many repetitions of the words "our father the Sun," that the phrase was used by the Incas to express respect whenever they mentioned the sun, for they boasted of descending from it, and none but Incas were allowed to utter the words: it would have been blasphemy and the speaker would have been stoned. The Inca said:

"Our father the Sun, seeing men in the state I have mentioned, took pity and was sorry for them, and sent from heaven to earth a son and a daughter of his to indoctrinate them in the knowledge of our father the Sun that they might worship him and adopt him as their god, and to give them precepts and laws by which they would live as reasonable and civilized men, and dwell in houses and settled towns, and learn to till the soil, and grow plants and crops, and breed flocks, and use the fruits of the earth like rational beings and not like beasts. With this order and mandate our father the Sun set these two children of his in Lake Titicaca, eighty leagues from here, and bade them go where they would, and wherever they stopped to eat or sleep to try to thrust into the ground a golden wand half a yard long and two fingers in thickness which he gave them as a sign and token: when this wand should sink into the ground at a single thrust, there our father the Sun wished them to stop and set up their court.

"Finally he told them: 'When you have reduced these people to our service, you shall maintain them in reason and justice, showing mercy, clemency, and mildness, and always treating them as a merciful father treats his beloved and tender children. Imitate my example in this. I do good to all the world. I give them my light and brightness that they may see and go about their business; I warm them when they are cold; and I grow their pastures and crops, and bring fruit to their trees, and multiply their flocks. I bring rain and calm weather in turn, and I take care to go round the world once a day to observe the wants that exist in the world and to fill and supply them as the sustainer and benefactor of men. I wish you as children of mine to follow this example sent down to earth to teach and benefit those men who live like beasts. And henceforward I establish and nominate you as kings and lords over all the people you may thus instruct with your reason, government, and good works.'

"When our father the Sun had thus made manifest his will to his two children he bade them farewell. They left Titicaca and travelled northwards, and wherever they stopped on the way they thrust the golden wand into the earth, but it never sank in. Thus they reached a small inn or resthouse seven or eight leagues south of this city. Today it is called Pacárec Tampu, 'inn or resthouse of the dawn.' The Inca gave it this name because he set out from it about daybreak. It is one of the towns the prince later ordered to be founded, and its inhabitants to this day boast greatly of its name because our first Inca bestowed it. From this place he and his wife, our queen, reached the valley of Cuzco which was then a wilderness."

■ Sor Juana Inés de la Cruz (1651–1691)
Mexico (poems, letter)

Scholar, intellectual, poet, and playwright, the Mexican nun Juana Inés de la Cruz is the outstanding writer of the long colonial period. Juana Ramírez de Asbaje was born on a hacienda in a village southeast of Mexico City called San Miguel de Nepantla. Nepantla in Nahuatl signifies "land in the middle," and her village lay between the great volcanoes of Popocatépatl and Ixtacíhuatal. Juana was a "daughter of the Church"—a euphemism of the day meaning that she was illegitimate. As a young child, she was precocious and has popularly been called a genius. She learned to read at three, she tells us in her largely autobiographical *Response to Sor Filotea,* and from very early was concerned with laws of the physical universe: "Once in my presence two young girls were spinning a top, and scarcely had I seen the motion and the figure described when I began, out of this madness of mine, to meditate on the effortless *motus* of the spherical form, and how the impulse persisted even when free and independent of its cause." Juana Inés's brief and acute observation about force and inertia anticipate contemporary laws of gravity and energy and precede Sir Isaac Newton's four laws of inertia elaborated in *Principia Mathematica.*

Juana Inés went to Mexico City as a child and there, in the house of an uncle who possessed a good library, she immersed herself in her readings and early literary writings. She was an avid autodidact. One delightful story, probably true, recounted by her contemporary biographer, the Jesuit father Diego Callejas, has the twelve-year-old Juana taken to the University of

Mexico, where, to test her knowledge and wisdom, the child is asked questions by the forty leading theologians, philosophers, and historians at the university. She outwitted them all, as Callejas states, "in the manner of a royal galleon fending off the attacks of a few canoes." But for all her knowledge and pleasure in accumulating it, she lacked companionship and the stimulation of fellow students. There were few choices for a talented young woman who wished to pursue artistic and intellectual aspirations: there was the court, the church, and marriage. Each had its price. Her first choice was the court, and at sixteen Juana Inés entered the court, where she became a lady-in-waiting to the viceroy's wife, the countess of Paredes, who cared for literature and was to encourage and facilitate Juana throughout her life.

At the worldly court, Juana was a brilliant figure and there was much elegant conversation and courting, *galaneo,* by would-be suitors who tended to be already well-married. From her autobiographical letter, we learn that amid the glamor and glitter of court activities, she possessed a gravity and determination of iron. But the wooing undoubtedly served, in disguised and invented form, as the basis of her love poems. With all her charm and brilliance, however, Juana Ramírez de Asbaje was still a fatherless orphan, without a dowry to obtain, through marriage, a life in which she might practice her literary pursuits. With no real future in the court or society, in 1669, at age twenty-one, at the height of her admiration by the literati and court society, Juana Inés took the veil in the relatively permissive Convent of Santa Paula of the Hieronymite order (the order of Saint Jerome).

In her quarters, she wrote poems that found publication and wrote her plays, including the extraordinary *The Divine Narcissus* that was published in 1689 in Madrid. Her convent was her library, workplace, literary salon, and *tertulia* (a literary discussion usually held in a cafe). As in the first- and second-century Hermetic and apocalyptic traditions, her great long poem "First Dream" describes the voyage of a soul soaring among superlunary spheres, while the harborer of the soul remains behind in deep bodily sleep. As such, it is a poem concerning ecstasy in its strictly etymological sense of "being outside oneself" or "being elsewhere." In her daring metaphysical meditation—the great extended poem of the Spanish baroque period—she attempts to find some philosophical explanation for this world of deceptive appearances and dream.

In reply to an oblique yet devastating letter from the Bishop of Puebla, who wrote her under the pseudonym of Sor Filotea, urging her to cease her creative work, she wrote her defiant *Response*. Her answer contains her threat of silence, which was to be executed, but the threat is not the essence of the *carta*. The letter is a biography of her life and mind, an assertion of her intellectual and creative freedom, and a refutation of censorial intrusion. It is also probably the world's first and extensive declaration of a woman's artistic and intellectual right to study, teach, write, and publish freely. Though she did not write anything new while under the constraints of the bishop, she did not order her works into silence. Indeed, Sor Juana oversaw and assiduously corrected the publication of the volumes of her collected works, which began a few years earlier in 1689 when her friend the countess of Paredes published the first volume of her poems in Spain. Four years later, after laying down her pen and selling off her library, she died on April 17, 1694, while nursing her sister nuns during an epidemic. The last high moment of poetry of the Spanish Golden Age was found in the first poetic figure of the New World.

FURTHER READING: Sor Juana Inés de la Cruz. *Sor Juana Inés de la Cruz, 1651–1691*. Bilingual. Translated by Margaret Sayers Peden, 1985; *A Sor Juana Anthology*. Translated by Alan S. Trueblood. Foreword by Octavio Paz, 1988. Paz, Octavio. *Sor Juana, or the Traps of Faith*, 1988.

To Her Self-Portrait

What you see here is colorful illusion,
an art boasting of beauty and its skill,
which in false reasoning of color will
pervert the mind in delicate delusion.
Here where the flatteries of paint engage   5
to vitiate the horrors of the years,
where softening the rust of time appears
to triumph over oblivion and age,
all is a vain, careful disguise of clothing,
it is a slender blossom in the gale,   10
it is a futile port for doom reserved,
it is a foolish labor that can only fail:
it is a wasting zeal and, well observed,
is corpse, is dust, is shadow, and is nothing.

TRANSLATED BY WILLIS BARNSTONE

To Hope

A green beguilement in our natural life,
mad hope and frenzy wrapped about with gold,
a dream by those awake, yet thinly cold
like dreams and treasures: mere gossip and rife.
Soul of the world, exuberant old age,   5
decrepit greenness of pure fantasy,
the now for which the happy ones rampage,
the future where the pitiful agree.
Clutching your name, seeking your day as real,

they stick green lenses in their glasses, and   *10*
the world they see is painted by command.
But I, much saner in my state of mind,
keep both eyes focused on my hands. Not blind,
I only see what I can touch and feel.

TRANSLATED BY WILLIS BARNSTONE

She Complains about Her Fate: She Asserts Her Aversion to Vices and Justifies Her Pleasure in the Muses

Why persecute me, world? To what effect?
Tell me how I offend. My sole intent
is to fix beauty to my intellect,
not hang my intellect in beauty's tent.
I do not care for emeralds or for gold,   *5*
and so I feel a happier effect
by fixing emeralds to my intellect
than to affix my intellect to gold.
I do not care for beauty that the knife
of age cuts into booty for the public hall,   *10*
nor can perfidious wealth please me at all.
The best I find of all my verities
is to consume my vanities in life
and not consume my life in vanities.

TRANSLATED BY WILLIS BARNSTONE

In Which She Morally Censures a Rose, and through the Rose Her Peers

Holy rose, who in genteel cultivation
you show in all your redolent finesse
a magisterial beauty in your station,
a snowy discourse in your loveliness,
a fearful sign to human architecture,   *5*
emblem of the vanity in grace's bloom,
whose being unites through trickery of nature
the joyous cradle and the sorrowing tomb.
How haughty in your pomp, how arrogant,
sovereign, while you disdain the risk of death;   *10*

and then, collapsing, shrinking, you are plucked
in feebleness of being, a withered plant!
And so through stupid life and dying breath,
in life you fool, in dying you instruct.

TRANSLATED BY ALIKI BARNSTONE AND WILLIS BARNSTONE

A Good Face One Should Choose before Dying Rather Than to Expose Oneself to the Outrages of Old Age

Celia looked at a rose proud in the field,
happily showing off its futile grace,
and, while adorned in rouge fully revealed,
it cheerfully was bathing its white face;
Courageously enjoy your destiny,   5
the brief migration of your fertile age;
then death that comes tomorrow will not be
in place to rob you of a joy, your wage
today. And though persistent death comes now
and your delicious life moves far from you,   10
and youth and beauty mix with death and fears,
see what experience informs, and how
it's best to die with youth and beauty too
than to observe the outrage of the years.

TRANSLATED BY WILLIS BARNSTONE

She Suspects That the Relief That Hope Gives Is Dissimulated Cruelty

With my one daily malady of hope
you plot to entertain my graying years
and in the scheme of goods and hangman's rope
you keep the scale in balance for all spheres;
and always hanging there (in the delay   5
before it tilts one way), your trickery
you won't let dominate to a degree
of posing crude belief or grave dismay.
Who stole the name from you of homicide?
You're it—severely so, if well observed—   10
and in the air you hang my laughing soul.

While between losing and your lucky side,
you do not work to keep a life preserved
but to give tolling death a lingering toll.

TRANSLATED BY WILLIS BARNSTONE

In Which She Satisfies a Fear with the Rhetoric of Tears

This afternoon, my love, speaking to you
since I could see that in your face and walk
I failed in coming close to you with talk,
I wanted you to see my heart. Love, who
supported me in what I longed to do,   5
conquered what is impossible to gain.
Amid my tears that were poured out in pain,
my heart became distilled and broken through.
Enough, my love. Don't be so stiff. Don't let
these maddening jealousies and arrogance   10
haunt you or let your quiet be upset
by foolish shadows: false signs of a man's
presence; and as you see my heart which met
your touch—now it is liquid in your hands.

TRANSLATED BY WILLIS BARNSTONE

In Which Her Fantasy Is Contented with Decent Love

Don't leave me, shadow of my love, elusive
and obsessed image which I care for most,
handsome deceit for whom I'd be a ghost,
sweet fiction for which pain is not abusive.
If my own body of obedient steel   5
serves as a magnet fated to your grace,
why flatter me with lover's commonplace,
only to drop me, run, while I congeal?
And yet you cannot brag of anything,
of any triumph through your tyranny.   10
If you elude the narrow noose I've set
to capture your fantastic form, and spring
out of my arms, who cares? You flee, and yet
I've got you locked up in my fantasy.

TRANSLATED BY WILLIS BARNSTONE

Concerning a Sage Reflection That Mitigates a Passion

With the affliction of a mortal wound
I brooded on a sore offense of love;
to see if death would drag me underground
I tried to make it grow and loom above.
The separated soul in clouds of pain,   5
counted its anguish one hurt at a time,
and with each second it was darkly plain
a thousand deaths dug one life into grime.
And after blows of battering a skull,
the ruptured heart discerned a maddening sign   10
that it had come to its last hopeless sigh —
and yet by some prodigious destiny
I woke, sensing: Am I not wonderful,
and who in love has happiness like mine?

TRANSLATED BY WILLIS BARNSTONE

She Continues with the Same Matter and Ends with Reason Prevailing over Pleasure

The ingrate dumping me I seek as lover,
seek me as lover, I'll throw him away.
I always worship one who runs for cover;
who worships me I bump out of my way.
Whom I beseech with love is hard as steel,   5
I'm hard as steel to you beseeching me.
Triumphant I want you who murder me,
I murder you who want my triumph real.
If someone wants me, my desire is gone.
If I want you, I crush my dignity;   10
and either way I end up feeling bashed.
So I choose as the better course to be
a violent curse on you who make me yawn,
than be for you who dump me vilely trashed.

TRANSLATED BY WILLIS BARNSTONE

Inés

When they revile you as sly and obscene,
you have no problem getting off the hook,
you launch into your gobbledygook,
knowing just how to wipe your asshole clean,
and when you grab the word, no magpie can   5
dish out such bad-year garbage from its throat:
you thunder and the clatter fills a moat,
stunning the world like pounding on a can.
That rumble jumbles all, one tumbling turd,
a con game making you a sweet Rebecca.   10
Though you, Inés, a wanton cuckoo bird,
must know my love and how to spot a sin;
your bumbling passion stumbles, fails to win,
though you're a holy saint and I'm from Mecca.

TRANSLATED BY WILLIS BARNSTONE

She Proves the Inconsistency of the Desires and Criticism of Men Who Accuse Women of What They Themselves Cause

Foolish men who accuse
women unreasonably,
you blame yet never see
you cause what you abuse

You crawl before her, sad,   5
begging for a quick cure;
why ask her to be pure
when you have made her bad?

You combat her resistance
and then with gravity,   10
you call frivolity
the fruit of your intents.

In one heroic breath
your reason fails, like a wild
bogeyman made up by a child   15
who then is scared to death.

With idiotic pride
you hope to find your prize:
a regal whore like Thaïs
and Lucretia for a bride.   20

Has anyone ever seen
a stranger moral fervor:
you who dirty the mirror
regret it is not clean?

You treat favor and disdain   25
with the same shallow mocking
voice: love you and you squawk,
demur and you complain.

No answer at her door
will be a proper part: 30
say no—she has no heart,
say yes—and she's a whore.

Two levels to your game
in which you are the fool:
one you blame as cruel,   35
one who yields, you shame.

How can one not be bad
the way your love pretends
to be? Say no and she offends.
Consent and you are mad.   40

With all the fury and pain
your whims cause her, it's good
for her who has withstood
you. Now go and complain!

You let her grief take flight   45
and free her with new wings.
Then after sordid things
you say she's not upright.

Who is at fault in all
this errant passion? She   50
who falls for his pleas, or he
who pleads for her to fall?

Whose guilt is greater in
this raw erotic play?
The girl who sins for pay   55
or man who pays for sin?

So why be shocked or taunt
her for the steps you take?
Care for her as you make
her, or shape her as you want,   60

but do not come with pleas
and later throw them in
her face, screaming of sin
when you were at her knees.

You fight us from our birth   65
with weapons of arrogance.
Between promise and pleading stance,
you are the devil, flesh, and earth.

TRANSLATED BY ALIKI BARNSTONE AND WILLIS BARNSTONE

from **First Dream**

But Venus first
with her fair gentle morning-star
shone through the dayspring,
and old Tithonus' beauteous spouse
—Amazon in radiance clad—   5
armed against the night,
fair though martial
and though plaintive brave,
showed her lovely brow
crowned with morning glimmers,   10
tender yet intrepid harbinger
of the fierce luminary
that came, mustering his van
of tiro gleams
and his rearward   15
of stouter veteran lights
against her, usurping tyrant
of day's empire, who,
girt with gloom's black bays
sways with dread nocturnal sceptre   20
the shades,
herself by them appalled.
But the fair forerunner,
herald of the bright sun,
scarce flew her banner in the orient sky,   25

calling all the sweet if warlike
clarions of the birds to arms,
their featly artless
sonorous bugles,
when the doomed tyrant, trembling,   30
distraught with dread misgiving,
striving the while
to launch her vaunted might, opposing
the shield of her funereal cloak
in vain to the unerring   35
shafts of light
with the rash unavailing
valiance of despair,
sensible of her faintness to withstand,
prone already to commit to flight,   40
more than to might, the means of her salvation,
wound her raucous horn,
summoning her black battalions
to orderly retreat.
Forthwith she was assailed   45
with nearer plenitude of rays
that streaked the highest pitch
of the world's lofty towers.
The sun in truth, its circuit closed, drew near,
limning with gold on sapphire blue a thousand   50
times a thousand points and gleaming scarves,
and from its luminous circumference
innumerable rays of pure light streamed,
scoring the sky's cerulean plain,
and serried fell on her who was but now   55
the baneful tyrant of their empire.
She, flying in headlong rout,
mid her own horrors stumbling,
trampling on her shade,
strove, with her now blindly fleeing host   60
of shadows harried by the overtaking light,
to gain the western verge which loomed at last
before her impetuous course.
Then, by her very downfall vivified,
plunging in ever more precipitant ruin,   65
with renewed rebellion she resolves,
in that part of the globe
forsaken by the day,
to wear the crown,
what time upon our hemisphere the sun   70
the radiance of his fair golden tresses shed,

with equable diffusion of just light
apportioning to visible things their colours
and still restoring
to outward sense its full efficacy,   *75*
committing to surer light
the world illuminated and myself awake.

TRANSLATED BY SAMUEL BECKETT

Sor Juana Inés de la Cruz's Response to Sor Filotea begins with a bitterly ironic humility, in which she states that she will open her heart to the bishop who has criticized her. Then she proceeds to tell her life and her struggle for intellectual and creative freedom. Here are excerpts from the Mexican nun's defense of her life as a student of books and a poet of unrestricted personal expression.

from Response to Sor Filotea

I have never written by my own choice but at the urgency of others to whom I can say truthfully: You have compelled me. What is true, and I will not deny the truth (first, because it is known publicly, and second, though it may be held against me God has granted me the mercy of a great love for the truth), which is that from the moment I was pierced with the first rays of reason, my inclination to letters has been so vehement and powerful that neither external reprimands, of which I have had many, nor my own meditations, and they have not been few, have been strong enough to make me abandon this natural impulse that God placed in me. The Lord's Majesty knows why and for what purpose, and he knows that I have prayed that he extinguish the light of my reason, leaving only what is necessary in me to obey his Law, for according to some there is too much reason in a woman. And there are even those who say that such knowledge does injury.

And his Majesty also knows that not being able to do this, I have tried to bury my knowledge along with my name, and to sacrifice it to him alone who gave it to me; and for no other reason I entered into religion, although the spiritual exercises and the company of a community were repugnant to the freedom and quiet that my intention to study required. Thereupon, and the Lord and only he in the world must know it, I *did* try to conceal my name, but they did not allow this, saying that my work was a temptation. And no doubt it was. If I could pay you what I owe you, my lady, I might do so by relating these matters to you, which earlier never escaped from my lips except to those who had to hear them. But in having thrown wide open the doors of my heart by making patent to you my most deeply hidden secrets, I want you to know that you must not disdain the belief I have in your venerable person and excessive favors toward me.

Continuing the narration of my inclinations, about which I wish to inform you fully, I was not yet three years old when my mother sent my sister, older than I was, to learn to read in one of those schools we call *Amigas*. Affection and mischief led me to follow her. And seeing that they were giving her lessons I was inflamed with desire to learn to read, and so by tricking the teacher, or so I thought, I told her that my mother had directed her to give me lessons. She did not believe it, because it was not believable, but to go along with my trick she gave me lessons. I continued to go there and she continued to teach me, but now no longer as a joke because the experience alerted her. And I learned to read in such a short time that I already knew how by the time my mother found out. The teacher had kept it from her in order to surprise her and receive a reward all at once. I kept still, thinking I would be whipped for having acted without her permission. The woman who taught me (God preserve her) is still alive and can attest to this.

I remember that in those days my love for eating being the same as children of my age, I abstained from eating cheese because I had heard that it made you stupid, and my desire to know was stronger than to eat. When I was six or seven, already knowing how to read and write along with all the other skills of sewing and needlework that women learn, I discovered that the University had schools in Mexico City where one studied the sciences. The moment I heard this, I began to batter my mother with constant and urgent pleas to change my manner of dress and send me to Mexico City, to the house of some relatives she had there, to study and be tutored at the University. She did not want to do so (and rightly so) but I satisfied my longings by reading many and diverse books in my grandfather's library, and there were not enough punishments or reprimands to stop me. Hence, when I came to the city of Mexico, people marveled, not so much at my intelligence as at my memory and store of knowledge I had at an age where it seemed that I had hardly had time to learn to speak.

I began to study Latin grammar, in which I think I did not have twenty lessons in all. So intense was my concern that although among women, and especially those in the flower of their youth, the natural adornment of one's hair is so highly esteemed, I cut four or five finger's width from mine, measuring the place it had reached before, and imposed a rule on myself that by the time it had grown back to its former length, if I had not learned such and such a thing that I had set out to learn while the hair was growing back, I would cut it again as punishment for my stupidity. It turned out that it grew out and I was learning slowly, and in fact I did cut it as a punishment for my dullness, for it did not seem to me right that the head should be dressed with hair when it was so naked of knowledge, which was the more desirable adornment.

I entered a religious order. Although I knew that the way of life had things about it (I speak of its secondary not its most formal qualities) many of them repugnant to my nature, but, given the total antipathy I had for marriage, it was the least unreasonable and most decent choice I could make to insure my salvation. To this first and finally most important end, all the trivial things that had dominated my nature I gave up: my desire to live alone—to have no duties that would interfere with the freedom of my studies, nor have the sounds of a community that would intrude upon the peaceful silence of my books. This made me hesitate in my determination until some learned persons enlightened me, explaining that my inclination was temptation; I overcame it with divine favor, and assumed the state which now I so unworthily hold. I thought that I was fleeing from myself, but, miserable person that I am, I brought to me and with me my worst enemy, which is this inclination to study and write—and I do not know whether this was a gift or punishment from Heaven—for though for a while it was dimmed and encumbered by the many duties of religious life, it exploded like gunpowder, proving that privation is the source of appetite.

I went back (I said it wrong, since I never stopped), I went on with my studious tasks (which for me were a respite in those moments not occupied by my religious duties) to reading and more reading, to studying and more studying, with no other master than the books themselves. And one can see how hard it is to study those soulless letters, lacking a live voice and the explanation of the teacher. But all this work I suffered with great pleasure for the love of letters. O had it been for the love God, which was the right way, how worthy it would have been! While I strove to elevate it as best I could and direct it to his service, since the goal I aspired to was to study Theology, and it seemed to me a diminishment for me as Catholic not to know all, through natural means, that this life in its divine mysteries can dissipate before us. Since I was a nun and not a lay person, it seemed right that I should profess my learning through ecclesiastical channels. Moreover, being a daughter of Saint Jerome and Saint Paula, it would be shameless for the daughter of such learned parents to be an idiot.[1] This is what I proposed for myself and it appeared reasonable, unless it was (and surely it was) that all these invented guides were to flatter and approve my own inclination and to enjoy what I offered as an obligation.

In this way I want on, directing as always, as I have said, the course of my studies toward the peak of Sacred Theology, and, in order to arrive there, it seemed necessary for me to climb the steps of human sciences and arts, since how can one understand the style of the queen of sciences if one does not also know the ancillary branches? How, without Logic, could I understand the general and specific ways in which the Holy Scripture is written? How, without Rhetoric, could I understand its figures, tropes, and locutions? How could I survive without Physics and so many natural questions

---

1. Paula (d. 414) was a Roman lady who became attached to Jerome. She and her daughters went with Jerome to Bethlehem, and she established and presided over the first nunneries of the Hieronymite order. Sor Juana's convent was Hieronymite and Paula was one of its patron saints.

concerning the nature of sacrificial animals, where many things are symbolized, many already explained, and others are waiting for explanation? How should I know whether Saul's being refreshed by the sound of David's harp was due to the virtue and natural force of music or to the supernatural powers that God wished to place in David? How without Arithmetic could one understand so many computations of years, of days, of months, of hours, of weeks, mysterious like those of Daniel, and others for the intelligence of which one must know the natures, concordances, and properties of numbers? How without Geometry could one measure the Holy Arc of the Covenant and the Holy City of Jerusalem, whose mysterious numbers form a cube in all its dimensions along with the marvelous proportions in the distribution of its parts? How without Architecture, could the great Temple of Solomon, where God himself was the artificer providing both the layout and design and the wise king Solomon, could only the overseer have carried it all out? No base was without its mystery, column without its symbol, cornice without its allusion, architrave without its significance, and so on with the other parts. . . . How without an expertise in music could one understand those delightful fine points of musical proportions that are in so many places, especially in Abraham's petitions to God for the cities, asking whether he would forgive them if they had fifty just men? And from this number he reduced it to forty-five, which is a ninth and goes from Mi to Re; then to forty, which is a tone and goes from Re to Mi; from forty to thirty, which is a diastesseron; then to twenty, which is the perfect fifth and from twenty to ten, which is the octave, the diapason. And since there are no more harmonic proportions it stopped there. Now how can one understand this without a knowledge of music?

* * *

I confess that I find myself very distant from the borders of wisdom and that I wish to follow her, even from far off. But everything has brought me into the fire of persecution, to the crucible of torture, and to such a degree that they have forbidden me my studies. At one time they managed to do so through the offices of a very saintly and ingenuous Abbess who believed that study was a matter for the Inquisition, and she commanded me to give up studying. I obeyed her (for some three months her power to command me endured) for I did not take up a book. But as for not studying at all that was not within my powers to satisfy, for while I did not study books, I studied all the things that God created, which served as my letters and as the book of the universal machine. I looked on nothing without reflecting on it. I heard nothing without considering it, even the tiniest material thing. For there is no creature, however lowly, in which one does not recognize that *God made me.* There is nothing that does not astonish reason, if one stops to observe it.

So, I repeat, I looked and admired all things. Thus even the people with whom I spoke, and what they were telling me, evoked a thousand meditations. Since we are from one species, where did that variety of geniuses and wit come from? What temperaments and hidden qualities brought this about? If I saw a figure, I was forever combining the proportion of its lines and measuring it with my reason and reducing it to new proportions. Sometimes I would walk back and forth along the far wall of our dormitory (which is a very large room) and noticed that though the lines of both sides were parallel and its ceiling level, one's vision made it appear that the lines sloped in toward each other and that the ceilings were lower at the far end, from which I inferred that visual lines run straight, but not parallel, and that they form a pyramidal figure. And I pondered whether this might be the reason that caused the ancients to question whether the world was spherical or not. Although straight lines appear to be bent, this could be a deception of vision,[2] showing concavities where none might have been.

This type of observation would occur to me about everything, and as it always occurs, without my being in control of it, I am constantly annoyed because this activity tires my mind. And I thought the same thing happened to everyone, also with regard to writing verse, until experience taught me otherwise. So it has become a habit that I can look at nothing without reflecting on it. Once in my presence, two young girls were playing with a top. As soon as I saw the motion and form, I began, with this madness of mine, to contemplate the easy motion of the spherical form, and how the impulse once given it persisted independent of the cause, since at a distance from the girl's hand, which was the causal force, the top went on dancing. And not content with this, I had flour brought in and spread so that one could know whether what described its movement were perfect circles. And I found that they were not, but were spiral lines that were losing their circular form as the impulse slowed down.

Other girls were playing with pins (surely childhood's most frivolous game). I came near to observe the figures they formed, and seeing that by chance three were placed in a triangle I began to connect one to the other, recalling that this was the shape that Solomon's mysterious ring was said to have and on which there were distant lights and depictions of the Most Holy Trinity by virtue of which it worked so many prodigies and marvels.[3] The same shape was said to form David's harp and that is why Saul was said to have been cured by its sound. And harps today conserve almost the same shape.

What shall I tell you, my lady, of the natural secrets that I have discovered while cooking? That an egg holds together and fries in butter or oil, but, by contrast, it comes apart in syrup. That in order to keep sugar liquid one need only add a few drops of water in which a quince or some other bitter fruit has been soaked. That the yolk and the white of the same egg are so different in nature that when eggs are used with sugar, it works when

---

2. An optical illusion.

3. There is no reference to such an incident in the Bible. It derives from a tradition of anecdotal commentary in which Old Testament Scripture is anachronistically given a level of Christian meaning.

using one (the yolk or the white), but not when using both. But I should not weary you with such trivia, which I relate only to give you a full idea of my nature and because I think that they might make you laugh. But, lady, what can women know other than philosophies of the kitchen? Lupercio Leonardo spoke well when he said how well one can philosophize while preparing the supper.[4]

I like to say, when seeing these small details: If Aristotle had been a cook, he would have written much more.

And going on with my cogitations, I say that this goes on so constantly in me that I do not need books. On one occasion, as a result of a gravely troubled stomach, the doctors forbade me from studying. I passed some days in this manner, and then I proposed that permitting me my books was less harmful and they conceded, for my meditations were so strong and vigorous that they consumed my spirit more in a quarter of an hour than four days of studying books. Moreover, my lady, not even my dreams have been freed from this ceaseless movement of my imagination. In fact, it seems to go on more openly and unimpeded, conferring a greater clarity and peace on the images that I have conserved from the day. I argue and make verses, of which I could offer you an extensive catalogue, including thoughts and subtleties that I have better achieved in sleep than when awake. I leave this matter now so as not to bore you, but the above is enough to allow your discretion and transcendent understanding to perceive and be perfectly informed about the nature, principle, means, and present state of my studies.

* * *

Oh, how much injury might have been avoided in our land if our old women were as learned as Laeta, and knew how to teach in the manner of Saint Paul and my Father Saint Jerome. And if this is not the case, if fathers wish to educate their daughters in a way beyond what is customary, because of the absence of wise older women, they are forced to bring in men teachers to teach reading, writing, calculating, the playing of musical instruments, and other skills. No little harm is done by this, as we witness every day in doleful examples of perilous association. Because of the immediate ease of contact and close company over a period of time, there come about things not thought possible. As a result many fathers prefer to leave their daughters barbaric and uncultivated rather than to expose them to the notorious danger that familiarity with men breeds. All of this would be eliminated if there were older women of learning, as Saint Paul wished, and if the teaching were handed down from one to another, as is the practice with needlework and other traditional skills.

* * *

---

4. The saying comes not from Lupercio Leonardo but from his brother, the Aragonese poet Bartolomé de Argensola (1562–1631).

If I turn my eyes to my habit of writing verses, which has been so chastised and persecuted, which in me is so natural that I must do violence to myself to keep this letter from turning into verse, I might cite that line from Ovid, "All I wished to say took the form of verse."[5] I see that my poetry is condemned and criticized by so many and I have attempted to find what harm there is in it, and I have found none. Rather, I see verse applauded on the lips of the Sybils, sanctified in the pens of the Prophets, and especially in King David of whom my great expositor and beloved Father Jerome, in explaining its metrical patterns, says, "in the manner of Horace and Pindar now it runs in iambs, now in alcaics, now it swells in sapphics, then it moves in half-feet."[6]

✳   ✳   ✳

In the end, if the wrong in me is that I a woman compose poems, since clearly many have done so and to great praise, what evil is there in my being a woman poet?

TRANSLATED BY WILLIS BARNSTONE

---

5. From Ovid's *Tristia* 4.10.26.

6. The application of Greek prosody, which is the later basis of Latin and most modern formal verse, to Hebrew poetry, such as the Psalms of David or Job, is wrong. Hebrew prosody, based on parallelism and closer to its imitators in William Blake and Walt Whitman, has nothing to do with Greek meter and prosody. Sor Juana gives a long list of those who have practiced verse, including passages in the books of Moses, the saints, and also the "Magnificat," a Greek poem of praise, which appears in Luke 1:46–55, and which is attributed to "Our Lady," meaning the Virgin Mary. The attribution to Mary is widely considered false in that Jesus' Aramaic-speaking mother was not likely to have been trained in writing Greek verse. The poem may have been a translation from a lost Hebrew or Aramaic source.

3

Nineteenth and Twentieth Centuries

■

INTRODUCTION

In Spain as well as Latin America, there is an artistic chasm between the sixteenth and seventeenth centuries (the *Siglo de Oro* or "Golden Age" of literature spanning the Renaissance and Baroque periods) and the nineteenth and twentieth centuries. The eighteenth century—the age of reason, encyclopedias, neoclassical imitations, and birth of modern democracy in document and practice—did not produce major literary figures in Spain or in its colonies. The great exception in the arts is the painter Francisco de Goya (1748–1828). With the nineteenth century came Romanticism, Realism, the beginnings of what we now call Modernism as found in the great Brazilian fiction writer Machado de Assis (1839–1908), and the notion of political engagement as in the popular poet-journalist José Martí (1867–1916) from Cuba. Latin American literature reaches its present zenith, however, after the first decades of the twentieth century with the explosion of major fiction writers in a group that has been called the "Boom" authors, ranging from Argentina and Chile to Mexico and Cuba, from Jorge Luis Borges to Carlos Fuentes. This astonishing group of authors has dominated fiction in Spanish in our century and, along with equally important poets, including Pablo Neruda (1904–1974) and Octavio Paz (1904–1998), has been awarded five Nobel Prizes in literature. Among Caribbean authors we have two other Nobel Prize winners, poet Derek Walcott (1924–) from Saint Lucia and V. S. Naipaul (1932–) from Trinidad; and other outstanding writers, including Aimé Césaire (1913–). Between the older recognized giants and more recent dazzling writers from Latin America and the Caribbean, the twentieth century has given us a new Golden Age in literature.

■ Domingo Faustino Sarmiento (1811–1888)
Argentina (biography)

TRANSLATED BY MRS. HORACE MANN

Journalist, professor, and later president of Argentina, Domingo Faustino Sarmiento drew a portrait of an evil, barbarous though secretly admired gaucho, the cowboy of the Argentine pampas, whom he called Facundo. Facundo was Sarmiento's vaguely disguised portrait of Juan Manuel Rosas, the more sinister Argentine dictator whom Sarmiento helped to overthrow. As a good, imaginative writer, Sarmiento depicted a gaucho more attractive than the figure he probably wished to portray, which paradoxically may explain why his writing has lived beyond the didactic purpose of the historical and political moment. Indeed, his fictitious Facundo survives in the Spanish-reading public more distinctly than the political leader and dictator Rosas.

Sarmiento is one of many statesman-writers whom Latin America has produced. In our day, Pablo Neruda, Octavio Paz, Carlos Fuentes, and Rosario Castellanos, former ambassadors to France, India, France, and Israel, continue that tradition. Sarmiento, however, went further. He not only became president (1868–1874) and participated in the defeat of the tyrant dictator Rosas, but his portrait of the gaucho leader Juan Facundo Quiroga became a force in shaping political and literary thought in Latin America.

Sarmiento's Facundo is a gaucho outsider and leader, ruthless yet with moments of Solomonic wisdom. Like Milton's Satan, this antihero did not lack appealingly romantic qualities. But for Sarmiento the gaucho was, as a wild force tearing up Argentina, an essential outlaw to be defeated militarily and crushed in the struggle of urban civilization against the wild and uncontrolled natural barbarian. Soon after the publication of *Facundo,* José Hernández's epic *Martín Fierro* would portray the gaucho with full sympathy in a literary masterpiece. But Sarmiento, who had a political motive in describing the gaucho, made his Facundo crude and cruel to better reflect the tyrant Rosas who was destroying the nation.

Sarmiento was born in the far province of San Juan, where, too poor to obtain a good formal education, he taught himself. He read everything of value he could find, from Spanish classics and Benjamin Franklin to French eighteenth-century encyclopedists and early nineteenth-century romantics. He taught elementary school and later worked as a political journalist. After his political journal *El Zonda* was closed by authorities in 1831, he went into exile in democratic Chile. In Chile, he found companionship and taught at the university. He returned to Argentina in 1837, only to be exiled again in 1840. During his second exile, he founded a newspaper *El Progreso,* in Santiago and, most important, wrote *Facundo* (1845), which had an enormous national and international impact. Sarmiento spent three years in Europe and the United States (1845–1848), where *Facundo* was translated into English and made famous internationally by Mrs. Horace Mann. In 1851, he returned to participate in the national struggle, joining General Urquiza in the march from Entre Ríos to Buenos Aires and was present when the dictator Rosas was defeated at the battle of Caseros in 1852. Thereafter, he was a congressman, ambassador to the United States, and eventually president of the Argentine Republic (1868–1874), whereupon he undertook a massive building program to modernize his nation. As elsewhere in North and South America, Sarmiento worked for "civilization" by supporting the suppression and killing of the Indian. Sarmiento was fascinated with the gaucho and the countryside, but ultimately he lacked sympathy for whatever was nonurban.

Facundo is a fierce, gripping portrait, as romantic as it is political. In its totality, it is naive, uneven, and brilliantly engaging and goes beyond its obvious message. The story of Facundo and the tiger has the parabolic ring of *A Thousand and One Nights.* It anticipates one of Sarmiento's later readers, Borges, lover of the tiger and portrayer of the gaucho. The gaucho to Argentina is comparable in many ways to the outsider, independent American cowboy. In each case, the figure is normally romanticized, seen as brave, tough, generous, or cruel; free of middle-class urban restraints; close to the land but not obedient to place or convention as is the farmer; and often beyond the law. Sarmiento was the first in Latin America to recognize this colorful and essential figure in a growing pioneer country and to convert the image into reportage and literature.

FURTHER READING: Sarmiento, Domingo Faustino. *Life in the Argentine Republic in the Days of the Tyrant,* 1868.

from *Life in the Argentine Republic in the Days of the Tyrant*

The Gaucho Outlaw

The example of this type of character, to be found in certain places, is an outlaw, a squatter, a kind of misanthrope. He is Cooper's Hawkeye or Trapper, with all the knowledge of the wilderness possessed by the latter; and with all his aversion to the settlements of the whites, but without his natural morality or his friendly relations with the savages. The name of gaucho outlaw is not applied to him wholly as an uncomplimentary epithet. The law has been for many years in pursuit of him. His name is dreaded—spoken under the breath, but not in hate, and almost respectfully. He is a mysterious personage; his abode is the pampa; his lodgings are the thistle fields; he lives on partridges and hedgehogs, and whenever he is disposed to regale himself upon a tongue, he lassos a cow, throws her without assistance, kills her, takes his favorite morsel, and leaves the rest for the carrion birds. The gaucho outlaw will make his appearance in a place just left by soldiers, will talk in a friendly way with the admiring group of good gauchos around him; provide himself with tobacco, yerba maté, which makes a refreshing beverage, and if he discovers the soldiers, he mounts his horse quietly and directs his steps leisurely to the wilderness, not even deigning to look back. He is seldom pursued; that would be killing horses to no purpose, for the beast of the gaucho outlaw is a bay courser, as noted in his own way as his master. If he ever happens to fall unawares into the hands of the soldiers, he sets upon the densest masses of his assailants, and breaks through them, with the help of a few slashes left by his knife upon the faces or bodies of his opponents; and lying along the ridge of his horse's back to avoid the bullets sent after him, he hastens towards the wilderness, until, having left his pursuers at a convenient distance, he pulls up and travels at his ease. The poets of the vicinity add this new exploit to the biography of the desert hero, and his renown flies through all the vast region around. Sometimes he appears before the scene of a rustic festival with a young woman whom he has carried off, and takes a place in the dance with his partner, goes through the figures of the *cielito,* and disappears, unnoticed. Another day he brings the girl he has seduced, to the house of her offended family, sets her down from his horse's croup, and reckless of the parents' curses by which he is followed, quietly betakes himself to his boundless abode.

This white-skinned savage, at war with society and proscribed by the laws, is no more depraved at heart than the inhabitants of the settlements. The reckless outlaw who attacks a whole troop, does no harm to the traveller. The gaucho outlaw is no bandit, or highwayman; murderous assaults do not suit his temper, as robbery would not suit the character of the *churriador* (sheep-stealer). To be sure, he steals; but this is his profession, his trade, his science. He steals horses. He arrives, for instance, at the camp of a train from the interior; its master offers to buy of him a horse of some unusual color, of a particular shape and quality, with a white star on the shoulder. The gaucho collects his thoughts, considers a moment, and replies, after a short silence: "There is no such horse alive." What thoughts have been passing through the gaucho's mind? In that moment his memory has traversed a thousand estates upon the pampa; has seen and examined every horse in the province, with its marks, color, and special traits, and he has convinced himself that not one of them has a star on its shoulder; some have one on their foreheads, others have white spots on their haunches. Is this power of memory amazing? No! Napoleon knew two hundred thousand soldiers by name, and remembered, when he saw any one of them, all the facts relating to him. Therefore, if nothing impossible is required of him, the gaucho will deliver upon a designated day and spot, just such a horse as has been asked for, and with no less punctuality if he has been paid in advance. His honor is as sensitive upon this point as that of a gambler about his debts.

Sometimes he travels to the country about Cordova or Santa Fé. Then he may be seen crossing the pampa behind a small body of horses; if any one meets him, he follows his course without approaching the newcomer unless he is requested to do so.

A Portrait of Facundo

Between the cities of San Luis and San Juan lies an extensive desert, called the Travesia, a word that signifies *want of water*. The aspect of that waste is mostly gloomy and unpromising, and the traveler coming from the east does not fail to provide his *chifles* with a sufficient quantity of water at the last cistern that he passes as he approaches it. This Travesia once witnessed the following strange scene. The consequences of some of the encounters with knives so common among our gauchos had driven one of them in haste from the city of San Luis and forced him to escape to the Travesia on foot, and with his riding gear on his shoulder, in order to avoid the pursuit of the law. Two comrades were to join him as soon as they could steal horses for all three. Hunger and thirst were not the only dangers which at that time awaited him in the desert; in these regions, where man must contend with the tiger for dominion over nature, the former sometimes falls a victim, upon which the tiger begins to acquire a preference for the taste of human flesh, and when it has once devoted itself to this novel form of chase, the pursuit of mankind, it gets the name of *man-eater*. The provincial justice nearest the scene of his depredations calls out the huntsmen of his district, who join, under his authority and guidance, in the pursuit of the beast, which seldom escapes the consequences of its outlawry.

When our fugitive had proceeded some six leagues, he thought he heard the distant roar of the animal, and a shudder ran through him. The roar of the tiger resembles the screech of the hog, but is prolonged, sharp, and piercing, and even when there is no occasion for fear, causes an involuntary tremor of the nerves as if the flesh shuddered consciously at the menace of death. The roaring was heard clearer and nearer. The tiger was already upon the trail of the man, who saw no refuge but a small carob tree at a great distance. He had to quicken his pace, and finally to run, for the roars behind him began to follow each other more rapidly, and each was clearer and more ringing than the last. At length, flinging his riding gear to one side of the path, the gaucho turned to the tree which he had noticed, and in spite of the weakness of its trunk, happily quite a tall one, he succeeded in clambering to its top and keeping himself half concealed among its boughs, which oscillated violently. Thence he could see the swift approach of the tiger, sniffing the soil and roaring more frequently in proportion to its increasing perception of the nearness of its prey. Passing beyond the spot where our traveler had left the path, it lost the track and, becoming enraged, rapidly circled about until it discovered the riding gear, which it dashed to fragments by a single blow. Still more furious from this failure, it resumed its search for the trail, and at last found out the direction in which it led. It soon discerned its prey, under whose weight the slight tree was swaying like a reed upon the summit of which a bird has alighted. The tiger now sprang forward, and in the twinkling of an eye its monstrous forepaws were resting on the slender trunk two yards from the ground, and were imparting to the tree a convulsive trembling calculated to act upon the nerves of the gaucho, whose position was far from secure. The beast exerted its strength in an ineffectual leap; it circled around the tree, measuring the elevation with eyes reddened by the thirst for blood, and at length, roaring with rage, it crouched down, beating the ground frantically with its tail, its eyes fixed on its prey, its parched mouth half open. This horrible scene had lasted for nearly two mortal hours; the gaucho's constrained attitude, and the fearful fascination exercised over him by the fixed and bloodthirsty stare of the tiger, which irresistibly attracted and retained his own glances, had begun to diminish his strength, and he already perceived that the moment was at hand when his exhausted body would fall into the capacious mouth of his pursuer. But at this moment the distant sound of the feet of horses on a rapid gallop gave him hope of rescue. His friends had indeed seen the tiger's footprints and were hastening on, though without hope of saving him. The scattered fragments of the saddle directed them to the scene of action, and it was the work of a moment for them to reach it, to uncoil their lassos, and to fling them over the tiger, now blinded by rage. The beast, drawn in opposite directions by the two lassos, could not evade the swift stabs by which its destined victim took his revenge for his prolonged torments. "On that occasion I knew what it was to be afraid," was the expression of Don Juan Facundo Quiroga, as he related this incident to a group of officers.

And here ends the private life of Quiroga, in which I have omitted a long series of deeds which only show his evil nature, his bad education, and his fierce and bloody instincts. . . . The fault is not his that thus he was born. In order to contend with, rule, and control the power of the city, and the judicial authority, he is willing to descend to anything. If he is offered a place in the army, he disdains it, because his impatience cannot wait for promotion. Such a position demands submission, and places fetters upon individual independence; the soldier's coat oppresses his body, and military tactics control his steps, all of which are insufferable! His equestrian life, a life of danger and of strong excitements, has steeled his spirit and hardened his heart. He feels an unconquerable and instinctive hatred for the laws which have pursued him, for the judges who have condemned him, and for the whole society and organism from which he has felt himself withdrawn from his childhood, and which regards him with suspicion and contempt. With these remarks is connected by imperceptible links the motto of this chapter, "He is the natural man, as yet unused either to repress or disguise his passions; he does not restrain their energy, but gives free rein to their impetuosity. This is the character of the human race." And thus it appears in the rural districts of the Argentine Republic. Facundo is a type of primitive barbarism. He recognized no form of subjection. His rage was that of a wild beast. The locks of his crisp black hair, which fell in meshes over his brow and eyes, resembled the snakes of Medusa's head. Anger made his voice hoarse, and turned his glances into dragons. In a fit of passion he kicked out the brains of a man with whom he had quarreled at play. He tore off both the ears of a woman he had lived with, and had promised to marry, upon her asking him for thirty dollars for the celebration of the wedding; and laid open his son John's head with an axe, because he could not make him hold his tongue. He violently beat a beautiful young lady at Tucuman, whom he had failed either to seduce or to subdue, and exhibited in all his actions a low and brutal yet not a stupid nature, or one wholly without lofty aims. Incapable of commanding noble admiration, he delighted in exciting fear; and this pleasure was exclusive and dominant with him to the arranging all his actions so as to produce terror in those around him, whether it was society in general, the victim on his way to execution, or his own wife and children. Wanting ability to manage the machinery of civil government, he substituted terror for patriotism and self-sacrifice. Destitute of learning, he surrounded himself with mysteries, and pretended to a foreknowledge of events which gave him prestige and reputation among the commonalty, supporting his claims by an air of impenetrability, by natural sagacity, an uncommon power of observation, and the advantage he derived from vulgar credulity.

The repertory of anecdotes relating to Quiroga, and with which the popular memory is replete, is inexhaustible; his sayings, his expedients, bear the stamp of an originality which gives them a certain Eastern aspect, a certain tint of Solomonic wisdom in the conception of the vulgar. Indeed, how does Solomon's advice for discovering the true mother of the disputed child differ from Facundo's method of detecting a thief in the following instances:

An article had been stolen from a band, and all endeavors to discover the thief had proved fruitless. Quiroga drew up the troops and gave orders for the cutting of as many small wands of equal length as there were soldiers; then, having had these wands distributed one to each man, he said in a confident voice, "The man whose wand will be longer than the others tomorrow morning is the thief." Next day the troops were again paraded, and Quiroga proceeded to inspect the wands. There was one whose wand was, not *longer,* but *shorter* than the others. "Wretch!" cried Facundo, in a voice which overpowered the man with dismay, "it is thou!" And so it was; the culprit's confusion was proof of the fact. The expedient was a simple one; the credulous gaucho, fearing that his wand would really grow, had cut off a piece of it. But to avail oneself of such means, a man must be superior in intellect to those about him, and must at least have some knowledge of human nature.

Some portions of a soldier's accouterments having been stolen and all inquiries having failed to detect the thief, Quiroga had the troops paraded and marched past him as he stood with crossed arms and a fixed, piercing, and terrible gaze. He had previously said, "I know the man," with an air of assurance not to be questioned. The review began; many men had passed, and Quiroga still remained motionless, like the statue of Jupiter Tonans or the God of the Last Judgment. All at once he descended upon one man and said in a curt and dry voice, "Where is the saddle?" "Yonder, sir," replied the other, pointing to a thicket. "Ho! Four fusiliers!" cried Quiroga. What revelation was this? That of terror and guilt made to a man of sagacity.

On another occasion, when a gaucho was answering to charges of theft which had been brought against him, Facundo interrupted him with the words, "This rogue has begun to lie. Ho, there! A hundred lashes!" When the criminal had been taken away, Quiroga said to someone present, "Look you, my master, when a gaucho moves his foot while talking, it is a sign he is telling lies." The lashes extorted from the gaucho the confession that he had stolen a yoke of oxen.

At another time he was in need of a man of resolution and boldness to whom he could entrust a dangerous mission. When a man was brought to him for this purpose, Quiroga was writing; he raised his head after the man's presence had been repeatedly announced, looked at him, and returned to his writing with the remark, "Pooh! That is a wretched creature. I want a brave man and a venturesome one!" It turned out to be true that the fellow was actually good for nothing.

Hundreds of such stories of Facundo's life, which show the man of superior ability, served effectually to give him a mysterious fame among the vulgar, who even attribute superior powers to him.

■ Ricardo Palma (1833–1919) *Peru* (tale)

TRANSLATED BY WILLIS BARNSTONE

A Peruvian historian of eighteenth-century life, Ricardo Palma wrote historical fictions based on research and the elegance of his imagination. His sources were libraries, archives, and monasteries; his means were re-creation and characterization, often through Goyaesque satire. Palma began his career as naval officer, journalist, and politician and, in 1863, published a significant historical volume on the Inquisition in Lima, Peru. After the War of the Pacific (1879–1884), he dedicated his time to rebuilding the destroyed national library. For many years he was its director. Palma converted a ruined structure into one of the finest libraries in South America. The library also served him perfectly for his research into a national past, which, through the invention of a new literary genre, the *tradición* (a historical anecdote), he converted into volumes of brief tales about colonial Peru. The *tradición* is historical, invented, fantastic, funny, and above all charmingly satiric. A favorite subject was Micaela Luján, La Perricholi (the bitch), concubine of the Viceroy in eighteenth-century Lima. She later appears in Thornton Wilder's *The Bridge of San Luis Rey.* In the historical re-creation "Of the Agony of Christ," Palma states in a deadpan, perhaps intentionally naive, manner, the grotesquely perverse morality of a painter who murders for art. "Margarita's Nightgown," which like many stories derides the colonial obsession with class and status, follows the psychological realism in Guy de Maupassant, with its classic epiphany. Ricardo Palma remains one of the most read earlier writers of Latin America.

FURTHER READING: Palma, Ricardo. *Peruvian Traditions,* 1872; *The Knights of the Cape.* Edited by Harriet de Onis, 1945.

Margarita's Chemise

Some of my readers may have heard of old women in Lima, speaking about the high prices of things, commenting: "Good lord, it costs more than Margarita Pareja's chemise."

Margarita's chemise was on everybody's tongue and my curiosity about it would surely never have been satisfied if I had not happened on an article in *La América* of Madrid, signed by Don Ildefonso Antonio Bermejo (author of an excellent book on Paraguay). Although Bermejo merely alluded to the young woman in the chemise, it gave me the clue I needed to find the story you are about to read.

I

Around 1765 Margarita Pareja was the pampered darling of her father, Don Raimundo Pareja, Knight of Santiago and a tax collector at the port of Callao.

The woman was one of those beauties Lima in famous for. She could have enchanted the Devil and made him cross himself and turn somersaults. Her black eyes were like dynamite charges that explode in the inner corners of the soul of the gallant men of her day.

Around this time a dashing young man from Spain turned up, a son of the royal villa of Madrid, whose name was Don Luis Alcázar. In Lima he had a rich bachelor uncle, of old Aragonese stock, escutcheons and all, and prouder than the sons of King Fruela.

Of course, until he became his uncle's heir, he was poorer than a church mouse. When I tell you that even his amorous escapes were on credit, I don't have to say more.

In a procession in honor of Santa Rosa, Alcázar met the lovely Margarita. The arrows of her eyes flew right into his heart. He poured compliments on her, and though she did not affirm or reject him, with all the other weapons in her feminine arsenal she made it clear that the young man was a dish exactly to her taste. The fact is they had fallen in love up to their eyelashes. I know it as if they themselves had told me.

Since lovers never remember there is something called arithmetic, Don Luis never imagined that his poverty could be an impediment to their desires. He went to Margarita's father, and, without any diversions, asked for her hand.

Don Raimundo didn't like the petition at all, and he politely dismissed the suitor, saying that Margarita was still very young to be choosing a husband, and that despite her eighteen summers she still played with dolls.

But this was not the real obstacle. Don Raimundo's refusal was because he did not want to be the father-in-law to a pauper, a fact that he confided in his friends, one of whom repeated the story to Don Honorato, the uncle from Aragon. When the uncle heard it, being prouder than the Cid, he fumed with rage, and said, "Who ever heard of something like this! Snubbing my nephew. There are many who would be out of their mind with joy to marry him. There is not a more elegant young man in all Lima. What insolence! I'll put this money-counting collector in his place."

Margarita, very much ahead of her time, was a high-strung young modern woman. She wept and tore her hair and fainted. And if she didn't threaten to poison herself, it was because matches with phosphorus tips had not yet been invented.

She lost weight and color. She began to fade, and spoke of entering a convent. Nobody could do anything with her.

"Luis or God," she cried every time her nerves overcame her, and this happened on the hour.

The Knight of Santiago, her adoring father, was alarmed and called in doctors and the curanderas. They all declared that the young woman was declining, that she looked consumptive, and the medicine she needed could not be found in a pharmacy.

They offered him his choice. Either he let her marry the man she desired or he would soon lay her out in her coffin. This was the doctor's ultimatum.

Don Raimundo—a father is always a father—raced out of the house like a lunatic, in such haste that he forgot his cape and cane, and came to

Don Honorato's home where he said to the gentleman, "I have come to ask you to give your consent for your nephew to marry Margarita tomorrow. Otherwise we are going to lose her, and very quickly."

"That's impossible," the uncle replied, sneering. "My nephew is just a pauper, and you need someone with his pockets full of gold for your daughter."

It was a stormy interview. The more Don Raimundo pleaded, the more stubborn the Aragonese became. Finally, as the father was about to give everything up as lost, Don Luis took a hand in the affair. He said, "Uncle, it's not Christian to kill a person who has done nothing wrong."

"Are you willing to have her?"

"O yes! With all my heart, my lord and uncle."

"Very well. I'll give my consent to make you happy, but on one condition. Don Raimundo must swear that he will not give his daughter a peseta or leave her five pesetas of his money."

Then an even more agitated argument took place.

"But, sir," Don Raimundo, countered, my daughter has a dowry of twenty thousand duros."

"We don't care for the dowry. The young woman will come to her husband with nothing but what she has on her back."

At least let me provide the furnishings for her house and a trousseau."

"Not a pin. If this doesn't meet with your approval, we can call it all off and let the young woman die."

"Don Honorato, be reasonable. My daughter at least needs to take along a change of chemise."

"Very well. I'll agree to that so you can't accuse me of being difficult. You may offer her a bridal chemise, but nothing else."

The following day Don Raimundo and Don Honorato went to the Church of San Francisco early in the morning, where they knelt to hear mass. Then, as they agreed the day before, when the priest raised the holy wafer, Margarita's father said, "I swear to give my daughter nothing but her bridal chemise. An may God damn my soul if I don't keep my word."

II

And Don Raimundo Pareja kept his oath to the letter. In his life and after his death he gave his daughter nothing.

The Brussels lace that trimmed the chemise cost 2,700 duros, according to Bermejo, who evidently gathered this information from *Secret Relations* by Ulloa and Don Jorge Juan. Moreover, the drawstring at the neck was a chain of diamonds worth 30,000 morlacas.

The newlyweds led the Aragonese uncle to believe that the chemise was worth a doubloon, since Don Honorato was so stubborn that if he found out the truth, he would have forced his nephew to get a divorce.

I am sure you will agree with me that Margarita Pareja's bridal chemise merited its widespread and enduring fame.

■ José Hernández (1834–1886) *Argentina* (epic verse)

TRANSLATED BY WALTER OWEN

Argentine soldier, journalist, and legislator, José Hernández is author of an epic of the pampas, *Martín Fierro* (1872), that redeems and glorifies the heroic outlaw gaucho at a moment when the gaucho was vanishing. The gaucho was disappearing because the rich soil of the pampas attracted industrious immigrant farmers who fenced off *estancias* (vast estates) with newly invented barbed wire. Hernández painted a golden age of the gauchos living free on their horses. His hero's name "Fierro" is an older spelling of "hierro," meaning "iron," a reference not lost to the Spanish reader. Fierro's iron will and body sum up the indomitable and adventurous qualities of the gaucho. The hero tells his own story as a *payador* (an improvising popular singer) as he moves from gaucho to badly treated military conscript to deserter and killer outlaw. Ultimately, to avoid persecution, he joins and becomes one with the Indians. In 1879, the sequel, *La vuelta de Martín Fierro (The Return of Fierro)*, was published, by which time life had become more tolerable and conscription less arbitrary and cruel. Fierro, who had lost everything, returns to find his family, reclaim his property, and begin a new life.

In the beginning, the epic of Martín Fierro had a popular following. It was printed in thin pamphlets, sold for pennies, and read aloud in country taverns. In its time, it was much appreciated, perhaps more by gauchos than by literary critics. Near the end of the century, the Spanish writer and philosopher Miguel de Unamuno discovered it as major literature and later the Argentines Leopoldo Lugones and Jorge Luis Borges declared it the national epic. It has become a Latin American classic. Unfortunately, the text, in colorful Argentine dialect, has not found a translation that transfers its literary qualities into English. The most successful version, tainted with archaisms, is by Walter Owen, which at its best, as in the selection here, has the rough darkness and simplicity of a Robert Frost narration.

FURTHER READING: Hernández, José. *Martín Fierro*, 1872; *The Gaucho Martín Fierro*. Translated by Walter Owen, 1936.

from *The Gaucho Martín Fierro*

Martín Fierro Relates His Meeting with Two of His Sons

Now pass me the crock and I'll take a swig
To cool my warmed-up throat;
And while my youngster tunes his strings
And finds his opening note,
I'll tell you how in my wanderings   *5*
I found my two lads once more.
        For many a day I roamed around
And stopped at many a door,
I wanted to know how matters went
In the pickle they call the Government,   *10*
But everything I very soon found
Was much as it was before.
So I just lay low and spied the land
And opened my eyes and ears;
It wasn't a bit of good I guessed   *15*
To meddle too much with a hornet's nest.
If you've been in trouble you'll understand
The law always holds the winning hand;
And whether it's weeks or months or years
If you're poor they get you in the end.   *20*
        But my luck held good—I found one day
A trusty old-time friend,
That put me wise how matters lay,
I was wasting my fears, he said;
For the judge whose nose had been on my trail   *25*
These many years was dead.
I had him to thank for ten long years
Of trials and sufferings sore,
And ten's a heap for a man like me
That hasn't got many more.   *30*
And this is the way I count my tale
Of trouble and misery;
Three years I lost at the frontier post,
Two years from the law I fled,
And five I spent in our little tent   *35*
In the hands of the infidel.
If I'm right, that's ten. And my friend said then,
I could put my mind at ease
That the Government had long forgot
All about my private row,   *40*
And none round there ever gave a thought

To the death of that nigger now.
   Though I snuffed his light, it's only right
To say he was part to blame;
I was middling tight—I picked the fight,   *45*
And he lost; but all the same
The brute got mad and he forced my hand
For he cut me first I'll swear,
He marked my face,—and you'll understand
That that's no light affair.   *50*
   The friend I'm telling of, told me more;
There was no more talk about
The gaucho killer that in a store
I had tumbled insides-out;
There was only one to blame for that   *55*
And that one wasn't me;
He dropped in there to look for a brawl
He got what was coming to him—that's all;
He thought I'd be good to practise on
And if I'd been slow, or a simpleton   *60*
It would have been him that hit the trail
And me that messed the floor.
   My old friend told me furthermore
That none even told the tale
Of the ding-dong fight I had the night   *65*
I met Cruz, with the police-patrol.
There's nothing in that to worry my soul,
To fight for his life is a man's first right;
They were out for my hide, and they sent a band
By night in the open, arms in hand;   *70*
They didn't arrest me in proper form,
But just came on in a yelling swarm,
And shouted out threats to have my life;
Was it any wonder I peeled my knife?
A gaucho outlaw I was, they said,   *75*
They were going to get me alive or dead
And it wasn't the Captain that told me that,
Although there was one commanding,
But the first that came up just barked at me,
And whatever I'd done, you'll all agree,   *80*
A man's got his rights, and that's no way
To come to an understanding.
   When I got such news I'm bound to say
I was pretty well content,
I felt I could show my face again,   *85*
And wherever I liked I went.
Of the little lads that long ago

From their mother and me were riven,
I've found but two; and thanks I owe
For that to the grace of heaven. 90
Though far and wide round the countryside
I hunted to find their trail,
Though I spared no dint I could get no hint
Of where they might hap to be,
And my hopes at last began to fail 95
When chance brought them back to me.
For not far off from this very spot
They were holding a racing-meet
And there I went though not a cent
To bless myself with, I'd got; 100
There were gauchos came from far and near
And many an 'estanciero'
And you'll guess no doubt there were lots about
That had heard of Martín Fierro.
There two of the sons I had thought were lost 105
Were dressing some mounts by the starting post,
When they heard my name, like a flash they came
And soon were at my side,
They shied a bit as they looked at me,
They had some excuse to stare; 110
I was tanned like a hide by the desert sun,
And was somewhat the worse for wear;
You can guess we didn't make any show
In front of the crowd. Few words we spoke,
For kisses and hugs are for women folk, 115
That are built that way; yet all men know
Though a man on his sleeve doesn't wear his heart,
There's a bit of a woman inside of him,
And he often sighs though his face be grim,
And his tears in secret start. 120
The only thing they've told me yet
Is that my poor wife is dead;
To look for her littlest lamb of all
She went to the town, they said.
And she who was prairie-born and bred 125
Must have suffered there full sore;
For all she was well set-up and strong,
She was in the hospital ere long,
And in that pen of pains and ills
Lay down to rise no more. 130
      There's not a thing in the whole wide earth
That will fill the gap she's left,
When they told me of her I was now bereft

I haven't cried bitterer since my birth;
But it's time to leave sadnesses aside,   *135*
Though my life doesn't hold for me much joy
It seems to me that my eldest boy
Is ready to sing us a stave or two;
Let's see how he handles the instrument
And the capers and paces he puts it through.   *140*
     Though both lads are strange to you,
Their father here's quite confident;
It's not because they bear my blood
That I think they've got their father's vein,
But because since they teethed they've chewed the cud   *145*
Of sorrow and suffering, want and pain;
They've both got spirit and like to play
With fire, more or less in their father's way,
Let them show us their paces, and if they're lame,
On their old crocked sire you can lay the blame.   *150*

■ Machado de Assis (1839–1908)
Brazil (novels)

Many speak of Joaquin Maria Machado de Assis as Latin America's most significant novelist. He was born in Rio de Janeiro, his mother a Portuguese, his father a Brazilian mulatto. The family was poor and literate and provided the future writer with conditions to encourage early expression. His early education was from a priest. Subsequently, he became a typesetter, proofreader, journalist, and accountant. He published his first poem at fifteen and wrote prolifically all his life—some two hundred short stories, nine novels, translations, journalism, plays, literary criticism—while working for thirty-four years as an accountant and finally director accountant at the Ministry of Agriculture, Commerce, and Public Works. He also became the first president of the Brazilian Academy of Letters. As he rose in the literary world, he always seemed to carry with him the psychological and social awareness of the insider-outsider looking in, with a clear and thorough knowledge of the social scene. During his lifetime, his stories were increasingly popular. His novels make him one of the nineteenth century's main fiction writers. Initially, it was the shocking realism and irony of his fiction—in contrast to contemporary romantic prose—that gained him his reputation. With the years, his innovative, sophisticated reader-narrator voice has caught our attention. Sharp and satiric as Goya, Machado de Assis anticipates Jorge Luis Borges and Italo Calvino in using metaliterary devices in an urbane fiction that self-consciously draws both reader and narrator into the text to speak about the activity of writing the novel. He became known internationally quite suddenly in 1952 when his novel *Epitaph of a Small Winner (Memórias póstumas de Braz Cubas,* 1881) was published in English (seventy-one years after its publication in Brazil). His popular fiction masterpiece *Dom Casmurro* appeared in 1900, but other works, such as *Philosopher or Dog* (translated in 1954) and *Quincas Borba* (1891), are distinctive and equally important. He must be considered one of the great fiction writers from any country in the nineteenth century. Susan Sontag speaks of him as the greatest writer ever produced by Latin America. *Epitaph of a Small Winner* is an imaginary autobiography, which might have been written in our postmodern era, more than a century after its publication. In the opening lines of this amusing, profound, and thoroughly ironic novel, the imaginary writer establishes the contours of his story: "I am a deceased writer not in the sense of one who has written and is now deceased, but in the sense of one who has died and is now writing." On the page before, in his "To the Reader," he also sets his mysteriously implausible tone, saying, "The work of a man already dead. I wrote it with the pen of Mirth and the ink of Melancholy, and no one can readily foresee what may come of such a union."

FURTHER READING: Machado de Assis, Joaquin Maria. *Dom Casmurro,* 1900 (tr. 1966); *The Psychiatrist and Other Stories; Devils Church and Other Stories,* 1977; *Epitaph of a Small Winner.* Foreword by Susan Sontag, 1990.

from Epitaph of a Small Winner

TRANSLATED BY WILLIAM L. GROSSMAN

To the Reader

When we learn from Stendhal that he wrote one of his books for only a hundred readers, we are both astonished and disturbed. The world will be neither astonished nor, probably, disturbed if the present book has not one hundred readers like Stendhal's, nor fifty, nor twenty, nor even ten. Ten? Maybe five. It is, in truth, a diffuse work, in which I, Braz Cubas, if indeed I have adopted the free form of a Sterne or of a Xavier de Maistre, have possibly added a certain peevish pessimism of my own. Quite possibly. The work of a man already dead. I wrote it with the pen of Mirth and the ink of Melancholy, and no one can readily foresee what may come of such a union. Moreover, solemn people will find in the book an aspect of pure romance, while frivolous folk will not find in it the sort of romance to which they have become accustomed; thus it is and will remain, disrespected by the solemn and unloved by the frivolous, the two great pillars of public opinion.

But I still entertain at least the hope of winning public favor, and the first step in that direction is to avoid a long and detailed prologue. The best prologue is the one that has the least matter or that presents it most briefly, even to the point of obscurity. Hence I shall not relate the extraordinary method that I used in the composition of these memoirs, written here in the world beyond. It is a most curious method, but its relation would require an excessive amount of space and, moreover, is unnecessary to an understanding of the work. The book must suffice in itself: if it please you, excellent reader, I shall be rewarded for my labor; if it please you not, I shall reward you with a snap of my fingers, and good riddance to you.

The Death of the Author

I hesitated some time, not knowing whether to open these memoirs at the beginning or at the end, i.e., whether to start with my birth or with my death. Granted, the usual practice is to begin with one's birth, but two considerations led me to adopt a different method: the first is that, properly speaking, I am a deceased writer not in the sense of one who has written and is now deceased, but in the sense of one who has died and is now writing, a writer for whom the grave was really a new cradle; the second is that the book would thus gain in merriment and novelty. Moses, who also related his own death, placed it not at the beginning but at the end: a radical difference between this book and the Pentateuch.

Accordingly: I expired at two o'clock of a Friday afternoon in the month of August, 1869, at my lovely suburban home in Catumby. I was sixty-four, sturdy, prosperous, and single, was worth about three hundred contos, and was accompanied to the cemetery by eleven friends. Only eleven! True, there had been no invitations and no notices in the newspapers. Moreover, there was a fine drizzle, steady and sad, so steady and so sad, in fact, that it led one of those faithful friends of my last hour to work this ingenious thought into the discourse that he offered at the edge of my grave: "You who knew him may well affirm with me that Nature herself appears to be weeping her lamentation over her irreparable loss, one of the most beautiful characters that ever honored humanity by his presence in our poor world. This sombre air, these drops from heaven, those dark clouds covering the blue like a crepe of mourning, all manifest the harsh and cruel grief that gnaws at her deepest entrails and the praise that heaven itself bestows upon our great and dear departed." Good and faithful friend! I shall never regret the legacy of twenty government bonds that I left him.

And thus I arrived at the end of my days; thus I started on the road to Hamlet's "undiscovered country," with neither the anxiety nor the doubts of the young prince, but slow and halting, like a person who has lingered in the theatre long after the end of the performance. Tardy and jaded. Some nine or ten people saw me go, among them three ladies: my sister Sabina, who was married to Cotrim; her daughter, a real lily of the valley; and . . .

Have patience! In a little while I shall reveal the identity of the third lady. Be content for the moment to know that this anonymous lady, although not a relative of mine, suffered more than the relatives. You must believe me: she really suffered more. I do not say that she tore her hair, nor that she rolled on the floor in convulsions. For there was nothing dramatic about my passing. The death of a bachelor at the age of sixty-four does not take on the proportions of high tragedy. And even if it did, nothing could have been more improper than that this anonymous lady display the intensity of her sorrow. Standing at the head of the bed, eyes glazed and mouth half open, she could hardly believe I had gone.

"Dead! Dead!" she repeated to herself.

And her imagination—like the storks that a famous traveler saw setting out in flight from the Ilissus to the African shores, heedless of the times and of the ruins—her imagination flew above the desolation of the moment to the shores of an ever youthful Africa.

Let her go; we shall go there later. We shall go there when I return to my early years. At present, I wish to die calmly, methodically, hearing the sobs of the ladies, the soft words of the men, the rain drumming on the taro leaves, and the piercing noise of a razor being sharpened by a knife-grinder outside in front of the door of a leather craftsman. I assure you that the music of this orchestra of death was much less sad than may appear. After a certain time, it was actually pleasurable. Life was shaking my body with the force of a great wave, my consciousness was fading away, I was descending to a physical and mental state of utter immobility, and my body was becoming a plant, a stone, clay, nothing at all.

I died of pneumonia; but, if I were to tell the reader that the cause of my death was less the pneumonia than a great and useful idea, possibly he would not believe me, yet it would be true. I am going to explain the matter to him briefly. Let him judge for himself.

On That Day

On that day, the Cubas tree brought forth a lovely flower: I was born. I was received in the arms of Paschoela, famous midwife from Minho, Portugal, who boasted that she had opened the doors to the world for a whole generation of noblemen. Quite possibly my father had heard her say this; I believe, however, that it was paternal sentiment that induced him to gratify her with two half-dobras. Washed and diapered, I immediately became the hero of the house. Everyone predicted for me what best suited his taste. Uncle João, the old infantry officer, found that I had a certain facial expression like Bonaparte's, a thing that my father could not hear without nausea. Uncle Ildefonso, then a plain priest, scented a future canon in me.

"He will most surely be a canon, and I shall say no more for fear of appearing prideful; but I should not be surprised in the least if God has destined him for a bishopric . . . Yes, a bishopric; it is by no means impossible. What is your opinion, brother Bento?"

My father replied to everyone that I would be what God desired. Then he would lift me high in the air, as if he wanted to show me to the whole city and, indeed, to the whole world. He asked everyone whether I looked like him, whether I was intelligent, pretty . . .

I relate these things briefly, just as I heard them related years later; I am uninformed about most of the details of that great day. I know that the neighbors came or sent their compliments to the new-born, and that during the first few weeks we had many visitors. There was no chair or stool that escaped service. Many Sunday coats and fine breeches put in an appearance. If I do not relate the caresses, the kisses, the admiration, the blessings, it is because, if I did so, I should never finish the chapter, and finish it I must.

Item: I can tell nothing about my baptism, for they told me nothing about it, except that it was the occasion for one of the jolliest parties of the following year, 1806. I was baptized in the church of Saint Dominic on a Tuesday in March, a fine, pure, clear day, with Colonel Rodrigues de Mattos and his wife as godparents. They were both descended from old families of the North, and did real honor to the blood that ran in their veins, blood that had once been spilled in the war against Holland. I believe that their names were among the first things that I learned; and surely I could repeat them with great charm, or I revealed a precocious talent in doing so, for I was obliged to recite them before every visitor.

"Nhonhô, tell these gentlemen the name of your godfather."

"My godfather? He is the Most Excellent Senhor Colonel Paulo Vaz Lobo Cesar de Andrade e Souza Rodrigues de Mattos. My godmother is the Most Excellent Senhora Dona Maria Luiza de Macedo Rezende e Souza Rodrigues de Mattos."

"Your little boy is so clever!" exclaimed the listeners.

"Very clever," my father agreed. His eyes spilled over with gratification, and, placing the palm of his hand on my head, he gazed at me a long time, lovingly, proudly.

Item: I began to walk—I do not know exactly when, but ahead of time. Perhaps to hurry nature, they had me hold on to chairs while they supported me by the diaper and promised me little wooden wagons as a reward. "There we go, Nhonhô, all alone now!" my Negro nurse would say to me. And I, attracted by the tin rattle that my mother shook in front of me, started forward, fell, arose, fell again; and walked, doubtless badly, but walked, and I have been walking ever since.

The First Kiss

I was seventeen; I was trying to convince the world and myself that the down on my upper lip was a mustache. My eyes, lively and resolute, were my most genuinely masculine feature. As I conducted myself with a certain arrogance, it was hard to know whether I was a child with manly ways or a man with childish ways. At all events, I was a handsome lad, handsome and bold, and I galloped into life in my boots and spurs, a whip in my hand and blood in my veins, riding a nervous, strong, high-spirited courser like the horse in the old ballads, which Romanticism found in the medieval castle and left in the streets of our own century. The Romanticists rode the poor beast until he was so nearly dead that he finally lay down in the gutter, where the realists found him, his flesh eaten away by sores and worms, and, out of pity, carried him away to their books.

Yes, I was good-looking, elegant, rich; and you may well believe that more ladies than one lowered before me a pensive brow or raised to me a pair of covetous eyes. Of all of them, however, the one who captivated me was a . . . a . . . I do not know whether to say it; this book is chaste, at least in intention; in intention, it is super-chaste. But come, I must tell either all or nothing. She who captivated me was a Spanish woman, Marcella, "the gorgeous Marcella," as the young blades used to call her. And the young blades were in the right. She was the daughter of an Asturian vegetable farmer; she told me this herself in a moment of sincerity, for the accepted belief was that she had been born to a Madrid lawyer, a victim of the French invasion, who had been wounded, imprisoned, and shot by a firing squad when she was only twelve years old. *Cosas de España.*

But whether her father was a vegetable farmer or a lawyer, the fact is that Marcella was wholly wanting in rustic innocence, and indeed it is doubtful whether she accepted even the modest ethics of the legal code. She was a beautifully built young lady, gay, without moral scruple, but inhibited a little by the austerity of the times, which did not permit her to parade her extravagances through the streets; luxurious, impatient, a lover of money and of young men. In that year, she was dying of love for a certain Xavier, a fellow who was both rich and consumptive—a gem.

I saw her for the first time in the Rocio Grande on the night of the fireworks after the announcement of the declaration of independence, a celebration of spring, of the awakening of the public soul. We were two young men, the people and I; we were fresh from childhood, with all the eagerness and fervor of youth. I saw her get out of a sedan chair; graceful and bewitching, she had a slim, undulating body, with a sauciness that I have never observed in chaste women. "Follow me," she said to her manservant. And I followed her, as much her servant as the other; I followed her lovingly, vibrantly, full of the first dawns. I heard someone say "the gorgeous Marcella," I remembered what I had heard about her from Uncle João, and I became, I confess it, actually dizzy.

Three days later, my uncle asked me in private whether I wished to go to a supper party in Cajueiros, with women. We went; it was in Marcella's house. Xavier, for all his tuberculosis, was presiding at the supper, of which I ate little or nothing, for I could take neither my eyes nor my thoughts away from the lady of the house. How lovely was this Spanish girl! There were seven or eight other women — all more or less loose — and they were pretty and charming, but the Spanish beauty . . . My ecstasy, several draughts of wine, my imperious, impulsive nature, all led me to do an unheard-of thing: as we were leaving, at the street door, I asked my uncle to wait a moment and went back up the stairs.

"Did you forget something?" asked Marcella, standing at the head of the stairway.

"My handkerchief."

She got out of my way so that I could return to the salon; I seized her hands, drew her to me, and kissed her. I do not know whether she said something, whether she shouted, whether she called anyone; I know only that I rushed down the stairs, fast as a whirlwind and stumbling like a drunk.

Vision in the Hallway

In the dark hallway at the bottom of the stairs, I stopped a minute to catch my breath, to compose myself, to collect my scattered thoughts — in short, to regain my self-possession after such deep and contrary emotional experiences. I decided that I was happy. Certainly the diamonds tainted my happiness a little; but it is certain also that a pretty woman can very well love both the Greeks and their gifts. Moreover, I had confidence in my Marcella; she may have had faults, but she loved me . . .

"An angel!" I murmured, looking at the ceiling of the hallway.

And there, mocking me, I saw Marcella's eyes, with the expression that had given me, a few minutes earlier, a shudder of distrust, and they were sparkling above a nose that was at once Bakbarah's nose and my own. Poor infatuated fool of *The Thousand and One Nights!* I saw you running the length of the gallery after the vizier's wife, she beckoning you to possess her and you running, running, running, until you came to the garden path and out into the street, where the leather venders laughed at you and beat you. Then it seemed to me that Marcella's hallway was the garden path and that the street outside was the one in Bagdad. Indeed, as I looked toward the street door, I saw three of the leather venders, one in a cassock, another in livery, and the third in ordinary clothes, come into the hallway; they seized me by the arms, put me in a chaise — my father on my right, my uncle, the canon, on my left, and the man in livery on the driver's box — and took me to the house of the local police captain, from which I was transported to a galleon that was to sail for Lisbon. You can imagine how I resisted; but all resistance was in vain.

Three days later, downcast and silent, I crossed the bar. I did not even cry; I had a fixed idea. Accursed fixed ideas! On this occasion, my idea was to repeat the name Marcella as I leaped into the ocean.

from **Dom Casmurro**

TRANSLATED BY HELEN CAULDWELL

Othello

I dined out; went to the theater in the evening. They happened to be playing *Othello,* which I had never seen or read. I was familiar only with its
theme, and rejoiced at the coincidence. I watched the Moor rage because
of a handkerchief—a simple handkerchief!—and here I furnish material
to be considered by psychologists of this and other continents, since I
could not escape the observation that a handkerchief was enough to kindle
the jealousy of Othello and fashion the most sublime tragedy of this world.
Handkerchiefs have passed out of use; today one must have nothing less
than sheets, at times it is not sheets but only shirts that matter. These were
the vague and muddled ideas that passed through my mind as the Moor
rolled convulsively and Iago distilled his calumny. During the intervals
between the acts I did not leave my seat. I did not wish to risk meeting
someone I knew. Most of the ladies remained in the boxes, while the men
went out to smoke. Then I asked myself if one of these women might not
have loved someone who now lay quiet in the cemetery; and there came to
me other incoherencies, until the curtain rose and the play went on. The
last act showed me that not I, but Capitú ought to die. I heard the prayers
of Desdemona, her pure and loving words, the fury of the Moor, and the
death he meted out to her amid the frantic applause of the audience.

"And she was innocent!" I kept saying to myself all the way down the
street. "What would the audience do if she were really guilty, as guilty as
Capitú? And what death would the Moor mete out to her then? A bolster
would not suffice; there would be need of blood and fire, a vast, intense fire
to consume her wholly, and reduce her to dust, and the dust tossed to the
wind, in eternal extinction. . . ."

I roamed through the streets the rest of the night. I had supper, it is
true, a trifle, but enough to live on till morning. I saw the last hours of
night and the first hours of day. I saw the late strollers and the first sweep-
ers, the first carts, the first noises, the first white streaks of day, a day that
came after the other and would see me depart never to return. The streets
I roamed seemed to flee from me of themselves. I would never again contemplate the sea beyond Gloria, nor the Serra dos Orgãos, nor the fortress
of Santa Cruz, and the rest. There were not so many people on the street as
on weekdays but there were quite a number off to tasks they would do
again; but I would never do anything again.

I reached home, opened the door very slowly, climbed the stairs on tip-
toe, and let myself into my study. It was almost six. I took the poison out of
my pocket, sat in my shirt sleeves and wrote one more letter, the last, directed to Capitú. None of the others were for her. I felt the necessity of writing some word which would leave her remorseful for my death. I wrote two

versions. I burned the first, thinking it too long and diffuse. The second contained only what was necessary, clear and brief. It did not remind her of our past, nor of the struggles we had had, nor of any joy: it spoke only of Escobar and of the necessity of dying.

■ José Martí (1853–1895) *Cuba* (poem)

TRANSLATED BY WILLIS BARNSTONE

Journalist, essayist, poet, and leader of the Cuban Revolutionary Party, which sought independence for Cuba from Spain (it came in 1898), José Martí was killed in a landing in Cuba in the last major battle against Spain. Politically active from an early age, at sixteen Martí was arrested and sent into exile. Thereafter, he lived in Mexico, Spain, Guatemala, Venezuela, and mainly, for a period of fourteen years, in the United States. In New York, where he had his longest residence, he earned his living as a newspaperman, writing for the *New York Sun* and foreign papers. He wrote about literary, social, and political matters in the United States and Latin America. Among the memorable writings in his *Chronicles* are pages on the life of Ulysses Grant and on the first exhibition of French impressionist paintings in New York. He admired and wrote about Whitman, whom he met in Camden, New Jersey, and he painted a vivid picture of the celebration of Whitman's seventieth birthday. In his last residence in New York (1891–1895), he founded the Cuban Revolutionary Party and led the liberation movement until his death, during an invasion attempt at Dos Ríos in 1895, the same year as the liberation. He is Cuba's national hero.

As a poet, he was schooled in Spanish and French classics. Like the Argentine writer and leader Sarmiento, Martí was a political journalist and in his fine essays and newspaper columns, he combined social ardor with a sure aesthetic hand. Because he rejected the stilted rhetoric of the past in favor of straightforward prose, he is usually credited with being one of the precursors of the *modernismo* movement. Yet only in that the modernistas, including their leader, the Nicaraguan poet Rubén Darío, were also interested in revolutionary politics, might he be included under the loose and ill-defined rubric of modernismo. He had none of the French Parnassian escapist aestheticism that permeated the work of Leopoldo Lugones or Rubén Darío; no symbolic peacocks, swans, or delicate princesses in glass towers enter his writing. On the contrary, in his best poetry, Martí is elegantly simple as in the brief lyrics of *Simple Lyrics,* the title of his best-known volume of verse. The revolutionary song "Guantanamera," made popular by Joan Baez in the 1960s, incorporates the famous line "I am a sincere man" from one of his "simple lyrics."

FURTHER READING: Martí, José. *Simple Lyrics,* 1891; *Free Lyrics,* ca. 1882, published 1913; *The America of José Martí: Selected Writings.* Translated by Juan de Onís, 1953.

I Am a Sincere Man

I am a sincere man
from where the palms grow,
and before I die I want
to spread my soul poems.

I come from everywhere   5
and to everywhere I go.
I am art among the arts.
In the hills I am a hill.

I know the exotic names
of grasses and flowers,   10
of fatal betrayals
and sublime sorrows.

In dark night I have seen
rays of pure fire
and holy beauty   15
rain upon my head.

I have seen wings born
in beautiful women's shoulders,
and butterflies flying
out of piles of rubble.   20

I have seen a man living
with a dagger in his side,
who will never say the name
of the woman who killed him.

Swiftly like a reflection   25
twice I saw the soul, twice:
when the old poor man died,
when she told me goodbye.

I shivered once on the grating
at the entrance to the vineyard   30
when I saw a barbarous bee
scratch a girl's forehead.

I enjoyed my fate
like never before when
the mayor weeping   35
read my sentence of death.

I hear a sigh across
the lands and the sea:
it is not a sigh. It is
my son about to wake   40

If they say I got the best
jewel from the jewelers,
I take on a sincere friend
and put love aside.

I have seen the wounded eagle   *45*
fly into a serene blue,
and a poisonous viper
die in its den.

I'm aware that when the world
yields lividly to rest,   *50*
a tame stream murmurs
over a profound silence.

I put a daring hand
stiff with horror and jubilation
over an extinct star   *55*
that fell before my door.

I conceal in my brave chest
a pain that wounds me:
the son of an enslaved people
lives for it, hushes and dies.   *60*

All is beautiful and constant,
all is music and reason,
and all, like the diamond,
before light is carbon.

I know that a fool is buried   *65*
with grand wealth and wailing,
and there is no earthly fruit
like the fruit of a peasant.

I shut up, catch on, and get rid
of a rhymer's pomp,   *70*
and hang my doctor's hood
on a withered tree.

■ Rubén Darío (1867–1916) *Nicaragua* (poems)

The Nicaraguan poet Rubén Darío was the founder and leader of the modernismo movement and, by his example, profoundly altered Spanish poetry in the Americas. Darío looked to France and particularly to the French poet Paul Verlaine in whose purity, perfection, ineffable sadness, and "music above all," he found a model for his own verse. He brought a Spanish form of French symbolism and Parnassian aestheticism to a worn out, dispirited poetry of Latin America and Spain, renovating its diction with exotic, clear imagery and sonorous rhythms. A prodigy, Darío was eighteen when he published Blue (1888), which made him famous. His next major work was Profane Proses (1896), a volume of poems that moved from "purity" of content and form to graceful exoticism. Yet artificiality and art-for-art's sake prevailed. In his later books, Songs of Life and Hope (1905), he initiated an anti–North American polemic, calling for the political, religious, and cultural independence of the Hispanic world. In Spanish America and Spain, early poets of our century initially embraced him for his fresh beauty and magic and later for his political word. The Spanish poet Antonio Machado and the Argentine Leopoldo Lugones were at first in debt to the Nicaraguan modernist, but soon, searching for their own voice, they rejected him as an Hispanic equivalent of fin de siècle French preciosity. Darío spent his later years in Nicaragua, Madrid, and Paris. Like his mentor Paul Verlaine, he embraced a bohemian lifestyle and in his last years was often sick from severe alcoholism. He died at age forty-nine. No poet in the Spanish language, on either side of the Atlantic, has so thoroughly changed the poetry of the Spanish language. His political poems have been rewritten by fellow Nicaraguan Ernesto Cardenal in his own modern idiom.

FURTHER READING: Darío, Rubén. *Blue,* 1888; *Profane Proses and Other Poems,* 1896; *Songs of Life and Hope,* 1905; *Selected Poems.* Translated by Lysander Kemp, 1965.

Symphony in Gray Major

The sea, great mercury mirror,
reflects the zinc sheet of sky;
stain of faraway birds
on pale burnished gray.

Opaque round window, the sun   5
at a sick pace totters to the zenith;
a sea wind stretches
in shade, pillowed on its black
trumpet.

Under the pier the waves   10
groan, twitching leaden bellies.
A sailor sits on a coil of rope,
smoking, remembering
distant landfalls, a misty country.

This sea dog is old. Fiery rays   *15*
of Brazilian sun have scorched his face;
vicious Chinese typhoons have seen him
tilting his gin bottle.

Foam infused with saltpeter and iodine
has long been familiar with his red nose,   *20*
his crisp curls and athlete's biceps,
his canvas cap and drill shirt.

In the tobacco smoke he sees
that far-off misty land for which,
one golden, hot afternoon,   *25*
his brig set out in full sail.

Tropical siesta. The old man sleeps.
The scale of gray major envelops him.
It's as if an enormous
soft charcoal had been rubbed   *30*
over where the horizon used to curve.

Tropical siesta. An old cigala
tries out her obsolete, hoarse guitar;
a grasshopper begins
a monotone on his one-stringed fiddle.   *35*

TRANSLATED BY DENISE LEVERTOV

To Roosevelt

The voice that would reach you, Hunter, must speak
in Biblical tones, or in the poetry of Walt Whitman.
You are primitive and modern, simple and complex;
you are one part George Washington and one part Nimrod.
          You are the United States,   *5*
future invader of our naïve America
with its Indian blood, an America
that still prays to Christ and still speaks Spanish.

You are a strong, proud model of your race;
you are cultured and able; you oppose Tolstoy.   *10*
You are an Alexander-Nebuchadnezzar,
breaking horses and murdering tigers.

(You are a Professor of Energy,
as the current lunatics say.)

You think that life is a fire,   *15*
that progress is an irruption,
that the future is wherever
your bullet strikes.
        No.

The United States is grand and powerful.   *20*
Whenever it trembles, a profound shudder
runs down the enormous backbone of the Andes.
If it shouts, the sound is like the roar of a lion.
And Hugo said to Grant: "The stars are yours."
(The dawning sun of the Argentine barely shines;   *25*
the star of Chile is rising . . .) A wealthy country,
joining the cult of Mammon to the cult of Hercules;
while Liberty, lighting the path
to easy conquest, raises her torch in New York.

But our own America, which has had poets   *30*
since the ancient times of Nezahualcóyotl;
which preserved the footprints of great Bacchus,
and learned the Panic alphabet once,
and consulted the stars; which also knew Atlantis
(whose name comes ringing down to us in Plato)   *35*
and has lived, since the earliest moments of its life,
in light, in fire, in fragrance, and in love—
the America of Moctezuma and Atahualpa,
the aromatic America of Columbus,
Catholic America, Spanish America,   *40*
the America where noble Cuauhtémoc said:
"I am not on a bed of roses"—our America,
trembling with hurricanes, trembling with Love:
O men with Saxon eyes and barbarous souls,
our America lives. And dreams. And loves.   *45*
And it is the daughter of the Sun. Be careful.
Long live Spanish America!
A thousand cubs of the Spanish lion are roaming free.
Roosevelt, you must become, by God's own will,
the deadly Rifleman and the dreadful Hunter   *50*
before you can clutch us in your iron claws.

And though you have everything, you are lacking one thing:
God!

TRANSLATED BY LYSANDER KEMP

Ramón López Velarde (1880–1921)
Mexico (poem)

TRANSLATED BY WILLIS BARNSTONE

Ramón López Velarde was born in a Mexican town, and though he moved to Mexico City, he never lost his feeling for the landscape and villages of his youth, and they remain the main references in his poems. He received a law degree from the University of San Luis Potosí. In 1919, he published *Zozobra* (*Worries*), which gave him an immediate reputation. *El son del corazón* (*Heartbeat*) appeared posthumously in 1932. Although influenced by Lugones and Latin American modernism, his natural affinity is with the Spanish nature poet Antonio Machado or the village poems about place, family, and friends in César Vallejo's compassionate early poems. López Velarde's poems are free of modernista preciosity. On the contrary, a grave simplicity and an elemental humanity run through them. A poet far ahead of his time, he has enduring qualities of ordinary, sensitive speech that have enhanced his readership and reputation and have made him today one of Latin America's most esteemed writers from the early part of the century.

FURTHER READING: López Velarde, Ramón. *Devoted Blood,* 1916; *Worries,* 1919; *Heartbeat,* 1932.

Our Lives Are Pendulums

Where is that girl, I wonder,
who one night at a dance
in a forsaken town
revealed how she had to
get out, to travel, and told me   5
her boredom?

The waltz was groaning for her,
and she was a languid artist's
plaster model: two amber
drop earrings, and a jasmine   10
in her hair.

Girl who told me
your secrets of boredom
one night at a dance

in that forsaken town,   *15*
wherever you're exhaling
your discreet sigh,
our lives are pendulums.

Two far off pendulums
swinging and parallel   *20*
in the same fog
of winter.

■ Ricardo Güiraldes (1886–1927) *Argentina* (novel)

TRANSLATED BY HARRIET DE ONÍS

An Argentine aristocrat who spent his life between Buenos Aires and Paris, Ricardo Güiraldes also traveled to the Far East, but in his writing he was perfectly at home in the pampas. Like José Hernández, the author of *Martín Fierro,* Güiraldes created a gaucho after the gaucho had effectively vanished, publishing his masterpiece of the gauchoesque novel in 1926, a year before his death. The hero Don Segundo Sombra, who is a "second shadow" of a disappeared gaucho reality, comes through as a poetically described hero of integrity, adventure, and sporadic epic qualities. Don Segundo is perceived largely through the eyes of the young boy Fabio Cáceres, who idealizes and mythologizes Don Segundo Sombra. At the same time, the boy is also a myth created by Güiraldes. The novel *Don Segundo Sombra* is an elaborate, beautifully crafted anachronism, a fairy tale for all ages like Antoine de Saint-Exupéry's *The Little Prince;* and, like Exupéry's fable or a tale from *A Thousand and One Nights,* it remains alive for each generation. Provided one does not look for fiction to replace history or chronicle, *Don Segundo* works as a finely wrought adventure story.

FURTHER READING: Güiraldes, Ricardo. *Don Segundo Sombra,* 1926. Translated by Harriet de Onís, 1935.

from *Don Segundo Sombra*

Slowly, with my fishing rod over my shoulder and dangling my small victims heartlessly at my side, I made my way toward town. The street still was flooded by a recent thundershower, and I had to walk carefully to keep from sinking in the mud that clung to my sandals and almost sucked them off my feet. My mind was a blank as I took the narrow path that crept along the hedges of prickly pear, thorn, myrrh, following the rise of the ground, like hares seeking a level place to run.

The lane ahead of me stretched dark. The sky, still blue with twilight, lay in reflected shards in the puddles or in the deep wagon ruts, where it looked like strips of carefully trimmed steel.

I had reached the first houses, where the hour put the dogs on the alert. Fear twitched in my legs as I heard the growl of a dangerous mastiff not far off, but without a mistake I called all the brutes by name: Sentinel, Captain, Watcher. When some mutt set up a barking as swift as it was inoffensive, I disdainfully shied a clod at it.

I passed the graveyard and a familiar tremor ran down my spine, radiating its pallid chill to my calves and forearms. The dead, will-o'-the-wisps, ghosts, scared me far more than any encounter I might have with mortals in that neighborhood. What could the greediest robber hope for from me? I was on good terms with the slyest of them; and if one was so careless as to hold me up, he would be the loser by a cigarette.

The lane became a street, the outlying farms thickened into blocks of houses; and neither walls nor bead-tree hedges held any secrets for me. Here was a stand of alfalfa, there a patch of corn, a barn lot, or just brush. Now I could make out the first shanties, silent in their squalor and illumined only by the frail glow of a candle or stinking kerosene lamps. As I crossed a street I frightened a horse whose step had sounded farther off than it was; and as fear is catching, even from animal to man, I stood stock-still in the mud without daring to move. The rider, who seemed to me enormous in his light poncho, urged the horse on, whirling the whiplash past its left eye; but as soon as I tried to take a step the scared beast snorted like a mule and reared. A puddle cracked beneath his hoof with the sound of breaking glass. A high-pitched voice spoke calmly, "Steady, boy. Steady, boy."

Then trot and gallop splashed through the sleek mud.

I stood still and watched the silhouette of horse and rider disappear strangely magnified against the glowing sky. It was as if I had seen a vision, a shade, a something that passes and is more a thought than a living thing, a something that drew me as a pool swallows the current of a river into its depths.

Filled with my vision, I reached the first sidewalks, where I could make better time. Stronger than ever was the need I felt to get away, to leave this paltry town forever. I had glimpsed a new life, a life of motion and space.

In a whirl of dreams and doubts I kept on through the town and down the blackness of another alley to La Blanqueada. As I entered, the light made me pucker up my eyes. Behind the counter, as usual, stood the owner, and in front of him the half-breed Burgos was just finishing off a brandy.

"Good evening, gentlemen."

"Evening," mumbled Burgos.

"What you got?" asked the owner.

"There you are, Don Pedro." I showed him my string of catfish.

"All right. Want some rock candy?"

"No, Don Pedro."

"Couple packages of La Popular?"

"No, Don Pedro. Remember the last money you gave me?"

"Sure."

"It was round."

"And you made it roll?"

"You said it."

"All right. Here you are." He clinked several nickel coins down on the counter.

"Gonna set up the drinks?" grinned the half-breed.

"Sure—in the *Wouldn't You Like It* café."

"Anything new?" asked Don Pedro, for whom I was a kind of reporter.

"Yes, sir; a stranger."

"Where'd you see him?"

"At the crossing, as I was coming in from the river."

"And you don't know who he is?"

"I know he's not from here. There's no man as big as him in this town."

Don Pedro frowned, as if trying to concentrate on some half-forgotten memory. "Tell me, was he very dark?"

"I think so—yes, sir. And strong!"

As though talking of something extraordinary, the saloonkeeper muttered, "Who knows if it isn't Don Segundo Sombra!"

"It is!" I said, without knowing why, and I felt the same thrill as when at nightfall I had stood motionless before the portentous vision of that gaucho stamped black on the horizon.

"You know him?" Don Pedro asked the half-breed, paying no attention to my exclamation.

"Only what I've heard tell of him. The devil, I reckon, ain't as fierce as he's painted. How about serving me another drink?"

"Hm," went on Don Pedro. "I've seen him more than once. He used to come in here, afternoons. He's a man you want to watch your step with. He's from San Pedro. Had a run in, they say, with the police some time ago."

"I suppose he butchered somebody else's steer."

"Yes. But, if I remember rightly, the steer was a Christian."

Burgos kept his stolid eyes on the glass, and a frown wrinkled his narrow forehead of a pampas Indian half-breed. The fame of another man seemed to lessen his own as an expert with the knife.

We heard a gallop stop short at the door, then the soft hiss with which the country folk quiet a horse, and Don Segundo's silent figure stood framed in the doorway.

"Good evening," came the high-pitched voice, and it was easy to recognize. "How's Don Pedro?"

"Good. And you, Don Segundo?"

"I can't complain, thank God."

As they greeted each other with the customary courtesies, I looked the man over. He was not really so big. What made him seem so, as he appears to me even today, was the sense of power flowing from his body. His chest was enormous and his joints big-boned like those of a horse. His feet were short and high-arched; his hands thick and leathery like the scales of an armadillo. His skin was copper-hued and his eyes slanted slightly toward his temples. To talk more at ease he pushed his narrow-brimmed hat back from his forehead showing bangs cut like a horse's, level with his eyebrows. His attire was that of a poor gaucho. A plain pigskin belt girded his waist. The short blouse was caught up by the bone-handled knife from which swung a rough, plaited quirt, dark with use. His chiripá was long and coarse, and a plain black kerchief was knotted around his neck with the ends across his shoulders. He had split his *alpargatas* at the instep to make room for the fleshy foot.

When I had looked my fill at him, I listened to the talk. Don Segundo was looking for work, and Don Pedro was telling him where to find it; his constant business with the country people made him know everything that was going on at the ranches.

"At Galván's there are some mares they want broke. A few days ago Valerio was here and asked me if there was anyone I could recommend. I told him about Mosco Pereira, but if it suits you—"

"Seems to me it might."

"Good. I'll tell the boy they send to town every day. He generally drops in."

"I'd rather you said nothing. If I can, I'll go by the ranch myself."

"All right. Like a drink?"

"Well, I don't mind," said Don Segundo, sitting down at a nearby table. "Give me a glass of brandy, and thanks for the invitation."

Everything that had to be said was said. A calm silence filled the place. Burgos poured out his fourth glass. His eyes were bleary and his face expressionless. Suddenly, and for no apparent reason, he said to me, "If I was a fisher like you, I'd want to haul in a great big mud-bottom catfish." A sarcastic giggle underlined his words, and he kept looking at Don Segundo out of the corner of his eye. "They seem tough because they flop around and make such a fuss. But what can they do when they're nothing but niggers."

Don Pedro gave the half-breed a sharp look. Both of us knew what Burgos was like and that nothing could hold him when he turned ugly. The only one of the four of us who didn't understand the drift of things was Don Segundo, who went on sipping his liquor, his thoughts far away. The half-breed giggled again; he was proud of the comparison he had hit on. I longed to do something—something terrible if need be—to break the strain. Don Pedro was humming to himself. And the air was tense for us all, except for the stranger, who seemed to have neither understood nor felt the chill of our silence.

"A big mud-bottom catfish," repeated the drunk again. "But nothing but a catfish, for all it's got whiskers and walks on two legs like Christians. . . . I've heard there's a lot of 'em in San Pedro. That's why they say:

'Anyone from San Pedro
Is either a chink or a mulatto.'"

Twice he repeated the rhyme in a voice that grew thicker and more insolent.

Don Segundo looked up and, as if just realizing that the half-breed's words were meant for him, said calmly, "Come, friend, I'll soon begin to think you're trying to start something."

So unexpected were the words, so amusing the expression of surprise on his face, that we had to smile despite the ugly turn the talk was taking. The drunk himself was nonplussed, but only for a moment.

"Yeah? I was beginning to think everybody around here was deaf."

"How could a catfish be deaf, with the big ears they got? But me? I'm a busy man and I can't take care of you now. When you want to fight with me, let me know at least three days in advance."

We burst out laughing, in spite of the amazement this calm that verged on foolhardiness aroused in us. Again he began to grow in my imagination. He was the "masked man," the "mystery man," the man of silence, who inspires a wondering admiration in the pampas.

The half-breed Burgos paid for his drinks, muttering threats. I followed him to the door and saw him hide in the shadow. Don Segundo got up and took his leave of Don Pedro, who was pale with fear. The drunk was going to kill this man to whom my heart went out! As if speaking to Don Pedro, I warned Don Segundo, "Watch out!"

And then I sat down on the doorsill, my heart in my mouth, waiting for the fight that was sure to come.

Don Segundo stood on the threshold, looking from side to side. I understood that he was getting his eyes used to the dark, so as not to be taken by surprise. Then, keeping to the wall, he started toward his horse.

The half-breed stepped from the shadow feeling sure of his man and let loose his knife aimed straight at the heart. I saw the blade cut the night like the flash of a gun. With incredible swiftness Don Segundo dodged, and the knife shattered against the brick wall with the clang of a bell. Burgos stepped back two paces and waited for what must be his death. The triangular blade of a small knife glittered in Don Segundo's fist. But the attack did not come. Don Segundo bent calmly over, picked the broken steel from the ground, and said in his ironic voice, "Here you are, friend. Better get it fixed. This way, it's no good even to skin a sheep."

The attacker kept his distance. Don Segundo put away his own little knife and again held out the fragments of the blade.

"Take it, friend."

The bully came forward, his head low, moved by a force stronger than his fear. His clumsy fist took the hilt of the knife, now harmless as a broken cross. Don Segundo shrugged and walked toward his horse. And Burgos followed him. Don Segundo mounted and made ready to move into the night. The drunk came close, seeming to have recovered the gift of speech.

"Listen, friend," he said and raised his sullen face, in which only the eyes were alive. "I'm gonna have this knife fixed for whenever you need me." The dull bully's mind could think of only one act of thanks: to offer his life to the other. "Now, shake."

"Sure thing," agreed Don Segundo, as calm as ever. "Put it there, brother."

And without further ado he went down the narrow street, while the half-breed stood seeming to struggle with a thought too great and radiant for him.

I went striding along beside Don Segundo, who kept his horse at a walk.

"You know that fellow?" he asked, muffling himself in his voluminous poncho with a leisurely gesture.

"Yes, sir. I know him well."

"Seems sort of foolish, don't he?"

■ Manuel Bandeira (1886–1968) *Brazil* (poems)

Manuel Bandeira was born in the north of Brazil, in Recife. His family moved to Rio de Janeiro when he was ten. In Rio, he attended a collegio and the Polytechnical School in São Paulo, where he studied architecture. Sick with turberculosis, in 1913 he went to Switzerland to a sanatorium near Davos-Platz. There he met the poet Paul Eluard, who was a patient in the same clinic. His early work was French Parnassian and symbolist—as were the poems of most of his Latin American and Iberian contemporaries. He found his own style in *The Dissolute Rhythm* (1924) and *Libertinism* (1930). The later ironic and semisurreal spirit of Guillaume Apollinaire was now in his poems, which became a model for later Brazilian masters. In *Territory*, he returned to the landscapes, people, and myths of rural northern Brazil. Eventually, he also moved to a more socially committed poetry.

Silence

In the complicit darkness of the room,
In the contact of my slow hands
with the substance of your flesh,
It was the same as silence.

It was a roaring of musical silence, 5
A grave feeling of enigma.
I was wounded by a grace
That came mortally sharp, and soft.

Ah, so soft and sharp!
It seemed to rise from death. 10
Silence was saying all
That before I could poorly guess.

Silence was your flesh,
Amber and naked body.
It is better to live in the mind 15
Than wait for tenderness.

TRANSLATED BY WILLIS BARNSTONE

Brazilian Tragedy

Misael, civil servant in the Ministry of Labor, 63 years old,
Knew Maria Elvira of the Grotto: prostitute, syphilitic, with ulcerated fingers, a pawned wedding ring and teeth in the last stages of decay.

Misael took Maria out of "the life," installed her in a two-storey house in Junction City, paid for the doctor, dentist, manicurist. . . . He gave her everything she wanted.

When Maria Elvira discovered she had a pretty mouth, she immediately took a boy-friend.

Misael didn't want a scandal. He could have beaten her, shot her, or stabbed her. He did none of these: they moved.

They lived like that for three years.

Each time Maria Elvira took a new boy-friend, they moved.

The lovers lived in Junction City. Boulder. On General Pedra Street, The Sties. The Brickyards. Glendale. Pay Dirt. On Marquês de Sapucaí Street in Villa Isabel. Niterói. Euphoria. In Junction City again, on Clapp Street. All Saints. Carousel. Edgewood. The Mines. Soldiers Home . . .

Finally, in Constitution Street, where Misael, bereft of sense and reason, killed her with six shots, and the police found her stretched out, supine, dressed in blue organdy.

TRANSLATED BY ELIZABETH BISHOP

■ Gabriela Mistral (1889–1957) *Chile* (poem)

TRANSLATED BY CHRISTIANE JACOX KYLE

Born in Chile as Lucila Godoy Alcayaga, the poet adopted the more euphonious name Gabriela Mistral. She took Gabriela from the Archangel Gabriel and Mistral from the mistral wind that blows over the south of France. In 1914, while a provincial schoolteacher in Chile, she issued her first poems, *Sonetos de la muerte* (The Sonnets of Death), which won her the Chilean National Prize for Poetry. These sonnets, along with some fifty stories and poems published in 1917, established her as an important national writer. Her lullabies and despairing love lyrics became extremely popular in her time. The poet speaks of elemental things—of nature, death, childbirth. Although she had no children of her own, maternity is an obsessive preoccupation in her poetry. Her best poems have a taut strength in their brevity and clarity. Yet, it is her very early series of the sonnets of death, included in *Desolación* (*Desolation,* 1992) that contains her most enduring poetry. She lived her later years in Long Island, New York, with her companion translator. For her educational labors on behalf of Indian adults and children in rural areas, she became known as the "Citizen of the Americas." In her lifetime, Gabriela Mistral received every external form of recognition a poet can have. In 1945, she was awarded the Nobel Prize for Literature. Her *Selected Poems* (1957) were translated by Langston Hughes.

FURTHER READING: Mistral, Gabriela. *Desolation,* 1922; *Tenderness,* 1924; *Feeling,* 1938; *Wine Press,* 1954; *Selected Poems.* Translated by Langston Hughes, 1957; *Complete Poems,* 1958.

Poems of the Saddest Mother

Cast Out

My father said he would throw me
out; he shouted at my mother that he
would cast me out this very night.

     The night is warm; by the clear light
of the stars, I could walk to the next   5
village; but what if he's born during
these hours? Maybe my sobs have
called him; maybe he would want to
come out to see my face. And he would
shiver in the raw wind, even though I   10
would cover him.

■ César Vallejo (1892–1938) *Peru* (poems)

Born in Santiago de Chuco, a remote mining town in Northern Peru, César Vallejo came from Spanish and Indian ancestors. Like the French poet Guillaume Apollinaire whom he admired and who claimed the pope as his father, Vallejo could claim at least one Spanish priest as a grandfather. He studied at the University of San Marcos in Lima (the oldest university in the Americas) and the University of Trujillo. After graduation, he taught elementary school and worked on his poems. In 1918, he published *Los heraldos negros* (*The Black Heralds*) in Lima, probably the first major book of truly modern poetry in the Spanish language in the Americas. This extraordinary volume of classically modeled poems, avant-garde in their lexicon, treats everyday life of family and the abused poor; Vallejo observes the black iron handiwork of a dispassionate God who distributes misery along the black coffin edges of the earth. The American poet Robert Bly, who, with another poet, James Wright, translated and introduced Vallejo into English, writes about the book: "It is a staggering book, sensual, prophetic, affectionate, wild. It has a kind of compassion for God, and compassion for death, who has so many problems, and it moves with incredible leaps of imagination. I think it is the greatest single collection of poems I have ever read." The first two lines of *The Black Heralds* in the poem "There Are Blows in Life" sets the powerful tone: "There are blows in life, so strong—I don't know!/Blows like the hatred of God."

On a visit in 1920 to the city of Trujillo, where he had studied, there was political turmoil. Vallejo was arrested on false charges (for which he was later exonerated) and spent nearly four months in jail. There, he wrote poems included in *Trilce* (1922), a radically experimental, surreal, humorous, and, at the same time, dark and tragic volume. The poems are direct, often difficult, and as powerful as any poems written in our century. (Only the Spanish poet Miguel Hernández, who died in 1942 in a Spanish prison at age thirty-two, composed verse of comparable strength in their surreal imagination, black-and-white imagery, immediacy, and searing humanity.) *Trilce,* despite its Joycean delight in creating outrageous neologisms and its obscurities that recall Paul Celan's last books of poems, elaborates the essential themes of family remembrances, poverty, and the great ideas of time and death, all with wit and depth. The next year, Vallejo lost his teaching job in Lima. In 1923, fearful and angry about his life in Peru, he obtained a job as a stringer in Paris for a Trujillo newspaper and left Peru, never to return.

In Paris, he married, was poor, even hungry, became a Communist, and twice visited the U.S.S.R., in 1928 and 1930. On the second visit, he interviewed the Russian poet Vladimir Mayakovsky in Moscow. On returning from Russia, he and his wife Georgette were deported from France. They spent two years (1930–1932) in Spain, during the furiously good days of the early thirties when the poets Federico García Lorca, Rafael Alberti,

Miguel Hernández, Vicente Aleixandre, Luis Cernuda, Jorge Guillén, and Pedro Salinas were creating the greatest flowering in Spanish poetry since the Golden Age. Soon, the Chilean Pablo Neruda would spend crucial years of his life in Madrid, writing his *Residencias* (*Residences*) and befriending Lorca, Aleixandre, and Hernández. With Vallejo, Neruda, and the Mexican poet Octavio Paz in Spain during those vital years, the best poets of Spain and Hispanic America came together in person and in poetic conspiracy. Vallejo wrote prolifically in Spain, completing, in addition to poems, a novel, *Tungsteno,* a play, *Lockout,* and a travel book about the Soviet Union, *Rusia.*

Back in Paris, César Vallejo wrote most of the poems for *Poemas humanos* (*Human Poems*), which, like all his poems after he left Peru in 1923, were to remain unpublished in book form until after his death. *Human Poems* contains verse interspersed with some prose poems. It has less experimentation than his earlier *Trilce,* which is a singular phenomenon among all books of poetry, but the same humanity and unsentimental sorrow persist. All the pathos and eloquent poignancy of the French nineteenth-century poet Charles Baudelaire (1821–1867), who wrote about the poor, the drunk, the prostitutes, the miserable of Paris, reappear in the Spanish poems of the Peruvian master. Like Baudelaire, who also led a bohemian life with little glamor and much sorrow, physical suffering, and sickness, Vallejo wrote himself out in Paris. When the Spanish Civil War (1936–1939) began, he threw himself into the Republican cause. In the second year of the war, he went to Spain and wrote *Spain, Let This Cup Pass from Me,* which, with *Human Poems,* was published posthumously in 1938, shortly after his death in the Parisian Clinique Aragon. Vallejo wrote a sonnet in Paris, "White Stone over a White Stone," in which he states that he will die one day in Paris, in the rain, on a day he can already remember. When death came, it took him, as it did Baudelaire, in his forty-sixth year. Vallejo, the poet of his generation of piercing compassion, caustic candor, and startling and original experimentation, died of undiagnosed causes in Paris on Holy Friday, April 15, 1938, during a rainfall.

FURTHER READING: Vallejo, César. *Black Heralds,* 1918; *Trilce,* 1922; *Human Poems,* 1938; *Spain, Let This Cup Pass from Me,* 1938; *Trilce.* Translated by David Smith, 1973; *Neruda and Vallejo: Selected Poems.* Translated by Robert Bly, John Knoepfle, and James Wright, 1971; *Spain, Take This Cup from Me.* Translated by Clayton Eshleman and José Rubia Barcia, 1974; *Spain, Take This Cup from Me.* Translated by Alvaro Cardona-Hine, 1972; *The Complete Posthumous Poetry.* Translated by Clayton Eshleman and José Rubia Barcia, 1978; *Selected Poems of César Vallejo.* Translated by E. Dorn and Gordon Brotherston, 1978; *Selected Poems.* Translated by H. R. Hays, 1981; *Black Heralds.* Translated by Kathleen Ross and Richard Schaaf, 1990; *Trilce.* Translated by Rebecca Seiferle, 1992.

There Are Blows in Life

There are blows in life, so strong . . . I don't know!
Blows like the hatred of God, as if before them
the undertow of everything suffered
puddled up in the soul . . . I don't know!

Just a few; but they are . . . They open dark trenches   5
on the fiercest face and on the strongest back.
Maybe they are the colts of barbarous Attilas
or the black heralds sent to us by Death.

They are deep plunges of the Christs in the soul,
of some worshipable faith that Destiny blasphemes.   10
Those bloody blows are the crackling sounds
of some bread burning up on us at the oven door.

And the man . . . poor . . . poor! He turns his eyes as
when over a shoulder a clapping of hands call us.
He turns his crazy eyes, and everything lived   15
puddles up like a pool of guilt in that glance.

There are blows in life, so strong . . . I don't know!

TRANSLATED BY WILLIS BARNSTONE

Agape[1]

Today no one has come to question me;
nor asked anything from me this evening.

I haven't seen even one cemetery flower
in so cheerful a procession of lights.
Forgive me, Lord, how little I have died!   5

This evening everyone, everyone passes me by
and no one begs or asks me for a thing.

I don't know what they're forgetting but it sits
wrong in my hands, like something alien.

I come to the door   10
and would like to scream at all of them:
If you're missing something, here it is!

Because through all the evenings of this life,

---

1. Agape is Greek for spiritual love.

I don't know what doors have slammed in a face
and my soul seizes on something alien.   *15*

Nobody came today;
and today how little I've died on this evening!

TRANSLATED BY TONY BARNSTONE AND WILLIS BARNSTONE

The Black Cup

The night is a cup of evil. A watchman's stinging
whistle pierces through it like a vibrating pin.
Listen, you little slut, how come, if you're already gone,
the wave is still black and still burning me up.

The Earth spreads coffin edges in its shadow.   *5*
Listen, you little tramp, don't come back.

My flesh swims, swims
in the cup of shadow that keeps on hurting me;
my flesh swims in it
as in the swampy heart of a woman.   *10*

Star coal . . . I've felt
the dry frictions of clay
fall across my diaphanous lotus.
Ah, woman! For you
this flesh of instinct exists. Ah, woman!   *15*

So, oh black chalice, even now with you gone
I choke on dust;
and more desires to drink paw inside my flesh.

TRANSLATED BY TONY BARNSTONE AND WILLIS BARNSTONE

In That Corner Where We Slept Together

In that corner where we slept together
so many nights, now I sit down
to take a walk. The bedstead of the dead lovers
was taken away, or something must have happened.

You came early for other matters   *5*
and now you're gone. It's the corner
where beside you I read one night

between your tender nipples
a story by Daudet. It is our lovers'
corner. Don't mistake it.   *10*

I've begun to remember the lost days
of summers, your coming and going,
small and fed up and pale in the rooms.

On this rainy night,
already far from them both, suddenly I jump up . . .   *15*
They are two doors coming open, shutting,
two doors that come and go with the wind
shadow   to   shadow.

TRANSLATED BY TONY BARNSTONE AND WILLIS BARNSTONE

Oh the Four Walls of the Cell

Oh the four walls of the cell,
the four whitening walls
inescapably facing themselves.

Hothouse of nerves, of terrible cracks,
my daily shackled limbs   *5*
drag from corner to corner.

Sweet keeper of unnumbered keys,
if you were here you'd see the time
of these four walls striking four.
We two would stand against them together,   *10*
more two than ever, and you wouldn't sob,
I swear it, my savior!

Ah the four walls of the cell.
I pity them and especially tonight
the two long ones somehow shaped   *15*
like mothers already dead
leading a child by the hand
down a slope of corrosive bromine.

And only I stay on here,
waving my right hand high (my only   *20*
working hand), seeking a third arm
to teach—between my where and my when—
the impotent majority of men.

TRANSLATED BY TONY BARNSTONE AND WILLIS BARNSTONE

White Stone over a White Stone

I will die in Paris during a heavy rain,
a day whose being already I recall.
I will die in Paris—and I won't escape—
perhaps a Thursday like today in fall.

It must be Thursday, since today, Thursday,   *5*
that I prose this verse, I've put my shoulder bones
on wrong, and turn—and never like today—
with all my road to see myself alone.

César Vallejo is dead. And everyone
beat him, though he never hurt anyone.   *10*
They clobbered him hard with a stick, also

hard with a rope. Among the witnesses
are the days Thursdays and the shoulder bones,
the rain, the roads, the loneliness . . .

TRANSLATED BY WILLIS BARNSTONE

Hat, Coat, Gloves

Before the Comédie Française is the Café
de la Regénce; in it behind the stair
there is a hidden room, a table and armchair.
When I come in, the lifeless dust stands up to play.
Between my lips turned rubbery, the smoldering tip   *5*
of a cigarette fumes. In the smoke lies the way
of two intense smokes, the thorax of the Café,
and in the thorax a rust deep with sorrow's lip.
It is important that the fall is caught in fall.
It is important the the fall consists of all   *10*
it shoots—clouds, months, its cheekbone and its wrinkle.
It is important to smell madly and guess then
how hot is the snow, how evasive the turtle,
the how so simple, lightning struck the when!

TRANSLATED BY WILLIS BARNSTONE

Our Daily Bread

I drink my breakfast . . . Damp earth
of the cemetery freezes the precious blood.
City of winter . . . the biting crusade
of a wheelbarrow appears, hauling
a feeling of starvation in chains.   5

I wish I could beat on all the doors,
and ask for somebody; and then
look at the poor, and, while they wept softly,
give bits of fresh bread to them.
And plunder the rich of their vineyards   10
with my two blessed hands
which, with one blow of light,
could blast nails from the Cross!

Eyelash of morning, Thou wilt not rise!
Give us our daily bread,   15
Lord . . . !
Every bone in me belongs to others;
and maybe I robbed them.

I came to take something for myself that maybe
was meant for some other man;   20
and so I start thinking that, if I had not been born,
another poor man could have drunk this coffee.
I feel like a dirty sneak-thief . . . Wherever I go!

And in this frigid hour, when the earth
transcends human dust and is so sorrowful,   25
I wish I could beat on all the doors
and beg pardon from someone,
and make bits of fresh bread with it
here, in the oven of my heart . . . !

TRANSLATED BY JAMES WRIGHT

Masses

When the battle ended
and the combatant was dead, a man came toward him
and said to him "Don't die, I love you too much!"
But the corpse, ay!, went on dying.

Two came up to him and repeated   5

"Don't leave us! Courage! Come back to life!"
But the corpse, ay!, went on dying.

Twenty came up to him, a hundred, a thousand, a hundred thousand,
clamoring, "So much love, and not able to do anything against death!"
But the corpse, ay!, went on dying.   *10*

Millions of people came around him,
with one common plea; the corpse gazed at them sadly, emotionally;
slowly he pulled his body up,
embraced the first man; and broke into a walk.

TRANSLATED BY TONY BARNSTONE AND WILLIS BARNSTONE

▪ Alfonsina Storni (1892–1938)
Switzerland/Argentina (poems)

TRANSLATED BY ALIKI BARNSTONE AND WILLIS BARNSTONE

Born in Sala Capriasca, Switzerland, of Italian-Swiss parents, Alfonsina
Storni lived in Argentina from the age of four. After the death of her father, she had various jobs to help support her family and worked as an actress, touring Argentina for a year. Then in 1910, she began to teach
elementary school in San Juan, Argentina. During this same year, she published her first poems and moved to Buenos Aires. In 1912, her illegitimate son was born. She supported herself and her son in Buenos Aires as
a journalist and held teaching positions in state schools. She was awarded
various prizes and, in 1923, was named professor of literature at the Normal School of Modern Languages. Then came disease. In 1935, she underwent cancer surgery for a breast tumor. In 1938, the cancer recurred
and on October 25 Alfonsina Storni walked into the ocean at Mar del Plata
and drowned. Storni's work developed from commonplace sentimental
poems with expected clichés to a poetry of surprise, ironic strength, and
gloomy vision. Indeed, she has the qualities of the Russian poet Anna
Akhmatova in combining extreme sensitivity with terrible power. Like
Vladimir Mayakovsky, she left a suicide poem that captures her various
moods and strengths. Not to be deprived of savage humor even in the
midst of death, she writes: ". . . Thank you. Oh, one request:/if he telephones again/tell him not to keep trying, for I have left. . . . "

FURTHER READING: Storni, Alfonsina. *The Disquiet of the Rosebush*, 1916; *Selected Poems*,
1940; *Poetry*, 1948.

My Sister

It's ten. Evening. The room is in half light.
My sister's sleeping, her hand on her chest; although
her face is very white, her bed entirely white,
the light, as if knowing, almost doesn't show.

She sinks into the bed the way pinkish fruit   5
does, into the deep mattress of soft grass.
Wind brushes her breasts, lifts them resolutely
chaste, measuring seconds as they pass.

I cover her tenderly with the white spread
and keep her lovely hands safe from the air.   10
On tiptoes I close all the doors near her bed,
leave the windows open, pull the curtain, prepare

for night. A lot of noise outside. Enough to drown
in: quarreling men, women with the juiciest
gossip. Hatred drifting upward, storekeepers shouting down   15
below. O voices, stop! Don't touch her nest.

Now my sister is weaving her silk cocoon
like a skillful worm. Her cocoon is a dream.
She weaves a pod with threads of a gold gleam.
Her life is spring. I am the summer afternoon.   20

She has only fifteen Octobers in her eyes
and so the eyes are bright, clear, and clean.
She thinks that storks from strange lands fly unseen,
leaving blond children with small red feet. Who tries

to come in? Is it you, now, the good wind?   25
You want to see her? Come in. But first cool
my forehead a second. Don't freeze the pool
of unwild dreams I sense in her. Undisciplined

they want to flood in and stay here, like you,
staring at that whiteness, at those tidy cheeks,   30
those fine circles under her eyes that speak
simplicity. Wind, you would see them and, falling to

your knees, cry. If you love her at all, be good
to her, for she will flee from wounding light.
Watch your word and intention. Her soul like wood   35
or wax is shaped, but rubbing makes a blight.

Be like that star which in the night stares at
her, whose eye is filtered through glassy thread.
That star rubs her eyelashes, turning like a cat
quiet in the sky, not to wake her in her bed.   40

Fly, if you can, among her snowy trees.
Pity her soul! She is immaculate.
Pity her soul! I know everything, but she's
like heaven and knows nothing. Which is her fate.

Lighthouse in the Night

The sky a black sphere,
the sea a black disk.

The lighthouse opens
its solar fan on the coast.

Spinning endlessly at night,   5
whom is it searching for

when the mortal heart
looks for me in my chest?

Look at the black rock
where it is nailed down.   10

A crow digs endlessly
but no longer bleeds.

I Am Going to Sleep (Suicide Poem)

Teeth of flowers, hairnet of dew,
hands of herbs, you, perfect wet nurse,
prepare the earthly sheets for me
and the down quilt of weeded moss.

I am going to sleep, my nurse, put me to bed.   5
Set a lamp at my headboard;
a constellation; whatever you like;
all are good: lower it a bit.

Leave me alone: you hear the buds breaking through . . .
a celestial foot rocks you from above   10
and a bird traces a pattern for you

so you'll forget . . . Thank you. Oh, one request:
if he telephones again
tell him not to keep trying, for I have left . . .

■ Vicente Huidobro (1893–1948)
Chile (poem)

TRANSLATED BY PAUL BLACKBURN

Poet and theoretician of the Dada-like experimental literary movement called *Creationism,* Vicente Huidobro changed modern poetry in Spanish. Unlike Rubén Darío, who gave Spanish letters a sugary taste of "purist" French Parnassian poetry under the misnomer of modernismo, Vicente Huidobro, in the Poundian sense, gave us the new, and he went further than Pound—as did the European avant-garde generally in rejecting the immediate past and turning poetic practice upside down. Octavio Paz speaks of Huidobro as the "magnificent bird," commenting: "He is everywhere and nowhere. He is the invisible oxygen of our poetry."

Huidobro was born García Fernández in Santiago, Chile. (Like his fellow Chilean poets Gabriela Mistral and Pablo Neruda, he assumed a more glamorous poetic name.) In 1916, he went to Europe and became one of the Paris school of writers, writing in both French and Spanish. He wrote poetry, plays, and novels, and even collaborated on a novel with the French avant-garde sculptor and painter Hans Arp. He was painted by the great modern painters Pablo Picasso, Robert Delaunay, and Juan Gris, who were, along with Guillaume Apollinaire, Jacques Lipchitz, Max Jacob, and Pierre Reverdy, his friends. He invented, or claimed to invent, Creationism and spent much of his later life writing manifestos about and lecturing on Creationism. He also feuded with fellow writers about his doctrine in Europe, and, on his triumphant return to Chile in 1933, he feuded with Pablo Neruda.

In Creationism, words radically create their own realities, which then clash and interact with other realities. Huidobro's Creationism—with its revolutionary, spoofing, radically unreferential symbolism and unpunctuated typography borrowed from Apollinaire—lies somewhere in the frame of the many similar experimental movements of Dadaism, Spanish *ultraísmo,* and surrealism. The poet in parachutes, as he describes himself in *Altazor,* goes to every extreme, breaks every rule and convention, and attempts a visionary transcendence in his parachute, which falls and rises at the same time. His literary monument is the book *Altazor.* In his very last years of seclusion near Cartegena on the coast of Chile, he wrote simple and moving verses—one might say wisdom poems about death—but always with the humor, irony, and outrageous imagery that pervade his poetry.

Huidobro's American editor David Guss describes the poet as the "animist, looking for God in trees and waves. The 'magician' imploring us to fly with him. The 'antipoet' giving us a new language. The one of the endless hunger 'to be the first free man, the first to break all the chains.'" The notion of chance, experiment, and buoyant faith in futurity is all contained in one line from Vicente Huidobro's 1925 *Manifestos,* "The wind points my flute toward the future."

FURTHER READING: Huidobro, Vincente. *Altazor,* 1931; *Complete Works,* 1964; *The Selected Poetry of Vicente Huidobro.* Translated by David M. Guss, 1981.

Glances and Souvenirs

    The sea
raising the sighs of travellers
runs in behind its waves swept by the wind
Infinity looks for a gull to hold aloft
one point of support, smooth and logical.   5
As we shall do

The sky clacks full of the wings it loves
        while I
look for my poem on foot
A star crunches like the wheel of   10
a car carrying away
the last souvenirs.

      Nothing will be encountered
The well of things lost will never be filled, never
with the glances and the echoes   15
      which move away
        above the fog
          and its great beasts.

▪ Miguel Angel Asturias (1899–1974)
Guatemala (story)

TRANSLATED BY HARDIE ST. MARTIN

Born in Guatemala and raised in the nightmarish times of dictator Estrada Cabrera, Miguel Angel Asturias went to London and Paris to study and there discovered Maya literature. He translated the Maya *Popol Vuh* into Spanish; Paul Valéry wrote the preface for his *Legends of Guatemala* (1930). He worked as a journalist, joined the diplomatic corps, and eventually was ambassador to El Salvador and to France. *El Señor Presidente* (1946), his grand uneven work, published in Mexico, depicts the prototypical Latin American dictatorship. It initiated a series of books on the perennial Latin

American dictator, including Gabriel García Márquez's *Autumn of the Patriarch* (1975). Asturias's master political novel was eventually translated widely and gained him world fame. In his highly praised second novel, *Man of Maize* (1949), Asturias brings Maya myths into a contemporary social setting. As such, he established a literary practice of resurrecting dramatic tales of Indian culture; years later, his Mexican neighbor, Carlos Fuentes, elaborated a tale of fearful mystery of the Maya raingod in his story "Chac-Mool." A prolific writer in many genres, including children's books, for many years Miguel Angel Asturias was a dominant figure in Latin American fiction. One of his last works was *The Bejeweled Boy* (tr. 1972), an allusive novel, mystical and rich in Guatemalan legend. His short stories appear in *A Week-end in Guatemala* (1956). He was awarded the Nobel Prize in 1967. He died in Madrid in 1974.

FURTHER READING: Asturias, Miguel Angel. *El Señor Presidente*, 1946, tr. 1963; *Man of Maize*, 1949; *Strong Wind*, 1950, tr. 1968; *The Green Pope*, 1954, tr. 1971; *The Eyes of the Interred*, 1955, tr. 1973; *A Week-end in Guatemala*, 1956; *The Bejeweled Boy*, tr. 1972.

Legend of "El Cadejo"

> *And El Cadejo, who steals girls with long braids and knots the manes of horses, makes his appearance in the valley.*

In the course of time, Mother Elvira of St. Francis, abbess of the monastery of St. Catherine, would be the novice who cut out the hosts in the convent of the Conception, a girl noted for her beauty and manner of speaking, so ingenuous that on her lips the word was a flower of gentleness and love.

From a large window without glass, the novice used to watch the flights of leaves dried by the summer's heat, the trees putting on their flowers and ripe fruit dropping in the orchards next to the convent, through the part that was in ruins, where the foliage, hiding the wounded walls and the open roofs, transformed the cells and the cloisters into paradises filled with the scent of *búcaro* clay and wild roses; bowers of feasting, as the chroniclers recorded, where nuns were replaced by pigeons with pink feet and their canticles by the warble of the cimarron mockingbird.

Outside her window, in the collapsed rooms, the warm shade, where butterflies worked the dust of their wings into silk, joined the silence of the courtyard, interrupted by the coming and going of the lizards, and the soft aroma of the leaves that multiplied the tender feelings of the trees whose roots were coiled into the very ancient walls.

And inside, in the sweet company of God, trimming the peel from the fruit of angels to disclose the meat and seed that is the Body of Christ, long as the orange's medulla — *vere tu es Deus absconditus!* —, Elvira of St. Francis reunited her spirit and her flesh to the house of her childhood, with its heavy locks and its light roses, its doors that split sobs into the loose seams of the wind, its walls reflected in the troughs of the fountains like clouds of breath on clean glass.

The voices of the city broke the peace of her window: last-minute blues of the passenger that hears the movement of the port at sailing time; a man's laughter as he brings his galloping horse to a stop, a cart wheeling by, or a child crying.

Horse, cart, man, child passed before her eyes, evoked in country settings, under skies whose tranquil appearance put under a spell the wise eyes of the fountain troughs sitting around the water with the long-suffering air of old women servants.

And the images were accompanied by odors. The sky smelled like a sky, the child like a child, the fields like fields, the cart like hay, the horse like an old rosebush, the man like a saint, the troughs like shadows, the shadows like Sunday rest and the Lord's day of rest like fresh washing. . . .

Dark was coming on. The shadows erased their thought, luminous mixture of dust particles swimming in a shaft of sunlight. The bells drew their lips towards the cup of evening without a sound. Who talks of kisses? The wind shook up the heliotropes. Heliotropes or hippocampi? And the hummingbirds quenched their desire for God in streams of flowers. Who talks of kisses?

The tap of heels hurrying brought her to herself. Their sound frilled along the corridor like drumsticks.

Could she be hearing right? Could it be the man with the long eyelashes who came by late on Fridays for the hosts to take them nine towns away from there, to the Valley of the Virgin, where a pleasant hermitage rested on a hill's top?

They called him the poppy-man. The wind moved in his feet. When the sound of his goat's footsteps stopped, there he would be, like a ghost: hat in hand, tiny boots, a goldish color, wrapped in his blue greatcoat; and he waited for the wafer boxes in the doorway.

Yes, it was he; but this time he rushed in looking very frightened, as if to prevent some catastrophe.

"Miss, oh miss!" he came in shouting, "they're going to cut off your hair! They're going to cut it off!"

When she saw him coming in, livid and elastic, the novice sprang to her feet intending to reach the door. But, wearing shoes she had charitably inherited from a paralytic nun who had worn them in life, when she heard his shout, she felt as if the nun who had spent her life motionless had stepped on her feet, and she couldn't move a step. . . .

. . . A sob, like a star, trembled in her throat. Birds scissored the twilight among the grey, crippled ruins. Two giant eucalyptus trees were saying prayers of penance.

Bound to the feet of a corpse, unable to move, she wept disconsolately, swallowing her tears silently as sick people whose organs begin to dry up and turn cold, bit by bit. She felt as if she were dead, covered with dirt; she felt that in her grave—her orphan's dress being filled with clay—rosebushes of white words bloomed and, little by little, her dismay changed into a quiet sort of happiness. Walking rosebushes, the nuns were cutting off one another's roses to dress the altars of the Virgin and the roses became the month of May, a spider web of fragrances that trapped Our Lady like a fly of light.

But the sensation of her body's flowering after death was a shortlived happiness.

Like a kite that suddenly runs out of string among the clouds, the weight of her braid pulled her headlong, with all her clothes, into hell. The mystery was in her braid. Sum of anguished instants. She lost consciousness for as long as a couple of her sighs lasted and felt herself back on earth only when she had almost reached the boiling pit where devils bubble. A fan of possible realities opened around her: the night sweetened with puff paste, pine trees that smell like altars, the pollen of life in the hair of the air, formless, colorless cat that scratches the waters of the fountain troughs and unsettles old papers.

The window and she herself became filled with heaven. . . .

"Miss, when I receive Holy Communion, God tastes like your hands!" the one in the greatcoat whispered, laying the grille of his lashes over the coals of his eyes.

The novice pulled her hands away from the hosts when she heard the blasphemy. No, it wasn't a dream! Then she touched her arms, her shoulders, her neck, her face, her braid. She held her breath one moment, long as a century, when she felt her braid. No, it wasn't a dream! Under the warm handful of hair she came alive, aware of her womanly charms, accompanied in her diabolic nuptials by the poppy-man and a candle burning at the end of the room, oblong as a coffin. The light supported the impossible reality of the lover, who stretched out his arms like a Christ who had turned into a bat in a viaticum, and this was her own flesh! She closed her eyes to escape, wrapped in her blindness, from that vision from hell, from the man who caressed her down to where she was a woman, simply by being a man—the most abominable of conscupiscences!—; but as soon as she lowered her round pale eyelids the paralytic nun seemed to step from her shoes, soaked in tears, and she quickly opened them. She tore through the darkness, opened her eyes, left their deep interior with their pupils restless as mice in a trap, wild, insensible, the color drained out of her cheeks, caught between the stertor of a strange agony she carried in her feet and her braid's stream of live coals twisted like an invisible flame on her back.

And that's the last she knew about it. Like someone under a spell that can't be broken, with a sob on her tongue which seemed to be filled with poison, like her heart, she broke away from the presence of the corpse and the man, half mad, spilling the wafers about, in search of her scissors and, finding them, she cut off the braid and, free of the spell, she fled in search of the sure refuge of the Mother Superior, no longer feeling the nun's feet on hers. . . .

But when the braid fell it was no longer a braid: it moved, undulated over the tiny mattress of hosts scattered on the floor.

The poppy-man turned to look for light. Tears quivered on his eyelashes like the last little flames on the black of the match that is about to go out. He slid along the side of the wall with bated breath, without disturbing the shadows, without making a sound, desperate to reach the flame he believed would be his salvation. But his measured step soon dissolved into a flight of fear. The headless reptile was moving past the sacred leaf-pile of hosts and filing towards him. It dragged itself right under his feet like the black blood of a dead animal and suddenly, as he was about to take hold of the light, leaped with the speed of water that runs free and light to coil itself like a whip around the candle which it caused to weep until it consumed itself for the soul of him who was being extinguished, along with it, forever. And so the poppy-man, for whom cactus plants still weep white tears, reached eternity.

The devil had passed like a breath through the braid which fell lifeless on the floor when the candle's flame went out.

And at midnight, changed into a long animal—twice as long as a ram by full moon, big as a weeping willow by new moon—with goat's hoofs, rabbit's ears and a bat's face, the poppy-man dragged down to hell the black braid of the novice who, in the course of time, would be Mother Elvira of St. Francis—that's how "El Cadejo" was born—while, on her knees in her cell, smiling like an angel, she dreamed of the lily and the mystic lamb.

■ Jorge Luis Borges (1899–1986) *Argentina* (parables, stories, poems)

Author of stories, poems, and essays, the great writer Jorge Luis Borges was born in Buenos Aires into a family whose ancestors included military heroes of Argentina's independence. His father, Jorge Guillermo Borges, however, was a gentle academic and the young boy grew up in the "paradise" of his father's ample personal library. He learned English natively from his paternal grandmother, Fanny Haslin, who was from Northumberland in England. As a child, he knew he was to be a writer, and at seven and eight he was rewriting Greek mythology in English and composing his own stories; at nine he published a translation of Oscar Wilde's fairy tale "The Happy Prince." His father retired from teaching because of failing eyesight (a problem his son was to inherit), and, in 1914, he moved the family to Geneva, where the younger Borges learned French and eventually German. His first publication was in French. In Geneva, Borges discovered "modern poetry" through Walt Whitman, whom he first encountered in German translation; Whitman, whom he later translated into Spanish, was to be a decisive influence in his poetry. He also developed his lifelong passion for the writings of the German philosopher Schopenhauer (1788–1860); Borges's metaphysical orientation and his meditations on time, being, and the "other" are related to his readings of Schopenhauer as well as to other philosophers, such as Baruch Spinoza (1632–1677), the reading of whose works became, to use his words, "his habit."

In 1919, the family moved to Spain where Borges, now twenty-one, became an active initiator of the avant-garde poetic movement of *ultraísmo*. When he returned to Argentina two years later, after seven formative years in Europe, he left *ultraísmo* and discovered his native city of Buenos Aires, which he documents in the poems of *Fervor of Buenos Aires* (1923). During the next decade, he met and collaborated with Victoria Ocampo, who had founded the famous literary review *Sur* (*South*), and for which he wrote book and film reviews and poems, edited manuscripts, and did translations. Borges was the first to translate into Spanish a volume of the stories of Franz Kafka, with whom he had a spiritual and literary affinity. He wrote seminal essays, which often read like philosophical fables or erudite stories, that he eventually gathered in *Other Inquisitions* (1937–1952) and in the fascinating and outrageous volume concerning "fictional historic figures," which he entitled *A Universal History of Infamy*. In 1930, he met Adolfo Bioy Casares, who would be his lifelong friend and literary partner. With Bioy Casares, he compiled original anthologies of the fantastic and also coauthored a series of comic detective books under the pseudonymn of H. Bustos Domecq.

When his father died in 1938, to earn his living, Borges became an assistant librarian in a modest public library. The same year, after hitting his head against an open stairway window and falling down the stairs, he nearly died from the subsequent septicemia that set in after a botched operation. On recovering, he wrote his first story, "El sur" ("The South"), which takes place either in the hospital under a surgeon's knife, or in the pampas during a knife fight among gauchos, or in a dream. His years in the library left him free to increase his learning, to write such stories as "The Library at Babylon," and, in the next decade, to compose most of the erudite, fantastic, and outlaw stories in *Ficciones* (1944) and *The Aleph* (1949), which were to revolutionize the Latin American and world short story.

A strong opponent of the Nazis during World War II, which was not a popular stance in the Argentina of those years, he equally opposed Juan Perón, who brought in a dictatorship (1946–1955) modeled after Mussolini's fascist blackshirts. Borges was dismissed from his library post and, by necessity, began a new career as public speaker in Buenos Aires and other cities, lecturing on his favorite ideas and literary and philosophical figures. Some of these essential talks would appear in *Seven Nights* (1977). They represent the oral or spoken Borges, who figures in the many brilliant *charlas* (chats) or dialogues, which have been gathered in books of interviews.

After the fall of Perón, Borges, now virtually blind, was appointed director of the National Library and began his study of Anglo-Saxon. Then, for nearly twenty years he taught Old English at the University of Buenos Aires, traveled frequently abroad, lectured, and was in residence at various American universities, including the University of Texas, Indiana University, and Michigan State. He received honorary degrees from the leading universities of Europe and the United States. In 1961, Borges shared the First Formentor Prize with Samuel Beckett, and prizes came plentifully, including the Cervantes Prize bestowed on him by King Juan Carlos of Spain and knighthood from the English monarchy. He died in Geneva, Switzerland, where on his deathbed he married María Kodama, his friend and collaborator for many years.

Along with the great modernists Kafka, Joyce, and Beckett, Borges transcends academic categories. He is one of the century's most profound and influential thinkers and writers. His themes and intellectual fancy have had a deep influence on a younger generation of experimental writers and filmmakers. Julio Cortázar's experimental novel *Hopscotch* was structured on Borges's notions in "The Garden of Bifurcating Paths" of the labyrinths of language and time that go off on infinitely tangential paths. Umberto Eco's internationally best-selling novel *The Name of the Rose* shares Borges's interest in obscure religious sects, creates its own version of the labyrinthine library in Borges's "The Library of Babylon," and even models the murderer of the novel, a blind librarian, on Borges himself. Borges was more than one person, as he suggests in his famous parable "Borges and I." He is the gentle, endlessly erudite academic and jeweler of language, a narrator named Borges trapped in his own stories, the author as maker and god, and, for generations of readers and artists, a Protean figure inhabiting the labyrinths of dream.

FURTHER READING: Borges, Jorge Luis. *Fervor of Buenos Aires*, 1923; *Ficciones*, 1944; *The Aleph*, 1949; *Other Inquisitions*, 1960, tr. 1964; *Labyrinths*, 1960; *A Personal Anthology*, 1961. Translated by Anthony Kerrigan, 1967; *The Book of Imaginary Beings*, 1967; *In Praise of Darkness*, 1969. Translated by Norman Thomas Di Giovanni, 1973; *Selected Poems*, 1923–1967. Translated by Norman Thomas Di Giovanni, 1981; *Dr. Brodie's Report*, tr. 1972; *The Gold of the Tigers: Selected Later Poems*, 1972; *The Book of Sand*, 1975. Burgin, Richard. *Conversations with Borges*, 1969. Barnstone, Willis. *Borges at Eighty: Conversations*, 1982; *With Borges on an Ordinary Evening in Buenos Aires*, 1993. Barrenechea, A. M. *Jorge Luis Borges*, 1965. Christ, Ronald. *Jorge Luis Borges*, 1969. Alazraki, Jaime. *Jorge Luis Borges*, 1971.

Borges and I

It's to the other man, to Borges, that things happen. I walk along the streets of Buenos Aires, stopping now and then—perhaps out of habit—to look at the arch of an old entranceway or a grillwork gate; of Borges I get news through the mail and glimpse his name among a committee of professors or in a dictionary of biography. I have a taste for hourglasses, maps, eighteenth-century typography, the roots of words, the smell of coffee, and Stevenson's prose; the other man shares these likes, but in a showy way that turns them into stagy mannerisms. It would be an exaggeration to say that we are on bad terms; I live, I let myself live, so that Borges can weave his tales and poems, and those tales and poems are my justification. It is not hard for me to admit that he has managed to write a few worthwhile pages, but these pages cannot save me, perhaps because what is good no longer belongs to anyone—not even the other man—but rather to speech or tradition. In any case, I am fated to become lost once and for all, and only some moment of myself will survive in the other man. Little by little, I have been surrendering everything to him, even though I have evidence of his stubborn habit of falsification and exaggerating. Spinoza held that all things try to keep on being themselves; a stone wants to be a stone and the tiger, a tiger. I shall remain in Borges, not in myself (if it is so that I am someone), but I recognize myself less in his books than in those of others or than in the laborious tuning of a guitar. Years ago, I tried ridding myself of him and I went from myths of the outlying slums of the city to games with time and infinity, but those games are now part of Borges and I will have to turn to other things. And so, my life is a running away, and I lose everything and everything is left to oblivion or to the other man.

Which of us is writing this page I don't know.

TRANSLATED BY ANTHONY KERRIGAN

Kafka and His Precursors

Once I planned to make a survey of Kafka's precursors. At first I thought he was as singular as the fabulous phoenix; when I knew him better I thought I recognized his voice, or his habits, in the texts of various literatures and various ages. I shall record a few of them here, in chronological order.

The first is Zeno's paradox against movement. A moving body at A (declares Aristotle) will not be able to reach point B, because before it does, it must cover half of the distance between the two, and before that, half of the half, and before that, half of the half of the half, and so on to infinity; the formula of this famous problem is, exactly, that of *The Castle;* and the moving body and the arrow and Achilles are the first Kafkian characters in literature.

In the second text that happened to come to my attention, the affinity is not of form but rather of tone. It is an apologue by Han Yu, a prose writer of the ninth century, and it is included in the admirable *Anthologie raisonnée de la littérature chinoise* by Margouliès (1948). This is the paragraph I marked, a mysterious and tranquil one:

It is universally admitted that the unicorn is a supernatural being and one of good omen; this is declared in the odes, in the annals, in the biographies of illustrious men, and in other texts of unquestioned authority. Even the women and children of the populace know that the unicorn constitutes a favorable presage. But this animal is not one of the domestic animals, it is not always easy to find, it does not lend itself to classification. It is not like the horse or the bull, the wolf or the deer. And therefore we could be in the presence of the unicorn and we would not know for certain that it was one. We know that a certain animal with a mane is a horse, and that one with horns is a bull. We do not know what the unicorn is like.[1]

The third text proceeds from a more foreseeable source: the writings of Kierkegaard. The mental affinity of both writers is known to almost everyone; what has not yet been brought out, as far as I know, is that Kierkegaard, like Kafka, abounded in religious parables on contemporary and middle-class themes. Lowrie, in his *Kierkegaard* (Oxford University Press, 1938), mentions two. One is the story of a forger who examines Bank of England notes while under constant surveillance; in the same way, God must have been suspicious of Kierkegaard and must have entrusted him with a mission simply because He knew that he was accustomed to evil. Expeditions to the North Pole are the subject of the other. Danish clergymen had announced from their pulpits that to participate in those expeditions would be beneficial for the eternal salvation of the soul. However, they admitted that it was difficult and perhaps impossible to reach the Pole, and that not everyone could undertake such an adventure. Finally, they announced that any journey—from Denmark to London, say, by ship—or a Sunday outing in a hackney coach, was in fact a real expedition to the North Pole.

The fourth prefiguration I found is the poem "Fears and Scruples," by Browning, which was published in 1876. A man has, or thinks he has, a famous friend. He has never seen this friend, and the latter has not yet been able to help him, but he is reputed to have very noble qualities, and letters he has written are circulated. Some question his good qualities, and handwriting experts assert that the letters are apocryphal. In the last verse the man asks: "What if this friend happens to be—God?"

My notes also include two short stories. One is from the *Histoires désobligeantes*, by Léon Bloy, and tells of people who have a collection of atlases, globes, train schedules, and trunks, and then die without ever having left the town where they were born. The other is entitled "Carcassonne" and is by Lord Dunsany. An invincible army of warriors departs from an enormous castle, subjugates kingdoms, sees monsters, conquers deserts and mountains, but never arrives at Carcassonne, although the men catch sight of the city once from afar. (This story is the exact opposite of the

---

1. The failure to recognize the sacred animal and its opprobrious or casual death at the hands of the populace are traditional themes in Chinese literature. See the last chapter of Jung's *Psychologie und Alchemie* (Zurich, 1944), which includes two curious illustrations.

other one; in the first story, a city is never departed from; in the second, a city is never reached.)

If I am not mistaken, the heterogeneous selections I have mentioned resemble Kafka's work: if I am not mistaken, not all of them resemble each other, and this fact is the significant one. Kafka's idiosyncrasy, in greater or lesser degree, is present in each of these writings, but if Kafka had not written we would not perceive it; that is to say, it would not exist. The poem "Fears and Scruples" by Robert Browning is like a prophecy of Kafka's stories, but our reading of Kafka refines and changes our reading of the poem perceptibly. Browning did not read it as we read it now. The word "precursor" is indispensable in the vocabulary of criticism, but one should try to purify it from every connotation of polemic or rivalry. The fact is that each writer *creates* his precursors. His work modifies our conception of the past, as it will modify the future.[2] In this correlation the identity or plurality of men matters not at all. The first Kafka of *Betrachtung* is less a precursor of the Kafka of the shadowy myths and atrocious institutions than is Browning or Lord Dunsany.

TRANSLATED BY RUTH L. C. SIMMS

The South

The man who landed in Buenos Aires in 1871 bore the name of Johannes Dahlmann and he was a minister in the Evangelical Church. In 1939, one of his grandchildren, Juan Dahlmann, was secretary of a municipal library on Calle Córdoba, and he considered himself profoundly Argentinian. His maternal grandfather had been that Francisco Flores, of the Second Line-Infantry Division, who had died on the frontier of Buenos Aires, run through with a lance by Indians from Catriel; in the discord inherent between his two lines of descent, Juan Dahlmann (perhaps driven to it by his Germanic blood) chose the line represented by his romantic ancestor, his ancestor of the romantic death. An old sword, a leather frame containing the daguerreotype of a blank-faced man with a beard, the dash and grace of certain music, the familiar strophes of *Martín Fierro,* the passing years, boredom and solitude, all went to foster this voluntary, but never ostentatious nationalism. At the cost of numerous small privations, Dahlmann had managed to save the empty shell of a ranch in the South which had belonged to the Flores family; he continually recalled the image of the balsamic eucalyptus trees and the great rose-colored house which had once been crimson. His duties, perhaps even indolence, kept him in the city. Summer after summer he contented himself with the abstract idea of possession and with

2. See T. S. Eliot, *Points of View* (1941), pages 25–26.

the certitude that his ranch was waiting for him on a precise site in the middle of the plain. Late in February, 1939, something happened to him.

Blind to all fault, destiny can be ruthless at one's slightest distraction. Dahlmann had succeeded in acquiring, on that very afternoon, an imperfect copy of Weil's edition of *The Thousand and One Nights*. Avid to examine this find, he did not wait for the elevator but hurried up the stairs. In the obscurity, something brushed by his forehead: a bat, a bird? On the face of the woman who opened the door to him he saw horror engraved, and the hand he wiped across his face came away red with blood. The edge of a recently painted door which someone had forgotten to close had caused this wound. Dahlmann was able to fall asleep, but from the moment he awoke at dawn the savor of all things was atrociously poignant. Fever wasted him and the pictures in *The Thousand and One Nights* served to illustrate nightmares. Friends and relatives paid him visits and, with exaggerated smiles, assured him that they thought he looked fine. Dahlmann listened to them with a kind of feeble stupor and he marveled at their not knowing that he was in hell. A week, eight days passed, and they were like eight centuries. One afternoon, the usual doctor appeared, accompanied by a new doctor, and they carried him off to a sanitarium on the Calle Ecuador, for it was necessary to X-ray him. Dahlmann, in the hackney coach which bore them away, thought that he would, at last, be able to sleep in a room different from his own. He felt happy and communicative. When he arrived at his destination, they undressed him, shaved his head, bound him with metal fastenings to a stretcher; they shone bright lights on him until he was blind and dizzy, auscultated him, and a masked man stuck a needle into his arm. He awoke with a feeling of nausea, covered with a bandage, in a cell with something of a well about it; in the days and nights which followed the operation he came to realize that he had merely been, up until then, in a suburb of hell. Ice in his mouth did not leave the least trace of freshness. During these days Dahlmann hated himself in minute detail: he hated his identity, his bodily necessities, his humiliation, the beard which bristled upon his face. He stoically endured the curative measures, which were painful, but when the surgeon told him he had been on the point of death from septicemia, Dahlmann dissolved in tears of self-pity for his fate. Physical wretchedness and the incessant anticipation of horrible nights had not allowed him time to think of anything so abstract as death. On another day, the surgeon told him he was healing and that, very soon, he would be able to go to his ranch for convalescence. Incredibly enough, the promised day arrived.

Reality favors symmetries and slight anachronisms: Dahlmann had arrived at the sanitarium in a hackney coach and now a hackney coach was to take him to the Constitución station. The first fresh tang of autumn, after the summer's oppressiveness, seemed like a symbol in nature of his rescue and release from fever and death. The city, at seven in the morning, had not lost that air of an old house lent it by the night; the streets seemed like long vestibules, the plazas were like patios. Dahlmann recognized the city with joy on the edge of vertigo: a second before his eyes registered the phenomena themselves, he recalled the corners, the billboards, the modest variety of Buenos Aires. In the yellow light of the new day, all things returned to him.

Every Argentine knows that the South begins at the other side of Rivadavia. Dahlmann was in the habit of saying that this was no mere convention, that whoever crosses this street enters a more ancient and sterner world. From inside the carriage he sought out, among the new buildings, the iron grille window, the brass knocker, the arched door, the entranceway, the intimate patio.

At the railroad station he noted that he still had thirty minutes. He quickly recalled that in a café on the Calle Brazil (a few dozen feet from Yrigoyen's house) there was an enormous cat which allowed itself to be caressed as if it were a disdainful divinity. He entered the café. There was the cat, asleep. He ordered a cup of coffee, slowly stirred the sugar, sipped it (this pleasure had been denied him in the clinic), and thought, as he smoothed the cat's black coat, that this contact was an illusion and that the two beings, man and cat, were as good as separated by a glass, for man lives in time, in succession, while the magical animal lives in the present, in the eternity of the instant.

Along the next to the last platform the train lay waiting. Dahlmann walked through the coaches until he found one almost empty. He arranged his baggage in the network rack. When the train started off, he took down his valise and extracted, after some hesitation, the first volume of *The Thousand and One Nights*. To travel with this book, which was so much a part of the history of his ill-fortune, was a kind of affirmation that his ill-fortune had been annulled; it was a joyous and secret defiance of the frustrated forces of evil.

Along both sides of the train the city dissipated into suburbs; this sight, and then a view of the gardens and villas, delayed the beginning of his reading. The truth was that Dahlmann read very little. The magnetized mountain and the genie who swore to kill his benefactor are—who would deny it?—marvelous, but not so much more than the morning itself and the mere fact of being. The joy of life distracted him from paying attention to Scheherazade and her superfluous miracles. Dahlmann closed his book and allowed himself to live.

Lunch—the bouillon served in shining metal bowls, as in the remote summers of childhood—was one more peaceful and rewarding delight.

Tomorrow I'll wake up at the ranch, he thought, and it was as if he was two men at a time: the man who traveled through the autumn day and across the geography of the fatherland, and the other one, locked up in a sanitarium and subject to methodical servitude. He saw unplastered brick houses, long and angled, timelessly watching the trains go by; he saw horsemen along the dirt roads; he saw gullies and lagoons and ranches; he saw great luminous clouds that resembled marble; and all these things were accidental, casual, like dreams of the plain. He also thought he recognized trees and crop fields; but he would not have been able to name them, for his actual knowledge of the countryside was quite inferior to his nostalgic and literary knowledge.

From time to time he slept, and his dreams were animated by the impetus of the train. The intolerable white sun of high noon had already become the yellow sun which precedes nightfall, and it would not be long before it would turn red. The railroad car was now also different; it was not the same as the one which had quit the station siding at Constitución; the plain and the hours had transfigured it. Outside, the moving shadow of the railroad car stretched toward the horizon. The elemental earth was not perturbed either by settlements or other signs of humanity. The country was vast but at the same time intimate and, in some measure, secret. The limitless country sometimes contained only a solitary bull. The solitude was perfect, perhaps hostile, and it might have occurred to Dahlmann that he was traveling into the past and not merely south. He was distracted from these considerations by the railroad inspector who, on reading his ticket, advised him that the train would not let him off at the regular station but at another: an earlier stop, one scarcely known to Dahlmann. (The man added an explanation which Dahlmann did not attempt to understand, and which he hardly heard, for the mechanism of events did not concern him.)

The train laboriously ground to a halt, practically in the middle of the plain. The station lay on the other side of the tracks; it was not much more than a siding and a shed. There was no means of conveyance to be seen, but the station chief supposed that the traveler might secure a vehicle from a general store and inn to be found some ten or twelve blocks away.

Dahlmann accepted the walk as a small adventure. The sun had already disappeared from view, but a final splendor exalted the vivid and silent plain, before the night erased its color. Less to avoid fatigue than to draw out his enjoyment of these sights, Dahlmann walked slowly, breathing in the odor of clover with sumptuous joy.

The general store at one time had been painted a deep scarlet, but the years had tempered this violent color for its own good. Something in its poor architecture recalled a steel engraving, perhaps one from an old edition of *Paul et Virginie*. A number of horses were hitched up to the paling. Once inside, Dahlmann thought he recognized the shopkeeper. Then he realized that he had been deceived by the man's resemblance to one of the male nurses in the sanitarium. When the shopkeeper heard Dahlmann's request, he said he would have the shay made up. In order to add one more event to that day and to kill time, Dahlmann decided to eat at the general store.

Some country louts, to whom Dahlmann did not at first pay any attention, were eating and drinking at one of the tables. On the floor, and hanging on to the bar, squatted an old man, immobile as an object. His years had reduced and polished him as water does a stone or the generations of men do a sentence. He was dark, dried up, diminutive, and seemed outside time, situated in eternity. Dahlmann noted with satisfaction the kerchief, the thick poncho, the long *chiripá*, and the colt boots, and told himself, as he recalled futile discussions with people from the Northern counties or from the province of Entre Rios, that gauchos like this no longer existed outside the South.

Dahlmann sat down next to the window. The darkness began overcoming the plain, but the odor and sound of the earth penetrated the iron bars of the window. The shop owner brought him sardines, followed by some roast meat. Dahlmann washed the meal down with several glasses of red wine. Idling, he relished the tart savor of the wine, and let his gaze, now grown somewhat drowsy, wander over the shop. A kerosene lamp hung from a beam. There were three customers at the other table: two of them appeared to be farm workers; the third man, whose features hinted at Chinese blood, was drinking with his hat on. Of a sudden, Dahlmann felt something brush lightly against his face. Next to the heavy glass of turbid wine, upon one of the stripes in the tablecloth, lay a spit ball of breadcrumb. That was all: but someone had thrown it there.

The men at the other table seemed totally cut off from him. Perplexed, Dahlmann decided that nothing had happened, and he opened the volume of *The Thousand and One Nights*, by way of suppressing reality. After a few moments another little ball landed on his table, and now the peones laughed outright. Dahlmann said to himself that he was not frightened, but he reasoned that it would be a major blunder if he, a convalescent, were to allow himself to be dragged by strangers into some chaotic quarrel. He determined to leave, and had already gotten to his feet when the owner came up and exhorted him in an alarmed voice:

"*Señor* Dahlmann, don't pay any attention to those lads; they're half high."

Dahlmann was not surprised to learn that the other man, now, knew his name. But he felt that these conciliatory words served only to aggravate the situation. Previously to this moment, the *peones'* provocation was directed against an unknown face, against no one in particular, almost against no one at all. Now it was an attack against him, against his name, and his neighbors knew it. Dahlmann pushed the owner aside, confronted the *peones,* and demanded to know what they wanted of him.

The tough with the Chinese look staggered heavily to his feet. Almost in Juan Dahlmann's face he shouted insults, as if he had been a long way off. His game was to exaggerate his drunkenness, and this extravagance constituted a ferocious mockery. Between curses and obscenities, he threw a long knife into the air, followed it with his eyes, caught and juggled it, and challenged Dahlmann to a knife fight. The owner objected in a tremulous voice, pointing out that Dahlmann was unarmed. At this point, something unforeseeable occurred.

From a corner of the room, the old ecstatic gaucho—in whom Dahlmann saw a summary and cipher of the South (his South)—threw him a naked dagger, which landed at his feet. It was as if the South had resolved that Dahlmann should accept the duel. Dahlmann bent over to pick up the dagger, and felt two things. The first, that this almost instinctive act bound him to fight. The second, that the weapon, in his torpid hand, was no defense at all, but would merely serve to justify his murder. He had once played with a poniard, like all men, but his idea of fencing and knife-play did not go further than the notion that all strokes should be directed upward, with the cutting edge held inward. *They would not have allowed such things to happen to me in the sanitarium,* he thought.

"Let's get on our way," said the other man.

They went out and if Dahlmann was without hope, he was also without fear. As he crossed the threshold, he felt that to die in a knife fight, under the open sky, and going forward to the attack, would have been a liberation, a joy, and a festive occasion, on the first night in the sanitarium, when they stuck him with the needle. He felt that if he had been able to choose, then, or to dream his death, this would have been the death he would have chosen or dreamt.

Firmly clutching his knife, which he perhaps would not know how to wield, Dahlmann went out into the plain.

TRANSLATED BY ANTHONY KERRIGAN

Death and the Compass

To Mandie Molina Vedia

Of the many problems which exercised the daring perspicacity of Lönnrot none was so strange—so harshly strange, we may say—as the staggered series of bloody acts which culminated at the villa of Triste-le-Roy, amid the boundless odor of the eucalypti. It is true that Erik Lönnrot did not succeed in preventing the last crime, but it is indisputable that he foresaw it. Nor did he, of course, guess the identity of Yarmolinsky's unfortunate assassin, but he did divine the secrete morphology of the vicious series as well as the participation of Red Scharlach, whose alias is Scharlach the Dandy. This criminal (as so many others) had sworn on his honor to kill Lönnrot, but the latter had never allowed himself to be intimidated. Lönnrot thought of himself as a pure thinker, an Auguste Dupin, but there was something of the adventurer in him, and even of the gamester.

The first crime occurred at the Hôtel du Nord—that high prism that dominates the estuary whose waters are the colors of the desert. To this tower (which most manifestly unites the hateful whiteness of a sanitorium, the numbered divisibility of a prison, and the general appearance of a bawdy house) on the third day of December came the delegate from Podolsk to the Third Talmudic Congress, Doctor Marcel Yarmolinsky, a man of gray beard and gray eyes. We shall never know whether the Hôtel du Nord pleased him: he accepted it with the ancient resignation which had allowed him to endure three years of war in the Carpathians and three thousand years of oppression and pogroms. He was given a sleeping room on floor R, in front of the suite which the Tetrarch of Galilee occupied not without some splendor. Yarmolinsky supped, postponed until the following day an investigation of the unknown city, arranged upon a cupboard his many books and his few possessions, and before midnight turned off the light. (Thus declared the Tetrarch's chauffeur, who slept in an adjoining room.) On the fourth, at 11:03 A.M., there was a telephone call for him from the editor of the *Yiddische Zeitung;* Doctor Yarmolinsky did not reply; he was found in his room, his face already a little dark, and his body, almost nude, beneath a large anachronistic cape. He was lying not far from the door which gave onto the corridor; a deep stab wound had split open his breast. In the same room, a couple of hours later, in the midst of journalists, photographers, and police, Commissioner Treviranus and Lönnrot were discussing the problem with equanimity.

"There's no need to look for a Chimera, or a cat with three legs," Treviranus was saying as he brandished an imperious cigar. "We all know that the Tetrarch of Galilee is the possessor of the finest sapphires in the world. Someone, intending to steal them, came in here by mistake. Yarmolinsky got up; the robber had to kill him. What do you think?"

"It's possible, but not interesting," Lönnrot answered. "You will reply that reality hasn't the slightest need to be of interest. And I'll answer you that reality may avoid the obligation to be interesting, but that hypotheses may not. In the hypothesis you have postulated, chance intervenes largely. Here lies a dead rabbi; I should prefer a purely rabbinical explanation; not the imaginary mischances of an imaginary robber."

Treviranus answered ill-humoredly:

"I am not interested in rabbinical explanations; I am interested in the capture of the man who stabbed this unknown person."

"Not so unknown," corrected Lönnrot. "Here are his complete works." He indicated a line of tall volumes: *A Vindication of the Cabala; An Examination of the Philosophy of Robert Fludd;* a literal translation of the *Sepher Yezirah;* a *Biography of the Baal Shem;* a *History of the Sect of the Hasidim;* a monograph (in German) on the Tetragrammaton; another, on the divine nomenclature of the Pentateuch. The Commissioner gazed at them with suspicion, almost with revulsion. Then he fell to laughing.

"I'm only a poor Christian," he replied. "Carry off all these moth-eaten classics if you like; I haven't got time to lose in Jewish superstitions."

"Maybe this crime belongs to the history of Jewish superstitions," murmured Lönnrot.

"Like Christianity," the editor of the *Yiddische Zeitung* dared to put in. He was a myope, an atheist, and very timid.

No one answered him. One of the agents had found inserted in the small typewriter a piece of paper on which was written the following inconclusive sentence.

The first letter of the Name has been spoken

Lönnrot abstained from smiling. Suddenly becoming a bibliophile — or Hebraist — he directed that the dead man's books be made into a parcel, and he carried them to his office. Indifferent to the police investigation, he dedicated himself to studying them. A large octavo volume revealed to him the teachings of Israel Baal Shem-Tob, founder of the sect of the Pious; another volume, the virtues and terrors of the Tetragrammaton, which is the ineffable name of God; another, the thesis that God has a secret name, in which is epitomized (as in the crystal sphere which the Persians attribute to Alexander of Macedon) his ninth attribute, eternity — that is to say, the immediate knowledge of everything that will exist, exists, and has existed in the universe. Tradition numbers ninety-nine names of God; the Hebraists attribute this imperfect number to the magical fear of even numbers; the Hasidim reason that this hiatus indicates a hundredth name — the Absolute Name.

From this erudition he was distracted, within a few days, by the appearance of the editor of the *Yiddische Zeitung*. This man wished to talk of the assassination; Lönnrot preferred to speak of the diverse names of God. The journalist declared, in three columns, that the investigator Erik Lönnrot had dedicated himself to studying the names of God in order to "come up with" the name of the assassin. Lönnrot, habituated to the simplifications of journalism, did not become indignant. One of those shopkeepers who have found that there are buyers for every book came out with a popular edition of the *History of the Sect of the Hasidim.*

The second crime occurred on the night of the third of January, in the most deserted and empty corner of the capital's western suburbs. Toward dawn, one of the gendarmes who patrol these lonely places on horseback detected a man in a cape, lying prone in the shadow of an ancient paint shop. The hard visage seemed bathed in blood; a deep stab wound had split open his breast. On the wall, upon the yellow and red rhombs, there were some words written in chalk. The gendarme spelled them out. . . .

That afternoon Treviranus and Lönnrot made their way toward the remote scene of the crime. To the left and right of the automobile, the city disintegrated; the firmament grew larger and the houses meant less and less and a brick kiln or a poplar grove more and more. They reached their miserable destination: a final alley of rose-colored mud walls which in some way seemed to reflect the disordered setting of the sun. The dead man had already been identified. He was Daniel Simon Azevedo, a man of some fame in the ancient northern suburbs, who had risen from wagoner to political tough, only to degenerate later into a thief and even an informer. (The singular style of his death struck them as appropriate: Azevedo was the last representative of a generation of bandits who knew how to handle a dagger, but not a revolver.) The words in chalk were the following:

The second letter of the Name has been spoken

The third crime occurred on the night of the third of February. A little before one o'clock, the telephone rang in the office of Commissioner Treviranus. In avid secretiveness a man with a guttural voice spoke: he said his name was Ginzberg (or Ginsburg) and that he was disposed to communicate, for a reasonable remuneration, an explanation of the two sacrifices of Azevedo and Yarmolinsky. The discordant sound of whistles and horns drowned out the voice of the informer. Then the connection was cut off. Without rejecting the possibility of a hoax (it was carnival time), Treviranus checked and found he had been called from Liverpool House, a tavern on the Rue de Toulon—that dirty street where cheek by jowl are the peepshow and the milk store, the bordello and the women selling Bibles. Treviranus called back and spoke to the owner. This personage (Black Finnegan by name, an old Irish criminal who was crushed, annihilated almost, by respectability) told him that the last person to use the establishment's phone had been a lodger, a certain Gryphius, who had just gone out with some friends. Treviranus immediately went to Liverpool House, where Finnegan related the following facts. Eight days previously, Gryphius had taken a room above the saloon. He was a man of sharp features, a nebulous gray beard, shabbily clothed in black; Finnegan (who put the room to a use which Treviranus guessed) demanded a rent which was undoubtedly excessive; Gryphius immediately paid the stipulated sum. He scarcely ever went out; he dined and lunched in his room; his face was hardly known in the bar. On this particular night, he came down to telephone from Finnegan's office. A closed coupe stopped in front of the tavern. The driver did not move from his seat; several of the patrons recalled that he was wearing a bear mask. Two harlequins descended from the coupe; they were short in stature, and no one could fail to observe that they were very drunk. With a tooting of horns they burst into Finnegan's office; they embraced Gryphius, who seemed to recognize them but who replied to them coldly; they exchanged a few words in Yiddish—he, in a low guttural voice; they, in shrill, falsetto tones—and then the party climbed to the upstairs room. Within a quarter hour the three descended, very joyous; Gryphius, staggering, seemed as drunk as the others. He walked—tall, dazed—in the middle, between the masked harlequins. (One of the women in the bar remembered the yellow, red and green rhombs, the diamond designs.) Twice he stumbled; twice he was held up by the harlequins. Alongside the adjoining dock basin, whose water was rectangular, the trio got into the coupe and disappeared. From the running board, the last of the harlequins had scrawled an obscene figure and a sentence on one of the slates of the outdoor shed.

Treviranus gazed upon the sentence. It was nearly foreknowable. It read:

The last of the letters of the Name has been spoken

He examined, then, the small room of Gryphius-Ginzberg. On the floor was a violent star of blood; in the corners, the remains of some Hungarian-brand cigarettes; in a cabinet, a book in Latin—the *Philologus Hebraeo-Graecus* (1739) of Leusden—along with various manuscript notes. Treviranus studied the book with indignation and had Lönnrot summoned. The latter, without taking off his hat, began to read while the Comissioner questioned the contradictory witnesses to the possible kidnapping. At four in the morning they came out. In the tortuous Rue de Toulon, as they stepped on the dead serpentines of the dawn, Treviranus said:

"And supposing the story of this night were a sham?"

Erik Lönnrot smiled and read him with due gravity a passage (underlined) of the thirty-third dissertation of the *Philologus:*

Dies Judaeorum incipit a solis occasu
usque ad solis occasum diei sequentis.

"This means," he added, "that *the Hebrew day begins at sundown and lasts until the following sundown.*"

Treviranus attempted an irony.

"Is this fact the most worthwhile you've picked up tonight?"

"No. Of even greater value is a word Ginzberg used."

The afternoon dailies did not neglect this series of disappearances. *The Cross and the Sword* contrasted them with the admirable discipline and order of the last Eremitical Congress; Ernest Palast, writing in *The Martyr,* spoke out against "the intolerable delays in this clandestine and frugal pogrom, which has taken three months to liquidate three Jews"; the *Yiddische Zeitung* rejected the terrible hypothesis of an anti-Semitic plot, "even though many discerning intellects do not admit of any other solution to the triple mystery"; the most illustrious gunman in the South, Dandy Red Scharlach, swore that in his district such crimes as these would never occur, and he accused Commissioner Franz Treviranus of criminal negligence.

On the night of March first, the Commissioner received an imposing-looking, sealed envelope. He opened it: the envelope contained a letter signed Baruj Spinoza, and a detailed plan of the city, obviously torn from a Baedeker. The letter prophesied that on the third of March there would not be a fourth crime, inasmuch as the paint shop in the West, the Tavern on the Rue de Toulon and the Hôtel du Nord were the "perfect vertices of an equilateral and mystic triangle"; the regularity of this triangle was made clear on the map with red ink. This argument, *more geometrico*, Treviranus read with resignation, and sent the letter and map on to Lönnrot—who deserved such a piece of insanity.

Erik Lönnrot studied the documents. The three sites were in fact equidistant. Symmetry in time (the third of December, the third of January, the third of February); symmetry in space as well. . . . Of a sudden he sensed he was about to decipher the mystery. A set of calipers and a compass completed his sudden intuition. He smiled, pronounced the word "Tetragrammaton" (of recent acquisition), and called the Commissioner on the telephone. He told him:

"Thank you for the equilateral triangle you sent me last night. It has enabled me to solve the problem. Tomorrow, Friday, the criminals will be in jail, we can rest assured."

"In that case, they're not planning a fourth crime?"

"Precisely because they *are* planning a fourth crime can we rest assured."

Lönnrot hung up. An hour later he was traveling in one of the trains of the Southern Railways, en route to the abandoned villa of Triste-le-Roy. South of the city of our story there flows a blind little river filled with muddy water made disgraceful by floating scraps and garbage. On the further side is a manufacturing suburb where, under the protection of a chief from Barcelona, gunmen flourish. Lönnrot smiled to himself to think that the most famous of them—Red Scharlach—would have given anything to know of this clandestine visit. Azevedo had been a comrade of Scharlach's; Lönnrot considered the remote possibility that the fourth victim might be Scharlach himself. Then, he put aside the thought. . . . He had virtually deciphered the problem; the mere circumstances, or the reality (names, prison records, faces, judicial and penal proceedings), scarcely interested him now. Most of all he wanted to take a stroll, to relax from three months of sedentary investigation. He reflected on how the explanation of the crimes lay in an anonymous triangle and a dust-laden Greek word. The mystery seemed to him almost crystalline now; he was mortified to have dedicated a hundred days to it.

The train stopped at a silent loading platform. Lönnrot descended. It was one of those deserted afternoons which seem like dawn. The air over the muddy plain was damp and cold. Lönnrot set off across the fields. He saw dogs, he saw a wagon on a dead road, he saw the horizon, he saw a silvery horse drinking the crapulous water of a puddle. Dusk was falling when he saw the rectangular belvedere of the villa of Triste-le-Roy, almost as tall as the black eucalypti which surrounded it. He thought of the fact that only one more dawn and one more nightfall (an ancient splendor in the east, and another in the west) separated him from the hour so much desired by the seekers of the Name.

A rust colored wrought-iron fence defined the irregular perimeter of the villa. The main gate was closed. Without much expectation of entering, Lönnrot made a complete circuit. In front of the insurmountable gate once again, he put his hand between the bars almost mechanically and chanced upon the bolt. The creaking of the iron surprised him. With laborious passivity the entire gate gave way.

Lönnrot advanced among the eucalypti, stepping amidst confused generations of rigid, broken leaves. Close up, the house on the estate of Triste-le-Roy was seen to abound in superfluous symmetries and in maniacal repetitions: a glacial Diana in one lugubrious niche was complemented by another Diana in another niche; one balcony was repeated by another balcony; double steps of stairs opened into a double balustrade. A two-faced Hermes cast a monstrous shadow. Lönnrot circled the house as he had the estate. He examined everything; beneath the level of the terrace he noticed a narrow shutter door.

He pushed against it: some marble steps descended to a vault. Versed now in the architect's preferences, Lönnrot divined that there would be a set of stairs on the opposite wall. He found them, ascended, raised his hands, and pushed up a trap door.

The diffusion of light guided him to a window. He opened it: a round, yellow moon outlined two stopped-up fountains in the melancholy garden. Lönnrot explored the house. He traveled through antechambers and galleries to emerge upon duplicate patios; several times he emerged upon the same patio. He ascended dust-covered stairways and came out into circular antechambers; he was infinitely reflected in opposing mirrors; he grew weary of opening or half-opening windows which revealed the same desolate garden outside, from various heights and various angles; inside, the furniture was wrapped in yellow covers and the chandeliers bound up with cretonne. A bedroom detained him; in the bedroom, a single rose in a porcelain vase—at the first touch the ancient petals fell apart. On the second floor, on the top story, the house seemed to be infinite and growing. *The house is not this large,* he thought. *It is only made larger by the penumbra, the symmetry, the mirrors, the years, my ignorance, the solitude.*

Going up a spiral staircase he arrived at the observatory. The evening moon shone through the rhomboid diamonds of the windows, which were yellow, red and green. He was brought to a halt by a stunning and dizzying recollection.

Two men of short stature, ferocious and stocky, hurled themselves upon him and took his weapon. Another man, very tall, saluted him gravely, and said:

"You are very thoughtful. You've saved us a night and a day."

It was Red Scharlach. His men manacled Lönnrot's hands. Lönnrot at length found his voice.

"Are you looking for the Secret Name, Scharlach?"

Scharlach remained standing, indifferent. He had not participated in the short struggle; he scarcely stretched out his hand to receive Lönnrot's revolver. He spoke; in his voice Lönnrot detected a fatigued triumph, a hatred the size of the universe, a sadness no smaller than that hatred.

"No," answered Scharlach. "I am looking for something more ephemeral and slippery, I am looking for Erik Lönnrot. Three years ago, in a gambling house on the Rue de Toulon, you arrested my brother and had him sent to prison. In the exchange of shots that night my men got me away in a coupe, with a police bullet in my chest. Nine days and nine nights I lay dying in this desolate, symmetrical villa; I was racked with fever, and the odious double-faced Janus who gazes toward the twilights of dusk and dawn terrorized my dreams and my waking. I learned to abominate my body, I came to feel that two eyes, two hands, two lungs are as monstrous as two faces. An Irishman attempted to convert me to the faith of Jesus; he repeated to me that famous axiom of the *goyim:* All roads lead to Rome. At night, my delirium nurtured itself on this metaphor: I sensed that the world was a labyrinth, from which it was impossible to flee, for all paths, whether they seemed to lead north or south, actually led to Rome, which was also the quadrilateral jail where my brother was dying and the villa of Triste-le-Roy. During those nights I swore by the god who sees from two faces, and by all the gods of fever and of mirrors, to weave a labyrinth around the man who had imprisoned my brother. I have woven it, and it holds: the materials are a dead writer on heresies, a compass, an eighteenth-century sect, a Greek word, a dagger, the rhombs of a paint shop.

"The first objective in the sequence was given me by chance. I had made plans with some colleagues—among them, Daniel Azevedo—to take the Tetrarch's sapphires. Azevedo betrayed us; with the money we advanced him he got himself inebriated and started on the job a day early. In the vastness of the hotel he got lost; at two in the morning he blundered into Yarmolinsky's room. The latter, harassed by insomnia, had set himself to writing. He was editing some notes, apparently, or writing an article on the Name of God; he had just written the words *The first letter of the Name has been spoken.* Azevedo enjoined him to be quiet; Yarmolinsky reached out his hand for the bell which would arouse all the hotel's forces; Azevedo at once stabbed him in the chest. It was almost a reflex action: half a century of violence had taught him that it was easiest and surest to kill. . . . Ten days later, I learned through the *Yiddische Zeitung* that you were perusing the writings of Yarmolinsky for the key to his death. For my part I read the *History of the Sect of the Hasidim;* I learned that the reverent fear of pronouncing the Name of God had given rise to the doctrine that this Name is all-powerful and mystic. I learned that some Hasidim, in search of this secret Name, had gone as far as to offer human sacrifices. . . . I knew you would conjecture that the Hasidim had sacrificed the rabbi; I set myself to justifying this conjecture.

"Marcel Yarmolinsky died on the night of December third; for the second sacrifice I selected the night of January third. Yarmolinsky died in the

North; for the second sacrifice a place in the West was preferable. Daniel Azevedo was the inevitable victim. He deserved death: he was an impulsive person, a traitor; his capture could destroy the entire plan. One of our men stabbed him; in order to link his corpse to the other one I wrote on the paint shop diamonds *The second letter of the Name has been spoken.*

"The third 'crime' was produced on the third of February. It was as Treviranus must have guessed, a mere mockery, a simulacrum. I am Gryphius-Ginzberg-Ginsburg; I endured an interminable week (filled out with a tenuous false beard) in that perverse cubicle on the Rue de Toulon, until my friends spirited me away. From the running board one of them wrote on a pillar *The last of the letters of the Name has been spoken.* This sentence revealed that the series of crimes was *triple.* And the public thus understood it; nevertheless, I interspersed repeated signs that would allow you, Erik Lönnrot, the reasoner, to understand that it is *quadruple.* A portent in the North, others in the East and West, demand a fourth portent in the South; the Tetragrammaton—the name of God, JHVH—is made up of four letters; the harlequins and the paint shop sign suggested *four* points. In the manual of Leusden I underlined a certain passage: it manifested that the Hebrews calculate a day counting from dusk to dusk and that therefore the deaths occurred on the *fourth* day of each month. To Treviranus I sent the equilateral triangle. I sensed that you would supply the missing point. The point which would form a perfect rhomb, the point which fixes where death, exactly, awaits you. In order to attract you I have premeditated everything, Erik Lönnrot, so as to draw you to the solitude of Triste-le-Roy."

Lönnrot avoided Scharlach's eyes. He was looking at the trees and the sky divided into rhombs of turbid yellow, green and red. He felt a little cold, and felt, too, an impersonal, almost anonymous sadness. It was already night; from the dusty garden arose the useless cry of a bird. For the last time, Lönnrot considered the problem of symmetrical and periodic death.

"In your labyrinth there are three lines too many," he said at last. "I know of a Greek labyrinth which is a single straight line. Along this line so many philosophers have lost themselves that a mere detective might well do so too. Scharlach, when, in some other incarnation you hunt me, feign to commit (or do commit) a crime at A, then a second crime at B, eight kilometers from A, then a third crime at C, four kilometers from A and B, halfway enroute between the two. Wait for me later at D, two kilometers from A and C, halfway, once again, between both. Kill me at D, as you are now going to kill me at Triste-le-Roy."

"The next time I kill you," said Scharlach, "I promise you the labyrinth made of the single straight line which is invisible and everlasting."

He stepped back a few paces. Then, very carefully, he fired.

TRANSLATED BY ANTHONY KERRIGAN

Poem of the Gifts

To María Esther Vásquez

Let no one with tears or disapproval slight
This declaration of the majesty
Of God, who with magnificent irony
Granted me books and, at the same time, night.

He made this set of lightless eyes the lord 5
In this city of books, and they can only read
In the library of dreams where the dawns cede
These senseless paragraphs to unexplored.

Wishful longings. Futilely the day
Squanders its infinite books on them in scripts 10
Elusive like the elusive manuscripts
Of Alexandria, which burned away.

A king among his fountains and greenery
Is dying of hunger and thirst (the Greek relates).
I lurch from side to side, lost in the straits 15
Of this towering, profound, blind library.

The encyclopedia, atlas, the Orient
And the West, centuries, the dynasties,
Symbols, cosmos, the cosmogonies
Salute the walls, yet all is impotent. 20

Slow in my darkness, I am exploring the
Thread of twilight with my faltering cane,
I who imagined Paradise was the domain
Under the heading of a library.

Something, which surely cannot be defined 25
By the word *chance,* presides over these things;
Some other man controlled, in shadowy evenings,
The multitude of books. He too was blind.

Straying through the slowness of these galleries
I often feel with unclear, holy dread 30
That I am the other, the dead man who tread
The same steps on the same days. Which of these

Two beings, which of us is writing this poem
Of a plural I and one lone shadow? I came
To ask: what difference if one name is my name 35
When our curse is indivisible, a single gloom?

Groussac[1] or Borges, now I look upon
A dear world coming apart like smoldering trash,
Formless, burning to a vague, pale ash
That looks like sleep and like oblivion.   *40*

TRANSLATED BY WILLIS BARNSTONE

The Labyrinth

Zeus, Zeus himself could not undo these nets
Of stone encircling me. My mind forgets
The persons I have been along the way,
The hated way of monotonous walls,
Which is my fate. The galleries seem straight   *5*
But curve furtively, forming secret circles
At the terminus of years; and the parapets
Have been worn smooth by the passage of days.
Here, in the tepid alabaster dust,
Are tracks that frighten me. The hollow air   *10*
Of evening sometimes brings a bellowing,
Or the echo, desolate, of bellowing.
I know that hidden in the shadows there
Lurks another, whose task is to exhaust
The loneliness that braids and weaves this hell,   *15*
To crave my blood, and to fatten on my death.
We seek each other. Oh, if only this
Were the last day of our antithesis!

TRANSLATED BY JOHN UPDIKE

In Praise of Shadow

Old age (this is the name that others give it)
may be the time of our happiness.
The animal is dead or nearly dead.

---

1. Groussac was the former director of the National Library and was, like Borges, blind.

Man and his soul remain.
I live among vague and luminous forms   5
that are not yet darkness.
Buenos Aires,
which once was torn into far suburbs
facing the endless plain,
is now the cemetery of the Recoleta, the Retiro square,   10
the dingy streets of the Eleventh district,
and the precarious old houses
that we still call the South.
Always there were too many things in my life;
Demokritos of Abdera tore out his eyes to think;   15
time has been my Demokritos.
This penumbra is slow and brings no pain;
it flows down a gentle slope
and resembles eternity.
My friends have no faces,   20
women are what they were so many years ago,
one street corner might be another,
there are no letters on the pages of books.
All this ought to unnerve me,
but it is a sweetness, a return.   25
From the generations of texts on the earth
I have read only a few,
the ones I keep reading in memory,
reading and distorting.
From the South, the East, the West, the North,   30
roads converge that have led me
to my secret center.
Those roads were echoes and footsteps,
women, men, agonies, resurrections,
days and nights,   35
half-dreams and dreams,
every obscure instant of yesterday
and of the world's yesterdays,
the firm sword of the Dane and the moon of the Persian,
the deeds of the dead,   40
shared love, words,
Emerson and snow and so many things.
Now I can forget them. I reach my center,
my algebra and my key,
my mirror,   45
Soon I will know who I am.

TRANSLATED BY TONY BARNSTONE AND WILLIS BARNSTONE

The Other Tiger

I think of a tiger. Half-light exalts
The vast busy Library
And seems to set the bookshelves back;
Strong, innocent, bloodstained, fresh,
It wanders through its jungle and its morning   5
And prints its tracks on the muddy
Banks of a river whose name it doesn't know
(In its world there are no names or past
Or future, only a certain now)
And slips through barbaric distances,   10
Sniffing smells in the braided labyrinth
Out of the smell of dawn
And the delicious smell of deer;
Among the stripes of the bamboo tree
I decipher the tiger's stripes and feel   15
Its bony frame under the splendid quivering hide.
The curving seas and deserts of the planet
Futilely intervene;
From this house in a remote port
In South America I track you and dream you,   20
O tiger of the Ganges's banks.

As evening fills my soul I think
The tiger addressed in my poem
Is a tiger of symbols and shadows,
A string of literary tropes   25
And scraps from the encyclopedia
And not the fatal tiger, the deadly jewel
That under the sun or changing moon
Goes on in Sumatra or Bengal fulfilling
Its rounds of love, indolence and death.   30
To the tiger of symbols I oppose
The real one, with hot blood,
Decimating a herd of buffalos,
And today, August 3rd. 1959,
A deliberate shadow spreads over the grass   35
Yet in the act of naming it
And conjecturing its word, it becomes
A fiction, art, and not a living beast
Among beasts roaming the earth.
We will seek a third tiger. Like   40
The others it will be a shape
From my dream, a system of human words,

And not the vertebrate tiger
Which beyond mythologies
Paces the earth. I know all this,   45
Yet something drives me to this vague,
Insane and ancient adventure, and I go on,
Searching through the hours of the afternoon
For the other tiger, not in the poem.

TRANSLATED BY WILLIS BARNSTONE

A Blindman

I do not know what face looks back at me
When I look at the mirrored face, nor know
What aged man conspires in the glow
Of the glass, silent and with tired fury.
Slow in my shadow, with my hand I explore   5
My invisible features. A sparkling ray
Reaches me. Glimmers of your hair are gray
Or some still gold. I say I've lost no more
Than just the useless surfaces of things.
This consolation is of great import,   10
A comfort had by Milton. I resort
To letters and the rose—my wonderings.
I think if I could see my face I'd soon
Know who I am on this rare afternoon.

TRANSLATED BY WILLIS BARNSTONE

Remorse

I have committed the worst sin of all
That a man can commit. I have not been
Happy. Let the glaciers of oblivion
Drag me and mercilessly let me fall.
My parents bred and bore me for a higher   5
Faith in the human game of nights and days;
For earth, for air, for water, and for fire.
I let them down. I wasn't happy. My ways
Have not fulfilled their youthful hope. I gave
My mind to the symmetric stubbornness   10
Of art, and all its webs of pettiness.

They willed me bravery. I wasn't brave.
It never leaves my side, since I began:
This shadow of having been a brooding man.

TRANSLATED BY WILLIS BARNSTONE

Spinoza

Here in the twilight the translucent hands
Of the Jew polishing the crystal glass.
The dying afternoon is cold with bands
Of fear. Each day the afternoons all pass
The same. The hands and space of hyacinth   5
Paling in the confines of the ghetto walls
Barely exists for the quiet man who stalls
There, dreaming up a brilliant labyrinth.
Fame doesn't trouble him (that reflection of
Dreams in the dream of another mirror), nor love,   10
The timid love women. Gone the bars,
He's free, from metaphor and myth, to sit
Polishing a stubborn lens: the infinite
Map of the One who now is all His stars.

TRANSLATED BY WILLIS BARNSTONE

Camden, 1892

The smell of coffee and of newspapers.
Sunday and its monotony. The morning,
Some allegoric verses are adorning
The glimpsed at page, the vain pentameters
Of a contented colleague. The old man lies   5
Stretched out and white in his respectable
Poor man's room. Then lazily he fills
The weary mirror with his gaze. His eyes
See a face. Unsurprised he thinks: That face
Is me. With fumbling hand he reaches out   10
To touch the tangled beard and ravaged mouth.
The end is not far off. His voice declares:
I'm almost gone and yet my verses scan
Life and its splendor. I was Walt Whitman.

TRANSLATED BY WILLIS BARNSTONE

Proteus

Before the oarsmen of Odysseus
strained their arms against the wine dark sea,
I try to guess the vague and shadowy
forms of that god whose name was Proteus.
He was the herdsman tending to the seas   5
and had the gift of reading omens too,
but he preferred to hide the things he knew
and wove odd scraps into his auguries.
When urged by people he would take upon
himself a lion's shape, be a huge blaze,   10
grow treelike by the river, giving shade,
and then like water in a wave be gone.
Don't shrink from Proteus the Egyptian,
you, who are one, and yet are many men.

TRANSLATED BY TONY BARNSTONE

I Am

I am a man who knows he's no less vain
than the observer on the mirror's other
side: crystal, silent, following his brother's
body or reflection (it is the same).
No other pardon and no other vengeance   5
than oblivion is what I see,
my silent friends. A god gave this strange key
to men to solve their hate of other men.
Time belongs to me as it does to all
and yet, in spite of wandering so far,   10
its labyrinth remains as singular,
as plural, harsh, distinct, as hard to solve.
No man of war, I am oblivion,
an echo, just a zero. I am no one.

TRANSLATED BY TONY BARNSTONE

To the Mirror

Why is it you persist, incessant mirror?
Why copy me, down to the smallest gesture of my hand? Why suddenly reflect

there in the shadows? You, uncanny brother,
you are the other me that ancient Greek   5
spoke of. You've watched forever. From a glaze
of old and watery crystal do you gaze
at me? It's useless to be blind. You seek
me and it's worse that I can't see, can't tell;
that really is your horror, magic thing   10
who multiplies the cipher of our being
then sucks our blessings into your strange well.
And when I'm dead, you'll duplicate another,
another, then another, and another . . .

TRANSLATED BY TONY BARNSTONE

■ Cecília Meireles (1901–1964) *Brazil* (poem)

TRANSLATED BY JAMES MERRILL

Born in Rio de Janeiro, Cecília Meireles worked as a primary school
teacher, librarian, journalist, and professor of comparative literature. A
playwright, translator of European and Indian writers into Portuguese, and
specialist in Brazilian folklore, she was once considered one of Brazil's
major poets. Unlike Manuel Bandeira and Carlos Drummond de Andrade,
she never fully altered her turn-of-the-century aesthetic of romanticism and
beauty into a speech of modernity. In her best poems, however, she is very
good and strong, and a social or metaphysical irony underlies the work.
She has been favored in English with masterful translations by Elizabeth
Bishop and James Merrill.

FURTHER READING: Meireles, Cecília. *Spectres,* 1919; *Collected Works,* 1958.

Ballad of the Ten Casino Dancers

Ten dancers glide
across a mirror floor.
They have thin gilt plaques on Egyptian bodies,
fingertips reddened, blue lids painted,
lift white veils naively scented,   5
bend yellow knees.

The ten dancers go
voiceless among customers,

hands above knives, teeth above roses,
little lamps befuddled by cigars.   *10*
Between the music and the movement flows
depravity, a flight of silken stairs.

The dancers now advance
like ten lost grasshoppers,
advance, recoil, avoiding glances   *15*
in the close room, and plucking at the din
they are so naked, you imagine
them clothed in the stuff of tears.

The ten dancers screen
their pupils under great green lashes.   *20*
Death passes tranquil as a belt around
their phosphorescent waists.
As who should bear a dead child to the ground
each bears her flesh that moves and scintillates.

Fat men watch in massive tedium   *25*
those cold, cold dancers,
pitiful serpents without appetite
who are children by daylight.
Ten anemic angles made of hollows,
melancholy embalms them.   *30*

Ten mummies in a band,
back and forth go the tired dancers.
Branch whose fragrant blossoms bend
blue, green, gold, white.
Ten mothers would weep at the sight   *35*
of those dancers hand in hand.

■ Carlos Drummond de Andrade
(1902–1987) *Brazil* (poems)

The Brazilian poet Carlos Drummond de Andrade was brought up in
the mining district of Minas Gerais, was educated in Belo Horizonte, studied pharmacy, but earned his living as a teacher and journalist. In 1930, he
settled in Rio de Janerio, where he spent his life. A poet always with a social
eye, he is at the same time personal both in voice and interest. Understated
and subtle, his difficult, elusive poems have been splendidly translated by
Mark Strand and Elizabeth Bishop. In his lifetime, he was Brazil's outstanding poet. Over the years, his reputation has continued to grow and now,

like his counterpart Fernando Pessoa in Portugal, he is esteemed as one of the twentieth century's major poetic voices.

FURTHER READING: Drummond de Andrade, Carlos. *The People's Rose,* 1945; *Lessons in Things,* 1962.

Seven-Sided Poem

When I was born, one of the crooked
angels who live in shadow, said:
Carlos, go on! Be *gauche* in life.

The houses watch the men,
men who run after women.   5
If the afternoon had been blue,
there might have been less desire.

The trolley goes by full of legs:
white legs, black legs, yellow legs.
My God, why all the legs?   10
my heart asks. But my eyes
ask nothing at all.

The man behind the moustache
is serious, simple, and strong.
He hardly ever speaks.   15
He has a few, choice friends,
the man behind the spectacles and the moustache.

My God, why hast Thou forsaken me
if Thou knew'st I was not God,
if Thou knew'st that I was weak?   20

Universe, vast universe,
if I had been named Eugene
that would not be what I mean
but it would go into verse
faster.   25

Universe, vast universe,
my heart is vaster.

I oughtn't to tell you,
but this moon
and this brandy   30
play the devil with one's emotions.

TRANSLATED BY ELIZABETH BISHOP

Widower's Song

At night the agony
Overtakes my soul.
I see a shadow coming,
Coming. She hugs me.

The shadow of my love   5
Who died long ago.

She hugs me gingerly
yet chains me with fire,
kisses and consoles me.

I grin. Slowly she   10
nods goodbye and walks
through the wall. I shut

the door, hearing her
clacking on the stairs.
Then nothing. Curtain.   15

TRANSLATED BY WILLIS BARNSTONE

Souvenir of the Ancient World

Clara strolled in the garden with the children.
The sky was green over the grass,
the water was golden under the bridges,
other elements were blue and rose and orange,
a policeman smiled, bicycles passed,   5
a girl stepped onto the lawn to catch a bird,
the whole world—Germany, China—
            all was quiet around Clara.

The children looked at the sky: it was not forbidden.
Mouth, nose, eyes were open. There was no danger.   10
What Clara feared were the flu, the heat, the insects.
Clara feared missing the eleven o'clock trolley:
She waited for letters slow to arrive,
She couldn't always wear a new dress. But
            she strolled in the garden, in the morning!   15
They had gardens, they had mornings in those days!

TRANSLATED BY MARK STRAND

Family Portrait

Yes, this family portrait
is a little dusty.
The father's face doesn't show
how much money he earned.

The uncles' hands don't reveal   5
the voyages both of them made.
The grandmother's smoothed and yellowed;
she's forgotten the monarchy.

The children, how they've changed.
Peter's face is tranquil,   10
that wore the best dreams.
And John's no longer a liar.

The garden's become fantastic.
The flowers are gray badges.
And the sand, beneath dead feet,   15
is an ocean of fog.

In the semicircle of armchairs
a certain movement is noticed.
The children are changing places,
but noiselessly! it's a picture.   20

Twenty years is a long time.
It can form any image.
If one face starts to wither,
another presents itself, smiling.

All these seated strangers,   25
my relations? I don't believe it.
They're guests amusing themselves
in a rarely-opened parlor.

Family features remain
lost in the play of bodies.   30
But there's enough to suggest
that a body is full of surprises.

The frame of this family portrait
holds its personages in vain.
They're there voluntarily,   35
they'd know how—if need be—to fly.

They could refine themselves
in the room's chiaroscuro,
live inside the furniture
or the pockets of old waistcoats.   40

The house has many drawers,
papers, long staircases.
When matter becomes annoyed,
who knows the malice of things?

The portrait does not reply,   45
it stares; in my dusty eyes
it contemplates itself.
The living and dead relations

multiply in the glass.
I don't distinguish those   50
that went away from those
that stay. I only perceive
the strange idea of family

travelling through the flesh.

TRANSLATED BY ELIZABETH BISHOP

Song for a Young Girl's Album

Good morning: I said to the girl
who smiled from far away.
Good morning: but she didn't
respond from the distance.
Eye contact was pointless   5
so I waved my arms
good morning to the girl who,
day or night,
was far out of my range,
far from my poor good morning.   10
Good morning forever: maybe
the answer will come cold
or come late, yet
I shall wait
for her good morning.   15
And over the rows of houses,
over the hills and valleys,
I shall lamely repeat
at whatever hour: good morning.
Maybe the time is wrong   20
and my sadness too great
to warrant
this absurd good morning.
The girl does not know,

or sense, or suspect   25
the tenderness within
the heart of my good morning.
Good morning: I repeat
in the afternoon;
at midnight: good morning.   30
And at dawn
I color my day
blue and pink:
so the girl can find it!
good morning.   35
Good morning: only an echo
in the bushes (but who can say)
makes out my message
or wishes me good morning.
Smiling from far away,   40
the girl in her joy
does not feel the violence
in the radiance of this
good morning.
Night that had betrayed   45
sadness, trouble, confusion,
wanders without fire
in the wildest nostalgia.
If only she would say
good morning to my good morning,   50
the night would change
to the clearest of days!

TRANSLATED BY MARK STRAND

■ Alejo Carpentier (1904–1980) *Cuba* (story)

TRANSLATED BY FRANCES PARTRIDGE

Born in Havana of a French father and Russian mother, Alejo Carpentier returned to Europe with his family in 1914. In the early 1920s, he returned to Cuba to study architecture and music and threw himself into literary and political activities. While in Cuba, he helped form the Cuban Communist Party. He was arrested in 1927, and in early 1928, after forty days in jail for opposition to the Machado dictatorship, he fled to Paris, posing as the French surrealist poet who had lent him his passport. In

Paris, he was immersed in French and Latin American literary ventures and ideological struggles, meeting André Breton and other surrealists through his friend Robert Desnos. He also came to know the Guatemalan political novelist Miguel Angel Asturias (who was to win the Nobel Prize in Literature in 1967). Like Asturias, who gave life to Maya legends, Carpentier discovered the precolumbian world and determined to revivify it in avant-garde fiction. At the start of World War II, he returned to Cuba, where he wrote his second novel, *The Kingdom of This World* (1949), which mythologizes the times of the Haitian King Henri Christoph (reigned 1811–1820), a former slave who helped secure independence from France and used compulsory labor to build the fabulous palace of Sans Souci and the gigantic mountain-top citadel of La Ferrière. Carpentier also began writing the stories that would later be published as *The War of Time* (1958). As a professor of music at the National Conservatory, he wrote a volume on Cuban music, *La música en Cuba* (1946). In 1946, he moved to Venezuela, where he wrote two more novels. After Fidel Castro's victory in 1959, he returned to Cuba, where he wrote *Explosion in a Cathedral* (1962) while working at the State Publishing House. He was posted in 1966 as cultural attaché to the Cuban embassy in Paris, where he stayed until his death in 1980. An author of impeccable and imaginative craft, whose historical re-creations live between dream and brutal reality, Carpentier is one of the most original and accomplished twentieth-century writers of fiction.

FURTHER READING: Carpentier, Alejo. *The Kingdom of This World,* 1949; *The Lost Steps,* 1953; *The Chase,* 1956; *The War of Time (Stories),* 1958; *Reasons of State,* 1974; *The Harp and the Shadow,* 1979.

Like the Night

> *And he traveled like the night.*
>
> —Iliad, *Book I.*

I

Although the headlands still lay in shadow, the sea between them was beginning to turn green when the lookout blew his conch to announce that the fifty black ships sent us by King Agamemnon had arrived. Hearing the signal, those who had been waiting for so many days on the dung-covered threshing floors began carrying the wheat toward the shore, where rollers were already being made ready so that the vessels could be brought right up to the walls of the fortress. When the keels touched the sand, there was a certain amount of wrangling with the steersmen, because the Mycenaeans had so often been told about our complete ignorance of nautical matters that they tried to keep us at a distance with their poles. Moreover, the beach was now crowded with children, who got between the soldiers' legs, hindered their movements, and scrambled up the sides of the ships to steal nuts from under the oarsmen's benches. The transparent waves of dawn were breaking amid cries, insults, tussles, and blows, and our leading citizens could not make their speeches of welcome in the middle of such pandemonium. I had been expecting something more solemn, more ceremonious, from our meeting with these men who had come to fetch us to fight for them, and I walked off, feeling somewhat disillusioned, toward the fig tree on whose thickest branch I often sat astride, gripping the wood with my knees, because it reminded me somewhat of a woman's body.

As the ships were drawn out of the water and the tops of the mountains behind began to catch the sun, my first bad impression gradually faded; it had clearly been the result of a sleepless night of waiting, and also of my having drunk too heavily the day before with the young men recently arrived on the coast from inland, who were to embark with us soon after dawn. As I watched the procession of men carrying jars, black wineskins, and baskets moving toward the ships, a warm pride swelled within me, and a sense of my superiority as a soldier. That oil, that resinated wine, and above all that wheat from which biscuits would be cooked under the cinders at night while we slept in the shelter of the wet prows in some mysterious and unknown bay on the way to the Great City of Ships—the grain that I had helped to winnow with my shovel—all these things were being put on board for me; nor need I tire my long, muscular limbs, and arms designed for handling an ashwood pile, with tasks fit only for men who knew nothing but the smell of the soil, men who looked at the earth over the sweating backs of their animals or spent their lives crouched over it, weeding, uprooting, and raking, in almost the same attitudes as their own browsing cattle. These men would never pass under the clouds that at this time of day darken the distant green islands, whence the acrid-scented silphium was brought. They would never know the wide streets of the Trojans' city, the city we were now going to surround, attack, and destroy.

For days and days, the messengers sent us by the Mycenaean king had been telling us about Priam's insolence and the sufferings that threatened our people because of the arrogant behavior of his subjects. They had been jeering at our manly way of life; and, trembling with rage, we had heard of the challenges hurled at us long-haired Achaeans by the men of Ilium although our courage is unmatched by any other race. Cries of rage were heard, fists clenched and shaken, oaths sworn with the hands palm upward, and shields thrown against the walls, when we heard of the abduction of Helen of Sparta. While wine flowed from skins into helmets, in loud voices the emissaries told us of her marvelous beauty, her noble bearing, and adorable way of walking, and described the cruelties she had endured in her miserable captivity. That same evening, when the whole town was seething with indignation, we were told that the fifty black ships were being sent. Fires were lighted in the bronze foundries while old women brought wood from the mountains.

And now, several days later, here I was gazing at the vessels drawn up at my feet, with their powerful keels and their masts at rest between the bulwarks like a man's virility between his thighs; I felt as if in some sense I was the owner of those timbers, transformed by some portentous carpentry unknown to our people into racehorses of the ocean, ready to carry us where the greatest adventure of all time was now unfolding like an epic. And I, son of a harness maker and grandson of a castrator of bulls, was to have the good fortune to go where those deeds were being done whose luster reached us in sailors' stories; I was to have the honor of seeing the walls of Troy, of following noble leaders and contributing my energy and strength to the cause of rescuing Helen of Sparta—a manly undertaking and the supreme triumph of a war that would give us prosperity, happiness, and pride in ourselves forever. I took a deep breath of the breeze blowing from the olive-covered hillside and thought how splendid it would be to die in such a just conflict, for the cause of Reason itself. But the idea of being pierced by an enemy lance made me think of my mother's grief and also of another, perhaps even profounder grief, though in this case the news would have to be heard with dry eyes because the hearer was head of the family. I walked slowly down to the town by the shepherds' path. Three kids were gamboling in the thyme-scented air. Down on the beach the loading of wheat was still going on.

II

The impending departure of the ships was being celebrated on all sides with thrumming of guitars and clashing of cymbals. The sailors from *La Gallarda* were dancing the zarambeque with enfranchised Negresses, and singing familiar *coplas*—like the song of the *Moza del Retoño,* wherein groping hands supplied the blanks left in the words. Meanwhile the loading of wine, oil, and grain was still going on, with the help of the overseer's Indian servants, who were impatient to return to their native land. Our future chaplain was on his way to the harbor, driving before him two mules loaded with the bellows and pipes of a wooden organ. Whenever I met any of the men from the ships, there were noisy embraces, exaggerated gestures, and enough laughter and boasting to bring the women to their windows. We seemed to be men of a different race, expressly created to carry out exploits beyond the ken of the baker, the wool carder, and the merchant who hawked holland shirts embroidered by parties of nuns in their patios. In the middle of the square, their brass instruments flashing in the sun, the Captain's six trumpeters were playing popular airs while the Burgundian drummers thundered on their instruments, and a sackbut with a mouth-piece like a dragon was bellowing as if it wanted to bite.

In his shop, smelling of calfskin and Cordovan leather, my father was driving his awl into a stirrup strap with the half-heartedness of someone whose mind is elsewhere. When he saw me, he took me in his arms with serene sadness, perhaps remembering the horrible death of Cristobalillo, the companion of my youthful escapades, whom the Indians of the Dragon's Mouth had pierced with their arrows. But he knew that everyone was wild to embark for the Indies then—although most men in possession of their senses were already realizing that it was the "madness of many for the gain of a few." He spoke in praise of good craftsmanship and told me that a man could gain as much respect by carrying the harness maker's standard in the Corpus Christi procession as from dangerous exploits. He pointed out the advantages of a well-provided table, a full coffer, and a peaceful old age. But, probably having realized that the excitement in the town was steadily increasing and that my mood was not attuned to such sensible reasoning, he gently led me to the door of my mother's room.

This was the moment I had most dreaded, and I could hardly restrain my own tears when I saw hers, for we had put off telling her of my departure until everyone knew that my name had been entered in the books of the Casa de la Contratación. I thanked her for the vows she had made to the Virgin of Navigators in exchange for my speedy return, and promised her everything she asked of me, such as to have no sinful dealings with the women of those far-off countries, whom the Devil kept in a state of paradisiac nakedness in order to confuse and mislead unwary Christians, even if they were not actually corrupted by the sight of such a careless display of flesh. Then, realizing that it was useless to make demands of someone who was already dreaming of what lay beyond the horizon, my mother began asking me anxiously about the safety of the ships and the skill of their pilots. I exaggerated the solidity and seaworthiness of *La Gallarda*, declaring that her pilot was a veteran of the Indies and a comrade of Nuño García. And to distract her from her fears, I told her about the wonders of the New World, where all diseases could be cured by the Claw of the Great Beast and by bezoar stones; I told her, too, that in the country of the Omeguas there was a city built entirely of gold, so large that it would take a good walker a night and two days to cross it, and that we should surely go there unless we found our fortune in some not-yet-discovered regions inhabited by rich tribes for us to conquer. Gently shaking her head, my mother then said that travelers returned from the Indies told lying, boastful stories, and spoke of Amazons and anthropophagi, of terrible Bermudan tempests and poisoned spears that transformed into a statue anyone they pierced.

Seeing that she confronted all my hopeful remarks with unpleasant facts, I talked to her of our high-minded aims and tried to make her see the plight of all the poor idol worshippers who did not even know the sign of the Cross. We should win thousands of souls to our holy religion and carry out Christ's commandments to the Apostles. We were soldiers of God as well as soldiers of the King, and by baptizing the Indians and freeing them from their barbarous superstitions our nation would win imperishable glory and greater happiness, prosperity, and power than all the kingdoms of Europe. Soothed by my remarks, my mother hung a scapulary around my neck and gave me various ointments against the bites of poisonous creatures, at the same time making me promise that I would never go to sleep without wearing some woolen socks she had made for me herself. And as the cathedral bells began to peal, she went to look for an embroidered shawl that she wore only on very important occasions. On the way to church I noticed that in spite of everything my parents had, as it were, grown in stature because of their pride in having a son in the Captain's fleet, and that they greeted people more often and more demonstratively than usual. It is always gratifying to have a brave son on his way to fight for a splendid and just cause. I looked toward the harbor. Grain was still being carried onto the ships.

III

I used to call her my sweetheart, although no one yet knew that we were in love. When I saw her father near the ships, I realized that she would be alone, so I followed the dreary jetty battered by the winds, splashed with green water, and edged with chains and rings green with slime until I reached the last house, the one with green shutters that were always closed. Hardly had I sounded the tarnished knocker when the door opened, and I entered the house along with a gust of wind full of sea spray. The lamps had already been lighted because of the mist. My sweetheart sat down beside me in a deep armchair covered in old brocade and rested her head on my shoulder with such a sad air of resignation that I did not dare question those beloved eyes, which seemed to be gazing at nothing, but with an air of amazement. The strange objects that filled the room now took on a new significance for me. Some link bound me to the astrolabe, the compass, and the wind rose, as well as to the sawfish hanging from the beams of the ceiling and the charts by Mercator and Ortelius spread out on either side of the fireplace among maps of the heavens populated by Bears, Dogs, and Archers.

Above the whistling of the wind as it crept under the doors, I heard the voice of my sweetheart asking how our preparations were going. Reassured to find that it was possible to talk of something other than ourselves, I told her about the Sulpicians and Recollects who were to embark with us, and praised the piety of the gentlemen and farmers chosen by the man who would take possession of these far-off countries in the name of the King of France. I told her what I knew of the great River Colbert, bordered with ancient trees draped in silvery moss, its red waters flowing majestically beneath a sky white with herons. We were taking provisions for six months.

The lowest decks of the *Belle* and the *Amiable* were full of corn. We were undertaking the important task of civilizing the vast areas of forest lying between the burning Gulf of Mexico and Chicagua, and we would teach new skills to the inhabitants.

Just when I thought my sweetheart was listening most attentively to what I was saying, she suddenly sat up, and said with unexpected vehemence that there was nothing glorious about the enterprise that had set all the town bells ringing since dawn. Last night, with her eyes inflamed with weeping, her anxiety to know something about the world across the sea to which I was going had driven her to pick up Montaigne's *Essais* and read everything to do with America in the chapter on Coaches. There she had learned about the treachery of the Spaniards, and how they had succeeded in passing themselves off as gods, with their horses and bombards. Aflame with virginal indignation, my sweetheart showed me the passage in which the skeptical Bordelais says of the Indians that "we have made use of their ignorance and inexperience to draw them more easily into fraud, luxury, avarice, and all manner of inhumanity and cruelty by the example of our life and pattern of our customs." Blinded by her distress at such perfidy, this devout young woman who always wore a gold cross on her bosom actually approved of a writer who could impiously declare that the savages of the New World had no reason to exchange their religion for ours, their own having served them very well for a long time.

I realized that these errors came only from the resentment of a girl in love—and a very charming girl—against the man who was forcing her to wait for him so long merely because he wanted to make his fortune quickly in a much-proclaimed undertaking. But although I understood this, I felt deeply wounded by her scorn for my courage and her lack of interest in an adventure that would make my name famous; for the news of some exploit of mine, or of some region I had pacified, might well lead to the King's conferring a title on me, even though it might involve a few Indians dying by my hand. No great deed is achieved without a struggle, and as for our holy faith, the Word must be imposed with blood. But it was jealousy that made my sweetheart paint such an ugly picture of the island of Santo Domingo, where we were to make a landing, describing it in adorably unsuitable words as "a paradise of wicked women." It was obvious that in spite of her chastity, she knew what sort of women they were who often embarked for Cap Français from a jetty nearby under the supervision of the police and amid shouts of laughter and coarse jokes from the sailors. Someone, perhaps one of the servants, may have told her that a certain sort of abstinence is not healthy for a man, and she was imagining me beset by greater perils than the floods, storms, and water dragons that abound in American rivers, in some Eden of nudity and demoralizing heat.

In the end I began to be annoyed that we should be having this wrangle instead of the tender farewells I had expected at such a moment. I started abusing the cowardice of women, their incapacity for heroism, the way their philosophy was bounded by baby linen and workboxes, when a loud knocking announced the untimely return of her father. I jumped out of a back window, unnoticed by anyone in the marketplace, for passersby, fishermen, and drunkards—already numerous even so early in the evening—had gathered around a table on which a man stood shouting. I took him at first for a hawker trying to sell Orvieto elixir, but he turned out to be a hermit demanding the liberation of the holy places, I shrugged my shoulder and went on my way. Some time ago I had been on the point of enlisting in Foulque de Neuilly's crusade. A malignant fever—cured thanks to God and my sainted mother's ointments—most opportunely kept me shivering in bed on the day of departure: that adventure ended, as everyone knows, in a war between Christians and Christians. The crusades had fallen into disrepute. Besides, I had other things to think about.

IV

The wind had died down. Still annoyed by my stupid quarrel with my betrothed, I went off to the harbor to look at the ships. They were all moored to the jetty, side by side, with hatches open, receiving thousands of sacks of wheat flour between their brightly camouflaged sides. The infantry regiments were slowly going up the gangways amid the shouts of stevedores, blasts from the boatswain's whistle, and signals tearing through the mist to set the cranes in motion. On the decks, shapeless objects and menacing machines were being heaped together under tarpaulins. From time to time an aluminum wing revolved slowly above the bulwarks before disappearing into the darkness of the hold. The generals' horses, suspended from webbing bands, traveled over the roofs of the shops like the horses of the Valkyries. I was standing on a high iron gangway watching the final preparations, when suddenly I became agonizingly aware that there were only a few hours left—scarcely thirteen—before I too should have to board one of those ships now being loaded with weapons for my use. Then I thought of women; of the days of abstinence lying ahead; of the sadness of dying without having once more taken my pleasure from another warm body.

Full of impatience, and still angry because I had not got even a kiss from my sweetheart, I struck off toward the house where the dancers lived. Christopher, very drunk, was already shut into his girl's room. My girl embraced me, laughing and crying, saying that she was proud of me, that I looked very handsome in my uniform, and that a fortuneteller had read the cards and told her that no harm would come to me during the Great Landing. She more than once called me a "hero," as if she knew how cruelly her flattery contrasted with my sweetheart's unjust remarks. I went out onto the roof. The lights were coming on in the town, outlining the gigantic geometry of the buildings in luminous points. Below, in the streets, was a confused swarm of heads and hats.

At this distance, it was impossible to tell women from men in the evening mist. Yet it was in order that this crowd of unknown human beings should go on existing, that I was due to make my way to the ships soon after dawn. I should plow the stormy ocean during the winter months and land on a remote shore under attack from steel and fire, in defense of my countrymen's principles. It was the last time a sword would be brandished over the maps of the West. This time we should finish off the new Teutonic Order for good and all, and advance as victors into that longed-for future when man would be reconciled with man. My mistress laid her trembling hand on my head, perhaps guessing at the nobility of my thoughts. She was naked under the half-open flaps of her dressing gown.

V

I returned home a few hours before dawn, walking unsteadily from the wine with which I had tried to cheat the fatigue of a body surfeited with enjoyment of another body. I was hungry and sleepy, and at the same time deeply disturbed by the thought of my approaching departure. I laid my weapons and belt on a stool and threw myself on my bed. Then I realized, with a start of surprise, that someone was lying under the thick woolen blanket; and I was just stretching out my hand for my knife when I found myself embraced by two burning-hot arms, which clasped me around the neck like the arms of a drowning man while two inexpressibly smooth legs twined themselves between mine. I was struck dumb with astonishment when I saw that the person who had slipped into my bed was my sweetheart. Between her sobs, she told me how she had escaped in the darkness, had run away in terror from barking dogs and crept furtively through my father's garden to the window of my room. Here she had waited for me in terror and impatience. After our stupid quarrel that afternoon, she had thought of the dangers and sufferings lying in wait for me, with that sense of impotent longing to lighten a soldier's hazardous lot which women so often express by offering their own bodies, as if the sacrifice of their jealously guarded virginity at the moment of departure and without hope of enjoyment, this reckless abandonment to another's pleasure, could have the propitiatory power of ritual oblation.

There is a unique and special freshness in an encounter with a chaste body never touched by a lover's hands, a felicitious clumsiness of response, an intuitive candor that, responding to some obscure promptings, divines and adopts the attitudes that favor the closest possible physical union. As I lay in my sweetheart's arms and felt the little fleece that timidly brushed against one of my thighs, I grew more and more angry at having exhausted my strength in all-too-familiar coupling, in the absurd belief that I was ensuring my future serenity by means of present excesses. And now that I was being offered this so desirable compliance, I lay almost insensible beneath my sweetheart's tremulous and impatient body. I would not say that my youth was incapable of catching fire once again that night under the stimulus of this new pleasure. But the idea that it was a virgin who was offering herself to me, and that her closed and intact flesh would require a slow and sustained effort on my part, filled me with an obsessive fear of failure.

I pushed my sweetheart to one side, kissing her gently on the shoulders, and began telling her with assumed sincerity what a mistake it would be for our nuptial joys to be marred by the hurry of departure; how ashamed she would be if she became pregnant and how sad it was for children to grow up with no father to teach them how to get green honey out of hollow tree trunks and look for cuttlefish under stones. She listened, her large bright eyes burning in the darkness, and I was aware that she was in the grip of a resentment drawn from the underworld of the instincts and felt nothing but scorn for a man who, when offered such an opportunity, invoked reason and prudence instead of taking her by force, leaving her bleeding on the bed like a trophy of the chase, defiled, with breasts bitten, but having become a woman in her hour of defeat.

Just then we heard the lowing of cattle going to be sacrificed on the shore and the watchmen blowing their conchs. With scorn showing clearly in her face, my sweetheart got quickly out of bed without letting me touch her, and with a gesture not so much of modesty as of someone taking back what he had been on the point of selling too cheap, she covered those charms which had suddenly begun to enflame my desire. Before I could stop her, she had jumped out of the window. I saw her running away as fast as she could among the olives, and I realized in that instant that it would be easier for me to enter the city of Troy without a scratch than to regain what I had lost.

When I went down to the ships with my parents, my soldier's pride had been replaced by an intolerable sense of disgust, of inner emptiness and self-depreciation. And when the steersmen pushed the ships away from the shore with their strong poles, and the masts stood erect between the row of oarsmen, I realized that the display, excesses, and feasting that precede the departure of soldiers to the battlefield were now over. There was no time now for garlands, laurel wreaths, wine drinking in every house, envious glances from weaklings, and favors from women. Instead, our lot would consist of bugle calls, mud, rainsoaked bread, the arrogance of our leaders, blood spilled in error, the sickly, tainted smell of gangrene. I already felt less confident that my courage would contribute to the power and happiness of the long-haired Achaeans. A veteran soldier, going to war because it was his profession and with no more enthusiasm than a sheep shearer on his way to the pen, was telling anyone prepared to listen that Helen of Sparta was very happy to be in Troy, and that when she disported herself in Paris' bed, her hoarse cries of enjoyment brought blushes to the cheeks of the virgins who lived in Priam's palace. It was said that the whole story of the unhappy captivity of Leda's daughter, and of the insults and humiliations the Trojans had subjected her to, was simply war propaganda, inspired by Agamemnon with the consent of Menelaus. In fact, behind this enterprise and the noble ideals it had set up as a screen, a great many aims were concealed which would not benefit the combatants in the very least:

above all, so the old soldier said, to sell more pottery, more cloth, more vases decorated with scenes from chariot races, and to open new ways of access to Asia, whose peoples had a passion for barter, and so put an end once and for all to Trojan competition.

Too heavily loaded with flour and men, the ship responded slowly to the oars. I gazed for a long time at the sunlit houses of my native town. I was nearly in tears, I took off my helmet and hid my eyes behind its crest; I had taken great trouble to make it round and smooth, like the magnificent crests of the men who could order their accouterments of war from the most highly skilled craftsmen and who were voyaging on the swiftest and longest ship.

■ João Guimarães Rosa (1908–1967)
Brazil (story)

TRANSLATED BY BARBARA SHELBY MERELLO

A Brazilian doctor from the Minas Gerais plateau, in his native state João Guimarães Rosa accumulated a knowledge of regional legends from working in libraries and long conversations with local storytellers. He transformed this material into his first collections of tales. Rosa entered the diplomatic service and was stationed in Germany, Colombia, Paris, and Rio. In 1942, while serving as the consular attaché in Hamburg, he was interned by the Nazis after Brazil broke diplomatic relations with Germany. He was eventually released in an exchange of diplomats. He was an extraordinary polyglot, with a fine knowledge of Russian, Japanese, English, German, French, Latin, and Greek. In 1946, he published his first collection of short stories, a difficult, extremely successful book, which effectively changed fiction writing in Brazil. The "saga" in *Sagarana* (1946) is an explicit reference to oral legendary saga, suggesting the mythical, magical yet historical basis for these interrelated tales. Guimarães's great novel is *Grande Sertão* (1956), a hypnotic narration, in the exquisite lucid language of his best tales. The Mexican novelist Juan Rulfo considered him the finest author produced by the Americas in our century. In his stories he plays with time and existence. The title of his most famous story, "The Third Bank of the River," is fascinatingly mysterious. It has many meanings as it describes the narrator's father in midstream, holding steady against the allegorical current. What is the third shore? Time, death, the planks of the boat, redemption after a new flood? The story ends, as great art often does, with an ending that is open and continuing like the river.

FURTHER READING: Rosa, João Guimarães. *Sagarana*, 1946; *Grande Sertão: Veredas* (*The Devil to Pay in the Backlands*), 1956; *First Tales*, 1962 (tr. as *The Third Bank of the River and Other Stories*); *Tutaméia*, 1967; *These Tales*, 1969.

The Third Bank of the River

Father was a reliable, law-abiding, practical man, and had been ever since he was a boy, as various people of good sense testified when I asked them about him. I don't remember that he seemed any crazier or even any moodier than anyone else we knew. He just didn't talk much. It was our mother who gave the orders and scolded us every day—my sister, my brother, and me. Then one day my father ordered a canoe for himself.

He took the matter very seriously. He had the canoe made to his specifications of fine *vinhático* wood; a small one, with a narrow board in the stern as though to leave only enough room for the oarsman. Every bit of it was hand-hewn of special strong wood carefully shaped, fit to last in the water for twenty or thirty years. Mother railed at the idea. How could a man who had never fiddled away his time on such tricks propose to go fishing and hunting now, at his time of life? Father said nothing. Our house was closer to the river then than it is now, less than a quarter of a league away: there rolled the river, great, deep, and silent, always silent. It was so wide that you could hardly see the bank on the other side. I can never forget the day the canoe was ready.

Neither happy nor excited nor downcast, Father pulled his hat well down on his head and said one firm goodbye. He spoke not another word, took neither food nor other supplies, gave no parting advice. We thought Mother would have a fit, but she only blanched white, bit her lip, and said bitterly: "Go or stay; but if you go, don't you ever come back!" Father left his answer in suspense. He gave me a mild look and motioned me to go aside with him a few steps. I was afraid of Mother's anger, but I obeyed anyway, that time. The turn things had taken gave me the courage to ask: "Father, will you take me with you in that canoe?" But he just gave me a long look in return: gave me his blessing and motioned me to go back. I pretended to go, but instead turned off into a deep woodsy hollow to watch. Father stepped into the canoe, untied it, and began to paddle off. The canoe slipped away, a straight, even shadow like an alligator, slithery, long.

Our father never came back. He hadn't gone anywhere. He stuck to that stretch of the river, staying halfway across, always in the canoe, never to spring out of it, ever again. The strangeness of that truth was enough to dismay us all. What had never been before, was. Our relatives, the neighbors, and all our acquaintances met and took counsel together.

Mother, though, behaved very reasonably, with the result that everybody believed what no one wanted to put into words about our father: that he was mad. Only a few of them thought he might be keeping a vow, or—who could tell—maybe he was sick with some hideous disease like leprosy, and that was what had made him desert us to live out another life, close to his family and yet far enough away. The news spread by word of mouth, carried by people like travelers and those who lived along the banks of the river, who said of Father that he never landed at spit or cove, by day or by night, but always stuck to the river, lonely and outside human society. Finally, Mother and our relatives realized that the provisions he had hidden in the canoe must be getting low and thought that he would have to either land somewhere and go away from us for good—that seemed the most likely—or repent once and for all and come back home.

But they were wrong. I had made myself responsible for stealing a bit of food for him every day, an idea that had come to me the very first night, when the family had lighted bonfires on the riverbank and in their glare prayed and called out to Father. Every day from then on I went back to the river with a lump of hard brown sugar, some corn bread, or a bunch of bananas. Once, at the end of an hour of waiting that had dragged on and on, I caught sight of Father; he was way off, sitting in the bottom of the canoe as if suspended in the mirror smoothness of the river. He saw me, but he did not paddle over or make any sign. I held up the things to eat and then laid them in a hollowed-out rock in the river bluff, safe from any animals who might nose around and where they would be kept dry in rain or dew. Time after time, day after day, I did the same thing. Much later I had a surprise: Mother knew about my mission but, saying nothing and pretending she didn't, made it easier for me by putting out leftovers where I was sure to find them. Mother almost never showed what she was thinking.

Finally she sent for an uncle of ours, her brother, to help with the farm and with money matters, and she got a tutor for us children. She also arranged for the priest to come in his vestments to the river edge to exorcise Father and call upon him to desist from his sad obsession. Another time, she tried to scare Father by getting two soldiers to come. But none of it was any use. Father passed by at a distance, discernible only dimly through the river haze, going by in the canoe without ever letting anyone go close enough to touch him or even talk to him. The reporters who went out in a launch and tried to take his picture not long ago failed just like everybody else; Father crossed over to the other bank and steered the canoe into the thick swamp that goes on for miles, part reeds and part brush. Only he knew every hand's breadth of its blackness.

We just had to try to get used to it. But it was hard, and we never really managed. I'm judging by myself, of course. Whether I wanted to or not, my thoughts kept circling back and I found myself thinking of Father. The hard nub of it was that I couldn't begin to understand how he could hold out. Day and night, in bright sunshine or in rainstorms, in muggy heat or in the terrible cold spells in the middle of the year, without shelter or any protection but the old hat on his head, all through the weeks, and months, and years—he marked in no way the passing of his life. Father never landed, never put in at either shore or stopped at any part of the river islands or sandbars; and he never again stepped onto grass or solid earth. It was true that in order to catch a little sleep he may have tied up the canoe at some concealed islet-spit. But he never lighted a fire on shore, had no lamp or candle, never struck a match again. He did no more than taste food; even the morsels he took from what we left for him along the roots of the fig tree or in the hollow stone at the foot of the cliff could not have been enough to keep him alive. Wasn't he ever sick? And what constant strength he must have had in his arms to maintain himself and the canoe ready for the piling up of the floodwaters where danger rolls on the great current, sweeping the bodies of dead animals and tree trunks downstream—frightening, threatening, crashing into him. And he never spoke another word to a living soul. We never talked about him, either. We only thought of him. Father could never be forgotten; and if, for short periods of time, we pretended to ourselves that we had forgotten, it was only to find ourselves roused suddenly by his memory, startled by it again and again.

My sister married; but Mother would have no festivities. He came into our minds whenever we ate something especially tasty, and when we were wrapped up snugly at night we thought of those bare unsheltered nights of cold, heavy rain, and Father with only his hand and maybe a calabash to bail the storm water out of the canoe. Every so often someone who knew us would remark that I was getting to look more and more like my father. But I knew that now he must be bushy-haired and bearded, his nails long, his body cadaverous and gaunt, burnt black by the sun, hairy as a beast and almost as naked, even with the pieces of clothing we left for him at intervals.

He never felt the need to know anything about us; had he no family affection? But out of love, love and respect, whenever I was praised for something good I had done, I would say: "It was Father who taught me how to do it that way." It wasn't true, exactly, but it was a truthful kind of lie. If he didn't remember us any more and didn't want to know how we were, why didn't he go farther up the river or down it, away to landing places where he would never be found? Only he knew. When my sister had a baby boy, she got it into her head that she must show Father his grandson. All of us went and stood on the bluff. The day was fine and my sister was wearing the white dress she had worn at her wedding. She lifted the baby up in her arms and her husband held a parasol over the two of them. We called and we waited. Our father didn't come. My sister wept; we all cried and hugged one another as we stood there.

After that my sister moved far away with her husband, and my brother decided to go live in the city. Times changed, with the slow swiftness of time. Mother went away too in the end, to live with my sister because she was growing old. I stayed on here, the only one of the family who was left. I could never think of marriage. I stayed where I was, burdened down with all life's cumbrous baggage. I knew Father needed me, as he wandered up and down on the river in the wilderness, even though he never gave a reason for what he had done. When at last I made up my mind that I had to know and finally made a firm attempt to find out, people told me rumor had it that Father might have given some explanation to the man who made the canoe for him. But now the builder was dead; and no one really knew or could recollect any more except that there had been some silly talk in the beginning, when the river was first swollen by such endless torrents of rain that everyone was afraid the world was coming to an end; then they had said that Father might have received a warning, like Noah, and so prepared the canoe ahead of time. I could half-recall the story. I could not even blame my father. And a few first white hairs began to appear on my head.

I was a man whose words were all sorrowful. Why did I feel so guilty, so guilty? Was it because of my father, who made his absence felt always, and because of the river-river-river, the river-flowing forever? I was suffering the onset of old age—this life of mine only postponed the inevitable. I had bad spells, pains in the belly, dizziness, twinges of rheumatism. And he? Why, oh why must he do what he did? He must suffer terribly. Old as he was, was he not bound to weaken in vigor sooner or later and let the canoe overturn or, when the river rose, let it drift unguided for hours downstream, until it finally went over the brink of the loud rushing fall of the cataract, with its wild boiling and death? My heart shrank. He was out there, with none of my easy security. I was guilty of I knew not what, filled with boundless sorrow in the deepest part of me. If I only knew—if only things were otherwise. And then, little by little, the idea came to me.

I could not even wait until next day. Was I *crazy*? No. In our house, the word crazy was not spoken, had never been spoken again in all those years; no one was condemned as crazy. Either no one is crazy, or everyone is. I just went, taking along a sheet to wave with. I was very much in my right mind. I waited. After a long time he appeared; his indistinct bulk took form. He was there, sitting in the stern. He was there, a shout away. I called out several times. And I said the words which were making me say them, the sworn promise, the declaration. I had to force my voice to say: "Father, you're getting old, you've done your part. . . . You can come back now, you don't have to stay any longer. . . . You come back, and I'll do it, right now or whenever you want me to; it's what we both want. I'll take your place in the canoe!" And as I said it my heart beat to the rhythm of what was truest and best in me.

He heard me. He got to his feet. He dipped the paddle in the water, the bow pointed toward me; he had agreed. And suddenly I shuddered deeply, because he had lifted his arm and gestured a greeting—the first, after so many years. And I could not. . . . Panic-stricken, my hair standing on end, I ran, I fled, I left the place behind me in a mad headlong rush. For he seemed to be coming from the hereafter. And I am pleading, pleading, pleading for forgiveness.

I was struck by the solemn ice of fear, and I fell ill. I knew that no one ever heard of him again. Can I be a man, after having thus failed him? I am what never was—the unspeakable. I know it is too late for salvation now, but I am afraid to cut life short in the shallows of the world. At least, when death comes to the body, let them take me and put me in a wretched little canoe, and on the water that flows forever past its unending banks, let me go—down the river, away from the river, into the river—the river.

■ Juan Carlos Onetti (1909–1994)
Uruguay (story)

TRANSLATED BY ANDREW HURLEY

Writer of novels and stories, Juan Carlos Onetti was born in Montevideo and divided most of his literary life between that city and Buenos Aires. As a child, he was a reader of popular novelists, including Jules Verne and, later, Knut Hamsun. He did not finish high school. In Montevideo and Buenos Aires, he did odd jobs, and when he returned to Montevideo in 1939, he worked as literary editor and contributor for *Marcha,* a weekly news magazine; at the same time, he wrote and published his first novel, *El pozo* (*The Pit*), which brought him limited acclaim in Uruguay. He spent most of his life as a journalist. As with many writers of his generation, he was clearly influenced by William Faulkner's *Sanctuary* and Louis Ferdinand Céline's *Voyage to the End of the Night.* In 1941, he moved back to Buenos Aires, where he published *Tierra de nadie* (*No Man's Land,* 1941), a book about Buenos Aires immigrant lowlife modeled on the American novelist John Dos Passos's *Manhattan Transfer,* which was a pivotal experimental book about street life, squalor, crime, and social conflict. Onetti absorbed the cinematic techniques, obscenities, and tough observer glance of *Manhattan Transfer,* a book that internationally established a tone among socially committed writers of France, Germany, Italy, and Spain, guiding, among others, the Spanish Nobel laureate novelist Camilo José Cela. Onetti's fiction has also led critics to speak of early Jean Paul Sartre and Dostoyevsky because of their dark themes of nihilistic loneliness, sexual obsession, humor, despair, and existential dream fantasy. In three novels written in Buenos Aires, Onetti created an imaginary town of Santa María for his distopian scenes in *A Brief Life* (1950), *The Shipyard* (1961), and *Juntacadáveres* (*Corpse Gatherers,* 1964). He returned to Montevideo in 1954, and, in 1957, he became the director of municipal libraries in the capital city. He was arrested in Uruguay in 1974 for his participation in a jury that awarded a prize for a novel that suggested sexual misadventures by a member of the ruling military junta. There was an international protest against his arrest organized by the Argentine novelist Adolfo Bioy Casares, and Onetti, in poor health, was released. He then retired to Spain, in 1976, where he continued writing. In 1980, Onetti received the Cervantes Award, Spain's highest literary honor. He died in Madrid in 1994, a grand master of the Latin American narrative.

FURTHER READING: Onetti, Juan Carlos. *A Brief Life*, 1950; *The Shipyard*, 1961; *Junta-cadáveres* (*Corpse Gatherers*, 1964); *Goodbye and Stories*, 1990.

The Dog Will Have Its Day

For my teacher, Enrico Cicogna

The overseer, his head bared in respect, was handing the pieces of bloody meat one by one to the man in the bowler hat and frock coat. At afternoon's end, in silence. The man in the bowler waved his arms in a circle above the kennel, and immediately there arose the dark hot wind of the four Dobermans, thin, almost skin and bone, and the blind avidity of their muzzles, their innumerable teeth.

The man in the bowler stood for a few moments watching them eat, swallow, then watched them beg for more meat.

"All right," he said to the overseer, "as I ordered. All the water they want, but no food. Today is Thursday. Let them out on Saturday at this same time, more or less—when the sun sets. And tell everyone to go to bed. Saturday I want everyone deaf even if you can hear it all the way from the peons' quarters."

"Sir," nodded the overseer.

Then the man in the bowler handed the overseer a few meat-colored bills, refusing to hear his words of thanks. He settled his gray bowler lower on his forehead and spoke as he continued to watch the dogs. The four Dobermans were kept separate by wire-mesh fences; the four Dobermans were male.

"I'll be up to the house in a half-hour or so. Have the coach ready. I'm going to Buenos Aires. Business. I don't know how long I'll be there. And don't forget. All his clothes have to be changed afterward. Burn the papers. The money is yours, and anything else you want—rings, cufflinks, watch. But don't wear anything for several months. I'll let you know when. The money is yours," he repeated. "City men always have plenty of money. And his hands—don't forget about his hands."

Then he was small and strong, dressed now in a gray embroidered shirt, a wide belt heavy with silver medallions, a dark poncho, and a black necktie. The color had been imposed on him when he was thirteen, and by now he had forgotten why or by whom. There was a big silver knife, sometimes, for show or for decoration, and the hat with the brim turned back. His eyes, like his moustache, were the color of new wire, and they had the same stiffness.

He gazed at the world without real hatred or pain, looked invariably to other men as though he were sure that life, his life, would unfold in pleasant routine until the last. But he was lying. Leaning on the mantelpiece, he saw the room lie: the silk-and-gilt armchairs he had never allowed himself to sit in, the cabinets and "curios" with their twisted, elaborate legs, their glass doors, their shelves full of tea services, coffee services, chocolate services which probably had never been used, the enormous birdcage with its dreadful cacophony, the curves of the loveseat, the low fragile tables of no known purpose. The heavy wine-colored drapes shut out the calm afternoon: all that existed was suffocating bric-a-brac.

"I'm going to Buenos Aires," the man was saying again, as he did every Friday afternoon, in his slow, solemn, deep voice. "The boat leaves at ten. Business, that swindle they're trying to pull on me with those lands of yours up north."

He looked at the bonbons, the thin slices of ham, the little triangles of cheese, the woman pouring tea: she was young, blond, forever pale, quite mistaken now about her immediate future.

He looked at the six-year-old child, nervous, speechless, whiter than its mother, always dressed by her in feminine clothes, profusions of velvet and lace. He said nothing, because everything had been said long before. The woman's repugnance, the man's growing hatred had both been born on that same extravagant wedding night they had conceived the girl-boy that now leaned open-mouthed against its mother's thigh, its restless fingers twirling the thick yellow curls that fell to its neck, to its necklace of little holy medals.

The coach was a shining black; it gleamed as though it were new—varnished every day. It bore two great carriage-lamps which years later would be disputed over by the wealthy of Santa María, who would want them (with lightbulbs now, instead of candles) to grace their front porches. The coach was drawn by a dapple-gray horse that could have been forged of silver, or of pewter. And the coach itself had not been made by Daglio; it had been brought from England.

Sometimes with envy, even almost with hate, he marked the speed, the blind youth of the animal; sometimes he imagined himself infected with its youth, its ignorance of its own future.

But once again that Friday—that Friday especially—he did not go to Buenos Aires. He wasn't even in Santa María, in fact; because as he came to the first houses outside Enduro he pulled the young dapple's head to the left, and the barouche swung around, its wheels kicking up clods as it spun down a dry-clay road that led through fields of burned hay and past a distant, solitary tree here and there, and that continued on toward the dirty beach which many years later would be a resort that bore his name, with beach houses and shops and summering people, another humble stone in the edifice of the achievement of his ambitions.

Farther on, through enormous flatlands, the horse trotted along a road flanked by the peaceableness of wheat fields, of seemingly deserted farms, all timidly washed-out, bleached, immersed in the growing heat of the afternoon.

He halted the coach in front of the largest building in the ramshackle settlement. He did not reply to the murmured words that greeted his arrival; into the hand of the dark man who emerged to meet him he counted out ten bills. He was paying for the animal's feed, the stable in the barn, the secret, the silence which both men knew was a lie.

Then he walked over to a new-looking, whitewashed shack. It was surrounded by pigweed, and a huge, straight pine planted by no one half a century before seemed to be what was keeping it upright.

As always, he knocked imperiously, coolly three times with the handle of the whip at the flimsy door. Perhaps that too was an implicit part of the ritual: the woman silent, maybe not even at home, taking her time. The man did not knock again. He waited there unmoving, drinking in, with his heavy breaths, this first dose of the weekly suffering that she, Josephine, obediently and generously served him up.

Submissive, the girl opened the door; hiding the revulsion and disgust that once had been pity, she unbuttoned her robe, let it fall to the floor, and turned and walked naked to the bed.

One Friday long ago, uneasy because she was afraid of another man, she had looked at her little clock: she knew, then, that this ritual took two hours. He took off his coat, laid it next to the whip and the hat, and then, trembling, went on folding things across a chair. Then he walked over to her and, as always, began at the girl's feet, sobbing in a hoarse, broken voice, begging forgiveness with incomprehensible moans for some old, old sin still unpardoned, his tears and saliva wetting the girl's red toenails.

For almost three whole days the girl had him underfoot about the place, rolling cigarettes, silent, emptying with no hurry, no drunkenness, the big bottles of gin, getting up to go to the bathroom or to come back, furious and docile, to the torture of the bed.

Carried by the seeds wrapped in filaments of white silk, flying on the wings of the capricious air, the news reached Santa María, reached Enduro, reached the little white house on the coast. When the man got it — the horse's caretaker stirred himself to scratch at the door and tell him the news, his eyes averted, his strangled cap in his huge dark hands — he realized that, incredibly, the naked woman imprisoned in the bed already knew it.

Standing there outside the door, his head still bowed from trying to catch the servile, less and less understandable words, the man with the wire-colored moustache, with the gleaming black barouche, with the pewter horse, with more than half the property in the settlement, spoke slowly and spoke too much:

"Fruit thieves. It's for them I've got the best dogs, the most murderous dogs there are. They don't attack. They defend." He looked an instant at the impassive sky, not smiling, not sad; he took more bills from his waist. "But I don't know anything, don't forget. I'm in Buenos Aires."

It was Sunday noon, but the man didn't leave the house until Monday morning. Now the little dappled horse was held back to a trot; it didn't need to be guided; it was trotting back home so rhythmically it had something of a wind-up animal, something of a toy about it.

"A soldier-boy," unconcernedly thought the man when he saw a bored young policeman leaning on the wall beside the great black wrought-iron gate with its ornate doubling swirls of a J overlaid with a P. The young man's uniform had once been blue; it had once belonged to a heavier, taller man.

"The first soldier-boy," the man thought almost smiling, feeling himself fill slowly with excitement, with something like the beginnings of amusement.

"Pardon, sir," said the uniformed young man, looking younger and shyer the closer the older man came, almost a boy at last. "Commissioner Medina told me to ask you to stop by the Station. I, I mean at your convenience."

"Another soldier-boy," murmured the man, his senses entangled in the steam and the smell of the horse. "But it's no fault of yours. Tell Medina that I'm home. I'll be in my house. All day. If he wants to see me."

He ticked the reins imperceptibly and the animal jubilantly drew him past the garden and the arbor out to the half-moon of dry earth and the coach house.

The men who came over to meet him and take charge of the carriage were glum yet experienced; none of them spoke of Saturday night or of Sunday morning.

Petrus didn't smile, because he had discharged his mockery years before, and perhaps forever, into the moustache the color of iron filings. He had a blurred memory of reaching fifty; he knew everything that he still had to do or try to do in that strange spot in the world not yet on any map; it was his opinion that he would never meet any obstacle more stubborn, more viscous and sticky, than the stupidity and incomprehension of other people, of all the other people he'd be obliged to come up against.

And so, that afternoon, when the suffocating heat began to soften a little under the trees, there came Medina, the Commissioner, a man timeless, heavy, and slothful, driving the first Model T Henry Ford had managed to sell in the country in 1907.

The overseer greeted him with a salute too slow and exaggerated. Medina measured him with a wry smile and spoke to him mildly.

"I expect you at the Station at seven, Petrus or no Petrus. It'll be to your advantage to come. I promise you it will not be to your advantage if you make me send somebody to get you."

The man dropped his arm and consented, nodding. He was not intimidated.

"The master said that if you came he was in the house."

Medina walked deliberately, planting his heels in the dried-out earth at each step, swaggering a little, and he went up the granite steps, too wide, too high. "A palace; this foreigner thinks he can live in a palace here. In Santa María."

All the doors were closed against the heat. Medina brushed off his hands as a kind of notice and he stepped into the large parlor with all the glass, all the fans, all the flowers. In a different suit from the morning's, and as neatly dressed as though he were about to go for an evening spin in his barouche, even wearing a hat, sitting with a cigarette in the only chair that looked able to support the weight of a man, Jeremías Petrus dropped onto the carpet the book he had been reading and raised two fingers in a kind of salute, a welcome.

"Take a seat, please, Commissioner."

"Thank you. Last time we saw each other my name was Medina."

"But today I promoted you. I already know what brought you here."

Medina looked doubtfully at the profusion of little gilt chairs.

"Any chair, any chair," Petrus insisted. "If you break it, you'll be doing me a favor. But first, what'll we drink? I'm sick of gin."

"I didn't come for a drink."

"Or to tell me no alcohol while you're on duty, either. No bottles from France have been delivered in months. Some little soldierboy must be drinking my Moët Chandon in some cathouse somewhere. But I've got some bitters—Campari—that I think would be about right for this time of day."

He rang a little bell, and the servant who had been waiting behind a curtain came. He was young, dark-skinned, his hair greased down on his skull. Medina knew him; he was reformatory fodder, a messenger-boy for secretive whores—and what woman isn't one?—a petty thief when the opportunity presented itself. He remembered, looking without triumph into the boy's eyes, the classic, if now butchered, phrase, "I know you, Mirabelles." The boy looked comical in his white waiter's jacket and black bow tie. "He brought furniture, a wife, a whore, and a little horse and buggy from Europe. But I guess he couldn't find an exportable servant. He had to pick one out of the garbage in Santa María."

A parade of memories had filed by—of ruined harvests, staggering harvests, rises and falls in the price of cattle; they had reminded each other of long-gone summers and winters, so worn and polished by time as to have become unreal, when the bottle showed only two glasses left of the red liquid as soft as sweet water. Neither of the two men had changed, neither showed a trace of mockery or of dominance.

"My wife and the boy went to Santa María. They may go on farther. I mean, you never know with women," Petrus said.

"I beg your pardon, I didn't ask how your wife was getting along," Medina replied.

"No matter. You aren't a doctor, anyway; you came because my dogs killed a chicken thief."

"No, don Jeremías, with respect. I came for two reasons. The corpse we carried away had been disguised. Your peons muddied his face and his hands, they dressed the body in the overseer's clothes, they stole his belongings. Rings—you could see the marks on the fingers. Wash off the mud, and you saw he'd been clean and sweet when he came; just out of the bath. They forgot the cologne, good cologne, as sweet and sissified as the cologne your own wife wears, don Jeremías. A clumsy trick, typical of these peons. But that's enough of that—I know the man's name now. It's very possible that you don't know who he was, or it's possible that you'll place him when I tell you the name or when you see—if you want to be troubled to come to the Station, of course—when you see the file. The dogs mangled his throat, his hands, half his face. But the dead man didn't come to steal your chickens. He came from Buenos Aires, and you didn't go to Buenos Aires on Friday."

A pause chewed over by both men, a shared apprehension.

Petrus smelled danger, but no fear. His peons had been stupid, clumsy, and so had he—he had trusted in them and this grotesque charade.

"Medina. Or Commissioner. I went to Buenos Aires on Friday. I go almost every Friday. I paid a lot of money so that everyone would swear to that."

"Which they did, don Jeremías. No one double-crossed you, no one cheated you out of so much as a single peso. They swore on their fear, on the Bible, on the ashes of their whoring mothers. Although not all of them were orphans. But anyway, and flattery aside, I felt like they were swearing out of some other respect, don Jeremías, something besides money."

"Thank you," Petrus said without moving his head, a slight line of dry amusement trying to push at his moustache. "The end, story over, case closed, then. I was in Buenos Aires."

"Case closed because the dead man was inside your house, your land, your sacred private property. And because it wasn't you that murdered him. It was the dogs. And I tried, don Jeremías, but your dogs refuse to testify."

"Dobermans," Petrus nodded. "Intelligent breed. Very refined. They don't talk to police dogs."

"Hah. Maybe not out of scorn for them, though. Discretion, maybe. Anyway—case closed. But there are some things I'd like clear. You weren't around here on Saturday night. But you weren't in Buenos Aires, either. You weren't anywhere, you weren't alive, you didn't exist from Friday to Monday. Curious. A story about a ghost, vanished. No one ever wrote that story, and nobody ever told it to me."

At that Jeremías Petrus left his chair and stood motionless, looking straight and hard at Medina's face, the useless riding-quirt dangling from his wrist.

"I have been patient," he said slowly, as though talking to himself, as though he were murmuring into the magnifying mirror he shaved at every morning. "All this bores me, it befuddles me, it makes me slow, it wastes my time. I want, I *have* to do so many things—there may not be room for them all in one man's life. Because in this work, I'm all alone. . . ." He broke off. He stood unmoving for a long time in the enormous parlor filled with things—objects born of and imposed by the never-defeated female sex. His voice had sounded, a little, like a prayer and a confession. Now it turned cold; he returned to everyday stupidity to ask without curiosity, without insult, "How much?"

Medina chuckled softly, making his poor hilarity fit the atmosphere of unbearable vitrines, japanned tables, fans, gilt settees, and dead butterflies under domes of crystal.

"Money? Nothing for me. If you want to pay off the mortgage, that's another thing, don Jeremías. It's the Bank's, or nobody's. I always have my cot at the Station."

"Done," Petrus said.

"As you like. In payment, I want to tell you something that will upset you maybe at first, tonight or tomorrow, say. . . ."

"You always hated to waste time. Me too. Maybe that's why we put up with each other for so many years. Maybe that's why I'm listening to you this minute. Say what you have to say."

"As you wish. I thought a little prologue, between two gentlemen whose hands are clean. . . . But as you wish. Mam'selle Josefina refused to say or listen to a single word. I beg your pardon, she did say one thing, I didn't quite catch it, just one thing, something like 'say petty car song.' I'm not sure. . . . She cried a little. Then she scattered a bagful of silver coins all over the bed. They're at the Station, with the file, waiting for the judge. He went to a horse race; he may stop by here on his way back."

"That's fine," Petrus said. "She was heard to say that—no matter. The money, a little under a hundred and thirty-seven—that's no matter, either, and it's got nothing to do with the case."

"I beg your pardon again," Medina said, trying to sweeten his voice. "Less than fifty."

"I understand. There are always expenses."

"Exactly. Especially for a trip. Because Mam'selle was using the telephone in the train station. You know poor old Masiota, you know how poor old Masiota treats all the women, as long as it's not his, of course, as we all know—all you have to do is look at his left eye on Monday after the conjugal spree every Saturday night. All the women except the one he puts up with and the one that was lucky enough to find him half awake this Monday morning at the train station, when you reappeared. A coin, a smile, a kind word was all it took for him to put all the telephone lines, all the freight cars full of bags and cows waiting on the siding, all the miles of rails going who knows where, the left ones and the right ones both—put all of it at her service."

"And so?" Petrus interrupted him, lashing at his boot with the whip impatiently.

"I was taking my time getting there because I thought we were gentlemen. I apologize. I know we don't like to waste time. So: Mam'selle must have worn out our station-master's batteries. But in an hour or two she got what she'd wanted. Train, hotel, ship for Europe. I learned all this a few minutes ago. There's never a want of a drunk or some layabout on a train-station bench."

Petrus had been nibbling at the whip-handle, pensive, all desire to lash out at something now gone, as Medina, not at ease, not entirely inattentive, rubbed his thumb over the trigger of the pistol at his waist. Without prior agreement, his mouth and his thumb, both slow, drew out the pause: it was too long at last to fit this story. At last it was Petrus who spoke; his voice was slow and hoarse, the voice of a woman about to be overtaken by menopause. He was too proud to ask.

"Josephine knew his name. She knew the name of the chicken thief and I'm sure much more besides. I see no other reason for her to have gone away."

"That may be, don Jeremías," Medina said syllable by syllable, watchful of the whip's verticality. "Why *would* she have gone?"

It had been so long since Petrus had laughed that his wide-open, black mouth began first with a long mooing sound and then tapered off into the bleat of a lost calf.

"Why explain, Commissioner? Women are whores. Every one of them. Worse than us. Mares, even better. Not even real whores. I've known a few I'd take my hat off to, I suppose. They were ladies. A long time ago. But women today are little whores, no better than that. Sad little whores."

"True, don Jeremías," Medina recoiled at the memory of Petrus's señora offering him tea and cake in that very parlor. "Almost all, anyway. Poor things, that's what they're born for. You fight to make a lumberyard. Fight against the whole world. I fight—Saturdays to go to bed drunk, sometimes to find out who the owner of the stolen sheep is. And I need time to paint. Paint the river, paint you."

"I bought two of your paintings," Petrus said. "Two or three."

"Yes, you did, don Jeremías, and you paid well for them. But they aren't here in the parlor. They're out in the peons' quarters. That's neither here nor there. You're right, what you were saying. They don't have an ounce of brain to be anything more than what you said they were."

The whip fell, tilted into the man's legs, then lay lengthwise on the floor. Petrus, sitting down, opened his hand:

"What do you say we have a drink, Commissioner?"

When he left, Medina saw one of the animals in the shade, out of the sun, taking a long siesta.

■ Jorge Amado (1912–2001) *Brazil* (novel)

TRANSLATED BY BARBARA SHELBY MERELLO

Jorge Amado, one of the most successful writers in Latin America, a precursor to the Boom novelists, has been translated into the main languages of the world. His fame rests on his literary qualities as well as on his immensely popular and colorful Brazilian love novels. His mother was part Indian, his father a backwoodsman landowner whose authority rested on his rifle. The family was made destitute first by the great flood of 1914 and later by the stock market crash of 1929; yet, Amado managed to attend a Jesuit boarding school, complete law school, and become an active journalist. He began his career as a journalist and was early interested in politics. He was arrested by the Getulio Vargas regime in 1936, and many times thereafter, because of his proletarian novels about life in the slums and shanty towns of Brazil. His books were banned, confiscated, and burned; and in 1942, he was arrested again for his participation in anti-Axis activities. In 1946, he was elected a Communist deputy to the Brazilian Congress, but he went into exile when the Communist Party was banned in 1948. After a few years in Paris, he was expelled from France and fled to Czechoslovakia. He won the Stalin Peace Prize in 1952; but in 1954, he spoke out in Moscow against the confines of socialist-realism, and, in 1955, he broke definitively with the party and communism. He returned to Brazil, disillusioned with the Soviet Union.

Amado has many voices: the conscience of and sharp eye for the city poor, the storytelling fabulist of popular love novels, a graceful allegorist in children's books. In the excerpts from *The Two Deaths of Quincas Wateryell*, we have a coherent picaresque novel, with full Cervantes-like exuberance, wildness, and existential absurdity, as Quincas, like a picaresque ruffian of individualist survival, chooses his own death, an appropriate one for his beliefs and condition.

FURTHER READING: Amado, Jorge. *Jubiabá*, 1935; *The Sea of Death*, 1936; *Captains of the Sands*, 1937; *The Violent Land*, 1943; *Gabriela, Clove and Cinnamon*, 1958; *Home Is the Sailor; Dona Flor and Her Two Husbands; The Two Deaths of Quincas Wateryell*, 1959; *Shepherds of the Night*, 1964; *The Tent of Miracles*, 1969; *Tereza Batista Home from the Wars*, 1972; *Pen Sword Camisole*, 1980; *Showdown*, 1985; *The War of the Saints: A Tale of Sorcery*, 1988.

from **The Two Deaths of Quincas Wateryell**

A Certain Amount of Confusion

A certain amount of confusion about the death of Quincas Wateryell persists even today. There are doubts to be explained away, ridiculous details, contradictory testimony from witnesses, divers gaps in the story. Time, place, and last words are uncertain. The family, backed up by neighbors and acquaintances, sticks to its version of a quiet death in the morning—with no witnesses, no fuss, and no last words—occurring almost twenty hours before that other, notorious death just before dawn, when the moon faded into the ocean and mysterious things took place on the docks of Bahia. Quincas's last words were sworn to nevertheless by reliable witnesses and passed on by word of mouth through steep streets and back alleys, and they meant far more to those who repeated them than a mere farewell to the world. They were a prophetic pronouncement, a message of deep significance (as one of our young contemporary authors would put it).

With so many reliable witnesses around—including Cap'n Manuel and Wide-Eyed Quitéria, a woman of her word—there are still those who deny any and all authenticity not only to the much-admired last words but also to everything that happened on that memorable night when, at an uncertain hour and in ambiguous circumstances, Quincas Wateryell dived into the gulf of Bahia and set off on his last journey, never to return. That's the world for you—swarming with doubters and skeptics who are yoked like oxen to law and order, due process, and notarized documents. These good people triumphantly display the death certificate signed by the doctor just before noon, and with that one scrap of paper—for no other reason than that it has printing and stamps on it—try to blot out the last few hours lived so intensely by Quincas Wateryell before he departed of his own free will, or so he proclaimed loud and clear to his friends and the others who were present.

The dead man's family—his respectable daughter and conventional son-in-law, a civil servant with a promising career; Aunt Marocas and her younger brother, a businessman with a modest bank account—stoutly asserts that the whole story is nothing but a gross falsehood concocted by inveterate drunkards, scoundrels on the fringes of lawful society, crooks who ought to be seeing the world from behind bars instead of enjoying the free run of the streets, the port of Bahia, the white sandy beaches, the vast friendly night. They unjustly lay at the door of these pals of Quincas all responsibility for the ill-fated life he had been leading during the past few years, to the grief and shame of his family. In fact, his name was never uttered and his deeds never were mentioned in the presence of the innocent children. As far as they were concerned, their Grandfather Joaquim, of fond memory, had decently passed away long ago, esteemed and respected by all who knew him. All of which leads us to deduce a first death, moral if not physical, dating from years back and bringing the total to three—thus making Quincas a record-holder for dying, and, justifying us in thinking that the events that took place afterward, from the signing of the death certificate to his dive into the ocean, were a farce acted out with the sole aim of mortifying his relatives one last time by turning their lives upside down, covering them with shame, and exposing them to malicious gossip. He was not a man to earn respect or keep up appearances, in spite of his gambling partners' respect for the lucky gambler and the fine-talking tippler.

I honestly don't know whether the mystery of Quincas Wateryell's death (or deaths) can ever be cleared up. But I am going to try my best, for as Quincas said himself, the important thing is to attempt even the impossible.

In the Opinion of the Family

In the opinion of the family, the rapscallions who reported Quincas's last moments in the streets and alleys, in front of the Trade Mart and in the open-air market of Água dos Meninos,[1] showed an appalling lack of respect for the dead. Furthermore, a leaflet containing doggerel verses composed by Cuica de Santo Amaro, the improviser, was enjoying a brisk sale. A dead man's memory is, as we all know, sacred and not meant to be bandied about in the dirty mouths of drunken sots, gamblers, and marijuana smugglers. Nor should it be turned into a subject for uninspired rhyming by folk singers at the entrance to the Lacerda Elevator, where so many of the best people pass by every day, including co-workers of Leonardo Barreto, Quincas's humiliated son-in-law. When a man dies, he is automatically restored to genuine respectability, no matter what sort of folly he may have indulged in when he was alive. Death wipes out the black marks of the past with an absentminded hand, and the memory of the dear departed shines flawless as a diamond. This at any rate was the family's theory, and it was applauded by their friends and neighbors. According to this theory, Quincas Wateryell, when he died, became once again the former respectable, well-born Joaquim Soares de Cunha, exemplary employee of the State Rent Board, with his measured step, his close-shaved beard, his black alpaca coat, and his briefcase under his arm; listened to respectfully by the neighbors when he chose to express his opinions on weather and politics; never seen in a bar; a temperate, home-loving drinker. The family had in fact, by dint of extremely praiseworthy efforts, succeeded in making Quincas's memory shine unimpaired for several years after declaring him dead to society. They spoke of him in the past tense when obliged by circumstances to speak of him at all. Unfortunately, every so often a neighbor, or some colleague of Leonardo, or a busybody friend of Vanda (the disgraced daughter), ran into Quincas or heard about him from someone else. Then it was

---

1. Salvador's most famous open-air market for generations, the Feira Água dos Meninos, was totally destroyed by fire in 1964.

as though the dead man had risen from his grave to defile his own memory —lying dead drunk in broad daylight in the marketplace; or, dirty and disheveled, hunched over a pack of greasy cards in the courtyard of the Church of the Pillar; or even singing in a hoarse voice in São Miguel Alley, chummily embracing Negro and mulatto women of doubtful virtue. It was simply dreadful!

When at last, on that particular morning, a man who sold religious articles on Tabuão Street hurried in distress to the Barretos' house, which was small but neat, and told daughter Vanda and son-in-law Leonardo that Quincas had definitely departed this life in the wretched pigsty he had been occupying, the couple let out a simultaneous sigh of relief. Never again would the memory of the retired employee of the State Rent Board be dragged in the mud by the wild, thoughtless behavior of the bum he had turned into at the end of his life. Their well-earned rest had come at last. Now they could talk freely about Joaquim Soares da Cunha, praise his conduct as an employee, as a husband and father, and as a citizen, point out his virtues as an example to the children, and teach them to honor their grandfather's memory without fear of contradiction.

The saint-seller, a skinny old man with a white woolly pate, expatiated on details of his story: a Negro woman who sold cornmeal mush, beancakes wrapped in banana leaves, and other delicacies, had had an important matter to bring up with Quincas that morning. He had promised to get hold of certain herbs for her that were hard to find but absolutely necessary for her voodoo devotions. She had come for the herbs; she just had to have them; the time for Xangô's sacred rites was at hand. The door of his room at the top of the steep flight of stairs was open as usual; Quincas had lost the big hundred-year-old key a long time before. It was believed that he had actually sold it to some tourists on a lean day when he had had no luck at cards, adding into the bargain a grand story, lavishly embellished with dates and details, of its being a blessed church key. The Negro woman called, got no answer, thought he was still asleep, and pushed the door open. The sheet black with dirt, a torn bedspread over his legs, Quincas was lying on the cot and smiling his usual welcoming smile. She didn't notice anything wrong. When she asked him about the herbs, he smiled and didn't answer. His right big toe stuck out through a hole in his sock, and his shabby shoes were on the floor. The woman, who knew Quincas well and was used to his jokes, sat down on the bed and told him she was in a hurry. She was surprised that he didn't put out his shameless hand, which never missed a chance to pinch and feel around. She had another look at his right big toe; it looked funny. She touched Quincas's body, jumped up in alarm, and felt his cold hand. Then she ran down the stairs and spread the news.

Daughter and son-in-law listened without relish to this detailed narration of Negro women and herbs, voodoo, and feeling around. They shook their heads impatiently, trying to get him to cut it short; but the saint-seller was a deliberate man and liked to tell a story with all the details. He was the only one who knew about Quincas's relatives, whose identity had been revealed one night during a monumental binge; that was why he had come. He composed his face into a suitably contrite expression to present "his heartfelt condolences."

It was time for Leonardo to go to work. He said to his wife: "You go on, I'll stop at the office. I have to sign in and explain to the boss."

They told the saint-seller to come in and showed him to a chair in the living room. Vanda went to change her clothes, and the old man told Leonardo about Quincas, about how there wasn't anybody on Tabuão Street who didn't like him. Why had a man from a good background, a man of means (the saint-seller could see he had been one, now that he had had the pleasure of making the acquaintance of his daughter and son-in-law), decided to live the life of a tramp? Had something happened at home to make him unhappy? That must be it. Maybe his wife had put horns on him; that happened pretty often. The saint-seller placed his forefingers on his forehead in sly interrogation. Had he guessed right?

"Dona Otacília, my mother-in-law, was a saintly woman!"

The saint-seller scratched his chin: why had he done it then? But instead of replying, Leonardo got up to join Vanda, who was calling him from the bedroom.

"We'll have to let people know."

"Let who know? What for?"

"Aunt Marocas and Uncle Eduardo and the neighbors. We'll have to invite them to the funeral."

"Why should we tell the neighbors right away? We can tell them later. Otherwise they'll talk their damned heads off."

"But what about Aunt Marocas?"

"I'll talk to her and Eduardo after I stop by the office. Hurry up. Otherwise that old guy'll be running around telling everybody he sees."

"Who would ever have thought he would die that way, all alone?"

"It was his own fault, the crazy screwball."

In the living room, the saint-seller was admiring a colored portrait of Quincas painted about ten years before. It showed him as a fine-looking gentleman with a high collar, a black necktie, pointed mustaches, slicked-down hair, and rosy cheeks. Next to him in an identical frame was Dona Otacília in a black lace dress, her eyes accusing, her mouth hard. The saint-seller examined her sour visage.

"She doesn't have a husband-cheating face, but she sure looks like a hard bone to gnaw on . . . saintly woman, my foot!"

Only a Few Friends from Tabuão Street

Only a few friends from Tabuão Street were keeping Quincas's body company when Vanda entered the room. The saint-seller explained to them in a low voice: "That's his daughter. And he had a son-in-law and a brother and sister, too, all high-class people. The son-in-law's a clerk and lives in Itapagipe, in a very fine house."

They made way for Vanda to pass, waiting expectantly for her to fling herself on the corpse and embrace it, to dissolve into tears, or to burst out sobbing. Quincas Wateryell, lying on the cot in his patched old trousers, tattered shirt, and enormous greasy vest, smiled as though enjoying himself hugely. Vanda stood stock still and stared at his unshaved face and dirty hands, and at the big toe sticking out through the hole in his sock. She had no tears left to shed, no sobs to fill the room with. All her tears and sobs had been used up long ago, when she had tried again and again to persuade Quincas to come back to the home he had abandoned. Now she could only stare at him, her face flushed with shame.

He made a most unpresentable corpse—the corpse of a bum who had died accidentally and indecently, laughing cynically at her, and no doubt at Leonardo and the rest of the family. That corpse belonged in a morgue; it should have been dumped into a police wagon to be cut up by the medical students and buried in a shallow grave, with no cross and no inscription. It was the body of Quincas Wateryell, rum-swiller, debauchee, and gambler, who had no family, no home, no flowers, and no one to pray for him. It was certainly not Joaquim Soares da Cunha, respectable functionary of the State Rent Board who had retired after twenty-five years of loyal service, or the model husband to whom people had tipped their hats and whose hand everyone had been proud to shake. How could a fifty-year-old man leave his home, his family, his lifelong habits, and his old acquaintances to wander the streets, drink in cheap bars, visit whorehouses, go around dirty and unshaved, live in a filthy hole in the worst part of town, and sleep on an old cot that was falling to pieces? Vanda racked her brains for a valid explanation. Often at night, after Otacília's death (not even on that solemn occasion had Quincas consented to return to the fold), she had talked it over with her husband. He wasn't crazy, at least not crazy enough to be put away; the doctors had been unanimous on that point. How on earth, then, could such behavior be accounted for?

Now it was all over at last—the nightmare that had dragged on for years, the blot on the family escutcheon. Vanda had inherited a good deal of her mother's practical common sense and was capable of making rapid decisions and carrying them out. As she gazed at the dead man, a disgusting caricature of what her father had been, she made up her mind what to do. First she would call in a doctor to write out the death certificate. Then she would have him dressed in decent clothes, take him home, and bury him next to Otacília. It would have to be a very modest funeral—times were hard—but good enough so they would not lose face in the eyes of their friends and neighbors and Leonardo's colleagues. Aunt Marocas and Uncle Eduardo would help. At this thought, Vanda, her eyes fixed on Quincas's smiling face, wondered what would become of the money from her father's retirement fund. Would they inherit it, or would they get only the life insurance? Maybe Leonardo would know.

She turned to the curious eyes gazing at her. It was that scruffy riffraff from Tabuão Street whose company Quincas had enjoyed so much. What on earth were they doing there? Didn't they realize that when Quincas Wateryell had breathed his last, that had been the end of him? That Quincas Wateryell had been an invention of the devil, a bad dream, a nightmare? Joaquim Soares da Cunha would come back now and stay for a little while with his own people in the comfort of a decent house, his respectability restored. It was time for him to come home. And this time Quincas couldn't laugh at his daughter and son-in-law, tell them to go jump in the lake, wave them an ironic farewell, and walk out whistling. He was lying on the cot, not making a move. Quincas Wateryell was gone for good.

Vanda lifted her head, scanned the faces before her defiantly, and gave an order in Otacília's voice: "Do you want anything? If not, you can leave." Then she addressed the saint-seller: "Would you kindly call a doctor to sign the death certificate?"

The saint-seller nodded, impressed; and the others filed slowly out. Vanda remained alone with the corpse. Quincas Wateryell was smiling, and his big right toe seemed to grow bigger through the hole in his sock.

■ Léon Damas (1912–1978)
French Guiana (poem)

TRANSLATED BY ROBERT BAGG

With Léopold Senghor and Aimé Césaire, Léon Damas was a founder of the Négritude movement, the important midcentury literary movement that emphasized black consciousness, pride, and the achievement of black culture in Africa and the Antilles. The three poets—each one was also to be a statesman—produced a magazine called *L'Étudiant noir* (*The Black Student*, 1934). Damas wrote an experimental syncopated verse in which he attempted to reproduce the musical sounds of his culture in such books as *Pigments* (1937) and *Graffiti* (1951). It is energetic and intense, like the persona of the poet. His *African Songs of Love, Grief, War, and Abuse* (1961) reveals life in an African village.

FURTHER READING: Damas, Léon. *Pigments*, 1937; *Graffiti*, 1951; *African Songs of Love, Grief, War, and Abuse*, 1961.

Position Paper

The days
shape themselves: African masks
aloof
from the quick-lime obscenities
enraging   5
a piano pounding with the same old wheeze—
Breathless Moonlight
in the shrubbery
in the gondolas
etc.   10

■ Vinícius de Morães (1913–) *Brazil* (poem)

TRANSLATED BY RICHARD WILBUR

Vinícius de Morães, born in Rio, studied law at the University of Brazil
and English literature at Oxford University. In England, he later worked
for the Brazilian program of the BBC. In 1943, he entered the diplomatic
service, serving in Los Angeles, Paris, and Montevideo. A versatile writer of
poetry, popular song, and filmscripts, he was at one time called the "Pope
of the Bossa Nova." He wrote the script for Marcel Camus's famous film
Black Orpheus.

Song

Never take her away,
The daughter whom you gave me,
The gentle, moist, untroubled
Small daughter whom you gave me;
O let her heavenly babbling   5
Beset me and enslave me.
Don't take her; let her stay,
Beset my heart, and win me,
That I may put away
The firstborn child within me,   10
That cold, petrific, dry
Daughter whom death once gave,
Whose life is a long cry
For milk she may not have,

And who, in the night-time, calls me   *15*
In the saddest voice that can be
Father, Father, and tells me
Of the love she feels for me.
Don't let her go away,
Her whom you gave—my daughter—   *20*
Lest I should come to favor
That wilder one, that other
Who does not leave me ever.

■ Aimé Césaire (1913–) *Martinique* (poems)

TRANSLATED BY CLAYTON ESHLEMAN AND ANNETTE SMITH

Aimé Césaire was born in Martinique in the West Indies. After an early career in politics in his native island, he has given himself to the writing and politics of literature. A poet above all, but also an essayist and playwright, very early in his career he was a surrealist following in the footsteps of the French poet Guillaume Apollinaire (1880–1918) and appropriately entitled his first famous book of poems *Soleil cou coupé* (*Sun Its Neck Cut Off*), taking the title from the last words of Apollinaire's surreal poem "Zone." When Césaire was a student in Paris, he was mortified by the colonial tradition, which denied a black heritage. Together with Léopold Senghor and Léon Damas he developed the notion of Négritude, which resisted assimilation and vaunted the accomplishments of black culture, especially in Africa, but also elsewhere in the world, as in Martinique, where there were large black communities. Among Aimé Césaire's writings are *Return to My Native Land*, 1969; *A Season in the Congo*, 1969; *Discourse on Colonialism*, 1972; and his very important *Collected Poetry*, 1984. Césaire remains one of the most important twentieth-century French poets.

FURTHER READING: Césaire, Aimé. *Return to My Native Land*, 1969; *A Season in the Congo*, 1969; *Discourse on Colonialism*, 1972; *Collected Poetry*. Translated by Clayton Eshleman and Annette Smith, 1984.

zaffer sun

at the foot of stammering volcanoes
earlier than the little violet fog arising from my fever
i am sitting in the middle of a courtyard
a horologer of three centuries accumulated in bat droppings
under the false hope of sweet grigris   *5*

already howling from a bitch soul
and carrying the true shackles
i have exchanged a thousand of my hearts
for the one today that
powerfully   10
rises in our throat
parakinesized by lofty bitter kingdoms
i
zaffer sun

abyss

he pondered the logic of the swamp's teeth
he pondered the molten lead in the Chimera's throat
he pondered a morgue of beaks in the coral dump for the dying
he pondered the boundless extension
of the century-old quarrel   5
across the beaches of time
(in the time it took a soul to vanish there went
through me the passion of a piton)
he pondered a mouse pitter-pattering through the palace of a royal
    soul
he pondered the voice of a galley slave strangled by a song   10
then by the soulless halt of a herd
an isolate of sea slugs coiffed with venom helmets

thus
    all nostalgia
      rolls   15
        into the abyss

■ Julia de Burgos (1914–1953)
Puerto Rico (poem)

TRANSLATED BY ALIKI BARNSTONE AND WILLIS BARNSTONE

Born in Carolina, Puerto Rico, the eldest of thirteen children, Julia de Burgos attended the University of Puerto Rico and taught school in Naranjito. After the publication of her first book in 1938, she taught at the University of Havana and then, in 1940, moved to New York, where she spent her remaining years. Her short life was tormented and chaotic, fraught with poverty and alcoholism. The harsh tone of her often self-demeaning verses reveals unusual force. Her nihilism, sometimes obscured by her rhetoric, breaks through the masks, even through the words, to reveal devastating humor and nothingness.

FURTHER READING: Burgos, Julia de. *Poems in Twenty Furrows*, 1938; *Collected Works*, 1961; *Collected Poems*, 1979.

Nothing

Since life is nothing in your philosophy,
let's drink to the fact of not being our bodies.

Let's drink to the nothing of your sensual lips,
which are sensual zeros in your blue kisses:
like all blue a chimerical lie   5
of white oceans and white firmaments.

Let's drink to the touchable decoy bird
sinking and rising in your carnal desire:
like all flesh, lightning, spark,
in the truth, unending lie of the universe.   10

Let's drink to nothing, the perfect nothing
of your soul, that races its lie on a wild colt:
like all nothing, perfect nothing, it's not even
seen for a second in sudden dazzle.

Let's drink to us, to them, to no one;   15
to our always nothing of our never bodies;
to everyone at least; to everyone so much nothing,
to bodiless shadows of the living who are dead.

We come from not being and march toward not being:
nothing between two nothings, zero between two zeros,   20
and since between two nothings nothing can be,
let's drink to the splendor of not being our bodies.

■ Julio Cortázar (1914–1988)
Argentina (story)

TRANSLATED BY PAUL BLACKBURN

Julio Cortázar was born in Brussels, but his Argentine parents moved back to Buenos Aires when he was four. After his parents' divorce, he was brought up by his mother. Fluent in French and English, he took a degree in literature and eventually became a teacher of French in Buenos Aires high schools. He began to translate literature, including the complete short stories of Edgar Allan Poe—a task Baudelaire performed as his livelihood in the mid-nineteenth century. Jorge Luis Borges published Cortázar's first story in the magazine *Sur,* which he was editing. In the late forties, unhappy with the dictatorship of Juan Perón and its oppression of intellectuals, he quit teaching and trained as an interpreter. He went to Paris in 1951 and began to work as a translator for UNESCO, a position he kept most of his life. Cortázar's first book of stories, *Bestiary,* came out that same year, but, since he was removed from Argentine letters, the book found no immediate resonance, and it disappeared into neglect. Then came two volumes of stories: *The End of the Game and Other Stories* (1956), including the story "Blow-up" (Spanish title *Las babas del diablo*) on which the Italian film director Michelangelo Antonioni based his film *Blow-up* (1966), and *Secret Weapons* (1959). Cortázar wrote an allegorical novel, *The Winners* (1961), which satirized the regime of the dictator Juan Perón. By now, the American poet and translator Paul Blackburn was translating Cortázar into English and publishing his stories widely. His world fame, however, was established by the experimental, ingenious novel *Rayhuela* (1963, translated as *Hopscotch* in 1965). The story, which takes place simultaneously in Paris and Buenos Aires, was inspired by Borges's story "The Garden of the Forking Paths." *Hopscotch* was followed by another experimental novel, *62: A Model Kit* (1968). Cortázar's last book, which he wrote in English with his young Canadian wife, is a collage of travel journals, *Around the Day in Eighty Worlds* (1967).

Despite the notoriety and praise for *Hopscotch* and his more Dadaist and nutty experimental tales as in *Cronopios and Famas* (1969), it is in the straight short story that his combination of Borgesian intellectual fantasy and his own grotesques and sexual obsessions makes him unique and one of the world's important storytellers. Julio Cortázar was for his works and person among the most appreciated authors. The Chilean poet Pablo Neruda said of him, "Anyone who doesn't read Cortázar is doomed. Not to read him is a serious invisible disease, which in time can have terrible consequences. Something similar to a man who has never tasted peaches. He would quietly become sadder, noticeably paler, and probably, little by little, he would lose his hair."

FURTHER READING: Cortázar, Julio. *Bestiary,* 1951; *The End of the Game and Other Stories,* 1956; *Secret Weapons,* 1959; *The Winners,* 1961; *Rayhuela,* 1963, tr. *Hopscotch; 62: A Model Kit,* 1968, tr. 1972; *Cronopios and Famas,* 1969; *All Fires the Fire and Other Stories,* 1966, tr. 1973; *A Manual for Manuel,* 1973; *A Change of Light and Other Stories,* 1977; *We Love Glenda So Much and Other Stories,* 1981.

Axolotl

There was a time when I thought a great deal about the axolotls. I went to see them in the aquarium at the Jardin des Plantes and stayed for hours watching them, observing their immobility, their faint movements. Now I am an axolotl.

I got to them by chance one spring morning when Paris was spreading its peacock tail after a wintry Lent. I was heading down the boulevard Port-Royal, then I took Saint-Marcel and L'Hôpital and saw green among all that grey and remembered the lions. I was friend of the lions and panthers, but had never gone into the dark, humid building that was the aquarium. I left my bike against the gratings and went to look at the tulips. The lions were sad and ugly and my panther was asleep. I decided on the aquarium, looked obliquely at banal fish until, unexpectedly, I hit it off with the axolotls. I stayed watching them for an hour and left, unable to think of anything else.

In the library at Sainte-Geneivève, I consulted a dictionary and learned that axolotls are the larval stage (provided with gills) of a species of salamander of the genus Ambystoma. That they were Mexican I knew already by looking at them and their little pink Aztec faces and the placard at the top of the tank. I read that specimens of them had been found in Africa capable of living on dry land during the periods of drought, and continuing their life under water when the rainy season came. I found their Spanish name, *ajolote,* and the mention that they were edible, and that their oil was used (no longer used, it said) like cod-liver oil.

I didn't care to look up any of the specialized works, but the next day I went back to the Jardin des Plantes. I began to go every morning, morning and afternoon some days. The aquarium guard smiled perplexedly taking my ticket. I would lean up against the iron bar in front of the tanks and set to watching them. There's nothing strange in this, because after the first minute I knew that we were linked, that something infinitely lost and distant kept pulling us together. It had been enough to detain me that first morning in front of the sheet of glass where some bubbles rose through the water. The axolotls huddled on the wretched narrow (only I can know how narrow and wretched) floor of moss and stone in the tank. There were nine specimens, and the majority pressed their heads against the glass looking with their eyes of gold at whoever came near them. Disconcerted, almost ashamed, I felt it a lewdness to be peering at these silent and immobile figures heaped at the bottom of the tank. Mentally I isolated one, situated on the right and somewhat apart from the others, to study it better. I saw a rosy little body, translucent (I thought of those Chinese figurines of milky glass), looking like a small lizard about six inches long, ending in a fish's tail of extraordinary delicacy, the most sensitive part of our body. Along the back ran a transparent fin which joined with the tail, but what obsessed me was the feet, of the slenderest nicety, ending in tiny fingers with minutely human nails. And then I discovered its eyes, its face. Inexpressive features, with no other trait save the eyes, two orifices, like brooches, wholly of transparent gold, lacking any life but looking, letting themselves be penetrated by my look, which seemed to travel past the golden level and lose itself in a diaphanous interior mystery. A very slender black halo ringed the eye and etched it onto the pink flesh, onto the rosy stone of the head, vaguely triangular, but with curved and irregular sides which gave it a total likeness to a statuette corroded by time. The mouth was masked by the triangular plane of the face, its considerable size would be guessed only in profile; in front a delicate crevice barely slit the lifeless stone. On both sides of the head where the ears should have been, there grew three tiny sprigs red as coral, a vegetal outgrowth, the gills, I suppose. And they were the only thing quick about it; every ten or fifteen seconds the sprigs pricked up stiffly and again subsided. Once in a while a foot would barely move, I saw the diminutive toes poise mildly on the moss. It's that we don't enjoy moving a lot, and the tank is so cramped—we barely move in any direction and we're hitting one of the others with our tail or our head—difficulties arise, fights, tiredness. The time feels like it's less if we stay quietly.

It was their quietness that made me lean toward them fascinated the first time I saw the axolotls. Obscurely I seemed to understand their secret will, to abolish space and time with an indifferent immobility. I knew better later; the gill contraction, the tentative reckoning of the delicate feet on the stones, the abrupt swimming (some of them swim with a simple undulation of the body) proved to me that they were capable of escaping that mineral lethargy in which they spent whole hours. Above all else, their eyes obsessed me. In the standing tanks on either side of them, different fishes showed me the simple stupidity of their handsome eyes so similar to our own. The eyes of the axolotls spoke to me of the presence of a different life, of another way of seeing. Glueing my face to the glass (the guard would cough fussily once in a while), I tried to see better those diminutive golden points, that entrance to the infinitely slow and remote world of these rosy creatures. It was useless to tap with one finger on the glass directly in front of their faces; they never gave the least reaction. The golden eyes continued burning with their soft, terrible light; they continued looking at me from an unfathomable depth which made me dizzy.

And nevertheless they were close. I knew it before this, before being an axolotl. I learned it the day I came near them for the first time. The anthropomorphic features of a monkey reveal the reverse of what most people believe, the distance that is traveled from them to us. The absolute lack of similarity between axolotls and human beings proved to me that my recognition was valid, that I was not propping myself up with easy analogies. Only the little hands . . . But an eft, the common newt, has such hands also, and we are not at all alike. I think it was the axolotls' heads, that triangular pink shape with the tiny eyes of gold. That looked and knew. That laid the claim. They were not *animals.*

It would seem easy, almost obvious, to fall into mythology. I began seeing in the axolotls a metamorphosis which did not succeed in revoking a mysterious humanity. I imagined them aware, slaves of their bodies, condemned infinitely to the silence of the abyss, to a hopeless meditation. Their blind gaze, the diminutive gold disc without expression and nonetheless terribly shining, went through me like a message: "Save us, save us." I caught myself mumbling words of advice, conveying childish hopes. They continued to look at me, immobile; from time to time the rosy branches of the gills stiffened. In that instant I felt a muted pain; perhaps they were seeing me, attracting my strength to penetrate into the impenetrable thing of their lives. They were not human beings, but I had found in no animal such a profound relation with myself. The axolotls were like witnesses of something, and at times like horrible judges. I felt ignoble in front of them; there was such a terrifying purity in those transparent eyes. They were larvas, but larva means disguise and also phantom. Behind those Aztec faces, without expression but of an implacable cruelty, what semblance was awaiting its hour?

I was afraid of them. I think that had it not been for feeling the proximity of other visitors and the guard, I would not have been bold enough to remain alone with them. "You eat them alive with your eyes, hey," the guard said, laughing; he likely thought I was a little cracked. What he didn't notice was that it was they devouring me slowly with their eyes, in a cannibalism of gold. At any distance from the aquarium, I had only to think of them, it was as though I were being affected from a distance. It got to the point that I was going every day, and at night I thought of them immobile in the darkness, slowly putting a hand out which immediately encountered another. Perhaps their eyes could see in the dead of night, and for them the day continued indefinitely. The eyes of axolotls have no lids.

I know now that there was nothing strange, that that had to occur. Leaning over in front of the tank each morning, the recognition was greater. They were suffering, every fiber of my body reached toward that stifled pain, that stiff torment at the bottom of the tank. They were lying in wait for something, a remote dominion destroyed, an age of liberty when the world had been that of the axolotls. Not possible that such a terrible expression which was attaining the overthrow of that forced blankness on their stone faces should carry any message other than one of pain, proof of that eternal sentence, of that liquid hell they were undergoing. Hopelessly, I wanted to prove to myself that my own sensibility was projecting a nonexistent consciousness upon the axolotls. They and I knew. So there was nothing strange in what happened. My face was pressed against the glass of the aquarium, my eyes were attempting once more to penetrate the mystery of those eyes of gold without iris, without pupil. I saw from very close up the face of an axolotl immobile next to the glass. No transition and no surprise, I saw my face against the glass, I saw it on the outside of the tank, I saw it on the other side of the glass. Then my face drew back and I understood.

Only one thing was strange: to go on thinking as usual, to know. To realize that was, for the first moment, like the horror of a man buried alive awaking to his fate. Outside, my face came close to the glass again, I saw my mouth, the lips compressed with the effort of understanding the axolotls. I was an axolotl and now I knew instantly that no understanding was possible. He was outside the aquarium, his thinking was a thinking outside the tank. Recognizing him, being him himself, I was an axolotl and in my world. The horror began—I learned in the same moment—of believing myself prisoner in the body of an axolotl, metamorphosed into him with my human mind intact, buried alive in an axolotl, condemned to move lucidly among unconscious creatures. But that stopped when a foot just grazed my face, when I moved just a little to one side and saw an axolotl next to me who was looking at me, and understood that he knew also, no communication possible, but very clearly. Or I was also in him, or all of us were thinking humanlike, incapable of expression, limited to the golden splendor of our eyes looking at the face of the man pressed against the aquarium.

He returned many times, but he comes less often now. Weeks pass without his showing up. I saw him yesterday, he looked at me for a long time and left briskly. It seemed to me that he was not so much interested in us any more, that he was coming out of habit. Since the only thing I do is think, I would think about him a lot. It occurs to me that at the beginning we continued to communicate, that he felt more than ever one with the mystery which was claiming him. But the bridges were broken between him and me, because what was his obsession is now an axolotl, alien to his human life. I think that at the beginning I was capable of returning to him in a certain way—ah, only in a certain way— and of keeping awake his desire to know us better. I am an axolotl for good now, and if I think like a man it's only because every axolotl thinks like a man inside his rosy stone semblance. I believe that all this succeeded in communicating something to him in those first days, when I was still he. And in this final solitude to which he no longer comes, I console myself by thinking that perhaps he is going to write a story about us, that, believing he's making up a story, he's going to write all this about axolotls.

■ Octavio Paz (1914–1998) *Mexico* (poems)

Octavio Paz was born in Mexico City. His father was from Jalisco and had Spanish and Indian blood. His paternal grandfather was a well-known journalist who fought against the French-imposed emperor Maximilian. His father, a lawyer, took part in the Mexican revolution and represented the Zapotec revolutionary leader Emiliano Zapata and was also an architect of agrarian reform. In 1937, Octavio Paz went to Spain for the Second International Conference of Anti-Fascist Writers and traveled around the war-ravaged country. Initially a participant in activities of Marxist writers, the Nazi-Soviet pact led him to break with the Stalinists—and, like the late painter Rufino Tamayo, he was often criticized for turning away from Communist orthodoxy and the doctrine of socialist-realism. Paz began a life of long journeys—to the United States on a Guggenheim fellowship (1944–1945); to Paris in 1945 where he met the surrealist poet André

Breton; and, a year later, he entered the Mexican diplomatic corps. In the next decades, he worked in Paris, New York, San Francisco, Geneva, and New Delhi, where he was the Mexican ambassador to India. There he met and married Marie-José Tramini and wrote *Eastern Rampart* (1968). He resigned his post to protest the 1968 slaughter by the Mexican government of student demonstrators. For some years after 1968, he spent part of each year as professor of comparative literature at Harvard University. On his permanent return to Mexico City, he founded the literary journal *Plural* and published *Salamander* (1962) and other books. Octavio Paz, like Borges, was a poet and essayist, and like Borges, though the areas are different, he had a global knowledge of diverse Eastern and Western literature, religion, and philosophy. He was particularly affected by Buddhism, including Buddhist art and religion. In addition to his poetry, he published many books of essays, notably *The Labyrinth of Solitude* and *Sor Juana Inés de la Cruz, or the Traps of Faith* (1988), important anthologies of Spanish and Mexican verse, and translations of William Carlos Williams, Pessoa, Apollinaire, and others. He founded many literary journals and collaborated with a number of artists such as Robert Motherwell, Henri Michaux, Robert Rauchenberg, and Rufino Tamayo. His books and essays represent the many aspects of a life devoted to the arts. In 1990, when he was in New York to open a great exhibition of ancient and contemporary Mexican art at the Metropolitan Museum of Art, he received word that he had been awarded the Nobel Prize for Literature.

FURTHER READING: Paz, Octavio. *The Labyrinth of Solitude* (essays), 1950. Translated by Lysander Kemp, 1961; *Sunstone.* Translated by Muriel Rukeyser, 1962; *Blanco, The Violent Season,* 1958; *Marcel Duchamp or the Castle of Purity,* 1966; *The Bow and the Lyre* (essays), 1967; *Eastern Rampart,* 1968; *Alternating Current.* Translated by Helen Lane, 1973; *The Grammatical Monkey* (essays), 1974; *Children of the Mire* (essays). Translated by Rachel Phillips, 1974; *A Draft of Shadows and Other Poems,* 1979; *On Poets and Others.* Translated by Michael Schmidt, 1986; *Convergences: Selected Essays on Art and Literature.* Translated by Helen Lane, 1987; *The Collected Poems of Octavio Paz: 1957–1987.* Edited by Eliot Weinberger, 1987; *Sor Juana Inés de la Cruz, or the Traps of Faith,* 1988; *The Other Voice: Essays on Modern Poetry.* Translated by Helen Lane, 1992.

Sight, Touch

For Balthus

Light holds between its hands
the white hill and black oaks,
the path that goes on,
the tree that stays;

light is a stone that breathes
by the sleepwalking river,

5

light: a girl stretching,
a dark bundle dawning;
light shapes the breeze in the curtains,
makes a living body from each hour,   10
enters the room and slips out,
barefoot, on the edge of a knife;

light is born a woman in a mirror,
naked under diaphanous leaves,
chained by a look,   15
dissolved in a wink;

it touches the fruit and the unbodied,
it is a pitcher from which the eye drinks clarities,
a flame cut in blossom, a candle watching
where the blackwinged butterfly burns;   20

light opens the folds of the sheets
and the creases of puberty,
glows in the fireplace, its flames become shadows
that climb the walls, yearning ivy;

light does not absolve or condemn,   25
is neither just or unjust,
light with impalpable hands raises
the buildings of symmetry;

light escapes through a passage of mirrors
and returns to light: 30
is a hand that invents itself,
an eye that sees itself in its own inventions.

Light is time reflecting on time.

TRANSLATED BY MARK STRAND

The Key of Water

After Rishikesh
the Ganges is still green.
The glass horizon
breaks among the peaks.
We walk upon crystals.   5
Above and below
great gulfs of calm.
In the blue spaces
white rocks, black clouds.

You said: *10*
>   *Le pays est plein de sources.*[1]
That night I dipped my hands in your breasts.

TRANSLATED BY ELIZABETH BISHOP

Wind from All Compass Points

The present is motionless
The mountains are of bone and of snow
they have been here since the beginning
The wind has just been born
>   ageless   5
as the light and the dust
>   A windmill of sounds
the bazaar spins its colors
>   bells motors radios
the stony trot of dark donkeys   10
songs and complaints entangled
among the beards of the merchants
the tall light chiselled with hammer-strokes
In the clearings of silence
>   boys' cries   15
>   explode
Princes in tattered clothes
on the banks of the tortured river
pray   pee   meditate
>   The present is motionless   20
The floodgates of the year open
>   day flashes out
>   agate
>   The fallen bird
between rue Montalambert and rue de Bac   25
is a girl
>   held back
at the edge of a precipice of looks
If water is fire
>   flame   30
>   dazzled
in the center of the spherical hour
>   a sorrel filly

---

1. The countryside is full of springs.

A marching battalion of sparks
   a real girl   *35*
among wraithlike houses and people
Presence a fountain of reality
I looked out through my own unrealities
I took her hand
    together we crossed   *40*
the four quadrants the three times
floating tribes of reflections
and we returned to the day of beginning
The present is motionless

    June 21st   *45*
today is the beginning of summer
    Two or three birds
invent a garden
    You read and eat a peach
on the red couch   *50*
    naked
like the wine in the glass pitcher
    A great flock of crows
Our brothers are dying in Santo Domingo
If we had the munitions   *55*
    You people would not be here
    We chew our nails down to the elbow
In the gardens of this summer fortress
Tipoo Sultan planted the Jacobin tree
then distributed glass shards among   *60*
the imprisoned English officers
and ordered them to cut their foreskins
and eat them
    The century
has set fire to itself in our lands   *65*
Will the builders of cathedrals and pyramids
charred hands
    raise their transparent houses
by its light?

    The present is motionless   *70*
The sun has fallen asleep between your breasts
The red covering is black and heaves
Not planet and not jewel
    fruit
you are named   *75*
    date
    Datia
castle of Leave-If-You-Can

scarlet stain
upon the obdurate stone 80
Corridors
terraces
stairways
dismantled nuptial chambers
of the scorpion 85
Echoes repetitions
the intricate and erotic works of a watch
beyond time
You
taciturn patios under the pitiless afternoon 90
a cloak of needles on your untouched shoulders
If fire is water
you are a diaphanous drop
the real girl
transparency of the world 95
The present is motionless
The mountains
quartered suns
petrified storm earth-yellow
The wind whips 100
it hurts to see
The sky is another deeper abyss
Gorge of the Salang Pass
black cloud over black rock
Fist of blood strikes 105
gates of stone
Only the water is human
in these precipitous solitudes
Only your eyes of human water
Down there 110
in the cleft
desire covers you with its two black wings
Your eyes flash open and close
phosphorescent animals
Down there 115
the hot canyon
the wave that stretches and breaks
your legs apart
the plunging whiteness
the foam of our bodies abandoned 120

The present is motionless
The hermit watered the saint's tomb
his beard was whiter than the clouds
Facing the mulberry

on the flank of the rushing stream 125
you repeat my name
　　　dispersion of syllables
A young man with green eyes presented you
with a pomegranate
　　　　On the other bank of the Amu-Darya 130
smoke rose from Russian cottages
The sound of an Usbek flute
was another river invisible clearer
The boatman
　　　　on the barge was strangling chickens 135
The countryside is an open hand
　　　its lines
　　　marks of a broken alphabet
Cow skeletons on the prairie
Bactria 140
　　　a shattered statue
I scraped a few names out of the dust
By these fallen syllables
seeds of a charred pomegranate
I swear to be earth and wind 145
　　　whirling
over your bones
　　　The present is motionless
Night comes down with its trees
night of electric insects and silken beasts 150
night of grasses which cover the dead
meeting of waters which come from far off
rustlings
　　　universes are strewn about
a world falls 155
　　　a seed flares up
each word beats
　　　I hear you throb in the shadow
a riddle shaped like an hour-glass
　　　woman asleep 160
Space living spaces
Anima mundi
　　　maternal substance
always torn from itself
always falling into your empty womb 165
　　　Anima mundi
mother of the nomadic tribes
　　　of suns and men
The spaces turn
　　　the present is motionless 170

At the top of the world
Shiva and Parvati caress
       Each caress lasts a century
for the god and for the man
       an identical time   *175*
an equivalent hurling headlong
       Lahore
          red river black boats
a barefoot girl
       between two tamarinds   *180*
and her timeless gaze
       An identical throbbing
death and birth
A group of poplars
suspended between sky and earth   *185*
they are a quiver of light more than a trembling of leaves
       Do they rise
        or fall?
The present is motionless
       It rains on my childhood   *190*
it rains on the feverish garden
flint flowers trees of smoke
In a fig-leaf you sail
       on my brow
The rain does not wet you   *195*
you are flame of water
       the diaphanous drop of fire
spilling upon my eyelids
I look out through my own unrealities
the same day is beginning   *200*
       Space wheels
the world wrenches up its roots
Our bodies
       stretched out
        weigh no more than dawn   *205*

TRANSLATED BY PAUL BLACKBURN

The Grove

Enormous and solid
       but swaying,
beaten by the winds
       but chained

to the soil, 5
     murmur of millions of leaves
against the window:
     the inextricable
mass
     woven dark green branches 10
and dazzling spaces.
     Fallen
into these nets
     there's a material
violent, resplendent, 15
     an animal
wrathful and swift,
     now immobile,
light that lights itself
     to extinguish itself. 20
To the left, above the wall,
     more idea than color,
the blue blue of a basin
   edged round by large rod
crumbling, 25
     sand silently precipitated
into the funnel of the grove.
     In the central
part
     thick drops of ink 30
     spattered
on a sheet of paper inflamed by the west,
     black
there, almost entirely,
     in the far southeast, 35
where the horizon breaks down.
     The grove
turns copper, shines.
     Three blackbirds
pass through the blaze and reappear, 40
     unharmed,
in an emptiness: neither light nor shade.
     Vegetation
on fire for its dissolution.
     In the houses 45
lights are lit.
     In the window
the sky gathers.
     In its walls of tile
the patio 50

```
        grows more and more
secluded:
        it perfects
its reality.
        And now                                                    55
on the opaque cement
        nothing but
sackfuls of shadow
        the trash-can,
the empty flower-pot.                                              60
        Space closes
over itself:
        inhuman.
Little by little, the names petrify.
```

TRANSLATED BY ELIZABETH BISHOP

The River

The restless city circles in my blood like a bee.
And the plane that traces a querulous moan in a long S, the trams
        that break down on remote corners,
that tree weighted with affronts that someone shakes at midnight in
        the plaza,
the noises that rise and shatter and those that fade away and whisper a
        secret that wriggles in the ear,
they open the darkness, precipices of a's and o's, tunnels of taciturn
        vowels,   5
galleries I run down blindfolded, the drowsy alphabet falls in the pit
        like a river of ink,
and the city goes and comes and its stone body shatters as it arrives at
        my temple,
all night, one by one, statue by statue, fountain by fountain, stone by
        stone, the whole night long
its shards seek one another in my forehead, all night long the city
        talks in its sleep through my mouth,
a gasping discourse, a stammering of waters and arguing stone, its
        story.   10
To stop still an instant, to still my blood which goes and comes, goes
        and comes and says nothing.
seated on top of me like a yogi in the shadow of a fig tree, like
        Buddha on the river's edge, to stop the instant,
a single instant, seated on the edge of time, to strike out my image of the
        river that talks in its sleep and says nothing and carries me with it,

seated on the bank to stop the river, to unlock the instant, to
  penetrate its astonished rooms reaching the center of water,
to drink at the fountain, to be the cascade of blue syllables falling
  from stone lips,   *15*
seated on the edge of night like Buddha on his self's edge, to be the
  flicker of the lidded instant,
the conflagration and the destruction and the birth of the instant, the
  breathing of night rushing enormous at the edge of time,
to say what the river says, a long word resembling lips, a long word
  that never ends,
to say what time says in hard sentences of stone, in vast gestures of sea
  covering worlds.

In mid-poem a great helplessness overtakes me, everything abandons
  me,   *20*
there is no one beside me, not even those eyes that gaze from behind
  me at what I write,
no one behind or in front of me, the pen mutinies, there is neither
  beginning nor end nor even a wall to leap,
the poem is a deserted esplanade, what's said is not said, the unsaid is
  unsayable,
towers, devastated terraces, Babylons, a sea of black salt, a blind
  kingdom,
        No,   *25*
to stop myself, to keep quiet, to close my eyes until a green spike
  sprouts from my eyelids, a spurt of suns,
and the alphabet wavers long under the wind of the vision and the
  tide rolls into one wave and the wave breaks the dike,
to wait until the paper is covered with stars and the poem a forest of
  tangled words,
        No,
I have nothing to say, no one has anything to say, nothing and nobody
  except the blood,   *30*
nothing except this coming and going of the blood, this writing over
  the written, the repetition of the same word in mid-poem,
syllables of time, broken letters, splotches of ink, blood that goes and
  comes and says nothing and carries me with it.

And I speak, my beak bent over the paper and someone beside me
  writes while the blood goes and comes,
and the city goes and comes through his blood, wants to say
  something, time wants to say something, the night wants to speak,
all night long the man wants to say one single word, to speak his
  discourse at last, made up of moldered stones,   *35*
and I whet my hearing, I want to hear what the man says, to repeat
  what the drifting city says,

all night the broken stones seek one another, groping in my forehead,
  all night the water fights the stone,
the words against the night, the night against the night, nothing lights
  up the opaque combat,
the shock of arms does not wrench away a single gleam to the stone,
  one spark to the night, no one grants a respite,
it is a fight to the death between immortals to offer retreat, to stop the
  river of blood, the river of ink,   *40*
to stop the river of words, to go back upstream, and that the night
  turn upon itself display its bowels of flaming gold,
and that the water show its heart, a cluster of drowned mirrors, a glass
  tree that the wind uproots
(and every leaf of the tree flutters and glints and is lost in a cruel
  light, as the words of the poet's image are lost),
may time thicken and its wound be an invisible scar, scarcely a delicate
  line upon the skin of the world,
let the words lay down their arms and the poem be one single
  interwoven word, an implacable radiance that advances   *45*
and may the soul be the blackened grass after fire, the lunar breast of
  a sea that's turned to stone and reflects nothing
except splayed dimension, expansion, space lying down upon itself,
  spread wings immense,
and may everything be like flame that cuts itself into and freezes into
  the rock of diaphanous bowels,
hard blazing resolved now in crystal, peaceable clarity.

And the river goes back upstream, strikes its sails, picks up its images
  and coils within itself.   *50*

TRANSLATED BY PAUL BLACKBURN

■ Nicanor Parra (1914–) *Chile* (poems)

Born to a poor family in southern Chile, Nicanor Parra used to play
with his brothers and sisters in a cemetery. Later, he studied mathematics
and astrophysics in Santiago and went abroad to study at Brown and Oxford Universities. At Oxford, he discovered the poems of John Donne; and
after reading the line "Death be not proud," he claims he could do no less
than devote his life to poetry. Nevertheless, he continued in his science
studies and became a professor of astrophysics at the University of Santiago. While at Oxford, he studied with A. A. Milne, the author of *Winnie-the-
Pooh*. His first book of poems was *Songbook without a Name* (1937), and it

would be seventeen years before he published his next book, *Poems and Antipoems* (1954), which won several national prizes, much acclaim, and denunciation for its shocking, funny, deep irreverence. It also catapulted him into worldwide fame. His sister was the famous Chilean folk singer Violeta Parra, whose song "Gracias a la vida" ("Thanks to Life") was made popular in the United States by Joan Baez. Later books were *Parlor Verses* (1962), *Russian Songs* (1967), and *Emergency Poems* (1972). On Sundays during the long Pinochet dictatorship, which began in 1973 with the overthrow of Salvador Allende, the poet would sit outside the entrance to the main cathedral in Santiago, with a hat for contributions, under a sign that said he was reading poems to collect money for the oppressed intellectuals of Chile. Nicanor Parra was perhaps the only Chilean intellectual who could do this with impunity. His most recent books *reflect* his opposition to the Pinochet regime or any overbearing police state: *Sermons and Homilies of the Christ of Elqui* (1984) and *Jokes for Disorienting Police about Poetry*.

Nicanor Parra has always written under the shadow of Neruda, with whom and about whom he wrote a fine critical book, *Discourses with Pablo Neruda* (1960). His poems, thoroughly framed in colloquial irony, social satire, and fantasy, mirror the humor of the great English modernists. His poems are antirhetorical; so he will not write with Nerudian prophetic ardor, yet he shares Neruda's wild and wicked wit and humor. His experimentation is not surrealist imagery or syntactic contortions or outrageous neologisms. Rather, he turns the absurdly prosaic, the folly, loneliness, and cruelty of ordinary life to his own mocking vision of humanity.

FURTHER READING: Parra, Nicanor. *Songbook without Title*, 1937; *Poems and Antipoems.* Translated by Miller Williams, 1954; *Discourses with Pablo Neruda*, 1960; *Parlor Verses*, 1962; *Russian Songs*, 1967; *Emergency Poems.* Translated by Miller Williams, 1972; *Sermons and Homilies of the Christ of Elqui.* Translated Sandra Reyes, 1984; *Jokes for Disorienting Police about Poetry.*

Viva Stalin

those motherfuckers
wouldn't give me time to get my overcoat
with no warning at all
they grabbed me and knocked me around
one got me in the chest with his gun butt   5
another son of a bitch spat on me
but I never lost patience

then they took me in a patrol car
to an abandoned street
close to the railroad station   10
they said ok now you can go free

I knew exactly what they meant by that

murderers!
    that's what I ought to have screamed
but I died screaming Viva Stalin.   15

TRANSLATED BY MILLER WILLIAMS

Warnings

No praying allowed, no sneezing.
No spitting, eulogizing, kneeling
worshipping, howling, expectorating.

No sleeping permitted in this precinct
No inoculating, talking, excommunicating   5
Harmonizing, escaping, catching.

Running is absolutely forbidden.

No smoking. No fucking.

TRANSLATED BY MILLER WILLIAMS

■ Juan Rulfo (1918–1986) *Mexico* (story)

TRANSLATED BY GEORGE D. SCHADE

Juan Rulfo, a child of the Mexican revolution, was born and brought up in the village of San Gabriel near Jaslisco. His father was murdered when he was seven. In the chaos of his orphan youth, he attended school in his village and then in Guadalajara. At fifteen, he went to Mexico City, where eventually he obtained a bureaucratic job. Later, he worked as an archivist at the Indian Institute in Mexico City. In 1953, he published a book of short stories, *The Burning Plain*. He received a Rockefeller grant to write a novel and three years later, in 1956, he came out with *Pedro Páramo*, which gained him national and very soon international acclaim. After the publication of these two volumes, a few short stories appeared, but during the last three decades of his life he drank heavily and never resumed his career as a writer of fiction. He did write a novel in the forties that he destroyed. His two books, however, are classics of contemporary Latin American fiction. In the burning plains and harsh rocks and tragically macabre atmosphere of his stories and novel, we discover that we are overhearing the confessions of a ghost speaking in a time of murder and personal and political corruption. Rulfo is a writer of great depth and burning accuracy. His modernist ruminations owe much to William Faulkner's *As I Lay Dying*, but his world is a Mexican wasteland of feudal landowners, desperate peasants, and bitterly furious personal conflicts. A master of the word, a writer of immense strength, one is in awe before his two volumes and wishes there had been more.

FURTHER READING: Rulfo, Juan. *The Burning Plain*, 1953; *Pedro Páramo*, 1956.

Talpa

Natalia threw herself into her mother's arms, crying on and on with a quiet sobbing. She'd bottled it up for many days, until we got back to Zenzontla today and she saw her mother and began feeling like she needed consolation.

But during those days when we had so many difficult things to do — when we had to bury Tanilo in a grave at Talpa without anyone to help us, when she and I, just the two of us alone, joined forces and began to dig the grave, pulling out the clods of earth with our hands, hurrying to hide Tanilo in the grave so he wouldn't keep on scaring people with his smell so full of death — then she didn't cry.

Not afterward either, on the way back, when we were traveling at night without getting any rest, groping our way as if asleep and trudging along the steps that seemed like blows on Tanilo's grave. At that time Natalia seemed to have hardened and steeled her heart so she wouldn't feel it boiling inside her. Not a single tear did she shed.

She came here, near her mother, to cry, just to upset her, so she'd know she was suffering, upsetting all the rest of us besides. I felt that weeping of hers inside me too as if she was wringing out the cloth of our sins.

Because what happened is that Natalia and I killed Tanilo Santos between the two of us. We got him to go with us to Talpa so he'd die. And he died. We knew he couldn't stand all that traveling; but just the same, we pushed him along between us, thinking we'd finished him off forever. That's what we did.

The idea of going to Talpa came from my brother Tanilo. It was his idea before anyone else's. For years he'd been asking us to take him. For years. From the day when he woke up with some purple blisters scattered about on his arms and legs. And later on the blisters became wounds that didn't bleed — just a yellow gummy thing like thick distilled water came out of them. From that time I remember very well he told us how afraid he was that there was no cure for him any more. That's why he wanted to go see the Virgin of Talpa, so she'd cure him with her look. Although he knew Talpa was far away and we'd have to walk a lot under the sun in the daytime and in the cold March nights, he wanted to go anyway. The blessed Virgin would give him the cure to get rid of that stuff that never dried up. She knew how to do that, by washing them, making everything fresh and new like a recently rained-on field. Once he was there before Her, his troubles would be over; nothing would hurt him then or hurt him ever again. That's what he thought.

And that's what Natalia and I latched on to so we could take him. I had to go with Tanilo because he was my brother. Natalia would have to go too, of course, because she was his wife. She had to help him, taking him by the arm, bearing his weight on her shoulders on the trip there and perhaps on the way back, while he dragged along on his hope.

I already knew what Natalia was feeling inside. I knew something about her. I knew, for example, that her round legs, firm and hot like stones in the noonday sun, had been alone for a long time. I knew that. We'd been together many times, but always Tanilo's shadow separated us; we felt that his scabby hands got between us and took Natalia away so she'd go on taking care of him. And that's the way it'd be as long as he was alive.

I know now that Natalia is sorry for what happened. And I am too; but that won't save us from feeling guilty or give us any peace ever again. It won't make us feel any better to know that Tanilo would've died anyway because his time was coming, and that it hadn't done any good to go to Talpa, so far away, for it's almost sure he would've died just as well here as there, maybe a little afterward, because of all he suffered on the road, and the blood he lost besides, and the anger and everything—all those things together were what killed him off quicker. What's bad about it is that Natalia and I pushed him when he didn't want to go on anymore, when he felt it was useless to go on and he asked us to take him back. We jerked him up from the ground so he'd keep on walking, telling him we couldn't go back now.

"Talpa is closer now than Zenzontla." That's what we told him. But Talpa was still far away then, many days away.

We wanted him to die. It's no exaggeration to say that's what we wanted before we left Zenzontla and each night that we spent on the road to Talpa. It's something we can't understand now, but it was what we wanted. I remember very well.

I remember those nights very well. First we had some light from a wood fire. Afterward we'd let the fire die down, then Natalia and I would search out the shadows to hide from the light of the sky, taking shelter in the loneliness of the countryside, away from Tanilo's eyes, and we disappeared into the night. And that loneliness pushed us toward each other, thrusting Natalia's body into my arms, giving her a release. She felt as if she was resting; she forgot many things and then she'd go to sleep with her body feeling a great relief.

It always happened that the ground on which we slept was hot. And Natalia's flesh, the flesh of my brother Tanilo's wife, immediately became hot with the heat of the earth. Then those two heats burned together and made one wake up from one's dreams. Then my hands groped for her; they ran over her red-hot body, first lightly, but then they tightened on her as if they wanted to squeeze her blood out. This happened again and again, night after night, until dawn came and the cold wind put out the fire of our bodies. That's what Natalia and I did along the roadside to Talpa when we took Tanilo so the Virgin would relieve his suffering.

Now it's all over. Even from the pain of living Tanilo found relief. He won't talk any more about how hard it was for him to keep on living, with his body poisoned like it was, full of rotting water inside that came out in each crack of his legs or arms. Wounds this big, that opened up slow, real slow, and then let out bubbles of stinking air that had us all scared.

But now that he's dead things are different. Now Natalia weeps for him, maybe so he'll see, from where he is, how full of remorse her soul is. She says she's seen Tanilo's face these last days. It was the only part of him she cared about—Tanilo's face, always wet with the sweat which the effort to bear his pain left him in. She felt it approaching her mouth, hiding in her hair, begging her, in a voice she could scarcely hear, to help him. She says he told her he was finally cured, that he no longer had any pain. "Now I can be with you, Natalia. Help me to be with you," she says he said to her.

We'd just left Talpa, just left him buried there deep down in that ditch we dug to bury him.

Since then Natalia has forgotten about me. I know how her eyes used to shine like pools lit up by the moon. But suddenly they faded, that look of hers was wiped away as if it'd been stamped into the earth. And she didn't seem to see anything any more. All that existed for her was her Tanilo, whom she'd taken care of while he was alive and had buried when his time came to die.

It took us twenty days to get to the main road to Talpa. Up to then the three of us had been alone. At that point people coming from all over began to join us, people like us who turned onto that wide road, like the current of a river, making us fall behind, pushed from all sides as if we were tied to them by threads of dust. Because from the ground a white dust rose up with the swarm of people like corn fuzz that swirled up high and then came down again; all the feet scuffling against it made it rise again, so that dust was above and below us all the time. And above this land was the empty sky, without any clouds, just the dust, and the dust didn't give any shade.

We had to wait until nighttime to rest from the sun and that white light from the road.

Then the days began to get longer. We'd left Zenzontla about the middle of February, and now that we were in the first part of March it got light very early. We hardly got our eyes closed at night when the sun woke us up again, the same sun that'd gone down just a little while ago.

I'd never felt life so slow and violent as when we were trudging along with so many people, just like we were a swarm of worms all balled together under the sun, wriggling through the cloud of dust that closed us all in on the same path and had us corralled. Our eyes followed the dust cloud and struck the dust as if stumbling against something they could not pass through. And the sky was always gray, like a heavy gray spot crushing us all from above. Only at times, when we crossed a river, did the dust clear up a bit. We'd plunge our feverish and blackened heads into the green water, and for a moment a blue smoke, like the steam that comes out of your mouth when it's cold, would come from all of us. But a little while afterward we'd disappear again, mixed in with the dust, sheltering each other from the sun, from that heat of the sun we all had to endure.

Eventually night will come. That's what we thought about. Night will come and we'll get some rest. Now we have to get through the day, get through it somehow to escape from the heat and the sun. Then we'll stop—afterward. What we've got to do now is keep plugging right along behind so many others just like us and in front of many others. That's what we have to do. We'll really only rest well when we're dead.

That's what Natalia and I thought about, and maybe Tanilo too, when we were walking along the main road to Talpa among the procession, wanting to be the first to reach the Virgin, before she ran out of miracles.

But Tanilo began to get worse. The time came when he didn't want to go any farther. The flesh on his feet had burst open and begun to bleed. We took care of him until he got better. But, he'd decided not to go any farther.

"I'll sit here for a day or two and then I'll go back to Zenzontla." That's what he said to us.

But Natalia and I didn't want him to. Something inside us wouldn't let us feel any pity for Tanilo. We wanted to get to Talpa with him, for at that point he still had life left in him. That's why Natalia encouraged him while she rubbed his feet with alcohol so the swelling would go down. She told him that only the Virgin of Talpa would cure him. She was the only one who could make him well forever. She and no one else. There were lots of other Virgins, but none like the Virgin of Talpa. That's what Natalia told him.

Then Tanilo began to cry, and his tears made streaks down his sweaty face, and he cursed himself for having been bad. Natalia wiped away the streaky tears with her shawl, and between us we lifted him off the ground so he'd walk on a little further before night fell.

So, dragging him along was how we got to Talpa with him.

The last few days we started getting tired too. Natalia and I felt that our bodies were being bent double. It was as if something was holding us and placing a heavy load on top of us. Tanilo fell down more often and we had to pick him up and sometimes carry him on our backs. Maybe that's why we felt the way we did, with our bodies slack and with no desire to keep on walking. But the people who were going along by us made us walk faster.

At night that frantic world calmed down. Scattered everywhere the bonfires shone, and around the fire the pilgrims said their rosaries, with their arms crossed, gazing toward the sky in the direction of Talpa. And you could hear how the wind picked up and carried that noise, mixing it together until it was all one roaring sound. A little bit afterward everything would get quiet. About midnight you could hear someone singing far away. Then you closed your eyes and waited for the dawn to come without getting any sleep.

We entered Talpa singing the hymn praising Our Lord.

We'd left around the middle of February and we got to Talpa the last days of March, when a lot of people were already on their way back. All because Tanilo took it into his head to do penance. As soon as he saw himself surrounded by men wearing cactus leaves hanging down like scapularies, he decided to do something like that too. He tied his feet together with his shirt sleeves so his steps became more desperate. Then he wanted to wear a crown of thorns. A little later he bandaged his eyes, and still later, during the last part of the way, he knelt on the ground and shuffled along on his knees with his hands crossed behind him; so that thing that was my brother Tanilo Santos reached Talpa, that thing so covered with plasters and dried streaks of blood that it left in the air a sour smell like a dead animal when he passed by.

When we least expected it we saw him there among the dancers. We hardly realized it and there he was with a long rattle in his hand, stomping hard on the ground with his bare bruised feet. He seemed to be in a fury, as if he was shaking out all the anger he'd been carrying inside him for such a long time, or making a last effort to try to live a little longer.

Maybe when he saw the dances he remembered going every year to Tolimán during the novena of Our Lord and dancing all night long until his bones limbered up without getting tired. Maybe that's what he remembered and he wanted to get back the strength he used to have.

Natalia and I saw him like that for a moment. Right afterward we saw him raise his arms and slump to the ground with the rattle still sounding in his bloodspeckled hands. We dragged him out so he wouldn't be tromped on by the dancers, away from the fury of those feet that slipped on stones and leaped about stomping the earth without knowing that something had fallen among them.

Holding him up between us as if he was crippled, we went into the church with him. Natalia had him kneel down next to her before that little golden figure of the Virgin of Talpa. And Tanilo started to pray and let a huge tear fall, from way down inside him, snuffing out the candle Natalia had placed in his hands. But he didn't realize this; the light from so many lit candles kept him from realizing what was happening right there. He went on praying with his candle snuffed out. Shouting his prayers so he could hear himself praying.

But it didn't do him any good. He died just the same.

"... *from our hearts filled with pain we all send her the same plea. Many laments mixed with hope. Her tenderness is not deaf to laments nor tears, for She suffers with us. She knows how to take away that stain and to leave the heart soft and pure to receive her mercy and charity. Our Virgin, our mother, who wants to know nothing of our sins, who blames herself for our sins, who wanted to bear us in her arms so life wouldn't hurt us, is right here by us, relieving our tiredness and the sicknesses of our souls and our bodies filled with thorns, wounded and supplicant. She knows that each day our faith is greater because it is made up of sacrifices ...*"

That's what the priest said from up in the pulpit. And after he quit talking the people started praying all at once with a noise just like a lot of wasps frightened by smoke.

But Tanilo no longer heard what the priest was saying. He'd become still, with his head resting on his knees. And when Natalia moved him so he'd get up he was already dead.

Outside you could hear the noise of the dancing, the drums and the hornpipes, the ringing of bells. That's when I got sad. To see so many living things, to see the Virgin there, right in front of us with a smile on her face, and to see Tanilo on the other hand as if he was in the way. It made me sad.

But we took him there so he'd die, and that's what I can't forget.

Now the two of us are in Zenzontla. We've come back without him. And Natalia's mother hasn't asked me anything, what I did with my brother Tanilo, or anything. Natalia started crying on her shoulder and poured out the whole story to her.

I'm beginning to feel as if we hadn't reached any place; that we're only here in passing, just to rest, and that then we'll keep on traveling. I don't know where to, but we'll have to go on, because here we're very close to our guilt and the memory of Tanilo.

Maybe until we begin to be afraid of each other. Not saying anything to each other since we left Talpa may mean that. Maybe Tanilo's body is too close to us, the way it was stretched out on the rolled petate, filled inside and out with a swarm of blue flies that buzzed like a big snore coming from his mouth, that mouth we couldn't shut in spite of everything we did and that seemed to want to go on breathing without finding any breath. That Tanilo, who didn't feel pain any more but who looked like he was still in pain with his hands and feet twisted and his eyes wide open like he was looking at his own death. And here and there all his wounds dripping a yellow water, full of that smell that spread everywhere and that you could taste in your mouth, like it was a thick and bitter honey melting into your blood with each mouthful of air you took.

I guess that's what we remember here most often—that Tanilo we buried in the Talpa graveyard, that Tanilo Natalia and I threw earth and stones on so the wild animals wouldn't come dig him up.

◾ Juan José Arreola (1918–2001) *Mexico* (fable)

TRANSLATED BY GEORGE D. SCHADE

Juan José Arreola was born in Ciudad Guzmán in Jalisco. Despite his worldliness, his years in Europe, the life in the province of Jalisco remained at the center of his work. In the 1940s, he went to Guadalajara where he began to work for journals. He met the famous actor Louis Jouvet, who took him to Paris. He returned to Mexico City to found a publishing house, *Los Presentes,* to introduce new writers, including Carlos Fuentes. He also began to publish his own inimitable stories and to work actively in the theater. *Various Inventions,* a book of stories, came out in 1949, followed by *Silvertip* in 1958. These stories and other writings were incorporated in *Confabulario and Other Inventions,* which appeared in English in 1964. Arreola was funny, savagely witty, a bit fantastically crazy in his satires and always revealed an immense grace. Like the contemporary playwright Eugène Ionesco, who invented the theater of the absurd in Paris, Arreola invented and was a master of the absurd, often in miniature. Whereas his fellow Mexican writer Juan Rulfo was fantastic and grave, Arreola beamed with mischievous life. *The Fair* was published in 1977.

FURTHER READING: Arreola, Juan José. *Various Inventions,* 1949; *Silvertip,* 1958; *Confabulario and Other Inventions.* Translated by George D. Schade, 1964; *The Fair.* Translated by John Upton, 1977.

I'm Telling You the Truth

Everybody who is interested in seeing a camel pass through the eye of the needle should inscribe his name on the list of patrons for the Niklaus Experiment.

Disassociated from a group of death-dealing scientists, the kind who manipulate uranium, cobalt, and hydrogen, Arpad Niklaus is guiding his present research toward a charitable and radically humanitarian end: the salvation of the souls of the rich.

He proposes a scientific plan to disintegrate a camel and make it pass in a stream of electrons through a needle's eye. A receiving apparatus (very similar to the television screen) will organize the electrons into atoms, the atoms into molecules, and the molecules into cells, immediately reconstructing the camel according to its original scheme. Niklaus has already managed to make a drop of heavy water change its position without touching it. He has also been able to evaluate, up to the point where the discretion of the material permits, the quantum energy discharged by a camel's hoof. It seems pointless here to burden the reader with that astronomical figure.

The only serious difficulty Professor Niklaus has run into is the lack of his own atomic plant. Such installations, extensive as cities, are incredibly expensive. But a special committee is already busy solving the problem by means of a world-wide subscription drive. The first contributions, still rather anemic, are serving to defray the cost of thousands of pamphlets, bonds, and explanatory prospectuses, as well as to assure Professor Niklaus the modest salary permitting him to continue with his calculations and theoretical investigations while the immense laboratories are being built.

At present, the committee can count only on the camel and the needle. As the societies for the prevention of cruelty to animals approve the project, which is inoffensive and even healthful for any camel (Niklaus speaks of a probable regeneration of all the cells), the country's zoos have offered a veritable caravan. New York City has not hesitated to risk its very famous white dromedary.

As for the needle, Arpad Niklaus is very proud of it and considers it the keystone of the experiment. It is not just any needle, but a marvelous object discovered by his assiduous talent. At first glance, it might be confused with a common ordinary needle. Mrs. Niklaus, displaying a fine sense of humor, takes pleasure in mending her husband's clothes with it. But its value is infinite. It is made from an extraordinary, as yet unclassified, metal, whose chemical formula, scarcely hinted at by Niklaus, seems to indicate that it involves a base composed exclusively of isotopes of nickel. This mysterious substance has made scientists ponder a great deal. There was even one who sustained the laughable hypothesis of a synthetic osmium or an abnormal molybdenum, or still another who dared to proclaim in public the words of an envious professor who was sure he had recognized Niklaus metal in the form of tiny crystalline clusters encysted in dense masses of siderite. What is known with certainty is that Niklaus' needle can resist the friction of a stream of electrons flowing at ultrasonic speed.

In one of those explanations so pleasing to mathematicians, Professor Niklaus compares the camel in its transit to a spider's thread. He tells us that if we were to use that thread to weave a fabric, we would need all of sidereal space to stretch it out in, and that the visible and invisible stars would be caught in it like sprays of dew. The skein in question measures millions of light years, and Niklaus is offering to wind it up in about three-fifths of a second.

As can be seen, the project is completely viable, and we might even say, overly scientific. It can already count on the sympathy and moral support (not officially confirmed yet) of the Interplanetary League, presided over in London by the eminent Olaf Stapledon.

In view of the natural expectation and anxiety that Niklaus' project has provoked everywhere, the committee is manifesting a special interest by calling the world powers' attention to it, so they will not let themselves be surprised by charlatans who are passing dead camels through subtle orifices. These individuals, who do not hesitate to call themselves scientists, are simply swindlers on the lookout for imprudent optimists. They proceed by an extremely vulgar method, dissolving the camel in sulphuric acid solutions each time lighter than the last. Then they distill the liquid through the needle's eye, using a steam clepsydra, believing that they have performed the miracle. As one can see, the experiment is useless, and there is no reason to finance it. The camel must be alive before and after the impossible transfer.

Instead of melting down tons of candle wax and spending money on indecipherable works of charity, persons interested in the eternal life who have more capital than they know what to do with should subsidize the disintegration of the camel, which is scientific, colorful, and, ultimately, lucrative. To speak of generosity in such a case is totally unnecessary. One must shut one's eyes and open one's purse generously, knowing full well that all expenses will be met pro rata. The reward for all the contributors will be the same; what is urgent is to hasten the date of payment as much as possible.

The total capital necessary cannot be known until the unpredictable end, and Professor Niklaus, in all honesty, refuses to work with a budget that is not fundamentally elastic. The subscribers should pay out their investment quotas patiently over the years. It is necessary to contract for thousands of technicians, managers, and workers. Regional and national subcommittees must be established. And the statute founding a school of successors for Professor Niklaus must not only be foreseen, but budgeted for in detail, since the experiment might reasonably extend over several generations. In this respect, it is not beside the point to indicate the ripe old age of the learned Niklaus.

Like all human plans, Experiment Niklaus offers two probable results: failure and success. Besides simplifying the problem of personal salvation, a success by Niklaus will convert the promoters of such a mystical experience into stockholders of a fabulous transport company. It will be very easy to develop the disintegration of human beings in a practical and economical way. The men of tomorrow will travel great distances in an instant and without danger, dissolved in electronic flashes.

But the possibility of a failure is even more attractive. If Arpad Niklaus is a maker of chimeras and is followed at his death by a whole line of impostors, his humanitarian work will only have increased in grandeur, like a geometric progression or the texture of a chicken bread by Carib. Nothing will keep him from passing into history as the glorious innovator of the universal disintegration of capital. And the rich, impoverished en masse by the draining investments, will easily enter the kingdom of heaven by the narrow gate (the eye of the needle), though the camel may not pass through.

■ João Cabral de Melo Neto (1920–1999)
Brazil (poems)

João Cabral de Melo Neto was born in Recife, to a wealthy family, and as a young man he entered the diplomatic service. He served largely in Europe. While in Spain, he became closely connected to Spanish poets. In 1950, he published a long poem, "The Dog without Feathers." After the appearance of his *Complete Poems* in 1968, he became his generation's natural heir to Carlos Drummond de Andrade, a social critic with modernist ways and strong, brilliant verse often framed in traditional ballad form. A major poetic voice in Latin America, he had, Elizabeth Bishop writes, "striking visual imagery and an insistent use of concrete, tactile nouns. He [was] 'difficult': but his work . . . [displayed] the highest development and the greatest coherency of style of any Brazilian poet."[1]

FURTHER READING: Cabral de Melo Neto, João. *Poems,* 1968.

Poem

My eyes have telescopes
trained on the street
trained on my soul
a mile away.

Women come and go swimming   5
in invisible rivers.
Cars like blind fish
compose my mechanical visions.

For twenty years I've not said the word
I always expect from me.   10
I'll go on indefinitely gazing
at the portrait of me, dead.

TRANSLATED BY W. S. MERWIN

---

1. Elizabeth Bishop, ed., *An Anthology of Twentieth-century Brazilian Poetry* (Middletown, CT: Wesleyan University Press, 1972), xxi.

The End of the World

At the end of a melancholy world
men read the newspapers.
Men indifferent to eating oranges
that flame like the sun.

They gave me an apple to remind me   5
of death. I know that cities telegraph
asking for kerosene. The veil I saw flying fell in the desert.

No one will write the final poem
about this particular twelve o'clock world.
Instead of the last judgment, what worries me   10
is the final dream.

TRANSLATED BY JAMES WRIGHT

Derek Walcott (1930–)
Saint Lucia/United States (epic poem)

The only American-born poet to win the Nobel Prize in Poetry is T. S. Eliot, although Eliot was by then an English citizen, who from graduate student days before World War I had lived in London. Three foreign-born poets, however (Josef Brodsky, a Russian; Czeslaw Milosz, a Pole; and Derek Walcott, a Saint Lucian), each a Nobel laureate, have lived in the United States. Unlike Eliot, who after "Prufock" scarcely alludes to the United States, Brodsky, Milosz, and Walcott write frequently about American life. To add another level of sophisticated, international complication to literatures without borders, Walcott's most impressive poem—which won the Swedish literary award—is *Omeros,* an epic in Dante-flowing tercets, tracing the life and adventures of a fisherman on a Caribbean island, based on Homer's *Odysseus.*

Derek Walcott was born in Castries, Saint Lucia. A poet and playwright from his undergraduate days, he published his first book, *25 Poems,* in 1948 when he was eighteen, and two years later his first play, *Henri Christophe,* was staged. He obtained his B.A. from the University College of the West Indies in Jamaica. In 1958, he went to New York on a Rockefeller Foundation Fellowship to study theater. Then, in Port of Spain, Trinidad, he founded and ran the Little Carib Theatre Workshop from 1959 to 1976. In his back-and-forth life between Trinidad and the United States, he wrote his early masterpiece, *Dream on Monkey Mountain* (1967), whose West Indian hero Makak has South Africa in his mind. Its 1971 version won an Obie Award. Walcott's first important volume of poems is *In a Green Night: Poems, 1948–1962* (1962), published in England by Cape.

Two years later, Farrar Straus published his *Selected Poems in America. Another Life* (1973), also with Farrar Straus, continues the autobiographical search for identity through a sequence of poems. His next two plays, *The Joker of Seville* and *O Babylon!*, came out together as a book of the same name. *The Joker,* with calypso music, retells the Spanish playwright Tirso de Molina's sixteenth-century play *The Trickster of Seville* as a modern version of the notorious Don Juan Tenorio in which both men and women are victimized by their socially imposed roles. *O Babylon!*, with music by Galt MacDermot, is, Walcott states, his first real musical; it dramatizes the Rastafarian cult in Jamaica. His plays prospered. *Pantomine* (1978) was premiered at Joseph Papp's Shakespeare Festival. In 1979, he was named an honorary member of the American Academy of Arts and Letters, and he began to teach at American universities: New York University, Yale, Columbia, and, ultimately, Boston University, where he accepted a permanent post.

Derek Walcott continued publishing volumes of poems, *Sea Grapes* (1976), *The Star-Apple Kingdom* (1979), and *The Fortunate Traveller* (1981). The latter, suggesting the traveler between United States urban centers and the Caribbean, feels increasingly like work by Josef Brodsky, to whom his work is dedicated. Both authors are cosmopolitan world travelers and commentators. A certain formal stiffness often characterizes their city and nature pictures. After *Collected Poems* in 1986, Derek Walcott turned to the two great epics of the West, Homer's *Odyssey* and Dante's *Comedy,* to find a Homeric narrative pitch and a version of Dante's flowing tercets to compose his New World epic, *Omeros* (1990), about a black Helen from Saint Lucia and the life of its dispossessed descendants of African slaves. As Gabriel García Márquez wrote the prose book of the Americas, so Walcott has given us the epic poem of the Americas in wondrously beautiful speech, with extraordinary local detail, and a masterly humane story engaging to the last page. Recognition of his multiple talents, which climax in *Omeros,* came with his 1991 Nobel Prize for Literature.

FURTHER READING: Walcott, Derek. *25 Poems*, 1948; *Henri Christophe*, 1950; *Dream on Monkey Mountain*, 1967; *In a Green Night: Poems, 1948–1962*, 1962; *Selected Poems*, 1964; *Another Life*, 1973; *The Joker of Seville and O Babylon!*, 1978; *Sea Grapes*, 1976; *The Star-Apple Kingdom*, 1979; *The Fortunate Traveller*, 1981; *Collected Poems*, 1986; *Omeros*, 1990.

from Omeros

Chapter XXXVII

I

I crossed my meridian. Rust terraces, olive trees,
the grey horns of a port. Then, from a cobbled corner
of this mud-caked settlement founded by Ulysses—

swifts, launched from the nesting sills of Ulissibona,
their cries modulated to "Lisbon" as the Mediterranean 5
aged into the white Atlantic, their flight, in reverse,

repeating the X of an hourglass, every twitter an aeon
from which a horizon climbed in the upturned vase.
A church clock spun back its helm. Turtleback alleys

crawled from the sea, not towards it, to resettle 10
in the courtyard under the olives, and a breeze
turned over the leaves to show their silvery metal.

Here, clouds read backwards, muffling the clash
of church bells in cotton. There, on an opposite wharf,
Sunday in a cream suit, with a grey horned moustache, 15

strolled past wooden crates, and the long-shadowed Sabbath
was no longer Lisbon but Port of Spain. There, time sifts
like grain from a jute sack under the crooning pigeons.

Sunday clicks open a gold watch, startling the swifts
from the opening eye of a tower, closes it, then slips the sun's 20
pendulum back into its fob, patting it with a nod.

Sunday strolls past a warehouse whose iron-ringed door
exhales an odour of coffee as a reek of salt cod
slithers through the railings. Sunday is a widower

in an ice-cream suit, and a straw with a mourning band, 25
an old Portugee leathery as Portugal, via Madeira,
with a stalled watch for a compass. When he rewinds its hand

it raises an uproar of docks, mulatto clerks cowed
by jets of abuse from wine-barrelled wholesalers.
winches and cranes, black drivers cursing black loaders, 30

and gold-manacled vendors teasing the Vincentian sailors
folded over the hulls. Then not a single word, as Saturday went home
    at one, except from the pigeons

and a boy rattling his stick along the rusted staves
of a railing, its bars caging him as he runs.
After that arpeggio, Sunday hears his own footsteps, 35

making centuries recede, the ebbing market in slaves
and sugar declining below the horizon. Then Sunday stops
to hear schooners thudding on overlapping wharves.

II

Across the meridian, I try seeing the other side,
past rusty containers, waves like welts from the lash
in a light as clear as oil from the olive seed.

Once the world's green gourd was split like a calabash
by Pope Alexander's decree. Spices, vanilla   *5*
sweetened this wharf; the grain of swifts would scatter

in their unchanging pattern, their cries no shriller
than they are now over the past, or ours, for that matter,
if our roles were reversed, and the sand in one half

replicated the sand in the other. Now I had come   *10*
to a place I felt I had known, an antipodal wharf
where my forked shadow swayed to the same brass pendulum.

Yes, but not as one of those pilgrims whose veneration carried
the salt of their eyes up the grooves of a column
to the blue where forked swifts navigated. Far from it; instead,   *15*

I saw how my shadow detached itself from them
when it disembarked on the wharf through a golden haze
of corn from another coast. My throat was scarred

from a horizon that linked me to others, when our eyes
lowered to the cobbles that climbed to the castle yard,   *20*
when the coins of the olives showed us their sovereign's face.

My shadow had preceded me. How else could it recognize
that light to which it was attached, this port where Europe
rose with its terrors and terraces, slope after slope?

III

A bronze horseman halts at a wharf, his green-bronze
cloak flecked with white droppings, his wedged visor
shading the sockets' hyphenating horizons,

his stare fixed like a helm. We had no such erections
above our colonial wharves, our erogenous zones   *5*
were not drawn to power, our squares shrank the directions

of the Empire's plazas. Above us, no stallions paw
the sky's pavement to strike stars from the stones,
no sword is pointed to recapture the port of Genoa.

There the past is an infinite Sunday. It's hot, or it rains;   *10*
the sun lifts the sheets of the rain, and the gutters
run out. For those to whom history is the presence

of ruins, there is a green nothing. No bell tower utters
its flotilla of swallows memorizing an alphabet,
no cobbles crawl towards the sea. We think of the past   *15*

as better forgotten than fixed with stony regret.
Here, a castle in the olives rises over the tiered roofs
of crusted tile but, like the stone Don in the opera,

is the ghost of itself. Over the flagstones, hooves
clop down from the courtyard, stuttering pennons appear   *20*
from the mouths of arches, and the past dryly grieves

from the O's of a Roman aqueduct; silver cuirasses
flash in the reversible olives, their silvery leaves,
and twilight ripens the municipal canvases,

where, one knee folded, like a drinking deer, an admiral   *25*
with a grey horned moustache and foam collar proffers a gift
of plumed Indians and slaves. The wharves of Portugal

were empty as those of the islands. The slate pigeons lift
from the roof of a Levantine warehouse, the castle in the trees
is its own headstone. Yet, once, Alexander's meridian   *30*

gave half a gourd to Lisbon, the seeds of its races,
and half to Imperial Spain. Now Sunday afternoon passes
the empty cafés, their beads hanging like rosaries,

as shawled fado singers sob in turn to their mandolins
while a cobbled lane climbs like a tortoise, and tiredly raises   *35*
its head of a pope at the limp sails on washing lines.

Chapter XXXVIII

I

In scorched summer light, from the circle of Charing Cross,
he arose with the Underground's grit and its embers of sparrows
in a bargeman's black greatcoat, clutching in one scrofulous

claw his brown paper manuscript. The nose, like a pharos,
bulbed from his cragged face, and the beard under it was   *5*
foam that exploded into the spray burst of eyebrows.

On the verge of collapse, the fallen sails of his trousers
were upheld by a rope. In the barges of different shoes
he flapped towards the National. The winch of his voice,

a fog still in its throat, barged through the queues   *10*
at the newspaper kiosks, then changed gears with the noise
of red double-deckers embarking on chartered views

from pigeon-stirred Trafalgar; it broke off the icing
from wedding-cake London. Gryphons on their ridge
of sandstone snarled because it had carried the cries in   *15*

the Isle of Dogs running over Westminster Bridge.
Today it would anchor in the stone waves of the entrance
of St. Martin-in-the-Fields. There, in tiered sunshine,

the black sail collapsed, face sunward with both hands
crossed over the shop-paper volume bound with grey twine.   *20*
He looked like a heap of slag-coal crusting the tiers

with their summering tourists. Eyes shut, the frayed lips
chewed the breeze, the beard curled like the dog's ears
of his turned-down Odyssey, but Omeros was naming the ships

whose oars spidered soundlessly over the sun-webbed calm   *25*
behind his own lashes. Then, suddenly, a raging sparrow
of a church-warden bobbed down the steps. It picked one arm.

The bargeman huddled. It screeched. It yanked an elbow,
then kicked him with polished pumps, and a curse as
Greek to the choleric cleric as one might imagine   *30*

sprayed the spluttering soutane. It showed him the verses
framed at the entrance announcing this Sunday's lesson
in charity, etc. Then, like a dromedary, over the sands

of the scorching pavement, the hump began to press on
back to the river. The sparrow, rubbing both hands,   *35*
nodded, and chirruped up the steps back to its sanctuary,

where, dipping one claw in the font, it vanished inside
the webbed stone. The bargeman tacked toward his estuary
of light. It was summer. London rustled with pride.

II

He curled up on a bench underneath the Embankment wall.
He saw London gliding with the Thames around its neck
like a barge which an old brown horse draws up a canal

if its yoke is Time. From here he could see the dreck
under the scrolled skirts of statues, the grit in the stone lions'   *5*
eyes; he saw under everything an underlying grime

that itched in the balls of rearing bronze stallions,
how the stare of somnolent sphinxes closed in time
to the swaying bells of "cities all the floure"

petalling the spear-railed park where a couple suns   *10*
near the angled shade of All-Hallows by the Tower,
as the tinkling Thames drags by in its ankle-irons,

while the ginkgo's leaves flexed their fingers overhead.
He mutters its fluent alphabet, the peaked A of a spire,
the half-vowels of bridges, down to the crumpled Z   *15*

of his overcoat draping a bench in midsummer's fire.
He read the inverted names of boats in their element,
he saw the tugs chirring up a devalued empire

as the coins of their wake passed the Houses of Parliament.
But the shadows keep multiplying from the Outer   *20*
Provinces, their dialects light as the ginkgo's leaf, their

fingers plucking their saris as wind picks at water,
and the statues raising objections; he sees a wide river
with its landing of pier-stakes flooding Westminster's

flagstones, and traces the wake of dugouts in the frieze   *25*
of a bank's running cornice, and whenever the ginkgo stirs
the wash of far navies settles in the bargeman's eyes.

A statue swims upside down, one hand up in response
to a question raised in the House, and applause rises
from the clapping Thames, from benches in the leaves.   *30*

And the sunflower sets after all, retracting its irises
with the bargeman's own, then buds on black, iron trees
as a gliding fog hides the empires: London, Rome, Greece.

III

Who decrees a great epoch? The meridian of Greenwich.
Who doles out our zeal, and in which way lies our
hope? In the cobbles of sinister Shoreditch,

in the widening rings of Big Ben's iron flower,
in the barges chained like our islands to the Thames.   *5*
Where is the alchemical corn and the light it yields?

Where, in which stones of the Abbey, are incised our names?
Who defines our delight? St. Martin-in-the-Fields.
After every Michaelmas, its piercing soprano steeple

defines our delight. Within whose palatable vault   *10*
will echo the Saints' litany of our island people?
St. Paul's salt shaker, when we are worth their salt.

Stand by the tilted crosses of well-quiet Glen-da-Lough.
Follow the rook's crook'd finger to the ivied grange.
As black as the rook is, it comes from a higher stock.   *15*

Who screams out our price? The crows of the Corn Exchange.
Where are the pleasant pastures? A green baize-table.   *20*
Who invests in our happiness? The Chartered Tour.

Who will teach us a history of which we too are capable?
The red double-decker's view of the Bloody Tower.
When are our brood, like the sparrows, a public nuisance?

When they screech at the sinuous swans on the Serpentine.   *25*
The swans are royally protected, but in whose hands
are the black crusts of our children? In the pointing sign

under the harps of the willows, to the litter of Margate Sands.
What has all this to do with the price of fish, our salary
tidally scanned with the bank-rate by waxworks tellers?   *30*

Where is the light of the world? In the National Gallery.
In Palladian Wren. In the City that can buy and sell us
the packets of tea stirred with our crystals of sweat.

Where is our sublunar peace? In that sickle sovereign
peeling the gilt from St. Paul's onion silhouette.   *35*
There is our lunar peace: in the glittering grain

of the coined estuary, our moonlit, immortal wheat,
its white sail cresting the gradual swell of the Downs,
startling the hare from the pillars on Salisbury Plain,

sharpening the grimaces of thin-lipped market towns,
whitewashing the walls of Brixton, darkening the grain
when coal-shadows cross it. Dark future down darker street.

Chapter LXIV

I

I sang of quiet Achille, Afolabe's son,
who never ascended in an elevator,
who had no passport, since the horizon needs none,

never begged nor borrowed, was nobody's waiter,
whose end, when it comes, will be a death by water   *5*
(which is not for this book, which will remain unknown

and unread by him). I sang the only slaughter
that brought him delight, and that from necessity—
of fish, sang the channels of his back in the sun.

I sang our wide country, the Caribbean Sea.   *10*
Who hated shoes, whose soles were as cracked as a stone,
who was gentle with ropes, who had one suit alone,

whom no man dared insult and who insulted no one,
whose grin was a white breaker cresting, but whose frown
was a growing thunderhead, whose fist of iron   *15*

would do me a greater honour if it held on
to my casket's oarlocks than mine lifting his own
when both anchors are lowered in the one island,

but now the idyll dies, the goblet is broken,
and rainwater trickles down the brown cheek of a jar   *20*
from the clay of Choiseul. So much left unspoken

by my chirping nib! And my earth-door lies ajar.
I lie wrapped in a flour-sack sail. The clods thud
on my rope-lowered canoe. Rasping shovels scrape

a dry rain of dirt on its hold, but turn your head   *25*
when the sea-almond rattles or the rust-leaved grape
from the shells of my unpharaonic pyramid

towards paper shredded by the wind and scattered
like white gulls that separate their names from the foam
and nod to a fisherman with his khaki dog   *30*

that skitters from the wave-crash, then frown at his form
for one swift second. In its earth-trough, my pirogue
with its brass-handled oarlocks is sailing. Not from

but with them, with Hector, with Maud in the rhythm
of her beds trowelled over, with a swirling log   *35*
lifting its mossed head from the swell; let the deep hymn

of the Caribbean continue my epilogue;
may waves remove their shawls as my mourners walk home
to their rusted villages, good shoes in one hand,

passing a boy who walked through the ignorant foam,   *40*
and saw a sail going out or else coming in,
and watched asterisks of rain puckering the sand.

II

You can see Helen at the Halcyon. She is dressed
in the national costume: white, low-cut bodice,
with frilled lace at the collar, just a cleft of a breast

for the customers when she places their orders
on the shields of the tables. They can guess the rest   *5*
under the madras skirt with its golden borders

and the flirtatious knot of the madras head-tie.
She pauses between the tables, holding a tray
over her stomach to hide the wave-rounded sigh

of her pregnancy. There is something too remote   *10*
about her stillness. Women study her beauty,
but turn their faces away if their eyes should meet,

like an ebony carving. But if she should swerve
that silhouette hammered out of the sea's metal
like a profile on a shield, its sinuous neck   *15*

longing like a palm's, you might recall that battle
for which they named an island or the heaving wreck
of the *Ville de Paris* in her foam-frilled bodice,

or just think, "What a fine local woman!" and her
head will turn when you snap your fingers, the slow eyes   *20*
approaching you with the leisure of a panther

through white tables with palm-green iron umbrellas,
past children wading with water-wings in the pool;
and Africa strides, not alabaster Hellas,

and half the world lies open to show its black pearl.   *25*
She waits for your order and you lower your eyes
away from hers that have never carried the spoil

of Troy, that never betrayed horned Menelaus
or netted Agamemnon in their irises.
But the name Helen had gripped my wrist in its vise   *30*

to plunge it into the foaming page. For three years,
phantom hearer, I kept wandering to a voice
hoarse as winter's echo in the throat of a vase!

Like Philoctete's wound, this language carries its cure,
its radiant affliction; reluctantly now,   *35*
like Achille's, my craft slips the chain of its anchor,

moored to its cross as I leave it; its nodding prow
lettered as simply, ribbed in our native timber,
riding these last worried lines; its rhythm agrees

that all it forgot a swift made it remember   *40*
since that green sunrise of axes and laurel-trees,
till the sunset chars it, slowly, to an ember.

And Achille himself had been one of those children
whose voices are surf under a galvanized roof;
sheep bleating in the schoolyard; a Caribbean   *45*

whose woolly crests were the backs of the Cyclops's flock,
with the smart man under one's belly. Blue stories
we recited as children lifted with the rock

of Polyphemus. From a plaster Omeros
the smoke and the scarves of mare's tails, continually   *50*
chalked associate phantoms across our own sky.

III

Out of their element, the thrashing mackerel
thudded, silver, then leaden. The vermilion scales
of snappers faded like sunset. The wet, mossed coral

sea-fans that winnowed weeds in the wiry water
stiffened to bony lace, and the dripping tendrils   *5*
of an octopus wrung its hands at the slaughter

from the gutting knives. Achille unstitched the entrails
and hurled them on the sand for the palm-ribbed mongrels
and the sawing flies. As skittish as hyenas

the dogs trotted, then paused, angling their muzzles   *10*
sideways to gnaw on trembling legs, then lift a nose
at more scavengers. A triumphant Achille's,

his hands gloved in blood, moved to the other canoes
whose hulls were thumping with fishes. In the spread seine
the silvery mackerel multiplied the noise   *15*

of coins in a basin. The copper scales, swaying,
were balanced by one iron tear; then there was peace.
They washed their short knives, they wrapped the flour-bag sails,

then they helped him haul *In God We Trust* back in place,
jamming logs under its keel. He felt his muscles   *20*
unknotting like rope. The nets were closing their eyes,

sagging on bamboo poles near the concrete depot.
In the standpipe's sandy trough aching Achille's
washed sand from his heels, then tightened the brass spigot

to its last drop. An immense lilac emptiness   *25*
settled the sea. He sniffed his name in one armpit.
He scraped dry scales off his hands. He liked the odours

of the sea in him. Night was fanning its coalpot
from one catching star. The No Pain lit its doors
in the village. Achille put the wedge of dolphin   *30*

that he'd saved for Helen in Hector's rusty tin.
A full moon shone like a slice of raw onion.
When he left the beach the sea was still going on.

■ Clarice Lispector (1925–1977)
Brazil (stories)

Born of Ukranian Jews, Clarice Lispector and her family emigrated to Recife, Brazil, when she was only two months old. She grew up in poverty. When she was nine, her mother died after two difficult childbirths. The family moved to Rio de Janeiro in 1937, where she completed secondary school and where, still a schoolgirl, she published her first short story. She did her law studies in Rio, where she married a fellow law student, who became a diplomat. In 1944, the year of her graduation, she published her first novel, *Near to the Wild Heart.* Soon thereafter, her husband was assigned to foreign posts, and she spent many years living abroad, in Switzerland, England, Italy, and the United States. After her marriage ended, she returned in 1959 to Rio, where she supported herself and her two children on what she earned as a journalist and author. Although she received much national and international recognition, she had financial and health problems during her difficult last years, finally dying of cancer in a public hospital.

Clarice Lispector seems equally indebted to Katherine Mansfield, Virginia Woolf, and the experimental New Wave French antinovel of Nathalie Sarraute. A splendid concise stylist and an outstanding short story writer in the Portuguese language, she creates lonely characters who sometimes even attempt to escape from the page into their own fictions. In the introduction to Alexis Levitin's masterful English translation of Lispector's stories in *Soulstorm,* Grace Paley writes:

> *Lispector was lucky enough to have begun to think about all these lives, men's lives as well as women's, in the early years of the women's movement—that is, at a time when she found herself working among the scrabbly low tides of that movement in the ignorance which is often essential to later understanding. That historical fact is what has kept her language crooked and clean.[1]*

In her "Explanation" that precedes the thirteen stories in *Soulstorm,* we have a short story in which the author herself writes a tale about writing her "bruising stories" and about her enigmatic and unresponsive encounters with would-be characters in her tales.

FURTHER READING: Lispector, Clarice. *Near to the Wild Heart,* 1944; *Besieged City,* 1949; *Family Links,* 1960; *The Foreign Legion,* 1964; *The Passion According to G. H.,* 1964; *The Apple in the Dark,* 1967; *Soulstorm,* 1989.

---

1. Clarice Lispector, *Soulstorm: Stories.* Translated by Alexis Levitin; introduction by Grace Paley (New York: New Directions, 1989), x.

Marmosets

The first time we had a marmoset was just before New Year's. We were without water and without a maid, people were lining up to buy meat, the hot weather had suddenly begun—when, dumbfounded, I saw the present enter the house, already eating a banana, examining everything with great rapidity, and with a long tail. It looked like a monkey not yet grown; its potentialities were tremendous. It climbed up the drying clothes to the clothesline, where it swore like a sailor, and the banana peelings fell where they would. I was exhausted already. Every time I forgot and absent-mindedly went out on the back terrace, I gave a start: there was that happy man. My younger son knew, before I did, that I would get rid of this gorilla: "If I promise that sometime the monkey will get sick and die, will you let him stay? Or if you knew that sometime he'd fall out the window, somehow, and die down there?" My feelings would glance aside. The filthiness and blithe unconsciousness of the little monkey made me responsible for his fate, since he himself would not take any blame. A friend understood how bitterly I had resigned myself, what dark deeds were being nourished beneath my dreaminess, and rudely saved me: a delighted gang of little boys appeared from the hill and carried off the laughing man. The new year was devitalized but at least monkeyless.

A year later, at a time of happiness, suddenly there in Copacabana I saw the small crowd. I thought of my children, the joys they gave me, free, unconnected with the worries they also gave me, free, and I thought of a chain of joy: "Will the person receiving this pass it along to someone else," one to another, like a spark along a train of powder. Then and there I bought the one who would be called Lisette.

She could almost fit in one hand. She was wearing a skirt, and earrings, necklace, and bracelet of glass beads. The air of an immigrant just disembarking in her native costume. Like an immigrant's, too, her round eyes.

This one was a woman in miniature. She lived with us three days. She had such delicate bones. She was of such a sweetness. More than her eyes, her look was rounded. With every movement, the earrings shook; the skirt was always neat, the red necklace glinted. She slept a lot, but, as to eating, she was discreet and languid. Her rare caress was only a light bite that left no mark.

On the third day we were out on the back terrace admiring Lisette and the way she was ours. "A little too gentle," I thought, missing the gorilla. And suddenly my heart said harshly: "But this isn't sweetness. This is death." The dryness of the message left me calm. I said to the children: "Lisette is dying." Looking at her, I realized the stage of love we had already reached. I rolled her up in a napkin and went with the children to the nearest first-aid station, where the doctor couldn't attend to her because he was performing an emergency operation on a dog. Another taxi—"Lisette thinks she's out for a drive, Mama"—another hospital. There they gave her oxygen.

And with the breath of life, a Lisette we hadn't known was revealed. The eyes less round, more secretive, more laughing, and in the prognathous and ordinary face a certain ironic haughtiness. A little more oxygen and she wanted to speak so badly she couldn't bear being a monkey; she was, and she would have had much to tell. More oxygen, and then an injection of salt solution; she reacted to the prick with an angry slap, her bracelet glittering. The male nurse smiled; "Lisette! Gently, my dear!"

The diagnosis: she wouldn't live unless there was oxygen at hand, and even then it was unlikely. "Don't buy monkeys in the street," he scolded me; "sometimes they're already sick." No, one must buy dependable monkeys, and know where they came from, to ensure at least five years of love, and know what they had or hadn't done, like getting married. I discussed it with the children a minute. Then I said to the nurse: "You seem to like Lisette very much. So if you let her stay a few days, near the oxygen, you can have her." He was thinking. "Lisette is pretty!" I implored.

"She's beautiful!" he agreed, thoughtfully. Then he sighed and said, "If I cure Lisette, she's yours." We went away with our empty napkin.

The next day they telephoned, and I informed the children that Lisette had died. The younger one asked me, "Do you think she died wearing her earrings?" I said yes. A week later the older one told me, "You look so much like Lisette!"

I replied, "I like you, too."

TRANSLATED BY ELIZABETH BISHOP

Explanation

My editor commissioned me to write three stories which, said he, had really happened. The facts I had, only imagination was missing. And the subject was dangerous. I told him that I didn't know how to write commissioned stories. But—even as he talked to me over the phone—I began to feel inspiration growing in me. The phone conversation was on Friday. I began on Saturday. Sunday morning the three stories were ready: "Miss Algrave," "The Body," and "The Way of the Cross." I myself, amazed. All the stories in this book are bruising stories. And the one who suffered most was me myself. I was shocked by reality. If there are indecencies in these stories, the fault is not mine. It's useless to say they didn't happen to me, my own family, and my friends. How do I know? I know. Artists know things. I just want to tell you that I don't write for money, but rather on impulse. They will throw stones at me. It hardly matters. I'm not playing games, I'm a serious woman. Besides, it was a challenge.

Today is the twelfth of May, Mother's Day. It wouldn't make sense to write stories on this day that I wouldn't want my children to read because I'd be ashamed. So I said to my editor: I'll only publish these under a pseudonym. I had, in fact, already chosen a very nice name: Cláudio Lemos. But he refused. He said that I ought to have the freedom to write whatever I wanted. I gave in. What could I do but be my own victim? I just pray to God that no one ever commissions anything from me again. For it looks as if I'm likely to rebelliously obey, I the unliberated one.

Someone read my stories and said that that wasn't literature, it was trash. I agree. But there's a time for everything. There's also a time for trash. This book is a bit sad because I discovered, like a foolish child, that it's a dog's world.

This is a book of thirteen stories. It could have been fourteen. But I didn't want it to be. It would have shown disrespect for the trust of a simple man who told me his life. He drives the cart on a farm. And he said to me: "In order not to spill blood, I separated from my woman. She had gone astray and had led my sixteen-year-old daughter astray." He has an eighteen-year-old son who doesn't even want to hear the sound of his own mother's name. And that's how things are.

P. S. — "The Man Who Appeared" and "For the Time Being" were also written on that same damned Sunday. Today, the thirteenth of May, Monday, the day of freedom for the slaves—therefore for me, too—I wrote "Day by Day," "Pig Latin," and "Plaza Mauá." "Footsteps" was written a few days later on a farm, in the darkness of the great night.

I've tried to look closely into someone else's face—a cashier at the movies. In order to learn the secret of her life. Useless. The other person is an enigma. And with eyes that are those of a statue: blind.

"My soul breaketh for longing of Thee."
Psalms 119:20

"I, who understand the body. And its cruel exigencies. I've always known the body. Its dizzying vortex. The solemn body."
One of my characters
still without a name

"Therefore do I weep, and my eyes run down with water."
Lamentations of Jeremiah

"And let all flesh bless his holy name for ever and ever."
Psalm of David

"Who has ever seen a love life and not seen it drown in tears of disaster or remorse?"

I don't know whose this is

TRANSLATED BY ALEXIS LEVITIN

◼ José Donoso (1924–1996) *Chile* (novel)

TRANSLATED BY HARDIE ST. MARTIN

José Donoso was born in Chile into a family of doctors and lawyers, and he studied at an English school in Santiago. In 1949, he went to Princeton University, where he studied English literature for two years. In 1974, he returned to Princeton as a visiting professor. During his two years at the Writers' Workshop in Iowa, he taught American students how to write and publish novels in English. Although his first stories were written and published in English, he never strayed from the Spanish language or his native Chile as his lifelong focus—even when living in Mexico, the United States, or Barcelona, where he wrote most of *The Obscene Bird of the Night* (1969). Donoso's first novel, *Coronation* (1957, translated in 1962), was awarded the 1962 Faulkner Foundation Prize for the best Latin American novel of the year. With *Coronation,* an "Upstairs/Downstairs" story contrasting a decaying aristocratic family with its vigorous servants, Donoso emerged as the breakthrough novelist of his generation. Donoso worked as a shepherd in southern Chile and a dock worker in Buenos Aires; these varied experiences are reflected in his books *Summer Vacation* (1955) and *Charleston* (1960). Donoso has many voices, all showing artistic mastery, as we hear in one of his most telling books, *Hell Has No Limits* (1966), an ironic, powerful tale of love in a small-town brothel. Of the generation of new novelists, all highly educated and rich in diverse cultures, Donoso may have the most subtle and intellectually inquisitive pen.

FURTHER READING: Donoso, José. *Summer Vacation,* 1955; *Coronation,* 1957, tr. 1962; *Charleston and Other Stories,* 1960; *Hell Has No Limits,* 1966; *The Obscene Bird of Night,* 1969, tr. 1973; *A House in the Country,* 1978, tr. 1984.

from The Obscene Bird of Night

Misiá Raquel Ruiz (Mistress Raquel Ruiz, that is) shed many tears when Mother Benita called up to tell her that Brígida had died in her sleep. Then she calmed down a little and asked for more details.

"Amalia, the little one-eyed woman who was a sort of servant to her, I don't know if you remember her . . ."

"Why, yes, Amalia . . ."

"Well, as I was saying, Amalia brewed Brígida her cup of tea, very strong, the way she liked it at night, and Amalia says that Brígida went right off to sleep, as peacefully as ever. It seems that before she went to bed she'd been darning a lovely nightgown, cream satin . . ."

"Oh, my God! It's a good thing you mentioned it, Mother! I've been so upset, it slipped my mind. Have them wrap it for me and tell Rita to hold it in the vestibule. It's my granddaughter Malú's bridal nightgown, she just got married, you remember how I was telling you all about it. The nightgown got caught in the zipper of her suitcase during the honeymoon. I used to like to take Brígida a little needlework, to give her something to do and make her still feel like part of the family. There was no one like Brígida for delicate work like that. How good she was at it! . . ."

Misiá Raquel took over the funeral arrangements. A wake in the chapel of the Casa de Ejercicios Espirituales de la Encarnación, the retreat house at La Chimba where Brígida spent the last fifteen years of her life, with High Mass for its forty women inmates, three nuns, and five young orphans, as well as Misiá Raquel's own children, daughters-in-law and granddaughters who attended the service. Since it was to be the last Mass celebrated in the chapel before it was deconsecrated by the Archbishop and the Casa was torn down, it was sung by Father Azócar. Then, burial in the Ruiz family's mausoleum, as she'd always promised her. Unfortunately, the mausoleum was very crowded. But, with a few phone calls, Misiá Raquel arranged things so that, by hook or by crook, they'd make room for Brígida. The blind faith the poor old woman had had in Misiá Raquel's promise to let her too rest under that marble enabled her to live out her last years in peace: in Mother Benita's archaic but still touching rhetoric, her death became a little flame that flickered out. One of these days, of course, they'd have to see to the weeding out of some of the remains interred in the mausoleum—all those babies from a time when they hadn't even found a cure for diphtheria, some French governess who died far from her own country, old bachelor uncles whose identities were fading—in order to store that miscellany of bones in a small box that would take up only a little space.

Everything went according to Misiá Raquel's plans. The inmates spent the entire afternoon helping me put up the black hangings in the chapel. Other old women, close friends of the deceased, washed the corpse, combed her hair, inserted her dentures, got her up in her finest underclothes and, lamenting and whimpering as they tried to decide the best way to dress her for the last time, finally chose her Oxford gray jersey dress and her pink shawl, the one Brígida kept folded in tissue paper and wore only on Sundays. We arranged the wreaths, sent by the Ruiz family, around the bier. We lit the candles . . . It's really worthwhile being a servant like that, with an employer like Misiá Raquel. Such a good lady! But how many of us women have Brígida's luck? None. Look at Mercedes Barroso, only last week. A public welfare truck came to carry off poor Menche, and we ourselves, yes, it's hard to believe that we ourselves had to pick a few red geraniums from the vestibule court to dress up her coffin, and her former employers, who, over the phone, kept promising poor Menche the sun, the moon and the stars . . . wait, woman, wait, have patience, better wait till summer, no, better still when we get back from the summer holidays since you don't like the beach, remember how the sea air always gives you a windburn, when we come back that's when, you'll see, you'll love the new chalet with its garden, it has a room over the garage that's ideal for you . . . and, you see, Menche's employers didn't even show up at the Casa when she died. Poor Menche! What hard luck! And she was so good at telling dirty jokes, and she knew so many of them. Who knows where she used to dig them up. But Brígida's funeral was something else again: she had real wreaths, with white flowers and all, the way funeral flowers ought to be, and with calling cards too. The first thing Rita did when they brought the coffin was to run her hand under it to check if that part of the box was well polished like first-class coffins in the old days. I watched her purse her lips and nod approval. Such a fine job was done on Brígida's coffin! Misiá Raquel even kept her word about that. Nothing disappointed us. Neither the hearse drawn by four black horses bedecked with caparison and tufts of feathers nor the Ruiz family's gleaming cars lined up along the sidewalk, waiting for the funeral procession to start.

But it can't start yet. Misiá Raquel remembers, at the very last minute, that she has a bicycle that's a bit damaged but, with a little fixing here and there, will make a perfect gift for her gardener on the feast day of St. Peter and Paul . . . go Mudito (I was *Mudito* to everyone because I was mute), take your cart and fetch it for me, my chauffeur can put it in the back of the station wagon and save an extra trip.

"Aren't you coming back to see us any more, Misiá Raquel?"

"I have to come when Inés gets back from Rome."

"Have you had any news from Misiá Inés?"

"Not a word. She hates writing letters. And now that the famous business of the beatification fell through and Jerónimo signed the chaplaincy of the Azcoitías over to the Archbishopric, she must be hiding her head and she's not even going to send postcards. If she stays in Rome much longer, it'll be a miracle if she finds the Casa still standing."

"Father Azócar's been showing me the plans for his Children's Village. They're lovely! You should see all the glass windows! The drawings made me feel a little better about . . . this being the last Mass in the chapel."

"One of Father Azócar's tall stories, Mother Benita. Don't be so naïve! He's the worst kind of scheming priest. This property Jerónimo signed over to the Archbishop is very, yes, very very valuable. Children's Village! I'll bet anything they divide all this into lots after they tear the Casa down and sell it, and the money will evaporate in smoke. Mudito's taking long, Mother, and with Brígida waiting for us to bury her! What can be holding him up? Of course the Casa's so big it takes all day to make your way through all the passageways and corridors that lead to the cell where I keep my stuff, and Mudito's so thin and sickly. But I'm tired, I want to go bury Brígida, I want to get away, this whole business is too much for me, I'm burying a whole life, poor Brígida, only a couple of years older than I, my God, and, to keep my word, I gave up my vault in the mausoleum for her to start rotting in my place, keeping it warm for me with her remains so that when they take them out mine won't get numb, won't be afraid, giving up my vault to her for the time being was the only way to keep my word, now that even relatives I haven't so much as said hello to in years come around claiming—I don't know what makes them think they have a leg to stand on—that they must be buried in the mausoleum, but I'm not afraid that they'll steal my place now, she'll be there, holding it for me, heating it with her body like in the days when she used to turn down the covers and slip a good hot water bottle under them, for me to go to bed early when I came in exhausted from running around on business errands in winter. But when I die she'll have to move out of my vault. What can I do? Yes, Brígida, yes, I'm going to hire lawyers to strip those relatives of their rights, but I doubt that we'll win the lawsuits . . . you'll have to get out. It won't be my fault. I won't have to answer for it anymore, Brígida, no one knows what they'll do after I'm gone. You can't say I haven't been good to you, I've done everything you told me, but I'm afraid because when they take you out I don't know what they're going to do with your bones, nobody will give a rap . . . who knows how many years from now I'll die, fortunately I'm in very good health, imagine, I haven't spent a single day in bed this winter, not even a chill, Mother Benita, not a thing, half of my grandchildren down with the flu and my daughters calling me up to please go over and help them because even their servants are sick . . ."

"How lucky! Almost all the orphans here came down with it. But then, the Casa's so cold, and coal is so expensive . . ."

"Imagine! It's the last straw! All this talk about a Children's Village, and look at the miserable conditions they keep them in. I'm going to send you a little contribution next time I go out to the farm. I have no idea what's left over from this year's crops, but I'll send you something so that you'll all remember poor Brígida. Were you able to get the bicycle in, Jenaro?"

The chauffeur sits next to Misiá Raquel. They can get under way now. The coachman climbs into the driver's seat of the hearse, Misiá Raquel's daughter-in-law puts on her perforated driving gloves, the black horses stamp, tears fill the eyes of the old women who go out on the sidewalk muffled up, shivering, coughing, to see the procession off. Before Misiá Raquel gives the order to get under way, I go over to her window and hand her the package.

"What's this?"

I wait.

"Malú's nightgown! My God! If this poor little man hadn't thought of it, I'd have forgotten, and he'd have had to pull the cart back here again for me . . . Thanks, Mudito . . . no, no, wait . . . have him wait, Mother . . . here, Mudito, for cigarettes, for your little vices, go on, take it . . . Blow the horn, Jenaro, get the procession started . . . Well, goodbye, Mother Benita . . ."

"Goodbye, Misiá Raquel . . ."

"Goodbye, Brígida . . ."

"Goodbye . . ."

When the last car disappears around the corner, we go in—Mother Benita, I, the old women who mumble as they slowly scatter to their courts. I bolt and lock the outside door. Rita closes the inner one with its rattly glass panes. Straggling behind, one of the old women picks up a white rose from the tile floor of the vestibule and, yawning and tuckered out from all the excitement, pins it on her bun before disappearing into the passage-ways to look for her friends, her bowl of watery soup, her shawl, her bed.

In a nook in one of the corridors, they stopped before the door I sealed off with two boards nailed crosswise. I'd loosened the nails, to make it easy for them to pry off the boards and go up to the next floor. The or-phans pulled out the nails, took the boards off and helped Iris Mateluna go up . . . Get a move on, chubby, I'm scared, these stairs don't have a railing, some of the steps are gone . . . hey, fatso's so heavy everything's creaking under her . . . They take their time going up, studying where to take each step so the whole works won't collapse, looking for solid places so as to get Iris to the next floor. Ten years ago Mother Benita had me board up those doors so as to forget about that section of the Casa once and for all and not have to think about cleaning and keeping it neat, because we just don't have the strength to do it anymore . . . Mudito, better let it go to pot and not lose any sleep over it . . . Until the five little girls, bored with wandering about the Casa with nothing to do, discovered that they could open this door and go up to the cloistered galleries on the next floor that surround the courts . . . let's go up, kids, don't be scared . . . scared of what, when it's still light out, let's go see what's there . . . like what, nothing, filth, same as all over the Casa, but at least it's fun because no one's allowed to roam there because they say it might cave in . . . Eliana warns them to watch their step and make sure nobody sees them from downstairs but it's not too risky today because they're at the doorkeeper's, seeing Brígida off. Still, they'd better not take chances, Mother Benita's in a nasty mood . . . make your-selves useful, you little pests, pick that up, help with this pile of spoons and plates, they have to be left clean, now that they're going to hold an auction, fold the napkins, count them, sweep, get some washing done, wash your own things at least, you've been going around filthy as pigs, don't spend all your time playing . . . shshshshshsh, kids, shshshshshsh . . . careful, or we'll get punished . . .

They round one court and then another, until they come to a door Eliana pushes open. A room with twenty rusty iron bedsteads, disassem-bled, others crippled—missing rollers, patched-up springs—but set up in two rows against the walls, like beds in a boarding school. Twin windows: high, narrow, deeply recessed, their glass painted a chocolate brown up to a person's height so that no one can see anything outside except the dark clouds veiled by chicken wire and iron bars. I also loosened the nails with which I myself sealed the two windows. The orphans already know how to open them and they did it in time to wave goodbye to Brígida's hearse led by the four plumed horses followed by nine automobiles. Eliana counts eight, Mirella nine . . . no, eight . . . no, nine . . . and when the procession disappears the little neighborhood children take over the middle of the street again, scrambling after the soccer ball . . . Good pass, Ricardo! Kick, Mito! Quick, after it, Lucho, pass it, now, kick, there, goal, goooooal . . . a shrill scream from Mirella, who cheers her friends' *goooooooooooal* and applauds and waves to them.

Iris has stayed behind, at the back of the dormitory, sitting sleepily on an innerspring. She yawns. She leafs through a magazine. The orphans make faces at people going by, talk in shouts to their friends, sit in the window recess, laugh at a woman passing by, yawn. When it begins to get dark Iris calls Eliana.

"What do you want?"

"You promised to read me this one with Pluto the dog and Popeye the sailor man."

"No. You owe me for two readings."

"I'm going to get together with the Giant this evening and play yumyum. I'll pay you tomorrow."

"Then I'll read for you tomorrow."

Eliana presses up against the window bars again. The street lamps begin to go on. A woman in the house across the street opens her balcony window. As she combs her long jet-black hair, looking into the street, she turns on a radio . . . ta-ra-tat-tat-tatatat-tat-tatat . . . syncopated piercing sounds from electric guitars and twanging voices pour into the dormitory, the orphans rouse Iris from the bedsprings and get her to stand up in the aisle between the two rows of beds when they hear *babalú, babalú ayé* . . . hey, do a little dance for us, Gina, they urge her, come on, do your stuff . . . tossing her neck back like a mare, she twirls her long wavy hair, swaggering down the aisle, a look of ecstasy in her eyes half-closed like those of actresses in cheap illustrated love stories . . . I don't feel lazy anymore, I'm not yawning, I want to get out and dance like Gina, the actress who lived in a convent run by bad nuns in the love story Eliana read to me . . . Iris stops. She digs in her pockets. She smears her lips with a purplish lipstick, the horrible dark color turns to unbaked dough . . . Come on, Gina, do your stuff, dance down the aisle for us, shake it, that's it, that's it, more, more . . . At the window, Eliana's lighting two candles she stole from the chapel where Brígida lay in state; all she can do is set the stage, she's too young, the youngsters in the street don't call up to her, they want Iris, Eliana doesn't have breasts to show off or thighs to put on display. She shoos the other orphans over to the farther window and helps Iris climb up on the window recess.

"Look, Gina, the Giant's here."

"Yell down to them that I'll go out as soon as the old ladies are in bed."

"The guys want you to dance for them."

She's the only one left at the lighted window. She grinds her hips. Sticking out her breasts, she smooths her sweater with a long caress that runs the whole length of her body and ends with her hiking her skirt to show her heavy thighs that are a quivering mass, while her other hand piles up her hair and she puckers her lips as if she were about to give someone a madly passionate kiss. The group gathering under the streetlight cheers her on. The woman combing her hair in the window across the way turns up the music, resting her elbows on the railing to get a good look. Iris begins to move very slowly, only rubbing her thighs together at first, then shaking her whole body to the wild beat of *babalú*, whirling, hair flying, arms out-stretched, hands open as if searching for something or someone, whirling again, again, bending, stretching; she tosses back her head and lets all her hair spill forward, her gyrating body moving to the rhythm of rock, the frug, anything, as long as she can rotate and show her thighs and her filthy panties and her bouncing breasts, her tongue hot and searching like her hands, as she dances at the window so that the people in the street will applaud and egg her on and yell up to her . . . come on, give, Gina baby, give it all you've got, good-lookin', shake those tits, shake your ass off, burn down the Casa, burn us all . . . And the Giant, with his enormous papier-mâché head, steps into the middle of the street and dances as if he were dancing with Iris, Iris sways, grinds her hips, gyrates, shakes and screams from her candlelit cage that seems to hang from the side of the Casa as she dances like a Virgin Mary gone berserk in her niche. The Giant stands on the sidewalk in front and calls to her: "Gina, Gina, come on down so we can play yumyum, hey kid, yell up at her, she can't hear me because I'm shut up inside this stinking head."

"He says for you to come down, Gina!"

"Hey, Eliana, ask him what kind of present he's brought me today. Other-wise I won't go down."

"Not money, he says, but he's got five love story magazines for you and a lipstick that's not new but's real good and comes in a gold case."

"It must be gold-plated, gold ones are very expensive."

"Don't accept any of his crappy stuff, Iris, don't be stupid. You gotta get money out of him so you can pay me for the readings."

"If you don't read to me Mirella will, so who cares."

"But you like how I read because I explain the story, otherwise you don't understand a thing. I've got you where I want you, Iris Mateluna, right where I want you, because if I don't read and explain the love stories and Donald Duck you get bored to death here in this shithouse . . ."

Iris hangs on to the bars to get a look at him . . . it's him with his eyes that are as big and round as saucers and his laugh that's always the same because he never gets mad, he's good, we play yumyum real nice and when he calls me Gina he raises his eyebrow and the wrinkles on his forehead hold up his silly little hat . . . it's him, he wants to marry me because he likes the way I play yumyum, he's going to take me to see movies that show real live actresses so that pain-in-the-ass Eliana won't have to read anything to me, the Giant's going to take me to one of those tall buildings downtown so I can dance in a contest and win the prize, and makeup kit they say they give to the girl who dances best, and afterwards her picture comes out in the love story magazines and that moron Eliana and Miss Rita and Mudito and Mother Benita and the girls and all the old bags will see my picture in the magazines.

"What are you gonna pay me with if the Giant doesn't give you money today?"

Iris shrugs.

"Because you've got to pay me before you get married, you hear, or else I'll get the cops after you, the same ones who carried off your old man, to make you pay up, and if you don't pay they'll drag you off to jail too. I'll settle for the lipstick and two of the magazines the Giant's going to give you today."

"Do you think I'm stupid? One magazine and you can use the lipstick twice, and that's it . . ."

"It's a deal. But you'll have to give me the lipstick case when it's all used up."

"It's a deal."

Mother Benita remains very still for a second in the vestibule, her hands together and her eyes closed. Rita and I wait for her to move, to open her eyes, and she opens them and motions me to follow her. I know very well that, stopped and rickety or not, I have to pull my little cart as if I were her idiot son pulling a toy. I know why she wants me to follow her. We've done it so many times: to clean up what the dead woman left behind. Misiá Raquel told her to divide Brígida's things among her friends. No, among her mates is what she said, as if this were a finishing school. I don't want to look at Brígida's room, Mother, for God's sake, I don't want to, I don't want to go over anything or look at anything, no, there can't be anything of value so I don't want to look at anything, I tell you, you can do what you like with her things, Mother Benita, give them away, these old women are so poor they'll be happy with anything they can remember Brígida by, she was so well liked here at the Casa.

I follow her down the corridors, pulling the platform on four wheels. I put brooms, buckets, rags, father dusters on. In the court where the kitchen is, a group of old women forming a circle around Mother Anselma peel potatoes into a huge pot . . . what a lovely funeral Brígida had! . . . Misiá Raquel's princesse overcoat, they say they're coming back . . . the coachman had a mustache, I'm not sure it's right to let coachmen who drive first-class hearses wear a mustache, it's a sort of lack of respect . . . the funeral would keep tongues wagging for months . . . another group of old women farther over have already forgotten about it, they've forgotten Brígida, they're playing cards on a sugar bin . . . Watch out for that step, Mother, it's a step, not a shadow, and we come out into still another court that's not the one where Brígida lived, so we have to go down other passageways . . . One, then a second empty room, rows of vacant rooms, more doors, some open, some closed, because it's all the same if they're open or closed, more rooms to cross, shattered windowpanes coated with dust, the semidarkness sticking to the dried-up walls where a hen pecks at the centuries-old adobe, hunting for specks of grain. Another court. The laundry court where no laundry's done anymore because only three of them are left now, the court with the palm tree, the one with the linden, this court without a name, Ernestina Gómez's court, the refectory court no one uses because the old women prefer to eat in the kitchen, endless courts and cloisters connected by corridors that never end, rooms we'll never try to clean again even if up until a short time ago you used to say, yes, Mudito, one of these days, the first chance we have, we're going to clean everything out with brooms and dusters and rags and pails and soap powder because it's such a filthy mess . . . Watch out, Mother, I'll give you a hand, let's step around this rubble, better walk down this corridor that leads into still another court that's on a different level because of the now-forgotten purposes it once served, and opens onto rooms where sounds are softened by cobwebs and onto galleries where the echoes of forgotten comings and goings linger, or perhaps it's mice and cats and chickens and pigeons chasing one another among the ruins of this wall no one ever finished tearing down.

I walk ahead of Mother Benita. I stop next to a cluster of shacks made of tin, boards, cardboards, branches—shacks as flimsy and gray as though they were build with the well-worn cards the old women use for playing their age-old games . . . You've tried so many times to convince them to sleep in the rooms. There are hundreds and hundreds of them, good, spacious, all vacant . . . pick the ones you like in whatever court you like, Mudito and I will make them comfortable for you . . . no, Mother, we're afraid they're much too big and the ceilings are too high and the walls too thick and someone may have died or spent her life praying in those rooms and that's enough to scare anybody, they're damp, bad for rheumatism, they're enormous and gloomy, all that space when we're not used to living in rooms with so much space because we're servants used to living in cubbyholes crammed with all kinds of things, in the back part of our employers' houses, no, no, Mother Benita, thanks just the same, we prefer these rickety shacks that are sheltered by the long balconies, because we want to be as close to one another as possible so as to hear someone else breathing in the shack next door and smell stale tea leaves and listen to another sleepless body like our own tossing and turning on the other side of the thin wall, and the coughing and farts and intestinal rumblings and nightmares; who cares about the cold coming in through the cracks in the badly fitted boards as long as we're all together, in spite of the envy and greed or the terror that shrivels our toothless mouths and makes our gummy eyes squint, we're together and toward evening can go to the chapel in groups, because it's terrifying to go all by yourself, we can cling to one another's rags, through the cloisters, down passageways like tunnels that never end, through unlit galleries where a moth may brush against my face and make me scream because I get frightened if anyone touches me in the dark when I don't know who it is, we're together and can drive off any shadows that drops from the beams and stretch out toward us when it begins to get dark . . . Here comes the crotchety old woman who lines her eyebrows with black crayon. And here's Amalia . . . good afternoon Amalia, cheer up, wait for me here, I want to talk to you when I've tidied up Brígida's cell . . . no, no thanks, Mudito will help me as usual, look he's opening the padlock on Brígida's door . . . And Rosa Pérez, who can stir up a courtyard full of women with her gossip . . . Good afternoon, Carmela . . . yes, yes, they'll come for you, wait, woman . . . but you've been waiting for ten years and nobody comes . . . they say Rafaelito rented a house with an extra room . . . this little lock of hair I keep here, look, Mother Benita, it's one of his as a little boy when I was bringing him up, blond as a corn tassel and none of that drugstore-blond stuff like other kids, that's what his hair used to be like before it started turning darker, what a pity he's bald now, so they say, I called him on the phone the other day but that new wife of his said to me, call him some other time . . . wait Carmela . . . but Carmela is waiting for what all of them are waiting for with their hands crossed in their laps, staring through the secretions that have collected in their eyes, to see if they can make out what's creeping up on them and growing and beginning to cover up the light, at little at first, not quite all the light, and then all of it, all, all, all, all, all, total darkness suddenly in which you can't cry out because in the dark you can't find your voice to call for help, and one fine night you sink and you're lost in the sudden darkness like Brígida night before last. And, while they wait, the old women sweep a little as they've done all their lives or darn or do their laundry or peel potatoes or whatever there is to peel or wash, as long as it doesn't require much strength because there's no strength left, one day exactly like the next, one morning repeating the one before, one afternoon the same as all the others, sunning themselves as they sit by the cloister's drainage ditch and drive away the flies that feast on their slobber or their sores, their elbows digging into their knees and their faces buried in their hands, tired of waiting for the moment none of them believes she's waiting for, waiting as they've always waited, in other courtyards, beside other pilasters, behind other windowpanes, or else whiling away their time picking red geraniums with which to decorate the wooden box in which they carted off Mercedes Barroso, so that poor Menche wouldn't leave this earth without so much as a single flower even if they could provide only those dusty geraniums . . . she was a scream when she did the dances Iris Mateluna taught her, the frug, rock, with the rest of the orphans and even we keeping time by clapping so that they could dance together, Iris and Menche . . . poor Menche . . . Mercedes Barroso must of died of sheer fatness on a night exactly like this one that's beginning to fall.

I step back a little so you can go in. The dresser with its mirror and the brass bed barely fit in here. The sheets are rumpled so little that no one would guess a woman passed away between them forty-eight hours ago. Brígida's still alive here. This place is still here, it keeps another Brígida alive while the body of the dead one is beginning to feed the worms: this peculiar arrangement, these objects she gradually wore out with her attachment to them and with her pursuits, this attempt at elegance . . . look, Mother Benita, at the way she attached the Easter palms to a corner of the print showing the Annunciation, how she used Christmas wrapping paper to cover the Coca-Cola bottle she turned into a vase. Photographs of the Ruiz family. Holy pictures. She was so painstaking at her needlework that she was able to restore the embroidery on some chasubles Father Azócar took away because, he said, they were eighteenth-century ones and were too precious to let go to ruin here at the Casa. They were the only things of any value here, Mother Benita, everything else is trash, it's hard to believe that this country's ruling families haven't been able to collect anything but filthy junk in this place. And, without disturbing anything on the dresser, you run your fingertips over the perfect row formed by the thimble, pincushion, nail file, small scissors, tweezers, buffer—everything neatly arranged on the fresh, starched white runner. Mother Benita, you and I have come here to carve up this Brígida who's still alive, to divide her up, to burn her, to throw her out, to eradicate the Brígida who hoped to live on in the orderliness of her possessions. To wipe out all traces of her so that tomorrow or the next day they can send us another old woman who can start leaving the particular imprint of her dying hour on this place, an imprint that's not much different but is unmistakably her own. She'll replace Brígida as Brígida replaced . . . I can't think of the name of the quiet old woman with hands disfigured by warts who lived in this shack before Brígida came here.

The news that Mother Benita's started cleaning out Brígida's hovel travels through the Casa. Old women come from other courts to snoop. Mother Benita never favors any of the beggars and that's why, at first, none of them comes too close, they maraud silently or muttering under their breaths, they go past the door for a second: she smiles at you sweetly, she winks at me, and I wink my Mudito's eye back at her. They go past the door, slowing down more gradually until they barely stir, darkening the doorway like flies glued to a drop of syrup, whispering, shuffling, shouting, till you finally beg me to chase them off . . . get them out of here, Mudito . . . get out, for God's sake, let us get our work done in peace, we'll call you later. Once more they fall back a little. They sit down on the side of the corridor, at the foot of the pilasters, their hands fidgeting in their laps . . . look at Brígida's blue satin quilt, I hear it's all down, I wonder who they're going to give it to, I think the one who'll get the good things like that is Misiá Raquel, she'll take them for her house . . . look at the radio, Zunilda, I'll bet they're going to send it to some auction, radios are expensive, I'd love to own a radio like Brígida did, because she used to stay in bed on Sunday and listen to the Mass sung in the cathedral, and I'd love to hear Mass in bed some Sunday when it's cold. And that black shawl, take a look, Clemencia, I tell you it's the black shawl I was telling you about the other day, see, the one Miss Malú gave her on her birthday and she never wore because, you see, Brígida didn't care for black . . . it must be like new . . .

You roll up her sheets along with the stains and odors of her final moment, a moment no one was there to witness . . . straight to the wash! I take up the two layers of the mattress to air them out in the passageway. You strip off the ticking that protects the mattress from the rust on the spring—a wire cage that's a den where flat, long, soft, square, shapeless creatures crouch: dozens, hundreds, of packages, cartons tied with strips of cloth, balls of string or wool, a broken soap dish, an odd shoe, a bottle, a dented lampshade, a raspberry-colored bathing cap. All of them are velvety to the touch, homogeneous, motionless under the soft dust that covers everything with the silky, delicate fuzz that the slightest movement, like the flicker of an eye or someone's breathing, could scatter through the room, choking and blinding us and causing all those creatures that are resting quietly in the momentarily gentle shapes of small bundles of rags, sheaves of old magazines, umbrella ribs, boxes, box tops, pieces of box tops, to spring to life and pounce on us. More and more packages under the bed, and . . . look, Mother Benita, under the dresser too, between it and the wall and behind the curtain in the corner . . . and everything hidden just below or beyond eye level.

Don't stand there dangling your arms. Don't you know this Brígida who tamed the dust and tamed uselessness itself? Does this Brígida disturb you? Ah, Mother, you don't know it but that old woman had more secret recesses in her than the Casa. The pincushion, the scissors, the buffer, the white thread—yes, to the eye, everything was in order on the runner. Very touching. But now, suddenly, you have to face this other unofficial Brígida, the one who didn't leave herself open to view on the starched runner, the one who was queen of the inmates, who had a queen's funeral, who, from the pulchritude of her embroidered sheets, with her perfect hands and pleasant look, passed judgment by simply dropping a hint, gave orders with a moan or a sigh, changed the course of other people's lives with the flick of a finger . . . no, you didn't know her and you could never have known her, Mother Benita's eyes don't reach under the beds or into the hiding places, it's preferable to feel sorry for people, to serve them, to stick to this, even if it means working yourself to the bone as you've done for years among these decrepit old ladies in this condemned place, surrounded by imbeciles, by the sick, by the wretched, by the abandoned, by executioner and victim you can't tell apart—all of them complaining and suffering from the cold and hunger you try desperately to relieve; they drive you crazy with the anarchy of old age, which has first call on everything . . . poor old things, something must be done for them, yes, you've worked yourself to death in order to ignore Brígida's other side.

She sighs as she bends over to fish out a square package, done up in manila paper and string, from under the bedspring. I dust it with my rag and we have to wrinkle our noses because the tiny room fills up with fuzz. You begin undoing the package; it contains one of those cardboard mats on which they used to mount studio photographs with raised garlands and the photographer's signature embossed in gold in one corner, but there's no photograph. I take the paper and the cardboard out to the middle of the court and start the pile of trash that will turn into a pyre. The old women move in to rummage and grab anything they can find, but there's little, very little. Nothing. Anyhow, this is only the beginning. And it's going to be something! Because Brígida was rich. A millionaire, they say. All they have to do is wait a bit longer. The old women who've stationed themselves in the corridor or mill around never take their eyes off us.

Everything you find is tied, packaged, wrapped in something, inside something else—tattered clothing wrapped in itself, broken objects that crumble as you unwrap them, the porcelain handle of a demitasse, ribbons from a First Communion sash, things saved for the sake of saving, packing, tying, preserving this static, reiterative community that never lets you in on its secret, Mother Benita, because it's too cruel for you to bear the notion that you and I and the old women who are still alive and those who are dead, and all of us, are tied up in these packages you want to force a meaning from because you respect human beings, and if poor Brígida made up all these little packages, Mother Benita muses, carried away by her feelings, it was in order to raise a banner reading, "I want to protect, I want to rescue, I want to preserve, I want to survive." But I can assure you, Mother, that Brígida had more complex methods to make sure of her survival . . . little packages, oh yes, all old women make little packages and stow them away under their beds.

Let's open the packages, Mudito, there may be something important here, something that . . . you can't finish what you started to say because you're afraid to tie it to an incoherent idea, and instead you begin to play the game of supposing that by undoing knots, unwrapping rags, opening envelopes and cartons, you're going to discover something worth saving. No, everything into the trash pile! Rags and more rags. Papers. Cotton brown with blood from some past wound. Bundle after bundle. Don't you see, Mother Benita, that the act of wrapping, and not what's inside the wrappings, is the important thing? I go on heaping up trash in the court. A steady hum swells from the hive of old women who, as they rummage, fight over a cork, a brass knob, buttons kept inside a tea tin, an insole, the top of a pen. Sometimes, when we clean out the hovel of an inmate who just died, some familiar object turns up among her things; this black wooden curtain ring, for instance, is the very one we threw in the trash last week when Mercedes Barroso died, and she, in turn, had salvaged it, for no particular reason, from another dead woman's belongings and that one from still another's, and another's . . .

The toothless crone who winked at me tries on the raspberry-colored bathing cap and struts to the applause of the others. Dora unravels the remains of a moth-eaten cardigan, rolling the curly wool into a ball and piecing it together so that she can wash and then knit it into a little sweater for the baby that's going to be born. This package: this one. You're becoming tense, impatient, it has to be the package with the key to what Brígida was trying to say. This one. Do you want to open it? All right. Yes, Mudito, open it with respect, because Brígida wrapped it so that I would understand . . . no, Mother Benita, no, don't be fooled, Brígida made this package and the others because she was afraid. She was queen, scourge, dictator, judge, but she tied things and saved them the same as the rest of the old women. I know you're praying for this package to have something other than junk in it. You strip off the brown paper and throw it out. There's more paper, finer stuff, all wrinkled up, you tear it and drop it on the floor. Why go on opening and tearing wrappings—this apple-green taffeta one with a piece of newspaper underneath showing Roosevelt and Fala and Stalin's smile on board a ship—if you surely know you won't find a thing? This gray cotton shoulder pad is what made the parcel soft and bulky. You search, your anxious fingernails pull the shoulder pad apart and let the padding fall to the floor. There's still another hard little package you hold between your forefinger and your thumb. You peel off the layer of rusty homespun and press gently . . . yes, yes, dear God, there's something inside, something solid, with a definite shape—this object I finger anxiously. Your fingers get all tangled up undoing the homespun, only to discover a ball of silver foil. You rip it to shreds that remain in the open palm of your trembling hand. I'm about to blow on those shreds and scatter them but you snap your fist shut just in time, grabbing it away from my breath, and your fingers reconstruct the silver ball in a second. You look at it and glance toward me, inviting me to accept the wholeness of this thing you've restored. You move to the door. The old women stop, quiet down, their eyes trace the swoop of your arm and then the arc of the shining little sphere as it falls. They run toward the trash pile and pounce on the silvery thing that streaked through the air. Don't worry, we'll find it again among some other dead old woman's things.

Why do you cover your face with your hands, Mother? You rush down the passages, the galleries, across the courts, the cloisters, with the old women tagging after you with their gnarled faces and pleading gummy eyes as they ask for things—one of the women in a voice that's muffled because of the shawl she wears to protect her mouth from some imaginary chill or some imaginary contagion, another in a voice that's harsh from smoking too much and drinking too much scalding-hot tea to warm her body that's stiff from the cold. They reach out to touch your habit, to hold you fast, to hang on to your denim apron, to your sleeve . . . don't go away, Mother, I want the brass bedstead . . . and me the glasses she sometimes let me wear because I don't have any and I like to read the papers even if they're old . . . a blanket for me because I can't stand the cold at night even in the summer, I was her friend, she liked me better, I was her neighbor to the right . . . I was to her left, I used to trim her nails, even her toenails and her corns too because I used to be a manicurist when I was young, she liked me much better than Amalia, who used to charge her too much to wash her clothes . . . hands like tongs with wooden claws grab me by the arms, wrinkled mouths claim things I don't know anything about . . . I'm a widow, the little scissors were mine . . . look at Rafaelito's lock of hair, Mother Benita, what a pity the boy's bald now, and they even say he's gotten fat . . . a needle I lent her just the other day, and me a piece of crochet work . . . and me some buttons . . . These withered hands are stronger than mine, their fingers shoot out like branches to hold me back, their pleas and litanies bind

me . . . for me, for me, Mother Benita . . . I want, I need . . . why don't you
give me the tea Brígida left, you know how poor I am . . . no, not to her, me,
give it to me, everybody knows she's a thief, keep an eye on the things
because she's liable to steal them . . . give it to me, to me . . . old women in
a corner, whose voices are as soft as balls of fluff, are stirred up by want or
greed, chipped fingernails, filthy rags that fall apart on their bodies, bodies
with the stench of old age that back me against this vestibule door with
broken panes. The key! I open, I slip out and shut the door. I turn the key
from the outside. I take it out and put it in my apron pocket. At last, dear
God! They remain on the other side of the door like prisoners, collecting
dust. Their arms, their faces twisted by grimaces, stick out through the broken panes . . . the wail of their pleading voices dies out.

■ Jaime Sabines (1925–1999) *Mexico* (poems)

Born in Tuxtla Gutiérrez in the southern province of Chiapas, Jaime
Sabines is a businessman in Mexico City. His encantatory poems combine
surreal images, nature, and the everyday life of city people and their surroundings, including God, whom he has snoring outside his grandmother's house. The poems treat serious themes, whether love, death, or the
Deity, with humor and piercing irony, yet within the fantasy he uses a highly lyrical language. Like a traditional poet from India, such as Mirabai, who
addresses her god at the end of each poem, Sabines, inventing his own universal tradition, addresses his mock god Tarumba. His tone is grave, ironic,
amusing; his sympathy is with the Indian, displaced in a society that cannot
handle the outsider.

FURTHER READING: Sabines, Jaime. *Collection of Poems,* 1962; *Bad Times,* 1972; *New
Collection of Poems,* 1972; *Tarumba: The Selected Poems of Jaime Sabines.* Translated by
Philip Levine and Ernesto Trejo, 1987.

Tarumba

Tarumba.
I go with the ants
among the feet of the flies.
I go with the ground, through the wind,
in the shoes of men,
in the cloven hooves, the leaves, the papers;
I go where you go, Tarumba,
where you come from, I'm coming.
I know the spider.
I know what you know of yourself
and what your father knew.

5

10

I know what you've told me of me.
I'm afraid not to know,
to be here like my grandmother
looking at the wall, good and dead.   *15*
I want to go out and piss in the moonlight.
Tarumba, it looks like rain.

TRANSLATED BY W. S. MERWIN

In the House of the Day

People and things enter the house of the day,
stinkweeds,
the horses of insomnia,
catchy tunes,
window dummies that are girls;   *5*
you and I enter, Tarumba.
The dance enters. The sun enters.
An insurance agent enters
and a poet.
A cop.   *10*
We're all going to sell ourselves, Tarumba.

TRANSLATED BY PHILIP LEVINE

■ Ernesto Cardenal (1925–)
Nicaragua (poems)

TRANSLATED BY JONATHAN COHEN

Poet, Catholic priest, former ruling member of the Sandinista government in Nicaragua, Ernesto Cardenal has become the best-known Marxist
social poet in Latin America after Pablo Neruda. His work has been translated into many languages, including English, where New Directions has
published his books of fabled and social expression. Born in Nicaragua, as a
young man he stayed with Thomas Merton in his seminary in Kentucky and
considered becoming a Trappist monk. But he returned to Nicaragua to
struggle against the dictatorship of Anastasio Samoza. Cardenal was, in the
Andy Warhol time sense, famous worldwide for those minutes when international television flashed clips of Pope John Paul rebuking the kneeling
but unrepentant priest for his Liberation Catholicism, a branch of Latin

American Catholicism in which the priests and their churches are socially committed and usually in sympathy with Marxist or revolutionary movements. Cardenal borrows from many traditions—surrealism, socialist realism, and fantasy literature—and continues as a leader of committed poetry in modernist dress.

FURTHER READING: Cardenal, Ernesto. *Apocalypse and Other Poems*, 1977; *Zero Hour and Other Documentary Poems*, 1980; *With Walker in Nicaragua*, 1984; *From Nicaragua with Love: Poems*, 1986; *Golden UFOs: The Indian Poems*, 1992.

19th-Century Traveler on the Río San Juan

The silent bungo was oared up the river
bordered by water lilies and rushes
     (as wide as the Seine in front of the Louvre).
The birds quit singing,
and all was quietness and endless verdure and echoless retreats.   5
At 6 o'clock night came without twilight.
Only the splash of oars in the river was heard . . .
And my thoughts filled with shadows,
     and I fell asleep.

When I awoke the bungo was motionless in the dark.   10
We were tied up to the trunk of a tree.
Thousands of fireflies in the black foliage
and the Southern Cross
     deep in the black sky . . .
And there was a clamor in the air: 15
the cry perhaps of a strange bird,
answering another cry like it farther off.
Sarapiqui!:
The water so clear
it was invisible.   20
Two green riverbanks
     and the riverbanks upside down.
Blue sky above
     and sky below
And the water in between, invisible   25

León

I used to live in a big house by the Church of St. Francis
which had an inscription in the entrance hall saying
    AVE MARIA

and red corridors of brick,
and old red-tiled roof, 5
      and windows with rusty iron grilles,
and a large courtyard just unbearable on stuffy afternoons
with a sad clock bird singing out the hours,
and someone's pale aunt in the courtyard reciting the rosary.
In the evenings I'd hear that angelus bell 10
      ("The Angel of the Lord declared unto Mary . . .")
the hand of a distant little girl playing a note on the piano,
      and the bugle from some barracks.
At night a huge red moon rose above Calvary
They told me stories of souls in purgatory and ghosts. 15
      At midnight
the shade of General Arechabala rode a horse through the streets.
And the noise of a door closing . . . A black coach . . .
An empty cart rattling as it rolled through the Calle Real.
And then all the roosters in the neighborhood crowing, 20
and the song of the clock bird,
and my aunt who'd leave each morning for mass at 4
with the bells ringing in St. Francis,
      ringing
in Calvary 25
      and in St. John's Hospital
and the jars of the milkmen clattering on the stone pavement
and a bread vendor knocking on a front door
and crying
    BREAD 30
      BREAD

▪ Rosario Castellanos (1925–1974) *Mexico* (poems)

TRANSLATED BY WILLIS BARNSTONE

Born in Mexico City, Rosario Castellanos was raised in Comitán, a small town in the province of Chiapas on the Guatemalan border, where much of the population was Indian. It is a region of great natural beauty—mountains, ruins of Maya civilizations, Indians in white pajamas, ox-bulls in rice paddies. Thus Indians are a main subject of her novels. She attended the University of Mexico, where she later taught; she also taught at Indiana University. But Rosario Castellanos supported herself mainly from her novels and other writings, the first Mexican woman to do so. Her best-known novel, *Labors of Darkness* (1962), was awarded the Sor Juana Inés de la Cruz Prize in the year of its publication. She began her literary career as a poet, and her lyrics explore the "geography of women." Her novels partake of both the social and the fantastic, yet in depicting the plight of the Indians she has strictly avoided sentimentalizing or romanticizing her subject; rather, she observes with a sharp and critical eye the tedium, the cruelty, as well as the diverse harshness and drama of Indian life. In the tradition that saw Octavio Paz ambassador to India and Carlos Fuentes ambassador to France, Rosario Castellanos was appointed Mexican ambassador to Israel. In a freak accident recalling the death of the American monk-poet Thomas Merton in Burma, she was killed in Jerusalem from a faulty electrical connection in her hotel room. Rosario Castellanos is one of the few writers in Latin America who is equally known as poet and novelist.

FURTHER READING: Castellanos, Rosario. *Balún-Canán*, 1951; *The Nine Guardians*, 1959; *Ciudad Real* (stories), 1960; *Labors of Darkness*, 1962; *A Rosario Castellanos Reader: An Anthology of Her Poetry, Short Fiction, Essays, and Drama.* Translated by Maureen Ahern, 1988; *The Selected Poems of Rosario Castellanos.* Translated by Magda Bogin, 1988; *Presentation in the Temple. Another Way to Be: Selections.* Translated by Marylyn F. Allgood, 1990.

Three Poems

I

What is weaker than a god? It groans hungry and smells out
its victim's blood,
eating sacrifices, and looks for the entrails
of what it created in order to sink
its hundred rapacious teeth in them.   *5*

(A god. Or certain men who have a destiny.)

Each morning it wakes
and the world is newly freshly devoured.

II

The great fish's eyes never shut.
It doesn't sleep. It always stares (at whom? where?)
in its bright and soundless universe.

Once its heart, beating
near a thorn, says: I want.   *5*

And the great devouring fish,
weighs down and dyes the water with its rage,
and moves with nerves of lightning,
can do nothing, not even shut its eyes.

It stares beyond the glass.   *10*

III

O cloud that wants to be the sky's arrow
or God's halo or lightning's fist!

Each wind alters its form and it vanishes,
and each gust drags it about and tricks it.

Unraveling rag, dirty fleece,   5
with no entrails, no force, nothing, cloud.

▪ René Dépestre (1926–) *Haiti* (poem)

TRANSLATED BY JAMES SCULLY

René Dépestre is a Haitian poet from the town of Jacmel on the southern coast of the island. His first book of poems was titled *Sparks* and was published when he was nineteen. He was co-founder of a Marxist magazine, *The Beehive,* which was closed down by the government, and in 1946 he went to Paris and Africa, in exile. He returned to Haiti in 1958 but soon went to Cuba, where his views were more welcome. He has published many books. His work is vibrantly influenced by French surrealism and political poetry. His strength lies in wild, in-your-face imagery, the depth of his political and racial anger, and his ability to sustain long and powerful poems.

FURTHER READING: Dépestre, René. *Sparks,* 1945; *Vegetations of Clarity,* 1951; *Black Ore,* 1956; *A Rainbow for the Christian West,* 1967.

Black Ore

When the sun, and it was abrupt, had dried up the sweat of the Indian
When gold fever had drained the last drop of Indian blood into the
          marketplace
So that, on the grounds of the gold mines, there wasn't an Indian left
They looked then to the muscular African river
Sure to be relieved of their despair   5
Then began the rush on the inexhaustible
Treasure of black flesh
Began then the mad scramble
Into the gleaming black tropical body
And throughout the earth echoed the clamor of picks   10
In packed black ore
Which would have been all wrong, if chemists hadn't thought up

Ways to make some precious alloy
With black metal, all wrong if ladies hadn't
Dreamed of a battery of cooks   15
In negrony from Senegal, of a tea service
In hulking niggerboy from the West Indies
All wrong if some priest
Hadn't promised his parish
A bell surging with the resonance of black blood   20
Or, again, if an irreproachable Santa Claus hadn't considered
For his annual visit
Little soldiers in black lead
Or if some brave captain
Hadn't sharpened his sword in the petrified ebony   25
And throughout the earth quivered with drills
In the bowels of my race
In the muscular strata of the black man
And so many centuries gone on quarrying
Marvels from this race   30
O metallic seams, veins of my people
Inexhaustible ore of human dew
How many pirates have forced
The dark depths of your flesh
How many marauders hacked a road   35
Through the lush vegetation of lights on your body
Strewing your years with dead stalks
Small pools of tears
A people plundered, a people turned over top to bottom
Like a laboring land   40
A people broken up to enrich
The great fair grounds of the world
Brood, deep in your flesh-and-blood night, on what will erupt
No one will dare cast cannon or pieces of gold
From the black metal of your wrath pouring out   45

■ Carlos Fuentes (1928–) *Mexico* (story)

TRANSLATED BY MARGARET SAYERS PEDEN

Carlos Fuentes was born in Panama City into a wealthy Mexican family.
His father was a diplomat and, consequently, Fuentes spent his childhood
in Mexico, Chile (where he was in school with José Donoso), Buenos Aires,
Washington, and Geneva (where he completed a law degree). He returned
to Mexico in the fifties and headed the cultural division of the Ministry of

Foreign Affairs. He also entered diplomacy and was the Mexican ambassador to France until the massacre of students in Mexico City led him, as it did Octavio Paz when he was ambassador to India, to resign his post. He has also been a professor at Cambridge, Princeton, and Harvard and is a frequent lecturer. As a result of his career as one of the most prolific and major authors of the Latin American "boom" novelists—a term applied to the phenomenon of the great international success and sale of Latin American novelists—he has been a candidate for the Nobel Prize. At the Frankfort International Book Fair and by the measure of world publication, Fuentes and his fellow novelists have been the most valuable commercial property of the past two decades. Among these ambitious and innovative writers, Fuentes has been among the most daring, following many masters—especially American, English, and French ones. His subject has always been Mexico. His characters range from postrevolutionary heroes, such as Artemio Cruz in the novel *The Death of Artemio Cruz* (1962), in which we see, through experimental splitting of voices and time, a figure move from revolutionary to the exploiting cacique (a local political boss), to the jaded international couples who populate *A Change of Skin* (1968). His monumental work is *Terra Nostra* (1975), in which the world, in a Cervantine and almost magically Borgesian way, is his domain. Not always easy to read, he moves on every level of intellect. His recent volume, *The Old Gringo,* based on the life of Ambrose Bierce, concerns a stubbornly individualist old American gringo living in Mexico during its revolution and a Mexican leader who yields to personal temptations at the expense of the revolution. His response to 1992, the five-hundredth anniversary of Columbus's voyage to America, was his illuminating historical-cultural television series on Spain and the New World, *The Buried Mirror,* which has since appeared in book form. His most famous short story, "Chac-Mool," takes its title from the Maya god of rain, who is depicted as a reclining figure in Maya statuary.

FURTHER READING: Fuentes, Carlos. *The Masked Days; Where the Air Is Clear,* 1960; *The Death of Artemio Cruz,* 1964; *A Change of Skin,* 1968; *Terra Nostra,* 1975; *Hydra Head,* 1978; *Burnt Water,* 1980; *Distant Relations,* 1981; *The Old Gringo,* 1985; *Christopher Unborn,* 1988; *Constancia and Other Stories for Virgins,* 1989; *The Buried Mirror,* 1993.

Chac-Mool

It was only recently that Filiberto drowned in Acapulco. It happened during Easter Week. Even though he'd been fired from his government job, Filiberto couldn't resist the bureaucratic temptation to make his annual pilgrimage to the small German hotel, to eat sauerkraut sweetened by the sweat of the tropical cuisine, dance away Holy Saturday on La Quebrada, and feel he was one of the "beautiful people" in the dim anonymity of dusk on Hornos Beach. Of course we all knew he'd been a good swimmer when he was young, but now, at forty, and the shape he was in, to try to swim that distance, at midnight! Frau Müller wouldn't allow a wake in her hotel—steady client or not; just the opposite, she held a dance on her stifling little terrace while Filiberto, very pale in his coffin, awaited the departure of the first morning bus from the terminal, spending the first night of his new life surrounded by crates and parcels. When I arrived, early in the morning, to supervise the loading of the casket, I found Filiberto buried beneath a mound of coconuts; the driver wanted to get him in the luggage compartment as quickly as possible, covered with canvas in order not to upset the passengers and to avoid bad luck on the trip.

When we left Acapulco there was still a good breeze. Near Tierra Colorada it began to get hot and bright. As I was eating my breakfast eggs and sausage, I had opened Filiberto's satchel, collected the day before along with his other personal belongings from the Müllers' hotel. Two hundred pesos. An old newspaper; expired lottery tickets; a one-way ticket to Acapulco—one way?—and a cheap notebook with graph-paper pages and marbleized-paper binding.

On the bus I ventured to read it, in spite of the sharp curves, the stench of vomit, and a certain natural feeling of respect for the private life of a deceased friend. It should be a record—yes, it began that way—of our daily office routine; maybe I'd find out what caused him to neglect his duties, why he'd written memoranda without rhyme or reason or any authorization. The reasons, in short, for his being fired, his seniority ignored and his pension lost.

"Today I went to see about my pension. Lawyer extremely pleasant. I was so happy when I left that I decided to blow five pesos at a café. The same café we used to go to when we were young and where I never go now because it reminds me that I lived better at twenty than I do at forty. We were all equals then, energetically discouraging any unfavorable remarks about our classmates. In fact, we'd open fire on anyone in the house who so much as mentioned inferior background or lack of elegance. I knew that many of us (perhaps those of most humble origin) would go far, and that here in school we were forging lasting friendships; together we would brave the stormy seas of life. But it didn't work out that way. Someone didn't follow the rules. Many of the lowly were left behind, though some climbed higher even than we could have predicted in those high-spirited, affable get-togethers. Some who seemed to have the most promise got stuck somewhere along the way, cut down in some extracurricular activity, isolated by an invisible chasm from those who'd triumphed and those who'd gone nowhere at all. Today, after all this time, I again sat in the chairs—remodeled, as well as the soda fountain, a kind of barricade against invasion—and pretended to read some business papers. I saw many of the old faces, amnesiac, changed in the neon light, prosperous. Like the café, which I barely recognized, along with the city itself, they'd been chipping away at a pace different from my own. No, they didn't recognize me now, or didn't want to. At most, one or two clapped a quick, fat hand on my shoulder. So long, old friend, how's it been going? Between us stretched the eighteen holes of the Country Club. I buried myself in my papers. The years of my dreams, the optimistic predictions, filed before my eyes, along with the obstacles that had kept me from achieving them. I felt frustrated that I couldn't dig my fingers into the past and put together the pieces of some long-forgotten puzzle. But one's toy chest is a part of the past, and when all's said and done, who knows where his lead soldiers went, his helmets and wooden swords. The make-believe we loved so much was only that, make-believe. Still, I'd been diligent, disciplined, devoted to duty. Wasn't that enough? Was it too much? Often, I was assaulted by the recollection of Rilke: the great reward for the adventure of youth in death; we should die young, taking all our secrets with us. Today I wouldn't be looking back at a city of salt. Five pesos? Two pesos tip."

"In addition to his passion for corporation law, Pepe likes to theorize. He saw me coming out of the Cathedral, and we walked together toward the National Palace. He's not a believer, but he's not content to stop at that: within half a block he had to propose a theory. If I weren't a Mexican, I wouldn't worship Christ, and . . . No, look, it's obvious. The Spanish arrive and say, Adore this God who died a bloody death nailed to a cross with a bleeding wound in his side. Sacrificed. Made an offering. What could be more natural than to accept something so close to your own ritual, your own life . . . ? Imagine, on the other hand, if Mexico had been conquered by Buddhists or Moslems. It's not conceivable that our Indians would have worshipped some person who died of indigestion. But a God that's not only sacrificed for you but has his heart torn out, God Almighty, checkmate to Huitzilopochtli! Christianity, with its emotion, its bloody sacrifice and ritual, becomes a natural and novel extension of the native religion. The qualities of charity, love, and turn-the-other-cheek, however, are rejected. And that's what Mexico is all about: you have to kill a man in order to believe in him.

"Pepe knew that ever since I was young I've been mad for certain pieces of Mexican Indian art. I collect small statues, idols, pots. I spend my weekends in Tlaxcala, or in Teotihuacan. That may be why he likes to relate to indigenous themes all the theories he concocts for me. Pepe knows that I've been looking for a reasonable replica of the Chac-Mool for a long time, and today he told me about a little shop in the flea market of La Lagunilla where they're selling one, apparently at a good price. I'll go Sunday.

"A joker put red coloring in the office water cooler, naturally interrupting our duties. I had to report him to the director, who simply thought it was funny. So all day the bastard's been going around making fun of me, with cracks about water. Motherfu . . ."

"Today, Sunday, I had time to go out to La Lagunilla. I found the Chac-Mool in the cheap little shop Pepe had told me about. It's a marvelous piece, life-size, and though the dealer assures me it's an original, I question it. The stone is nothing out of the ordinary, but that doesn't diminish the elegance of the composition, or its massiveness. The rascal has smeared tomato ketchup on the belly to convince the tourists of its bloody authenticity.

"Moving the piece to my house cost more than the purchase price. But it's here now, temporarily in the cellar while I reorganize my collection to make room for it. These figures demand a vertical and burning-hot sun; that was their natural element. The effect is lost in the darkness of the cellar, where it's simply another lifeless mass and its grimace seems to reproach me for denying it light. The dealer had a spotlight focused directly on the sculpture, highlighting all the planes and lending a more amiable expression to my Chac-Mool. I must follow his example."

"I awoke to find the pipes had burst. Somehow, I'd carelessly left the water running in the kitchen; it flooded the floor and poured into the cellar before I'd noticed it. The dampness didn't damage the Chac-Mool, but my suitcases suffered; everything has to happen on a weekday. I was late to work."

"At last they came to fix the plumbing. Suitcases ruined. There's slime on the base of the Chac-Mool."

"I awakened at one; I'd heard a terrible moan. I thought it might be burglars. Purely imaginary."

"The moaning at night continues. I don't know where it's coming from, but it makes me nervous. To top it all off, the pipes burst again, and the rains have seeped through the foundation and flooded the cellar."

"Plumber still hasn't come; I'm desperate. As far as the City Water Department's concerned, the less said the better. This is the first time the runoff from the rains has drained into my cellar instead of the storm sewers. The moaning's stopped. An even trade?"

"They pumped out the cellar. The Chac-Mool is covered with slime. It makes him look grotesque; the whole sculpture seems to be suffering from a kind of green erysipelas, with the exception of the eyes. I'll scrape off the moss Sunday. Pepe suggested I move to an apartment on an upper floor, to prevent any more of these aquatic tragedies. But I can't leave my house; it's obviously more than I need, a little gloomy in its turn-of-the-century style, but it's the only inheritance, the only memory, I have left of my parents. I don't know how I'd feel if I saw a soda fountain with a jukebox in the cellar and an interior decorator's shop on the ground floor."

"Used a trowel to scrape the Chac-Mool. The moss now seemed almost a part of the stone; it took more than an hour and it was six in the evening before I finished. I couldn't see anything in the darkness, but I ran my hand over the outlines of the stone. With every stroke, the stone seemed to become softer. I couldn't believe it; it felt like dough. That dealer in La

Lagunilla has really swindled me. His 'pre-Columbian sculpture' is nothing but plaster, and the dampness is ruining it. I've covered it with some rags and will bring it upstairs tomorrow before it dissolves completely."

"The rags are on the floor. Incredible. Again I felt the Chac-Mool. It's firm, but not stone. I don't want to write this: the texture of the torso feels a little like flesh; I press it like rubber, and feel something coursing through that recumbent figure . . . I went down again later at night. No doubt about it: the Chac-Mool has hair on its arms."

"This kind of thing has never happened to me before. I fouled up my work in the office: I sent out a payment that hadn't been authorized, and the director had to call it to my attention. I think I may even have been rude to my coworkers, I'm going to have to see a doctor, find out whether it's my imagination, whether I'm delirious, or what . . . and get rid of that damned Chac-Mool."

Up to this point I recognized Filiberto's hand, the large, rounded letters I'd seen on so many memoranda and forms. The entry for August 25 seemed to have been written by a different person. At times it was the writing of a child, each letter laboriously separated; other times, nervous, trailing into illegibility. Three days are blank, and then the narrative continues:

"It's all so natural, though normally we believe only in what's real . . . but this is real, more real than anything I've ever known. A water cooler is real, more than real, because we fully realize its existence, or being, when some joker puts something in the water to turn it red . . . An ephemeral smoke ring is real, a grotesque image in a fun-house mirror is real; aren't all deaths, present and forgotten, real . . . ? If a man passes through paradise in a dream, and is handed a flower as proof of having been there, and if when he awakens he finds this flower in his hand . . . then . . . ? Reality: one day it was shattered into a thousand pieces, its head rolled in one direction and its tail in another, and all we have is one of the pieces from the gigantic body. A free and fictitious ocean, real only when it is imprisoned in a seashell. Until three days ago, my reality was of such a degree it would be erased today; it was reflex action, routine, memory, carapace. And then, like the earth that one day trembles to remind us of its power, of the death to come, recriminating against me for having turned my back on life, an orphaned reality we always knew was there presents itself, jolting us in order to become living present. Again I believed it to be imagination: the Chac-Mool, soft and elegant, had changed color overnight; yellow, almost golden, it seemed to suggest it was a god, at ease now, the knees more relaxed than before, the smile more benevolent. And yesterday, finally, I awakened with a start, with the frightening certainty that two creatures are breathing in the night, that in the darkness there beats a pulse in addition to one's own. Yes, I heard footsteps on the stairway. Nightmare.

Go back to sleep. I don't know how long I feigned sleep. When I opened my eyes again, it still was not dawn. The room smelled of horror, of incense and blood. In the darkness, I gazed about the bedroom until my eyes found two points of flickering, cruel yellow light.

"Scarcely breathing, I turned on the light. There was the Chac-Mool, standing erect, smiling, ocher-colored except for the flesh-red belly. I was paralyzed by the two tiny, almost crossed eyes set close to the wedge-shaped nose. The lower teeth closed tightly on the upper lip; only the glimmer from the squarish helmet on the abnormally large head betrayed any sign of life. Chac-Mool moved toward my bed; then it began to rain."

I remember that it was at the end of August that Filiberto had been fired from his job, with a public condemnation by the director, amid rumors of madness and even theft. I didn't believe it. I did see some wild memoranda, one asking the Secretary of the Department whether water had an odor; another, offering his services to the Department of Water Resources to make it rain in the desert. I couldn't explain it. I thought the exceptionally heavy rains of that summer had affected him. Or that living in that ancient mansion with half the rooms locked and thick with dust, without any servants or family life, had finally deranged him. The following entries are for the end of September.

"Chac-Mool can be pleasant enough when he wishes . . . the gurgling of enchanted water . . . He knows wonderful stories about the monsoons, the equatorial rains, the scourge of the deserts; the genealogy of every plant engendered by his mythic paternity: the willow, his wayward daughter; the lotus, his favorite child; the cactus, his mother-in-law. What I can't bear is the odor, the nonhuman odor, emanating from flesh that isn't flesh, from sandals that shriek their antiquity. Laughing stridently, the Chac-Mool recounts how he was discovered by Le Plongeon and brought into physical contact with men of other gods. His spirit had survived quite peacefully in water vessels and storms; his stone was another matter, and to have dragged him from his hiding place was unnatural and cruel. I think the Chac-Mool will never forgive that. He savors the imminence of the aesthetic.

"I've had to provide him with pumice stone to clean the belly the dealer smeared with ketchup when he thought he was Aztec. He didn't seem to like my question about his relation to Tlaloc, and when he becomes angry his teeth, repulsive enough in themselves, glitter and grow pointed. The first days he slept in the cellar; since yesterday, in my bed."

"The dry season has begun. Last night, from the living room where I'm sleeping now, I heard the same hoarse moans I'd heard in the beginning, followed by a terrible racket. I went upstairs and peered into the bedroom: the Chac-Mool was breaking the lamps and furniture; he sprang toward the door with outstretched bleeding hands, and I was barely able to slam the door and run to hide in the bathroom. Later he came downstairs, panting and begging for water. He leaves the faucets running all day; there's not a dry spot in the house. I have to sleep wrapped in blankets, and I've asked him please to let the living room dry out."[1]

"The Chac-Mool flooded the living room today. Exasperated, I told him I was going to return him to La Lagunilla. His laughter—so frighteningly different from the laugh of any man or animal—was as terrible as the blow from that heavily braceleted arm. I have to admit it: I am his prisoner. My original plan was quite different. I was going to play with the Chac-Mool the way you play with a toy; this may have been an extension of the security of childhood. But—who said it?—the fruit of childhood is consumed by the years, and I hadn't seen that. He's taken my clothes, and when the green moss begins to sprout, he covers himself in my bathrobes. The Chac-Mool is accustomed to obedience, always; I, who have never had cause to command, can only submit. Until it rains—what happened to his magic power?—he will be choleric and irritable."

"Today I discovered that the Chac-Mool leaves the house at night. Always, as it grows dark, he sings a shrill and ancient tune, older than song itself. Then everything is quiet. I knocked several times at the door, and when he didn't answer I dared enter. The bedroom, which I hadn't seen since the day the statue tried to attack me, is a ruin; the odor of incense and blood that permeates the entire house is particularly concentrated here. And I discovered bones behind the door, dog and rat and cat bones. This is what the Chac-Mool steals in the night for nourishment. This explains the hideous barking every morning."

"February, dry. Chac-Mool watches every move I make; he made me telephone a restaurant and ask them to deliver chicken and rice every day. But what I took from the office is about to run out. So the inevitable happened: on the first they cut off the water and lights for nonpayment. But Chac has discovered a public fountain two blocks from the house; I make ten or twelve trips a day for water while he watches me from the roof. He says that if I try to run away he will strike me dead in my tracks; he is also the God of Lightning. What he doesn't realize is that I know about his nighttime forays. Since we don't have any electricity, I have to go to bed about eight. I should be used to the Chac-Mool by now, but just a moment ago, when I ran into him on the stairway, I touched his icy arms, the scales of his renewed skin, and I wanted to scream.

"If it doesn't rain soon, the Chac-Mool will return to stone. I've noticed his recent difficulty in moving; sometimes he lies for hours, paralyzed, and almost seems an idol again. But this repose merely gives him new strength to abuse me, to claw at me as if he could extract liquid from my flesh. We

---

1. Filiberto does not say in what language he communicated with the Chac-Mool.

don't have the amiable intervals any more, when he used to tell me old tales; instead, I seem to notice a heightened resentment. There have been other indications that set me thinking: my wine cellar is diminishing; he likes to stroke the silk of my bathrobes; he wants me to bring a servant girl to the house; he has made me teach him how to use soap and lotions. I believe the Chac-Mool is falling into human temptations; now I see in the face that once seemed eternal something that is merely old. This may be my salvation: if the Chac becomes human, it's possible that all the centuries of his life will accumulate in an instant and he will die in a flash of lightning. But this might also cause my death: the Chac won't want me to witness his downfall; he may decide to kill me.

"I plan to take advantage tonight of Chac's nightly excursion to flee. I will go to Acapulco; I'll see if I can't find a job, and await the death of the Chac-Mool. Yes, it will be soon; his hair is gray, his face bloated. I need to get some sun, to swim, to regain my strength. I have four hundred pesos left. I'll go to the Müllers' hotel, it's cheap and comfortable. Let Chac-Mool take over the whole place; we'll see how long he lasts without my pails of water."

Filiberto's diary ends here. I didn't want to think about what he'd written; I slept as far as Cuernavaca. From there to Mexico City I tried to make some sense out of the account, to attribute it to overwork, or some psychological disturbance. By the time we reached the terminal at nine in the evening, I still hadn't accepted the fact of my friend's madness. I hired a truck to carry the coffin to Filiberto's house, where I would arrange for his burial.

Before I could insert the key in the lock, the door opened. A yellow-skinned Indian in a smoking jacket and ascot stood in the doorway. He couldn't have been more repulsive; he smelled of cheap cologne; he'd tried to cover his wrinkles with thick powder, his mouth was clumsily smeared with lipstick, and his hair appeared to be dyed.

"I'm sorry . . . I didn't know that Filiberto had . . ."

"No matter. I know all about it. Tell the men to carry the body down to the cellar."

■ Gabriel García Márquez (1928–)
Colombia (novel, story)

Born in Azacataca on the Caribbean coast of Colombia, Gabriel García Márquez became a journalist and remains a productive one in Latin America and Spain, despite his highly successful novels and short stories and a Nobel Prize in Literature. After living and writing many years in Spain, he now makes his home in Mexico. When in 1967 he published *One Hundred Years of Solitude,* García Márquez had written the "great American novel," that is, of all the Americas. Only John Dos Passos's *U.S.A.* equals its scope and linguistic and thematic achievement. In addition to the instant international sensation of *One Hundred Years of Solitude* that his narration created, like Melville's *Moby Dick,* it is a monumental achievement. Combining Rabelaisian grotesque and hyperbole and a cyclical Borgesian manipulation of time and mythical storytelling, the author uses his extraordinary skills and magical fantasy to paint a fabulous one hundred years of adventures and misadventures in Macondo, his invented tropical town in Colombia. García Márquez had already written superb books prior to *One Hundred Years of Solitude,* his fourth novel, notably, the haunting novella, *No One Writes to the Colonel,* a movingly fantastic story of a colonel decaying with age and revolutionary memories as he waits for a long delayed government pension. *The Autumn of the Patriarch* (1967) is one long sentence, an experimental novel about a Latin American dictator. It is brilliant. *The Autumn of the Patriarch* is a document of the essential problems of power, corruption, and the perennial strongman leader in Latin American politics. There followed wonderful short stories, a riveting confession of crime in the novella *Chronicle of a Death Foretold* (1981, tr. 1983), and the continuation of *One Hundred Years* in *Love in the Time of Cholera* (1988). This generational book reveals all the old graces, archaic habits, personal passions, and societal bigotries. It centers upon two separated lovers who must wait through most of the novel to attain—in their very last years when age has reduced most of their physical forces and their handsome façades—a full and complete passion of love, intensified by the lifelong delay and seeming impossibilities of its realization. It is another tour de force. And as with few authors of his sophistication, García Márquez has retained the writer's cunning to trap the reader and not allow escape until the last page. García Márquez's books, despite his profound view of society and history (including a novel based on the life of Simón Bolívar) do not pretend to the intellectual dimensions of a Borges, Donoso, Cortázar, or Fuentes. His books operate always as story and as a complete and entrancing original world. He is an extraordinarily skilled natural writer, and ambience, intuition, spirit, and life-and-death attitudes overtake the more recognizably conceptual writing of his contemporaries. His magic is in his fabulous imagination. Gabriel García Márquez is a fabulist and there is none like him. His very title, *One Hundred Years of Solitude,* initiates the mystery and metaphysical wonder of life in Macondo.

FURTHER READING: García Márquez, Gabriel. *The Leaf Storm,* 1955; *No One Writes to the Colonel,* 1962, tr. 1968; *An Evil Hour,* 1962; *Big Mama's Funeral* (stories), 1962; *One Hundred Years of Solitude,* 1967. Translated by Gregory Rabassa, 1970; *The Autumn of the Patriarch,* 1975; *Chronicle of a Death Foretold,* 1981, tr. 1983; *Love in the Time of Cholera,* 1985, tr. 1988.

from *One Hundred Years of Solitude*

The Founding of Macondo

Many years later, as he faced the firing squad, Colonel Aureliano Buendía was to remember that distant afternoon when his father took him to discover ice. At that time Macondo was a village of twenty adobe houses, built on the bank of a river of clear water that ran along a bed of polished stones, which were white and enormous, like prehistoric eggs. The world was so recent that many things lacked names, and in order to indicate them it was necessary to point. Every year during the month of March a family of ragged gypsies would set up their tents near the village, and with a great uproar of pipes and kettledrums they would display new inventions. First they brought the magnet. A heavy gypsy with an untamed beard and sparrow hands, who introduced himself as Melquíades, put on a bold public demonstration of what he himself called the eighth wonder of the learned alchemists of Macedonia. He went from house to house dragging two metal ingots and everybody was amazed to see pots, pans, tongs, and braziers tumble down from their places and beams creak from the desperation of nails and screws trying to emerge, and even objects that had been lost for a long time appeared from where they had been searched for most and went dragging along in turbulent confusion behind Melquíades' magical irons. "Things have a life of their own," the gypsy proclaimed with a harsh accent. "It's simply a matter of waking up their souls." José Arcadio Buendía, whose unbridled imagination always went beyond the genius of nature and even beyond miracles and magic, thought that it would be possible to make use of that useless invention to extract gold from the bowels of the earth. Melquíades, who was an honest man, warned him: "It won't work for that." But José Arcadio Buendía at that time did not believe in the honesty of gypsies, so he traded his mule and a pair of goats for the two magnetized ingots. Úrsula Iguarán, his wife, who relied on those animals to increase their poor domestic holdings, was unable to dissuade him. "Very soon we'll have gold enough and more to pave the floors of the house," her husband replied. For several months he worked hard to demonstrate the truth of his idea. He explored every inch of the region, even the riverbed, dragging the two iron ingots along and reciting Melquíades' incantation aloud. The only thing he succeeded in doing was to unearth a suit of fifteenth-century armor which had all of its pieces soldered together with rust and inside of which there was the hollow resonance of an enormous stone-filled gourd. When José Arcadio Buendía and the four men of his expedition managed to take the armor apart, they found inside a calcified skeleton with a copper locket containing a woman's hair around its neck.

In March the gypsies returned. This time they brought a telescope and a magnifying glass the size of a drum, which they exhibited as the latest discovery of the Jews of Amsterdam. They placed a gypsy woman at one end of the village and set up the telescope at the entrance to the tent. For the price of five reales, people could look into the telescope and see the gypsy woman an arm's length away. "Science has eliminated distance," Melquíades proclaimed. "In a short time, man will be able to see what is happening in any place in the world without leaving his own house." A burning noonday sun brought out a startling demonstration with the gigantic magnifying glass: they put a pile of dry hay in the middle of the street and set it on fire by concentrating the sun's rays. José Arcadio Buendía, who had still not been consoled for the failure of his magnets, conceived the idea of using that invention as a weapon of war. Again Melquíades tried to dissuade him, but he finally accepted the two magnetized ingots and three colonial coins in exchange for the magnifying glass. Úrsula wept in consternation. That money was from a chest of gold coins that her father had put together over an entire life of privation and that she had buried underneath her bed in hopes of a proper occasion to make use of it. José Arcadio Buendía made no attempt to console her, completely absorbed in his tactical experiments with the abnegation of a scientist and even at the risk of his own life. In an attempt to show the effects of the glass on enemy troops, he exposed himself to the concentration of the sun's rays and suffered burns which turned into sores that took a long time to heal. Over the protests of his wife, who was alarmed at such a dangerous invention, at one point he was ready to set the house on fire. He would spend hours on end in his room, calculating the strategic possibilities of his novel weapon until he succeeded in putting together a manual of startling instructional clarity and an irresistible power of conviction. He sent it to the government, accompanied by numerous descriptions of his experiments and several pages of explanatory sketches, by a messenger who crossed the mountains, got lost in measureless swamps, forded stormy rivers, and was on the point of perishing under the lash of despair, plague, and wild beasts until he found a route that joined the one used by the mules that carried the mail. In spite of the fact that a trip to the capital was little less than impossible at that time, José Arcadio Buendía promised to undertake it as soon as the government ordered him to so that he could put on some practical demonstrations of his invention for the military authorities and could train them himself in the complicated art of solar war. For several years he waited for an answer. Finally, tired of waiting, he bemoaned to Melquíades the failure of his project and the gypsy then gave him a convincing proof of his honesty: he gave him back the doubloons in exchange for the magnifying glass, and he left him in addition some Portuguese maps and several instruments of navigation. In his own handwriting he set down a concise synthesis of the studies by Monk Hermann, which he left José Arcadio so that he would be able to make use of the astrolabe, the compass, and the sextant. José Arcadio Buendía spent the long months of the rainy season shut up in a small room that he had built in the rear of the house so that no one would disturb his experiments. Having completely abandoned his domestic obligations, he spent entire nights in the courtyard watching the course of the stars and he almost contracted sunstroke from trying to establish an exact method to ascertain noon. When he became an expert in the use and manipulation of his instruments, he conceived a notion of space that allowed him to navigate across unknown seas, to visit uninhabited territories, and to establish relations with splendid beings without having to leave his study. That was the period in which he acquired the habit of talking to himself, of walking through the house without paying attention to anyone, as Úrsula and the children broke their backs in the garden, growing banana and caladium, cassava and yams, ahuyama roots and eggplants. Suddenly, without warning, his feverish activity was interrupted and was replaced by a kind of fascination. He spent several days as if he were bewitched, softly repeating to himself a string of fearful conjectures without giving credit to his own understanding. Finally, one Tuesday in December, at lunchtime, all at once he released the whole weight of his torment. The children would remember for the rest of their lives the august solemnity with which their father, devastated by his prolonged vigil and by the wrath of his imagination, revealed his discovery to them:

"The earth is round, like an orange."

Úrsula lost her patience. "If you have to go crazy, please go crazy all by yourself!" she shouted. "But don't try to put your gypsy ideas into the heads of the children." José Arcadio Buendía, impassive, did not let himself be frightened by the desperation of his wife, who, in a seizure of rage, smashed the astrolabe against the floor. He built another one, he gathered the men of the village in his little room, and he demonstrated to them, with theories that none of them could understand, the possibility of returning to where one had set out by consistently sailing east. The whole village was convinced that José Arcadio Buendía had lost his reason, when Melquíades returned to set things straight. He gave public praise to the intelligence of a man who from pure astronomical speculation had evolved a theory that had already been proved in practice, although unknown in Macondo, until then, and as a proof of his admiration he made him a gift that was to have a profound influence on the future of the village: the laboratory of an alchemist.

By then Melquíades had aged with surprising rapidity. On his first trips he seemed to be the same age as José Arcadio Buendía. But while the latter had preserved his extraordinary strength, which permitted him to pull down a horse by grabbing its ears, the gypsy seemed to have been worn down by some tenacious illness. It was, in reality, the result of multiple and rare diseases contracted on his innumerable trips around the world. According to what he himself said as he spoke to José Arcadio Buendía while helping him set up the laboratory, death followed him everywhere, sniffing at the cuff of his pants, but never deciding to give him the final clutch of its claws. He was a fugitive from all the plagues and catastrophes that had ever lashed mankind. He had survived pellagra in Persia, scurvy in the Malayan archipelago, leprosy in Alexandria, beriberi in Japan, bubonic plague in Madagascar, an earthquake in Sicily, and a disastrous shipwreck in the Strait of Magellan. That prodigious creature, said to possess the keys of

Nostradamus, was a gloomy man, enveloped in a sad aura, with an Asiatic look that seemed to know what there was on the other side of things. He wore a large black hat that looked like a raven with widespread wings, and a velvet vest across which the patina of the centuries had skated. But in spite of his immense wisdom and his mysterious breadth, he had a human burden, an earthly condition that kept him involved in the small problems of daily life. He would complain of the ailments of old age, he suffered from the most insignificant economic difficulties, and he had stopped laughing a long time back because scurvy had made his teeth drop out. On that suffocating noontime when the gypsy revealed his secrets, José Arcadio Buendía had the certainty that it was the beginning of a great friendship. The children were startled by his fantastic stories. Aureliano, who could not have been more than five at the time, would remember him for the rest of his life as he saw him that afternoon, sitting against the metallic and quivering light from the window, lighting up with his deep organ voice the darkest reaches of the imagination, while down over his temples there flowed the grease that was being melted by the heat. José Arcadio, his older brother, would pass on that wonderful image as a hereditary memory to all of his descendants. Úrsula, on the other hand, held a bad memory of that visit, for she had entered the room just as Melquíades had carelessly broken a flask of bichloride of mercury.

"It's the smell of the devil," she said.

"Not at all," Melquíades corrected her. "It has been proven that the devil has sulphuric properties and this is just a little corrosive sublimate."

Always didactic, he went into a learned exposition of the diabolical properties of cinnabar, but Úrsula paid no attention to him, although she took the children off to pray. That biting odor would stay forever in her mind linked to the memory of Melquíades.

The rudimentary laboratory—in addition to a profusion of pots, funnels, retorts, filters, and sieves—was made up of a primitive water pipe, a glass beaker with a long, thin neck, a reproduction of the philosopher's egg, and a still the gypsies themselves had built in accordance with modern descriptions of the three-armed alembic of Mary the Jew. Along with those items, Melquíades left samples of the seven metals that corresponded to the seven planets, the formulas of Moses and Zosimus for doubling the quantity of gold, and a set of notes and sketches concerning the processes of the Great Teaching that would permit those who could interpret them to undertake the manufacture of the philosopher's stone. Seduced by the simplicity of the formulas to double the quantity of gold, José Arcadio Buendía paid court to Úrsula for several weeks so that she would let him dig up her colonial coins and increase them by as many times as it was possible to subdivide mercury. Úrsula gave in, as always, to her husband's unyielding obstinacy. Then José Arcadio Buendía threw three doubloons into a pan and fused them with copper filings, orpiment, brimstone, and lead. He put it all to boil in a pot of castor oil until he got a thick and pestilential syrup which was more like common caramel than valuable gold. In risky and desperate processes of distillation, melted with the seven planetary metals, mixed with hermetic mercury and vitriol of Cyprus, and put back to cook in hog fat for lack of any radish oil, Úrsula's precious inheritance was reduced to a large piece of burnt hog cracklings that was firmly stuck to the bottom of the pot.

When the gypsies came back, Úrsula had turned the whole population of the village against them. But curiosity was greater than fear, for that time the gypsies went about the town making a deafening noise with all manner of musical instruments while a hawker announced the exhibition of the most fabulous discovery of the Naciancenes. So that everyone went to the tent and by paying one cent they saw a youthful Melquíades, recovered, unwrinkled, with a new and flashing set of teeth. Those who remembered his gums that had been destroyed by scurvy, his flaccid cheeks, and his withered lips trembled with fear at the final proof of the gypsy's supernatural power. The fear turned into panic when Melquíades took out his teeth, intact, encased in their gums, and showed them to the audience for an instant—a fleeting instant in which he went back to being the same decrepit man of years past—and put them back again and smiled once more with the full control of his restored youth. Even José Arcadio Buendía considered that Melquíades' knowledge had reached unbearable extremes, but he felt a healthy excitement when the gypsy explained to him alone the workings of his false teeth. It seemed so simple and so prodigious at the same time that overnight he lost all interest in his experiments in alchemy. He underwent a new crisis of bad humor. He did not go back to eating regularly, and he would spend the day walking through the house. "Incredible things are happening in the world," he said to Úrsula. "Right there across the river there are all kinds of magical instruments while we keep on living like donkeys." Those who had known him since the foundation of Macondo were startled at how much he had changed under Melquíades' influence.

At first José Arcadio Buendía had been a kind of youthful patriarch who would give instructions for planting and advice for the raising of children and animals, and who collaborated with everyone, even in the physical work, for the welfare of the community. Since his house from the very first had been the best in the village, the others had been built in its image and likeness. It had a small, well-lighted living room, a dining room in the shape of a terrace with gaily colored flowers, two bedrooms, a courtyard with a gigantic chestnut tree, a well-kept garden, and a corral where goats, pigs, and hens lived in peaceful communion. The only animals that were prohibited, not just in his house but in the entire settlement, were fighting cocks.

Úrsula's capacity for work was the same as that of her husband. Active, small, severe, that woman of unbreakable nerves who at no moment in her life had been heard to sing seemed to be everywhere, from dawn until quite late at night, always pursued by the soft whispering of her stiff, starched petticoats. Thanks to her the floors of tamped earth, the unwhitewashed mud walls, the rustic, wooden furniture they had built themselves were always clean, and the old chests where they kept their clothes exhaled the warm smell of basil.

José Arcadio Buendía, who was the most enterprising man ever to be seen in the village, had set up the placement of the houses in such a way that from all of them one could reach the river and draw water with the same effort, and he had lined up the streets with such good sense that no house got more sun than another during the hot time of day. Within a few years Macondo was a village that was more orderly and hard-working than any known until then by its three hundred inhabitants. It was a truly happy village where no one was over thirty years of age and where no one had died.

Since the time of its founding, José Arcadio Buendía had built traps and cages. In a short time he filled not only his own house but all of those in the village with troupials, canaries, bee eaters, and redbreasts. The concert of so many different birds became so disturbing that Úrsula would plug her ears with beeswax so as not to lose her sense of reality. The first time that Melquíades' tribe arrived, selling glass balls for headaches, everyone was surprised that they had been able to find that village lost in the drowsiness of the swamp, and the gypsies confessed that they had found their way by the song of the birds.

That spirit of social initiative disappeared in a short time, pulled away by the fever of the magnets, the astronomical calculations, the dreams of transmutation, and the urge to discover the wonders of the world. From a clean and active man, José Arcadio Buendía changed into a man lazy in appearance, careless in his dress, with a wild beard that Úrsula managed to trim with great effort and a kitchen knife. There were many who considered him the victim of some strange spell. But even those most convinced of his madness left work and family to follow him when he brought out his tools to clear the land and asked the assembled group to open a way that would put Macondo in contact with the great inventions.

José Arcadio Buendía was completely ignorant of the geography of the region. He knew that to the east there lay an impenetrable mountain chain and that on the other side of the mountains there was the ancient city of Riohacha, where in times past—according to what he had been told by the first Aureliano Buendía, his grandfather—Sir Francis Drake had gone crocodile hunting with cannons and that he repaired them and stuffed them with straw to bring to Queen Elizabeth. In his youth, José Arcadio Buendía and his men, with wives and children, animals and all kinds of domestic implements, had crossed the mountains in search of an outlet to the sea, and after twenty-six months they gave up the expedition and founded Macondo, so they would not have to go back. It was, therefore, a route that did not interest him, for it could lead only to the past. To the south lay the swamps, covered with an eternal vegetable scum, and the whole vast universe of the great swamp, which, according to what the gypsies said, had no limits. The great swamp in the west mingled with a boundless extension of water where there were soft-skinned cetaceans that had the head and torso of a woman, causing the ruination of sailors with the charm of their extraordinary breasts.

The gypsies sailed along that route for six months before they reached the strip of land over which the mules that carried the mail passed. According to José Arcadio Buendía's calculations, the only possibility of contact with civilization lay along the northern route. So he handed out clearing tools and hunting weapons to the same men who had been with him during the founding of Macondo. He threw his directional instruments and his maps into a knapsack, and he undertook the reckless adventure.

During the first days they did not come across any appreciable obstacle. They went down along the stony bank of the river to the place where years before they had found the soldier's armor, and from there they went into the woods along a path between wild orange trees. At the end of the first week they killed and roasted a deer, but they agreed to eat only half of it and salt the rest for the days that lay ahead. With that precaution they tried to postpone the necessity of having to eat macaws, whose blue flesh had a harsh and musky taste. Then, for more than ten days, they did not see the sun again. The ground became soft and damp, like volcanic ash, and the vegetation was thicker and thicker, and the cries of the birds and the uproar of the monkeys became more and more remote, and the world became eternally sad. The men on the expedition felt overwhelmed by their most ancient memories in that paradise of dampness and silence, going back to before original sin, as their boots sank into pools of steaming oil and their machetes destroyed bloody lilies and golden salamanders. For a week, almost without speaking, they went ahead like sleepwalkers through a universe of grief, lighted only by the tenuous reflection of luminous insects, and their lungs were overwhelmed by a suffocating smell of blood. They could not return because the strip that they were opening as they went along would soon close up with a new vegetation that almost seemed to grow before their eyes. "It's all right," José Arcadio Buendía would say. "The main thing is not to lose our bearings." Always following his compass, he kept on guiding his men toward the invisible north so that they would be able to get out of that enchanted region. It was a thick night, starless, but the darkness was becoming impregnated with a fresh and clear air. Exhausted by the long crossing, they hung up their hammocks and slept deeply for the first time in two weeks. When they woke up, with the sun already high in the sky, they were speechless with fascination. Before them, surrounded by ferns and palm trees, white and powdery in the silent morning light, was an enormous Spanish galleon. Tilted slightly to the starboard, it had hanging from its intact masts the dirty rags of its sails in the midst of its rigging, which was adorned with orchids. The hull, covered with an armor of petrified barnacles and soft moss, was firmly fastened into a surface of stones. The whole structure seemed to occupy its own space, one of solitude and oblivion, protected from the vices of time and the habits of the birds. Inside, where the expeditionaries explored with careful intent, there was nothing but a thick forest of flowers.

The discovery of the galleon, an indication of the proximity of the sea, broke José Arcadio Buendía's drive. He considered it a trick of his whimsical fate to have searched for the sea without finding it, at the cost of countless sacrifices and suffering, and to have found it all of a sudden without looking for it, as if it lay across his path like an insurmountable object. Many years later Colonel Aureliano Buendía crossed the region again, when it was already a regular mail route, and the only part of the ship he found was its burned-out frame in the midst of a field of poppies. Only then, convinced that the story had not been some product of his father's imagination, did he wonder how the galleon had been able to get inland to that spot. But José Arcadio Buendía did not concern himself with that when he found the sea after another four days' journey from the galleon. His dreams ended as he faced that ashen, foamy, dirty sea, which had not merited the risks and sacrifices of the adventure.

"God damn it!" he shouted. "Macondo is surrounded by water on all sides."

The idea of a peninsular Macondo prevailed for a long time, inspired by the arbitrary map that José Arcadio Buendía sketched on his return from the expedition. He drew it in rage, evilly, exaggerating the difficulties of communication, as if to punish himself for the absolute lack of sense with which he had chosen the place. "We'll never get anywhere," he lamented to Úrsula. "We're going to rot our lives away here without receiving the benefits of science." That certainty, mulled over for several months in the small room he used as his laboratory, brought him to the conception of the plan to move Macondo to a better place. But that time Úrsula had anticipated his feverish designs. With the secret and implacable labor of a small ant she predisposed the women of the village against the flightiness of their husbands, who were already preparing for the move. José Arcadio Buendía did not know at what moment or because of what adverse forces his plan had become enveloped in a web of pretexts, disappointments, and evasions until it turned into nothing but an illusion. Úrsula watched him with innocent attention and even felt some pity for him on the morning when she found him in the back room muttering about his plans for moving as he placed his laboratory pieces in their original boxes. She let him finish. She let him nail up the boxes and put his initials on them with an inked brush, without reproaching him, but knowing now that he knew (because she had heard him say so in his soft monologues) that the men of the village would not back him up in his undertaking. Only when he began to take down the door of the room did Úrsula dare ask him what he was doing, and he answered with a certain bitterness. "Since no one wants to leave, we'll leave all by ourselves." Úrsula did not become upset.

"We will not leave," she said. "We will stay here, because we have had a son here."

"We have still not had a death," he said. "A person does not belong to a place until there is someone dead under the ground."

Úrsula replied with a soft firmness:

"If I have to die for the rest of you to stay here, I will die."

José Arcadio Buendía had not thought that his wife's will was so firm. He tried to seduce her with the charm of his fantasy, with the promise of a prodigious world where all one had to do was sprinkle some magic liquid on the ground and the plants would bear fruit whenever a man wished, and where all manner of instruments against pain were sold at bargain prices. But Úrsula was insensible to his clairvoyance.

"Instead of going around thinking about your crazy inventions, you should be worrying about your sons," she replied. "Look at the state they're in, running wild just like donkeys."

José Arcadio Buendía took his wife's words literally. He looked out the window and saw the barefoot children in the sunny garden and he had the impression that only at that instant had they begun to exist, conceived by Úrsula's spell. Something occurred inside of him then, something mysterious and definitive that uprooted him from his own time and carried him adrift through an unexplored region of his memory. While Úrsula continued sweeping the house, which was safe now from being abandoned for the rest of her life, he stood there with an absorbed look, contemplating the children until his eyes became moist and he dried them with the back of his hand, exhaling a deep sigh of resignation.

"All right," he said. "Tell them to come help me take the things out of the boxes."

José Arcadio, the older of the children, was fourteen. He had a square head, thick hair, and his father's character. Although he had the same impulse for growth and physical strength, it was early evident that he lacked imagination. He had been conceived and born during the difficult crossing of the mountains, before the founding of Macondo, and his parents gave thanks to heaven when they saw he had no animal features. Aureliano, the first human being to be born in Macondo, would be six years old in March. He was silent and withdrawn. He had wept in his mother's womb and had been born with his eyes open. As they were cutting the umbilical cord, he moved his head from side to side, taking in the things in the room and examining the faces of the people with a fearless curiosity. Then, indifferent to those who came close to look at him, he kept his attention concentrated on the palm roof, which looked as if it were about to collapse under the tremendous pressure of the rain. Úrsula did not remember the intensity of that look again until one day when little Aureliano, at the age of three, went into the kitchen at the moment she was taking a pot of boiling soup from the stove and putting it on the table. The child, perplexed, said from the doorway, "It's going to spill." The pot was firmly placed in the center of the table, but just as soon as the child made his announcement, it began an unmistakable movement toward the edge, as if impelled by some inner dynamism, and it fell and broke on the floor. Úrsula, alarmed, told her husband about the episode, but he interpreted it as natural phenomenon. That was the way he always was, alien to the existence of his sons, partly because he considered childhood as a period of mental insufficiency, and partly because he was always too absorbed in his fantastic speculations.

But since the afternoon when he called the children in to help him unpack the things in the laboratory, he gave them his best hours. In the small separate room, where the walls were gradually being covered by strange maps and fabulous drawings, he taught them to read and write and do sums, and he spoke to them about the wonders of the world, not only where his learning had extended, but forcing the limits of his imagination to extremes. It was in that way that the boys ended up learning that in the southern extremes of Africa there were men so intelligent and peaceful that their only pastime was to sit and think, and that it was possible to cross the Aegean Sea on foot by jumping from island to island all the way to the port of Salonika. Those hallucinating sessions remained printed on the memories of the boys in such a way that many years later, a second before the regular army officer gave the firing squad the command to fire, Colonel Aureliano Buendía saw once more that warm March afternoon on which his father had interrupted the lesson in physics and stood fascinated, with his hand in the air and his eyes motionless, listening to the distant pipes, drums, and jingles of the gypsies, who were coming to the village once more, announcing the latest and most startling discovery of the sages of Memphis.

They were new gypsies, young men and women who knew only their own language, handsome specimens with oily skins and intelligent hands, whose dances and music sowed a panic of uproarious joy through the streets, with parrots painted all colors reciting Italian arias, and a hen who laid a hundred golden eggs to the sound of a tambourine, and a trained monkey who read minds, and the multiple-use machine that could be used at the same time to sew on buttons and reduce fevers, and the apparatus to make a person forget his bad memories, and a poultice to lose time, and a thousand more inventions so ingenious and unusual that José Arcadio Buendía must have wanted to invent a memory machine so that he could remember them all. In an instant they transformed the village. The inhabitants of Macondo found themselves lost in their own streets, confused by the crowded fair.

Holding a child by each hand so as not to lose them in the tumult, bumping into acrobats with gold-capped teeth and jugglers with six arms, suffocated by the mingled breath of manure and sandals that the crowd exhaled, José Arcadio Buendía went about everywhere like a madman, looking for Melquíades so that he could reveal to him the infinite secrets of that fabulous nightmare. He asked several gypsies, who did not understand his language. Finally he reached the place where Melquíades used to set up his tent and he found a taciturn Armenian who in Spanish was hawking a syrup to make oneself invisible. He had drunk down a glass of the amber substance in one gulp as José Arcadio Buendía elbowed his way through the absorbed group that was witnessing the spectacle, and was able to ask his question. The gypsy wrapped him in the frightful climate of his look before he turned into a puddle of pestilential and smoking pitch over which the echo of his reply still floated: "Melquíades is dead." Upset by the news, José Arcadio Buendía stood motionless, trying to rise above his affliction, until the group dispersed, called away by other artifices, and the puddle of the taciturn Armenian evaporated completely. Other gypsies confirmed later on that Melquíades had in fact succumbed to the fever on the beach at Singapore and that his body had been thrown into the deepest part of the Java Sea. The children had no interest in the news. They insisted that their father take them to see the overwhelming novelty of the sages of Memphis that was being advertised at the entrance of a tent that, according to what was said, had belonged to King Solomon. They insisted so much that José Arcadio Buendía paid the thirty reales and led them into the center of the tent, where there was a giant with a hairy torso and a shaved head, with a copper ring in his nose and a heavy iron chain on his ankle, watching over a pirate chest. When it was opened by the giant, the chest gave off a glacial exhalation. Inside there was only an enormous, transparent block with infinite internal needles in which the light of the sunset was broken up into colored stars. Disconcerted, knowing that the children were waiting for an immediate explanation, José Arcadio Buendía ventured a murmur:

"It's the largest diamond in the world."

"No," the gypsy countered. "It's ice."

José Arcadio Buendía, without understanding, stretched out his hand toward the cake, but the giant moved it away. "Five reales more to touch it," he said. José Arcadio Buendía paid them and put his hand on the ice and held it there for several minutes as his heart filled with fear and jubilation at the contact with mystery. Without knowing what to say, he paid ten reales more so that his sons could have that prodigious experience. Little José Arcadio refused to touch it. Aureliano, on the other hand, took a step forward and put his hand on it, withdrawing it immediately. "It's boiling," he exclaimed, startled. But his father paid no attention to him. Intoxicated by the evidence of the miracle, he forgot at that moment about the frustration of his delirious undertakings and Melquíades' body, abandoned to the appetite of the squids. He paid another five reales and with his hand on the cake, as if giving testimony on the holy scriptures, he exclaimed:

"This is the great invention of our time."

TRANSLATED BY GREGORY RABASSA

A Very Old Man with Enormous Wings

A Tale for Children

On the third day of rain they had killed so many crabs inside the house that Pelayo had to cross his drenched courtyard and throw them into the sea, because the newborn child had a temperature all night and they thought it was due to the stench. The world had been sad since Tuesday. Sea and sky were a single ash-gray thing and the sands of the beach, which on March nights glimmered like powdered light, had become a stew of mud and rotten shellfish. The light was so weak at noon that when Pelayo was coming back to the house after throwing away the crabs, it was hard for him to see what it was that was moving and groaning in the rear of the courtyard. He had to go very close to see that it was an old man, a very old man, lying face down in the mud, who, in spite of his tremendous efforts, couldn't get up, impeded by his enormous wings.

Frightened by that nightmare, Pelayo ran to get Elisenda, his wife, who was putting compresses on the sick child, and he took her to the rear of the courtyard. They both looked at the fallen body with mute stupor. He was dressed like a ragpicker. There were only a few faded hairs left on his bald skull and very few teeth in his mouth, and his pitiful condition of a drenched great-grandfather had taken away any sense of grandeur he might have had. His huge buzzard wings, dirty and half-plucked, were forever entangled in the mud. They looked at him so long and so closely that Pelayo and Elisenda very soon overcame their surprise and in the end found him familiar. Then they dared speak to him, and he answered in an incomprehensible dialect with a strong sailor's voice. That was how they skipped over the inconvenience of the wings and quite intelligently concluded that he was a lonely castaway from some foreign ship wrecked by the storm. And yet, they called in a neighbor woman who knew everything about life and death to see him, and all she needed was one look to show them their mistake.

"He's an angel," she told them. "He must have been coming for the child, but the poor fellow is so old that the rain knocked him down."

On the following day everyone knew that a flesh-and-blood angel was held captive in Pelayo's house. Against the judgment of the wise neighbor woman, for whom angels in those times were the fugitive survivors of a celestial conspiracy, they did not have the heart to club him to death. Pelayo watched over him all afternoon from the kitchen, armed with his bailiff's club, and before going to bed he dragged him out of the mud and locked him up with the hens in the wire chicken coop. In the middle of the night, when the rain stopped, Pelayo and Elisenda were still killing crabs. A short time afterward the child woke up without a fever and with a desire to eat. Then they felt magnanimous and decided to put the angel on a raft with fresh water and provisions for three days and leave him to his fate on the high seas. But when they went out into the courtyard with the first light of dawn, they found the whole neighborhood in front of the chicken coop having fun with the angel, without the slightest reverence, tossing him things to eat through the openings in the wire as if he weren't a supernatural creature but a circus animal.

Father Gonzaga arrived before seven o'clock, alarmed at the strange news. By that time onlookers less frivolous than those at dawn had already arrived and they were making all kinds of conjectures concerning the captive's future. The simplest among them thought that he should be named mayor of the world. Others of sterner mind felt that he should be promoted to the rank of five-star general in order to win all wars. Some visionaries hoped that he could be put to stud in order to implant on earth a race of winged wise men who could take charge of the universe. But Father Gonzaga, before becoming a priest, had been a robust woodcutter. Standing by the wire, he reviewed his catechism in an instant and asked them to open the door so that he could take a close look at that pitiful man who looked more like a huge decrepit hen among the fascinated chickens. He was lying in a corner drying his open wings in the sunlight among the fruit peels and breakfast leftovers that the early risers had thrown him. Alien to the impertinences of the world, he only lifted his antiquarian eyes and murmured something in his dialect when Father Gonzaga went into the chicken coop and said good morning to him in Latin. The parish priest had his first suspicion of an impostor when he saw that he did not understand the language of God or know how to greet His ministers. Then he noticed that seen close up he was much too human: he had an unbearable smell of the outdoors, the back side of his wings was strewn with parasites and his main feathers had been mistreated by terrestrial winds, and nothing about him measured up to the proud dignity of angels. Then he came out of the chicken coop and in a brief sermon warned the curious against the risks of being ingenuous. He reminded them that the devil had the bad habit of making use of carnival tricks in order to confuse the unwary. He argued that if wings were not the essential element in determining the difference between a hawk and an airplane, they were even less so in the recognition of angels. Nevertheless, he promised to write a letter to his bishop so that the latter would write to his primate so that the latter would write to the Supreme Pontiff in order to get the final verdict from the highest courts.

His prudence fell on sterile hearts. The news of the captive angel spread with such rapidity that after a few hours the courtyard had the bustle of a marketplace and they had to call in troops with fixed bayonets to disperse the mob that was about to knock the house down. Elisenda, her spine all twisted from sweeping up so much marketplace trash, then got the idea of fencing in the yard and charging five cents admission to see the angel.

The curious came from far away. A traveling carnival arrived with a flying acrobat who buzzed over the crowd several times, but no one paid any attention to him because his wings were not those of an angel but, rather, those of a sidereal bat. The most unfortunate invalids on earth came in search of health: a poor woman who since childhood had been counting her heartbeats and had run out of numbers; a Portuguese man who couldn't sleep because the noise of the stars disturbed him; a sleepwalker who got up at night to undo the things he had done while awake; and many others with less serious ailments. In the midst of that shipwreck disorder that made the earth tremble, Pelayo and Elisenda were happy with fatigue, for in less than a week they had crammed their rooms with money and the line of pilgrims waiting their turn to enter still reached beyond the horizon.

The angel was the only one who took no part in his own act. He spent his time trying to get comfortable in his borrowed nest, befuddled by the hellish heat of the oil lamps and sacramental candles that had been placed along the wire. At first they tried to make him eat some mothballs, which, according to the wisdom of the wise neighbor woman, were the food prescribed for angels. But he turned them down, just as he turned down the papal lunches that the penitents brought him, and they never found out whether it was because he was an angel or because he was an old man that in the end he ate nothing but eggplant mush. His only supernatural virtue seemed to be patience. Especially during the first days, when the hens pecked at him, searching for the stellar parasites that proliferated in his wings, and the cripples pulled out feathers to touch their defective parts with, and even the most merciful threw stones at him, trying to get him to rise so they could see him standing. The only time they succeeded in arousing him was when they burned his side with an iron for branding steers, for he had been motionless for so many hours that they thought he was dead. He awoke with a start, ranting in his hermetic language and with tears in his eyes, and he flapped his wings a couple of times, which brought on a whirlwind of chicken dung and lunar dust and a gale of panic that did not seem to be of this world. Although many thought that his reaction had been one not of rage but of pain, from then on they were careful not to annoy him, because the majority understood that his passivity was not that of a hero taking his ease but that of a cataclysm in repose.

Father Gonzaga held back the crowd's frivolity with formulas of maidservant inspiration while awaiting the arrival of a final judgment on the nature of the captive. But the mail from Rome showed no sense of urgency. They spent their time finding out if the prisoner had a navel, if his dialect had any connection with Aramaic, how many times he could fit on the head of a pin, or whether he wasn't just a Norwegian with wings. Those meager letters might have come and gone until the end of time if a providential event had not put an end to the priest's tribulations.

It so happened that during those days, among so many other carnival attractions, there arrived in town the traveling show of the woman who had been changed into a spider for having disobeyed her parents. The admission to see her was not only less than the admission to see the angel, but people were permitted to ask her all manner of questions about her absurd state and to examine her up and down so that no one would ever doubt the truth of her horror. She was a frightful tarantula the size of a ram and with the head of a sad maiden. What was most heartrending, however, was not her outlandish shape but the sincere affliction with which she recounted the details of her misfortune. While still practically a child she had sneaked out of her parents' house to go to a dance, and while she was coming back through the woods after having danced all night without permission, a fearful thunderclap rent the sky in two and through the crack came the lightning bolt of brimstone that changed her into a spider. He only nourishment came from the meatballs that charitable souls chose to toss into her mouth.

A spectacle like that, full of so much human truth and with such a fearful lesson, was bound to defeat without even trying that of a haughty angel who scarcely deigned to look at mortals. Besides, the few miracles attributed to the angel showed a certain mental disorder, like the blind man who didn't recover his sight but grew three new teeth, or the paralytic who didn't get to walk but almost won the lottery, and the leper whose sores sprouted sunflowers. Those consolation miracles, which were more like mocking fun, had already ruined the angel's reputation when the woman who had been changed into a spider finally crushed him completely. That was how Father Gonzaga was cured forever of his insomnia and Pelayo's courtyard went back to being as empty as during the time it had rained for three days and crabs walked through the bedrooms.

The owners of the house had no reason to lament. With the money they saved they build a two-story mansion with balconies and gardens and high netting so that crabs wouldn't get in during the winter, and with iron bars on the windows so that angels wouldn't get in. Pelayo also set up a rabbit warren close to town and gave up his job as bailiff for good, and Elisenda bought some satin pumps with high heels and many dresses of iridescent silk, the kind worn on Sunday by the most desirable women in those times. The chicken coop was the only thing that didn't receive any attention. If they washed it down with creolin and burned tears of myrrh inside it every so often, it was not in homage to the angel but to drive away the dungheap stench that still hung everywhere like a ghost and was turning the new house into an old one. At first, when the child learned to walk, they were careful that he not get too close to the chicken coop. But then they began to lose their fears and got used to the smell, and before the child got his second teeth he'd gone inside the chicken coop to play, where the wires were falling apart. The angel was no less standoffish with him than with other mortals, but he tolerated the most ingenious infamies with the patience of a dog who had no illusions. They both came down with chicken pox at the same time. The doctor who took care of the child couldn't resist the temptation to listen to the angel's heart, and he found so much whistling in the heart and so many sounds in his kidneys that it seemed impossible for him to be alive. What surprised him most, however, was the logic of his wings. They seemed so natural on that completely human organism that he couldn't understand why other men didn't have them too.

When the child began school it had been some time since the sun and rain had caused the collapse of the chicken coop. The angel went dragging himself about here and there like a stray dying man. They would drive him out of the bedroom with a broom and a moment later find him in the kitchen. He seemed to be in so many places at the same time that they grew to think that he'd been duplicated, that he was reproducing himself all through the house, and the exasperated and unhinged Elisenda shouted that it was awful living in that hell full of angels. He could scarcely eat and his antiquarian eyes had also become so foggy that he went about bumping into posts. All he had left were the bare cannulae of his last feathers. Pelayo threw a blanket over him and extended him the charity of letting him sleep in the shed, and only then did they notice that he had a temperature at night, and was delirious with the tongue twisters of an old Norwegian. That was one of the few times they became alarmed, for they thought he was going to die and not even the wise neighbor woman had been able to tell them what to do with dead angels.

And yet he not only survived his worst winter, but seemed improved with the first sunny days. He remained motionless for several days in the farthest corner of the courtyard, where no one would see him, and at the beginning of December some large, stiff feathers began to grow on his wings, the feathers of a scarecrow, which looked more like another misfortune of decrepitude. But he must have known the reason for those changes, for he was quite careful that no one should notice them, that no one should hear the sea chanteys that he sometimes sang under the stars. One morning Elisenda was cutting some bunches of onions for lunch when a wind that seemed to come from the high seas blew into the kitchen. Then she went to the window and caught the angel in his first attempts at flight. They were so clumsy that his fingernails opened a furrow in the vegetable patch and he was on the point of knocking the shed down with the ungainly flapping that slipped on the light and couldn't get a grip on the air. But he did manage to gain altitude. Elisenda let out a sigh of relief, for herself and for him, when she saw him pass over the last houses, holding himself up in some way with the risky flapping of a senile vulture. She kept watching him even when she was through cutting the onions and she kept on watching until it was no longer possible for her to see him, because then he was no longer an annoyance in her life but an imaginary dot on the horizon of the sea.

TRANSLATED BY GREGORY RABASSA AND J. S. BERNSTEIN

■ Guillermo Cabrera Infante (1929–)
Cuba (novel)

TRANSLATED BY DONALD GARDNER AND SUZANNE JILL LEVINE

Guillermo Cabrera Infante came from the correct proletarian family background to justify a place for the young intellectual novelist in postrevolutionary Cuba. His parents were Communists, and they had worked for the overthrow of the Batista regime. With Castro's triumph, Cabrera Infante was appointed director of the nation's most prestigious literary magazine buoyed by the large circulation of the newspaper *Revolución,* in which it appeared as the weekly literary supplement. But as Cabrera Infante's writing, with its Joycean flow and pure love of the word as word and his retelling of the eve of the Cuban revolution, became less tolerated, the magazine lacked paper and was killed. Cabrera Infante was then appointed cultural attaché in Brussels. Soon the mutual disenchantment between author and regime was reached as the writer's acerbic pen sharpened and he went from nonperson to enemy of the state. The Cuban writer—one of five major boom novelists from Cuba: the others are Alejo Carpentier, José Lezama Lima, Reinaldo Arenas, and Severo Sarduy—likened the writer to a translator. In a larger sense all writing is translation of experience and imagination into text, of tradition into one's originality; in Cabrera Infante's instance, the epithet "translator" is specifically appropriate for his transformation (the essential activity of translating or "carrying over") of Latin, English, American, and Latin American authors into his authors, who are, as Rodriguez Monegal and others have suggested, Petronius, Sterne, Joyce, Mark Twain, Lewis Carroll, and Borges. If two writers were to be chosen from these as the master source of Cabrera Infante's translations, they would have to be Joyce and Borges, along with the slick, slangy, overheard talk of contemporary fiction. When into all this we add Spanish and Cuban tropical rhythmic black speech, we have the inimitable voices of this Fellini of the Cuban *La dolce vita,* transformed into English masterfully by the author and Jill Levine.

Author of many books, short stories, film reviews, political and social essays, Guillermo Cabrera Infante's masterpiece is the tongue-twister titled novel *Tres tristes tigres* (1967; *Three Trapped Tigers,* 1971), which in Spanish means literally "three sad tigers," containing a multitude of puns, associations, and the obvious alliterative, childlike, mocking wordplay of the three *t*'s and *s*'s in *tres tristes tigres.* The book uses every Joycean and Cabrera Infante trick of the trade in the way of monologue, collage, and extraneous documentation. The word *deconstruction* as it applies to architecture and narration is perhaps rarely apt in his case—not as a critic's tool but the author's. Yet, as in all his mixtures of fact, fiction, and metafiction, there is a sensual and exciting engagement between interesting characters and sharp dialogue, and the novel never descends into mere tour de force tedium.

FURTHER READING: Cabrera Infante, Guillermo. *Así en la paz como en la guerra (In Peace as in War)* (short stories), 1961; *Vista del amanecer en el trópico (A View of Dawn in the Tropics),* 1965; *A Twentieth Century Job* (film reviews), 1963; *Tres tristes tigres,* 1967 (*Three Trapped Tigers,* 1971); *Habana para un infante difunto,* 1979; *Infante's Inferno.* Translated by Suzanne Jill Levine with author, 1984.

from *Three Trapped Tigers*

I Heard Her Sing

I dreamed I was an old man who'd gone out on a skiff into the Gulf Stream of the night and had gone 68 days now without catching any fish, not even a damselfish or a sardine. Silvestre had been with me for the first 66 days.

After 67 days without a single fish Bustrófedon and Eribó and Arsenio Cué had told Silvestre that I was now definitely and finally *salao,* which is the worst form of salty. But on day number 69 (which is a lucky number in Havana-by-night: Bustrófedon says that it's because it's a capicúa, that's Cuban for a palindrome number, Arsenio Cué for a thing or two he knows about it and Rine for other reasons: it's the number of his house) on day or rather on night number 69 I was really at sea and all alone, when through the deep blue, violet, ultraviolet waters a phosphorescent fish came swimming. It was very large and bosomy and it looked like Cuba and then it became small and toothy and it was Irenita and then it got dark, blackish, pitch black and lissome and it was Magalena and when it bit my line and I caught it, it began to grow and grow and grow and it fought the line as it grew and it was as big as the boat now and it stayed there floating with strange sounds coming from its liver-lipped mouth, purring, groaning beside the boat, gasping, palpitating, making funny noises, noises more weird than funny like somebody choking as he swallows, and then the big fish was quite still, and then predatory fish began to arrive, sharks and barracudas and piranhas, all of them with faces I could recognize, in fact one of them looked very much like Gianni Boutade and another like the Emcee and it had a star on its mouth and yet another fish was Vítor Perla and I knew it was him because it had a throat like a tie made of blood and a pearl pinned on it, and I pulled the line quickly and fastened it to the side and, funny thing, I started talking to it, to the fish, Big fish, I said, fish that you are, fish, Nobel fish, I have lampooned you, harpooned I mean, it's true I caught you but I'm not going to let them eat you, and I began to haul it into the boat in a slow frenzy and I managed to get its tail into the boat and it was a radiant white now, the fish tail only, the rest of it being jet black, and suddenly I began to struggle with its soft, sticky, gelatin-flanks, gelatin because that side of it wasn't a fish but a jellyfish, an *aguamala,* but all the same I kept on pulling and suddenly I lost my balance and fell back into the boat, still pulling at its jelly side and the whole whale of a fish fell on top of me and the boat was too small for both of us and it, the fish not the boat, gave me no room to breathe and I was suffocating because its gills had landed on my face and over my mouth and nostrils and as this fish was all blubber it was spreading over me, smothering me as it sucked in my air, all the air, not only the air for breathing, the air outside but the already breathed air, the air *inside* as well, the air from my nostrils and from my mouth and from my lungs, and it left me with no air to breathe and I was suffocating badly, choking, asphyxiated. I was about to drown or choke when I woke up.

I stopped fighting the noble fish that was in my dream to begin another struggle, kicking and wrestling with a villainous sperm whale in real life which was lying on top of me and *kissing me* with its immense lunglike lips, kissing me all over my face, kissing my eyes and nose and mouth and who was now chewing my ear and biting my neck and sucking my breast and La Estrella kept sliding off my body and climbing back onto it again making unbelievably weird noises, as if she were singing and snoring at the same time and in between her groans she was speaking to me, whispering, gasping in her rasping baritone *mi amor* please kiss me *ni negro* please kill me *mi chino* come come come, things which would have made me die laughing if I'd been able to breathe and I pushed her with what strength I had left, using a half-crushed leg as a fulcrum and making a springboard not of the bed but of the wall (because I'd been driven back against the wall by that expansion wave of fat, flattened, almost obliterated by that black universe that was expanding in my direction at the speed of love), I managed to give her a final big push and succeeded in putting her off balance and out of bed, *my* bed. She fell on the floor and there she stayed puffing and panting and sobbing but I leaped out of bed and switched on the light and then I *saw* her. She was stark naked and her breasts were as fat as her arms and twice as large as my head, and one of them fell over on one side and touched the floor and the other jutted out over the central breaker of the three great rollers that separated her legs from what would have been her neck if she had had one and the first roller above her thighs was a sort of canopied extension of her mons veneris and I could see how right Alex Bayer was when he said that "she depilated herself completely" because there wasn't a single trace of hair, pubic or otherwise, on her whole body and that couldn't have been natural, but then nothing was natural about La Estrella. It was then that I began to wonder whether she came from outer space.

If the dreams of reason beget monsters, what do the dreams of unreason beget? I dreamed (because I had fallen asleep again: sleep can be as stubborn as insomnia) that UFOs were invading the earth, not as Oscar Hurtado threatened in ships that touched down noiselessly on the rooftops or like Arsenio Cué's creatures quote hurld headlong flaming from th'Ethereal Skie/ with hideous ruin and combustion down unquote or as Silvestre feared infiltrating our lives in the form of microbes reproducing silently, but with definitely Martian shapes, creatures with suckers that could create total suction, as Rine would say, and adhere to walls made of air and then descend or ascend invisible steps and with majestic footfall could spread terror like an overflow of their black, brilliant, silent presences. In another dream or perhaps another form of the same dream these alien beings were sound waves which mingled with us and haunted us and enchanted us, like unseen sirens: from every corner a music gushed out that made men stupid, a paralysing song ray which nobody could resist and nobody could in fact do anything to fight this invasion from outer space because nobody knew that music could be the secret and final weapon, so nobody was going to stop his ears with wax or even with his fingers and at the end of that dream I was the only man on earth who could realize what was actually happening and I tried to lift my hands to my ears and I couldn't because my hands were tied and even my neck and shoulders were tied to the ground by some invisible menders and it happened that I must have fallen off the bed because I woke in a pool of sweat on the floor. I remembered then that

I'd dragged myself right across the floor to the opposite end of the room and had gone to sleep right there near the door. Did I wake up with a motorman's glove in my mouth? I can't tell but I can tell that I had a taste of bile on my lips, and was terribly thirsty, and I didn't even drink so much as a cup of coffee because I felt like vomiting, but I thought twice before getting up. I wasn't at all keen to see La Estrella whether she was freak or foe, sleeping in my bed, snoring with her mouth open and half-closed eyes, rolling from side to side: nobody ever wants to meet the nightmare of the night before when he wakes up. So I began to work out how I could get to the bathroom to wash and return to look for my clothes and put them on and go out into the street without disturbing her. When I'd done all this in my mind I began to write a mental note to La Estrella to ask her more or less when she got up to do me the favor of leaving without letting anyone see her, no that was no good: of leaving everything as she'd found it, no that was no good either: of closing the door behind her: shit, all this was childish and besides it was quite useless because La Estrella might not know how to read, o.k. I'd write it in big bold caps with my grease pencil but who told me she couldn't read? Racial segregation, that's who, I said to myself as I was making up my mind to get up and wake her up and talk to her openly. Of course I had to get dressed first. I staggered to my feet and looked at the Castro convertible and she wasn't there and I didn't have to look for her very far because I could see that empty kitchen right in front of me and the bathroom door was open so I could see the bath was empty as well: she wasn't here, she'd gone. I looked at my watch which I had forgotten to take off last night and it was two o'clock (in the afternoon?) and I thought she must have gotten up early and left without making any noise. Very considerate of her. I went to the bathroom and as I was sitting on the can, reading those instructions that come with every roll of Kodak film which had been left on the floor I don't know by whom, reading this conveniently simple division of life into Sunny, Cloudy, Shade, Beach or Snow (snow in Cuba, they must be joking!) and finally Clear Well-lighted Indoors, reading these instructions without understanding them, I heard the doorbell ringing and if I'd been able to jump up without foul consequences, I'd have done so because I was sure it was La Estrella's triumphal comeback, so I let the bell ring and ring and ring and I managed to silence my gut and my lungs and the rest of my body so I became the Silent ???Doni. But a Cuban friend is more adhesive than a Scotch tape and someone shouted my name through the airshaft between the kitchen and bathroom, not a difficult operation for someone who knows the building, has the physique of a trapeze artiste, the chest of an opera singer, the persistence of memory and a stunt man's daring to risk his neck by sticking his head through the corridor window. It wasn't the voice of a Martian. I opened the door after performing some hygienic rituals and Silvestre burst through the doorway like a white tornado, livid, shouting excitedly that Bustro was sick, seriously ill. Who? I said, picking up the debris of my hair after the wind of his entry had scattered it over a radius of my face, and he said, Bustrófedon, I left him in his house early this morning because he was feeling sick, throwing up and all that and I laughed at him because I thought he was able to take his drink better than that but he told me to leave him alone and take him to his place and not disturb him but this morning when I went to look for him to go to the beach the maid told me there was nobody at home neither the señor nor the señora nor Bustrófedon because they'd taken him to the hospital so Silvestre told me all in one breath without a comma. And the maid called him Bustrófedon, just like that? A question that was my token gift of shit to this morning already brimming with drowsiness, hangover and diarrhea. No, you cunt, she didn't say Bustrófedon but of course it was Bustrófedon, who else. Did they tell you what was wrong with him? I said on my way to the kitchen to drink a glass of milk, that oasis well in the morning-after desert of us nomad drinkers. I didn't know, Silvestre said, I don't believe it's serious but I don't think he's at all well either. I don't like the sound of his symptoms, it could very well be aneurysm. A new *rhythm?* I asked in mock disbelief. No, hell no! Cerebral *aneurysm,* an embolism of the brain arteries, I don't know, and I laughed at his words just before he said I don't know. What the fuck are you laughing at now? Silvestre said. You're on your way to becoming a famous diagnostician, *viejito,* I said. Why, he shouted and I could see he was getting angry, why did you say that? Forget it, I said. So you think I'm a hypochondriac too? he said and I said I didn't, I was merely laughing at his vocabulary but admiringly, dazzled by his instant diagnosis and stunned by his scientific knowledge. He smiled but didn't say anything and I narrowly missed hearing yet again his story of how he'd already started or was about to start studying medicine when he'd gone with a classmate of his to the faculty and straight into the dissection room and had seen the corpses and smelled the smell of formaldehyde and dead flesh and heard the ghastly sound of bones creaking when a professor cut them up with a saw, a *common* saw for chrissake! And so on and so forth. I offered him a grateful glass of milk and he said, No thank you I've already had breakfast and from the word breakfast he went on to what comes before breakfast—which is not the morning after but the night before.

What happened to you last night? he asked and I've never known anyone to ask more questions than Silvestre: Why should be his middle name. I went out, I said. For a walk. Where? Nowhere special I said. Are you sure? What do you mean, am I sure? Of course I'm sure! At least nobody else was in my shoes, or were they? Ah! he said, making a guttural noise to show he understood what I meant, how interesting! I didn't want to ask him any questions and he took advantage of my disadvantage to ask me some more. So you don't know what happened last night? Here, I said, trying not to make it sound like a question. No, not here, he said, in the street. We were the last to leave, I believe. Yes, the last because Sebastián Morán left before you returned with La Estrella as he still had to do his show (I thought I heard a musical note of sarcasm in his voice) and then Gianni and Franemilio left and we stayed and by we I mean Eribó and Cué and Bustrófedon and me, talking, shouting rather above La Estrella's snores and Eribó and

Cué and Piloto & Vera left together and Rine had gone earlier with Jesse and Juan Blanco, I think, I'm not sure, so Bustrófedon and I took Ingrid and Edith with us. I mean, what happened was that after closing up shop in your place Bustro and I picked up Ingrid and Edith as we planned to go to the Chori and on our way to La Playa Bustrófedon was in true form, you should have heard him, but we were already on the heavy side of the river when he began to feel ill and we had to go back and Edith finally told the driver to stop on the corner and she went to bed all by herself, Silvestre said.

In the room I come and go talking to my guardian angelo as I look for my socks which only last night came in pairs and have now all managed to become single specimens. When I got tired of searching for them through the universe of my studio I returned to my own private galaxy and went to the closet and pulled out a new pair and put them on while Silvestre went on talking, telling me his story, and I was working out what do with the rest of that Sunday. The thing is, he said, that I was making out with Ingrid (and now I should explain that Ingrid is Ingrid Bergamo but that's not her name, that's her nickname, we gave it to her because that's how she pronounces the name Ingrid Bergman: she's a *mulata adelantada,* as she herself puts it when she's in a good mood, meaning she can easily pass for white, and she dyes her hair ash blond and puts on lots of makeup and wears the tightest skirts of anyone on this island where the women don't wear dresses in any case but body gloves, and she's a very easy lay, which didn't do anything to diminish Silvestre's pleasure because no woman is easy on the eve of her bedding), so I picked her up and took her to the *posada* on 84th Street, he said, and after we were already inside the patio she started saying no, no and no, and I had to tell the driver to please drive on. But, he said, when we were back in El Vedado and the taxi had gone through the tunnel for the fourth or fifth time, we started kissing and all that and she let me take her to the *posada* on 11th and 24th Street and the same thing happened there except that the driver said he was a cab driver not a pimp and that I should pay him there and then so he could go away and then Ingrid started arguing with him for not taking her home and the guy was so cut up that I paid him quickly and he shot off. Of kosher, he said, Silvestre said, I took Ingrid with me and there in the intimate darkness she staged a big row and we went out onto the street again arguing with each other or rather she was doing all the arguing as I was trying to calm her down, as reasonable and cool as George Sanders in *All About Eve* (Silvestre always talks like that in filmese: once he had a frame with his hands playing the photographer, and he said to me, Whoa! Budge an inch and you go out of frame! and another time I arrived at his house, which was dark, with the doors of the balcony closed because the evening sun hit them hard and I inadvertently opened the balcony and he said, You've just exploded twenty thousand full candles in my face! and the time he and Cué and I were talking about jazz and then Cué said something pedantic about its origins in New Orleans and Silvestre told him, Don't cut in with that flashback now, viejito! and other things I forget or can't remember now), and there we were walking and quarreling and crossing El Vedado from north to south, you know where we finally ended up? he asked but didn't wait for my answer. We arrived at the posada on 31st Street and went in as though there was nothing to it. I believe, he told me, I won the game by default but this was only the first round and inside, once we were in the room there was a wrestling match between a heroine from Griffith and a Von Stroheim villain to get her to sit down, are you listening? just to get her to sit down and not even on the bed but in a chair! After she'd sat down she didn't want to let go of her handbag. Finally, he said, I got her to calm down and sit quietly, almost relaxed and I go and take off my jacket and she's up like a shot and runs to open the door to leave the room and I zoom in on the door and see her hand in big close-up on the bolt and I put my jacket back on and calm her down once more but in calming her down she gets so nervous she makes a mistake and sits on the bed and no sooner is she sitting than she leaps up as though it was a fakir's bed of nails and I, playing the part of a man of the world, very much a la Cary Grant, I manage to persuade her not to be frightened, there's nothing to be afraid of, sitting on the bed is only sitting, and the bed is just like any other bit of furniture, namely a chair, and like a chair the bed could just as well be a seat and she's much quieter now, so she gets up and leaves her handbag on the table and sits back on the bed again. I don't know why, Silvestre told me, but I guessed I could now take my jacket off, so I took it off and sat beside her and began to caress and kiss her and having got this far I push her back, so she would lie down, and she lies down only a second because up she pops like on a spring again and I go on pushing her down and she goes on sitting up and I insist she lie down until something's got to give and this time she lies down and stays down for good, very quiet and very much the ingenue in a romantic-but-risqué scene, so I decide to take a chance and begin telling her how hot it is and that it's a pity she's going to fuck—pardon—to wreck her dress and how it's getting all rumpled and how elegant it indeed is and she says, It's cute, isn't it? And with no heralding effect whatsoever she tells me she's going to take it off so as not to crease it, but that she won't take off anything more, that she will definitely keep her slip on, and then she takes her dress off. She gets back on the bed again and I've already taken my shoes off and I forget the Hays code, I start working on her body in medium shot, and I plead with her, I beg her, and I almost go down on my knees on the bed, asking her to take off her slip and I tell her I want to see her beautiful starlet's body, that she needn't wear more than just panties and bra, that it's only the same as a swimsuit except she's in bed not on the beach and I succeed in convincing her with this argument, viejito, and she takes her slip off though first she tells me that's all, she's not taking off anything more. But nothing. So then we start kissing and caressing and I tell her I'm going to get my pants rumpled unless I take them off so I take them off and I take my shirt off too and now I've got nothing on but my shorts and when I scramble back on the bed again she starts getting angry or pretends she's angry already and she won't let me caress her like before. But a minute later I'm touching her hand with a finger and then the finger climbs on top of her hand and then climbs up her arm not only one finger but two and then my hand climbs up the south face of her tit because it's there, and then I caress her body and we start feeling and fondling each other again and then I ask her, beginning in a whisper, almost in voice off, telling her, pleading with her to take off the rest of her clothes, or just her bra so I can see her marvelous breasts but she won't let me convince her and then just when I'm on the point of losing my cool, she says, O.K. and suddenly she's taken her bra off and what do you guess I'm seeing in the dim red light in the bedroom? That was the subject of another public debate: switching off the overhead light and switching on the bedside lamp. What I'm seeing is the eighth wonder of the world, the eighth and the ninth because there are *two* of them! And I start going crazy over them, and she starts going crazy and the whole atmosphere switches from suspense to euphoria like in a Hitchcock movie. The end of the sequence was, so as not to bore you with any more detail shots, that with the same or similar arguments that had become standard treatment by now I succeeded in persuading her to take off her pants, *but,* BUT, where old Hitch would have cut to insert an intercut of fireworks, I'll give it to you straight—I didn't get any further than that. Not even the Great Cary would have been able to persuade this poor man's Ingrid to do a love scene, torrid or horrid, and I came to the conclusion that rape is one of the labors of Hercules and that really there's no such thing as rape, because it can't be called a crime if the victim is conscious and only one person commits the act. No, that's quite impossible, dear De Sad.

I begin to laugh seismically but Silvestre interrupts me. Wait a moment, hang on a sec, as Ingrid says, that's not the end of the film. We spent the night, Silvestre tells me, or the bit of the night that was left on the best of terms and succored by her expert hands, satisfied more or less and in *Ecstasy,* a state of, I fell asleep and when I wake up it's already light and I look for my loved one and I see my costar has changed with the night, that sleep has transformed her and like poor Franz Kafka I call it a metamorphosis and even though it's not Gregor Samsa whom I find beside me it sure is another woman: night and kisses and sleep have removed not only her lipstick but the whole of her makeup, the lot: the once perfect eyebrows, the large thick lovely black lashes, the phosphorescent and pale complexion that was so kissable the night before are no more, and, wait a moment, don't laugh please: you ain't heard nothing yet, so hold on, I'll be rocking the boat: there, by my side, between her and me like an abyss of falsyhood, there's a yellowish object, round more or less and silky in appearance but not in texture, and as I touch it I almost leap out of bed: it's hairy! I pick it up, he says, in my hands, very cautiously, and hold it up to the morning light to see it better and it is, a last tremolo of strings attached plus a clash of cymbals, yes, a wig: my leading lady becomes the American eagle because she is hairless or, he said, bald, bald, bald, bald! Well, not *completely* bald, which is even worse because she has a few bits of colorless fuzz here and there, quite disgusting I must say. So there I was, Ionesco Malgré Louis, Silvestre said, in bed with the bald soprano. I must have been thinking this so hard I said it out loud, because she began to stir and then woke up. In the immediately preceding shot I'd left the wig where it was, had lain down again and feigned sleep, and as she wakes up now the first thing she does is to put a hand to her head and in a frenzy she frisks around, she leaps around, looking for her hairpiece everywhere and she finds it and puts it on — but *upside down, chico,* upside down! Then she gets up, goes to the bathroom, closes the door and turns on the light and when she opens it again everything's in its place. She looks at me and then she does a double take because she was so worried about losing her hair she forgot I existed and it's only now she remembers she's in a posada and with me. She looks at me twice, Silvestre said, to make sure I'm sleeping, but she looks at me from a distance and there I am fast asleep with my eyes half opened, seeing everything: I'm a film camera. She picks up her handbag and her clothes and goes into the bathroom again. When she comes out she's another woman. Or rather she's the same woman you and I and everybody else know and who gave me such a hard time last night before she consented to let me be present at her unveiling, at her total striptease, *au dépouillement à la Allais.*

All this time I couldn't contain my laughter and Silvestre had to narrate his *Odyssey* above my guffaws and now the two of us laughed together. But then he signaled me to stop and said, But don't you laugh at Barnum, old Bailey, because we're both partners of Browning in Freaks. What do you mean, I say. Yes siree, you've been making love with the Negro nation's answer to Oliver Hardy. What do you mean, I repeat. Yes, yes. Listen, after I'd left the lie-detector chamber I took that delectable little blonde back to where she once belonged in an early taxi and after I'd seen her safely home I went off toward the sunrise and beyond, where my house is, and as I was passing here, it must have been about 5 o'clock A.M., there was La Estrella walking along the sidewalk up 23rd Street, looking real cross, and I don't mean her hair but her looks. So I called her and picked her up and took her home but along the way, my friend and lighting cameraman, she told me that a horrible thing happened to her on her way to stardom and she proceeded to tell me that she'd fallen asleep in your camera obscura and that you came back drunk and had tried to sodomize her, and she ended by swearing to me that she'd never never never put a foot inside your house again, and I'm telling you, she was really mad at you. So you see one freak equals another and a farce mirrors a fiasco or *fracaso,* failure's saddest form. Did she actually say that? I asked. No, not her but probably Carlos or Ernesto. Come on! Is that what she told you, is that what she said? Well, said Silvestre, she said you tried to bugger her, that's what she told me but I'm not keeping to the text. I'm giving you a fair film copy instead.

As I had no more laughter left in my body, I left Silvestre sitting on the bed or the sofa and went to brush my teeth. From the bathroom I asked him which hospital Bustrófedon was in and he told me he was in Antomarchi. I asked him if he was going to see him in the evening and he shook his head and said that at four o'clock he had a date with Ingrid the woman from Bergamo and he thought that today he shouldn't put off till tomorrow what he should have done yesterday. I smiled but without conviction now and Silvestre told me I shouldn't smile like that because it wasn't her body he was after but only that naked soul of hers and that I should also bear in mind her antecedents in film myth: Jean Harlow also wore a wig. Made by Max Factor of Hollywood.

■ V. S. Naipaul (1932–) *Trinidad* (novel)

The novelist, essayist, and memoirist Vidiadhar Surajprasad Naipaul was born in Chaguanas, Trinidad, to which his grandfather had come. He was educated at Queen's Royal College in Trinidad and later at University College, Oxford, where he was an outstanding student, praised by one of his famed examiners, J. R. R. Tolkien. For some years, he worked for the BBC's Caribbean Voices. Naipaul has traveled extensively in the Americas, Europe, Africa, and Asia but has lived in Britain since 1950. Given his dispersed background, of East Indian ancestry, born in the West Indies, and living in London, he has the ambivalent sensibility of the exile, whose insight and sardonic humor inform his work and take him from the Indies to India and down to the back streets of Buenos Aires where he scorns the pretentious Catholic city's big red light district and the corrupt politicians who rob and degrade the culture. He is a magnificent stylist, and few people and places escape his irony and satire. Nothing is sacred—particularly the sacred mysteries of Hinduism—before his pen, although a more compassionate Naipaul at times emerges when he explores his own troubled, complex cultural identity. He attacks the deeds of the colonial British Empire as well as its present or former subjects, beginning with his fellow Trinidadians whom he seems to dismiss as the "Third World's third world," yet Trinidad enriched him with the material for his early novels.

His first three novels, *The Mystic Masseur* (1957), *The Suffrage of Elvira* (1958), and *Miguel Street* (1958) (the following self-contained segments about an antihero trickster are taken from *Miguel Street*), comically and genially describe personal and political life in Trinidad and the Caribbean, showing the cultural provincialism and economic ruin of the area, and the survival of the trickster. His *A House for Mr. Biswas* (1961), also set in the Caribbean, is his longest novel and his early masterpiece, establishing his world reputation. He turns his moralistic eye and ear to Africa in *In a Free State* (1971), a book of short fiction. The superb style and polished narrations of *In a Free State* won him the Booker Prize. He wrote about Africa again in *A Bend in the River* (1979), a political satire about the messes and contradictions of revolutionary politics. Less than a decade later in 1983, he was awarded the prestigious Jerusalem Prize. He was knighted in 1990. In 2001, he received the Nobel Prize for Literature. While Naipaul has been criticized for his acid pen, he has, in fiction, travel book, or essay, followed the ways of virtually all leading authors of Asia, Africa, and Latin America in the severity of his criticism. He does not sentimentalize and aggrandize revolutionary folk heroes; rather, he attacks their fraudulent offspring. V. S. Naipaul, a figure ever displaced, rooted in his rootlessness, has taken the world as his subject and is of the handful of truly major twentieth-century novelists. He provides cunning, often devastating observations of mythical or real nations caught in their chaos and pathos.

FURTHER READING: Naipaul, V. S. *The Mystic Masseur,* 1957; *The Suffrage of Elvira,* 1958; *A House for Mr. Biswas,* 1961; *In a Free State,* 1971; *Guerrillas,* 1975; *India: A Wounded Civilization,* 1977; *A Bend in the River,* 1979; *The Return of Eva Peron,* 1980; *Among the Believers: An Islamic Journey,* 1981; *The Loss of El Dorado: A History,* 1984; *Mr. Stone and the Knight's Companion,* 1985; *The Enigma of Arrival: A Novel,* 1987; *Finding the Center: Two Narratives,* 1984; *A Turn in the South,* 1989; *India: A Million Mutinies Now,* 1990; *A Way in the World: A Novel,* 1994.

from *Miguel Street*

The Thing without a Name

The only thing that Popo, who called himself a carpenter, ever built was the little galvanized-iron workshop under the mango tree at the back of his yard. And even that he didn't quite finish. He couldn't be bothered to nail on the sheets of galvanized-iron for the roof, and kept them weighted down with huge stones. Whenever there was a high wind the roof made a frightening banging noise and seemed ready to fly away.

And yet Popo was never idle. He was always busy hammering and sawing and planing. I liked watching him work. I liked the smell of the woods—cyp and cedar and crapaud. I liked the colour of the shavings, and I liked the way the sawdust powdered Popo's kinky hair.

'What you making, Mr Popo?' I asked.

Popo would always say, 'Ha, boy! That's the question. I making the thing without a name.'

I liked Popo for that. I thought he was a poetic man.

One day I said to Popo, 'Give me something to make.'

'What you want to make?' he said.

It was hard to think of something I really wanted.

'You see,' Popo said. 'You thinking about the thing without a name.'

Eventually I decided on an egg-stand.

'Who you making it for?' Popo asked.

'Ma.'

He laughed. 'Think she going use it?'

My mother was pleased with the egg-stand, and used it for about a week. Then she seemed to forget all about it; and began putting the eggs in bowls or plates, just as she did before.

And Popo laughed when I told him. He said, 'Boy, the only thing to make is the thing without a name.'

After I painted the tailoring sign for Bogart, Popo made me do one for him as well.

He took the little red stump of a pencil he had stuck over his ear and puzzled over the words. At first he wanted to announce himself as an architect; but I managed to dissuade him. He wasn't sure about the spelling. The finished sign said:

BUILDER AND CONTRACTOR
Carpenter
And Cabinet-Maker

And I signed my name, as sign-writer, in the bottom right-hand corner.

Popo liked standing up in front of the sign. But he had a little panic when people who didn't know about him came to inquire.

'The carpenter fellow?' Popo would say. 'He don't live here again.'

I thought Popo was a much nicer man than Bogart. Bogart said little to me; but Popo was always ready to talk. He talked about serious things, like life and death and work, and I felt he really liked talking to me.

Yet Popo was not a popular man in the street. They didn't think he was mad or stupid. Hat used to say, 'Popo too conceited, you hear.'

It was an unreasonable thing to say. Popo had the habit of taking a glass of rum to the pavement every morning. He never sipped the rum. But whenever he saw someone he knew he dipped his middle finger in the rum, licked it, and then waved to the man.

'We could buy rum too,' Hat used to say. 'But we don't show off like Popo.'

I myself never thought about it in that way, and one day I asked Popo about it.

Popo said, 'Boy, in the morning, when the sun shining and it still cool, and you just get up, it make you feel good to know that you could go out and stand up in the sun and have some rum.'

Popo never made any money. His wife used to go out and work, and this was easy, because they had no children. Popo said, 'Women and them like work. Man not make for work.'

Hat said, 'Popo is a man-woman. Not a proper man.'

Popo's wife had a job as a cook in a big house near my school. She used to wait for me in the afternoons and take me into the big kitchen and give me a lot of nice things to eat. The only thing I didn't like was the way she sat and watched me while I ate. It was as though I was eating for her. She asked me to call her Auntie.

She introduced me to the gardener of the big house. He was a good-looking brown man, and he loved his flowers. I liked the gardens he looked after. The flower-beds were always black and wet; and the grass green and damp and always cut. Sometimes he let me water the flower-beds. And he used to gather the cut grass into little bags which he gave me to take home to my mother. Grass was good for the hens.

One day I missed Popo's wife. She wasn't waiting for me.

Next morning I didn't see Popo dipping his finger in the glass of rum on the pavement.

And that evening I didn't see Popo's wife.

I found Popo sad in his workshop. He was sitting on a plank and twisting a bit of shaving around his fingers.

Popo said, 'Your auntie gone, boy.'

'Where, Mr Popo?'

'Ha, boy! That's the question,' and he pulled himself up there.

Popo found himself then a popular man. The news got around very quickly. And when Eddoes said one day, 'I wonder what happen to Popo. Like he got no more rum,' Hat jumped up and almost cuffed him. And then all the men began to gather in Popo's workshop, and they would talk about cricket and football and pictures—everything except women—just to try to cheer Popo up.

Popo's workshop no longer sounded with hammering and sawing. The sawdust no longer smelled fresh, and became black, almost like dirt. Popo began drinking a lot, and I didn't like him when he was drunk. He smelled of rum, and he used to cry and then grow angry and want to beat up everybody. That made him an accepted member of the gang.

Hat said, 'We was wrong about Popo. He is a man, like any of we.'

Popo liked the new companionship. He was at heart a loquacious man, and always wanted to be friendly with the men of the street and he was always surprised that he was not liked. So it looked as though he had got what he wanted. But Popo was not really happy. The friendship had come a little too late, and he found he didn't like it as much as he'd expected. Hat tried to get Popo interested in other women, but Popo wasn't interested.

Popo didn't think I was too young to be told anything.

'Boy, when you grow old as me,' he said once, 'you find that you don't care for the things you thought you woulda like if you coulda afford them.'

That was his way of talking, in riddles.

Then one day Popo left us.

Hat said, 'He don't have to tell me where he gone. He gone looking for he wife.'

Edward said, 'Think she going come back with he?'

Hat said, 'Let we wait and see.'

We didn't have to wait long. It came out in the papers. Hat said it was just what he expected. Popo had beaten up a man in Arima, the man had taken his wife away. It was the gardener who used to give me bags of grass.

Nothing much happened to Popo. He had to pay a fine, but they let him off otherwise. The magistrate said that Popo had better not molest his wife again.

They made a calypso about Popo that was the rage that year. It was the road-march for the Carnival, and the Andrews Sisters sang it for an American recording company:

> A certain carpenter feller went to Arima
> Looking for a mopsy called Emelda.

It was a great thing for the street.

At school, I used to say, 'The carpenter feller was a good, good friend of mine.'

And, at cricket matches, and at the races, Hat used to say, 'Know him? God, I used to drink with that man night and day. Boy, he could carry his liquor.'

Popo wasn't the same man when he came back to us. He growled at me when I tried to talk to him, and he drove out Hat and the others when they brought a bottle of rum to the workshop.

Hat said, 'Woman send that man mad, you hear.'

But the old noises began to be heard once more from Popo's workshop. He was working hard, and I wondered whether he was still making the thing without a name. But I was too afraid to ask.

He ran an electric light to the workshop and began working in the night-time. Vans stopped outside his house and were always depositing and taking away things. Then Popo began painting his house. He used a bright green, and he painted the roof a bright red. Hat said, 'The man really mad.'

And added, 'Like he getting married again.'

Hat wasn't too far wrong. One day, about two weeks later, Popo returned, and he brought a woman with him. It was his wife. My auntie.

'You see the sort of thing woman is,' Hat commented. 'You see the sort of thing they like. Not the man. But the new house paint up, and all the new furniture inside it. I bet you if the man in Arima had a new house and new furnitures, she wouldnta come back with Popo.'

But I didn't mind. I was glad. It was good to see Popo standing outside with his glass of rum in the mornings and dipping his finger into the rum and waving at his friends; and it was good to ask him again, 'What you making, Mr Popo?' and to get the old answer, 'Ha, boy! That's the question. I making the thing without a name.'

Popo returned very quickly to his old way of living, and he was still devoting his time to making the thing without a name. He had stopped working, and his wife got her job with the same people near my school.

People in the street were almost angry with Popo when his wife came back. They felt that all their sympathy had been mocked and wasted. And again Hat was saying, 'That blasted Popo too conceited, you hear.'

But this time Popo didn't mind.

He used to tell me, 'Boy, go home and pray tonight that you get happy like me.'

What happened afterwards happened so suddenly that we didn't even know it had happened. Even Hat didn't know about it until he read it in the papers. Hat always read the papers. He read them from about ten in the morning until about six in the evening.

Hat shouted out, 'But what is this I seeing?' and he showed us the headlines: CALYPSO CARPENTER JAILED

It was a fantastic story. Popo had been stealing things left and right. All the new furnitures, as Hat called them, hadn't been made by Popo. He had stolen things and simply remodelled them. He had stolen too much as a matter of fact, and had had to sell the things he didn't want. That was how he had been caught. And we understood now why the vans were always outside Popo's house. Even the paint and the brushes with which he had redecorated the house had been stolen.

Hat spoke for all of us when he said, 'That man too foolish. Why he had to sell what he thief? Just tell me that. Why?'

We agreed it was a stupid thing to do. But we felt deep inside ourselves that Popo was really a man, perhaps a bigger man than any of us.

And as for my auntie . . .

Hat said, 'How much jail he get? A year? With three months off for good behaviour, that's nine months in all. And I give she three months good behaviour too. And after that, it ain't going to have no more Emelda in Miguel Street, you hear.'

But Emelda never left Miguel Street. She not only kept her job as cook, but she started taking in washing and ironing as well. No one in the street felt sorry that Popo had gone to jail because of the shame; after all that was a thing that could happen to any of us. They felt sorry only that Emelda was going to be left alone for so long.

He came back as a hero. He was one of the boys. He was a better man than either Hat or Bogart.

But for me, he had changed. And the change made me sad.

For Popo began working.

He began making morris chairs and tables and wardrobes for people.

And when I asked him, 'Mr Popo, when you going start making the thing without a name again?' he growled at me.

'You too troublesome,' he said. 'Go away quick, before I lay my hand on you.'

George and the Pink House

I was much more afraid of George than I was of Big Foot, although Big Foot was the biggest and the strongest man in the street. George was short and fat. He had a grey moustache and a big belly. He looked harmless enough but he was always muttering to himself and cursing and I never tried to become friendly with him.

He was like the donkey he had tied in the front of his yard, grey and old and silent except when it brayed loudly. You felt that George was never really in touch with what was going on around him all the time, and I found it strange that no one should have said that George was mad, while everybody said that Man-man, whom I liked, was mad.

George's house also made me feel afraid. It was a brokendown wooden building, painted pink on the outside, and the galvanized-iron roof was brown from rust. One door, the one to the right, was always left open. The inside walls had never been painted, and were grey and black with age. There was a dirty bed in one corner and in another there was a table and a stool. That was all. No curtains, no pictures on the wall. Even Bogart had a picture of Lauren Bacall in his room.

I found it hard to believe that George had a wife and a son and a daughter.

Like Popo, George was happy to let his wife do all the work in the house and the yard. They kept cows, and again I hated George for that. Because the water from his pens made the gutters stink, and when we were playing cricket on the pavement the ball often got wet in the gutter. Boyee and Errol used to wet the ball deliberately in the stinking gutter. They wanted to make it shoot.

George's wife was never a proper person. I always thought of her just as George's wife, and that was all. And I always thought, too, that George's wife was nearly always in the cow-pen.

And while George sat on the front concrete step outside the open door of his house, his wife was busy.

George never became one of the gang in Miguel Street. He didn't seem to mind. He had his wife and his daughter and his son. He beat them all. And when the boy Elias grew too big, George beat his daughter and his wife more than ever. The blows didn't appear to do the mother any good. She just grew thinner and thinner; but the daughter, Dolly, thrived on it. She grew fatter and fatter, and giggled more and more every year. Elias, the son, grew more and more stern, but he never spoke a hard word to his father.

Hat said, 'That boy Elias have too much good mind.'

One day Bogart, of all people, said, 'Ha! I mad to break old George tail up, you hear.'

And the few times when Elias joined the crowd, Hat would say, 'Boy, I too sorry for you. Why you don't fix the old man up good?'

Elias would say, 'It is all God work.'

Elias was only fourteen or so at the time. But that was the sort of boy he was. He was serious and he had big ambitions.

I began to be terrified of George, particularly when he bought two great Alsatian dogs and tied them to pickets at the foot of the concrete steps.

Every morning and afternoon when I passed his house, he would say to the dogs, 'Shook him!'

And the dogs would bound and leap and bark; and I could see their ropes stretched tight and I always felt that the ropes would break at the next leap. Now, when Hat had an Alsatian, he made it like me. And Hat had said to me then, 'Never fraid dog. Go brave. Don't run.'

And so I used to walk slowly past George's house, lengthening out my torture.

I don't know whether George disliked me personally, or whether he simply had no use for people in general. I never discussed it with the other boys in the street, because I was too ashamed to say I was afraid of barking dogs.

Presently, though, I grew used to the dogs. And even George's laughter when I passed the house didn't worry me very much.

One day George was on the pavement as I was passing; I heard him mumbling. I heard him mumble again that afternoon and again the following day. He was saying, 'Horse-face!'

Sometimes he said, 'Like it only have horse-face people living in this place.'

Sometimes he said, 'Short-arse'

And, 'But how it have people so short-arse in the world?'

I pretended not to hear, of course, but after a week or so I was almost in tears whenever George mumbled these things.

One evening, when we had stopped playing cricket on the pavement because Boyee had hit the ball into Miss Hilton's yard, and that was a lost ball (it counted six and out) — that evening, I asked Elias, 'but what your father have with me so? Why he does keep on calling me names?'

Hat laughed, and Elias looked a little solemn.

Hat said, 'What sort of names?'

I said, 'The fat old man does call me horse-face.' I couldn't bring myself to say the other name.

Hat began laughing.

Elias said, 'Boy, my father is a funny man. But you must forgive him. What he say don't matter. He old. He have life hard. He not educated like we here. He have a soul just like any of we, too besides.'

And he was so serious that Hat didn't laugh and whenever I walked past George's house, I kept on saying to myself, 'I must forgive him. He ain't know what he doing.'

And then Elias's mother died, and had the shabbiest and the saddest and the loneliest funeral Miguel Street had ever seen.

That empty front room became sadder and more frightening for me.

The strange thing was that I felt a little sorry for George. The Miguel Street men held a post-mortem outside Hat's house. Hat said, 'He did beat she too bad.'

Bogart nodded and drew a circle on the pavement with his right index finger.

Edward said, 'I think he kill she, you know. Boyee tell me that the evening before she dead he hear George giving the woman licks like fire.'

Hat said, 'What you think they have doctors and magistrates in this place for? For fun?'

'But I telling you,' Edward said. 'It's really true. Boyee wouldn't lie about a thing like that. The woman dead from blows. I telling you. London can take it; but not George wife.'

Not one of the men said a word for George.

Boyee said something I didn't expect him to say. He said, 'The person I really feel sorry for is Dolly. You suppose he going to beat she still?'

Hat said wisely. 'Let we wait and see.'

Elias dropped out of our circle.

George was very sad for the first few days after the funeral. He drank a lot of rum and went about crying in the streets, beating his chest and asking everybody to forgive him, and to take pity on him, a poor widower.

He kept up the drinking into the following weeks, and he was still running up and down the street, making everyone feel foolish when he asked for forgiveness. 'My son Elias,' George used to say, 'my son Elias forgive me, and he is a educated boy.'

When he came to Hat, Hat said, 'What happening to your cows? You milking them? You feeding them? You want to kill your cows now too?'

George sold all his cows to Hat.

'God will say is robbery,' Hat laughed. 'I say is a bargain.'

Edward said, 'It good for George. He beginning to pay for his sins.'

'Well, I look at it this way,' Hat said, 'I give him enough money to remain drunk for two whole months.'

George was away from Miguel Street for a week. During that time we saw more of Dolly. She swept out the front room and begged flowers of the neighbours and put them in the room. She giggled more than ever.

Someone in the street (not me) poisoned the two Alsatians.

We hoped that George had gone away for good.

He did come back, however, still drunk, but no longer crying or helpless, and he had a woman with him. She was a very Indian woman, a little old, but she looked strong enough to handle George.

'She look like a drinker sheself,' Hat said.

This woman took control of George's house, and once more Dolly retreated into the back, where the empty cowpens were.

We heard stories of beatings and everybody said he was sorry for Dolly and the new woman.

My heart went out to the woman and Dolly. I couldn't understand how anybody in the world would want to live with George, and I wasn't surprised when one day, about two weeks later, Popo told me, 'George new wife leave him, you ain't hear?'

Hat said, 'I wonder what he going do when the money I give him finish.'

We soon saw.

The pink house, almost overnight, became a full and noisy place. There were many women about, talking loudly and not paying too much attention to the way they dressed. And whenever I passed the pink house, these women shouted abusive remarks at me; and some of them did things with their mouths, inviting me to 'come to mooma'. And there were not only these new women. Many American soldiers drove up in jeeps, and Miguel Street became full of laughter and shrieks.

Hat said, 'That man George giving the street a bad name, you know.'

It was as though Miguel Street belonged to these new people. Hat and the rest of the boys were no longer assured of privacy when they sat down to talk things over on the pavement.

But Bogart became friendly with the new people and spent two or three evenings a week with them. He pretended he was disgusted at what he saw, but I didn't believe him because he was always going back.

'What happening to Dolly?' Hat asked him one day.

'She dey,' Bogart said, meaning that she was all right.

'Ah know she dey,' Hat said. 'But how she dey?'

'Well, she cleaning and cooking.'

'For everybody?'

'Everybody.'

Elias had a room of his own which he never left whenever he came home. He ate his meals outside. He was trying to study for some important exam. He had lost interest in his family, Bogart said, or rather, implied.

George was still drinking a lot; but he was prospering. He was wearing a suit now, and a tie.

Hat said, 'He must be making a lot of money, if he have to bribe all the policemen and them.'

What I couldn't understand at all, though, was the way these new women behaved to George. They all appeared to like him as well as respect him. And George wasn't attempting to be nice in return either. He remained himself.

One day he said to everyone, 'Dolly ain't have no mooma now. I have to be father and mother to the child. And I say is high time Dolly get married.'

His choice fell on a man called Razor. It was hard to think of a more suitable name for this man. He was small. He was thin. He had a neat, sharp moustache above neat, tiny lips. The creases on his trousers were always sharp and clean and straight. And he was supposed to carry a knife.

Hat didn't like Dolly marrying Razor. 'He too sharp for we,' he said. 'He is the sort of man who wouldn't think anything about forgetting a knife in your back, you know.'

But Dolly still giggled.

Razor and Dolly were married at church, and they came back to a reception in the pink house. The women were all dressed up, and there were lots of American soldiers and sailors drinking and laughing and congratulating George. The women and the Americans made Dolly and Razor kiss and kiss, and they cheered. Dolly giggled.

Hat said, 'She ain't giggling, you know. She crying really.'

Elias wasn't at home that day.

The women and the Americans sang *Sweet Sixteen* and *As Time Goes By*. Then they made Dolly and Razor kiss again. Someone shouted, 'Speech' and everybody laughed and shouted, 'Speech! Speech!'

Razor left Dolly standing by herself giggling.

'Speech! Speech' the wedding guests called.

Dolly only giggled more.

Then George spoke out. 'Dolly, you married, it true. But don't think you too big for me to put you across my lap and cut your tail.' He said it in a jocular manner, and the guests laughed.

Then Dolly stopped giggling and looked stupidly at the people.

For a moment so brief you could scarcely measure it there was absolute silence; then an American sailor waved his hands drunkenly and shouted. 'You could put this girl to better work, George.' And everybody laughed.

Dolly picked up a handful of gravel from the yard and was making as if to throw it at the sailor. But she stopped suddenly, and burst into tears.

There was much laughing and cheering and shouting.

I never knew what happened to Dolly. Edward said one day that she was living in Sangre Grande. Hat said he saw her selling in the George Street Market. But she had left the street, left it for good.

As the months went by, the women began to disappear and the numbers of jeeps that stopped outside George's house grew smaller.

'You gotta be organized,' Hat said.

Bogart nodded.

Hat added, 'And they have lots of nice places all over the place in Port of Spain these days. The trouble with George is that he too stupid for a big man.'

Hat was a prophet. Within six months. George was living alone in his pink house. I used to see him then, sitting on the steps, but he never looked at me any more. He looked old and weary and very sad.

He died soon afterwards. Hat and the boys got some money together and we buried him at Lapeyrouse Cemetery. Elias turned up for the funeral.

■ Luisa Valenzuela (1938–) *Argentina* (story)

TRANSLATED BY MARGARET SAYERS PEDEN

Born in Argentina, Luisa Valenzuela became a writer at an early age. Her mother, Luisa Mercedes Levinson, was a well-known Argentine novelist. As a teenager, Valenzuela worked with Jorge Luis Borges when he was director of the National Library and also for the newspaper *La Nación*. She has traveled widely and lived in Paris, New York, and Mexico City. She published her first novel, *You Have to Laugh* (1969), in her twenties. Her world fame came with the publication in English and other languages of a series of novels and books of short stories, including *Clara: Thirteen Short Stories and a Novel* (1976), *Other Weapons* (1985), *Open Door Stories* (1988), and *The Lizard's Tail*. The political events of her country during the "Dirty War" led her, like Isabel Allende, to work and write abroad, and she has become an extremely well-known contemporary woman writer, translated by Helen Lane and Gregory Rabassa, among others. Her skilled narrative techniques and her use of multiple voices, elusive time, and always a metaphysical thread have contributed to winning her both critical and popular acclaim. She has taught at Columbia University and lives mainly in the United States.

FURTHER READING: Valenzuela, Luisa. *Clara: Thirteen Short Stories and a Novel*. Translated by Hortense Carpentier and J. Jorge Castello, 1976; *Strange Things Happen Here: Twenty-six Short Stories and a Novel*. Translated by Helen Lane, 1979; *The Lizard's Tail*. Translated by Gregory Rabassa, 1983; *Other Weapons*. Translated by Deborah Bonner, 1985; *Open Door*. Translated by Hortense Carpentier et al., 1988.

Up among the Eagles

You're going to find it hard to believe what I tell you because these days who knows anything about life in the country? And up there, life on the mountain, up among the eagles? But you get used to it. Oh, yes. I can say that, I who never knew anything but the city, see how I am now, the color of earth, carrying my pails of water from the public fountain. Water for myself and water for others. I do it to eke out a living; I've done it ever since the day I made the foolish mistake of climbing the path that borders the cliff. I climbed up, and when I looked down and saw the green dot of the valley far below, I decided to stay here forever. It wasn't that I was afraid, I was just being prudent, as they say: threatening cliffs, beyond imagination; impossible even to consider returning. I traded everything I had for food; my shoes, my wrist watch, my key chain with all my keys (I wouldn't be needing them now), a fountain pen that was almost out of ink.

The only thing of any value I have left is my polaroid camera; no one wanted it. Up here they don't believe in preserving images; just the opposite: every day they strive to create new images, they invent new images only for the moment. Often they get together to tell one another about the incorporeal images they've been entertaining. They sit in a circle on the dirt floor in the darkness of their communal building—a kind of hut—and concentrate on making the vision appear. One day, out of nothing, they materialized a tapestry of non-existent colors and ineffable design, but they decided that it was but a pale reflection of the mental image, and they broke the circle in order to return the tapestry to the nothingness from which it had come.

They are strange creatures; normally they speak a language whose meaning they themselves have forgotten. They communicate by interpreting pauses, intonations, facial expressions, and sighs. I tried to learn this language of silences, but it seems that my tongue is not meant for such subtleties. At any rate, they speak our language when they refer to trivial matters, the daily needs that have nothing to do with their images. Even so, some words are missing from their vocabulary. For example, they have no word for yesterday or tomorrow, before and after, or one of these days. Here everything is now, and always. An unsatisfactory imitation of eternity, like the tapestry I've already mentioned. Have mentioned? Oh, yes, I'm the only one that uses that verb tense; I may also be the only one who has any notion of conjugations. A vice left over from the world down there, knowledge I can't trade anyone, because no one wants it.

"Will you trade me a few beans for a notion of time?" I went around asking the women in the marketplace, but they shook their heads emphatically. (A notion of time? They were incredulous; a way of being, of moving on a different plane? That has nothing to do with the knowledge we're after.)

Who dares speak of the passage of time to the inhabitants of this high place where everything endures? Even their bodies endure. Death neither decays nor obliterates them; it merely stops them in their path. Then the others, with exquisite delicacy—a delicacy I've seen only in connection with newly dropped kids or certain mushrooms—carry the body beyond the rushing stream and with precise symmetry arrange it in the exact place it had in life. With infinite patience they have succeeded in creating, on the other side, a second population, one that obliterates time, an unmoving reflection of themselves that is secure because it is mummified, unmodifiable.

The only change they permit themselves is with their images. They grow, yes, they grow, and reach adulthood with a suspicion of implicit old age, and they stay that way until they die. In contrast, I note with horror that I have a sprinkling of gray hairs, and wrinkles are lining my face, premature, of course, but who could keep her youth in this dry air, beneath skies like these? What will become of me when they discover that time passes in my life, and is leaving its mark?

They are absorbed in other concerns, in trying to retain visions seemingly of jewelled palaces and splendors unknown on this earth. They glide through their astounding worlds while it is all I can do—very infrequently and with extreme stealth—to take a photograph of myself. I crawl along at ground level, in spite of the fact that I am in an elevated land floating in clouds. They say that the altitude deranges those of us who come here from sea level. But it is my belief, my fear, that they are the ones who are deranged, that it's something ancestral, inexplicable—especially when I see them sitting on their haunches, as they almost always are, looking inward in contemplation. I'm always looking outward, I search every path, almost nonchalantly nourishing my fear, something silent and my own. They watch me go by carrying water, with the pole across my shoulders and the two pails dangling from the pole, and I would like to think they do not suspect my fear. This is twinned, it has two faces, not at all like the fear that kept me from returning after I had climbed the mountain. No, this is not simple fear; it reflects others, and becomes voracious.

On the one hand, I am here, now. A now that grows and changes and expands with time and, if I am lucky, will continue to evolve. I do not want them to be aware of this evolving, as I have already said, and even less do I want to be like them, exempt from time. For what would become of me if I kept this face forever, as if surprised between two ages? I think about the mummies in the mirror city, oh yes, absolutely, only mummies are unchanged by time. Time does not pass for the dead. I told myself one day, and on a different day (because I, if not they, am very careful to relate question to calendar) I added: nor does it pass for those who have no concept of death. Death is a milestone.

The inhabitants here, with their language of silence, could teach me the secrets of immobility that so closely resemble immortality, but I am not eager to learn. Life is a movement toward death; to be static is already to be dead.

"Stay here, little lady, nice and quiet here with us," is one of the few things they consent to say to me in my own language, and I shake my head energetically (one more way of insuring movement), and as soon as I am out of their vision, I begin to run like a madwoman along the neglected paths. More often than not I run up, not down, but either way, I don't want to get too far from the town, I don't want to stumble into the still city and find myself face to face with the mummies.

The secret city. I don't know its exact location, but I know everything about it—or maybe I only suspect. I know it has to be identical to this humble little clump of huts where we live, a faithful replica with the exact same number of bodies, for when one of them dies the oldest mummy is thrown into the void. It's noisy in the secret city. The noise announces its proximity, but it also serves a basic purpose: scraps of tin, of every size and shape, hang from the rafters of the huts to scare away the buzzards. They are all that moves in the secret city, those scraps of tin to scare away the vultures, the only thing that moves or makes a sound, and on certain limpid nights the wind carries the sound to where we the living dwell, and on those nights they gather in the plaza, and dance.

They dance, but oh so slowly, almost without moving their feet, more as if they were undulating, submerged in the dense water of sound. This happens only rarely, and when it does I feel an almost uncontrollable urge to join in the dance—the need to dance soaks into my bones, sways me—but I resist with all my power to resist. I am afraid that nothing could be more paralyzing than to yield to this music that comes from death. So that I won't be paralyzed, I don't dance. I don't dance and I don't share their visions.

I have not witnessed a birth since I have been here. I know they couple, but they don't reproduce. They do nothing to avoid it, simply the stillness of the air, the immobility, prevents it. As for me, at this point, I don't even go near men. It must be admitted that men don't come near me either, and there must be a reason, considering how often and how closely they approach almost everything else. Something in my expression must drive them away, but I've no way of knowing what it is. There are no mirrors here. No reflections. Water is either glaucous or torrential white. I despair. And every so often in the privacy of my cave, sparingly and with extreme caution, I take a new photograph.

I do this when I can't stand things any longer, when I have an overwhelming need to know about myself, and then no fear, no caution, can hold me back. One problem is that I am running out of film. In addition, I know perfectly well that if they find my photographs, if they place them in chronological order, two things can happen: they will either abominate or adore me. And neither possibility is to be desired, both are too much like being stone. There are no alternatives. If they put the photographs in order and draw the conclusions. If they see that when I arrived, my face was smoother, my hair brighter, my bearing more alert. If they discover the marks of time, they will know that I have not controlled time even for a moment. And so if they find I am growing older, they will not want me to continue to live among them, and they will stone me from the town and I will have to face the terrifying cliffs.

I don't even want to think about the other possibility. That they will adore me because I have so efficiently and so concretely materialized these images of myself. I would then be like stone to them, like a statue forever captive and contained.

Either of these two quite lapidary prospects should be sufficient reason to restrain my suicidal impulse to take yet another photograph, but it isn't. Each time, I succumb, hoping against hope that they will not be alerted by the glare of the flash. Sometimes I choose stormy nights; perhaps I conjure the lightning with the pale simulacrum of its rays. Other times I seek the protection of the radiance of dawn, which at this altitude can be incendiary.

Elaborate preparations for each of my secret snapshots, preparations charged with hope and danger. That is, with life. The resulting picture does not always please me but the emotion of seeing myself—no matter how horrible or haggard I appear—is immeasurable. This is I, changing, in a static world that imitates death. And I feel safe. Then I am able to stop and speak of simple things with the women in the market and even understand their silences, and answer them. I can live a little longer without love, without anyone's touch.

Until another relapse, a new photo. And this will be the last. On a day with the sound of death, when the minimal activity of the town has come to a halt and they have all congregated to dance in the market plaza. That deliberate dancing that is like praying with their feet, a quiet prayer. They will never admit it, but I suspect that they count to themselves, that their dance is an intricate web of steps like stitches, one up, two stitches backward, one to the right. All to the tinkling of the faroff tin scraps: the wind in the house of the dead. A day like any other; a very special day for them because of the sound that they would call music; if they were interested in making such distinctions. But all that interests them is the dance, or believing they are dancing, or thinking of the dance, which is the same thing. To the pulse of the sound that floods over us, whose origins I cannot locate, though I know it comes from the city of the dead. A sound that threatens to engulf me.

They do not call to me, they don't even see me. It's as if I didn't exist. Maybe they're right, maybe I don't exist. Maybe I am my own invention, or a peculiar materialization of an image they have evoked. That sound is joyful, and yet the most mournful ever heard. I seem to be alive, and yet . . .

I hid in my cave trying not to think about these things, trying not to hear the tinkling; I don't know from where it comes, but I fear toward what it may lead me. With the hope of setting these fears to rest, I begin my preparations for the last photo. A desperate attempt to recover my being, to return to myself, which is all I have.

Anxiously, I await the perfect instant, while outside, darkness is weaving its blackest threads. Suddenly, an unexpected radiance causes me to trip the shutter before I am ready. No photograph emerges, only a dark rectangle which gradually reveals a blurred image of a wall of stone. And that's all. I have no more film so I may as well throw away the camera. A cause for weeping were it not for the fact the radiance is not fading. A cause for uneasiness, then, because when I peer out I see that the blazing light is originating from the very place I wanted not to know about, from the very heart of the sound, from a peak just below our feet, and that now the radiance comes from millions of glittering scraps of tin in the moonlight. The city of the dead.

Spontaneously, I set forth with all my stupid photos, responding to an unfathomable impulse that may be a response to a summons from the sonorous radiance. They are calling me from down there, over to the left, and I answer, and at first I run along the treacherous path and when the path ends I continue on. I stumble, I climb and descend, I trip and hurt myself; to avoid hurtling into the ravine I try to imitate the goats, leaping across the rocks; I lose my footing, I slip and slide, I try to check my fall, thorns rake my skin but at the same time save me. Rashly, I rush ahead, because I must, I will reach the city of the mummies, I will give my faces to them, I will place my successive faces on the mummies and then at last I will be free to take the path to the valley without fearing stone, because I will take the last photograph with me and I am myself in that photograph and I am stone.

■ José Emilio Pacheco (1939–) *Mexico* (poems)

Mexican poet, novelist, and short story writer, José Emilio Pacheco has earned his living as journalist and professor. His early novel, *The Principle of Pleasure,* contains the craft, painful and ecstatic emotion, and sun-cut imagery that will show in his poems. A poet of poets and place, he experiences the work of the poets he loves as a personal document of experience, and so we hear poets from Cavafy to Vallejo and accompany the poet's eyes as he moves from the Mexican tropics to New Orleans, Paris, Rio, and the Canadian northwest.

FURTHER READING: Pacheco, José Emilio. *Principio del placer* (novel) (*The Principle of Pleasure*), 1972; *No me preguntes como pasa el tiempo* (*Don't Ask Me How the Time Goes By*), 1977. Translated by Alastair Reid, 1978; *Selected Poems*, 1987.

from Some Time to This Place

I

It's the sun with its single eye, the fire-spitting mouth that never tires of charring eternity. Like a broken king who looks from his throne at the rout of his vassals.

Sometimes, the poor sun, the herald of the day who insults and slanders you, settled on your body, adorning with light all you loved.

Today it limits itself to coming in through the window and letting you know that it's already seven o'clock and you still have your sentence to serve: the papers floating in the office, the smiles that others spit on you, hope, memory . . . and the word: your enemy, your death, your origin.

II

The day of your ninth birthday you built a sand castle at the beach. Its moats connected with the sea, its patios lodged the shimmer of the sun, its turrets were incrustations of coral and reflected light.

An army of strangers gathered around to admire your work. You saw their potbellies chewed by curls, the legs of the women gnawed by bloody nights and by desires.

Stuffed with hearing about your perfect castle, you returned home, ripe with conceit. Twelve years have passed since then, and often you return to the beach and try to find the ruins of the castle.

The ebb and flow are blamed for wearing it away. But the tides aren't guilty: you know that someone stamped it down to nothing—and one day the sea will build it again.

III

On the last day of the world—when there is no longer hell, time, or to-morrow—you will say her name uncontaminated by ashes, pardons, and fear. Her name, high and pure, like that split second that brought her to your side.

IV

The sea sounds. The old lamp of dawn fires the breast of the dark islands. The great ship founders and drowns in solitude. On the break-water, wounded by the hours and standing like an open minute, the night takes its time.

The creatures of the shore weaved labyrinths in the eye of the ship-wrecked one, on his way to becoming a surge of waves, a flock faithful to time. Algae, green shore, ruined girl who dances and gleams when the sun visits her.

V

From some time to this place, things have for you the sour taste of the dying or beginning. Hard triumph of your own defeat, you lived each day in an armor of illusion. The sick year left as hostages days that enclose and humiliate you, hours that won't come back but still live their confusion in your memory.

You began to die and to realize that the mystery will never be easier. Awakening is a forest of findings, a miracle that finds the lost and destroys the found. And that future day, a misery that finds you alone: inventing and burnishing your words.

Come, chase after and enter your own past. Look at yourself, strange and alone, from some time to this place.

TRANSLATED BY PHILIP LEVINE

Whistler's London

Unreal in the water
the *unreal city* is duplicated[1]

---

1. An allusion to section III. The fire sermon in T. S. Eliot's *The Waste Land*.

Stacked shadows overflow the wharves
> The river
bears them along on a quivering shaft of air   *5*

Like a ghost on the other bank
> you observe
blurred lights in the gray mass
of buildings and warehouses

> The night too   *10*
is gray
The darkness thinned out
The moon burns deep down in the water.

TRANSLATED BY GEORGE MCWHIRTER

■ Gustavo Sainz (1940–) *Mexico* (novel)

TRANSLATED BY ANDREW HURLEY

After studying law and humanities at the National University and film at the University Center of Cultural Studies, where film became one of his literary instruments, Gustavo Sainz published his first novel, *Gazapo* (1965). He found himself, at the age of twenty-five, the leader of the younger experimental novelists and a new star in Latin American fiction. In *Gazapo,* he is a parodic painter of ordinary people in all stratas of Mexico City society. The film, James Joyce, and European vanguardist fiction all leave their traces in his work, which plays with narrative voices and includes, as its material, tape-recorded events, diaries, and overheard phone conversations. He focuses on con games, small conspiracies, sex, and multiple seduction, which he records with fascinating bravura. The novel not only was an instant local success but was quickly translated into English, Italian, German, French, and Portuguese.

FURTHER READING: Sainz, Gustavo. *Gazapo,* 1965; *The Princess in the Glass Cage.* Translated by Helen Lane, 1987.

from The Princess of the Iron Palace

He Had a Chivas Regal Face

Gabriel Infante had been such a drunk, he'd been so drunk for so long that he even had a face like a bottle. And he started getting attached to me, you know, like hanging on me, he conceived this deep attachment for me, there was this whole dependence thing. Maybe because I'd listen to him . . .

Like this one time he was going to commit suicide. He called me on the telephone, and he told me to get a pencil and paper, he had something for me to write down. He was crying like crazy, right?, and it was raining cats and dogs outside. You know who was there visiting me for the first time? That was the first day Alexis Stamatis ever came to visit me. He came to visit me for the first time that night, and there was this rainstorm you wouldn't believe—torrents!—and what happened was, that the Jalisco Monk had called me to tell me all about how the maître d' with those gorilla hands didn't work in the restaurant anymore, that he'd gone over there to tell him where to stick it, and he wasn't there, he'd run off or escaped or something with one of the whores, did you ever hear such a story?, but I didn't want to hear about it, although at the same time I was sort of interested, you know? But anyway, we got cut off. It was a terrible storm, like one of those ones in the Bible or something, so we got cut off, and then in about two seconds the telephone rings again, and I say to the other people, Oh, come with me, because on top of everything else, the lights had gone out. So I say to Alexis, to the maids, to everybody, Oh, come with me to answer the telephone. And Gabriel starts talking, I mean, it was Gabriel.

With him, well, there were a lot of things that kept us together. Not love, of course, not really love, but sort of the fact that he talked to me. Was it you that said that love is the wordiest of all passions? Because if that's true, then it was love. I let him talk to me when he was high as a kite on drugs, right? He talked and talked and talked. I even had problems because of that. I got into big trouble, because see he lived with these two women, these two women shared him, you might say. He was real in love with one of them, and he got a lot of money out of the other one. Anyway, the one he was so in love with—how can I put this delicately? She was a whore. I mean she was the biggest whore you could ever imagine in all your wildest dreams of whoredom. And he was madly in love with her, right?, but she told him, one day she said this wouldn't work, she couldn't live just for him, she liked to go out with other men. Other men . . . He suffered something awful. Just like the hairy maître d' I was telling you about, right?, that later on I found out his name was Tarcisio and he had run off with Carmelita Longlegs. He'd kidnapped her. And they lived together in hiding, from the gang, I mean, and since he couldn't go back to the restaurant he became a taxi driver. Anyway, that's what I heard, because they were hunting for him like he was Pancho Villa or somebody. Seems he had stolen a lot of money or some papers or something that was worth a lot of money to somebody. And whoever it was that told me also said that this guy wanted to marry Carmelita, but she said 'Fraid not, I'm a whore through and through, from my hormones to the tip of my lower lips, man, woman, or tableleg, it's all the same to me, I'll run around on you, and you won't be able to take it. She had a tarantula tatooed on the inside of one of her thighs as big as your hand. And Handsome to the Maximum told me once that whenever he went out with her, he put on spiked underwear, on top of a chastity belt, because she'd eat you alive, a devow, devowsomethingess, with teeth in her vagina and prehensile lips . . . Uh . . .

So anyway, Gabriel was telling me that this woman that gave him all this money, that they had had this big terrible scene, and he'd hit her and practically blinded her in one eye. So she'd gone to her mother and told her. This woman had run home and told her mother, and her mother it turns out is the lover of some big bigshot. Anyway, on and on like that. But I couldn't believe it was Gabriel on the phone, because the last time he had called me, I made him promise, he promised he'd never ever call me on the telephone again, because I was like tortured by all these telephone calls, you know? So I had decided to cut him off, right? I mean all the things he'd tell me about were making me sick, literally . . . Anyway, so this day with all the rain and the storm to beat all storms, terrible, terrible rain and then on top of everything the blackout, who should call but him, and he just starts talking. But meanwhile, my mother is on the phone upstairs, right?, waiting for me to pick up the telephone downstairs for her to hang up. So I answer the phone and it's him, so I go Gabriel, you said you weren't going to call me anymore. So he goes Yes, but listen, I've got to talk to you, I just had this big fight with what's-her-name, do you know what what's-her-name did. And then he told me all the gory details. And of course, my mother is listening to all this stuff on the extension absolutely appalled, and just about then my father comes home, and he yells Come up here right this minute. So I went upstairs, right? My father had barely taken off his raincoat, and he says to me, You tell me right now who this Gabriel is. What Gabriel?, I say. The person that just called you, he says, because I'm going to kill him. What do you mean you're going to kill him? I mean just what I said—I'm going to go find him and I'm going to kill him. Now, I'm going to kill him right now, this instant, because you know as well as I do that stained honor can only be washed in blood. It was just that simple, right? . . . He was good as gold, really he was, but he always swore he had Sicilian blood. So that's why stained honor had to be washed in blood, because that's the way his ancestors washed it, right?

What Gabriel was telling me was how this girl had run to her mother and told her he was a drug addict, he was always on something, plus all this other stuff, right? Like that she kept him, she worked in a house of ill repute so she could keep him, so she could give him the money he needed. And she's standing there telling her mother all this with her face all banged up to boot, from the beating he had given her. Terrible, right? So imagine what this girl's family thought about all this—I mean it was a big-deal family. Not to mention what my family thought. When they heard all this stuff you can picture the fit they threw. So anyway, he had called me to tell me all this stuff, right?, but also to leave a message in case something happened to his other woman. But mostly he called me to tell me all this stuff because his brain was . . . He took cocaine and marijuana. He was this very, very intelligent boy, too. Not to mention very handsome—he had this great body,

I mean has, and one time he won the national auto racing championship. He won I don't know how much money. But he was one of those Viva México! types, you know, he drove down the road with his nose sucking up the white line. If he'd been Japanese, he'd have been a kamikaze pilot, right? Couldn't care less. I mean he'd say he'd rather live for five days on drugs than twenty years as a jerk. He was just a drug addict at heart, that's all there was to it. So anyway, my father, as soon as he found out about Gabriel, my father swore he was going to kill him. Wildwigged urologists!

You know the type—as far as my father was concerned there were two kinds of women, two count 'em two, kinds or classes or types or categories—good girls and prostitutes. A good girl, like me for example, could never have friends her family didn't know, she had to go out solely and exclusively with one guy, from whom she had to remain aloof and, as the maids and one or another of my squarer friends would say, not get hot. They had to get to know my boyfriends in all these family gettogethers and stuff, and I was never supposed to go to the movies or bars or parties by myself. That's what my brother was for. To chaperone me? Even when I went on a date with a guy, my brother went with me, can you imagine? My father liked to listen to music like Agustín Lara, you know, Mexico's own Lawrence Welk, and before that he used to like to go out dancing with my mother to Ciro's. He also liked the idea of quote, purely masculine pursuits, unquote; so there'd be these nights, it didn't have to be Friday but it helped, when he'd take a night out with the boys, just whoosh! and he'd be gone, to some boxing match or a real Friday bash with some of his noisy friends—The Bad Boys . . . And then he has the gall to tell me he's going to go out and kill Gabriel. He swore up and down that he was going to kill him. So of course, I got real depressed, and really disappointed in my mother and father, right?, because on top of everything I never told who it was. They'd seen him a couple of times, we'd even gone out together, but they were so forgetful about names, they could never seem to get faces and names together or anything, so these guys would always be my anonymous "friends," and that was that. So anyway, Alexis left and I never told. They knew his name was Gabriel Infante, but they had no idea where to find him, right? But by this time I felt so awful, so awful, I mean so depressed and awful, that I ran to my room and slammed the door and started to cry. I cried so hard, I cried so hard my tears were actually splashing, like this, I was crying with my breasts and my throat, torrents were running out my nose—tears even came out my navel. I kid you not. And nobody came in to check on me, so I just cried all night.

So then the next day, in the afternoon, I still didn't come out of my room or eat, all I did was cry, right? The floodgates of tears had opened, and I hadn't been able to go to sleep all night. So when I saw that everybody in my family had left the house, I decided to take a sleeping pill. . . . What I'm going to tell you I swear to God happened just like I'm going to tell you, okay? I'm not trying to hide anything or change anything around, I swear. This is how it was. . . . I took a phenobarbitol about three o'clock in the afternoon. Actually I took two, because I figured two of them would put me out till the next day, right? To just get some rest, to sleep. But then about two hours later this girlfriend of mine came by to bring me an invitation to her wedding. She came over, she gave it to me, and we cried for a while. Because this girl was, well I'd practically been sisters with her for years and years and years, and we'd lost touch with each other because we'd made all these new friends. When I became friends with Handsome to the Maximum and Tito Caruso and those people, she lost touch with me, right? So when she left, I thought the effect had worn off, I decided the effect of the phenobarbitol had worn off, so I popped in two more and went back to bed. . . .

In fact . . . I'll tell you, this girl, you know who it was? Mercedes, the one that had been my brother's girlfriend . . . And one day she was driving up the Acapulco highway, coming to Mexico City, right? She had two beautiful little twin boys, about five years old, all smiling and pretty, right?, with little rabbit teeth. And all of a sudden, a trailer truck is coming the wrong, this big huge truck comes down the highway the wrong way and there's no way to get out of its way. It runs right over them and it doesn't even slow down. She had this sports car, a little tiny thing, about this high off the ground, you know?, I don't know the name of it, and their heads were cut off. Decapitated? Decapitated, her and the two little boys. It was tragic. I didn't want to go to the funeral or the funeral home or anything. It was so horrible that they buried all three of them in the same coffin and welded the coffin shut. They screwed on the top, they closed up the coffin, and then on top of that they welded it closed. . . . Why do people like to look at dead people? Why do they leave this hole in their memory, this peephole in their memory? . . .

So anyway, a little while later I woke up. I felt great, I was happy, I felt fine. It was like everything was over, the problem had passed, Gabriel Infante was behind me, Alexis Stamatis was behind me, Handsome to the Maximum was behind me. So I got in the shower, took a shower, put on a new nightgown, I put on the best nightgown I owned. Of course, also always thinking, thinking, thinking, about all these things that were happening. But I wanted to snap out of it completely, be just fine. When my parents came home I planned for everything to be okeydokey, hunky-dory, terrific, because I thought No problem, right? What's the problem? But then I saw these four pills lying beside the bottle. There were four of them. And I didn't even give it a second thought, didn't bat an eye, I just picked them up and popped them in my mouth and swallowed them. Like you're walking by and you see this piece of candy, and you pick it up and pop it in your mouth and eat it, and you never think it might be bad for you, you know? I mean, later I found out about a lot of stuff there was no way I could know back then, right? But anyway, I took these pills and just went on as happy and calm as anybody could be . . . And I went back to sleep.

While I was asleep, then, one of the Jalisco Sisters called, and they told her I was asleep. But she knew that if I was asleep, all you had to do was scratch at the door and I'd wake up, right? I mean I was an *extremely* light sleeper. So the maid goes and tells her The señorita is asleep, she must be very tired, because I knocked on the door and she didn't answer. So she figures, I mean by intuition, that something's wrong, right? So she went and got this guy she was going out with at the time. He was a doctor, a pediatrician I think. Anyway, he was hilarious because he kept trying to brainwash my girlfriend. You're not the kind to go out with just one man, he'd tell her, no, not you, you have to go out with lots of men, that's in your personality. And he'd make her dates with other men himself, so she'd go out with two men at the same time. I mean even with one of his brothers, right? But Big Jalisco was a real bitch, I'm telling you, and I'm not real sure what happened exactly, but she'd do very weird things to these people. For example, she tried to get all these relationships to turn out so the guy would ask her to marry him. Then when he did, she'd calmly tell the guy to go screw himself. It was like a bet she had with herself, right? Well, so in those days she was going out with this doctor and with this friend of Handsome to the Maximum's named Andrés. . . . While you were having one drink, he'd have three. Or anyway that's what she said all the time. . . .

So, uh . . . Where was I? Oh yeah, so she ran to get these two guys, and they all came to my house. The first thing I knew about them being there, we were all in the living room, and they were trying to wake me up. They'd tried to get into the bedroom through this big window, they thought they could get in from the pool, the garden side, you know?, but they finally gave up and broke in the door. Andrés and this doctor dragged me out of the bedroom, holding me up like this, and they walked me past my parents' bedroom, who were watching some program on television and hadn't even realized that any of this was going on. They were dragging me out of my bedroom and everything, breaking down the door. So then Alberto, or whatever his name was, started giving me coffee and helping me walk. He'd ask me my name and all, right? So then he started trying to find out, with me dead asleep, find out how many pills I'd taken. Big Jalisco was terribly worried and she kept shrieking like a bluejay, Aiee baby, you're soooo asleep. That's the way they were treating me, right, like a lost cause or something, right? How many pills did you take? And I'd say One. Then they'd say Oh no, we think you took more than one. So then I went Two. So then a little time went by, and finally they said Listen sweetheart, listen kiddo, we think you probably took quite a few more than that . . . Three, at least, you must have taken. And I shook my finger at them, like this, right?, saying No, more than three, more than four. Then things sort of started making sense to me, right?, and it turned out I'd taken I don't know how many, but a lot. They were really scared now, because, or anyway that's what I remember, the mortal or lethal or whatever it is dosage is ten pills. *Ten* is the number that poisons you, and I'd taken I think eight. So then they made me swear that when they left I'd go get into bed and not get out again till the next day. They said I had to stay as calm as possible, and rest, and I ought to read something. So of course, I said Okay, right? So I went right to my bedroom. I was pretty sleepy anyway . . . As you can imagine . . .

So now I'd been in my room for two days already, two days, and all of a sudden my mother comes. She hadn't noticed that I'd been in my room or that Andrés, Alberto, and Big Jalisco had come over. Incredible, but she hadn't noticed a thing. So she comes into my bedroom. It was strange as everything for her, because she was so tough, so hard-hearted I mean that, for example, when she saw the headless corpses of my friend and her little boys and all, all she said was Look how innocent they look. And I mean they were still a little burned-looking, right?, but How nice that they'll all go to heaven together, my mother says. And the corpses without any heads, okay? . . . She was so hard-hearted she could see you lying there in the middle of the street and not blink an eyelash. A strong character, horrible, *cold*, right? So anyway, I was lying there in my room, and she comes in to tell me I should have a glass of milk. Well, she wasn't quite so hard-hearted in those days, right? The lights were off, and I said No, Mama, listen, I don't, . . . no, thanks. So then she says Why are you talking like that? And I go How? I'm talking all right, I say to her . . . in the dark . . . She says No you aren't . . . So she flips on the light, and she yells, in horror, I mean she lets out such a scream—AAAAAGGGGGHHHHH! Like that, more or less, and she shoots out of the room in absolute terror. So I got scared myself, then, you know?, I got really really scared. . . .

Am I dragging this out too long?

So instead of staying in bed I went downstairs. I thought I'd watch television, see my father and mother, be a little sociable, you know? That'll cheer me up, I said to myself. So I walked in the TV room, and the two of them were sitting there, sitting there like . . . I mean they just sat there like a ghost had walked in. My own mother and father. So I say Well, okay, hey, everything's okay, don't get upset, I'm going to go lie down, I'm real sleepy. And my mother walks along behind me and helps me get into bed, right? And so then she told me about the glass of milk again. And I go No thanks again. So then she starts crying and moaning. Oh please drink a glass of milk! Just one glass of milk, for all you hold dearest! I mean there was my mother kneeling beside the bed crying and begging me to drink just a little something, if I loved her. I beg you, as you love me! She was so *servile* about the whole thing, you know, and this was such an old-fashioned way to . . . well. Drink a glass of milk! Please! So finally to make her happy I said Okay, and in less than three minutes she was back with the glass of milk. I drank it slowly, until she finally gave this sigh of relief, because while I was drinking the milk she had been holding her breath. You don't know how much I thank you, she said, reaching for the glass automatically. Now sleep.

As soon as she was out of the room, I got up and looked at myself in the mirror, first just to see why they were all so shocked, but second to splash a little water on my face. Because they'd looked at me, and like that!, they'd started screaming to high heaven and acting like I was this horrible-looking monster or something, and that worried me, you know? So I'm standing there looking at myself, and I see these spots on my face. Because I'd gotten poisoned, right? My face was practically completely deformed, all swollen up, like this, and there were these huge blotches like bruises, purple and white and all different colors. I was a rainbow all to myself. I looked like I'd bumped into a clown. . . . You could hear the voices from the television 'way off, so I went to bed, right? I just went to bed and nobody ever mentioned the subject again. . . .

But all the razor blades disappeared from my house, all the kitchen knives disappeared, all the sleeping pills, the bottles of strychnine, everything. *Every*thing. Because I think they thought I'd tried to commit suicide, which was not what it was at all, right? I was just trying to get some sleep and forget some of the things I was going through, you know, forget your troubles. But mostly just sleep. Afterwards this doctor guy explained it all to me. He said I got a little under the influence, you know, from those first phenobarbitols, and then I got so drunk it was like I'd drunk a whole bottle of whisky all by myself. So what happened to me then was, that I lost consciousness. It was like *snap!*, and I was out. So then you don't know what's good for you and what's not. They say when I got up and took those four phenobarbitols, when I got out of bed to take a shower, when I tell you I felt like a million dollars, well . . . They say that when I went to the bathroom I had to hold on to the walls, that I must have had to work myself along like this, against the wall?, because I'd taken such a bunch of pills that I must have been completely, completely drunk, right? So anyway, that went away. I was okay in no time . . . I was sort of stupid and blah for two or three days, but I didn't have any trouble, I mean I don't have any complexes or anything or any psychological hang-ups or frustrations or maladjustments because I wanted to kill myself and didn't—no, none of that stuff, forget it. I mean, I didn't want to poison myself at all, right? All I wanted to do was sleep it off, rest, just sleep for a while. . . .

("From that moment on, even the most remote figures suggested the idea of death so violently, so urgently, that a can of sardines—for example—brought up the memory of the lining of a coffin, or the stones in a sidewalk, noticed for the first time, revealed their kinship to the marble markers of a vault. In the thrall of this macabre vision, one's eyes simply saw that the plaster of façades was of the very color and texture of bones, and at last, just as stepping into a bath, sinking into the waters of a bath inescapably led to the posture one would adopt in a coffin, likewise not a person buried his body between the sheets without brooding on the pattern which the folds and creases of his shroud would take.")

■ **Isabel Allende (1942–)** *Chile* **(story)**

TRANSLATED BY MARGARET SAYERS PEDEN

Isabel Allende, daughter of Chilean diplomats and niece of President Salvador Allende, was born in Lima, Peru. She was taken back to Chile at three to live with her mother and grandparents after her parents divorced.

After her mother's marriage to another diplomat, she spent part of her childhood in Europe and the Middle East. She left school at sixteen to work. She had a job with the United Nations Food and Agricultural Organization in Santiago and later as a journalist, a talk show host, and a newscaster. She married at twenty and became an author of children's tales. Since her uncle Salvador Allende was murdered during the coup led by General Pinochet in 1973, she has lived abroad, for a long time in Venezuela, and presently in the San Francisco Bay area. She is one of Latin America's most important younger writers, which became internationally apparent with the publication of her best-known novel, *The House of Spirits* (1982), which appeared in more than twenty languages. She is a feminist who brings political concerns to her work. *The House of Spirits* was followed by *Of Love and Shadows* (1984, tr. 1987) and the novel *Eva Luna* (1987, tr. 1988). Her short story collection is called *The Stories of Eva Luna* (1991). She has also been a spokesperson for the political novel in her *Paths of Resistance and the Art and Craft of the Political Novel* (1989). Isabel Allende, a magical writer, is a frequent lecturer in classrooms and on public radio. She is one of the most popular women novelists Latin America has ever had, and, presently, she ranks among the most translated and enjoyed writers in the world.

FURTHER READING: Allende, Isabel. *The House of Spirits*, 1982, tr. 1985; *Of Love and Shadows*, 1984; *Eva Luna*, 1987, tr. 1988; *Paths of Resistance and the Art and Craft of the Political Novel*, 1989; *The Stories of Eva Luna*, 1991.

Gift for a Sweetheart

Horacio Fortunato was forty-six when the languid Jewish woman who was to change his roguish ways and deflate his fanfaronade entered his life. Fortunato came from a long line of circus people, the kind who are born with rubber bones and a natural gift for somersaults, people who at an age when other infants are crawling around like worms are hanging upside down from a trapeze and brushing the lion's teeth. Before his father made it into a serious enterprise, rather than the idle fancy it had been, the Fortunato Circus experienced more difficulty than glory. At different times of catastrophe and turmoil the company was reduced to two or three members of the clan who wandered the byways in a broken-down gypsy wagon with a threadbare tent they set up in godforsaken little towns. For years Horacio's grandfather bore the sole responsibility for the spectacle: he walked the tightrope, juggled with lighted torches, swallowed Toledo swords, extracted oranges and serpents from a top hat, and danced a graceful minuet with his only companion, a female monkey decked out in ruffles and a plumed hat. His grandfather, however, managed somehow to survive bad times, and while many other circuses succumbed, obliterated by more modern diversions, he saved his circus and, at the end of his life, was able to retire to the south of the continent and cultivate his garden of asparagus and strawberries, leaving a debt-free enterprise to his son Fortunato II. The scion lacked his father's humility, nor was he disposed to perform a balancing act on a tightrope or do pirouettes with a chimpanzee; on the other hand, he was gifted with the unshakable prudence of a born businessman. Under his direction the circus grew in size and prestige until it was the largest in the nation. Three colossal striped tents replaced the modest tarp of the earlier hard times; various cages sheltered a traveling zoo of tamed wild animals; and other fanciful vehicles transported the artists, who included the only hermaphroditic and ventriloquist dwarf in history. An exact, wheeled replica of Christopher Columbus's caravel completed the Fortunato Family Famous International Circus. This enormous caravan no longer drifted aimlessly, as it had in his father's day, but steamed purposefully along the principal highways from the Rio Grande to the Straits of Magellan, stopping only in major cities, where it made an entrance with such a clamor of drums, elephants, and clowns—the caravel at the lead, like a miraculous reenactment of the Conquest—that no man, woman, or child could escape knowing the circus had come to town.

Fortunato II married a trapeze artist, and they had a son they named Horacio. But one day wife-and-mother stayed behind, determined to be independent of her husband and support herself through her somewhat precarious calling, leaving the boy in his father's care. Her son held a rather dim picture of her in his memory, never completely separating the image of his mother from that of the many acrobats he had known. When he was ten, his father married another circus artist, this time an equestrienne able to stand on her head on a galloping steed or leap from one croup to another with eyes blindfolded. She was very beautiful. No matter how much soap, water, and perfume she used, she could not erase the last trace of the essence of horse, a sharp aroma of sweat and effort. In her magnificent bosom the young Horacio, enveloped in that unique odor, found consolation for his mother's absence. But with time the horsewoman also decamped without a farewell. In the ripeness of his years, Fortunato II entered into matrimony, for the third and final time, with a Swiss woman he met on a tour bus in America. He was weary of his Bedouin-like existence and felt too old for new alarms, so when his Swiss bride requested it, he had not the slightest difficulty in giving up the circus for a sedentary life, and ended his days on a small farm in the Alps amid bucolic hills and woods. His son Horacio, who was a little over twenty, took charge of the family business.

Horacio had grown up with the instability of moving every few days, of sleeping on wheels and living beneath a canvas roof, but he was very conformed to his fate. He had never envied other little boys who wore gray uniforms to school and who had their destinies mapped out before they were born. By contrast, he felt powerful and free. He knew all the secrets of the circus, and with the same confidence and ease he mucked out the animal cages or balanced fifty meters above the ground dressed as a hussar and charming the audience with his dolphin smile. If at any moment he longed for stability, he did not admit it, even in his sleep. The experience of having been abandoned first by his mother and then by his stepmother had left him slightly insecure, especially with women, but it had not made him a cynic, because he had inherited his grandfather's sentimental heart. He had an enormous flair for the circus, but he was fascinated by the commercial aspect of the business even more than by the art. He had intended to be rich from the time he was a young boy, with the naïve conviction that money would bring the security he had not received from his family. He increased the number of tentacles spreading from the family enterprise by buying a chain of boxing arenas in several capital cities. From boxing he moved naturally to wrestling, and as he was a man of inventive imagination he transformed that gross sport into a dramatic spectacle. Among his initiatives were the Mummy, who appeared at ringside in an Egyptian sarcophagus; Tarzan, who covered his privates with a tiger skin so tiny that with every lunge the audience held its breath, expecting some major revelation; and the Angel, who every night bet his golden hair and lost it to the scissors of the ferocious Kuramoto—a Mapuche Indian disguised as a Samurai—but then appeared the following day with curls intact, irrefutable proof of his divine condition. These and other commercial ventures, along with public appearances with a pair of bodyguards whose role it was to intimidate his competitors and pique the ladies' curiosity, had earned him a reputation of being a shady character, a distinction he reveled in. He lived a good life, traveled through the world closing deals and looking for monsters, frequented clubs and casinos, owned a glass mansion in California and a retreat in the Yucatán, but lived most of the year in luxury hotels. He bought the temporary company of a series of blondes. He liked them soft, with ample bosoms, in homage to the memory of his stepmother, but he wasted very little energy on amorous affairs, and when his grandfather urged him to marry and bring sons into the world so the Fortunato name would not vanish without an heir, he replied that not even out of his mind would he ascend the matrimonial gallows. He was a dark-skinned, hefty man with thick hair slicked back with brilliantine, shrewd eyes, and an authoritative voice that accentuated his self-satisfied vulgarity. He was obsessed with elegance and he bought clothes befitting a duke—but his suits were a little too shiny, his ties verging on the audacious, the ruby in his ring too ostentatious, his cologne too penetrating. He had the heart of a lion tamer, and no English tailor alive would ever disguise that fact.

This man, who had spent a good part of his existence cutting a wide swath with his lavish lifestyle, met Patricia Zimmerman on a Tuesday in March, and on the spot lost both unpredictability of spirit and clarity of thought. He was sitting in the only restaurant in the city that still refused to serve blacks, with four cohorts and a diva whom he was planning to take to the Bahamas for a week, when Patricia entered the room on her husband's arm, dressed in silk and adorned with some of the diamonds that had made the Zimmerman firm famous. Nothing could have been further from the unforgettable stepmother smelling of horses, or the complacent blondes, than this woman. He watched her advance, small, refined, her chest bones bared by her décolletage and her chestnut-colored hair drawn back into a severe bun, and he felt his knees grow heavy and an insufferable burning in his breast. He preferred uncomplicated women ready for a good time, whereas this was a woman who would have to be studied carefully if her worth was to be known, and even then her virtues would be visible only to an eye trained in appreciating subtleties—which had never been the case with Horacio Fortunato. If the fortune-teller in his circus had consulted her crystal ball and predicted that Fortunato would fall in love at first sight with a fortyish and haughty aristocrat, he would have had a good laugh. But that is exactly what happened as he watched Patricia walk toward him like the shade of a nineteenth-century widow-empress in her dark gown with the glitter of all those diamonds shooting fire at her neck. As Patricia walked past, she paused for an instant before that giant with the napkin tucked into his waistcoat and a trace of gravy at the corner of his mouth. Horacio Fortunato caught a whiff of her perfume and the full impact of her aquiline profile and completely forgot the diva, the bodyguards, his business affairs, everything that interested him in life, and decided with absolute seriousness to steal this woman from her jeweler and love her to the best of his ability. He turned his chair to one side and, ignoring his guests, measured the distance that separated her from him, while Patricia Zimmerman wondered whether that stranger was examining her jewels with some evil design.

That same night an extravagant bouquet of orchids was delivered to the Zimmerman residence. Patricia looked at the card, a sepia-colored rectangle with a name from a novel written in golden arabesques. What ghastly taste, she muttered, divining immediately it had come from the man with the plastered-down hair she had seen in the restaurant, and she ordered the gift to be tossed into the street, with the hope that the sender would be circling the house and thus learn the fate of his flowers. The following day a crystal box arrived bearing a single perfect rose, without a card. The majordomo also placed this offering in the trash. Different bouquets followed for the rest of the week: a basket of wild flowers on a bed of lavender, a pyramid of white carnations in a silver goblet, a dozen black tulips imported from Holland, and other varieties impossible to find in this hot climate. Each suffered the fate of the first, but this did not discourage the gallant, whose siege was becoming so unbearable that Patricia Zimmerman did not dare answer the telephone for fear of hearing his voice whispering indecent proposals, as had happened the previous Tuesday at two in the morning. She returned his letters unopened. She stopped going out, because she ran into Fortunato in the most unexpected places: observing her from the adjoining box at the opera; in the street, waiting to open the door of her car before the chauffeur could reach it; materializing like an illusion in an elevator or on some stairway. She was a prisoner in her own home, and frightened. He'll get over it, he'll get over it, she kept telling herself, but Fortunato did not evaporate like a bad dream; he was always there, on the other side of the wall, breathing heavily. She thought of calling the police, or telling her husband, but her horror of scandal prevented her. One morning she was attending to her correspondence when the majordomo announced the visit of the president of Fortunato and Sons.

"In my own house, how dare he!" Patricia muttered, her heart racing. She had to call on the implacable discipline she had acquired in years of small dramas played in salons to disguise the trembling of her hands and voice. For an instant she was tempted to confront this madman once and for all, but she realized that her strength would fail her; she felt defeated even before she saw him.

"Tell him I'm not in. Show him the door, and inform the servants that the gentleman is not welcome in this house," she ordered.

The next day there were no exotic flowers at breakfast, and Patricia thought with a sigh of relief, or dejection, that the man must finally have understood her message. That morning she felt free for the first time in a week, and she went out for a game of tennis and a trip to the beauty salon. She returned home at two in the afternoon with a new haircut and a bad headache. On the hall table she saw a royal purple velvet jewel box with the name Zimmerman printed in gold letters. She opened it rather absently, thinking that her husband had left it there, but found a necklace of emeralds accompanied by one of those pretentious sepia cards she had come to know and detest. Her headache turned to panic. This adventurer seemed prepared to ruin her life; as if it wasn't enough to buy a necklace from her own husband, he then had the gall to send it to her house. She could not throw this gift into the trash, as she had done with the flowers. With the case clutched to her bosom, she locked herself in her writing room. A half-hour later, she called the chauffeur and ordered him to deliver a package to the same address to which he had returned several letters. As she handed him the jewels she felt no relief; to the contrary, she had the impression that she was sinking into a quagmire.

At the same time, Fortunato was slogging through his own swamp, getting nowhere, feeling his way blindly. He had never spent so much money and time to court a woman, although it was true, he admitted, that all his women had been quite different from this one. For the first time in his life as a showman, he felt ridiculous. He could not go on this way; always strong as an ox, his health was suffering, he slept only a few hours at a time, he was short of breath, he had heart palpitations, he felt fire in his stomach and ringing in his temples. His business was similarly suffering the impact of his love fever; he was making hasty decisions, and losing money. Good Christ, I don't know who I am or what I'm doing here; damn it all, he grumbled, sweating, but not for a minute did he consider abandoning the chase.

Slumped in an armchair in the hotel where he was staying, the purple jewel box back in his hands, Fortunato remembered his grandfather.

He rarely thought of his father, but his memory often dwelt on that formidable ancestor who at ninety-some years was still cultivating his garden. He picked up the telephone and asked for long distance.

The elder Fortunato was nearly deaf and, in addition, unable to adapt to the mechanism of that devilish apparatus that carried voices halfway around the planet, but the years had not affected his lucidity. He listened carefully to his grandson's sorrowful tale, speaking only at the end.

"So, the sly vixen is giving herself the luxury of snubbing my boy, is that it, eh?"

"She won't even look at me, Nono. She's rich, she's beautiful, she's classy. . . . She has everything."

"Ummm . . . including a husband."

"Yes, but that's not important. If I could only speak to her."

"Speak to her? What about? You have nothing to say to a woman like that, son."

"I gave her a necklace fit for a queen and she returned it without a word."

"Well, give her something she doesn't have."

"What, for example?"

"A good excuse to laugh, that always gets 'em." And his grandfather nodded off with the receiver in his hand, dreaming of the pretty things who had given him their hearts as he performed his death-defying acrobatics on the trapeze or danced with his monkey.

The next day in his office the jeweler Zimmerman received a splendid young woman, a manicurist by trade, she said; she had come, she explained, to sell back at half price the very emerald necklace he had sold only forty-eight hours before. The jeweler remembered the purchase very well; impossible to forget such a conceited boor.

"I need something that will crumble the defenses of a haughty lady," he had said.

Zimmerman had studied him a moment, and decided he must be one of those new oil or cocaine millionaires. He could not tolerate vulgarity; he was accustomed to a different class of customer. He rarely served clients himself, but this man had insisted on speaking to him and seemed prepared to spend an unlimited amount of money.

"What do you recommend?" the man had asked before the tray where the most valuable jewels sparkled.

"It depends upon the lady. Rubies and pearls look good on dark skin; emeralds on someone fairer; and diamonds are perfect for anyone."

"She has too many diamonds. Her husband gives them to her as if they were candy."

Zimmerman coughed. He disliked this kind of confidence. The man picked up a necklace, held it to the light with no respect, shook it like a sleigh bell, and the air filled with tinkling and green sparks as the jeweler's ulcer twitched within him.

"Do you think emeralds bring good luck?"

"I suppose that all precious stones fit that description, sir, but I am not superstitious."

"This is a very special woman. I don't want to make any mistake with the gift, you understand?"

"Perfectly."

But apparently that was precisely what had happened, Zimmerman told himself, unable to restrain a scornful smirk when the girl returned the necklace. No, there was nothing wrong with the jewels, the mistake was the girl. He had imagined a more refined woman, certainly not a manicurist carrying a plastic handbag and wearing a cheap blouse. He was, nonetheless, intrigued by the girl, there was something vulnerable and pathetic about her, poor child; she would not fare well in the hands of that bandit, he thought.

"Why don't you tell me the whole story, my dear," said Zimmerman finally.

The girl spun him the tale she had memorized, and an hour later left the shop with a light step. According to plan, the jeweler had not only bought back the necklace, he had invited her to dinner as well. It was plain to her that Zimmerman was one of those men who are astute and suspicious in business dealings but naïve in every other regard; she would have no difficulty distracting him the amount of time Horacio Fortunato needed and was prepared to pay for.

That was a memorable night for Zimmerman; he had planned on dinner but found himself in the grip of an unexpected passion. The next day he saw his new friend again and by the end of the week he was stammering to Patricia something about going to New York for a few days to attend a sale of Russian jewels saved from the massacre of Ekaterinburg. His wife was totally unmoved.

∗   ∗   ∗

Alone in her house, too listless to go out and suffering that headache that came and went without respite, Patricia decided to devote her Saturday to recouping her strength. She settled on the terrace to leaf through some fashion magazines. It had not rained for a week and the air was still and hot. She read awhile, until the sun made her drowsy; her body grew heavy, her eyes closed, and the magazine slipped from her hands. At that moment she heard a sound from deep in the garden; she thought it must be the gardener, a headstrong old man who in less than a year had transformed her property into a tropical jungle, ripping out pots of chrysanthemums to make way for an efflorescence gone wild. She opened her eyes, stared half-seeing against the sun, and saw something unusually large moving in the top of the avocado tree. She removed her dark glasses and sat up. No doubt about it, a shadow was moving up there, and it was not part of the foliage.

Patricia Zimmerman rose from her chair and walked forward a step or two; then she saw it clearly: a ghostly blue-clad figure with a golden cape flew several meters over her head, turned a somersault in the air and, for an instant, seemed to freeze at the moment of waving to her from the sky. She choked back a scream, sure that the apparition would plummet like a stone and be pulverized on contact with the ground, but the cape filled with air and that gleaming coleopteran stretched out its arms and swung into a nearby medlar tree. Immediately, a second blue figure appeared, hanging by its legs in the top branches of another tree, swinging by the wrists a young girl wearing a flower crown. The first gave a signal and the holder released the girl, who scattered a rain of paper butterflies before being caught by the ankles. Patricia did not dare move while those silent, gold-caped birds flew through the air.

Suddenly a whoop filled the garden, a long, barbaric yowl that tore Patricia's attention from the trapeze artists. She saw a thick rope fall from the rear wall of the property and, climbing down it, Tarzan, in person, the same Tarzan of the matinées and comic books of her childhood, with his skimpy loincloth and live monkey on his hip. The King of the Jungle leapt gracefully to earth, thumped his chest with his fists, and repeated the visceral bellow, attracting all the servants, who rushed out to the terrace. With a wave of the hand, Patricia gestured to them to stay where they were, while the voice of Tarzan gave way to a lugubrious drumroll announcing a retinue of four Egyptian dancers who advanced as if trapped in a frieze, head and feet at right angles to their bodies; they were followed by a hunchback wearing a striped hooded cape and leading a black panther at the end of a chain. Then came two monks carrying a sarcophagus and, behind them, an angel with long golden locks and then, bringing up the rear, an Indian disguised as a Japanese wearing a dressing gown and wooden clogs. All of them paused behind the swimming pool. The monks deposited the coffin on the grass and, while the Egyptian maidens chanted softly in some dead tongue and the Angel and Kuramoto rippled their prodigious muscles, the lid of the sarcophagus swung open and a nightmarish creature emerged from inside. Once revealed, swathed in gauze, it was obvious that this was a mummy in perfect health. At this moment, Tarzan yodeled another cry and, with absolutely no provocation, began hopping around the Egyptians, brandishing the simian. The Mummy lost its millenary patience, lifted one rigid arm and let it swing like a cudgel against the nape of the savage's neck, who fell to the ground, his face buried in the lawn. The monkey screamed and scrambled up a tree. Before the embalmed pharaoh could deliver a second blow, Tarzan leapt to his feet and fell upon the Mummy with a roar. Locked in legendary combat, their rolling and thrashing freed the panther; the characters in the parade ran to hide in the garden and all the servants flew back to the safety of the kitchen. Patricia was about to jump into the pool when, as if by magic, an individual in tails and a top hat appeared and with one snap of his whip stopped the cat, who fell to the ground purring like a pussycat, with all four paws in the air; the hunchback recaptured the chain, as the ringmaster swept off his hat and pulled from it a meringue torte that he carried to the terrace and deposited at the feet of the lady of the house.

This was the signal for the remainder of the cast to march in from the rear of the garden: musicians playing military marches, clowns assaulting one another with slapsticks, dwarfs from medieval courts, an equestrienne standing on her mount, a bearded lady, dogs on bicycles, an ostrich costumed as Columbine and, finally, a team of boxers in satin trunks and boxing gloves pushing a wheeled platform crowned by a painted cardboard arch. And there, on the dais of a stage-set emperor, sat Horacio Fortunato, his mane slicked down with brilliantine, grinning his irrepressible gallant's grin, pompous beneath his triumphal dome, surrounded by his outrageous circus, acclaimed by the trumpets and cymbals of his own orchestra, the most conceited, most lovesick, and most entertaining man in the world. Patricia laughed, and walked forward to meet him.

■ Reinaldo Arenas (1943–1990) *Cuba* (novel)

TRANSLATED BY ANDREW HURLEY

Born in Oriente province, as a youth Reinaldo Arenas joined Fidel Castro's revolutionary movement. He worked as a researcher for some years in Havana, and in 1966 his first novel, *The Pit,* was published and sold out in a week. It is the story of a poor family during the Batista period as told by the idiot son. His postmodernist second novel, *Hallucinations* (1968), is a parodic treatment of a monk's hallucinatory life in Spain, London, and elsewhere. The monk on whose life his novel is based was two centuries earlier imprisoned in the same El Morro prison where Arenas was held a few years after having written his semifictitious story. Although he could not publish it in Cuba (where it remains unpublished), it was translated into most European languages, and, in 1969, it won the Prix Medici in France for the best foreign novel of the year. His impressive later novels, which won him international recognition, are *Farewell to the Sea* (1982, tr. 1986), *The Palace of the White Skunks* (1980, tr. 1990), and *The Doorman* (1987, tr. 1991).

Although Arenas's manuscripts were often seized by the police, he managed to smuggle most of his writing out of the country. In 1970, he spent time in a forced labor camp, where, as in China during the Cultural Revolution, intellectuals were sent for moral and political re-education. Despite increasing world fame, from 1974 to 1976 he was sent to the harsh El Morro prison. By luck and a bureaucratic mistake, he managed to leave Cuba in 1980 during the Mariel exodus. Greatly esteemed by writers of all political sides while in Cuba, even while in prison, once he went abroad as an exile he found his works and person deemed controversial and his books often dropped from the curriculum in Latin American and U.S. universities. He moved to France, where he was well received. He worked with great difficulty to finish his last novels and memoir, and in December 1990, suffering from AIDS, he committed suicide. Since his death, several new volumes have appeared, and his reputation has soared.

FURTHER READING: Arenas, Reinaldo. *The Pit,* 1966; *Hallucinations,* 1968; *Farewell to the Sea,* 1982; *The Palace of the White Skunks,* 1980; *The Doorman,* 1987.

from Singing from the Well

There went my mother, she just went running out the door. She was screaming like a crazy woman that she was going to jump down the well. I see my mother at the bottom of the well. I see her floating in the greenish water choked with leaves. So I run for the yard, out to where the well is, that's fenced around with a wellhead of naked-boy saplings so rickety it's almost falling in.

I run up and peek over. But just like always—the only one down there is me. Me being reflected from way down there up to me above. Me—and I disappear if you so much as spit into the oozy green water.

Madre mía, Mama! This is not the first time you've tricked me—every day you say you're going to jump headfirst down the well, but ha! You never do it. You think you're going to drive me crazy, making me run these wild-goose chases from the house to the well and the well to the house. Well, no. I'm getting tired of this. If you're not going to jump, it's all right with me. But don't say you're going to jump and then not do it.

We're out here crying, behind the old thicket of prickly wild pineapples. My mother and I, we're crying. The lizards are so big in this pineapple thicket! You ought to see them! The lizards here are in all different shapes. I just saw one with two heads. Two heads on that lizard slithering along.

Most of these lizards know me, and they hate me. I know they hate me, and they're just waiting for the day . . . Bastards!, I say to them, and I dry my eyes. And then I pick up a stick and go for them. But they know a lot more than you'd give them credit for, and the second they see me stop crying they run into the thicket, and they disappear. What really makes me mad is that I know that all the time I can't see them and I'm thrashing around looking for them, to try to catch them, they're watching me. They're probably laughing at me.

Finally I catch one. I whack him with the stick and break him in half. But he's still alive, and one half runs off while the other piece jumps up and down in front of me like it was saying, You little crybaby, don't think you can kill me *that* easy . . .

"You beast!" says my mother to me, and she throws a rock at me and hits me in the head. "Let those poor lizards live in peace!" My head has split into two halves and one of them has run off. The other half, though, stays there in front of my mother. Dancing. Dancing. Dancing.

Now all of us are dancing, up here on the roof of the house. What a lot of people on the roof! I love to climb up onto the palm branches of the thatch, and I always find one or two nests of shiny little green-and-purple blackbirds up here. I don't eat the blackbirds' eggs, because people say they're always rotten, so what I do is throw them at my grandfather's head, because every time he sees me up on top of the house he picks up the long pole he uses to cut off palm leaves way up on the tree and he starts poking at me like I was a bunch of coconuts. One of the eggs has splattered in my grandfather's eye, and I'm not sure, but it looks to me like it put his eye out. One-eyed Grandpa. But no—you'd have to poke that old coot's eyes out with a spear, because his eyeballs are tougher than the bottom of a bucket.

Dancing all by myself on the roof. I made my cousins get down, and now they're asleep under the pine trees. Inside the white brick wall. And the crosses.

"What are there so many crosses for?" I asked Mama the day we went to see my cousins.

"It's so they'll rest in peace and go to heaven," my mother told me, while she cried her eyes out and stole a fresh wreath off one of the crosses a little way away. So I pulled up seven crosses and carried them home with me under my arm. And I kept them in bed with me, so that way I could sleep when I went to bed and not even feel the mosquitoes, and mosquitoes here have worse stingers than scorpions.

"These crosses are so I can sleep," I told my grandmother when she came into my room. My grandmother is an old, old woman, I thought, while I squatted under the bed. "Take these crosses for you," I told Grandma, handing her the crosses. But she carried them *all* off. "We've got a shortage of firewood today," she said. And when she got to the cookstove she chopped them into kindling and threw them in the fire.

"What have you done with my crosses, you old nanny goat!" I said, and I grabbed a piece of smoking cross and went at her. I was going to poke out her eyes. But that old biddy wasn't born yesterday, and when I picked up the burning stick she grabbed the pot of scalding water that was on top of the cookstove and threw it on me. If I hadn't jumped back I'd have been cooked alive. "Don't fool with me," said Grandma, and then she gave me a roasted sweet potato to eat. I took the half-eaten sweet potato out to the bileweed plant and I dug a hole there and I put it in the ground. Then I made a cross out of a dry bileweed plant and put it in the ground, too, next to the dead sweet potato.

But now I better stop thinking about those things and see about getting down off the roof without Grandpa running me through with the pole. I know—I'll slip down the zinc rain gutters like I was a cat, and when he's not looking I'll jump out of the rain gutter and run off. Oh, I wish I could jump on top of my grandfather and squash him! Everything is all *his* fault. His fault. That's why I and all my cousins all meet here. Up here on the roof of the house. Like we've done so many times—we have to plan a way to have Grandpa die before his time.

This house has always been a hell. Even before everybody died all anybody ever talked about was dead people. And more dead people. And Grandma outprayed everybody, crossing herself in every corner of the house. But when things got really bad was when Celestino took it into his head to write poems. Poor Celestino! I can see him now—sitting on the parlor doorsill beam and pulling off his arms.

Poor Celestino! Writing. Writing and writing and writing, and never stopping, even on the spines of the account books where Grandpa writes down the dates the cows got pregnant. On yucca leaves and even on the hard round husks of the palm trees the horses didn't get there soon enough to eat.

Writing. Writing. And when not a single yucca leaf is left to mess up— or a single palm leaf husk, or Grandpa's ledger books—Celestino starts writing on the trunks of the trees.

"That's what girls do," said my mother, when she found out Celestino had got it into his head to start writing. And that was the first time she jumped down the well.

✳ ✳ ✳

"I'd rather die than have a son like that," and the water level in the well rose.

Mama was so fat in those days! Really really fat. So when she dived into the water it came way up. You ought to have seen it! I ran out to the well and I could wash my hands in the water and I got a drink almost without bending over. I just stretched out my neck a little. And then I started drinking, using my two hands like they were dippers. The water was so cool and clear! I love drinking out of my hands and getting them all wet. Like birds do. But of course, since birds don't have hands, they drink with their beaks . . . What if they did have hands, though, and we were the ones that were mixed up? . . . I don't even know what to say. In this house things have gone from bad to worse—I don't even know, really and truly, what to think. But I still think anyway. And worry. And think. And worry . . . And now Celestino comes up to me again with all the palm branches under his arms and the carpenter's pencils sticking out the middle of his stomach.

"Celestino! Celestino!"

"Carmelina's child has gone crazy!"

"He's gone crazy! He's gone crazy!"

"He's scribbling on the trunks of the trees!"

"He's batty as a loon!"

"What a disgrace! My God! This kind of thing could only happen to me!"

"What a disgrace!"

We went down to the river. The boys' voices kept getting louder and louder, and finally they were yelling. They pushed Celestino out of the water and told him to go swim with the women. I got out of the water too, right behind Celestino, and then the boys caught me and kicked my behind eight times—four on each side. I felt like I wanted to cry. But he cried for me too.

✳ ✳ ✳

And night caught us in the middle of the pasture. Boom, just like that, night falls around here. Just when you'd least expect it, here it comes. It wraps all around us and then it won't go away. The sun almost never comes up here. Oh, of course a lot of people say the sun comes up, or morning comes. I say the same thing once in a while.

"When we get to the house, don't let them find out what the boys did," Celestino said, and he dried his eyes with a guava leaf. But when we got to the house they were already waiting for us at the door. Nobody said a word. Not a peep. We came to the house, went into the dining room, and at that, she ran out through the kitchen door. She gave a shriek behind the cookstove and started running all over the yard, and finally she jumped down the well again . . . When I was littler, Grandma gave me a hen and told me, "Follow her till you find her nest, and don't come back to this house till your pockets are full of eggs." I turned the hen loose in the middle of the yard. She took off. She flapped her wings and flew three circles in the air. And she disappeared, cackling through the thicket of wild pineapples.

"The hen got away from me, Grandma."

"Son of a bitch! We'd all be better off if you just died!"

Celestino came up to me and put his hand on my head. I was so sad. It was the first time anybody had ever cursed at me. I was so sad I started crying. Celestino lifted me up in the air, and he said to me, "What foolishness, but you might as well get used to it." I looked at Celestino, and I realized that he was crying too, but he was trying not to show it. So that made me realize that he still hadn't got used to it either. I stopped crying a second. And the two of us went out into the yard. It was still daylight.

It was still daylight.

✳ ✳ ✳

There had been a rainstorm. But the lightning bolts hadn't been satisfied with just that, so they kept on winking and flashing behind the clouds and way up in the highest leaves of the shower-of-gold bushes. What a nice smell there is after it rains . . . I had never noticed things like that before. Now I did. So I took air in through my nose and mouth, both. And then I filled my stomach up again with the smell and the air. The sun wasn't going to come back out anymore now, there were too many clouds. But it was still light out. We walked along under the sugar apple trees, and I could feel the mud with leaves all mixed up in it coming up through the holes in my shoes. The mud was cold, and all of a sudden I got the idea of playing like I was walking through snow and that the sugar apple trees were Christmas trees and pines and evergreens and that the whole family was in the house buzzing and clattering and laughing, which up to then I'd never heard before. "What a shame there's no snow here where we live," I said to Celestino. But he wasn't with me anymore. "Celestino! Celestino!" I called, very very softly, trying not to wake myself up and find myself in the middle of a mud puddle.

Celestino! Celestino!

The lightning bolts came back again. My mother ran across the snow and hugged me tight. And she said "son" to me. I smiled at my mother, and then I jumped and hugged her around the neck. And the two of us started to dance on the ground, all dressed in white. At that, the noise of the people singing and making such a hubbub in the house got closer and closer to us; they were coming towards us with a whole roast pig on a spit, and they were singing all the way. All my cousins made a chorus and danced around us in a ring. Mama lifted me way up in the air. As high as her arms could reach. And from up there I could see the sky getting darker and darker, and a shower bigger and whiter than the one that had come down before starting to work its way out of the clouds. So I wiggled out of my mother's arms and ran over to where my cousins were, and we started jumping up and down in the snow as high as we could and we sang and sang and sang, and little by little we turned transparent—as transparent as the snow that didn't get mixed up with the mud, it just spread out white and pure and clean no matter how much we jumped around.

For one second there was a great big loud clap of thunder. I saw the lightning melt every bit of the snow as quick as you could snap your fingers. And before I could yell and close my eyes, I saw myself—walking through a big mud puddle—and saw Celestino writing poems on the sugar apple trees, and their bark is as hard as iron. And my grandfather came out of the kitchen with a hatchet and started cutting down all the trees Celestino had written on, even if it was just one word.

I watched him swinging his hatchet, whacking away at the tree trunks, and I said to myself, "The time has come. I'm going to break his back with a rock." But I didn't. What if I miss and it doesn't kill him? If the rock doesn't hit him just right, then I'm done for, because Grandpa will jump on me like a mad dog and make mincemeat out of me with the hatchet.

There's not a thing I can do all by myself. Sometimes there are a whole lot of things I wish I could do. But I don't do a single solitary thing. One day I told myself I was going to set the house on fire. I climbed up one of the forked props for the wall, up to the roof, and I had already struck the match and all I had to do was hold it to the palm thatch for the whole house and everything to go up like gunpowder, and not a black smudge of what had been the house be left, and all of a sudden I remembered the baby blackbirds. They had just pecked out of their shells and they were asleep all nice and still in the nest over by the rain gutters. I remembered them and that made me feel so sad. So I didn't do it. I didn't do a thing. I got down off the roof saying to myself, "Well, when the baby blackbirds grow up and fly away from the nest I'll set fire to the house, and there won't be any problem with doing it then at all." And when I got to the ground I felt the hard crack of a big thick switch that rattled my ribs and almost broke my back.

"Son of a bitch! I told you not to climb up on the roof of the house—it stops raining faster outside than it does inside these days, with you climbing all over the thatch and shinnying down the rain gutters all the time and punching holes in the roof. You goose! Get to work!"

And another crack. And another. And another. Grandpa had been waiting for me, just biding his time, under the rainspout, and he had taken such good aim when I was climbing down that there was no way I could duck the switch cracking and then cracking again, going "psssst-ch!" through the air from the mad blind rage Grandpa was taking out on my back. The stinking old coot! He caught me by surprise, and I didn't know what to do when I saw that switch coming at me. Something just came over me, and I really felt like crying. But then I started getting so mad, so mad inside that I bet I even turned all different colors and everything. So at that I gave a great big huge scream and ran for the meadow on the mountainside as fast as I could go, with the old coot after me, cursing and muttering and stumbling over the tree stumps he had cut down his own evil self. The high meadow is so beautiful! I love it.

When I got there I jumped into the first clump of tall grass I could find. And I didn't even feel the chiggers biting me, or even the ticks there are on the mountain. I lay on my back and made myself as comfortable as I could and watched the clouds. And I started eating some little wild persimmons I could just reach and pull off from a persimmon tree. Two great big clouds ran into each other and smashed into a million pieces.

The pieces fell on my house and squashed it, right down to the ground. I never thought pieces of cloud would be so big and heavy. They're sharp as a knife, too. One of them just sliced my grandfather's head right off. My cousins were down at the river, so they managed to escape. Not hide nor hair of my grandmother has been found, so I guess the clouds broke her to smithereens and ants came and carried off the pieces. I run down from the high meadow to the house, buried under the rubble of clouds, and when I get there all I can see is one of my mother's arms and one of Celestino's. My mother's arm is moving a little in the rubble and soot and ashes. (Because in this house the smoke from the cookstove has no place to go, because there's just one window and it's in the dining room, so that's why the house is always as black as the bottom of a kettle.)

"Get me out of here, I'm suffocating!" the voice of my mother tells me, and her arm waves around and jumps and twitches.

I can't hear Celestino say a word. Not a peep. His arm is barely sticking out of the soot and ashes and palm branches, and it's moving so very very slow and still that it's almost like his hand is petting the beams and the pieces of black thatch that have buried him alive.

"Get me out of here, goddammit! I'm your mother!"

"I'll be right there. I'll be right there!"

And I smile as I go over to where Celestino's still, cold hand is, and I start lifting up the big boulders of cloud from on top of him. Until finally, at just about nightfall, I've finally got him free.

The storm of clouds has let up a little, and a fine fine shower is little by little turning everything an almost transparent white white color. Out of that mist of water just barely barely falling I see my mother coming towards me carrying the ox prod in her hands. Sharpened to a fine point.

The chiggers have almost eaten my whole back, but I didn't feel them biting me, I was in such a daze. My mother walks right across the top of the wild pineapple thicket, not even watching out for thorns, and then she takes off flying.

Now she's right in front of me. In the middle of the high meadow, and pointing the prod straight at my throat.

"Why didn't you save me? You jackass!"

Mama grips the prod tighter, and I can feel a cold tickle that starts going right through the skin of my throat.

"I am your mother."

My cousin Eulogia got lost in this meadow one time. Poor Eulogia! She went out to get firewood and she never came back to the house again. With or without the firewood.

"Answer me—why didn't you save me, if I'm the woman that brought you into the world!"

Something must have happened to my cousin Eulogia that she still hasn't come back. We all waited for her in the dining room, not saying a word to one another. Looking at the floor or out the only window. But not saying a single word to one another.

Eulogia!

Eulogia!

Grandma cries because she says she knows that if Eulogia's lost Grandpa will hang himself. I feel sorry for Eulogia. But if it's true about Grandpa then I'd be very happy if she were to get lost.

"You're no son of mine! What you are is a beast!"

Hail Mary, full of grace. Blessed be the fruit of thy womb. Virgin Mary, please let Eulogia show up, because if she doesn't I'll pitch you into that cookstove . . .

Our Father, Who art in heaven . . .

*   *   *

"You beast! You beast! Instead of saving your own mother, you'd let her suffocate in that ash heap."

Poor Eulogia . . . When she went off to the mountain I saw that she was crying. She had just come out of Grandpa's room. Poor Eulogia! If she wasn't the goose she is she wouldn't have let Grandpa get up on top of her like he did. But she's the slave for this whole house and everybody gets on top of her. And does whatever they want to her. Even me. One afternoon I tripped her and pulled her down out behind the bileweed patch and got up on top of her. She didn't make the slightest peep. She brayed like a mule when you give it three or four slaps with a stick of wood, and she broke out in big drops of sweat.

Poor Eulogia! She left the house crying while Grandma was throwing the biggest fit you ever saw. As soon as she turned her back Mama slushed the dirty dishwater on her head.

"Goddamn you! My only son, and he's turned out to be as thick as a mule! Was there ever a sadder fate than mine! I knew I should've died before I came into the world!"

It's as plain as day that Eulogia didn't really get lost on the mountain, like my whole family would like me to think. And if she didn't, then they'll see—one day we'll find her hanging from a tree with a vine around her neck, hanging almost as high as the parson birds, and they *never* come down to the ground, except to get a drink of water, maybe, when they can't find a drop on the leaves of the trees and they're so thirsty they can't even fly. If it weren't for that, they'd never *ever* come down!

What I wouldn't give to be a parson bird! I wouldn't drink water even if my throat got as dry as a rock.

❋ ❋ ❋

The point of the prod goes in very very cool right through my throat. I hang on to the rocks and grass for dear life and I can feel that coolness all the way to my tonsils.

I wish I could escape.

Except really, I'm not so sure I do. And I think, If they let me go I'd tell Mama to stab me again with the stick. I would—I'd even get down on my knees to her and beg her to do it, and tell her to make the stick sharper, too.

"Goddamn you! Goddamn you!"

As the cool feeling fills my whole throat I gradually realize that my mother isn't mean. I look at her, standing over me, and she looks like a giant, or like a great big huge crepe myrtle bush like the ones people tie animals to. Never noticing that the crepe myrtle is all dried up from so many reins and ropes being tied around it.

My mother gets prettier and prettier and prettier. How beautiful! She's so pretty in her burlapbag skirt and the big blouse she stole from Eulogia. I love my mother and I know she's good and that she loves me. I have never seen my mother. But I always picture her like she is now—crying and running her fingers over my throat in the coolest, nicest tickling way you can imagine.

I should picture her like that, not the other way.

"You miserable child! What I really ought to do is hang myself this very instant!"

I feel like getting up and hugging her. Telling her I'm sorry and carrying her off far away where neither Grandma nor Grandpa could ever bother us anymore. I feel like saying, "*Madre mía! Madre mía, Mama!* You're so pretty today with that honeysuckle in your hair! You look like one of those women that you only see on Christmas cards. Let's get out of here, let's leave right this second. Let's get our things together and just take off. Let's not stay another minute in this horrible horrible house that looks like the bottom of a kettle. Let's leave now, before that jackass of a grandfather wakes up and makes us get out of bed and milk the cows."

"Let's leave right this minute, because in the daytime we won't be able to get away."

"*Madre mía! Madre mía!*"

But I don't say another single word. What I was planning to say got stuck in my throat. It hit the point of the stick that ran all the way through me now. And it didn't come out my mouth. For a second my mother stood there paralyzed—listening to me. The whole high meadow knows now that I said my mother. The whole hill knows it too, and now it repeats it in a very strange echo that's almost as close as my own voice.

Mama just stands there with her mouth open. She pulls the prod out of my throat. She throws it into the grass. She puts her hands to her face and lets out a huge huge wail.

Huge.

And she takes off flying, across the old thicket of wild pineapples and into the house, through those big holes in the roof that I've made climbing up and down looking for baby blackbirds or meeting my dead cousins.

I don't know what to do. My throat stings like the dickens. I run my hand over it and it turns out it's nothing. Not even a scratch. The fire ants have eaten my whole back away and the chiggers are starting to get on my face. My mother has disappeared and it's getting to be almost night now. I wish I could make it to the house without anybody seeing me and without her starting to poke me with the prod again or Grandma throwing scalding water on my back.

"You can, you can. Tonight you can," a band of blackbirds tells me, flying over way up high, all in rows, one after another. But how in the world could those blackbirds have been talking to me! I don't believe it. I look up at the sky again, and the black line of their wings is as straight and perfect as could be—the birds' trip has just gone right on and I'll never find out the truth.

Then I start crying.

I like to walk at night, when nobody can see me. I do. I like to because that's when I can hop on just one foot. Get up on a tree stump and spread out my arms and let myself go and dance on it, with my arms out to keep my balance. Do all kinds of somersaults and tricks, and all of them different. Roll around on the ground and take off running again, until I disappear into the fog and in the branches of the Indian laurel tree, which is still standing. I like to be by myself and just break out singing. Celestino has come up to me and asked me for a drink of water. Where from. "Where from," I ask him, and I hold out my empty hands. But the real truth is that I have a terrible memory and I can never remember a song. And so that's why I make them up. I almost like making them up better than learning them by heart.

I'm making one up now.

I hope nobody hears me, because I don't know if this song is any good. I hope nobody hears me, because I'd hate for them to hear me. How embarrassing if my cousins were to surprise me singing made-up songs and hopping through the tree stumps! How embarrassing it would be if somebody heard me!

■ Jamaica Kincaid (1949–) Antigua/United States (story)

Jamaica Kincaid was born in St. John's on the Caribbean island of Antigua. She came to the United States when she was sixteen to go to school and later had success as a freelance writer, a staff writer for the *New Yorker*, and a novelist. Her stories have appeared in *Rolling Stone* and *The Paris Review*. In addition to her highly successful book of short stories, *At the Bottom of the River* (1983), she has written two novels, *Annie John* (1983) and *Lucy* (1990), as well as a prose piece about Antigua titled *A Small Place* (1988). She is an extraordinary writer, peculiar, experimental, magical, and postmodern. Her stories dissect themselves as they speak to us. Or they exist in a dreamscape where anything can and does happen. Each of her brief tales surprises, perplexes, and acrobatically saves itself from its own narrative plunge.

FURTHER READING: Kincaid, Jamaica. *Annie John*, 1983; *At the Bottom of the River*, 1983; *A Small Place*, 1988; *Lucy*, 1990.

Girl

Wash the white clothes on Monday and put them on the stone heap; wash the color clothes on Tuesday and put them on the clothesline to dry; don't walk barehead in the hot sun; cook pumpkin fritters in very hot sweet oil; soak your little clothes right after you take them off; when buying cotton to make yourself a nice blouse, be sure that it doesn't have gum on it, because that way it won't hold up well after a wash; soak salt fish overnight before you cook it; is it true that you sing benna in Sunday school?; always eat your food in such a way that it won't turn someone else's stomach; on Sundays try to walk like a lady and not like the slut you are so bent on becoming; don't sing benna in Sunday school; you mustn't speak to wharf-rat boys, not even to give directions; don't eat fruits on the street—flies will follow you;

but I don't sing benna on Sundays at all and never in Sunday school; this is how to sew on a button; this is how to make a button-hole for the button you have just sewed on; this is how to hem a dress when you see the hem coming down and so to prevent yourself from looking like the slut I know you are so bent on becoming; this is how you iron your father's khaki shirt so that it doesn't have a crease; this is how you iron your father's khaki pants so that they don't have a crease; this is how you grow okra—far from the house, because okra tree harbors red ants; when you are growing dasheen, make sure it gets plenty of water or else it makes your throat itch when you are eating it; this is how you sweep a corner; this is how you sweep a whole house; this is how you sweep a yard; this is how you smile to someone you don't like too much; this is how you smile to someone you don't like at all; this is how you smile to someone you like completely; this is how you set a table for tea; this is how you set a table for dinner; this is how you set a table for dinner with an important guest; this is how you set a table for lunch; this is how you set a table for breakfast; this is how to behave in the presence of men who don't know you very well, and this way they won't recognize immediately the slut I have warned you against becoming; be sure to wash every day, even if it is with your own spit; don't squat down to play marbles—you are not a boy, you know; don't pick people's flowers—you might catch something; don't throw stones at blackbirds, because it might not be a blackbird at all; this is how to make a bread pudding; this is how to make doukona; this is how to make pepper pot; this is how to make a good medicine for a cold; this is how to make a good medicine to throw away a child before it even becomes a child; this is how to catch a fish; this is how to throw back a fish you don't like, and that way something bad won't fall on you; this is how to bully a man; this is how a man bullies you; this is how to love a man, and if this doesn't work there are other ways, and if they don't work don't feel too bad about giving up; this is how to spit up in the air if you feel like it, and this is how to move quick so that it doesn't fall on you; this is how to make ends meet; always squeeze bread to make sure it's fresh; *but what if the baker won't let me feel the bread?;* you mean to say that after all you are really going to be the kind of woman who the baker won't let near the bread?

Laura Esquivel (1950–) *Mexico* (novel)

TRANSLATED BY CAROL CHRISTIANSEN AND THOMAS CHRISTIANSEN

Laura Esquivel was originally a screenwriter, and her screenplay *Chido One* was nominated for the highest award from the Mexican Academy of Motion Pictures. Her film version of *Like Water for Chocolate* won awards in all categories, ten altogether, including one for Esquivel's screenplay, which was based on her best-selling international novel. The frame of Laura Esquivel's novel is cooking, and she precedes each month of the year with a recipe. So January's recipe is Christmas Rolls. There is a curious tradition of cooking, food, and literature of which a fine example is the Byzantine volume *Doctors at Dinner*. In it, the author gathered gems of Ancient Greek lyric poetry containing references to food and cooking. As a result, we possess many poems by Alkman and Sappho that would otherwise have been lost. Had Laura Esquivel composed her novel in Byzantine or Classical Greek times, *Doctors at Dinner* would be replete with Mexican spices and sauces.

Esquivel's story is more fantastic than her recipes. In the first pages, we read about Tita, whose mother was cutting onions in the kitchen, which brought on early labor and caused Tita to be "literally washed into this world on a great tide of tears that spilled over the edge of the table and flooded across the kitchen floor." We learn that when the tears dried and were swept up there was enough salt to fill a ten-pound sack. Esquivel's magic realism gives a mythic quality to the book, which scintillates with family drama, stupidity, and anger born of a traditionally tyrannical mother and a sickly farting sister who marries Pedro whom Tita is mad about. The book flows, like Tita's salt tears at her birth. Esquivel, in lucid, spare language, re-creates a historic rural Mexico during its revolution, and with humor and pain she fuels the domestic love tragedies to the story's burning climax. With a single spellbinding novel, her first, Laura Esquivel has taken her place as a writer read all over the world.

FURTHER READING: Esquivel, Laura, *Like Water for Chocolate*, 1992.

from *Like Water for Chocolate*

January

Christmas Rolls

INGREDIENTS:
1 can of sardines
½ chorizo sausage
1 onion
oregano
1 can of chiles serranos
10 hard rolls

Preparation

Take care to chop the onion fine. To keep from crying when you chop it (which is so annoying!), I suggest you place a little bit on your head. The trouble with crying over an onion is that once the chopping gets you started and the tears begin to well up, the next thing you know you just can't stop. I don't know whether that's ever happened to you, but I have to confess it's happened to me, many times. Mama used to say it was because I was especially sensitive to onions, like my great-aunt, Tita.

Tita was so sensitive to onions, any time they were being chopped, they say she would just cry and cry; when she was still in my great-grandmother's belly her sobs were so loud that even Nacha, the cook, who was half-deaf, could hear them easily. Once her wailing got so violent that it brought on an early labor. And before my great-grandmother could let out a word or even a whimper, Tita made her entrance into this world, prematurely, right there on the kitchen table amid the smells of simmering noodle soup, thyme, bay leaves, and cilantro, steamed milk, garlic, and, of course, onion. Tita had no need for the usual slap on the bottom, because she was already crying as she emerged; maybe that was because she knew then that it would be her lot in life to be denied marriage. The way Nacha told it, Tita was literally washed into this world on a great tide of tears that spilled over the edge of the table and flooded across the kitchen floor.

That afternoon, when the uproar had subsided and the water had been dried up by the sun, Nacha swept up the residue the tears had left on the red stone floor. There was enough salt to fill a ten-pound sack—it was used for cooking and lasted a long time. Thanks to her unusual birth, Tita felt a deep love for the kitchen, where she spent most of her life from the day she was born.

When she was only two days old, Tita's father, my great-grandfather, died of a heart attack and Mama Elena's milk dried up from the shock. Since there was no such thing as powdered milk in those days, and they couldn't find a wet nurse anywhere, they were in a panic to satisfy the infant's hunger. Nacha, who knew everything about cooking—and much more that doesn't enter the picture until later—offered to take charge of feeding Tita. She felt she had the best chance of "educating the innocent child's stomach," even though she had never married or had children. Though she didn't know how to read or write, when it came to cooking she knew everything there was to know. Mama Elena accepted her offer gratefully; she had enough to do between her mourning and the enormous responsibility of running the ranch—and it was the ranch that would provide her children the food and education they deserved—without having to worry about feeding a newborn baby on top of everything else.

From that day on, Tita's domain was the kitchen, where she grew vigorous and healthy on a diet of teas and thin corn gruels. This explains the sixth sense Tita developed about everything concerning food. Her eating habits, for example, were attuned to the kitchen routine: in the morning, when she could smell that the beans were ready; at midday, when she sensed the water was ready for plucking the chickens; and in the afternoon, when the dinner bread was baking, Tita knew it was time for her to be fed.

Sometimes she would cry for no reason at all, like when Nacha chopped onions, but since they both knew the cause of those tears, they didn't pay them much mind. They made them a source of entertainment, so that during her childhood Tita didn't distinguish between tears of laughter and tears of sorrow. For her laughing was a form of crying.

Likewise for Tita the joy of living was wrapped up in the delights of food. It wasn't easy for a person whose knowledge of life was based on the kitchen to comprehend the outside world. That world was an endless expanse that began at the door between the kitchen and the rest of the house, whereas everything on the kitchen side of that door, on through the door leading to the patio and the kitchen and herb gardens was completely hers—it was Tita's realm.

Her sisters were just the opposite: to them, Tita's world seemed full of unknown dangers, and they were terrified of it. They felt that playing in the kitchen was foolish and dangerous. But once, Tita managed to convince them to join her in watching the dazzling display made by dancing water drops dribbled on a red hot griddle.

While Tita was singing and waving her wet hands in time, showering drops of water down on the griddle so they would "dance," Rosaura was cowering in the corner, stunned by the display. Gertrudis, on the other hand, found this game enticing, and she threw herself into it with the enthusiasm she always showed where rhythm, movement, or music were involved. Then Rosaura had tried to join them—but since she barely moistened her hands and then shook them gingerly, her efforts didn't have the desired effect. So Tita tried to move her hands closer to the griddle. Rosaura resisted, and they struggled for control until Tita became annoyed and let go, so that momentum carried Rosaura's hands onto it. Tita got a terrible spanking for that, and she was forbidden to play with her sisters in her own world. Nacha became her playmate then. Together they made up all sorts of games and activities having to do with cooking. Like the day they saw a man in the village plaza twisting long thin balloons into animal shapes, and they decided to do it with sausages. They didn't just make real animals, they also made up some of their own, creatures with the neck of a swan, the legs of a dog, the tail of a horse, and on and on.

Then there was trouble, however, when the animals had to be taken apart to fry the sausage. Tita refused to do it. The only time she was willing to take them apart was when the sausage was intended for the Christmas rolls she loved so much. Then she not only allowed her animals to be dismantled, she watched them fry with glee.

The sausage for the rolls must be fried over very low heat, so that it cooks thoroughly without getting too brown. When done, remove from the heat and add the sardines, which have been deboned ahead of time. Any black spots on the skin should also have been scraped off with a knife. Combine the onions, chopped chiles, and the ground oregano with the sardines. Let the mixture stand before filling the rolls.

Tita enjoyed this step enormously; while the filling was resting, it was very pleasant to savor its aroma, for smells have the power to evoke the past, bringing back sounds and even other smells that have no match in the present. Tita liked to take a deep breath and let the characteristic smoke and smell transport her through the recesses of her memory.

It was useless to try to recall the first time she had smelled one of those rolls—she couldn't, possibly because it had been before she was born. It might have been the unusual combination of sardines and sausages that had called to her and made her decide to trade the peace of ethereal existence in Mama Elena's belly for life as her daughter, in order to enter the De la Garza family and share their delicious meals and wonderful sausage.

On Mama Elena's ranch, sausage making was a real ritual. The day before, they started peeling garlic, cleaning chiles, and grinding spices. All the women in the family had to participate: Mama Elena; her daughters, Gertrudis, Rosaura, and Tita; Nacha, the cook; and Chencha, the maid. They gathered around the dining-room table in the afternoon, and between the talking and the joking the time flew by until it started to get dark. Then Mama Elena would say:

"That's it for today."

For a good listener, it is said, a single word will suffice, so when they heard that, they all sprang into action. First they had to clear the table; then they had to assign tasks: one collected the chickens, another drew water for breakfast from the well, a third was in charge of wood for the stove. There would be no ironing, no embroidery, no sewing that day. When it was all finished, they went to their bedrooms to read, say their prayers, and go to sleep. One afternoon, before Mama Elena told them they could leave the table, Tita, who was then fifteen, announced in a trembling voice that Pedro Muzquiz would like to come and speak with her. . . .

After an endless silence during which Tita's soul shrank, Mama Elena asked:

"And why should this gentleman want to come talk to me?"

Tita's answer could barely be heard:

"I don't know."

Mama Elena threw her a look that seemed to Tita to contain all the years of repression that had flowed over the family, and said:

"If he intends to ask for your hand, tell him not to bother. He'll be wasting his time and mine too. You know perfectly well that being the youngest daughter means you have to take care of me until the day I die."

With that Mama Elena got slowly to her feet, put her glasses in her apron, and said in a tone of final command:

"That's it for today."

Tita knew that discussion was not one of the forms of communication permitted in Mama Elena's household, but even so, for the first time in her life, she intended to protest her mother's ruling.

"But in my opinion . . . "

"You don't have an opinion, and that's all I want to hear about it. For generations, not a single person in my family has ever questioned this tradition, and no daughter of mine is going to be the one to start."

Tita lowered her head, and the realization of her fate struck her as forcibly as her tears struck the table. From then on they knew, she and the table, that they could never have even the slightest voice in the unknown forces that fated Tita to bow before her mother's absurd decision, and the table to continue to receive the bitter tears that she had first shed on the day of her birth.

Still Tita did not submit. Doubts and anxieties sprang to her mind. For one thing, she wanted to know who started this family tradition. It would be nice if she could let that genius know about one little flaw in this perfect plan for taking care of women in their old age. If Tita couldn't marry and have children, who would take care of her when she got old? Was there a solution in a case like that? Or are daughters who stay home and take care of their mothers not expected to survive too long after the parent's death? And what about women who marry and can't have children, who will take care of them? And besides, she'd like to know what kind of studies had established that the youngest daughter and not the eldest is best suited to care for their mother. Had the opinion of the daughter affected by the plan ever been taken into account? If she couldn't marry, was she at least allowed to experience love? Or not even that?

Tita knew perfectly well that all these questions would have to be buried forever in the archive of questions that have no answers. In the De la Garza family, one obeyed—immediately. Ignoring Tita completely, a very angry Mama Elena left the kitchen, and for the next week she didn't speak a single word to her.

What passed for communication between them resumed when Mama Elena, who was inspecting the clothes each of the women had been sewing, discovered that Tita's creation, which was the most perfect, had not been basted before it was sewed.

"Congratulations," she said, "your stitches are perfect—but you didn't baste it, did you?"

"No," answered Tita, astonished that the sentence of silence had been revoked.

"Then go and rip it out. Baste it and sew it again and then come and show it to me. And remember that the lazy man and the stingy man end up walking their road twice."

"But that's if a person makes a mistake, and you yourself said a moment ago that my sewing was . . . "

"Are you starting up with your rebelliousness again? It's enough that you have the audacity to break the rules in your sewing."

"I'm sorry, Mami. I won't ever do it again."

With that Tita succeeded in calming Mama Elena's anger. For once she had been very careful; she had called her "Mami" in the correct tone of voice. Mama Elena felt that the word *Mama* had a disrespectful sound to it, and so, from the time they were little, she had ordered her daughters to use the word *Mami* when speaking to her. The only one who resisted, the only one who said the word without the proper deference was Tita, which had earned her plenty of slaps. But how perfectly she had said it this time! Mama Elena took comfort in the hope that she had finally managed to subdue her youngest daughter.

Unfortunately her hope was short-lived, for the very next day Pedro Muzquiz appeared at the house, his esteemed father at his side, to ask for Tita's hand in marriage. His arrival caused a huge uproar, as his visit was completely unexpected. Several days earlier Tita had sent Pedro a message via Nacha's brother asking him to abandon his suit. The brother swore he had delivered the message to Pedro, and yet, there they were, in the house. Mama Elena received them in the living room; she was extremely polite and explained why it was impossible for Tita to marry.

"But if you really want Pedro to get married, allow me to suggest my daughter Rosaura, who's just two years older than Tita. *She* is one hundred percent available, and ready for marriage. . . . "

At that Chencha almost dropped right onto Mama Elena the tray containing coffee and cookies, which she had carried into the living room to offer don Pascual and his son. Excusing herself, she rushed back to the kitchen, where Tita, Rosaura, and Gertrudis were waiting for her to fill them in on every detail about what was going on in the living room. She burst headlong into the room, and they all immediately stopped what they were doing, so as not to miss a word she said.

They were together in the kitchen making Christmas Rolls. As the name implies, these rolls are usually prepared around Christmas, but today they were being prepared in honor of Tita's birthday. She would soon be sixteen years old, and she wanted to celebrate with one of her favorite dishes.

"Isn't that something? Your ma talks about being ready for marriage like she was dishing up a plate of enchiladas! And the worse thing is, they're completely different! You can't just switch tacos and enchiladas like that!"

Chencha kept up this kind of running commentary as she told the others—in her own way, of course—about the scene she had just witnessed. Tita knew Chencha sometimes exaggerated and distorted things, so she held her aching heart in check. She would not accept what she had just heard. Feigning calm, she continued cutting the rolls for her sisters and Nacha to fill.

It is best to use homemade rolls. Hard rolls can easily be obtained from a bakery, but they should be small; the larger ones are unsuited for this recipe. After filling the rolls, bake for ten minutes and serve hot. For best results, leave the rolls out overnight, wrapped in a cloth, so that the grease from the sausage soaks into the bread.

When Tita was finishing wrapping the next day's rolls, Mama Elena came into the kitchen and informed them that she had agreed to Pedro's marriage—to Rosaura.

Hearing Chencha's story confirmed, Tita felt her body fill with a wintry chill: in one sharp, quick blast she was so cold and dry her cheeks burned and turned red, red as the apples beside her. That overpowering chill lasted a long time, and she could find no respite, not even when Nacha told her what she had overheard as she escorted don Pascual Muzquiz and his son to the ranch's gate. Nacha followed them, walking as quietly as she could in order to hear the conversation between father and son. Don Pascual and Pedro were walking slowly, speaking in low, controlled, angry voices.

"Why did you do that, Pedro? It will look ridiculous, your agreeing to marry Rosaura. What happened to the eternal love you swore to Tita? Aren't you going to keep that vow?"

"Of course I'll keep it. When you're told there's no way you can marry the woman you love and your only hope of being near her is to marry her sister, wouldn't you do the same?"

Nacha didn't manage to hear the answer; Pulque, the ranch dog, went running by, barking at a rabbit he mistook for a cat.

"So you intend to marry without love?"

"No, Papa, I am going to marry with a great love for Tita that will never die."

Their voices grew less and less audible, drowned out by the crackling of dried leaves beneath their feet. How strange that Nacha, who was quite hard of hearing by that time, should have claimed to have heard this conversation. Still, Tita thanked Nacha for telling her—but that did not alter the icy feelings she began to have for Pedro. It is said that the deaf can't hear but can understand. Perhaps Nacha only heard what everyone else was afraid to say. Tita could not get to sleep that night; she could not find the words for what she was feeling. How unfortunate that black holes in space had not yet been discovered, for then she might have understood the black hole in the center of her chest, infinite coldness flowing through it.

Whenever she closed her eyes she saw scenes from last Christmas, the first time Pedro and his family had been invited to dinner; the scenes grew more and more vivid, and the cold within her grew sharper. Despite the time that had passed since that evening, she remembered it perfectly: the sounds, the smells, the way her new dress had grazed the freshly waxed floor, the look Pedro gave her . . . That look! She had been walking to the table carrying a tray of egg-yolk candies when she first felt his hot gaze burning her skin. She turned her head, and her eyes met Pedro's. It was then she understood how dough feels when it is plunged into boiling oil. The heat that invaded her body was so real she was afraid she would start to bubble—her face, her stomach, her heart, her breasts—like batter, and unable to endure his gaze she lowered her eyes and hastily crossed the room, to where Gertrudis was pedaling the player piano, playing a waltz called

"The Eyes of Youth." She set her tray on a little table in the middle of the room, picked up a glass of Noyo liquor that was in front of her, hardly aware of what she was doing, and sat down next to Paquita Lobo, the De la Garzas' neighbor. But even that distance between herself and Pedro was not enough; she felt her blood pulsing, searing her veins. A deep flush suffused her face and no matter how she tried she could not find a place for her eyes to rest. Paquita saw that something was bothering her, and with a look of great concern, she asked:

"That liquor is pretty strong, isn't it?"

"Pardon me?"

"You look a little woozy, Tita. Are you feeling all right?"

"Yes, thank you."

"You're old enough to have a little drink on a special occasion, but tell me, you little devil, did your mama say it was okay? I can see you're excited—you're shaking—and I'm sorry but I must say you'd better not have any more. You wouldn't want to make a fool of yourself."

That was the last straw! To have Paquita Lobo think she was drunk. She couldn't allow the tiniest suspicion to remain in Paquita's mind or she might tell her mother. Tita's fear of her mother was enough to make her forget Pedro for a moment, and she applied herself to convincing Paquita, any way she could, that she was thinking clearly, that her mind was alert. She chatted with her, she gossiped, she made small talk. She even told her the recipe for this Noyo liquor which was supposed to have had such an effect on her. The liquor is made by soaking four ounces of peaches and a half pound of apricots in water for twenty-four hours to loosen the skin; next, they are peeled, crushed, and steeped in hot water for fifteen days. Then the liquor is distilled. After two and a half pounds of sugar have been completely dissolved in the water, four ounces of orange-flower water are added, and the mixture is stirred and strained. And so there would be no lingering doubts about her mental and physical well-being, she reminded Paquita, as if it were just an aside, that the water containers held 2.016 liters, no more and no less.

So when Mama Elena came over to ask Paquita if she was being properly entertained, she replied enthusiastically.

"Oh yes, perfectly! You have such wonderful daughters. Such fascinating conversation!"

Mama Elena sent Tita to the kitchen to get something for the guests. Pedro "happened" to be walking by at that moment and he offered his help. Tita rushed off to the kitchen without a word. His presence made her extremely uncomfortable. He followed her in, and she quickly sent him off with one of the trays of delicious snacks that had been waiting on the kitchen table.

She would never forget the moment their hands accidentally touched as they both slowly bent down to pick up the same tray.

That was when Pedro confessed his love.

"Señorita Tita, I would like to take advantage of this opportunity to be alone with you to tell you that I am deeply in love with you. I know this declaration is presumptuous, and that it's quite sudden, but it's so hard to get near you that I decided to tell you tonight. All I ask is that you tell me whether I can hope to win your love."

"I don't know what to say . . . give me time to think."

"No, no, I can't! I need an answer now: you don't have to think about love; you either feel it or you don't. I am a man of few words, but my word is my pledge. I swear that my love for you will last forever. What about you? Do you feel the same way about me?"

"Yes!"

Yes, a thousand times. From that night on she would love him forever. And now she had to give him up. It wasn't decent to desire your sister's future husband. She had to try to put him out of her mind somehow, so she could get to sleep. She started to eat the Christmas Roll Nacha had left out on her bureau, along with a glass of milk; this remedy had proven effective many times. Nacha, with all her experience, knew that for Tita there was no pain that wouldn't disappear if she ate a delicious Christmas Roll. But this time it didn't work. She felt no relief from the hollow sensation in her stomach. Just the opposite, a wave of nausea flowed over her. She realized that the hollow sensation was not hunger but an icy feeling of grief. She had to get rid of that terrible sensation of cold. First she put on a wool robe and a heavy cloak. The cold still gripped her. Then she put on felt slippers and another two shawls. No good. Finally she went to her sewing box and pulled out the bedspread she had started the day Pedro first spoke of marriage. A bedspread like that, a crocheted one, takes about a year to complete. Exactly the length of time Pedro and Tita had planned to wait before getting married. She decided to use the yarn, not to let it go to waste, and so she worked on the bedspread and wept furiously, weeping and working until dawn, and threw it over herself. It didn't help at all. Not that night, nor many others, for as long as she lived, could she free herself from that cold.

■ Giannina Braschi (1953–)
Puerto Rico/New York (prose poem)

TRANSLATED BY TESS O'DWYER

Giannina Braschi's collected poems, an epic-length sequence of prose poems, *The Empire of Dreams* (*El imperio de los sueños*), was published to acclaim in Barcelona in 1988. In 1994, Yale University Press, which usually publishes no poets other than those in the yearly Yale Younger Poets Series, chose to bring out *Empire of Dreams*. Alicia Ostriker wrote an illuminating introduction. In substantial ways, Braschi is the brightest new voice in her generation in the Spanish language. She was born in Puerto Rico and has lived in New York since 1977. She took her Ph.D. from State University of New York at Stony Brook and presently teaches at Queens College and John Jay College, City University of New York. She published a critical volume on the poetry of the nineteenth-century Spanish poet Gustavo Bécquer, *La poesía de Bécquer: el tiempo de los objetos o los espacios de la luz* (1982). Her focus now is her poetry and drama.

Braschi is a Spanish Arthur Rimbaud, re-inventing surrealism, creating a maze of characters—clowns, shepherds, magicians madmen, witches, and artists who perform their fantasies in city streets. The shepherds spread straw over New York and enter triumphantly with their herds. Her language is erotic, linguistically innovative, sexually ambiguous, postmodern, fluid, inevitable. She gives meaning to the meaningless as she creates, identifies, and slides between them. She is cosmopolitan—of the great cities of Europe and the Americas—and above all magical. *The Empire of Dreams* has been called a modern classic.

FURTHER READING: Giannina Braschi. *La poesía de Bécquer: el tiempo de los objetos o los espacios de la luz*, 1982; *El imperio de los sueños*, 1988; *Empire of Dreams*, 1994.

from *Empire of Dreams*

Behind the word is silence. Behind what sounds is the door. There is a back and a fold hiding in everything. And what was approaching fell and stopped far away in proximity. An expression falls asleep and rises. And what was over there returns. It's a way to put the world back in its place. And something comes back when it should remain remembering.

But if I ring the bell, water jumps and a river falls out of the water again. And the body rises and shakes. And the rock wakes and says, I'm singing. And a hand turns into a kerchief. And twilight and wind are companions. And this twilight appears amidst lightning. Outside there is a bird and a branch and a tree and that lightning. Above all, there is noon without form. And suddenly everything acquires movement. Two travelers meet and their shoes dance. And breeze and morning clash. And the seagull runs and the rabbit flies. And runs and runs, and the current ran. Behind what runs is life. Behind that silence is the door.

* * *

I want to be rid of this corpse that murders my soul. I have other things to say. Get away from me. Leave me alone. I request another name, another clown. Too many buffoons, too many dead dwarves. I want a giant. Get out of my body. Don't take the corpse away from me, let it walk. Swing with the trapeze, glide. Make me a shoe or dig the sole into me. Become a stocking and fill me. I have a nickel for the dance and the comedy. You see, that's just what I was telling you. I have no comedies. Kill me if you want. But do for me the black, the white, the void. Absence, as though it were the death of absence. As though absence could drop dead, dead. Of course, the corpse is a stick that walks. Of course, the stick gives you a blow on the head. Of course, you should never play with death.

* * *

On the top floor of the Empire State a shepherd has stood up to sing and dance. What a wonderful thing. That New York City has been invaded by so many shepherds. That work has stopped and there is only singing and dancing. And that the newspapers—the *New York Times,* in headlines, and the *Daily News*—call out: New York. New York. New York. Listen to it. Hear it on the radio. And on television. Listen to the loudspeakers. Listen to it. The buffoons have died. And the little lead soldier. Shepherds have invaded New York. They have conquered New York. They have colonized New York. The special of the day in New York's most expensive restaurant is golden acorns. It's an egg. It's an apple. It's a bird. Fish. Melody. Poetry. And epigram. Now there is only song. Now there is only dance. Now we do whatever we please. Whatever we please. Whatever we damn well please.

* * *

I love hiccups and I love sneezes and I love blinks and I love belches and I love gluttons. I love hair. I love bears. For me, the round. For me, the world. Round is the happy face. And round is the midday. And when the moon is most beautiful is when it's round. Sex is round. And the heart also. The hand is round. The mouth also. Sneezes are round. And hiccups also. The milk from the breast of Lady Macbeth was also round. I would have liked to be like her and be bad. I am good. I am shepherd. I am sex. And I am hiccup. And I am sneeze. And I am cough. Hoarse. Hoarse. Hoarse. I am thunder. I am voice. I am Obscene. Obscene. Obscene. I am pure like the tit or the milk. I am water, sea, or fish, or tadpole. I am round.

* * *

I'm really sorry, folks, but the shepherds are also farting in New York. I'm sorry. But they're gross. And the cops are chiming in. And they're farting too. And they're competing to see who can fart the loudest. So there's fart traffic. And burps. Traffic of bulls and cows and ambrosia and water. And bulls are pissing on buildings. And cows are shitting in shops. And all the shops are filled with shepherds. And all the mannequins are shepherds. I'm really sorry, folks, but shepherds are gross. Dirt. Dirt. Everything is dirty. Everything is disgusting. Everything is full of crap. Cow crap. Worm crap. Lizard crap. Santa Claus crap. Vulture crap. Beetle crap. The streets are full of crap. And the food too. I'm sorry, folks, but these New Yorkers are pigs. Pigs. Pigs.

* * *

Memories walk around dressed up as old men. But they're not old. They're hypocrites and gossipers. I love gossip. But I hate memories and sorrows. I like the things he told me and I told him, and we fell in love, and rode off into the sunset, and lived happily ever after. I like the sun and the beach. I like sidewalks. And soup and beets. I like men and women. And I like mountains and seas. I like fire and water. I like trashy movies and novels. I like tackiness and gossip. Most of all, I like to forget everything. Especially memories. I am forgetfulness. And nothingness. I am joy, well-being, and happiness. I am laughter, gossip, and pantomime. I am the idiot and the prince. I am the grain of rice and the bean. I am the chickpea and the casserole. I am the red apple. And salt and pepper. I am the shepherd of life. I am the shepherd of memories, which I love despite everything. Affirming is everything I love and everything I hate. Affirming. And living. And denying. Affirming everything.

* * *

A little while longer. Ten days repeated. I'm looking at the moon. The highest star. The solution to the same math problem. On a pile of conjectures. Polysynchronized colors. And the answer ten kilometers from my house. Proof for a theorem. I'll supply you with all the necessary material. I'll give you a certificate. A science diploma. Some goggles. From the time before iguanas and the world. A frog croaks. A cricket sings. I love bird nests from the time before life. I love frog dreams. Toad interpretations. I come whenever I hear iguana concerts. My orgasm is an organ. An organism. A simple tadpole that becomes a frog. A mouse has his own way of fighting a cat. He takes him out of context. The cat's text meows. Mice want cheese. Cows eat lots of meat. Polychromatic urban cows. Green. Orange. Or yellow. The piano, softly. Or the C in E-flat. In A minor. Still listening to the symphony. Still. Allegretto. Fugue. Scherzo. Or andante con moto, or andante con brio, or rondo burlesco. In the rondo of the minuet or the waltz. A C in E-flat. Ten days of fugue. Music vacations. An ironic fit of laughter rules over the sea. And a stupid drool.

ACKNOWLEDGMENTS

Section 1: Native American Literature of Precolumbian and Later Periods

Apu Inca, from "The Elegy for the Great Inca Atawallpa" (Anonymous, Quechua, Peru), tr. W. S. Merwin. English translation copyright © 1958 by W. S. Merwin. Reprinted by permission of Georges Borchardt, Inc. for W. S. Merwin.

The Huarochiri Manuscript, excerpts from *The Huarochiri Manuscript: A Testament of Ancient and Colonial Andean Religion*, translated and edited by Frank Salomon and George L. Urioste. Copyright © 1991. Reprinted by permission of the authors and the University of Texas Press.

Zithuwa Hymns, "Harvest," tr. J. H. Rowe, from *Kroeber Anthropological Society Papers Nos. 8–9* (University of California, Berkeley, 1953).

Zithuwa Hymns, "Sister Rain," tr. Gordon Brotherston, after tr. by Garcilaso de la Vega Inca. Reprinted by permission of Gordon Brotherston.

Afu Ollantay, "Song," tr. Mark Strand from *Eighteen Poems from the Quechua*. Copyright 1971. Reprinted by permission of Mark Strand.

"Like a Feather in the Air" (anonymous, Quechua), tr. W. S. Merwin. English translation copyright © 1958 by W. S. Merwin. Reprinted by permission of Georges Borchardt, Inc. for W. S. Merwin.

"I Have Lost My Dove" (anonymous, Quechua, Peru), tr. W. S. Merwin from *Selected Translations 1948–1968* (New York: Atheneum, 1968). Copyright 1948, 1949, 1950, 1954, © 1956, 1957, 1958, 1959, 1960, 1961, 1962, 1965, 1966, 1967, 1968 by W. S. Merwin. Reprinted by permission of Georges Borchardt, Inc. for W. S. Merwin.

"Where Are You" (Anonymous, Quechua, Peru), tr. W. S. Merwin from *Selected Translations 1968–1978* (New York: Atheneum, 1980). Copyright © 1979 by W. S. Merwin. Reprinted by permission of Georges Borchardt, Inc. for W. S. Merwin.

"War Song" (Cuzco), "To This Song," "Song," and "I Am Raising a Fly," tr. Mark Strand from *Eighteen Poems from the Quechua*. Copyright 1971. Reprinted by permission of Mark Strand.

"Ichi the Dwarf" (Anonymous, Quechua, Peru), tr. W. S. Merwin from *Selected Translations 1968–1978* (New York: Atheneum, 1980). Copyright © 1979 by W. S. Merwin. Reprinted by permission of Georges Borchardt, Inc. for W. S. Merwin.

"Kuchi, Who Brought Trees and Fruit to the Dirt Earth" and "Semenia, the Bird Who Showed How to Plant," from *Watunna: An Orinoco Creation Cycle* by Marc de Civrieux, edited and translated by David M. Guss. Copyright © 1980. Reprinted by permission of the University of Texas Press.

"The Interrogation of the Chiefs," tr. Ralph Roys from *The Book of Chilam Balam of Chumayel* by Ralph L. Roys. New edition copyright © 1967 by the University of Oklahoma Press, reproduced from the first edition published by the Carnegie Institution of Washington in 1933.

Chilam Balam, *Book of Chumayel*, "How Human Time Begins" and "Last Words," tr. Gordon Brotherston and Ed Dorn. Reprinted by permission of the translators.

Ritual of the Bacabs, "This Is to Cool Burning Fever," tr. Gordon Brotherston. Reprinted by permission of Gordon Brotherston.

X-Kolom-che, "The Archer's Dance Song," tr. Ann London, published in *Shaking the Pumpkin*, edited by Jerome Rothenberg (Doubleday, 1972 and University of New Mexico Press, 1991). Compiled, commented and translated from Maya by Alfredo Barrera Vásquez. © 1965 Instituto Nacional de Antropología e Historia, México. The Ann London Scott papers are located at Schlesinger Library, Radcliffe College. Translation reprinted by permission of Thomas Scott.

"Preamble: Silence of Sea and Sky," from *Popol Vuh*, translated by Dennis Tedlock. Copyright © 1985 by Dennis Tedlock. Reprinted by permission of Simon & Schuster.

Popol Vuh, "The End of the Doll People," tr. Munro Edmunson. Reprinted by permission of Munro Edmundson.

Tlatelolco Annals, "All This Happened among Us," tr. Gordon Brotherston. Reprinted by permission of Gordon Brotherston.

The Aztec Priests' Speech, tr. Gordon Brotherston and Edward Dorn. Reprinted by permission of the translators.

Twenty Sacred Hymns, "Tlaloc (Hymn 3)," tr. Gordon Brotherston and Edward Dorn. Reprinted by permission of the translators.

Twenty Sacred Hymns, "To the Mother of the Gods (Hymn 4)," tr. Edward Kissam from *Poems of the Aztec Peoples*, translated by Edward Kissam and Michael Schmidt. Copyright 1983. Reprinted by permission of Bilingual Press / Editorial Bilingue, Arizona State University, Tempe, AZ.

Twenty Sacred Hymns, "To Ease Birth (Hymn 12)" and "For Eating Unleavened Tamales (Hymn 14)," tr. Anselm Hollo after Edward Seler, published in *Shaking the Pumpkin*, edited by Jerome Rothenberg (Doubleday, 1972). Translations © 1972, 1998 by Anselm Hollo. Reprinted by permission of Anselm Hollo.

Legend of the Suns, "Quetzalcoatl Descends to Mictlan," tr. Gordon Brotherston. Reprinted by permission of Gordon Brotherston.

Legend of the Suns, "The Fifth Sun," tr. John Bierhorst from *History and Mythology of the Aztecs: The Codex Chimalpopoca*, translated from the Nahuatl by John Bierhorst. Copyright © 1992 by John Bierhorst. Reprinted by permission of the University of Arizona Press.

Cuauhtitlán Annals, "The Five Suns," tr. Gordon Brotherston. Reprinted by permission of Gordon Brotherston.

Florentine Codex, "The Toltecs Were Certainly Rich (Book III)" tr. Gordon Brotherston and Edward Dorn. Reprinted by permission of the translators.

Florentine Codex, "The Deadly Dance (Book III)," tr. Edward Kissam from *Poems of the Aztec Peoples*, translated by Edward Kissam and Michael Schmidt. Copyright 1983. Reprinted by permission of Bilingual Press / Editorial Bilingue, Arizona State University, Tempe, AZ.

Florentine Codex, "The Artist (Book X)," tr. Denise Levertov from *Collected Earlier Poems 1940–1960*. Copyright © 1949, 1979 by Denise Levertov. Reprinted by permission of New Directions Publishing Corp.

Cantares Mexicanos, "Orphan Song," tr. Luis Reyes and Gordon Brotherston. Reprinted by permission of the translators.

Cantares Mexicanos, "Could It Be True We Live on Earth?" tr. Edward Kissam from *Poems of the Aztec Peoples*, translated by Edward Kissam and Michael Schmidt. Copyright 1983. Reprinted by permission of Bilingual Press / Editorial Bilingue, Arizona State University, Tempe, AZ.

Cantares Mexicanos, "Death and Rebirth of Tula," tr. Gordon Brotherston. Reprinted by permission of Gordon Brotherston.

Cantares Mexicanos, "Three Nahuatl Poems," tr. William Carlos Williams from *Collected Poems: 1909–1939*, Vol. 1. Copyright © 1938 by New Directions Publishing Corp. Reprinted by permission of New Directions Publishing Corp.

Yancuic Tlahtolli: The New Word, "Bird," by J. Fausto Hernández Hernández, tr. Gordon Brotherston. Reprinted by permission of Gordon Brotherston.

Section 2: Discovery, Conquest, and the Colonies

Christopher Columbus, excerpts from *The Log of Christopher Columbus*, tr. Robert H. Fuson (Camden, ME: International Marine Publishing, a Division of The McGraw-Hill Companies). Reprinted by permission of The McGraw-Hill Companies.

"The Conquest of Cuba" and "Are Not the Indians Men?" tr. George Sanderlin from *Bartolomé de las Casas: A Selection of His Writings* by Bartolomé de las Casas, translated by George Sanderlin. Copyright © 1971 by Alfred A. Knopf Inc. Reprinted by permission of the publisher.

"The Entrance into Mexico" and "The Stay in Mexico," tr. J. M. Cohen from *The Conquest of New Spain* by Bernal Díaz, translated by J. M. Cohen (Penguin Classics, 1963). Copyright © J. M. Cohen, 1963. Reprinted by permission of Penguin Books Ltd.

Excerpts from *Royal Commentaries of the Incas and General History of Peru*, Part One, by Garcilaso de la Vega, translated by Harold V. Livermore. Copyright © 1996. Reprinted by permission of University of Texas Press.

Sor Juana Inés de la Cruz, "In Which She Morally Censures a Rose, and through the Rose Her Peers," tr. Aliki Barnstone and Willis Barnstone. Reprinted by permission of Aliki Barnstone.

Sor Juana Inés de la Cruz, "She Proves the Inconsistency of the Desires and Criticism of Men Who Accuse Women of What They Themselves Cause," tr. Aliki Barnstone and Willis Barnstone. Reprinted by permission of Aliki Barnstone.

Sor Juana Inés de la Cruz, from "First Dream," tr. Samuel Beckett from *An Anthology of Mexican Poetry* by Octavio Paz. © Samuel Beckett and Octavio Paz 1958, 1986. Reprinted by permission of Indiana University Press.

Section 3: Nineteenth and Twentieth Centuries

José Hernández, from *The Gaucho Martín Fierro*, "Martín Fierro Relates His Meeting with Two of His Sons," tr. Walter Owen. Copyright 1936, © 1964 by Henry Holt & Company, Inc. Reprinted by permission of Henry Holt & Company, Inc.

Excerpts from *Epitaph of a Small Winner* by Machado de Assis, translated by William L. Grossman. Translation copyright © 1952 by William Leonard Grossman. Translation copyright renewed © 1980 by Mignon S. Grossman. Reprinted by permission of Farrar, Straus & Giroux, Inc.

Machado De Assis, from *Dom Casmurro*, "Othello," tr. Helen Cauldwell. Translation copyright © 1953 and translation copyright renewed © 1981 by Helen Caldwell. Reprinted by permission of Farrar, Straus & Giroux, Inc.

Rubén Darío, "Symphony in Gray Major," tr. Denise Levertov from reverted rights of Levertov's translations. Copyright © 1961 by Denise Levertov. Reprinted by permission of New Directions Publishing Corp. Also from *An Anthology of Spanish Poetry from Garcilaso to García Lorca*, edited by Angel Flores. Copyright © 1961 by Angel Flores. All Rights Reserved. Reprinted by permission of the Estate of Angel Flores.

"To Roosevelt," by Rubén Darío, translated by Lysander Kemp. In *An Anthology of Spanish Poetry from Garcilaso to García Lorca*, edited by Angel Flores. Copyright © 1961 by Angel Flores. All Rights Reserved. Reprinted by permission of the Estate of Angel Flores. And in *Selected Poems of Rubén Darío*. Copyright © 1965, renewed 1993. Reprinted by permission of the University of Texas Press.

468 Acknowledgments

From *Don Segundo Sombra (Shadows on the Pampas)* by Ricardo Güiraldes, translated by Harriet de Onis. Copyright 1935, © 1963 by Henry Holt & Co., Inc. Reprinted by permission of Henry Holt & Co., Inc.

Manuel Bandeira, "Brazilian Tragedy," tr. Elizabeth Bishop from *An Anthology of Twentieth-Century Brazilian Poetry* edited by Elizabeth Bishop and Emanuel Brasil. © 1972 by Wesleyan University. Reprinted by permission of University Press of New England.

"Poems of the Saddest Mother: Cast Out" from *The Mothers' Poems/Poemas de las Madres* by Gabriela Mistral, edited by Margaret Sayers Peden, translated by Christiane Jacox Kyle. English translation copyright 1996 by Christiane Jacox Kyle. Reprinted by permission of Eastern Washington University Press.

César Vallejo, "Our Daily Bread," tr. James Wright from *Above the River: The Complete Poems* by César Vallejo, translated by James Wright. © 1990 by Anne Wright, Wesleyan University Press. Reprinted by permission of University Press of New England.

Alfonsina Storni, "My Sister," "Lighthouse in the Night," and "I Am Going to Sleep," tr. Aliki Barnstone and Willis Barnstone. Reprinted by permission of Aliki Barnstone.

Vincente Huidobro, "Glances and Souvenirs" tr. Paul Blackburn from *Modern European Poetry*, edited by Willis Barnstone. Copyright © 1966 by Bantam Books, a division of Bantam Doubleday Dell Publishing Group, Inc. Used by permission of Bantam Books, a division of Bantam Doubleday Dell Publishing Group, Inc.

Miguel Angel Asturias, "Legend of 'El Cadejo,'" tr. Hardie St. Martin. Reprinted by permission of Hardie St. Martin.

"Borges and I" from *A Personal Anthology* by Jorge Luis Borges, translated by Anthony Kerrigan. Copyright © 1967 by Grove Press, Inc. Used by permission of Grove/ Atlantic, Inc.

"Kafka and His Precursors," from *Other Inquisitions: 1937–1952* by Jorge Luis Borges, translated by Ruth L. C. Simms. Copyright © 1964, renewed 1993. Reprinted by permission of the University of Texas Press.

"The South" and "Death and the Compass," from *Ficciones* by Jorge Luis Borges, translated by Anthony Kerrigan. Copyright © 1962 by Grove Press, Inc. Used by permission of Grove/ Atlantic, Inc.

"Poem of the Gifts," tr. Willis Barnstone from *The Collected Works of Jorge Luis Borges*, 3 Vols., by Jorge Luis Borges. Translation copyright © 1967 by Willis Barnstone. Used by permission of Viking Penguin, a division of Penguin Putnam Inc.

Jorge Luis Borges, "The Labyrinth," tr. John Updike. Copyright © 1972 by Emece Editores, S.A. and Norman Thomas di Giovanni, English translation. Used by permission of Viking Penguin, a division of Penguin Putnam Inc.

Acknowledgments **469**

"In Praise of Shadow," tr. Tony Barnstone and Willis Barnstone from *The Collected Works of Jorge Luis Borges*, 3 Vols., by Jorge Luis Borges. Translation copyright © 1998 by Willis and Tony Barnstone. Used by permission of Viking Penguin, a division of Penguin Putnam Inc.

Jorge Luis Borges, "The Other Tiger," "A Blind Man," and "Remorse," tr. Willis Barnstone. Copyright © 1998 by Willis Barnstone. Used by permission of Viking Penguin, a division of Penguin Putnam Inc.

"Spinoza," tr. Willis Barnstone from *The Collected Works of Jorge Luis Borges*, 3 Vols., by Jorge Luis Borges. Translation copyright © 1998 by Willis and Tony Barnstone. Used by permission of Viking Penguin, a division of Penguin Putnam Inc

Jorge Luis Borges, "Camden," tr. Willis Barnstone. Copyright © 1998 by Willis and Tony Barnstone. Used by permission of Viking Penguin, a division of Penguin Putnam Inc.

Jorge Luis Borges, "Proteus," "I Am," "To the Mirror," tr. Tony Barnstone. Copyright © 1998 by Tony and Willis Barnstone. Used by permission of Viking Penguin, a division of Penguin Putnam Inc.

Cecilia Meireles, "Ballad of the Ten Casino Dancers," tr. James Merrill from *An Anthology of Twentieth-Century Brazilian Poetry* edited by Elizabeth Bishop and Emanuel Brasil. © 1972 by Wesleyan University. Reprinted by permission of University Press of New England.

Carlos Drummond de Andrade, "Seven-Sided Poem," tr. Elizabeth Bishop; "Widower's Song," tr. Willis Barnstone; "Souvenir of the Ancient World," tr. Mark Strand; "Family Portrait," tr. Elizabeth Bishop; and "Song for a Young Girl's Album," tr. Mark Strand from *Travelling in the Family* by Carlos Drummond de Andrade (various translators). Copyright © 1986 by Carlos Drummond de Andrade and Thomas Colchie. Reprinted by permission of Random House Inc.

Alejo Carpentier, "Like the Night," tr. Frances Partridge. Reprinted by permission of Fundación Alejo Carpentier, Havana.

João Guimarães Rosa, "The Third Bank of the River," tr. Barbara Shelby Merello from *The Third Bank of the River and Other Stories* by João Guimarães Rosa, translated by B. Shelby. Copyright © 1968 by Alfred A. Knopf Inc. Reprinted by permission of the publisher.

Juan Carlos Onetti, "The Dog Will Have Its Day," tr. Andrew Hurley. In *Tan triste como ella y otros cuentos*, by Juan Carlos Onetti, translated by Andrew Hurley. Reprinted by permission of Agencia Literaria Carmen Balcells, agent for the estate of Juan Carlos Onetti. And in *A Hammock beneath the Mangoes*, edited by Thomas Colchie. Copyright 1992. Reprinted by permission of Andrew Hurley.

Jorge Amado, from *The Two Deaths of Quincas Wateryell*, "A Certain Amount of Confusion," tr. Barbara Shelby Merello. Copyright © 1965 by Alfred A. Knopf, Inc. Reprinted by permission of Alfred A. Knopf, Inc.

Leon Damas, "Position Paper," tr. Robert Bagg from *The Contemporary World of Poetry,* edited by Donald Junkins. Reprinted by permisison of Donald Junkins.

Vinícius de Morães, "Song," tr. Richard Wilbur from *An Anthology of Twentieth-century Brazilian Poetry,* edited by Elizabeth Bishop and Emanuel Brasil. © 1972 by Wesleyan University. Reprinted by permission of University Press of New England.

Aimé Césaire, "zaffer sun" and "abyss," tr. Clayton Eshelman and Annette Smith from *Lyric and Dramatic Poetry, 1946–82 (moi, luminaire . . .).* Copyright © Editions du Seuil, 1982. Reprinted by permission of Georges Borchardt, Inc.

Julia de Burgos, "Nothing," tr. Aliki Barnstone and Willis Barnstone. Reprinted by permission of Aliki Barnstone.

Julio Cortázar, "Axolotl," tr. Paul Blackburn from *End of the Game and Other Stories* by Julio Cortázar, translated by P. Blackburn. Copyright © 1967, 1963 by Random House Inc. Reprinted by permission of Pantheon Books, a Division of Random House Inc.

Octavio Paz, "Sight, Touch," tr. Mark Strand from *Selected Poems* by Octavio Paz, translated by Mark Strand. Copyright © 1979 by Octavio Paz and Mark Strand. Reprinted by permission of New Directions Publishing Corp.

Octavio Paz, "The Key of Water," tr. Elizabeth Bishop from *Collected Poems 1957–1987.* Copyright © 1972, 1975 by Octavio Paz and Elizabeth Bishop. Used by permission of Farrar, Straus & Giroux. Reprinted by permission of New Directions Publishing Corp.

Octavio Paz "Wind from All Compass Points," tr. Paul Blackburn from *Collected Poems 1957–1987.* Copyright © 1970 by Octavio Paz and Paul Blackburn. Reprinted by permission of New Directions Publishing Corp.

Octavio Paz, "The Grove," tr. Elizabeth Bishop from *Collected Poems 1957–1987.* Copyright © 1972, 1975 by Octavio Paz and Elizabeth Bishop. Used by permission of Farrar, Straus & Giroux. Reprinted by permission of New Directions Publishing Corp.

Octavio Paz, "The River," tr. Paul Blackburn from *Early Poems of Octavio Paz.* Copyright © 1959 by Octavio Paz and Jean Miller Blackburn. Reprinted by permission of New Directions Publishing Corp.

Nicanor Parra, "Viva Stalin" and "Warnings," tr. Miller Williams from *Emergency Poems.* Copyright © 1972 by Nicanor Parra and Miller Williams. Reprinted by permission of New Directions Publishing Corp.

Juan Rulfo, "Talpa," tr. George D. Schade from *The Burning Plain and Other Stories.* Copyright © 1953, translation copyright © 1967, renewed 1966. Reprinted by permission of University of Texas Press.

Juan José Arreola, "I'm Telling You the Truth," tr. George D. Schade from *Confabulario and Other Inventions.* Copyright © 1964. Reprinted by permission of the University of Texas Press.

João Cabral de Melo Neto, "Poem," tr. W. S. Merwin; "The End of the World," tr. James Wright from *An Anthology of Twentieth-Century Brazilian Poetry* edited by Elizabeth Bishop and Emanuel Brasil. © 1972 by Wesleyan University. Reprinted by permission of University Press of New England.

Derek Walcott, excerpts from *Omeros*. Copyright © 1990 by Derek Walcott. Reprinted by permission of Farrar, Straus & Giroux, Inc.

Clarice Lispector, "Marmosets," tr. Elizabeth Bishop. First published in *The Kenyon Review*, Summer 1964, OX Vol. XXVI, No. 3. Copyright 1964 by Kenyon College. Reprinted by permission of The Kenyon Review.

Clarice Lispector, "Explanation," tr. Alexis Levitin from *Soulstorm*. Copyright © 1974 by Clarice Lispector, © 1989 by Alexis Levitin. Reprinted by permission of New Directions Publishing Corp.

From *The Obscene Bird of Night* by José Donoso, translated by Hardie St. Martin and Leonard Mades. Copyright © 1973 by Alfred A. Knopf Inc. Reprinted by permission of the publisher.

Jaime Sabines, "Tarumba," tr. W. S. Merwin; "In the House of the Day," tr. Philip Levine from *New Poetry of Mexico* by Octavio Paz and Mark Strand. Translation copyright © 1970 by E. P. Dutton & Co., Inc. Copyright © 1966 by Siglo XXI Editores, S.A. Used by permission of Dutton Signet, a division of Penguin Books USA Inc.

Ernesto Cardenal, "19th-Century Traveler on the Rio San Juan" and "Léon," tr. Jonathan Cohen from *With Walker in Nicaragua and Other Early Poems 1949–1954*. Translation © 1984 by Jonathan Cohen, Wesleyan University. Reprinted by permission of University Press of New England.

René Dépestre, "Black Ore," tr. James Scully from *The Massachusetts Review*, Vol. 15, No. 4, Autumn 1974. © 1975 The Massachusetts Review, Inc. Reprinted by permission of The Massachusetts Review.

"Chac-Mool," from *Burnt Water* by Carlos Fuentes, translated by Margaret Sayers Peden. Translation copyright © 1980 by Farrar, Straus & Giroux, Inc. Reprinted by permission of Farrar, Straus & Giroux, Inc.

"The Founding of Macondo," tr. Gregory Rabassa and J. S. Bernstein from *One Hundred Years of Solitude* by Gabriel García Márquez. English translation copyright © 1970 by Harper & Row Publishers, Inc. Reprinted by permission of HarperCollins Publishers, Inc.

"A Very Old Man with Enormous Wings," from *Leaf Storm and Other Stories* by Gabriel García Márquez, translated by Gregory Rabassa. Copyright © 1971 by Gabriel García Márquez. Reprinted by permission of HarperCollins Publishers, Inc.

"I Heard Her Sing," tr. Donald Gardner and Suzanne Jill Levine, from *Three Trapped Tigers* by Guillermo Cabrera Infante. English translation copyright © 1971 by Harper & Row, Publishers, Inc. Reprinted by permission of HarperCollins Publishers, Inc.

V. S. Naipaul, from *Miguel Street*, "The Thing without a Name" and "George and the Pink House." Copyright © 1959 by V. S. Naipaul. Used by permission of Viking Penguin, a division of Penguin Books USA Inc., and Wylie, Aitken & Stone.

"Up among the Eagles," from *Open Door: Stories* by Luisa Valenzuela, translated by Margaret Sayers Peden (San Francisco: North Point Press). Copyright 1988. Reprinted by permission of Rosario Santos, agent for Luisa Valenzuela.

José Emilio Pacheco, "From Some Time to This Place," tr. Philip Levine from *New Poetry of Mexico*, edited by Mark Strand (Farrar, Straus & Giroux, 1970). © Philip Levine. Reprinted by permission of Philip Levine.

José Emilio Pacheco, "Whistler's London," tr. George McWhirter from *Selected Poems*. Copyright © 1975, 1987 by George McWhirter. Reprinted by permission of New Directions Publishing Corp.

Gustavo Sainz, from *The Princess of Iron Palace*, "He Had a Chivas Regal Face," tr. Andrew Hurley. English translation copyright © 1987 by Andrew Hurley. Used by permission of Grove/Atlantic, Inc.

"Gift for a Sweetheart," from *The Stories of Eva Luna* by Isabel Allende, translated from Spanish by Margaret Sayers Peden. Copyright © 1989 by Isabel Allende, English translation copyright 1991 by Macmillan Publishing Company. Reprinted by permission of Scribner, a Division of Simon & Schuster.

From *Singing from the Well*, by Reinaldo Arenas, translated by Andrew Hurley. Translation copyright © 1987 by Andrew Hurley and Reinaldo Arenas, English translation. Used by permission of Viking Penguin, a division of Penguin Books USA Inc.

Jamaica Kincaid, "Girl," from *At the Bottom of the River*. Copyright © 1983 by Jamaica Kincaid. Reprinted by permission of Farrar, Straus & Giroux, Inc.

Laura Esquivel, from *Like Water for Chocolate*, tr. Carol Christiansen and Thomas Christiansen. Translation copyright © 1992 by Doubleday, a div. of Bantam, Doubleday, Dell Publishing Group Inc. Used by permission of Doubleday, a division of Bantam Doubleday Dell Publishing Group, Inc.

Giannina Braschi, from *Empire of Dreams*, tr. Tess O'Dwyer. Copyright 1994 by Yale University. Reprinted by permission of Yale University Press.

1 ✓
2 ✗
3 ✓
4 ✓
5 ✗
6 ✓
7 ✗
8 ✓
9 ✓
10 ✓